TESCO

The ESSENTIAL GUIDE — TO — W I N E

JOSEPH STEPHENSON

TESCO

The
ESSENTIAL
GUIDE
— TO —
WINE

ROBERT JOSEPH

CONTENTS

Published in the UK exclusively for
Tesco Stores Limited, Cheshunt,
Waltham Cross, Hertfordshire EN8 9SL by
Joseph Stephenson, 28 Fairholme Road,
London W14 9JX.

First published 1990
Copyright © 1990 Joseph Stephenson
Text copyright © 1990 Robert Joseph
Artwork and maps copyright © 1990 Joseph Stephenson

ISBN 1 873143 001

Text processed by Active Image, Unit 8, Worton Hall Industrial
Estate, Worton Road, Isleworth.
Printed and bound in the UK by Jarrold Printing, Norwich

Editor   *Louise Abbott*
Design   *Casebourne Rose Design Associates*
Assistant Editor   *Anne McDowall*
Editorial Assistants   *Simon Woods, Sophie Abbott,*
Samantha Murphy
Researchers   *Patrick Porritt, Ruth Sheard, Tara McTaggart,*
Darren Conquest
Wine Consultants   *David Gleave MW, Charles Metcalfe,*
Angela Muir MW, Anthony Rose,
Food Consultant   *Michael Stephenson*
Illustrations   *Sue Rose*
Cartographer   *Jonathan Phillips*
Indexer   *Jill Ford*

INTRODUCTION

Wine was one of the things no one ever taught me about at school. Like learning how to dance without stepping on anybody's toes, how to tell a weed from a baby geranium and how to match the right shoes to the right trousers, the trick of how to choose a bottle of wine was just one of those adult skills I was supposed to pick up as I went along. At first, though, wine seemed rather easier to bluff my way around than the dance floor; like most other people, I simply found a few styles I liked – red Rioja, Muscadet, Côtes du Rhône – and stuck to them.

But nevertheless I couldn't prevent my attention wandering across to all those other names on the wine list, to that bewildering parade of labels and bottle shapes on the off-licence shelf. What was I missing by playing safe?

So, I decided to learn about wine. And then almost gave up before I even began. The people who 'knew' about it all seemed the same to me – men (very few women were then acknowledged to be experts) who had all been to the right school, where they had presumably learned all about such impenetrable wine expressions as 'bouquet', 'elegant' and 'austere', and who knew without thinking whether a Bordeaux château was a third or fifth 'growth'.

But what I wanted to know was *why* the wines I liked tasted the way they did, why they all tasted so deliciously different from each other, and why their prices varied so widely. And when I went looking for the answers to these kinds of question, the pinstriped experts, as 'elegant' and 'austere' as they were themselves, didn't seem able to help me very much.

Then I met my first winemaker – a whiskery old Frenchman in Burgundy, with more chins than fingers. He spoke no English, and my schoolbook French was no match for the situation. But he was an enthusiast. As he drew a glassful of his wine from a barrel, sniffed it as if it were some new kind of flower and took a copious mouthful, licking his lips thoughtfully to savour every drop, he came alive. Eagerly, he led me out into the vineyard behind his house, trying to make me understand what it was that made his wine taste the way it did, and why he thought that the Chardonnay grape was the best variety in the world. Our communication difficulties seemed to melt away – here, at last, was someone who spoke my language.

That old Frenchman had probably rarely tasted a wine produced more than a few kilometres from his cellar door; the idea that winemakers in Australia might be making good wine from

the Chardonnay in almost precisely the same way, ageing it in the same kinds of barrels, made out of oak from the same French forests, as he was would almost certainly have made him break out in one of his rare, disbelieving smiles.

Today, the Burgundy from his estate – now made by his son – is sold in Britain alongside Chardonnays from Australia, California, Chile, Bulgaria, Italy and apparently almost everywhere else on earth.

But wherever it comes from and whatever grape it is made from, wine is all manner of things at once. On the one hand, it can be the most basic of drinks, served in French cafés from a cracked jug or, as in South America, from the waxed cartons we more often expect to contain milk. And on the other, in a dust-caked bottle with a scarcely-legible label, it can be an investment, an object of mystery to be sipped at with reverence.

And wine has a weird and unique relationship with time. If you can afford the few hundred thousand dollars it would cost, you could buy yourself a bottle of the wine Thomas Jefferson bought by the barrel two centuries ago. For a thousand dollars, you could have made a successful bid at the Sotheby's auction of pre-Revolutionary Russian wines from the Czar's own cellars.

For the price of a dinner for two in a London restaurant, you can still buy a bottle of 1963 port, made at a time when the world was still reeling from the news of Kennedy's assassination. And even when you spend a modest £3 or so on a 1989 Cabernet Sauvignon from Bulgaria or Hungary, you're buying wine made from grapes that were picked by men and women whose harvest songs celebrated the taste of freedom.

Old wine buffs reminisce about the 'good old days' when 2/3d would buy a pint of vintage port and still leave change for a glass or two of Lafite, but it is the wine drinkers of the 1990s who can have the greater fun – and the greater value for money.

In the pages that follow, we will travel around the world of wine, from grape to glass, from Albania to Zimbabwe, from the grandest of Bordeaux châteaux to the tiniest, most traditional estate in Chianti and the most high-tech of million-dollar wineries in California's Napa Valley. I can't say that the journey will turn you into an instant wine expert, but it will, I hope, give you confidence when buying your wine and more enjoyment in drinking it, as well as introducing you to thousands of different wines and producers and, most importantly, flavours.

Robert Joseph

Above: Burgundy is full of confusions. Did you know that Pouilly-Fuissé comes from two different villages?

Left: A classic in the making - new wine at Château Haut-Brion

Far left: A blend of new and old at the entrance to the tasting room at the Forestier winery in Brazil. Still almost unknown among wine drinkers in Europe, Brazil's winemakers are readying themselves to compete with their neighbours to the north and south in California and Chile

FROM OLD TO NEW

Some things never change. Thousands of years separate the couple depicted in the ancient Greek mosaic shown here from the group of cheerful grape-pickers photographed in Burgundy at the end of the great 1985 harvest. During that time man has mastered the art of walking on the moon, of flying at the speed of sound and of burning holes in the ozone layer. But the fundamental ways in which he enjoys eating and drinking haven't really altered at all.

Winemaking is probably the world's second oldest profession. For at least the last 7,000 years, wine of one kind or another has made people throughout most of the civilised world uproariously drunk, gloriously poetic and thoroughly romantic. More often than not, though, it has quite simply slaked their thirst and made them rather happy.

An essential thing to remember about wine is that, despite the eager efforts of the anti-alcohol campaigners to associate wine with tobacco and almost every other kind of health-endangering drug, it is – or at least it should be – one of the most natural substances man consumes.

Unlike cigarettes, which are a relatively sophisticated human invention, wine created itself. A grape is a self-contained, do-it-yourself winemaking kit; just crush it and leave the juice to its own devices and eventually, given half a chance, it will ferment into some sort of alcoholic, wine-like liquid. Man's only involvement in the process is to try to ensure that the liquid tastes good.

No one knows quite when man first discovered that grapes turned into wine, but it could have been at any time since he was capable of picking and appreciating fruit. According to one legend, it was Noah who, soon after grounding his ark in what we would now call Turkey, noticed that one of his flock of goats was behaving even more giddily than usual. Watching the animal closely, he discovered that it was getting its kicks by nibbling at a vine whose grapes had begun to ferment in the sun. Noah became not only the first winemaker, but also the first wine drinker; as the Bible says, he 'planted a vineyard: and he drank of the wine, and was drunken; and he was uncovered within his tent...'

The Persians agree that the joys of wine were discovered by accident, but disagree on the sex of the discoverer. King Jamshid apparently used to store grapes in jars where they were supposed to turn into raisins that could be eaten during the winter. One jar was set aside as poisonous because its contents were frothy, and it was from this unprepossessing liquid that a young girl, bent on suicide, drew what she thought would be her last drink. Needless to say, a few sips were enough to give her a taste for both life and wine. From those earliest vintages in what we now call the Middle East, and the first attempts at winemaking in Soviet Georgia – where vines are thought to have been cultivated by man in 5,000 BC – the story of wine has unfolded alongside the history of most of the civilised world.

Egypt has never enjoyed a particularly dazzling international reputation for its wines, though archaeologists know they have been made for at least 3,000 years. Nor, for that matter, has China. Vines were imported here from Persia in 128 BC; Marco Polo enjoyed drinking their fruits in the 13th century. However, many of the other regions we know today, such as Bordeaux, the Rhine and Mosel, had already been established by the time the Romans arrived in Britain in 55 AD.

The Romans took both their wines and their winemaking skills with them wherever they went, even planting vines in England – in Wiltshire, Gloucestershire and London – in an attempt to save the trouble of importing wine from other parts of the empire. (Unfortunately for those who claim a Roman heritage for English wine, archaeological remains suggest that, then as now, imported wine – principally from Italy, Spain and Germany, and possibly Bordeaux – was far more popular than the stuff made in the English vineyards.)

A thousand years later, in 1154, King Henry II married Eleanor of Aquitaine and took control of the part of France that would later be known as the greatest wine region on earth. Although that region fell out of English hands 300 years later, the relationship was established and 'claret' became the 'Englishman's drink' it has always remained. Indeed, in the mid-13th century, imports of Bordeaux wine reached the heady figure of over 30 million bottles per year.

As countries and regions quarrelled, made treaties and expelled their religious minorities, wine travelled. While the English pursued their love affair with Bordeaux, the Belgians were introduced to Burgundy when, during that Duchy's brief heyday, its dukes extended their territory to take in almost all of Flanders.

Throughout this time, most vineyards were in the hands of the church – which explains why English winemaking came to such an abrupt halt in the 16th century when Henry VIII dissolved the monasteries, and why, 200 years later, many of France's wine regions were thrown into such turmoil by the anti-clerical decrees of the Revolution.

Politics of another kind helped to create a wholly new style of wine when, following a falling out between England and France in the 17th century, the importing of claret was banned and the merchants had to look elsewhere for their red wine. The country they turned to was Portugal, and the wine they found and fortified to make it more stable for the long sea journey home was port.

Port was thus essentially an English invention – hence the survival today of British-owned port houses such as Cockburn, Dows and Taylor's. But this was not the only fortified wine into which the British were dipping their toes. In Jerez, merchants named Williams, Humbert and Harvey created the market for sherry; in Madeira it was a soldier called Blandy; in Marsala, a Liverpudlian called Woodhouse.

It was also the English – and more particularly the Irish – who built up some of the best estates in Bordeaux, as is clear from the names of such illustrious châteaux as Lynch-Bages, Léoville-Barton, Smith-Haut-Lafitte and Cantenac-Brown.

Elsewhere, immigrants from a wide range of countries began making wine in the New World. In Australia's Barossa Valley, some of the winemakers still speak a dialect of German; in New Zealand, after pioneering work by an Englishman called Busby, it was Yugoslavian gum-diggers who made the first commercial wines; and in California, newcomers such as Joe Heitz, Robert Mondavi and Paul Masson soon had wine-making roots just about everywhere.

By the late 19th century, political disputes notwithstanding, it appeared as though nothing could stop the progress of wine-making and the trading of wine throughout the western world. Then disaster struck – in the shape of a tiny louse, *Phylloxera vastatrix*, whose ideal diet consisted of fresh vine roots.

In its native North America, phylloxera caused little damage; there was almost no wine being produced and much of what was made came from a species of vine that was naturally resistant to the louse. The moment it arrived in Europe, however, the louse started behaving like a cake addict in a pâtisserie. Gradually but inexorably, it munched its way across the continent.

For years the Europeans vainly sought ways to counter it, before finally admitting defeat and accepting that the only way they could protect their livelihood was by grafting the types of

LEFT, ABOVE: Pickers celebrate the end of the harvest in Volnay

LEFT, BELOW: Ancient mosaics like this one in Cyprus offer ample evidence of the way wine was enjoyed in the past

ABOVE: The way wine is made and drunk may not have changed much, but storage tanks like these at Cooks in New Zealand might still surprise a Rip Van Winkle winemaker who had missed the developments of the last 100 years

vine they had traditionally grown onto the same kind of resistant stock that flourished naturally in North America, and completely replanting their vineyards. Since the beginning of this century, almost every vine in the world – with the exception of those planted in a few vineyards that enjoy some kind of natural protection (the phylloxera louse hates sand, for example) – has been grafted onto American rootstock.

The provision of resistant rootstock was the Americans' first contribution to the way wine was made around the world. During this century, since the repeal of Prohibition in 1933, the influence of America – to be more precise, California – has been felt almost everywhere; it is the Californians, more than anyone else, who have developed grape-growing and winemaking from a form of agriculture into a science.

But although the number of places where wine is produced has increased enormously, and scientific knowledge and equipment have enabled modern wineries to make more and better wine more consistently than in the past, the fundamental principles are still the same as they were 3,000 years ago, when a man called Kha'y was producing wine for Tutankhamun.

To make good wine, you need the right kind of grapes, the right piece of land, the right climate and the right skills. Today, a Californian winemaker who talks proudly about his new French oak barrels is, in fact, using pretty much the same kind of casks as the Romans. Some things never change.

THE GRAPES

The flavour of any wine will depend on its primary ingredient, the grape. Or, to be more precise, the variety of grape.

There are about 20 different species within the grape vine family, but only one, *Vitis vinifera*, seems to be any good for making wine (though *Vitis labrusca* makes passable wine in the Americas, none of it is of any great quality). And inside this one species there are some 4,000 varieties. So, you might suppose, wine could have 4,000 different flavours? No. Although scientists have isolated thousands of different flavour traces present in wine, there are only as few as 50 grape varieties which can really give a recognisable taste to wine, and less than half of these are of anything more than local importance.

The names of some of these varieties, however, would seem strange to the winemakers of a couple of centuries ago, who, accustomed to growing the grape varieties of their ancestors, might view some of today's hybrids and clones with as great an astonishment and suspicion as we might have for a blue rose. But just as 20th-century man has mastered the way in which the most successful beef herds should be bred and apples grown, so he has also not only isolated and husbanded the most successful types of grape variety — as clones — but also, by crossing, developed completely new vines.

To many people, some of these hybrids — heavy-cropping, dull-tasting — are about as welcome an arrival as the Golden Delicious apple. Properly used, however, and in well-judged blends, these grapes — such as the Müller-Thurgau — have permitted winemakers to produce a regular stream of reliable, if sometimes unexciting wine. It is varieties such as these which have at last made it possible for English wine-growers to make successful and more reasonably priced wines.

Vine growing is not unlike gardening. The answer 'lies in the soil'. And just as you can't grow roses in a sunless garden with unsuitable soil, most varieties of vine have historically proven to have strong preferences as to where they like growing.

The Pinot Noir, for example, is a notoriously finicky grape. For years it has resisted attempts to turn it into successful wine anywhere other than Burgundy. Only now does it seem that suitable homes may have been found for it — in places as far from the heart of France as Oregon and New Zealand. The Cabernet Sauvignon, on the other hand, is happily grown almost anywhere that is reasonably warm. And the Chardonnay is equally at home on the famous Kimmeridgian limestone of Chablis, the chalk of Champagne and the clay — you can almost taste the heaviness of the soil in the wine — of California.

In many areas of the world, great importance is attached to the mixture of varieties. This is particularly true in Bordeaux, where clarets are almost always blends of two or more grape varieties, principally the Cabernet Sauvignon, Merlot and Cabernet Franc. And most countries' wine laws (Germany being a notable exception) approve and proscribe certain varieties for each of their designated quality wine areas, based on experience of what grows best there, so that only certain grapes — or blends of grapes — may be used to produce a wine labelled with that appellation.

Such laws do a good job, overall, in protecting regional styles and typicity — an invaluable aid to the wine drinker. But there are loopholes. In Italy, for example, adventurous winemakers are producing some superb wines from unauthorised grape varieties — but, because they are stepping outside Italy's wine laws, may only label them as humble *vini da tavola*.

In the New World, producers have started an infectious trend for 'varietal' wines — sold simply under the name of the grape from which they are made (though the growers of Alsace have been quietly doing just this for centuries). In most cases the grapes they have chosen to grow are the classic, or 'noble' varieties from the great wine areas of Europe. But, thankfully for those of us who want as much variety as possible in the wines we drink, not all winemakers in these 'new' areas use these classic grapes merely to mimic the classic European styles. In Australia, for example, growers have discovered that Bordeaux's Sémillon — known in that region as the grape for great sweet white wines, and as a good mate for the Sauvignon in dry ones — can produce big, rich, dry wines, rivalling the Chardonnay.

The key to all this effort lies not only in the choice of the right grape for the particular piece of soil and climate, but in knowing how best to turn that particular grape into wine. With the exception of California, where a living can be made as a grower selling to wineries, most of the world's winegrowers have to be winemakers too. Or vice versa. Which is a little like a farmer having to harvest his corn, grind it into flour, and then bake that flour into perfect bread. It's little wonder that the French vigneron looks at his cattle-tending neighbour and wrily envies him his easy life.

Red Grape Varieties

Barbera

A grape native to *Piedmont*, but probably now the most prolifically grown throughout *Italy*, and second in importance there only to the Nebbiolo. However, it has in recent years suffered a slump in popularity and prestige, and many growers are replanting — a pity, because the grape can make good, fruity, chewy wines, with firm acidity, which need far less ageing than many quality Italian reds to show at their best. It's also very versatile, lending itself to a myriad of styles; light or full, dry or sweet, rosé and *frizzante* — even *spumante* — wine.

Some *Californian* producers, tired of the French grape bandwagon that grinds remorselessly through that state, are having great, if unappreciated success with the Barbera; it is also found in *South America* and *Yugoslavia*.

Cabernet Franc

A lesser grape than its 'noble' brother, the Cabernet Sauvignon, the Franc usually makes wine with less colour and tannin than the Cabernet Sauvignon, tasting like a rather 'greener', 'grassier' version of that grape. Imagine the smell of blackcurrant leaves, or the taste of unripe blackcurrant fruit, and you're well on the way to recognising Cabernet Franc; or possibly Cabernet Sauvignon grown in a cool climate or picked early.

It is grown throughout *Bordeaux*, to be used in blends with the Cabernet Sauvignon, Merlot, Malbec and Petit Verdot, and is particularly important in the Merlot-dominated vineyards of *Pomerol* and *St Emilion*, where some properties (most notably Château Cheval Blanc) make superb wine using it and the Merlot alone from vineyards unsuited to the Cabernet Sauvignon.

In the *Loire*, both Cabernets are grown and often blended to make red and rosé wines labelled simply as 'Cabernet'. These blends can be delicious; but the big names in Loire reds, *Chinon* and *Bourgueil*, are pure Cabernet Franc, as are, the locals say, the best wines of the *Touraine* region. Here the grape can take on notes of raspberry and strawberry, particularly when it is used in the region's sparkling rosés, most notably *Saumur*.

In Italy, the Cabernet Franc is grown throughout the north, making wines which are dry and light but seem almost sweet in their ripeness. Look out for Grave del Friuli.

Cabernet Sauvignon

The king of red grapes. In the *Médoc*, in *Bordeaux*, it is blended with the softer Merlot to produce some of the world's finest, most complex, longest-lived (and most expensive) wines, rich yet dry, tasting of blackcurrants and cedarwood, with the tannic backbone necessary for long life deriving from the grapes' thick skins.

Possibly the most widely planted — in terms of distribution, not quantity — grape in the world, it makes reliable wine wherever it will ripen. Perhaps surprisingly, it is little seen in France outside Bordeaux, except for the *Loire*, where the cooler climate gives it a grassier tang and, many tasters claim, a char-

FACING PAGE: Freshly picked Pinot Noir and Chardonnay grapes in Burgundy. Both these varieties are also used in Champagne

ABOVE: Cabernet Sauvignon grapes in Margaux after hot, dry weather. This drying-out of the skins will make for wines with more evident tannin

acteristic note of green pepper. In *Italy* it is increasingly used, and increasingly successful; Italian wine laws often preclude its wines, and the blends in which it is used, from carrying any designation other than *vino da tavola*, but some — particularly the 'super-Tuscans' made by *Chianti* estates who wish to use more Cabernet Sauvignon than the 10% permitted under the Chianti label — are nevertheless becoming increasingly sought-after.

Progressive producers in *Spain* and *Portugal*, and even *Greece*, are using the grape to great effect too, but the most remarkable European Cabernet Sauvignon success story of recent years has been *Bulgaria*, both in its inexpensive, simple, jammy form and in some rather more serious examples from, for example, the Sakar Mountain region.

Not surprisingly, most New World winemakers — in *California*, *South Africa*, *Australia* and *New Zealand* — want to succeed with it, and the grape has shown itself remarkably amenable to their efforts. New World Cabernets range from the ultra-classy to the jammily simple, depending on the prevailing climate and style of winemaking. As a rule, however, Australia makes big, approachable Cabernet, California a more tannic style and New Zealand light, green, grassy examples.

Carignan

A black grape widely used for table and dessert wines, mainly in the *south of France*. Though lacking any precise flavour, it is used in many *Rhône* appellations, in *Provençal* rosés and in red and rosé *Languedoc* wines, being the major grape used for *Fitou* — one of the best wines of the region — and the strong, full-bodied *Minervois* and *Corbières*.

The grape is also grown in a variety of hot-climate regions, for example *South America*, *North Africa* and *Israel*; it is also widely planted in *southern Spain* and more particularly in the Cariñena area of Aragon, where it is said to have originated.

Cinsault

Grown in almost exactly the same countries as the Carignan, this is a similarly useful, but if anything even less interesting grape, imparting no more than a spicy, attractive warmth to blends. It is one of the parents of the Pinotage cross grown in *New Zealand* and *South Africa*, where the Cinsault is also widely grown, though here it is confusingly known as the Hermitage. A blend of Cabernet, Syrah and Cinsault is proving successful for *Australian* and *southern French* producers, and for Serge Hochar of Château Musar in the *Lebanon*.

Dolcetto

The Gamay of Italy's *Piedmont* region, making cheerful, full, fruity reds which can be drunk young or after a little wood-ageing and don't tax the intellect or the pocket too much. Its wines are often named after the grape — for example, Dolcetto d'Alba — and it is also used to make Lambrusco-style *frizzante* wine, though this is rarely encountered outside Italy.

Gamay

Gamay is *Beaujolais*. How it is that it can be delicious when grown in a hilly region south of Burgundy, but flat and soupy virtually everywhere else, is a mystery. But in Beaujolais, the Gamay makes a stunningly fresh red which, even when it isn't labelled '*Nouveau*', epitomises new, youthful wine. The colour ranges from darkest pink to medium red, and an unusually blue pigment in the grapes' skins gives young Beaujolais a charac-teristic violet hue. Its acidity is high, and its taste a mouthful of almost any fresh, ripe red fruit, though cherry is a frequently-found flavour. Gamay is best drunk young, though some of the Beaujolais *crus* age well; with maturity, the Gamay takes on chocolatey-raspberry flavours not dissimilar to the Pinot Noir, to which it is thought to be related.

Passable Gamay can also be found in the *Loire*, most success-fully as *Gamay de Touraine* and, curiously, blended with Pinot Noir in *Switzerland*. It is grown in *northern Italy, Eastern Europe* and, in tiny quantities, *California*, though most of the wines make one wonder why.

Grenache

With the Cinsault grape, this provides the big, soft, easy reds and rosés of the *south of France*. Widely planted in the *Rhône*, it contributes, on average, a full-flavoured, ripely alcoholic 60% of any *Châteauneuf-du-Pape* and, with the Syrah, is the chief component of *Côtes du Rhône*. Elsewhere in this region, it is at its most characterful in the herby rosés of *Provence, Lirac* and *Tavel*, where its essentially peppery tang also occasionally shows through, and in the extraordinary red dessert wines of *Banyuls* in Roussillon.

This pepperiness will also be recognised by *Rioja* fans; grown widely in *Spain*, it is known there as the Garnacha and, together with the Tempranillo, is one of Rioja's major grapes. *California* also uses the variety to make 'blush' rosés.

Merlot

Merlot wines are buttery, plummy, toffeed and sometimes slightly minty too. Almost always soft, they can be dull or delicious. Used throughout *Bordeaux* and now elsewhere to temper the tough Cabernet Sauvignon, the Merlot dominates the *St Emilion* and *Pomerol* regions with, in good winemaking hands, its intense, supple, velvety fruit; Château Pétrus, which commands prices higher than any Médoc *premier cru*, is 95% Merlot. Outside France, any country growing Cabernet Sauvi-gnon will usually grow Merlot too. The *Italians* have been doing so for longer than most, vinifying it singly to make light, juicy wines (as do *Eastern European* winemakers) and, more re-cently, blending it with Cabernet to make wines with more depth and complexity.

New World winemakers, having triumphed with the Caber-net, are also cottoning on to the idea of blending it with the Merlot, particularly in *California* and *Australia*, and are increas-ingly using it as a single varietal. Likewise, *Washington State* and *New Zealand* are both having success with varietal wines from this attractive grape.

Mourvèdre

Originally from *Spain*, this black grape is now most commonly found in the *south of France*, contributing colour and spice to

Châteauneuf-du-Pape, and making solid, fruity, 'café' wines in many other Rhône appellations. In *Provence*, it provides the fruit in the wines of *Cassis, Palette* and, notably, *Bandol*, whose fresh, spicy reds are best drunk young. It has been introduced to the *Languedoc* to improve its *vins de pays*, is also grown in *Algeria*, and can occasionally now be found in *California*.

Nebbiolo

Italy's answer to the Syrah — but more so, making tremen-dously black, dry, tannic wines in the *Piedmont* hills, often hard to enjoy when young, but with age emerging as some of Italy's best wines — *Barolo* and *Barbaresco*. Rich, with incredibly complex bouquets, their flavour is a unique, chocolatey, pruney sweetness — rather like long-forgotten homemade jam. More approachable versions are produced — Nebbiolo d'Alba, for example; elsewhere in Italy, the Nebbiolo swaggers under tough, provocative names like Spanna, Grumello and Inferno.

Pinot Meunier

So-called because the leaves are powdery white underneath, as if dusted with flour (*meunier* is French for 'miller'), this is an inferior strain of the Pinot Noir whose use is no longer allowed in Burgundy, though it does still make rosés in the *Loire*, and is used in *Champagne* blended with Pinot Noir and Chardon-nay. It is also grown in *England*, where it is known either as Wrotham Pinot or Dusty Miller.

Pinot Noir

Probably the world's most sulky and infuriating variety, only in

LEFT: Unripe Merlot grapes at Château Ausone, one of the greatest châteaux in St Emilion, traditional home of this variety

BELOW: Grenache grapes being unloaded in the Rhône, where they will give their peppery flavour to Côtes du Rhône and Tavel Rosé

RIGHT: Baby vines at Brown Brothers in Victoria, Australia. In Australia, as in Europe, almost all newly–planted vines are grafted onto American rootstock, which is resistant to phylloxera

Burgundy does the Pinot Noir regularly deliver the goods. An agoraphobic grape, it hates to stray outside its Burgundian home, as New World producers, anxious to emulate France's most aristocratic of red wines, are discovering. Ironically, Burgundy is one of France's rare great reds that qualify under the New World's favoured banner, the 'varietal' wine; this single grape takes all the credit for every great (and less good) red of the *Côte d'Or*, as well as the slightly less fine wines of the *Côte Chalonnaise* to the south. Fine Burgundian Pinot Noir displays extraordinary delicacy and elegance, and characteristic flavours of wild raspberry, strawberry and, occasionally, black cherry when young. With age, it takes on chocolatey, gamey, 'farm-yard' overtones.

If a *Champagne* has raspberry-chocolatey flavours there's a good chance that it contains a fair proportion of Pinot Noir. In this northerly region of France, most producers don't even begin to try to turn the grape into a red wine, but blend its clear juice with that of the Chardonnay to spectacular effect.

In all but the very warmest years *Alsace* and the *Loire* make thin but passable reds from this variety, but vinify it far more successfully as rosé, particularly in *Sancerre*. In *Oltrepò Pavese* the Italians coax it into giving light, smoky, Burgundian-style reds; in *Germany* and *Switzerland* it also makes light, often almost rosé wines.

The New Worlders persevere, in *California, Australia, New Zealand, South Africa* and *Oregon*, on their uphill task. Their chief problem is that, in their generally hotter climates, the grape just makes soupy wine. The trick, as an increasing number are discovering, is to choose areas that are just too cool for the Cabernet Sauvignon.

Sangiovese

Chianti, Brunello di Montalcino and *Vino Nobile di Montepulciano* would be lost without this *Tuscan* grape, which proliferates throughout Italy yet only achieves greatness in these wines. Its quality and complexity varies between the three, largely because the Sangiovese presents one of the earliest illustrations of what is now called 'cloning' — specific vine-types having been isolated and jealously husbanded in their Tuscan sub-region or even individual estate. Biondi-Santi in Montalcino has for centuries had its own, unique strain of the grape for its Brunello; many other Chianti producers are improving their own quality clones.

At its best, the Sangiovese — or the Sangioveto or Morellino, as two of its clones are known — can be the most exciting,

herby-spicy grape in Italy. However, only the best of its wines can take being aged.

Syrah

Black, tannic wine, tasting of smoke, tar and creosote, but inside the forbidding frame lurks a deep, sweet, raspberry richness, needing age to show itself. The Syrah, used throughout *southern France* to give colour and body to blends, is vinified singly to give the great reds of the *northern Rhône, Hermitage* and *Côte Rôtie*, where its fruit can take on almost Cabernet Sauvignon-like characteristics within the framework of these deep, smoky wines. However, the Syrah demands much more of the skills of the winemaker than does the Cabernet. It also needs a hot climate, and as such is widely grown in *Australia*, where it is vinified either 'neat', as in Penfolds' great Grange, or in blends with the Cabernet Sauvignon. More recently a number of wineries in *California* have introduced the Syrah — to much critical acclaim.

Tempranillo

A pale, soft grape which, when aged in new oak barrels, gives red *Rioja* its character. But it can also be found all over *Spain* under a variety of names, and explains the soft, relatively light, toffeeish taste of much Spanish red. In the hands of a gifted winemaker like Miguel Torres, who uses it as a Merlot-like foil to the Cabernet Sauvignon, it shows at its best, but such producers are rare, particularly in Spain.

The Tempranillo can also be found in *Portugal*, where it is occasionally used for port, and in *Argentina*, where it changes character to produce rather hefty, rough wine. Plantations of it in *France* are on the increase.

Zinfandel

Thank goodness *California* has something to call its own — this is it. A black grape, which some think could be the Italian Primitivo, though others say Yugoslavia may have been its homeland, it is used and abused in California, so abundant is it, and performs the great vinous feat of being all things to all men. It makes jug wine, fine wine, red, white and rosé ('blush'), dry or sweet, still or sparkling, and even fortified wine.

But, when well treated, its best wines are bright, fruity reds which age into richer, spicy maturity. These come from the cooler areas, where the juice and fruit is not dried out. The grape is also found in small pockets in *Australia, South America* and *South Africa*.

White Grape Varieties

Aligoté
A *Burgundy* grape which makes freshly acidic and good, though not earth-shattering, still white wines that are generally named after the grape. These are best drunk young. The most traditional way to drink Aligoté is with cassis (blackcurrant liqueur) in the form of 'Kir'. In *Lorraine*, it is used in the production of *vin gris*, the traditional light rosé of the area, and in *Switzerland*, in the canton around Geneva, produces lovely light whites which are rarely seen overseas — dry and rather *pétillant*. It is also grown for still whites in *Romania* and *Russia*.

Alvarinho
A *Vinho Verde* bearing the name of this grape is likely to be a cut above the rest: recognised as producing the finest wines of Portugal's northerly Moncão region, it gives not only the dry, lively freshness that Vinho Verde should (though it all too rarely does) have, but also imparts more complex flavours and higher alcohol, in part due to the fact that it is, for Portugal, a low-yielding variety. In *Spain* it is known as the Albariño and is similarly successful, though sadly not very widely planted.

Bacchus
A cross derived from the Riesling, Sylvaner and Müller-Thurgau, displaying many of the characteristics of the last of these, but with a more pronounced, almost Muscatty grapiness. Grown throughout *Germany*, it is also proving successful for *England's* winemakers.

Chardonnay
By a whisker, the greatest of white wine grapes — and certainly currently the most fashionable. Now grown throughout the world, it is thought to have originated in the Lebanon; but it is in *Burgundy* that it has traditionally, and indisputably, achieved its finest potential. Even in this region, its flavours can vary enormously from village to village; butter and hazelnut in *Meursault;* the buttered-digestive-biscuit and ripe fruit of *Montrachet;* pineappley-fresh in the *Mâconnais;* flinty and steely in *Chablis*. When mature, fine Burgundian Chardonnay can also take on a not unpleasant rotty, vegetal richness. The grape also has a natural affinity with oak, which can lend a delicious, toasty complexity to the wine.

Elsewhere in France, the Chardonnay also achieves greatness in *Champagne*, to which it gives lightness and a yeasty, sometimes buttery fragrance. Here it can be vinified separately, without the depth provided by the Pinot Noir, to make *Blanc de Blancs*, a more delicate, refreshing style. It is grown in the *Loire* for still and sparkling wines, in the *Ardèche* and the *Jura*, and, by Listel, on the sands of the Mediterranean shore.

In *Eastern Europe*, the grape has yet to fulfil its hoped-for promise; in *Germany*, it can be found in various blends, but is often confused with the Weissburgunder — the Pinot Blanc. The same is true in *Italy*, where the muddling of the two grapes often obscures the fact that some fine Chardonnay is produced. *Switzerland* and *Austria* also make passable Chardonnay.

In *Spain*, the grape is increasingly used by forward-looking producers such as Raimat, Jean Léon and Torres, the last using it to give fatness and fruit to wine from the native Parellada grape. There are good Chardonnays being made in *South America*, *South Africa* and, increasingly, *New Zealand*, and even *India* is growing the variety for *méthode champenoise* wines, but it is in *North America* and *Australia* that world-class non-Burgundian Chardonnay is to be found.

The grape's quality, and its affinity wih oak, make it a natural choice for the *Californians*, who make richly oaky wines, packed with sweet, tropical fruit; these blockbusting flavours are also brought out by the warm climate of Australia. More European in style are the Chardonnays produced in America's *Pacific North-West* and *New York State*.

Chasselas
The widely-grown Chasselas produces rather ordinary, though pleasant white wines. It seems to do best in *Switzerland*, where it is known as the Dorin or Fendant and, in the *Vaud* region, makes some dry, sturdy whites. It's also grown on the west shore of Lake Geneva, at Neuchâtel in the north and in the *Valais*, where it is believed to have been introduced by mercenaries returning from France. It is grown in *Alsace*, is used for the dry *Pouilly-sur-Loire*, sparkling *Seyssel* in the *northern Rhône* and is found dotted throughout the north and centre of France. It is known as the Gutedel in *Germany* and grown chiefly in *Baden*; it is also found in *California*, under the name Chasselas Doré, and in *Algeria* and *Hungary*.

Chenin Blanc
One of the world's trickier grapes, but very widely planted. It ripens late and has a great deal of acidity, matched by relatively little taste. In the *Loire* it usually makes unexceptional dry whites, but its acidity and its vulnerability to botrytis — noble rot — provide the essential components for ageing and complexity in that region's great, sweet wines, in which the grape reveals honeyed, appley and apricotty flavours, and ocasionally a smell and taste of wet straw. It also makes an ideal, high-acid base for the Loire's fine sparkling wines.

A little Chenin is to be found in the *south-west of France*; elsewhere, the New World is its stamping ground. It makes vast quantities of unexciting wine in *North* and *South America* and *the Antipodes*; and some good, uncharacteristic, spicy wines in *South Africa*, where it is called the Steen. Some adventurous *Californian* and *Australian* producers are experimenting with oak-aged Chenin Blanc, with promising results.

Colombard
Originally from the *Charentais* in France, where it is still used in Cognac and Armagnac production, the Colombard is now grown in *south-west France* and *Provence* to make simple, fresh, fruity wines, some of which — for example, *vin de pays des Côtes de Gascogne* — can be excellent value. It has also been widely adopted in *California*, where it is blended in 'Chablis' and 'Rhine'-type wines, and also sparkling wine.

Gewürztraminer
One of the most difficult wines to sell, because of its unpronounceability, but one of the easiest grapes of all to recognise 'blind', with its perfumed (Parma violets), spicy, exotic fruit (lychee) smells and flavours and oily richness. Supposedly it is

a spicy variant of the Traminer grape of Italy's Alto Adige — hence the addition of the German word 'Gewürz', or 'spice'. There is now some confusion over the two names, which may be applied to the same grape; some Italian and New World labels opt for the more easily pronounced Traminer.

The Gewürztraminer is successfully grown in *Germany*, but is without doubt at its greatest in *Alsace*, particularly in the *vendange tardive* — late-picked — style. Outside France, in *Australia* and more particularly in *New Zealand*, some good Gewürz is being made in cooler areas. Experimentation with the grape is promising in *North America* and *Chile*, and in *Spain* it is a key component of Torres' delicious Viña Esmeralda.

Malvasia

The grape that produced the vat of Malmsey in which the Duke of Clarence drowned, the Malvasia still makes this rich, sweet wine on *Madeira*, but this originally Greek variety has also for centuries been grown in *Rioja*, where it not only makes good white wine but is also blended into some reds; the Malvasia is also used in this way in *France* and *Italy* — it is an ingredient of DOC *Chianti* — and now *California*.

It also makes a wide range of white wines in *Italy*, *Spain* and the *south of France* — dry and sweet, still and frothing — and is used in *Portugal* for white port. There are plantings, too, of this versatile grape in *South Africa* and *South America*.

Marsanne

Chiefly found in the *Rhône* valley, where it is used for the distinctive *Hermitage*, one of the longest-lived white wines in the world, and in *Côtes du Rhône*. It makes strong, fleshy whites in *Cassis* in *Provence*, and dry and sweet, still and sparkling *St-Péray*. Rare but good, fat *Australian* Marsanne can also be found, and it is widely planted (to little effect) in *Algeria*.

Moscatel

The Muscat's more workaday brother, with a wide variety of synonyms including Muscat of Alexandria, Gordo Blanco ('the big fat white one') and *South Africa*'s Hanepoot ('honeypot'). It is best used to produce sweet wines, often high in natural alcohol or fortified; some *Australian* late-harvest Muscats are made from this variety, as is the Portuguese *Moscatel de Setúbal*, Spain's *Malaga*, the dessert wines of *North Africa* and the French *vins doux naturels* of *Lunel* and *Rivesaltes*, which rarely compare with those of Beaumes de Venise and Frontignan, made from the 'true' Muscat, but can be powerful, if rather heavy-handed, good-value alternatives.

Müller-Thurgau

'Invented' in 1872 by a Dr Müller of Thurgau in Switzerland, who crossed Riesling and Sylvaner vines, this is *Germany*'s most widely planted grape and gives that soft, flowery gulpability to the great mass of ordinary Liebfraumilch and Niersteiner. It can be capable of more, sometimes managing a passable thumbnail sketch of the Riesling it would like to be, though with a touch of the 'cat's pee' smell more usually associated with Sauvignon Blanc. However, it is much to be regretted that so many German producers have felt themselves constrained to uproot their Riesling vines and plant this more manageable, heavy-cropping, rather dull newcomer in its stead.

Perversely, the better examples often come not from the variety's native land but from *England*, *north-east Italy* and *New Zealand*, where producers treat it with more care.

Muscat

More accurately called the *Muscat Blanc à Petits Grains*, this goes under a huge variety of names and is grown all over the world, though the wine it makes tends to share one overriding characteristic — it actually tastes of grapes.

In *Alsace* it is very dry, but as perfumed and crunchy-fresh as a bunch of the best from the hothouse in high summer. Rosenmuskateller wines from Italy's *Alto Adige* are less fat, but equally delicious and some pleasant dry Muscats have been made in the New World.

More successful here, though, as elsewhere outside Alsace, is the Muscat vinified to produce sweet, sometimes fortified wines. It can make some of the most distinctive styles in any country; the delicious, honeyed French Muscats of *Beaumes de Venise* and *Frontignan*; the golden, liquorous Greek Muscats of *Samos* and *Patras* and the lusciously powerful, often magnificent liqueur Muscats of *Australia*.

The Muscat is also used to make the mouthwateringly grapey French fizz, *Clairette de Die Tradition*, while *Piedmont* in Italy makes a variant on the grape, the Moscato, into deliciously sweet, much underrated 'playpen' sparkling wines, *Asti* and *Moscato Spumante*.

Muscat Ottonel

Just as *Eastern* and *Middle Europe* have an inferior version of the Riesling, the Welschriesling, so they make wine from this lesser version of the Muscat, the Ottonel. However, in *Austria*, where it is a particularly important variety, it can make fresh, pleasant wine, and it can also produce very acceptable dessert wines in *Romania*.

LEFT: Gewürztraminer vines in Alsace. Despite the pink colour of their skins, these grapes will produce white wine

RIGHT: Palomino grapes in Jerez, where they make great sherry and very dull table wine

Palomino

A *Spanish* grape which is enormously important in Jerez, where it is the principal variety for *sherry*, but grown all around the country for fair white table wine.

Pedro Ximénez

A very sweet *Spanish* grape, grown mainly in *Andalusia*. It makes strong, rich, dark dessert wines, often reaching 16° in alcohol, in *Malaga* and, sun-dried and concentrated, produces a sweetening wine for *sherry*. In *Moriles*, *Cordoba* and other areas of Spain it can be completely fermented to give dry, powerful aperitifs and table wines.

Pinot Blanc/Pinot Bianco

A grape found in almost every wine-growing region of the world and, nearly everywhere, producing different flavours and textures. In France, it is occasionally found in white *Burgundies*, but is at its rich, slightly nutty best in *Alsace* and in the *Jura*, where it makes the unusual *vin de paille*. It is becomingly increasingly popular in *Germany*, where it is used both for dry whites and the more traditional Germanic styles, and over the border in Italy's *Alto Adige* it makes some good, fragrant, dry wines. It is also used for Italian *spumante*, is on the increase in *Lombardy* and the *Marches*, is used in blends all over the central west of Italy and is currently thriving in *Puglia*. *California*, too, has seen rather more of it in recent years (it goes into the making of some Californian sparkling wines) and it is an important white grape variety in *Luxembourg*, *Austria*, *Chile*, *Hungary*, *Uruguay* and *Yugoslavia*.

Pinot Gris/Pinot Grigio/Tokay-Pinot Gris

In Italy and Alsace this is rapidly becoming a new superstar. As the Pinot Gris it makes pleasant rosés in *Touraine*, but as Tokay-Pinot Gris in *Alsace*, it produces lovely, full, golden wines, dry or slightly sweet, excellent with food. In *Germany* it makes good juicy wines in *Wurttemberg*, the *Rheinpfalz* and *Baden*, and is important, too, for the dry whites from Geneva and the soft dessert wines of the Valais in *Switzerland*. In *Italy*, 'neat' Pinot Grigios are deliciously fresh and, blended with Pinot Nero (Pinot Noir), it makes a lovely white from *Oltrepò Pavese*. It is also found in *Abruzzi*, and is creeping into the central west area. In *Mexico*, it makes the 'Hidalgo' wines, and it is also grown in the *Crimea* and for dessert wines in the *Murfatlar* vineyards of *Romania*.

Riesling

Chardonnay's only rival as the world's top white grape. Certainly it is more versatile, because it manages to make some of the world's greatest sweet wines as well as some of the steeliest and driest. In *Germany* virtually all the great wines, from dry

to sweet, are Riesling — the grape is thought to have originated in the Rhine Valley, hence its often-used pseudonyms, Rhine and Johannisberg Riesling.

Its flavours combine grape, apple and spice — sometimes baked apple (complete with brown sugar and cloves) can be a very apt description. The variety's great quality is its ability to preserve acidity while building up grapy, honeyed ripeness, enabling fine German wine to age and develop stunningly (and, to many people, surprisingly) well. When mature, really good Riesling can take on a spicy-oily character most usually, and accurately, described as 'petrolly' — and delicious.

The Riesling makes lovely, steely, lemon-fresh wine in Italy's *Trentino-Alto Adige* region, as it does, to a lesser extent, in *Austria* and *Switzerland*. The 'Riesling' grown in Eastern Europe, however, is almost invariably not this noble grape but the inferior Welschriesling (*q.v.*). Its French home is *Alsace*, where growers consider it their finest variety. Here it can make wine with all the freshness, fruit and complexity of German Riesling, but with added weight and dry, fatty fullness.

The Californians would like to make Riesling, but the grape is unhappy in their climate, tending only to give of its best in regions with chilly, crisp winters. A late ripener, it is also intolerant of too much rain. Grown throughout *South America*, however, it finds the high-altitude vineyards of *Chile* congenial; it also makes good wine in *New York State*'s Finger Lakes area; it is to be found in other US states as diverse as *Michigan* and *Colorado*, and on Canada's *Niagara* peninsula.

Elsewhere, *Australia* and *New Zealand* are proving the most successful countries, the latter making characterful, green-fresh wine often sold very shortly after the harvest, the former leaner, flintier wine to be kept longer, often becoming smoky with age.

Sauvignon Blanc

The last decade has seen a minor upsurge in popularity for this simple, fresh grape, with the greenest flavour of them all. Few are the restaurants whose wine lists do not include a *Sancerre* or the finer, smoky-flavoured *Pouilly Fumé*, which, together with their *Loire* neighbours *Quincy*, *Rully*, *Ménétou-Salon* and, on a simpler level, *Touraine*, have long made a virtue of its uncluttered, gooseberry-flinty flavour, which combines the freshness of newly-mown grass with a hint of blackcurrant fruit or, more commonly, blackcurrant leaf.

In *Bordeaux*, too, it has for centuries been used in blends with the Sémillon and Muscadelle in the dry whites of the *Graves* and the dessert wines of *Sauternes*. However, it is increasingly (some say less pleasantly) being vinified as a single variety, not only for its own inherent qualities but in response to the huge growth in demand for wines bearing the name Sauvignon on their label. This can be attributed to the espousal of the variety by New World winemakers, and the success they have had in producing varietal Sauvignon Blanc — sometimes called Fumé Blanc, particularly by the *Californians*, who often make it slightly sweet. They and the *South Africans* make wine from the grape in two styles — lemon-fresh or oaky, honeyed and rather heavy. The *Australians* and *Chileans* have yet to completely master the grape; more successful than all but the very best winemakers in these countries have been the *New Zealanders*. The grape seems ideally suited to their climate, producing stunning wines the equal of the best Sancerre and Pouilly Fumé.

LEFT: Rhine Riesling at Orlando's Steingarten vineyard in the Barossa Valley, where this variety makes wine that is quite unlike the Rieslings of Germany

RIGHT: After the crush, the skins and pips – the 'marc' – are used as fertiliser. In some regions, they are also used in the making of brandy

Scheurebe

A Riesling/Sylvaner cross invented in 1916 by George Scheu, this *German* grape makes wine with good fruit and acidity, with a pronounced smell and taste of grapefruit. It used in blends, but is often made into a varietal wine, particularly in the *Auslese* style. *English* winemakers are now growing it successfully.

Sémillon

A split-personality grape, as capable of flabby old table wine, in various regions of France and most of the southern hemisphere, as it is of reaching buttery heights in *Australia*'s *Hunter* and *Barossa Valley*s; exquisite, complex sweetness in *Sauternes*; flinty greenness in cool *New Zealand*; elegant, golden dry wine in *Bordeaux* and great dessert styles in the neighbouring regions of *south-west France*.

The environment and prevailing climate exert enormous influence over this variety. Its thin skin makes it susceptible to rot, which in certain areas, obviously, is welcomed; Sauternes would never have achieved greatness as a style without the rich, unctuous, golden-sweet wine from shrivelled, botrytised Sémillon grapes. *California* winemakers are having some success in emulating this style, though they have had to search hard for vineyard areas where conditions come close to matching Sauternes' unique, delicately balanced micro-climate.

Sylvaner

A big grape in terms of planting and production, but a minor variety as regards quality. Its flavour can be rather bland, and its chief virtue is its ability to provide body and firmness in blends, for which purpose it is widely used in *Eastern Europe*. Its best wines are made in *Alsace* (where it is increasingly rare); *Germany* (particularly in *Franken*); Italy's *Alto Adige, Switzerland* and *Austria*, thought to be its country of origin.

Trebbiano/Ugni Blanc

Italy and *southern France* (where it is called the Ugni Blanc) are heavily planted with this grape, which is one of the most important in Europe in terms of production figures, but not, alas, in quality. It may make superlative Cognac in the Charentais, but it is difficult to make table wine from the Trebbiano that is not neutral in flavour — hence the vine is the mainstay of white French plonk and Italian whites like *Orvieto, Soave* and *Frascati*. A good wine from any of these appellations will owe very little to the Trebbiano, and much to a skilful winemaker who has blended it with more flavoursome varieties: look also for *Tuscany*'s *Galestro*, or the superior French dry whites of *Bandol* and *Palette*.

Verdelho

A *Portuguese* grape which lends its name to a delicious, dry style of *Madeira*, the variety is also used in its native country for dry table wine and white port. In *Australia*, where it is often spelt Verdello, it produces some good, dry, lime-flavoured wines.

Viognier

This white *French* grape gives weight to the maxim that 'the best things come in small packages'. Planted in only 80 acres, nearly all in the *Rhône* at *Château Grillet* and *Condrieu*, it produces golden wines whose aroma enthusiasts have likened to peaches and apricots. However, canny producers in other countries are latching on to its potential — it is beginning to appear in *California*, and is the subject of experimentation in *Tuscany*.

Welschriesling

In *Hungary*, where it is called the Olasz Rizling, and in *north-east Italy*, as the Riesling Italico, this grape can produce some sprightly, floral whites; in *Austria*, it is used not only for light, perfumed dry wines but, when attacked by noble rot, for their versions of *Germany*'s rich, sweet, late-picked styles. But it should never be mistaken for true Rhine Riesling, though its wealth of pseudonyms do their best to encourage confusion; most Welschriesling is at its best acceptable, quaffing 'party wine' — for example, *Yugoslavia*'s Laski Rizling, when well-made — and at its worst, a flabby, sugary disgrace.

HOW WINE IS MADE

Wine is, of course, an alcoholic drink made from grapes. Freshly-gathered grapes, that is, fermented in the region where they grow. In Britain, the word is used to describe alcoholic drinks made from rhubarb or elderflowers as well – anything that will ferment, in fact – but these 'country wines' are not really wines in the strictest sense of the word, any more than are 'British' wines, made from grape concentrate imported from abroad. Wine must be made from grapes, and it is important that these grapes be fresh.

From vine to bottle, the process of winemaking is a natural one. *Vitis vinifera*, the wine-making vine species, holds in each berry everything necessary for perfect fermentation into wine.

Quite simply, during fermentation, yeast attacks sugar and converts it into alcohol and carbon dioxide. Look at any grape, and you will see a whitish bloom on the skin (this is easier to see on black grapes). This waxy substance contains millions of yeast cells.

Bite through the skin and you will immediately taste a fruity sweetness – and there you have your sugar. Normally, hanging in bunches on the vine, these two cataclysmic components are kept apart. But pick the bunch and gently crush the grapes, and the two come into contact with each other and start to react.

When tasting a grape – any grape – you will notice that the skin itself will seem bitter, as will the stalk. This bitterness comes from tannin, which is particularly important in making red wines intended to mature, because it acts as a preservative. If you accidentally bite into the pip, you will regret it. The taste is very sharp, and so care is taken never to crush the pips when making wine.

Left alone, grape juice will ferment either until all the sugar has been used up, or the level of alcohol becomes so high that it kills off the remaining yeasts. Very sweet grapes, with a high concentration of sugar, are therefore capable of producing pretty strong wine; if the sugar level is exceptional, this wine will be alcoholic and sweet as well. More usually, the sugar has all been used up before the alcohol represents more than 8-12%

Above: Pruning in Champagne. The way in which this frequently miserable winter task is performed can make all the difference between intense and dilute-flavoured wine

Below: The decision on when to pick depends on the sugar content of the grapes; here, in the Alto Adige in Italy, Herbert Tiefenbrunner measures the sweetness of his Müller-Thurgau

(average strength), making a naturally dry wine. Sometimes sweetness is put back after the yeasts have been filtered out to produce a cheaper type of low- or average-strength medium or sweet wine.

There are all sorts of ways of influencing vinification to achieve a particular style of wine. The job of the winemaker is a very important one, because he can alter the course of nature to make good, indifferent or even bad wine. But nothing he does influences the taste as much as the raw materials and the conditions in which they are grown.

The variety, or varieties, of grapes (wines are often blends of more than one type) used for making any wine influence the flavour substantially. If you were to taste several single-variety wines, the differences would be apparent – just as it would if you tasted the different grapes from which the wines were made.

Like most living things (ourselves included) grapes consist largely of water, and so, in turn, does wine. The water content of a grape originates from the soil in which the vine has planted its roots. Different soil types therefore affect the taste of wine as well. Around the world, the structure of the earth varies considerably. Conditions may repeat themselves, but often a particular region's geology is unique and accounts for the individuality of its wine.

The climatic conditions demanded by winemaking vines are pretty precise. Ideally, winters should be cold – cold enough for the vine to lie dormant and conserve all its growing energy until the spring. In the spring the vine flowers, and from this moment until the harvest the most important element is the sun. But not too much sun; no temperate fruit responds well to too much luxury. Too long or hot a blast encourages growth to be too prolific and too quick to concentrate the subtleties of flavour. Look at French Golden Delicious apples, for example, grown in ceaselessly hot southern sun; cotton wool compared to the complex flavours of a delicious English Cox.

So the wine-producing regions of the world lie in two quite sharply-defined bands around the globe; the moderate, temperate zones between 50° and 30° in the northern hemisphere, and 30° and 50° in the southern hemisphere. Within these bands, in general, fine wines are made in the cooler areas furthest removed from the equator, leaving the hotter terrain for the production of high-yield wines of lower quality.

Because the best vineyards are sited in relatively cool areas, to prevent the vine from over-stretching itself, maximum use must be made of the precious – sometimes elusive – summer sun. To make wine, enough sugar must be present in the grape to be converted, by yeast, into alcohol. And the sugar content is put in the grapes by the sun. So the best location for a vineyard in the northern hemisphere is normally on a south-facing slope which, from dawn until dusk, catches as many of the sun's rays as possible. (The principle is the same as a sun-worshipper lying on a raked sun bed).

Hot Country or Cool Country?

Hot countries yield riper grapes, which in turn make wine with a greater weight of flavour and a higher level of alcohol. Unless they are well made, these wines may also suffer from low acidity. Think of the jammy, full flavour of many Californian red wines, the mouthfilling character of Chardonnays from Australia, and compare them with the lighter taste of wines produced in the cooler regions of Italy, Burgundy and New Zealand.

Here, too, you must be wary of jumping to conclusions. The best winemakers in hot countries are doing their utmost to pick earlier, mimicking the condition of cooler climates – and those supposedly cooler countries can have abnormally warm summers and autumns. So that deeply fruity Cabernet Sauvignon you were sure came from California might just be the fruit of the ripe 1982 harvest in Bordeaux after all.

If you're trying to guess a wine's origins 'blind', you're going to have to look for the characteristic flavours which individual grape varieties can display when grown in particular soils and climates. The only way to do that is to taste as many different, representative examples as you can.

Siting the Vineyard

This is where the whole story of wine begins, and it is crucially important to remember that good wine cannot be made out of bad grapes. A wine's life-cycle starts in the vineyard, and the

---

THE LANGUAGE OF THE VINEYARD

Botrytis cinerea Often called noble rot; in France, *pourriture noble,* and in Germany, *Edelfäule.* Fungus which dehydrates grapes, not only concentrating sugars and acids but imparting its own characteristic flavour to sweet wines.

Black rot Fungal disease of both grape and vine due to humid weather conditions.

Bordeaux mixture Copper sulphate and lime compound used against vine disease.

Chlorosis Yellowing of the vine leaves through mineral deficiency.

Clone A selection within a variety of vine taken from one plant exhibiting desirable characteristics.

Coulure The shedding of flowers or berries, caused by over-vigorous growth, disease or rainstorms at flowering.

Cross Vine whose parents are two or more varieties within the same species.

Débourrement The budding of the vines after leaf formation.

Downy mildew *Peronospera,* a fungal disease. Treated with *Bordeaux mixture.*

Drip Irrigation New World method (sometimes computerised) of watering.

Espalier A method of training vines. Vertical shoots lead off a central trunk of two horizontal stems.

Eutypiose A fungal infection which withers the vine. Threatens to decimate the world's vineyards as *phylloxera* did in the late 19th century.

Floraison Flowering of the vine.

Geneva Double Curtain Method involving training vines along high trellises to maximise sunshine.

Gobelet Training and pruning of the vine into a bush-like form.

Grafting The process of attaching new vines to (*phylloxera*-resistant) rootstock.

Grey Rot or *pourriture gris.* Unwanted *botrytis* infection.

Guyot (Single or Double) Common vine training systems; growth is concentrated into one or two stems.

Hectare Metric measure equivalent to 10,000 square metres or 2.47 acres.

Hybrid A *cross* between two or more grape species.

Micro-climate A climate within the immediate area of the vineyard, an essential determinant of its unique aspects.

Millerandage Uneven development of grapes within a bunch as a result of cold or wet weather at flowering.

Oidium (Powdery mildew) A fungal disease controlled by sulphur spraying.

Phylloxera vastatrix Parasitic louse that attacks the roots of the *Vitis vinifera* grapevine. It devastated the world's vineyards in the late 19th century. Now controlled by *grafting.*

Pruning The selective trimming of a vine to control its shape and the quantity and quality of its produce.

Rootstock The rooted part of the vine on to which the scion is grafted.

Training The way in which a vine is forced to grow to optimise yield, ripening, ease of harvest etc.

Trie Selective harvesting of grapes to pick them at their optimum condition.

Véraison Final stage in the ripening of the grapes.

Vitis labrusca US vine species making undistinguished wine; can parent some tolerable hybrids which are usefully hardy.

Vitis riparia Vine species native to the US and Canada. The wine it produces smells weirdly 'foxy'. Important for its *phylloxera*-resistant rootstock and thus used around the world.

Vitis vinifera The botanical name of the wine-making vine; European varieties are nearly always members of this species.

Yeasts The 'bloom' on grapes is an accumulation of wild yeasts which, left to their own devices, will naturally but unpredictably begin fermentation. Winemakers usually prefer to use cultured yeasts.

way in which the vines are selected, planted and looked after dictates the quality of the fruit they will yield.

The ideal vineyard is set part-way up a hillside. Vines planted in flat land receive less sunshine, are badly drained, and are prone to frost. The lowest part of the slope is better off, but will suffer from any damp conditions prevailing on the flat land, particularly if there happens to be a stream or river running through it. Vines half-way up the hill receive the most direct sunlight and are well-drained. Higher up, altitude causes cooler temperatures which inhibit ripening. The top of the hill is thus no better than the bottom, suffering from cool temperatures, wind and reduced direct sunlight. In the best wine-growing areas of France, the hilltops are covered by trees.

Different soils suit different vines, and the styles of wine made from their grapes. The Chardonnay of Chablis may thrive on limestone there, and on chalk in Champagne, but in California, where it makes some excellent, full-bodied wines, most Chardonnay is grown on clay. You can almost taste the heavier soil in the wine.

The same is true of other varieties. Despite learned disputes which seek to prove the contrary, it is beyond question that certain patches of land have, over the centuries, produced better wines than their immediate neighbours, no matter how much care – and money – has been lavished on attempts to improve the rivals. The names of the great first growth clarets of Bordeaux have been revered since the 17th century and, in an age when practically every wine imported into England was referred to generically as 'claret', those names, and those names alone, were specific exceptions. And even in those days they cost more than the others.

Climate And Microclimate

In England, we grumble about the difficulty of growing grapes ripe enough to make decent wine. Or that we have to use varieties which ripen specially early, but don't possess the qualities which make for really great wine. These grouches are true, to a certain extent, but that doesn't mean that the best wines come from the hottest climates.

What vines really need to produce grapes capable of making first-class wine is a climate that allows the final, important ripening of the grapes to happen in the cooler months of autumn, not all in a rush in the blazing heat of high summer. Then the balance of grape-sugar to acidity is better, and the slower ripening has permitted the fruit to develop all the other subtle flavour components which can contribute to a great wine.

Rain is a relevant factor too, particularly in the quality wine regions of Europe where irrigation is forbidden. Too much rain can dilute wine and possibly facilitate rot; too little will parch the grapes, making for tough, tannic wine.

Frost is an ever-present enemy. It can damage or kill the leaves and shoots of vines just at the most vulnerable point in their development, so frost-free sites are desirable. If a vineyard is inevitably prone to frost, measures can be taken to combat this: water-sprinklers, oil burners, or wind machines to mix in warm air and dispel the cold air lying close to the vines.

Tending The Vines

If the struggle to produce fine wine starts with the selection of a suitable site for the chosen grape varieties, it continues with hard work in the vineyard. Growing vines is farming, just as much as growing barley or rearing pigs, and demands long hours and dedicated attention if the harvest of grapes is to be worth waiting for.

Before a vineyard can be planted it must be prepared. In

ABOVE: In cool regions, rotten grapes can be a problem. Here, in Burgundy, the Duke of Magenta is checking that no rotten fruit makes its way into his Puligny Montrachet

LEFT: Mechanical harvesters – which shake the grapes off the vines – are gradually replacing human pickers throughout the world

The Varieties of Soil

Gravel
A great number of vineyards are perched on the side of river valleys, in well-drained gravel deposits. Vines do better in poor, well-drained soils which make them plunge their roots deeper to find water and goodness. The great wines of Bordeaux come from gravel soils (Graves means gravel) which particularly suits the Cabernet Sauvignon. Much depends, however, on the other kinds of soil with which the gravel is combined. If it is over clay the wine will have less acidity than if it is over limestone.

Granite
The granite vineyards of the southern Rhône, home of Châteauneuf-du-Pape and Tavel rosé, are littered with huge 'pudding stones', making the cultivation of anything seem virtually impossible. Once vines are established, however, the stones act as reflectors, bouncing the heat from the sun back on to the grapes, giving big, high-in-alcohol reds and the world's most famous dry rosé. In the Beaujolais, granite suits the Gamay; its chemical properties reduce the wines' natural acidity.

Chalk
Chalk, too, makes for very good drainage and forces the vines to work hard for a living. Not all vine varieties like predominantly alkaline soil (vines are every bit as fussy as roses or hydrangeas). Those that do best on chalky hillsides produce white wines of unique character such as the Chardonnay, which forms part of the inimitable blend for Champagne. The keynote of wines made from grapes grown on chalky – limestone – soil is their acidity, a characteristic that links Champagne, Chablis and Sancerre.

Slate
The richer minerals found in slaty soils suit some vines admirably. The alluvial deposits on the banks beside the Rhine and Mosel rivers in Germany are responsible for the delicate fragrance of the 'gently fruity local wines, produced on the precipitous, barren-looking slopes. The locals say: 'Where the plough may go, no great wines grow.' The main advantage of slate in regions like the Mosel is its heat retention, which compensates for the low temperatures in which the grapes have to ripen.

THE LANGUAGE OF THE WINERY

Acid Essential component of wine, giving freshness and bite. Malic and tartaric acid occur naturally in grapes. Malic acid may be converted to the softer lactic acid via the *malolactic fermentation*. Tartaric acid is often added in warm regions.

Alcohol The by-product of fermentation, created by yeasts working on sugar. It is also added during or after fermentation to produce fortified wines. Measured as a percentage of volume.

Anthocyanin Grape skin tannin responsible for colour and flavour in red wines.

Autolysis Interaction between wine and solid yeast matter giving a distinctive flavour, encouraged by ageing wine on its *lees* in Muscadet and Champagne.

Back-blending See *süssreserve*.

Barrel-ageing Maturing of wine in cask.

Barrel-fermented Fermented in barrel in order to intensify oak and vanilla flavours.

Barrique The traditional Bordelais oak barrel, now widely adopted elsewhere, with a capacity of 225 litres.

Baumé See *sugar*.

Bentonite Clay used for *fining*.

Blending The mixing of several wines to create balanced *cuvée*. Also called *assemblage*.

Brix See *sugar*.

Cap The floating skins in a red wine must.

Capsule The lead, foil or plastic covering cork and bottle neck.

Carbon dioxide (CO_2) By-product of fermentation, trapped in wine by the *méthode champenoise* as bubbles and otherwise induced in or injected into all sparkling wines.

Carbonic Maceration Uncrushed grapes ferment under a blanket of CO_2, intensifying fruit flavours.

Centrifuge Machine used to separate wine from the lees after fermentation. Also used in production of low-alcohol wines.

Champagne Method See *méthode champenoise*.

Chaptalisation See *sugar*.

Concentrated grape must Grape juice that has been reduced by heating to 20% of its volume. If rectified, it has also had its acidity neutralised.

Congeners The colouring and flavouring matter in wines.

Cool fermentation Temperatures are kept below 18°C (64°F).

Crushing The gentle breaking of berries before fermentation.

Cuvaison Period of time a red wine spends in contact with its skins.

Cuve A vat generally made of wood used for storage or fermentation.

Cuvée A specific blend.

Débourbage Period during which the sediments settle out from the fresh must.

Egrappoir Machine which removes stalks from grapes before they are crushed.

Elevage The 'rearing' or maturing of wines before bottling.

Fermentation The conversion of sugars into alcohol through the action of yeasts.

Filtration Passing the wine through a medium to remove bacteria and solids (and possibly flavour – which is why some top class wines aren't filtered).

Fining The clarification of must or wine, usually using natural agents such as egg white, gelatine, isinglass or *bentonite* which, as they sink, attract and drag down impurities with them.

Fortification The addition of alcohol to certain wines (e.g. sherry and port) either before or after fermentation is complete.

Free-run juice The clear juice which runs from the crushed grapes before they are pressed. The best quality juice.

Harvest Dictated by ripeness. Occurs in the vintage year indicated on the label.

Hectolitre 100 litres.

Isinglass Fining agent derived from fish.

Lees Dead yeasts left after fermentation.

Maceration Period of contact between wine and skins in red wines.

Maderisation Term for heat-induced oxidation e.g. in Madeira.

Made wine Wine made from concentrated must – not fresh grapes.

Malolactic Fermentation Natural or induced conversion of malic acid to the softer lactic by specialised bacteria.

Marc Skins, stalks and pips left after pressing. May be distilled into brandy.

Méthode champenoise Secondary fermentation induced within the bottle in which the wine is sold.

Must Unfermented grape juice.

Must weight Amount of sugar in the must.

Mutage The addition of alcohol to stop fermentation – used to make sweet fortified wines.

Oak Preferred type of wood in which to mature wine. Provides character, imparts flavour, and softens the wine.

Oechsle See *sugar*.

Oenology The science of winemaking.

Oxidation Result of air contact with wine. Controlled in the maturation process; destructive in excess.

Pasteurisation Sterilising wine by heating.

pH (number) Measure of acidity (low) or alkalinity (high).

Press Machine used to gently squeeze out juice remaining in skins.

Press wine Blending wine obtained by pressing the grape skins after *maceration*.

Pumping over The process of pumping the must over the floating cap of skins to obtain more colour and flavour.

Racking Decanting from one vessel to another leaving the lees behind.

Skin contact See *maceration*.

Sugar The sugar in fresh grape juice is measured prior to fermentation as this will determine the alcohol content and style of wine. Scales of sugar measurement are: in France, Baumé; in the New World, Brix; in Germany, Oechsle. In some regions, sugar may be added to *chaptalise* the must – to raise its potential alcoholic strength, but not to sweeten it.

Sulphur dioxide (SO_2) Invaluable antiseptic, antioxidant and preservative. Used sparingly by wise winemakers.

Süssreserve In Germany, England and a few other regions, wines can be sweetened by the addition – back-blending – of sweet, unfermented grape juice.

Tannins Extracts from red grape skins and oak which give a red wine backbone. The mouth-drying quality of cold black tea is due to tannin.

Tartaric acid See *Acid*.

Tartrates Potassium bitartrate is naturally present in all wine. Most is removed before bottling but some may linger in the form of harmless tartrate crystals.

Ullage The air space between the wine and roof of cask or, in bottle, cork.

Varietal Wine made and named after one or more grape varieties.

Yeast Naturally present on grapes, or added in cultured form, this is what makes grape juice ferment.

LEFT: New oak barrels are a crucial component of most top-quality wines nowadays. These are at Cos d'Estournel, probably the best – and best equipped – château in St Estèphe in Bordeaux

RIGHT: For more commercial wine, large stainless steel tanks, like these at the Almeirim cooperative in Portugal, perform the same storage task as the barrels

BELOW: Egg whites are still used for fining by top-quality wine producers throughout the world, though it is possible to use such alternatives as milk protein and bentonite, a kind of clay

most of the world's wine-growing areas, vineyards are devoted solely to the growing of vines. (This is not as tautological as it sounds; there are some countries in which it is customary to grow other crops in the vineyards as well – olive trees in Tuscany, cabbages in Portugal, and artichokes in northern Spain.)

The vineyard cleared, the vines must be planted. Choice of vines is not a straightforward business nowadays. Not only do you have to choose a variety, but also the rootstock on which to graft it, and the actual 'clone' of the variety itself.

Every grape variety has many different forms. Some are high yielders, others low; some have thick skins, others thin. Depending upon where the vine has been grown, the local climate, and how it has been cultivated, a single variety can give rise to a bewildering number of forms.

The development of a particular example of a vine with certain desirable characteristics is known as clonal selection. The example may have started its life as a Chardonnay vine in the great Le Montrachet Burgundy vineyard, for instance. It has been reproduced by taking cuttings, growing them, taking cuttings from this second generation, and rejecting any that do not have precisely the same features as the original. Several generations of vines later, after ruthless elimination of any 'dissident' examples, cuttings taken from the successful strain will always have the desirable features of that original Le Montrachet vine. Except possibly the price of the finished wine.

If vines are cultivated to give the maximum possible yield, the grapes will be feeble-flavoured, low in tannins and other essential ageing and flavouring components, and make undistinguished wine. Yield is partly a matter of choosing the right clone of a particular grape variety; partly of how a grower trains and prunes his vines. The purpose of care in training and pruning vines is, quite simply, to concentrate all the vine's energies into producing grapes, and the better the grapes, the better the resulting wine.

Methods of training are traditionally adapted to the climates of the countries where the vines are grown, though experimentation with 'new' styles is common. In hot countries with limited rainfall, vines are likely to be trained to grow relatively close to the ground, so that the limited moisture available does not have to waste itself on producing too many shoots and leaves, but can be directed into the grapes. In cooler climates, with more rainfall and less sun, priorities are different. Here grapes are usually trained higher, to catch the limited sun more effectively, and reduce the risks of mildew and rot by permitting a free flow of air around the bunches of grapes.

Inevitably, this paints a very simple picture of what is an

extremely complicated subject, with innumerable methods of training and pruning vines. Among those frequently encountered are the Single and Double Guyot, Gobelet, Lenz Moser, and the exotically named Geneva Double Curtain, which, needless to say, has nothing to do with Switzerland, but originated in New York State.

From Vineyard To Winery

Making wine from grapes follows a natural process. Certain refinements are necessary, however, to make sure that you make only good wine.

Present in the white bloom on the skin of grapes are not only

good wine yeasts, but tricky wild yeasts and bacteria as well. These are brought to the grapes by insects, or just carried in the air, and are fashionably aerobic – meaning they need plenty of oxygen to work.

If you were to leave fermentation to take place unaided in the open air, the wild yeasts would set to work in a furious rush until they were overcome by alcohol (at a strength of about four per cent). The slower-working, but more persistent wine yeasts would then take over until they had completed the job, leaving the fruits of their labours exposed to the bacteria which feed on alcohol, turning it into vinegar.

Obviously, the bacteria must be prevented from taking a grip, along with the wild yeasts, which work too quickly for the good of the wine. There are two ways of doing this; one, to seal the tanks and starve them of oxygen, and the other, to add sulphur dioxide to the wine juice (or *must*), which feeds on oxygen and forms an oxygen-exclusive coating on top of the must. These precautions taken, vinification is quite straightforward.

Winemaking is rather like cooking. If the ingredients are fresh and of good quality, and if the basic rules are followed, the final result should be good wine. But just as each cook may have an individual touch, every winemaker will aim to produce wines which bear his own stamp. This he can do by following the rules in his own way.

The temperature of the fermentation, the length of time it is allowed to carry on, the choice of wooden barrels or stainless steel tanks, the age and size of the casks, the period before bottling: all these are factors over which the winemaker has complete control and which will influence the character of the finished wine.

Much of the fascination of wine-tasting lies in guessing exactly how each particular wine was made. Every glass of wine you are likely to encounter will have gone through one of the processes described on these pages.

How White Wine Is Made

1. Grapes are picked, possibly by mechanical harvesters which shake them from the vines. They may be sorted; rotten ones are removed. The rest are taken quickly back to the winery. The longer the journey, the greater the risk of oxidation by heat and air.

2. For heavier-bodied wines, grapes may be crushed and allowed to macerate for 24 hours in a cool tank. This 'skin-contact' is particularly popular in California.

3. For crisp, fruity wines, grapes are lightly crushed and the solid matter passed straight into the press. Winemakers may control the temperature, keeping it cool for enhanced crispness.

4. The more you press, the more bitter the result. Some pressed juice is generally added to the 'free-run' juice drawn off from the crusher, and the mixture passed into vats. Sulphur is added to kill off bacteria and prevent oxidation.

5. In the vat, suspended matter will drop out of the juice, which can then be allowed to ferment – in vat or in wooden barrels. Modern wineries may use vacuum pumps or centrifuges to separate solids from liquid.

6. Fermentation may be fast or slow, warm or cool. 'Warm' means between 18-25°C; 'cool', 8-18°C. The cooler the fermentation, the fruitier, but possibly less complex, the wine. Extra yeast may help to get the process going.

7. Barrel fermenation – particularly in small, new oak barrels, as in Burgundy – will give the wine an oaky vanilla character and some longevity-bearing tannin. This is only appropriate for certain grapes, notably the Chardonnay and Sémillon. Tank-fermented wine may then go into barrel, or stay in tank.

8. If there is insufficient grape sugar, (powdered) sugar may be added. If there's too little acidity, tartaric or citric acid can correct the balance; if there's too much, chalk will remove it. Sweet grape juice may also be added, as in Germany.

9. Malolactic fermentation will normally take place, except where producers want to retain that appley malic acidity – as in some New World styles and Vinho Verde.

10. The wine will then be fined, probably with bentonite, a powdery clay which drags any remaining solid matter, or 'lees', to the bottom of the vat or barrel. It will then be 'racked' – passed into another vat – before filtering and bottling months or, in some cases, years after the harvest.

11. Some wines, notably Muscadet, are left *'sur lie'* – on their lees – and so taste slightly yeasty.

12. White wine is often 'cold stabilised': chilled so that its tartaric acid forms crystals which can be filtered out rather than be allowed to form in the bottle.

13. Sulphur is added before bottling to protect the wine. The dose must be carefully judged, otherwise the wine will suffer from a 'bad egg' or 'sulphuric acid' smell which will tickle the back of the throat

14. If barrels are used, there is the choice of how long the wine remains in them, and what kind and size of barrel to use. Chardonnay gains from being matured in small new oak barrels. White Dão tends to remain for a long time in large old ones.

How Red Wine Is Made

Red wine is made almost exclusively from black grapes, the colour coming from the skins.

1. The freshly-picked bunches of grapes are first put through a crusher, which just breaks the skins. Depending on the sort of wine to be made, and the amount of tannin required, the stalks may or may not be discarded at this stage.

2. From the crusher, the grapes go straight into the fermentation vats, skins and all. Fermentation can take up to four weeks or longer to complete. The higher the temperature, the more colour and tannin is extracted.

3. To produce youthful, soft, light-in-style red wines, whole grapes are fermented in sealed vats. Carbon dioxide trapped in the vat forces the grapes to ferment quickly – sometimes inside their skins – under pressure, and the whole process can be completed in as few as five days.

4. A wine's colour and tannin content is dictated partly by the length of time the fermenting must remains in contact with the skins and pips. Unless these are restrained under the surface of the must, by a mesh or other device, they will be carried to the surface of the vat by the carbon dioxide formed during fermentation, and form a 'cap' there. If there is no such device, the must is pumped up and over the cap from time to time, to break it up and leach out colour.

5. The weight of the mass of grapes is sufficient to squeeze the fermented juice out of grapes, and this is then allowed to run into a cask as free-run wine.

6. The rest of the bulk goes into a press and is crushed to produce a highly tannic, dark wine. This may be added to the free-run wine to add structure to the blend. The wine from both vat and press are mixed and transferred to tanks or barrels where a second, malolactic fermentation will occur.

7. Red wine generally needs more time to mature than white. The tannin is very bitter at first, but mellows in time, while the other components of the wine have time to blend together harmoniously. Wood barrels are often used for the maturation of red wines and the oak contributes not only additional flavour and complexity but also greater staying power to the wine.

8. 'Fine' wine almost always spends at least a year in barrels, large or small, new or old. The wine is 'fined' with egg-white, which drags suspended yeasts and other solids in the wine downwards, before being 'racked' (passed from one container to another, leaving the solids behind), filtered and bottled.

9. Finally, time spent in bottle is important, but not every wine needs it. A complex (and expensive) bottle of red will almost certainly benefit from bottle ageing, as will whites with both body and high enough acidity. Simple wines, intended for prompt drinking, will lose colour, freshness and just about everything that makes wine enjoyable, if left for too long.

How Rosé Is Made

The classic way of making rosé wines is to follow the red wine process until about 24 hours into step two. The wine is thus in contact with the black skins for just long enough to become delicately coloured. It is then racked off to complete fermentation on its own. Alternatively, the grapes may be allowed to macerate on the skins for a few hours before they are pressed and vinified like a white wine. The simple addition of red wine to white is illegal for quality still wines – but permitted for rosé Champagne.

Sparkling Wine

Sparkling wines are made by every wine-producing country in the world. The carbon dioxide which creates the bubbles in the wine is a natural by-product of fermentation.

If the winemaker intends his produce to be sparkling, he traps the gas in the wine. There it remains dissolved until the pressure is released, when it rapidly makes its way to the surface in the form of tiny bubbles.

There are various ways of capturing fizz in a wine. The best is the *méthode champenoise*, used not only in Champagne but throughout the winemaking world. The way in which the gas is trapped can vary, from a highly skilled, labour-intensive science to a heavy-handed, mass-produced routine, as can the quality of the base wine itself. The best base wines for sparkling wine are those with high acidity and little character. That the soil (chalk) and climate (cool) of Champagne are ideally suited to producing wines of this type is a major factor in explaining Champagne's pre-eminence among sparkling wines.

However, it is the Champagne method, or *méthode champenoise*, that brings out their character and flavours. Pinot Noir and Chardonnay are the only grape varieties, together with the lesser Pinot Meunier, permitted to be grown in Champagne, and each has its own role to play in the finished product.

Some areas (such as California) frequently use the same mix as Champagne, but in general each of the world's regions makes sparkling wine from its own choice of grapes. At the cheaper end of the scale, base wines to make mass-produced inexpensive sparklers are bought not by grape variety, but by acidity and price.

There are however, exceptions: in northern Italy's Piedmont, the highly scented, honey-sweet Muscat grape is vinified into the delicately sweet Asti Spumante, showing off its fragrance and character admirably. Another is old-style German Sekt. Made from Riesling grown in a cool climate, it gains high levels of acidity and finesse.

Two good families of Champagne-method sparkling wines

LEFT: *In Champagne, having caused the wine to go through its second fermentation, the dead yeasts are made to collect in the necks of the bottles before being disgorged*

ABOVE: *Most grapes are now crushed mechanically; in some traditional fortified wine regions, however, they are still crushed by foot. These boots have just been used to tread sherry grapes in Jerez*

are Saumur and cava. Saumur wines come from the area south of Saumur on the Loire in France, where the soil structure is like that in Champagne.The grape varieties used are two white, the Chardonnay and the Chenin Blanc, and one red, the Cabernet Franc,producing a lighter style than Champagne.

Any French *appellation contrôlée* fizz must , by law, be made by the Champagne method. Many are called Crémant, a term that, confusingly, is traditionally used to describe a less vigorously sparkling Champagne.

'Cava' is the Spanish word for wines made by the Champagne method. These come mainly from around San Sadurní de Noya in the Penedés region.The principal grape varieties are the Xarel-lo, the Macabeo and the Parellada – all white grapes, with occasionally a small amount of black Monastrell.

Sweet And Fortified Wines

Sweet wines are the most difficult of wines to make and yet are probably the best value of any wines in the world. Out of fashion for many years, good, rich, honeyed white wine is beginning to enjoy a comeback. Winemakers in countries as diverse as France, Austria, Israel and America are increasingly surprising us with their mastery of the art of making sweet wine. Quality wine depends on grape varieties which naturally contain a lot of sugar, picked late to get all the sweetness of really ripe fruit.

It also needs a high degree of balancing acidity to prevent the wines from tasting treacly or cloying. Those grapes affected by 'noble rot' – a fungus correctly known as *Botrytis cinerea* – make the very finest of all dessert wines, the Trockenbeerenauslesen of Germany and the great Sauternes of Bordeaux. Mysteriously, and despite its name, the fungus doesn't actually rot the grapes as much as dehydrate them, breaking through their skins, allowing the water content to evaporate and thus concentrating the richness of the sugar which remains.

The sugar contained in any grape will, given half a chance and a bit of yeast, ferment into alcohol. The sweeter the grape, the stronger the wine – in theory. In practice, once the strength rises to 15-16%, the alcohol itself will kill off the yeast, leaving you with rather sweet, very alcoholic wine.

So, the key is to stop the fermentation before it gets to this stage. This can be achieved in one of two tricky ways. One method inevitably involves the use of the winemaker's friend and, occasionally, wine drinker's enemy – sulphur. Sulphur is needed for almost all white wines, but the sweeter examples need very large doses which, unless they are handled very carefully, give the wines an irritating throat-tickling character.

HOW WINE IS MADE TO SPARKLE

The Méthode Champenoise
Used for: Champagne; Cava; Crémant de Loire, de Bourgogne and d'Alsace; Blanquette de Limoux; Quality New World sparkling wines; Italian 'Metodo Classico'; Quality German Sekt.

After the blending of the base wines, a solution of wine and sugar is added, along with specially cultured yeasts, to provoke a secondary fermentation. The bottles are then stacked on their sides in a cool cellar and left for the second fermentation slowly to run its course. The bottles are then placed, neck first, into specially-designed sloping racks called *pupitres*.

It is the skilled job of the *remueur* to shake the sediment down so that it rests on the cork, by gently rotating and tilting each bottle many times over. The whole job takes about a month but is now often done by machines called giropalettes.

Finally the necks of the bottles are chilled, freezing the sediment into a solid plug. When the corks are removed and the plug of sediment pops out under pressure, the wine remaining in the bottle is topped up with more of the same wine and a little liquid sugar, known as the *dosage*, before being corked with the traditional Champagne cork tied down with wire.

The Transfer Method
Used for: French Kriter; Some New World fizz.

This is essentially a 'second-best' cross between the Champagne and *cuve close* (see below) methods. The second fermentation takes place in the bottle and the wine is transferred under pressure to tanks for dosage, filtering and re-bottling.

The Cuve Close, Charmat or Tank Method
Used for: Basic French sparklers; All but the best German Sekt; Most Asti Spumante; Spanish 'Granvas' fizz.

Invented by the Frenchman Charmat, this method can make tolerable sparkling wine – ideal, perhaps for mixing with orange juice for a Buck's Fizz. The base wine is run into huge stainless steel tanks where secondary fermentation takes place at a controlled temperature, then dosage, filtering and bottling.

METHODS OF FORTIFICATION

With a few exceptions, fortified wines tend to be sweet. This is either because the addition of alcohol was made whilst there was still sugar in the grapes, or because in a few cases – most notably certain sherries – the final result is sweetened.

Alcohol is added to the grape juice either before it has begun to ferment, or during its fermentation process in order to halt the fermentation. The result is a wine varying in strength from under 16% to as much as 25%.

The French distinguish between *vins de liqueur,* which are made by the first of these two methods, and *vins doux naturels,* which are made by the second. Least prestigious of the *vins de liqueur* are the *mistelles* which are used as the base for aperitifs and vermouths. The best known are Pineau des Charentes, made in Cognac; Ratafia de Champagne and Floc de Gascogne.

Of the *vins doux naturels,* the most popular in Britain are the Muscats from the Rhône, Roussillon and Languedoc regions, such as Beaumes de Venise, Rivesaltes and most notably Banyuls, made in Roussillon from the Grenache grape.

Of the other fortified wines, port and Madeira are made by the *vin doux naturel* method. Sherry is fermented to dryness, then fortified before oxygen and yeasts start to act on the wine.

The other way to halt fermentation is to add more alcohol. Those who fortify wine in this way can also produce great wines: they include port, Marsala, Madeira, the delicious fortified Muscats of Australia and the *vins doux naturels* of France: Muscat de Beaumes de Venise and Rivesaltes.

In California, where winemakers have already learnt to master the yeasts which make wine ferment, the aim now is to create great sweet wine every year by *spraying* rot onto the grapes. Scientists are eagerly attempting to devise methods of duplicating exactly the effect of the mould as it creeps over the vines of Bordeaux and the Rhine. No-one yet knows whether this will work, and there are purists who believe that such pre-empting of nature is cheating.

VINTAGES

One of the greatest areas of wine mystery and mystique is the difference between vintages. Was 1985 a good year for Châteauneuf-du-Pape? When ought I to drink my 1986 Bordeaux? Which was better for Burgundy – 1982 or 1983?

Unfortunately, the closer you look at vintages, the more confusing the subject tends to become; if you want a simple, reliable, easy-to-follow vintage chart that will fit on the back of a credit card, I'm afraid that you are out of luck. If, on the other hand, what you are looking for is good flavour and good value, you've come to the right place – because it's surprising how often the best buys are to be found in years that get the cold shoulder from most vintage charts. The chart on the following pages is different because it looks at drinkability – the readiness of the wine to be enjoyed – as well as quality.

When thinking about vintages, it is worth bearing the following points in mind.

* 'Great' vintages aren't always the ones you want to buy – particularly if the wines are young and you are going to open them soon. Many 'lesser' vintages – such as 1980, 1984 and 1987 for red Bordeaux – are much more enjoyable when they are only a few years old, at an age at which 'better' ones – such as 1982, 1983 or 1986 – are not yet ready to drink.

* The quality of a vintage – or lack of it – is only partly dependent on the weather during the summer. The clock begins ticking in the spring when the first leaves appear on the vines, and continues right up until the moment when the last grapes are safely picked and carried into the winery. A spring frost can harm the vines; bad weather at the flowering in the early summer can cut down the size of the crop; rain coupled with warm weather in the summer may lead to rot developing on the fruit; cold temperatures at summer's end may prevent the

grapes from ripening properly; storms during the harvest may dilute the wine; hail can tear the bunches from the vines.

* Weather conditions can vary widely within the same country and even region. So, a great year for Burgundy in the east of France may be a rotten one for Bordeaux, down in the south-west. Chablis can have markedly better weather than Chassagne Montrachet, 100 miles further south – despite the fact that both are usually given the same 'White Burgundy' rating on most vintage charts.

* Different grape varieties react in different ways. In Bordeaux, for example, the Merlot – which is the predominant grape in St Emilion and Pomerol – ripens earlier than the Cabernet Sauvignon, which is the main variety in the Médoc. So, in years like 1964, when rain storms ruined the harvest in the Médoc, the Merlot grapes of the former areas had already been picked in perfectly dry weather.

Similarly, the varieties used to make Sauternes and Barsac need damp weather to develop noble rot – the very same damp weather that can cause havoc in neighbouring vineyards where the grapes for dry red wine are grown. Both 1967 and 1965, which were disastrous years for claret, produced stunning Château d'Yquem. Great years for white Burgundy – 1973, 1979, 1982 and 1986 – are often less impressive for red, partly because the Chardonnay is happier than the Pinot Noir in cooler weather, and partly because, unlike that variety, it has the capacity to produce good wine in heavily productive vintages.

* Winemakers can get it right in bad years – and wrong in good ones. A week's holiday taken during the crucial week when neighbouring growers discover they have to spray against rot can make all the difference between making great wine and

FACING PAGE: Bottles of Château Lafite from the 18th century still come under the auctioneer's hammer and, thanks to the original quality of the wine and the careful way in which at least some of the bottles have been kept in the château's cellars, they can still taste extraordinarily good

ABOVE: In the traditional vine-yards of Europe, the quality of a vintage depends enormously on there being the right amount of rain at the right time of the year; irrigation is illegal. Here in Washington State, however, regular watering is not only legal but indispensable

LEFT: The weather during the early stages of the grape's development can be just as crucial as that which prevails during the final months of ripening

poor, rotty stuff. Similarly, growers who do not prune tightly enough can allow their vines to over-produce in potentially good vintages (as in red Burgundy in 1982) and will make thin, dilute wine; if the weather during the harvest is too hot, winemakers who do not have cooling equipment can see their fermenting vats overheat and their wine irredeemably spoiled.

* Wines can behave unpredictably once they are bottled. Vintages thought to be 'built to last' can fail to live up to their promise; others that are initially dismissed as being too good young to be worth keeping may mature for decades; occasionally, wines from cool wet vintages – like 1972 red Burgundy – that are so acidic as to be almost undrinkable when they are first bottled can, like ugly ducklings, briefly develop into tasty swans a decade or so later.

* Wines from a given vintage can, just like racehorses, perform well or badly 'on the day' and they can even go through the equivalent of a poor season; winemakers and wine merchants are ceaselessly both fascinated and exasperated by the way in which wines can apparently go into a sulk for as little as a few months or as long as a few years. For example, in the late 1980s many wine drinkers began to despair of their tough-tasting 1966 clarets, which seemed to have come to the end of their drinking lives. Two years later, the people who hadn't drunk up their remaining bottles or sold them at auction discovered that most of those 1966s had returned from the dead with all their fruit intact.

Throughout the following chart, the ratings given are for good examples of wines from the regions in question. Always bear in mind, however, that in any year individual producers can out and underperform the vintage as a whole.

FRANCE

Bordeaux (Red) Bear in mind the differences between the different regions of Bordeaux – and the differences between what particular winemakers are trying to produce. A wine simply labelled as Bordeaux Rouge is made for fairly immediate consumption, however good the vintage. At the other end of the scale, a top-class château will normally be aiming to make long-lived wines in good vintages; their 'second label' wines (like Château Margaux's 'Pavillon Rouge du Château Margaux' and Château Léoville Las Cases's 'Clos du Marquis') are usually made to be drunk younger than the 'first label' wines from the same property and the same vintage.

	89	88	87	86	85	84	83	82	81	80	79	78	77	76	75	74	73	72	71	70			
Northern Haut-Médoc (Pauillac, St Estèphe, St Julien)	9△	8△	6△	8△	8△	5▲	8△	10△	8△	6●	7▲	9▽	4●	6●	7▲	3▼	3▼	3▼	6▼	8●			
Southern Haut-Médoc (Margaux)	7△	7△	5△	8△	8△	5▲	9△	8△	7▲	5●	6●	8▲	4▼	5▼	8●	2▼	2▼	2▼	5▼	7▼			
Graves	8△	8△	6△	8△	8△	5▲	9△	9△	7▲	6●	7▲	8▲	4●	6●	7▲	4▼	4▼	4▼	6●	8●			
St. Emilion/Pomerol	9△	8△	6△	7△	9△	3▲	8△	10△	7▲	4●	7●	8●	4▼	7●	8●	3▼	3▼	3▼	6●	8●			

Bordeaux (White) Until recently, there was very little dry white Bordeaux worth drinking at all – let alone cellaring. Sweet wines from Sauternes and Barsac can, however, last for an extraordinarily long time when they are from top-class châteaux.

	89	88	87	86	85	84	83	82	81	80	79	78	77	76	75	74	73	72	71	70			
Graves	7△	9△	8▲	9▲	8▲	6▲	8▲	7▲	6▲	5▲	8▲	7●	4●	8▲	8●	4▼	4▼	4▼	8●	8●			
Sauternes/Barsac	8△	9△	5△	9△	7△	3△	9△	4△	6△	5●	6●	5●	2●	8●	8●				8●	7●			

Burgundy (Red) Burgundy is possibly the most varied (in quality terms) region in France. As a general rule, the reds of the Côte de Nuits live longer than those of the Côte de Beaune, while the Côte Chalonnaise and the Mâconnais tend to produce wines for younger drinking.

	89	88	87	86	85	84	83	82	81	80	79	78	77	76	74	73	72	71	70	69			
Côte de Nuits	8△	9△	7▲	7△	9△	6●	7▲	7●	4▼	8●	7●	8●	4▽	7▼	4▼	4▼	8●	9●	6▼	8▼			
Côte de Beaune	8△	9△	7▲	7△	9▲	5●	7△	6●	4▼	7●	6●	8●	3▽	6▼	3▽	3▼	9▼	9▼	6▼	8▼			
Côte Chalonnaise/Maconnais	8△	8△	7▲	7△	8▲	5●	6●	6●	3▼	7●	6●	8●	3▽	6▼	3▽	3▼	8▼	8▼	5▽	8▽			

Burgundy (White) Top-class white Burgundy can last supremely well – but don't push your luck by trying to cellar most basic examples for longer than four or five years. In Burgundy, a good vintage for reds can, confusingly, be a poor one for whites – and vice versa.

	89	88	87	86	85	84	83	82	81	80	79	78	77	76	74	73	72	71	70	69			
Chablis	8△	8△	7●	9▲	8▲	7▲	6●	8▼	7●	5▼	8●	8●	6▼	6▼	5▽	5▽	8▼	9▼	6▼	8▼			
Côte d'Or	7△	8△	7▲	9▲	8▲	7▲	5●	8●	7●	5▼	9●	8●	6●	6▼	4▽	6▽	8▼	8▼	6▼	8▼			
Côte Chalonnaise/Maconnais	7△	8△	7●	9●	8●	7●	5●	6▼	7▼	5▽	8▼	8▼	5▽	5▽									

Alsace Good examples of Alsace can be extraordinarily long-lived – particularly the late-picked Vendange Tardive and Sélection de Grains Nobles wines. However, the region's reds, relatively delicate wines from the Pinot Noir, are for early consumption.

	89	88	87	86	85	84	83	82	81	80	79	78	77	76	75	74	73	71	70	69	67		
Gewürztraminer	9△	7△	5△	8△	9△	3▲	8▲	4▼	6●	4▼	6▼	4▼	2▽	8●	7▼	5▼	5▼	8●	5▼	5▼	8●		
Riesling	9△	8△	6△	8△	9△	4▲	9▲	5●	7▲	5●	7●	5●	5●	9▲	8●	6●	6●	9▲	6●	6●	8●		
Tokay-Pinot Gris	9△	8△	5△	7△	9△	3▲	9▲	4●	7▲	4●	6▼	5●	3▼	8●	7▼	5▼	5▼	8●	6●	6●	7●		

Rhone (Red) Basic Côtes du Rhône, like Beaujolais, is made to be drunk young. Châteauneuf and Gigondas will age better, but for real keeping potential, you have to head north to Hermitage, Côte Rôtie and Cornas, some of whose wines are almost undrinkably tough when they are less than five or even 10 years old. These wines, however, are very vintage-dependent, and from lesser years will drink younger.

	89	88	87	86	85	84	83	82	81	80	79	78	77	76	75	74	73	72	71	70	69	67	66	64
Hermitage	8△	8△	6△	7△	8△	7●	10△	8▲	6●	6●	6▲	10▲	3▼	7▲	6●	6●	9●	8●	8●	7●	8●	9●		
Côte Rôtie	7△	8△	6△	7△	9▲	6●	9△	8●	6●	6●	6●	10▲	3▼	8▲	5▼	5▼	9●	7●	9●	6▼	8▼	9▼		
Cornas	7△	8△	6△	7△	9▲	7●	9▲	7●	5●	5●	6●	9▲	3▼	6▼	5▽	5▽	8▼	7▽						
Châteauneuf-du-Pape	7△	8△	5△	8△	8▲	6●	8▲	6●	8●	7●	7●	9▲	4▼	6▼	5●	5●	7▽	8▼	8▼	9▼	8▼	8▼		

Rhone (White) White Rhônes can be gloriously fragrant when they are young and richly exotic when they are at least a decade old. Between the two stages, although perfectly drinkable, they are for some reason far less attractive than when at either.

	89	88	87	86	85	84	83	82	81	80	79	78	77	76									
Hermitage/Condrieu	9△	8△	8▲	7△	8▲	6●	9▲	8▲	7●	5●	7●	9●	4▼	7▼									

Champagne Until the 1970s, Champagne vintages were rare; they were only 'declared' by producers in what they believed to be exceptional years. Today, thanks to better weather and a keen market, at least a few examples of vintage Champagnes are available almost every year.

	89	88	87	86	85	84	83	82	81	80	79	78	77	76	75	73	71	70	69	66	64		
Champagne	8△	7△	6△	7△	9△	4▲	9▲	8●	5●	8●	7●	2▼	7▼	7●	8▼	8●	9●	9▼	9▼	9▼	10▼		

Loire (Red) Although they can have an attractive youthful fruitiness when they are young, good-quality red Loires really do repay keeping.

	89	88	87	86	85	84	83	82	81	80	79	78	77	76	75	74	73	71	69				
Chinon, Bougueil etc.	9△	8△	6▲	8▲	9▲	6▼	8▲	7●	6▼	5▼	4▼	7●	4▼	8●	9▼	7▼	6▽	7▽	8▽				

Loire (White) Good examples of dry white Loires (Muscadet, Sancerre, Savennières etc) can last well, but they rarely improve beyond the first few years. Sweet Loires often need age to tame their acidity. Many appear to last indefinitely.

	89	88	87	86	85	84	83	82	81	80	79	78	77	76	75	74	73	71	69				
Coteaux du Layon	9△	9△	6△	7△	9△	4△	8▲	6▲	6▲	5▲	6▲	6▲		9●	8●	4▼	6▼	9●	8●				
Vouvray	9△	8△	6△	7●	9●	4●	8●	7●	6●	4▼	6▼	5▼	2▽	9●	8●	4▼	7▼	9●	8●				

Beaujolais (Crus) Basic Beaujolais and Beaujolais Nouveau should usually be drunk in the year or so after the harvest (nothing awful happens to Nouveau if you don't uncork it before the Christmas following the harvest). Of the ten Beaujolais *cru* villages, the ones to keep longest are Moulin-à-Vent and Morgon, followed by Juliénas and Chénas. Regnié, Chiroubles and Brouilly need drinking up first.

	89	88	87	86	85	84	83	82	81	80													
Cru Beaujolais	8△	8△	8▲	5▲	9▲	4▼	7●	6▼	6▼	5●													

ITALY

Piedmont Most Barolo needs at least five, if not 10, years to soften enough to be enjoyable. Barbaresco is usually approachable younger.

	89	88	87	86	85	84	83	82	81	80	79	78	77	76	75	74	73	72	71	70	69	68	67	66
Barolo	9△	7△	6△	8△	10△	6▲	7▼	10▲	5●	7●	7▼	9△	3▽	5▽	4▽	8▼	4▽		9●	8▼	6▽	6▽	8▼	3▽
Barbaresco	9△	8△	7△	8△	10△	6▲	7▼	10▲	6●	6●	7●	9●	3▽	5▽	4▽	7▼	4▽		9●	8▼	6▽	6▽	7▼	3▽

Veneto Valpolicella and Bardolino are generally made to be drunk young (though a few exceptions are breaking that rule). Amarone and Recioto keep well.

	89	88	87	86	85	84	83	82	81	80	79	78	77	76	75	74	73	72	71	70	69	68	67	
Amarone/Recioto	6△	9△	3△	8△	9△	5▲	9▲	6▲	10△	7▲	8●	8●	9●		9●			8●	8●			9▼		

Tuscany While Tuscany is usually thought to be the land of Chianti, it is increasingly the place to find exciting wines made from the same varieties as red Bordeaux. These (Sassicaia is a good example) often continue to mature for longer than all but the very best Chianti, most of which is made to be drunk quite young. Many are labelled merely '*vino da tavola*', so the name of the wine and producer are important.

	89	88	87	86	85	84	83	82	81	80	79	78	77	76	75	74	73	72	71	70	69	68	67	66
Chianti	6△	9△	7△	7▲	10△	5▼	9▲	8●	7▼	6▼	8▼	7▼	8▼	2▽	8▼	6▼	5▽	4▽	9▼	7▼	7▼	6▼	8▼	6▽
Montalcino	7△	9△	7△	7▲	10△	5▲	9△	9△	7●	6●	8▼	7▼	9●	3▽	9●	5▽	4▽	2▽	9●	5▽	5▽	6▽		4▽
Montepulciano	6△	9△	7△	7▲	10△	5●	9▲	8▲	6●	7▼	7▼	8▼	3▽	8▼	5▽	5▽	2▽	6▽	6▽	5▽		8▽	6▽	7▽
Sassicaia	7△	9△	7△	7△	10△	5▲	7▲	9△	8▲	6●	7●	7●	7●	5●	8●	6●		7●	8●	7●		9●		

SPAIN

In general Spanish producers indicate their best and better vintages by calling them 'Gran Reserva' and 'Reserva' respectively. Both these terms will indicate longer oak-ageing and – in theory – greater potential longevity. Spain produces very few white wines that are built to last.

	89	88	87	86	85	84	83	82	81	80	79	78	77	76	75	74	73	72	71	70	69	68	67	66
Rioja Reserva/Gran Reserva	7△	6△	8△	8△	8△	5▲	8▲	9△	8▲	7●	6●	7●	3▽	7▼	7▼	6▽	8▼	3▽	4▽	9▼	7▽	8▽	6▽	7▽
Penedés Red	7△	7△	9△	6△	8△	5▲	6▲	7▲	8▲	8▲	7●	8●	6●	7●										
Ribera del Duero	7△	4△	6△		7△	6▲	7▲	9▲	8▲	7●														
Penedés White	6▲	8▲	7▲	6●	6●	8●	7▼	7▼	8▼	6▼	6▼	8▼	6▽	7▽										

PORTUGAL

Like Spain, Portugal makes few long-lived whites. Its reds last better – and are often sold when they are already mature. The term 'Garrafeira' indicates a reserve wine that ought to last well. Vintage port, though always supposedly intended for cellaring, does vary in its likely longevity. Curiously, top-class houses never 'declare' a vintage two years running. Most Late Bottled vintage port does not develop or improve with age.

	89	88	87	86	85	84	83	82	81	80	79	78	77	76	75	70	67	66	63	60	55	45	35
Bairrada	7△	6△	6△	5△	9△	6▲	9▲	5●	5●	8●	5▼	8●	5▼	5▼	9▼								
Dão	7△	6△	6△	5△	9△	6▲	9▲	5●	5●	8●	5▼	5▼	5▼	7▼	8▼								
Vintage Port					8△		7△	6△		6△		6△	10△		6●	9▲	6●	●	10▲	7●			

GERMANY

The new trend towards dry, 'Trocken' wines in Germany complicates the life of anyone trying to draw up a chart like this. These wines – particularly the Rieslings – often take longer to be pleasurably drinkable than their sweeter equivalents, but they don't live as long. Germany's sweetest whites – Beerenauslesen and Trockenbeerenauslesen, which are mostly made only in the best vintages – can last almost indefinitely.

QBA, Kabinett, Spätlese

	89	88	87	86	85	84	83	82	81	80	79	78	77	76	75	74	73	72	71	70
Mosel-Saar Ruwer	9△	9▲	8▲	7▲	9▲	5●	9▲	5●	6●	4▼	6▼	4▽	3▽	9●	9●	3▽	7▽	3▽	9▼	8▼
Nahe	9△	8▲	7▲	7▲	8▲	4●	9▲	5▼	6▼	5▼	7▼	4▽	3▽	9●	9●	3▽	7▽	3▽	9▼	8▼
Rheingau	9△	7▲	7▲	7▲	8▲	4●	10▲	6▼	6▼	4▼	6▼	4▽	3▽	9●	9●	3▽	7▽	3▽	9▼	8▼
Rheinhessen	9△	8▲	7▲	7▲	8▲	5●	8●	6▼	6▼	5▼	7▼	4▽	4▽	8▼	9▼	2▽	6▽	3▽	9▼	7▼
Rheinpfalz	9△	8▲	7▲	7▲	9▲	5●	8●	6▼	7●	5▼	6▼	4▽	3▽	8▼	9▼	2▽	6▽	3▽	9▼	7▼

Auslese, Beerenauslese, TBA

	89	88	86	85	83	76	75	71	67	66	64	61
Mosel-Saar Ruwer	9△	9△		9△	9△	9●	9●	10●	8●	9●	9▼	9▼
Nahe	9△	8△		8△	10△	9●	8●	9●	9●	9●		9▼
Rheingau	9△	8△	5▼	8△	10△	9●	8●	10●	9●	8▼	9▼	
Rheinhessen	9△	8△	6●	9△	9△	8●	7▼	9●				
Rheinpfalz	9△	8△	6●	9△	8▲	9●	8▼	9●				

USA

The variation between producers' styles and between grape varieties makes it very difficult to generalise in the USA. And, of course, it is a huge country – California is large and varied enough in itself to warrant an extensive vintage chart of its own. Even so, the following should provide useful guidelines for the more commonly-seen wines. The ageability of all but a very few US wines is, as yet, unproven.

	89	88	87	86	85	84	83	82	81	80	79	78	77	76	75	74
California Red	7△	7△	9△	9△	10△	8▲	7●	7●	6▼	7▼	6▼	7●	6▼	7▼	7▼	9●
California White	7△	7△	9△	9△	8●	9●	7●	7▼	8●							
Pacific NW Red	7△	8▲	8△	7△	9▲	5▲	9▲	7●	8●	8●	7●	8●	7▼	8▼	9●	
Pacific NW White	7△	8▲	8△	8▲	9▲	6●	9▲	7●								

AUSTRALIA (Red)

As in the USA, styles and regions can vary enormously. However, it is fair to say that while few Australian Chardonnays have been built to last, old Semillons, Cabernet Sauvignons and Shirazes (and blends of the latter two) can be the longest-lived of all New World wines.

	89	88	87	86	85	84	83	82	81	80	79	78	77	76	75
New South Wales	6△	7▲	8▲	9▲	8▲	7▲	7●	8●	7●	8●	9●	7▼	7▼	6▼	10▼
Queensland	6△	8▲	8▲	6▲	7●	8▲	6●	7●							
South Australia	6△	8▲	8▲	8▲	9▲	9▲	7●	8●	7●	7●	8▼	7▼	7▼	8▼	7▼
Tasmania	6△	8▲	6▲	8▲	8▲	7▲	8●	8●							
Victoria	7△	8▲	7▲	7▲	7▲	8▲	6●	8●							
Western Australia	6△	7▲	8▲	8▲	9▲	8▲	7●	8●	7●	8●	7▼	9▼	5▽	3▽	

AUSTRALIA (White)

	89	88	87	86	85	84	83	82	81	80	79	78	77	76	75	74
New South Wales	5△	8▲	8▲	9●	8●	7●	8●	8●	8▼	9●	8▽	6▽	6▽	7▽	6▽	7▽
Queensland	6△	8▲	8▲	6●	7●	8▼	6▼	7▼								
South Australia	5△	8▲	7▲	8●	8●	9●	7●	8●	7▼	8▼	9▼	8▽	7▽	8▽	7▽	2▽
Tasmania	6△	7▲	6▲	8●	8●	7●	8▼	8▼								
Victoria	7△	8▲	7▲	7●	7●	8●	6▼	8●								
Western Australia	6△	8▲	8▲	8●	9●	8●	7▼	8●	8▼	9▼	8▽	4▽	7▽	5▽	2▽	4▽

NEW ZEALAND

Reds here are still rarely built to keep successfully, but Chardonnays are already top-class and worth cellaring and Sauvignons last surprisingly well.

	89	88	87	86	85	84
Red	8△	7▲	7▲	7●	9●	8●
White	9△	8▲	8▲	9●	8▼	7▼

KEY

△ Still needs keeping	▲ Can be drunk but will improve	● Ready now but no hurry
▼ Should be drunk now	▽ Probably over the hill	

READING THE LABEL

Wine labels are a cross between a passport, with all its legally required information, a visiting card, and a full-scale advertisement for the contents of the bottle. Some are so overloaded with techno-speak that they are evidently aimed at people whose main interest in wine is scientific; others are coy; and some seem to aspire to be thought works of art. But even a label that appears to tell you the bare minimum can be quite revealing: read it carefully and you should know the name of the wine, where and possibly when it was made, the identity of the person or company that produced and/or bottled it, its alcoholic strength and the amount you are getting for your money. And, if you live in an EC country, you will be protected from the kind of labelling featured in our African example below.

Other labels, more helpfully, may reveal a whole lot more. In the traditional countries of Europe, they might indicate the officially-designated quality of the wine (such as *appellation contrôlée*, *Premier* or *Grand Cru*) and the style in which it has been made (its sweetness or dryness, and the fact that it was aged in oak barrels for instance). 'New World' wines from the USA or Australia are more likely to tell you the name of the grape variety from which they are made.

Whatever the wine, and however many helpful or baffling words appear on the label, don't forget that once you know its style, the most important fact about any wine is the name of its producer. Over 1,000 different people make wine labelled as Beaujolais. And they make it to very different standards.

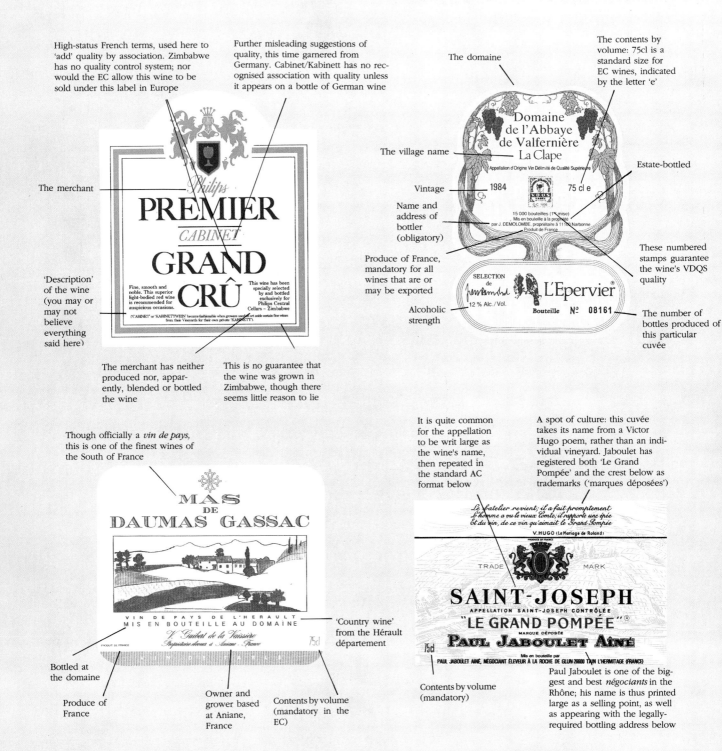

High-status French terms, used here to 'add' quality by association. Zimbabwe has no quality control system; nor would the EC allow this wine to be sold under this label in Europe

Further misleading suggestions of quality, this time garnered from Germany. Cabinet/Kabinett has no recognised association with quality unless it appears on a bottle of German wine

The merchant

'Description' of the wine (you may or may not believe everything said here)

The merchant has neither produced nor, apparently, blended or bottled the wine

This is no guarantee that the wine was grown in Zimbabwe, though there seems little reason to lie

The contents by volume: 75cl is a standard size for EC wines, indicated by the letter 'e'

The domaine

The village name

Vintage

Name and address of bottler (obligatory)

Produce of France, mandatory for all wines that are or may be exported

Alcoholic strength

Estate-bottled

These numbered stamps guarantee the wine's VDQS quality

The number of bottles produced of this particular cuvée

Though officially a *vin de pays*, this is one of the finest wines of the South of France

'Country wine' from the Hérault département

Bottled at the domaine

Produce of France

Owner and grower based at Aniane, France

Contents by volume (mandatory in the EC)

It is quite common for the appellation to be writ large as the wine's name, then repeated in the standard AC format below

A spot of culture: this cuvée takes its name from a Victor Hugo poem, rather than an individual vineyard. Jaboulet has registered both 'Le Grand Pompée' and the crest below as trademarks ('marques déposées')

Contents by volume (mandatory)

Paul Jaboulet is one of the biggest and best *négociants* in the Rhône; his name is thus printed large as a selling point, as well as appearing with the legally-required bottling address below

Morgon is one of the ten Beaujolais crus: since each has an *appellation contrôlée* in its own right, there is no need to mention Beaujolais at all on the label.

The 'old parchment' look is characteristic of labels from Burgundy.

Like all Beaujolais *Nouveau* or *Primeur* this is in fact merely Beaujolais that is sold soon after the harvest.

Wine from the first pressing of the grapes, as youthful and lively as the hard-working babes pictured, and as full of fruit as their baskets.

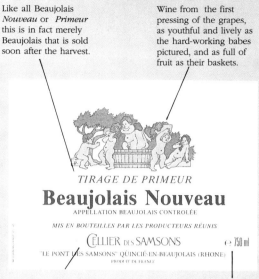

Name and address of the grower

Bottled at the property

Contents by volume (obligatory)

Bottled by a growers' cooperative called the Cellier des Samsons.

Contents by volume: 750ml (75cl) is also a standard EC measurement, hence the 'e'

The brand name. This is a *Prestige Cuvée*.

The town where it was made.

The wine is solely from this Premier Cru vineyard, one of only 14 sites so designated. A blend of wine from two or more of them may still be labelled 'Premier Cru'

High-quality, though not the very best (Grand Cru) Chablis; however, Premier Cru is prestigious enough to warrant mentioning here as well as within the standard AC format below

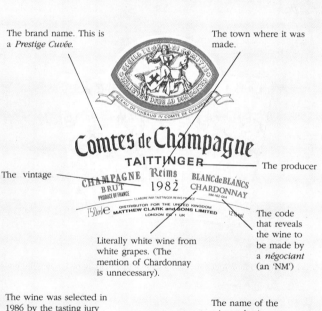

The vintage

The producer

Literally white wine from white grapes. (The mention of Chardonnay is unnecessary).

The code that reveals the wine to be made by a *négociant* (an 'NM')

Alcoholic strength:

Evidently made for the English speaking market

The signature of the 'owner-grower', William Fèvre

The wine was selected in 1986 by the tasting jury of the Confrérie des Chevaliers de Tastevin, a Burgundian brotherhood that seeks to maintain quality standards.

The name of the wine, a basic Appellation which can promote some good wines

Crémant, means sparkling, usually – appellation Contrôlée– 'Méthode Champenoise

Produced by the Champagne method. From 1992, only wines from Champagne will be allowed to use this term.

Dry

Contents

Contents

Wines given the tastevinage label are individually numbered

Rodet is a *négociant* - merchant - based at Mercurey

Appellation Contrôlée

Producer

Alcohol by volume

The producer: the Samur co-operative

The name of the appellation

The name of the particular *cuvée* (or bottling)

The well-known brand name is often mistaken for that of the finer, pricier, Château Mouton Rothschild.

A *Cru Bourgeois* – not included in the 1855 classification, but potentially good value.

The vintage

The name is trade-marked

Contents

Bottled by Baron Phillipe de Rothschild - or rather by his merchant business

Alcoholic content

English shipper

The name of the château

The vintage,

Contents — 750 ml

Bottled at the château

From the fairly basic Médoc appellation

The owners (Gilbeys) are based at St Yzans

Bottled at the château

Appellation and name of commune

Pauillac is a commune - like an English parish

Contents

The vintage

A classed growth included in the 1855 classification

The owner of the property, M Cazes, owns a number of top Bordeaux châteaux

The domaine

The Muscadet appellation

The name of the château.

French note for the English speaking drinkers.

Contents

Village.

Bottled on its 'lees', this wine has gained extra weight and flavour.

Bottled at the château

The wine name.

The appellation

Vintage

Late Harvest

The name of the cooperative

Bottled at the domaine.

Literally 'half-dry' These wines can be quite sweet and rich, especially given bottle age. May also say 'sec' – dry – or 'moelleux' – soft, sweet.

The name of the domaine.

Appellation.

Contents

Alcoholic strength

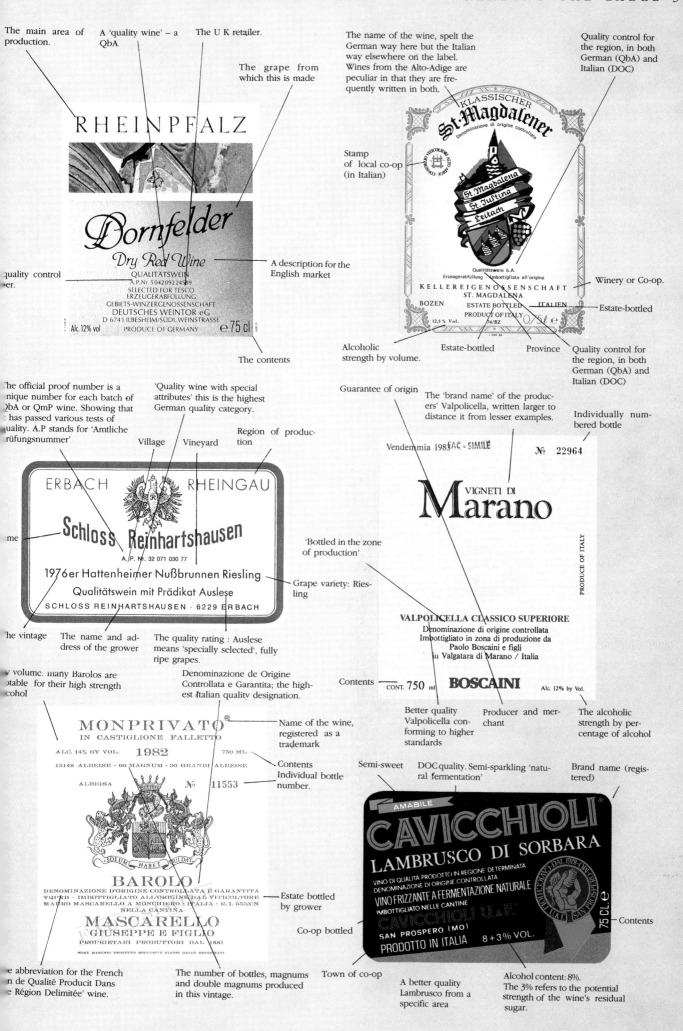

The main area of production.

A 'quality wine' – a QbA.

The U K retailer.

The grape from which this is made

The name of the wine, spelt the German way here but the Italian way elsewhere on the label. Wines from the Alto-Adige are peculiar in that they are frequently written in both.

Quality control for the region, in both German (QbA) and Italian (DOC)

RHEINPFALZ

Dornfelder
Dry Red Wine
QUALITÄTSWEIN
A.P.Nr. 504209224589
SELECTED FOR TESCO
ERZEUGERABFÜLLUNG
GEBIETS-WINZERGENOSSENSCHAFT
DEUTSCHES WEINTOR eG
D 6741 ILBESHEIM/SÜDL.WEINSTRASSE
Alc. 12% vol   PRODUCE OF GERMANY   e 75 cl

quality control ...er.

A description for the English market

The contents

KLASSISCHER
St·Magdalener
Denominazione di origine controllata

Stamp of local co-op (in Italian)

St. Magdalena
St. Justina
Leitach

Qualitätswein b.A.
Erzeugerabfüllung · Imbottigliato all'origine
KELLEREIGENOSSENSCHAFT
ST. MAGDALENA
BOZEN   ESTATE BOTTLED   ITALIEN
PRODUCT OF ITALY
12,5 % Vol.   76/BZ   0,75 l e

Winery or Co-op.

Estate-bottled

Alcoholic strength by volume.

Estate-bottled

Province

Quality control for the region, in both German (QbA) and Italian (DOC)

The official proof number is a unique number for each batch of QbA or QmP wine. Showing that it has passed various tests of quality. A.P stands for 'Amtliche Prüfungsnummer'

'Quality wine with special attributes' this is the highest German quality category.

Village   Vineyard

Region of production

Guarantee of origin

The 'brand name' of the producers' Valpolicella, written larger to distance it from lesser examples.

Individually numbered bottle

ERBACH   RHEINGAU
Schloss Reinhartshausen
A./P. Nr. 32 071 030 77
1976er Hattenheimer Nußbrunnen Riesling
Qualitätswein mit Prädikat Auslese
SCHLOSS REINHARTSHAUSEN · 6229 ERBACH

me

he vintage

The name and address of the grower

The quality rating : Auslese means 'specially selected', fully ripe grapes.

Denominazione de Origine Controllata e Garantita; the highest Italian quality designation.

Vendemmia 1985   FAC - SIMILE   № 22964

VIGNETI DI
Marano

'Bottled in the zone of production'

Grape variety: Riesling

PRODUCE OF ITALY

VALPOLICELLA CLASSICO SUPERIORE
Denominazione di origine controllata
Imbottigliato in zona di produzione da
Paolo Boscaini e figli
in Valgatara di Marano / Italia
BOSCAINI

y volume: many Barolos are ...table for their high strength ...cohol

MONPRIVATO ®
IN CASTIGLIONE FALLETTO
ALC. 14% BY VOL.   1982   750 ML
13148 ALBEISE - 66 MAGNUM - 30 GRANDI ALBEISE
ALBEISA   № 11553

Name of the wine, registered as a trademark

Contents

Better quality Valpolicella conforming to higher standards

Producer and merchant

The alcoholic strength by percentage of alcohol

Contents Individual bottle number.

Semi-sweet

DOC quality. Semi-sparkling 'natural fermentation'

Brand name (registered)

AMABILE
CAVICCHIOLI ®
LAMBRUSCO DI SORBARA
VINO DI QUALITA PRODOTTO IN REGIONE DETERMINATA
DENOMINAZIONE DI ORIGINE CONTROLLATA
VINO FRIZZANTE A FERMENTAZIONE NATURALE
IMBOTTIGLIATO NELLE CANTINE
CAVICCHIOLI U.&F.
SAN PROSPERO (MO)
PRODOTTO IN ITALIA   8 + 3% VOL.   75 CL e

BAROLO
DENOMINAZIONE D'ORIGINE CONTROLLATA E GARANTITA
VQPRD - IMBOTTIGLIATO ALL'ORIGINE DAL VITICOLTORE
MAURO MASCARELLO A MONCHIERO - ITALIA - R.1. 555/CN
NELLA CANTINA
MASCARELLO
GIUSEPPE E FIGLIO
PROPRIETARI PRODUTTORI DAL 1881

Estate bottled by grower

Co-op bottled

Contents

e abbreviation for the French n de Qualité Produit Dans e Région Delimitée' wine.

The number of bottles, magnums and double magnums produced in this vintage.

Town of co-op

A better quality Lambrusco from a specific area

Alcohol content: 8%. The 3% refers to the potential strength of the wine's residual sugar.

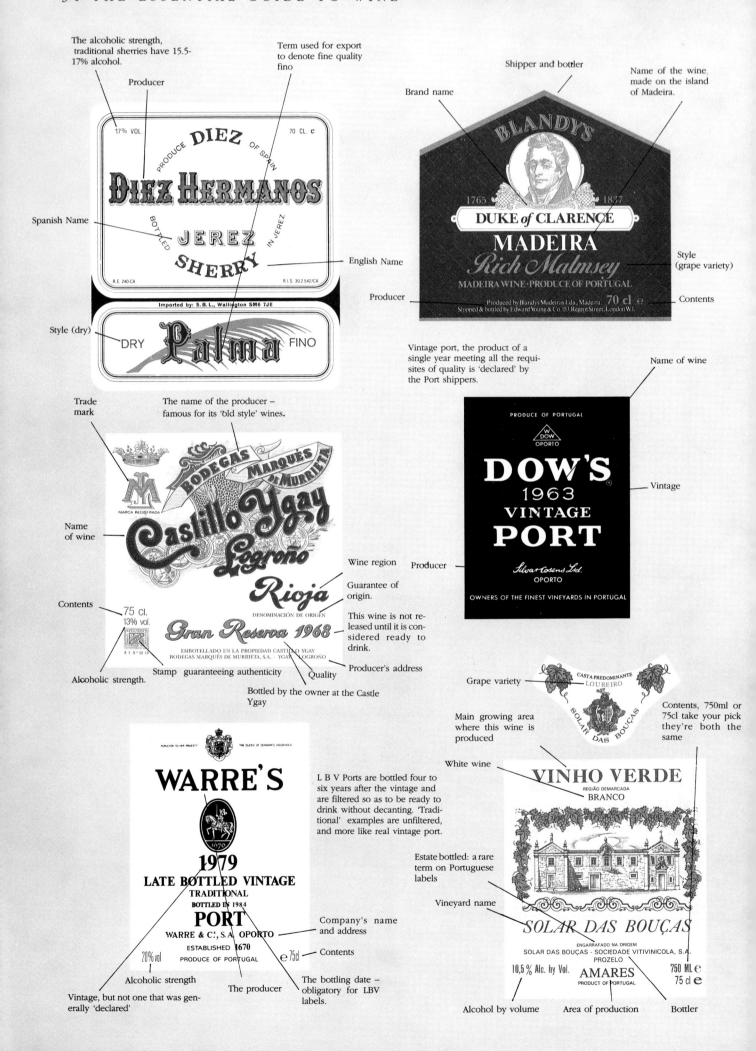

The alcoholic strength, traditional sherries have 15.5-17% alcohol.

Term used for export to denote fine quality fino

Producer

Shipper and bottler

Name of the wine, made on the island of Madeira.

Brand name

Spanish Name

BLANDY'S

1765   1837

DUKE of CLARENCE

MADEIRA

Rich Malmsey

MADEIRA WINE · PRODUCE OF PORTUGAL

Produced by Blandys Madeiras Lda, Madeira. 70 cl e

Shipped & bottled by Edward Young & Co. 153 Regent Street, London W.1.

PRODUCE OF SPAIN

DIEZ

DIEZ HERMANOS

BOTTLED   IN JEREZ

JEREZ

SHERRY

17% VOL.   70 CL. e

R.E. 240-CA   R.I.S. 30.2.542/CA

Imported by: S.B.L., Wallington SM6 7JE

DRY   Palma   FINO

English Name

Style (dry)

Producer

Style (grape variety)

Contents

Vintage port, the product of a single year meeting all the requisites of quality is 'declared' by the Port shippers.

Trade mark

The name of the producer – famous for its 'old style' wines.

Name of wine

BODEGAS

MARQUÉS DE MURRIETA

MARCA REGISTRADA

Castillo Ygay

Logroño

Rioja

DENOMINACIÓN DE ORIGEN

Gran Reserva 1968

EMBOTELLADO EN LA PROPIEDAD CASTILLO YGAY

BODEGAS MARQUÉS DE MURRIETA, S.A. · YGAY LOGROÑO

R.E. N.º 53 LO

Name of wine

PRODUCE OF PORTUGAL

DOW

OPORTO

DOW'S

1963

VINTAGE

PORT

Silva & Cosens Ltd.

OPORTO

OWNERS OF THE FINEST VINEYARDS IN PORTUGAL

Vintage

Contents

75 cl.

13% vol.

Wine region

Guarantee of origin.

This wine is not released until it is considered ready to drink.

Producer's address

Producer

Alcoholic strength.

Stamp guaranteeing authenticity

Quality

Quality

Bottled by the owner at the Castle Ygay

CASTA PREDOMINANTE

LOUREIRO

SOLAR DAS BOUÇAS

Grape variety

Contents, 750ml or 75cl take your pick they're both the same

Main growing area where this wine is produced

White wine

PURVEYOR TO HER MAJESTY   THE QUEEN OF DENMARK'S HOUSEHOLD

WARRE'S

1670

1979

LATE BOTTLED VINTAGE

TRADITIONAL

BOTTLED IN 1984

PORT

WARRE & C.º, S.A. OPORTO

ESTABLISHED 1670

PRODUCE OF PORTUGAL

20% vol   e 75cl

L B V Ports are bottled four to six years after the vintage and are filtered so as to be ready to drink without decanting. 'Traditional' examples are unfiltered, and more like real vintage port.

VINHO VERDE

REGIÃO DEMARCADA

BRANCO

SOLAR DAS BOUÇAS

ENGARRAFADO NA ORIGEM

SOLAR DAS BOUÇAS - SOCIEDADE VITIVINICOLA, S.A.

PROZELO

10,5 % Alc. by Vol.   AMARES   750 ML e

PRODUCT OF PORTUGAL   75 cl e

Estate bottled: a rare term on Portuguese labels

Vineyard name

Company's name and address

Contents

Alcoholic strength

Vintage, but not one that was generally 'declared'

The producer

The bottling date – obligatory for LBV labels.

Alcohol by volume   Area of production   Bottler

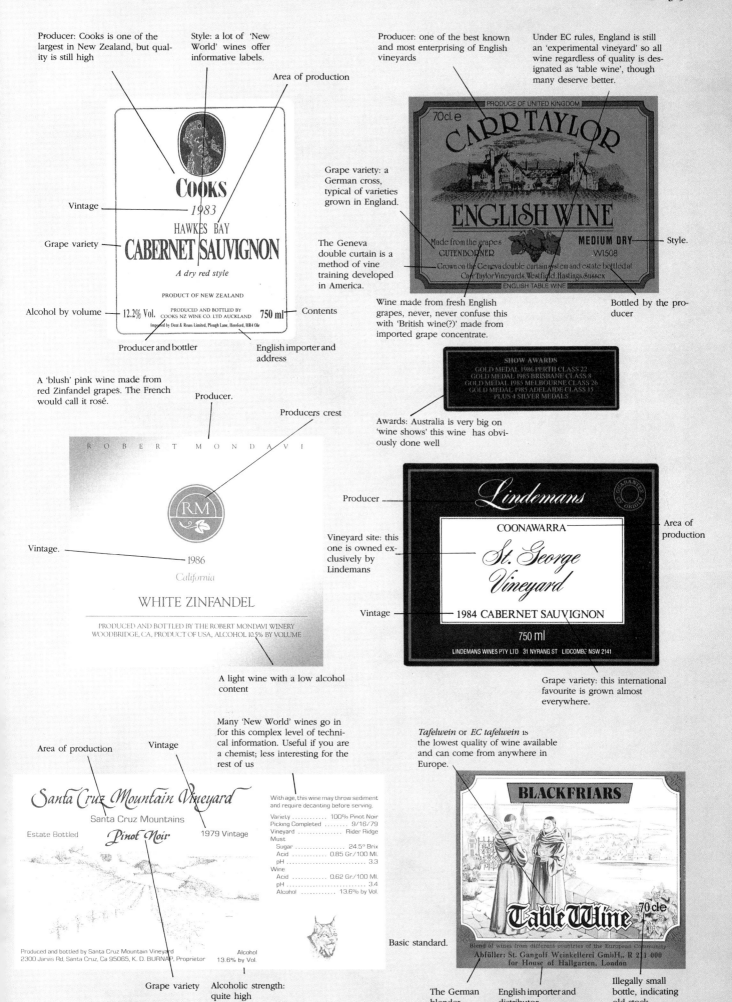

Producer: Cooks is one of the largest in New Zealand, but quality is still high

Style: a lot of 'New World' wines offer informative labels.

Area of production

Vintage

Grape variety

Alcohol by volume

Producer and bottler

English importer and address

COOKS
1983
HAWKES BAY
CABERNET SAUVIGNON
A dry red style
PRODUCT OF NEW ZEALAND
12.2% Vol. PRODUCED AND BOTTLED BY COOKS NZ WINE CO. LTD AUCKLAND
Imported by Deut & Reuss Limited, Plough Lane, Hereford, HR4 Ole
750 ml

Contents

Producer: one of the best known and most enterprising of English vineyards

Under EC rules, England is still an 'experimental vineyard' so all wine regardless of quality is designated as 'table wine', though many deserve better.

PRODUCE OF UNITED KINGDOM
70cl. e
CARR TAYLOR
ENGLISH WINE
Made from the grapes
GUTENBORNER
MEDIUM DRY
W1508
Grown on the Geneva double curtain system and estate bottled at
Carr Taylor Vineyards, Westfield, Hastings, Sussex
ENGLISH TABLE WINE

Grape variety: a German cross, typical of varieties grown in England.

Style.

The Geneva double curtain is a method of vine training developed in America.

Wine made from fresh English grapes, never, never confuse this with 'British wine(?)' made from imported grape concentrate.

Bottled by the producer

A 'blush' pink wine made from red Zinfandel grapes. The French would call it rosé.

Producer.

Producers crest

SHOW AWARDS
GOLD MEDAL 1986 PERTH CLASS 22
GOLD MEDAL 1985 BRISBANE CLASS 8
GOLD MEDAL 1985 MELBOURNE CLASS 26
GOLD MEDAL 1985 ADELAIDE CLASS 15
PLUS 4 SILVER MEDALS

Awards: Australia is very big on 'wine shows' this wine has obviously done well

ROBERT MONDAVI
RM
1986
California
WHITE ZINFANDEL
PRODUCED AND BOTTLED BY THE ROBERT MONDAVI WINERY
WOODBRIDGE, CA, PRODUCT OF USA, ALCOHOL 10.5% BY VOLUME

Vintage.

A light wine with a low alcohol content

Producer

Lindemans
GUARANTEED ORIGIN
COONAWARRA
St. George Vineyard
1984 CABERNET SAUVIGNON
750 ml
LINDEMANS WINES PTY LTD 31 NYRANG ST LIDCOMBE NSW 2141

Area of production

Vineyard site: this one is owned exclusively by Lindemans

Vintage

Grape variety: this international favourite is grown almost everywhere.

Area of production

Vintage

Many 'New World' wines go in for this complex level of technical information. Useful if you are a chemist; less interesting for the rest of us

Tafelwein or *EC tafelwein* is the lowest quality of wine available and can come from anywhere in Europe.

Santa Cruz Mountain Vineyard
Santa Cruz Mountains
Estate Bottled *Pinot Noir* 1979 Vintage

With age, this wine may throw sediment and require decanting before serving.

Variety .... 100% Pinot Noir
Picking Completed 9/16/79
Vineyard .... Rider Ridge
Must
 Sugar .... 24.5° Brix
 Acid .... 0.85 Gr/100 Ml.
 pH 3.3
Wine
 Acid .... 0.62 Gr/100 Ml.
 pH 3.4
 Alcohol .... 13.6% by Vol.

Produced and bottled by Santa Cruz Mountain Vineyard
2300 Jarvis Rd, Santa Cruz, Ca 95065, K. D. BURNAP, Proprietor
Alcohol 13.6% by Vol.

BLACKFRIARS
Table Wine 70 cle
Blend of wines from different countries of the European Community
Abfüller: St. Gangolf Weinkellerei GmbH., R 2/1 000
for House of Hallgarten, London

Basic standard.

Grape variety

Alcoholic strength: quite high

The German blender

English importer and distributor

Illegally small bottle, indicating old stock.

CHOOSING A STYLE

Buying wine today is much more enjoyable – and challenging – than it ever used to be. Of course, there are people who find the style of wine they like, and stick to it, picking up the same bottle of Rioja or Côtes du Rhône every time, confident in the knowledge that they know what they are getting – just as there are people who invariably go to the same restaurant and order the same dishes, and office managers who unquestioningly buy all their computers from IBM.

Of course, playing safe does have its advantages, but for every occasion that it protects you from disappointment, there are probably at least a couple of times when it'll stop you from discovering a delicious wine – and, quite probably, a bargain.

But being adventurous doesn't have to mean buying wine at random. An office manager who's decided that he might like to buy a computer from a manufacturer other than IBM will probably turn his attention towards 'IBM-compatible' equipment which will be similar to the system he's used to.

Wine is very similar. Once you have decided that you like your white wine to have a particular level of sweetness, or your red to be medium- rather than full-bodied – or if you need a particular style of wine to match a dish you are preparing – there are now two widely-used scales to guide you towards the style of wine you are most likely to enjoy.

The white wine scale – extending from '1' for a bone-dry Muscadet to '9' for an ultra-sweet Muscat de Beaumes de Venise – was first promoted by the Wine Development Board, an organisation devoted to converting the population of the United Kingdom to the joys of wine. At first, some of the traditionalists in the wine trade mumbled and grumbled that one really oughtn't to be categorising – and thus 'demystifying' – wine in this way but, within a very short while, most major retailers adopted the codes as, from its first issue in 1983, did *WINE Magazine* when reporting on its tastings.

The success of the white-wine scale and its popularity among the general public led inevitably to calls for a similar set of codes for reds. This proved to be rather more contentious at first, partly because it was suggested that any such innovation might contravene one of the EC's more arcane regulations. Fortunately, however, by the beginning of the 1990s, an A-E scale was being widely introduced that now allows wine buyers a good idea of whether the wine they are looking at is as light-weight as a Beaujolais or as much of a bruiser as a Barolo.

Clearly, any such codes inevitably tend both to simplify and to generalise. Some Beaujolais may be a great deal more muscular than others – and there are some middle-weight modern Barolos; although most wines of a particular style or appellation can be fitted into the niche of a single code number or letter, there will always be exceptions to prove the rule. Most wine retailers handle these anomalies by allocating codes to specific wines rather than styles, describing one red Burgundy, for example, as a 'B' and another, bigger, one as a 'C'.

As an illustration of how these codes work, I have chosen a broad selection of wines to which each number or letter might be applied.

WHITES AND ROSES : BONE DRY (1) - VERY SWEET (9)

— 1 —

Amontillado sherry *(Spain)*
Anjou Blanc *(France)*
Bergerac *(France)*
Bordeaux Sauvignon *(France)*
Bordeaux Sec *(France)*
Brut Champagne *(France)*
Dry English Table Wine
Fino sherry (Spanish style)
Loire Chardonnay *(France)*
Chablis *(France)*
California Dry Rosé
Chiaretto di Bardolino *(Italy)*
Côtes du Rhône Rosé *(France)*
Dry Oloroso sherry
Dry Vouvray *(France)*
Entre-deux-Mers *(France)*
Lirac Rosé *(France)*
Loire Chardonnay *(France)*

Manzanilla sherry *(Spain)*
Muscadet *(France)*
New Zealand Sauvignon
NE Italy Chardonnay
NE Italy Pinot Grigio
NE Italy Riesling
NE Italy Sauvignon
Pouilly Blanc Fumé *(France)*
Quincy *(France)*
Rioja Rosado *(Spain)*
Rosé de Provence *(France)*
Sancerre *(France)*
Sauvignon de St Bris *(France)*
Sauvignon de Touraine/du
  Haut Poitou *(France)*
Savennières *(France)*
Sparkling Vouvray Brut
  (France)
Tavel Rosé *(France)*

RIGHT: Just over the border, many Bergerac producers also have land in Bordeaux. When well-made, the former wine can be a good, inexpensive alternative to the latter

LEFT: The Marlborough Valley on the South Island of New Zealand has become the source of great Sauvignon Blancs, flavour-packed alternatives to Sancerre and Pouilly Fumé

— 2 —

Anjou Blanc *(France)*
Arneis *(Italy)*
Australian/California Riesling
Australian/California Sauvignon
Australian Semillon
Bianco di Custoza *(Italy)*
Blanquette de Limoux *(France)*
California Chardonnay
Cava *(Spain)*
Chilean Chardonnay
Clairette de Die *(France)*
Côtes du Jura *(France)*
Crémant d'Alsace *(France)*
Crémant de Bourgogne *(France)*
Dry Montilla *(Spain)*
Dry Sherry – UK style *(Spain)*
Frascati Secco *(Italy)*
Graves *(France)*

Italian Pinot Bianco
New Zealand Chardonnay
New Zealand 'Fumé Blanc'
Modern-style Rioja *(Spain)*
Orvieto Secco *(Italy)*
Pinot Blanc d'Alsace *(France)*
Prosecco *(Italy)*
Riesling d'Alsace *(France)*
Saumur Mousseux *(France)*
Sekt *(Germany)*
Sercial Madeira *(Portugal)*
Soave *(Italy)*
German *trocken* wines
Tuscan Chardonnay *(Italy)*
Verdicchio *(Italy)*
Vernaccia di San Gimignano
   (Italy)
White Burgundy *(France)*
White Rhône *(France)*

— 3 —

Australian Chardonnay
Australian/New Zealand Riesling
Australian Sparkling Wines
Austrian Grüner Veltliner
Brut Sparkling Wines
California Chardonnay
California/New Zealand Chenin
   Blanc
Dry White Port *(Portugal)*
German Gewürztraminer
German *halbtrocken* Wines
Goldmuskateller *(Italy)*

Gewürztraminer d'Alsace
   (France)
Hungarian Dry Olasz Rizling
Medium-dry English Wine
Mosel Kabinett *(Germany)*
Mosel QbA *(Germany)*
Mosel Tafelwein *(Germany)*
Muscat d'Alsace *(France)*
NE Italy Gewürztraminer
Pomino *(Italy)*
Rioja - traditional style *(Spain)*

— 4 —

Amontillado UK-style *(Spain)*
Anjou Rosé *(France)*
Australian/New Zealand/
   Bulgarian Riesling
Austrian Gewürztraminer
California Chenin Blanc
California Gewürztraminer
EEC Tafelwein
Hungarian Olasz Rizling
Medium-dry Sherry

New Zealand Gewürztraminer
Orvieto Abbocato *(Italy)*
Portuguese Rosé
Rhine and Nahe Kabinett
   (Germany)
Rhine QbA *(Germany)*
Vinho Verde – commercial
   style *(Portugal)*
Yugoslavia Laski Rizling

— 5 —

'Hock' *(Germany)*
Liebfraumilch *(Germany)*
Medium 'British' Sherry (any-
   where in Europe

Demi-Sec Sparkling Wines
German Spätlese
Verdelho Madeira *(Portugal)*
Demi-Sec Vouvray *(France)*

— 6 —

Amontillado sherry (UK-style)
Demi-Sec Champagne *(France)*
Lambrusco Bianco *(Italy)*

Quarts de Chaume *(France)*
Tokay Szamarodni *(Hungary)*

— 7 —

Asti Spumante *(Italy)*
Bual Madeira *(Portugal)*
Clairette de Die Tradition
   (France)
Monbazillac *(France)*

Moscato d'Asti *(Italy)*
Mosel Auslese *(Germany)*
Pale Cream Sherry *(Spain)*
Premières Côtes de Bordeaux
   (France)
Tokay Aszu *(Hungary)*

— 8 —

Australian/US late-picked
   Riesling
Barsac *(France)*
Cream and Rich Cream Sherry
   (Spain)
Loupiac *(France)*
Moscatel *(Spain)*

Beerenauslese
   (Austria, Germany)
Recioto di Soave *(Italy)*
Ste-Croix-du-Mont *(France)*
Sauternes *(France)*
Torcolato *(Italy)*

— 9 —

Australian Liqueur Muscat/Tokay
Eiswein *(Germany)*
Greek Muscat
Malmsey Madeira *(Portugal)*
Marsala *(Italy)*
Moscatel *(Spain)*
Moscato Passito di Pantelleria
   (Italy)

Muscat de Beaumes de Venise
   (France)
Muscat de Frontignan*(France)*
Muscat de Rivesaltes *(France)*
Trockenbeerenauslesen
   (Austria, Germany)
Sweet Sherry *(Spain)*
Vin Santo – sweet style *(Italy)*

RED WINES : VERY LIGHT (A) – VERY FULL (E)

— A —

Alsace Pinot Noir *(France)*
Bardolino *(Italy)*
Beaujolais *(France)*
Freisa *(Italy)*
Gaillac Gamay *(France)*

Gamay de Touraine *(France)*
German Spätburgunder
Lambrusco Rosso *(Italy)*
Sancerre Rouge *(France)*
Valdepeñas *(Spain)*

— B —

Bourgueil *(France)*
Chianti *(Italy)*
Chinon *(France)*
Corbières *(France)*
Costières du Gard *(France)*
Côte de Beaune Burgundy
  (France)
Côtes du Roussillon *(France)*
Cru Beaujolais *(France)*
Bouzy Rouge *(France)*

Dolcetto *(Italy)*
Fitou *(France)*
Grave del Friuli *(Italy)*
Hungarian Pinot Noir
NE Italian Merlot
Oregon Pinot Noir *(USA)*
Teroldego Rotaliano *(Italy)*
Valencia *(Spain)*
Valpolicella *(Italy)*

— C —

Bairrada *(Portugal)*
Barbera d'Alba / d'Asti *(Italy)*
Bergerac *(France)*
Bordeaux Rouge *(France)*
Bulgarian Cabernet Sauvignon
Cahors *(France)*
Chilean Cabernet Sauvignon
Côte de Nuits Burgundy
  (France)
Bourgogne Rouge *(France)*

Côtes du Rhône *(France)*
Dão *(Portugal)*
Gigondas *(France)*
New Zealand Cabernet
  Sauvignon
Rioja *(Spain)*
Rosso di Montalcino *(Italy)*
Washington State Cabernet/
  Merlot *(USA)*

— D —

Australian Cabernet Sauvignon
Brunello di Montalcino *(Italy)*
California Cabernet Sauvignon
Carmignano *(Italy)*
Château Musar *(Lebanon)*
Châteauneuf-du-Pape *(France)*
Classed Growth Bordeaux
  (France)
Crozes Hermitage *(France)*
Douro *(Portugal)*

Fuller-style 'Ripasso'
  Valpolicella *(Italy)*
Gattinara *(Italy)*
Madiran *(France)*
Nebbiolo d'Alba *(Italy)*
Rosso Conero *(Italy)*
St Joseph *(France)*
'Super-Tuscans' – Sassicaia,
  Tignanello etc *(Italy)*
Toro *(Spain)*

— E —

Aglianico del Vulture *(Italy)*
Australian Shiraz or
  Shiraz/Cabernet
Barolo *(Italy)*
Californian Zinfandel –
  traditional style

Côte Rôtie *(France)*
Hermitage *(France)*
Recioto della Valpolicella/
  Amarone *(Italy)*

ABOVE: Relaxed Australian labelling laws permit 'sherry', 'Champagne' and 'port' to be made. Australian 'Vintage' is rather like an Oporto Tawny, seen here (FACING PAGE) maturing in barrel

Alternatives

The sweetness and heaviness of a wine is, of course, just one aspect of its character. A Tavel rosé and a *trocken* wine from Germany may be equally dry, but their flavour is as different as their colour. The best indications of the way in which a wine is likely to taste, and of the other wine styles to which it will bear the closest resemblance, can be derived from its grape variety (or varieties), the climate and soil of its vineyard and the way in which it was made.

If you like Bordeaux, the flavour you enjoy is largely that of the Cabernet Sauvignon, Merlot and Cabernet Franc grapes; if your favourite wine is Barolo, you clearly relish the toughish, tannic, spicy character of the Nebbiolo grape. In both cases, there is a long list of similar alternatives that should suit your taste.

Oaky White Wine

Traditional Rioja
Chardonnay – from just about
  everywhere
Classy white Burgundy *(France)*

Graves – new style *(France)*
Fumé Blanc *(California,
  Australia)*

Fresh/Grassy Whites

Most Bordeaux Blanc *(France)*
New Zealand Sauvignon Blanc
Pouilly Blanc Fumé
  (France)
Sauvignon de Touraine
  (France)

Sancerre *(France)*
German *trocken* Müller-
  Thurgau
German *trocken* Scheurebe
English dry Müller-Thurgau
Grüner Veltliner *(Austria)*

Aromatic/Spicy Whites

Alsace Gewürztraminer
  (France)
Alsace Tokay-Pinot Gris
  (France)
Condrieu *(France)*

Arneis *(Italy)*
Pinot Grigio *(Italy)*
Grüner Veltliner *(Austria)*
Viña Esmeralda *(Spain)*
New Zealand Traminer

Rich, Unoaked Whites

Alsace Pinot Blanc *(France)*
Most Mâcon Villages *(France)*
Alsace Muscat *(France)*
Hermitage *(France)*
Graves (old-style) *(France)*
Gavi *(Italy)*
Frascati – at rare best *(Italy)*
Austrian Kabinett
New Zealand Riesling
Trocken Riesling
Dry English WInes
Australian Riesling
Australian dry Muscat
Australian Semillon
Off-dry, Grapey Whites

Dry Grapy Whites

Alsace Riesling *(France)*
English medium
German Kabinett
German Halbtrocken

Sweet Grapy Wines (Still and Sparkling)

Clairette de Die Tradition *(France)*
Muscat de Beaumes de Venise, Rivesaltes etc *(France)*
Alsace Riesling Sélection de Grains Nobles *(France)*
Alsace Muscat Vendange Tardive *(France)*
Auslese Riesling (Germany, (Austria)
Moscato d'Asti *(Italy)*
Moscatel de Setúbal *(Portugal)*
Moscatel de Valencia *(Spain)*
Samos Muscat *(Greece)*
Australian Fruity Gordo
Muscat Canelli *(California)*

Sweet Honeyed Whites

Sauternes *(France)*
Vouvray Demi Sec *(France)*
Jurançon *(France)*
Monbazillac *(France)*
Moelleux Vouvray, Quarts de Chaume etc *(France)*
Ste-Croix-du-Mont *(France)*
Orvieto Amabile *(Italy)*

Botrytised Whites

Alsace Vendange Tardive or Sélection de Grains Nobles *(France)*
Barsac or Sauternes *(France)*
German or Austrian Auslese or Beerenauslese
Moelleux Bonnezeaux/ Vouvray/Quarts de Chaume *(France)*
Any 'Bunch Select' wine
Edelbeerenlese *(Romania)*
Hungarian Tokay Trockenbeerenauslese

Dry Sparkling Whites

Brut Champagne *(France)*
Crémant de Bourgogne *(France)*
Crémant d'Alsace/Loire *(France)*
Blanquette de Limoux *(France)*
Prosecco *(Italy)*
Cava *(Spain)*
California sparkling wine
Australian sparkling wine

Medium Sparkling Wines

Demi-Sec from just about any- where.
White Lambrusco
Sekt *(Germany)*

Dry Rosé

Burgundy *(France)*
Côtes du Rhône *(France)*
Lirac *(France)*
Provence *(France)*
Rioja *(Spain)*
Chiaretto di Bardolino *(Italy)*

Medium Rosé

'Blush' wine from California – or just about anywhere else
Portuguese Rosé
Rosé d'Anjou

Beaujolais Style/Light Reds

Alsace Pinot Noir *(France)*
Bourgogne Passetoutgrains *(France)*
Côtes du Rhône Nouveau/ Primeur *(France)*
Gamay from Gaillac, Anjou and Touraine *(France)*
Bardolino *(Italy)*
Sancerre Rouge (light example) *(France)*
Teroldego Rotaliano *(Italy)*
Dornfelder *(Germany)*
German Spätburgunder
Lemberger
Gamay and Pinot Noir *(Switzerland)*

Bordeaux Style

Buzet *(France)*
Chinon *(France)*
Pécharmant *(France)*
St-Nicolas-de-Bourgueil *(France)*
Bergerac *(France)*
Australian Cabernet Sauvignon
Bulgarian Cabernet Sauvignon / Merlot
Spanish Cabernet Sauvignon (Torres, Marqués de Griñon and Jean León)
Italian Merlot / Cabernet
Italian 'super-Tuscans' (such as Tignanello, Sassicaia etc)
California Cabernet Sauvignon
Château Musar *(Lebanon)*
Chilean Cabernet Sauvignon
New Zealand Cabernet Sauvignon
Washington State Merlot/ Cabernet Sauvignon
Yugoslavian Merlot and Cabernet
Hungarian Merlot

Tough, Tannic Reds

Barolo *(Italy)*
Barbaresco *(Italy)*
Cahors *(France)* - though only old-fashioned examples
Hermitage *(France)*
St-Estèphe *(France)*
Douro *(Portugal)*
Priorato *(Spain)*
Bigger Californian Zinfandel
Some Australian Shiraz

Rustic Reds

Cahors *(France)*
Corbières/Minervois *(France)*
Corvo/Taurasi *(Italy)*
Dão *(Portugal)*

Sweet and Off-Dry Reds

Piat d'Or *(France)*
Lambrusco *(Italy)*
Recioto di Valpolicella *(Italy)*
Some Russian reds

Burgundy-Style

Older Cru Beaujolais *(France)*
Bouzy Rouge *(France)*
US Pinot Noir
Antipodean Pinot Noir

Rich and Raisiny Wines

Malaga *(Spain)*
Malmsey Madeira *(Portugal)*
Marsala *(Italy)*
Recioto *(Italy)*
Mavrodaphne *(Greece)*
Australian Liqueur Muscat

Medium -Bodied Spicy Reds

Côtes du Rhône *(France)*
Crozes Hermitage *(France)*
St Joseph *(France)*
Nebbiolo d'Alba *(Italy)*
Lighter-bodied Zinfandel *(California)*

Fuller-Bodied Spicy Reds

Côte Rôtie *(France)*
Hermitage *(France)*
Barolo *(Italy)*
Priorato *(Spain)*
Australian Shiraz
Australian Shiraz/Cabernet
Fuller-bodied Zinfandel *(California)*

Sherry-like Wines

Vin Santo *(Italy)*
Montilla *(Spain)*
Sercial Madeira *(Portugal)*
Vin Jaune *(France)*

Port-like Wines

Banyuls *(France)*
Anghelu Ruju *(Italy)*
Commandaria *(Cyprus)*
Recioto della Valpolicella *(Italy)*
New World 'Port'

STORING

There is a certain amount of snobbery attached to storing wine. It's as though the flashiness of the storing system somehow reflects the seriousness of the wine collection. Expensive glass-fronted refrigerated cabinets, or shelving with mahogany doors, often have more to do with impressing visitors than appropriate storage. You don't need to throw money at the problem.

However, some people do still go to enormous lengths to build a clinically perfect cellar in which all the factors which affect wine are in perfect control. If you've got several thousand bottles of priceless old claret, you might do the same. The rest of us, in our modern, cellarless houses or flats, have to rely on our ingenuity.

Storing wine doesn't have to be complicated – indeed, it is astonishing how well even fine wine will put up with less than ideal conditions. Provided your bottles are left lying horizontally in a draught-free (but not airless), reasonably cool, damp-ish, rather dark place, the wine in them should develop and survive as its makers originally intended.

All that is necessary is to decide how many bottles you are likely to want to store, then find a suitable space which you can assign to them. There are then any number of simple ways to give your wine the necessary protection from the effects of light, heat and dehydrated air.

An old fireplace, a wall in the spare room, beneath the staircase, a box-room, an unused cupboard... all kinds of places can be turned into useful wine stores with a little imagination and, on occasion, a touch of do-it-yourself. Then comes the fun part – deciding what you're going to put into it, and how much you're going to spend. We've given suggestions for some well-balanced selections here, but you'll have your own tastes and needs to accommodate. Any good wine merchant should be pleased to advise you if you want to splash out on a 'ready-made' cellar – or you may want to build up your selection slowly. With suitable storage space to hand, you'll be able to stock up on good buys as and when you come across them – and store up a great deal of future drinking pleasure.

ABOVE: Wine racks can be improvised in all sorts of ways. This one was made from pieces of terracotta pipe

RIGHT: One of the grandest cellars in the world, but also one of the most sensibly laid out, this is beneath the offices of Bouchard Père et Fils in Burgundy

CREATING A CELLAR

The practicalities of creating and maintaining a wine store range from the simple to the ingenious. What you're aiming for is not only an environment in which your wine will be happy, but one which, by being well-kept, will never have you searching frantically for a wine you think you still have a bottle of... somewhere.

If you haven't an actual cellar, similar conditions can be obtained either by building one of the kit versions now available into the floor of your house, or by buying a thermostatically-controlled cabinet such as the French Eurocave. But if, like the majority of us, you are converting a spare boxroom or cupboard into your wine store, you'll need to start with the basics.

Light is easy to keep out; insulation can help to maintain a steady temperature; and a damp sponge left on a saucer will provide essential humidity. Don't make it too airtight – you should avoid your store smelling musty – but draughts are to be prevented too.

The temperature to aim for is between 7-10°C – about as cool as you will normally want to drink your white wines. In general terms, and over a period of several years, the warmer the cellar, the faster your wine will develop or – possibly – decay.

Racks

Wooden folding and self-assembly racks are inexpensive and readily obtainable. Avoid models which have sharp metal edges — these tend to tear labels as bottles are being inserted or removed. Handier folk can, given the space, build bin-units using wooden shelving or breeze blocks in which several bottles of the same wine can be kept in a pile. It is useful to be able to attach cards with numbers or wine names to the rack so that un-

necessary searching is reduced to a minimum. If you buy purpose-made racks, remember that they are not suited to half-bottles, magnums and larger bottles. Leave space for these. Save rack space by not unpacking any wine or port which has arrived in wooden cases (important in any event if you subsequently decide to resell the wine). By the same token, cheap daily-drinking wine can be left in stout cardboard cartons, provided the store is not too damp.

Cellar Book

Essential, as is a well-kept plan showing exactly where all the wines have been placed. A good cellar book will remind you of when you bought particular wines and how they tasted last time you opened a bottle. If you do have a real cellar, or a reasonably damp store, avoid leaving the book in it — otherwise the paper can disintegrate and the ink can run. A chinagraph pencil or laundry marker and white plastic cards can be useful for this reason. Similarly, Hugh Johnson suggests spraying wine labels with *scentless* hair lacquer to protect them from the damp.

Order

Try to establish a pattern for where you store each wine type. One easy system is that used in the old game of 'Battleships' – number and letter your wine racks vertically and horizontally, so that each 'hole' has a code that you can assign to the bottle it contains in your cellar book.

Insurance

One final point. Your cellar will be worth a certain amount when you start to fill it. With luck, that value will rise – perhaps considerably so – over the years. Forgetting to be properly insured would be a pity.

A CLASSIC CELLAR
A selection that offers years of drinking from Europe's top vineyards. It combines the best of tradition with some of the 'new classics' with which European winemakers have been showing the New World that they still haven't lost their spark.

* **Bordeaux** Médoc *Châteaux Léoville Las Cases, Léoville-Barton, Pichon-Lalande, Lynch-Bages, Ducru-Beaucaillou, Cos d'Estournel, Palmer, La Gurgue, Haut-Bages-Libéral, Chasse-Spleen.* Graves *Dom. de Chevalier; Châteaux la Louvière, Fieuzal, Haut-Bailly* (red). Pomerol and St Emilion *Châteaux Pavie, Figeac, Lafleur, Le Bon Pasteur, Certan-de-May; Vieux-Château-Certan.* Sauternes *Châteaux Rieussec, Gilette, Bastor-Lamontagne, Doisy-Daëne.*
* **Burgundy** Nuits St Georges *A Michelot.* Vosne Romanée *D Rion.* Volnay *Lafarge.* Meursault *Michelot-Buisson; Lafon.* Puligny Montrachet *Leflaive; Chartron et Trébuchet.* Chassagne Montrachet *Carillon; Sauzet.*
* **Rhône** Hermitage, Côte Rôtie *Guigal; Jaboulet Aîné.* Châteauneuf-du-Pape *Domaine du Vieux Télégraphe.*
* **Southern French superstars** *Mas de Daumas Gassac; Domaine de Trevallon*
* **Barolo** *Ceretto; Borgogno; Aldo Conterno.*
* **Italian superstars** *Gaja Chardonnay; Sassicaia; Tignanello; Solaia; Pomino.*
* **Rioja** Gran Reserva *Marqués de Murrieta; CVNE; La Rioja Alta; Contino; Remelluri.*
* **Spanish superstars** *Jean León ; Marqués de Griñon; Torres Black Label.*
* **Germany** Mosel *Egon Müller; Deinhard; F W Gymnasium .* Rhine/Nahe *Balthasar Ress; Bürklin-Wolf; Bassermann-Jordan.*

Champagne *Pol Roger; Alfred Gratien; Gosset; Boizel; Deutz; Krug.*
Port *Dows; Grahams; Taylors; Noval.*

A 'WORKING' CELLAR
No priceless dust-gatherers here, but a good-value cellar that ensures you'll have a bottle packed with flavour and interest for all but the most special occasion.

* **Daily Drinking** Vin de Pays des Côtes de Gascogne; Touraine Sauvignon; Australian Chenin/Semillon/Colombard; Bulgarian Cabernet Sauvignon and Merlot; Romanian Pinot Noir.
* **Bordeaux** Bergerac; Côtes de Castillon; Côtes de Francs; Lalande de Pomerol. Entre-deux-Mers (*Château Bonnet*).
* **Burgundy** Bourgogne Rouge; Côte de Beaune- or Nuits-Villages; St Aubin; St Romain; Mercurey; Rully; Givry; St-Véran; St Romain; Pernand-Vergelesses (*Jaffelin; Drouhin; Vallet Frères; Louis Jadot*).
* **Cru Beaujolais** Fleurie; Morgon; Moulin-à-Vent (*Duboeuf, Loron; Drouhin*).
* **Alsace** Pinot Blanc (*Kuentz Bas; Cave Vinicole de Turckheim; Hugel*).
* **Rhône** Côtes du Rhône-Villages; Côtes du Ventoux; Coteaux du Tricastin; Lirac (*Guigal; Jaboulet Aîné; Delas*); Côtes du Lubéron (*Val Joanis*).
Italy Pinot Grigio; Dolcetto d'Asti (*Bava*) Pinot Bianco (*Tiefenbrunner*); Barbera d'Asti (*Viticoltori dell'Acquese; Gaja; Fontanafredda*); Teroldego (*Gaierhof*).
* **Spain** Toro (*Gran Colegiata*); Navarra (*Chivite*)
* **Portugal** Pasmados, Periquita, Camarate (all *Fonseca*); Tinta da Anfora (*João Pires*);

Vinho Verde (*Aveleda; Solar das Boucas*).
* **Australia** Chardonnay (*Rosemount; Wynns; Orlando RF*); Shiraz (*Penfolds; Wynns; Brown Bros*).
* **New Zealand** Sauvignon Blanc (*Montana; Cooks*).
* **Chile** Cabernet Sauvignon (*Santa Rita; Errazuriz Panquehe; Nogales*).
* **Sparkling Wine** Crémant d'Alsace, de Loire & Bourgogne.
Port Tawny (*Dows; Noval; Cockburns; Noval; Ramos Pinto*); Crusted (*Cockburns; Churchill Graham*).

A NEW WORLD CELLAR
A completely different approach – a cellar arranged by grape variety and style, just as the New Worlders do their wines.

* **Cabernet Sauvignon** Wynns Coonawarra (*Australia*); Mondavi Reserve (*California*); Cousino Macul Antiguas Reservas (*Chile*).
* **Chardonnay** Rosemount Roxburgh (*Aus*); Inniskillin (*Canada*); Hargrave (*Long Island*); Sonoma Cutrer (*Cal*).
* **Sauvignon Blanc** Cloudy Bay (*NZ*).
* **Semillon** Rothbury (*Aus*).
* **Riesling** Hardy's Siegersdorf (*Aus*); Kiona (*Washington*).
* **Pinot Noir** Cameron (*Oregon*); Hamilton Russell (*South Africa*); Au Bon Climat (*Cal*).
* **Merlot** Newton (*Cal*).
* **Shiraz** Grange (*Aus*); Bonny Doon (*Cal*).
* **Zinfandel** Ridge (*Cal*).
* **Sparkling Wine** Petaluma (*Aus*); Iron Horse (*Cal*).
* **Late-Harvest and Fortified** Brown Bros Orange Muscat and Flora; Morris Liqueur Muscat (*Aus*); Phelps Riesling (*Cal*).

SERVING

Some people see the serving of wine as an etiquette minefield – as if, were the port to be passed the wrong way or a red opened before a white, the sky would fall on their heads. But the guidelines here have nothing to do with 'table manners' – we'll leave the social dilemmas to Debrett's and concentrate instead on simple (and by no means hard and fast) rules by which to ensure that the wine you are opening tastes at its best.

Temperature

For reds, the word *chambré* – meaning at room temperature – is rather misleading. Which room? What temperature? Supposedly 'standard' conditions can vary a great deal. And remember that a century ago, when the French coined the term *chambré*, the chances were that even the wealthiest of wine drinkers lived in homes which were far less warm than our centrally-heated cocoons. To them 'room temperature' often meant only a few degrees warmer than the cellar from which the wine was brought.

Served too warm, even the finest red wine can seem heavy and rather dull. In fact, some red wines are best drunk slightly chilled – fresh, fruity Beaujolais and light red Loires desperately need to be served at temperatures only slightly higher than that at which you would serve a white Burgundy.

SERVING TEMPERATURES

Not many of us can think automatically in degrees Centigrade; 'hours in the fridge' or 'hours open' are usually quite adequate units of measurement when gauging serving temperatures for wine. If you really want to be precise, one can now buy floppy plastic thermometers which, though intended for recalcitrant children's foreheads, will wrap round and adhere to the neck of a bottle very satisfactorily.

Remember, incidentally, that the term 'wine cooler' is a misnomer: these insulated bags and buckets will keep a chilled wine cold, but do not actually chill it.

Red Wine
* Chill lightly (11-14°C, or no more than an hour in the door of the fridge): Beaujolais Nouveau, Beaujolais and Beaujolais-Villages – but not the *crus* (Fleurie, Morgon etc.); red Loire (Gamay and Cabernet); French *vins de pays*; Bardolino; Valpolicella.
* 'Room Temperature' (15-16°C, which is actually rather cooler than most living rooms; your wine should certainly not be stored anywhere warmer than this, and if you are bringing it up from a chilly cellar it may need a little standing time): most other reds, though older Bordeaux and Burgundy may be served a trifle warmer.
* Open at least an hour before serving: bigger, older Burgundy; Rhônes; New World Cabernet Sauvignon; Rioja.
* Decant an hour or so before serving: young claret; heavy Portuguese reds; bigger Italians such as Barolo and Barbaresco (though older ones should be decanted just before the meal); Australian Shiraz.

Rosé
* Chill, but don't over-chill, particularly if the wine is dry; two hours in the door of the fridge is ample.

White Wine
* Serve coldest: dessert and the more everyday sparkling wines – around 4°C, or a good two or three hours in the fridge.
* Most dry and semi-dry whites and Champagne should be drunk a little less cool (8-10°C), but richer dry wines such as Burgundy are best at around 12-13°C – about an hour in the fridge door.

Bear in mind that the colder a wine is, the less one can taste it – and that this can have a positive side. If you have no alternative to a wine which you know from experience isn't very nice, chill it down with a vengeance.

What about chilling white wine? Many restaurants seem to believe that a Mosel which hasn't been left in the freezer until icicles form isn't fit to serve. In fact, the only reason to treat a wine that brutally is to make it more drinkable – or less undrinkable – than it might otherwise be. Chilled heavily enough, Coca-Cola would be almost indistinguishable from Champagne.

Sweet wines such as Sauternes can take being served vodka-cold; dry ones, particularly rich dry ones like white Burgundy, deserve gentler handling – chill them too hard and they will lose half their flavour. If you're chilling in a hurry, an ice bucket filled with cold water and generous handfuls of ice cubes is far more successful than ice alone – and so much easier to get the bottle back into. Serve only small portions at first to allow the rest of the wine to cool down further. If you need to warm a wine up, stand it in a bucket of tepid water for ten minutes. If this isn't possible, pour the wine, then swish it around in the glass, cupping it in your hands to warm it.

Uncorking

The best corkscrew by far is the American Screwpull. Any other types should be formed like a spiral, rather than the screw after which they are named. The device with two flat prongs rather than a screw or spiral is called a 'Butler's Friend', because it supposedly allowed deceitful servants to appropriate a glass or two of wine, top the bottle up with water and replace the undamaged cork without detection. The trick of using it – sliding the prongs down between cork and bottle, then pressing them together as you draw the cork – takes a bit of mastering: practise on an already-opened and recorked bottle.

Ironically, the tool which no traditional cellar or sommelier once lacked, a knife to cut the foil, is much more necessary today than it ever was in the past, now that tinfoil and infuriatingly shrink-fitted plastic are increasingly replacing the easily peelable – but medically suspect – lead capsule.

Decanting

There's a great deal of nonsense talked about the importance of letting a wine 'breathe' – and a fair bit of sense too. In fact, the principal reason for decanting wine, or port, should be to remove sediment, which many wines – Rioja and red Burgundy, for example – do not have. It's an unsettling procedure for the wine itself, which will need time to calm down before being drunk – and indeed, a delicate red wine like Burgundy can be quite spoiled by decanting. But wines with a lot of tannin (for example, claret and most Portuguese reds) certainly benefit

fizz as flat as a pancake within minutes, the bubbles escaping rapidly from the wine's huge surface area. And any Jerezano would be appalled by the thought that the delicate aromas of his elegant fino were destined to evaporate from the brimming surface of a tiny, overfilled 'schooner'.

If you haven't got the 'right' shape of glass, make sure the one you have got is smaller at the rim than across the bowl, which will prevent the bouquet of the wine from escaping. Whatever the wine and whatever the glass, under no circumstances over-pour. A third to half full is just about right.

from being decanted – or at least uncorked and simply left open for a while before they are drunk. A rather astringent cheaper wine may soften up too.

So, how do you do it? For the nervous, muslin or a coffee filter paper will effectively separate sediment from liquid; for the steadier of hand, a candle flame, a torch or a piece of white card held just behind the neck of the bottle should enable you to see when the trickle of transparent wine begins to become thicker sludge. Be certain not to shake up the bottle before decanting and pour slowly, keeping the flow constant. If it's a really special bottle – a birthday port, for example – and you're filled with trepidation, many specialist wine merchants offer a decanting service.

Glasses

However exquisite, a glass can't make the wine taste better – or can it? There's no doubt that a beautifully made and shaped glass can make the drinking of a finer wine seem just that bit more special than simply slugging it down from a beaker. But Keats's 'beaker full of the warm South' – a solid, chunky glass filled with a rustic Provence red – can turn a picnic into a *déjeuner sur l'herbe.*

Certain glass shapes are by tradition associated with certain types of wine – but remember that this, again, is only tradition, not law. Moreover, some of these traditions are actually bad for the wine. The saucer-shaped Champagne glass will make your

Order

There exists a set of principles which dictate the most sensible order in which wines should be served during the course of a meal. Basically they are: white before red; dry before sweet; light before heavy; young before old; ordinary before fine. The underlying aim is to lead your palate gently up the scale of increasing fullness, 'flavoursomeness' and quality, rather than swinging wildly between styles.

But it's sometimes impossible to observe one of these rules without breaking another – so check against the rest of the list. The more that 'agree', the better; a mature, full California Chardonnay can safely follow a young, light Beaujolais, for example, even though this breaks the white/red rule.

It's a good idea anyway to make sure there is a jug or bottle of water on the table, so that palates can be cleansed and refreshed between wines.

These 'rules' also govern the order in which wines are arranged at professional tastings. In the following pages, as we go into detail about what you're going to find inside the bottles you open, we'll also look at the way those 'professionals' taste wine, why they do it, what they're looking for and the skills and language they use to identify what they find.

TASTING

There are three basic reasons for tasting wine:
* To decide whether or not you like it.
* To judge whether it is a good example of its type.
* To guess its identity and vintage in a 'blind' tasting.
Most people are only usually concerned with the first of these. But the second can be as important to the wine drinker as it is, say, to a wine merchant or restaurateur. Is the wine a 'good buy'? And does it taste as it should? Of course, wines that are atypical of their style or region can be delicious, too, but if that glass of 'house French Sauvignon' is actually filled with an inferior EC *Tafelwein*, it should only have cost you half the price. A little knowledge and practice will enable you to recognise and memorise styles and flavours.

But being able to tell a Rioja from a claret when you have both in front of you is far easier than guessing the precise identity and age of a single glass of wine 'blind'. This is the skill professional tasters develop – not as a glorified party trick, but to help them assess each wine they encounter quite simply on its own merits. It's quite amazing how much influence the knowledge, prior to tasting, of a wine's provenance, quality and price can have on a taster's reaction to it. For instance, knowing that the wine you are about to taste is of a style you disapprove of, or hails from one of Bordeaux's most prestigious châteaux, could naturally predispose you to criticism or praise even before the first sip.

Blind tasting is a skill that only comes with practice, even for the most naturally gifted of tasters, but, like any skill, it can be learnt and, once mastered, can give a great deal of pleasure.

The key to identifying a wine lies in its combination of visual, smell and taste 'triggers' – the ones you remember from the last time you tasted it. By the same token, you can probably recognise a Strauss waltz by its distinctive lilt, orchestration and harmonies, quite apart from the actual melody.

These triggers often work unconsciously – but they do rely on the information having been stored in the first place. So concentrate for a moment or two on every glass of wine you drink. Will you recognise it next time you taste it?

Colour

First of all, scrutinise the colour, holding the wine, if possible, against a well-lit white surface. Since white wines tend to darken as they age, paleness will suggest youthfulness. A pale wine, perhaps with greenish glints, will be light in body and may well be from a cool climate – grapes grown in hot climates such as Australia or California have deeper pigmentation and so impart more colour to the fermenting juice. A wine of great depth of yellow-tinged colour could be a recent vintage from a very hot climate, or it might be a moderately mature wine with long barrel-ageing such as an old-style Rioja. Alternatively, fine

LEFT: The colour of a wine can tell you a lot about its provenance, age and style

ABOVE: In Australia and New Zealand, wine competitions are taken extremely seriously. Here, at the Rutherglen Show in Victoria, judges taste their way through as many as 200 wines in a day

RIGHT: The tasting room at Sotheby's, one of London's major auction houses. David Molyneux–Berry, the head of the department, judges the quality of old wines that can sell for thousands of pounds per bottle

old Chardonnays darken when in an advanced state of maturity, while dessert wines often look golden.

With red wines, the general colour depends on where the grapes are from, regardless of age. So look at the rim: an intense purple is indicative of a young full-bodied wine, perhaps from the very warm Rhône, while a fresh, ruby colour is characterisic of a lighter wine and might suggest, for example, a Beaujolais. A chestnut rim suggests a more mature wine but beware – wines mature at different rates. It could be a relatively young Rioja that has had long barrel-ageing, or a young wine from a poor vintage near the end of its foreshortened life. Or it could be a very mellow Burgundy or claret.

Then, swirl the wine in the glass (the increased air contact makes the wine release more of its aromas), and take a big sniff.

Smell

The smell of a wine is its taste. Just as you can tell that a piece of meat is 'off' by sniffing it, you can also judge whether there is anything wrong with a wine simply by the way it smells. On the other hand, there are some perfectly normal wine smells which you simply may not like. White Sancerre is often said to smell of cat's pee; Australian Shiraz of 'sweaty saddle'; and old red Burgundy, 'farmyardy'. None of these are odours many people find pleasant as such, but they can be likened to (hopefully not too exactly) characteristic traits of an old friend: essential facets of his or her personality.

The majority of good wines, however, display a wonderfully diverse collection of pleasant smells. Few of these appear to

have any direct relation to grapes – indeed, it's astonishing how this single fruit, grown and vinified in different ways, manages to produce not only so many aromas, but in blends of a complexity and success a perfumier would be hard pressed to match.

And just as a perfumier divides scents into groups, so wine smells fall into categories – fruity, floral, spicy, vegetal, earthy and woody. So when you sniff a wine and find apricot where someone else has found plum, don't worry, neither of you is wrong, you've both choosing nuances you recognise from the same 'fruity' group. And if you think that a wine smells of something truly bizarre – Chablis of wet wool, for instance – take note of it; it's your personal key to picking out Chablis 'blind' next time.

The glossary of tasting terms here will give you an indication of smells often associated with particular wines. But if your Cabernet Sauvignon doesn't smell of blackcurrants, don't worry; not all Swedes áre tall and blonde.

For some reason, women are often better at this aspect of wine tasting than men. The female nostril may well naturally be more sensitive than the male – after all, women choose perfume much more carefully than most men select their aftershave – or it may be that they are simply more used to paying attention to the way things smell.

The key to being able to identify wines by their smell lies in constucting your own smell vocabulary, which can be built up by practising on the aromas you encounter every day. Do Golden Delicious apples smell the same as Cox's? Compare the smell of new and old leather...

A final point: what if a wine doesn't appear to smell of anything at all? Well, it's either a very boring wine, or one that is very reluctant to release its bouquet; professional tasters will simply describe it as a 'dumb nose' and move on to the taste in order to find out why.

Taste

Take a generous sip – and roll it around in your mouth. When winetasters suck in air through their teeth and make slurping noses, they're aerating the wine in their mouth just as one swirls it in the glass before sniffing.

What your mouth – your 'palate' – is going to tell you about the wine is not its flavour – the flavours you 'taste' in your mouth are actually being 'smelt' in your nasal cavity above – but its structure; that is, its texture (rough or smooth), its 'body' (light or full), and its 'balance' – whether elements such as sweetness,

---

TRAINING YOUR TASTEBUDS

Taste buds are like muscles; so I've devised a few exercises – comparative tastings – with which to keep them in trim.
* **Fruity Reds** Taste a range of blackcurranty Cabernet Sauvignons and Cabernet Francs, such as Bordeaux from the Médoc, red Loires such as Chinon or Bourgueil, and examples from Bulgaria, California and Australia. Then move on to the more cherry-like flavours of Beaujolais and good young Bardolino. and the raspberry taste of the Pinot Noir (from Burgundy, Sancerre, Alsace, California or Oregon).
* **Oaky Wines** For this, you'll need a bottle or two of red Rioja *con crianza*, a traditional white Rioja such as the one made by Marqués de Murrieta, a Chardonnay from Australia (such as Rosemount's 'Show Reserve') and a classy Bordeaux (such as Pavillon Rouge du Château Margaux).
* **Spicy Wines** The pepper of any Grenache from the southern Rhône (ideally Gigondas or Châteauneuf-du-Pape) can be compared with the deeper spice of the Syrah from further north (in Côte Rôtie or Hermitage) or Australia (where it's called the Shiraz) and with the tobaccoey flavours of good Nebbiolo from Barolo or Barbaresco.
* **Botrytis** Take a good Sauternes, a *beerenauslese* from Germany or Austria and a 'late-picked' Riesling from California or Australia – and look for that flavour of dried apricots.

acidity, fruit, alcohol and, in red wine, tannin come together in harmonious combination.

The first question to ask yourself when tasting any wine is 'does it taste good?' If it does, it's a fairly good indication that it has been well made. Of course, if you absolutely detest sweet wine, the finest Sauternes or Trockenbeerenauslese isn't going to give you much pleasure. Even so, most people can give a fair judgement on whether a piece of music is played well or not, even if it isn't to their taste.

The essential quality of any good wine – cheap or expensive – is its balance. A young wine can appear to be unbalanced, most commonly because high acidity or tannin are obscuring the flavour of the fruit. When they are first made, red wines which have been built to last can be very tannic. Experienced tasters should be able to discern future quality nevertheless, but even they can get it wrong sometimes. A very tannic, apparently fruitless young wine can develop into a rich and complex mature one, but the fruit has to be in there somewhere.

Young white wines can taste very acidic but, similarly, it is this acidity which will enable them to age – provided they are of a style which needs maturity. White wines intended to be drunk young – Muscadet, Frascati, Vinho Verde – need acidity to give them freshness, but in these cases that tang must be balanced by fruit – if your bottle tastes tart and fruitless, you simply have an inferior example which is unlikely to improve.

No wine should ever taste sharp or bitter – although some Italian whites seem to be resolutely sour. If you think it tastes of vinegar, it may well have been got at by 'acetobacters' – vinegar bacteria. On the other hand, wines which seem flabby are probably suffering from too little acidity, often the result of the vines having been grown in too warm a climate.

Inexperienced tasters often imagine that poor wine tends to be acidic and vinegary; generally though, far too many poor wines are simply dull and inoffensive, tasting of nothing at all. These should not, however, be confused with some good wines which are reticent with their flavours, just as they were 'dumb'

THE LANGUAGE OF WINETASTING

Acetic Vinegary – the wine has been got at by bacteria.

Acidity The essential natural component which gives wine freshness and zing and prevents it from *cloying*.

Aggressive Over-*tannic* or over-acidic.

Alcoholic Over-alcoholic wine tastes 'hot', burns the palate.

Almond Bitter almond can announce Tocai from Italy.

Aniseed Found in red Burgundy and – to a lesser extent – Bordeaux and some Northern Italian whites.

Apple A smell often found in young white wines, from the Bramley freshness of Vinho Verde, young Loire, Chardonnay and English wines, through the ripe Cox's of more mature white Burgundies, Champagne and some white Bordeaux. Stewed or baked apple can be a sure sign of Riesling. Unripe apple is often a sign that a wine has not undergone its malolactic fermentation.

Apricot Common in the white Rhônes of Condrieu and Château-Grillet (made from the Viognier grape) and in wine from botrytis-affected grapes.

Aromatic Often associated with wines from the Gewürztraminer and Muscat.

Artificial Also **Contrived, Confected**. Used to describe wines whose taste appears to have been created chemically.

Attack The quality in a wine which makes you sit up and take notice.

Attenuated Thin, drawn out; often associated with tired wines.

Austere A wine difficult to approach, with fruit not obvious. Wait for the flavour to open out in the mouth.

Backward Not as developed as its age would lead you to expect.

Bad eggs Presence of hydrogen sulphide, usually a result of faulty cellaring or winemaking.

Baked Like hot, sunned earth. Common in New World wines.

Balance A balanced wine has its fruitiness, acidity, alcohol and tannin (for reds) in pleasant harmony. Balance may develop with age.

Banana A smell usually associated with young wine, fermented at low temperatures and – in the case of reds – in an oxygen-free environment. A sign of *macération carbonique*.

Beefy Big, hearty, meaty wine.

Beeswing A skin which forms on certain old ports, leaving a characteristic residue in the glass.

Beetroot One of the lesser characteristics of the Pinot family.

Big Mouth-filling, full-flavoured, possibly strongly alcoholic.

Biscuity Often used to describe the bouquet of Champagne.

Bite High acidity, good in young wine.

Blackcurrant Found in Cabernet Sauvignon and Pinot Noir wines.

Blowsy Exaggeratedly fruity, lacking *bite*.

Body A full-bodied wine fills the mouth with flavour.

Bottle Sick Newly-bottled wines may take some time (sometimes months) to recover from the shock of air-contact and sulphuring at bottling.

Bottle Stink Wines which have just been opened may have a musty smell – bottle stink – which disappears in the glass.

Bouquet Smell of a wine with bottle-age.

Breathing Opening a red wine prior to serving to allow slight oxidation. Can enhance nose and flavours.

Butter A richness of aroma and texture found in mature Chardonnay.

Caramel A buttery toffee smell in wines like Madeira.

Cassis Literally, blackcurrant; used when the sensation is of an intense, heady syrup rather than the fresh fruit.

Cat's Pee The pungent smell of Sauvignon Blanc.

Cedar An aroma of oak-aged claret.

Chaptalised Chaptalisation is the process of adding sugar to fermenting must to increase the alcoholic strength. If overdone, a wine tastes *hot*.

Cherry A characteristic of Beaujolais – particularly Morgon.

Chocolate For some people, a sure sign of the Pinot Noir grape.

Cigar-box See *cedar*.

Closed Has yet to show its quality.

Cloudy A sign of a faulty wine.

Cloying A sickly taste, sweetness without *acidity*.

Clumsy An unbalanced wine.

Coarse Rough-tasting wine.

Coffee Special characteristic of old, great Burgundy.

Commercial Light, drinkable, undemanding wine.

Complex Having a diverse, well-blended mixture of smells and flavours.

Cooked A 'warm' stewed-fruit flavour –

may suggest the use of grape concentrate.

Corked A wine spoiled by a bad cork has a musty smell and flavour.

Crisp Fresh, lively, with good acidity.

Crust Deposit thrown by a mature port.

Depth Wine with depth fills the mouth with lingering flavour.

Dirty Badly made wine can taste unclean.

Dirty Socks Cheesy sourness accompanying badly-made white wine.

Dry Having no obvious sweetness.

Dried out A wine which has lost its fruit as it has aged.

Dumb No apparent smell.

Dusty Sometimes used to describe tannic Bordeaux – literally the 'dusty' smell of an attic.

Earthy Not as unpleasant as it sounds – an 'earthy' flavour can characterise certain fine Burgundy.

Eggy Carelessly-handled sulphur can produce an eggy smell.

Elegant Restrained, classy.

Esters Sweet-smelling, often fruity compounds.

Eucalyptus A flavour and smell found in certain clarets (e.g. Château Latour), Californian Cabernet Sauvignon (Martha's Vineyard), Italian and Australian wines and (very occasionally) Burgundy .

Extract The concentration of the grape's flavours in a wine.

Farmyard A good sign of pungent young Burgundian Pinot Noir.

Fat Used to describe mouth-filling white Burgundy, for example.

Finesse Understated, classy.

Finish How a wine's flavour ends in the mouth. Can be 'long' or 'short'.

Flabby Lacking balancing acidity.

Flat Short of acidity and fruit.

Flinty/Gunflint 'Stonily' crisp, used of whites; Pouilly Fumé, for example.

Flor A yeast film which grows on top of the fermenting must of fino sherry.

Forward A precocious wine showing its qualities earlier than expected.

Foxy A peculiar 'wild' smell found in *labrusca* grapes and wine in the U.S.

Gamey Used of mature Burgundy, Rhône Syrah and Australian Shiraz. It's a smell that combines meat and spice.

Generous Big, mouthfilling, round.

Geraniums The smell of the leaves of this flower indicates the presence of an unwelcome micro-organism formed during fermentation.

Glycerine The 'fatty' constituent in some

on the nose – these are described as 'closed', needing more time in bottle, or a little contact with oxygen to 'bring them out'. How do you tell the difference? It's like guessing whether a shy person has anything to say. Does there seem to be something worth digging out? If so, leave the wine in the glass for a while and come back to it.

Finally, the 'finish'. Tasters often describe wines as 'long' or 'short' – meaning that the wine's flavour either lingers pleasantly in the mouth after the wine is swallowed, or seems rapidly to melt away. If a wine is slightly faulty or off-balance, you may find that it is the flawed or excessive element that comes out most strongly on the finish – the dry-mouthed sensation created by high tannins, for example.

So, your tasting armoury is complete. Your smell and taste 'triggers' will have helped you make a guess at the wine's origin and grape variety; the colour, its age; qualities of its structure may help to verify both, and tell you whether the wine is too young, too old, or ready to drink. If all (or nearly all) of these elements are pleasing and, essentially, they come together to give balance, you have a good wine.

But what makes a good wine 'great'? Well, everything that makes it good must be there in spades – but then one moves on into less easily definable territory. Tasters may use words like 'classy' or 'elegant' to describe a fine wine; a great wine's key characteristic is complexity — the perception of a host of nuances and flavours, perfectly interwoven, to which one wants to return to again and again. Many people scoff at the artistic analogies tasters use – indeed, the whole concept of the 'art of the winemaker' – as pretentious nonsense. But they can be useful when trying to place a wine on the quality scale, and when remembering that one doesn't necessarily want 'greatness' and complexity every time one has a glass of wine. A country church can be just as pleasing, in its own way, as St Paul's Cathedral – perhaps even more so on a beautiful summer's afternoon; musically, most of us would prefer, after a hard day, to unwind with Sondheim, not Stravinsky.

---

wines, making them taste richer – the 'legs' which flow down the inside of the glass.

Gooseberry The smell of Sauvignon, especially Loire and New Zealand.

Grapey It's surprising how rare this flavour is: Muscat and Riesling are often grapey; so is good Beaujolais.

Grassy 'Green' smell of young wine, esp. Sauvignon Blanc and Cabernet Franc.

Green Pepper Can be the sign of Cabernet Sauvignon – in Bordeaux, or indeed anywhere else.

Grip Firm wine has 'grip'. Essential to some styles.

Gris Very pale pink.

Hazelnut Along with toasted almonds, can indicate rich maturing Chardonnay.

Herbaceous Think of a cross between grass and flowers – 'planty'.

Herby Some wines from the south-west of France, as well as from Italy, can smell positively herby – almost like a pizza, fresh from the grill.

Hollow Lacking depth and roundness.

Honey An obvious description for most of the great sweet white wines of the world, but also a characteristic – in its richness rather than its sweetness – of some mature white Burgundy and much Chenin Blanc from the Loire.

Hot Used to describe over-chaptalised, over-alcoholic wine.

Iodine A smell and taste sometimes encountered in wines made from grapes grown close to the sea.

Jammy A jammy fruit smell often signifies red wines from hot countries.

Lanolin Some white wines have an oily softness reminiscent of lanolin.

Legs The visible evidence of *glycerine* in a wine, these are the 'tears' that run down the glass's side after swirling.

Lemon 'New-style' Spanish white wines are recognisable by their lemony smell and taste. Other young whites may similarly display a lemony freshness.

Length The time the flavour stays in the mouth.

Liquorice Encountered in all sorts of wine – from claret and port to Burgundy.

Lychees Common in wines made from the Gewürztraminer grape.

Maderised The *rancio* character of heat-induced oxidation.

Malic Acid The component of wine converted by malolactic fermentation into softer lactic acid. Smells like green apples in young white wines.

Meaty A wine to get your teeth into – like a good Châteauneuf or Australian Shiraz.

Mellow Soft and mature.

Mercaptans A smell of rotten eggs or burnt rubber, stemming from the mishandling of sulphur dioxide.

Metallic Taste/smell arising from the use of poor equipment.

Mint Often found in Cabernet Sauvignons.

Mouldy Taste/smell arising from rotten grapes, poor winemaking or a bad cork.

Mouth-puckering Young, tannic or over-acidic wine has this effect.

Mulberry The ripe berry flavour of some Pomerol.

Mushroom Can indicate quality reds, but also a wine past its prime.

Nose The smell of a wine.

Nutty Esp. of Chardonnay and sherry.

Oaky In moderation, pleasant, like vanilla. Esp. New World wines and Rioja.

Old Socks (Clean) A promising sign of young white Burgundy, particularly Chablis.

Oxidised If a table wine looks and smells of sherry, it's oxidised – a diagnosis confirmed by its colour: brown for red wines, deep yellow for whites.

Palate The flavour, and what you taste it with.

Pear drops Smell which is usually the mark of a very young wine.

Pepper Black, not green: the sign of the Grenache or Syrah in the Rhône.

Pétillant Slight sparkle or spritz.

Petrol A desirable aroma of mature Riesling.

Pine Aroma found in retsina.

Plum Esp. clarets, Rioja and Burgundy.

Quaffing, quaffable Everyday wine, usually soft, fruity and undemanding.

Rancio Rich, distinctive flavour of certain wines, particularly southern French *vins doux naturels* stored in barrels exposed to heat.

Raspberry Aroma associated with Syrah, Gamay and much Pinot Noir.

Residual sugar The natural grape sugar left in a wine which has not been fermented into alcohol.

Ripe Grapes were fully ripe when picked.

Robust Solid, full-bodied.

Rose Often the choicest clarets, some *cru* Beaujolais and Côte de Beaune.

Rough Unbalanced and coarse.

Round Smooth and harmonious.

Rubber Some wines can smell rubbery, though not unpleasant. This is an aroma often associated with red wines from South Africa, Beaujolais, Californian Zinfandel and American Pinot Noir.

Salt A salty tang, almost like iodine, associated with manzanilla sherry.

Sediment Precipitation of tannins in red wine due to ageing.

Short Wine with a short *finish*.

Silky Exceptionally smooth.

Smoke The most famous smoky wine is Pouilly Blanc Fumé, made from the Sauvignon Blanc. Alsace Tokay-Pinot Gris, Corsican rosés, some Bordeaux, and Syrah from the Rhône may also be smoky.

Sorbic Acid Preservative in wine.

Spicy Wines from the Rhône, made from a variety of different grapes, can be positively spicy. Also whites from the Gewürztraminer.

Spritz Slight sparkle. Or faint fizz. Similar to *pétillant*.

Stalky or **Stemmy**. The flavour of the stem rather than of the juice.

Steely Attractively crisp, with a firm backbone of acidity.

Strawberry The taste of some Gamay, Pinot Noir and Rioja.

Structure Wine with good structure has, or will have, all its elements in harmony.

Sulphur The antiseptic used to protect wine from bacteria. Its throat-tickling aroma should disappear after the wine has been swirled in the glass for a moment, or left in the open bottle for a while. Often, however, it is 'locked in' and prevents the wine from ever being pleasant.

Tannin The mouth-puckering ingredient in red wine. Softens with age.

Tobacco Like *cigar box*, found in oak-aged reds, especially clarets.

Toffee Often indicates the presence of the Merlot grape in red Bordeaux.

Truffles Mushroom and vegetal aromas, especially in red wines.

Vanilla Aromas of wines matured in American oak casks; also white Burgundy and oak-aged Rioja.

Vegetal Earthy, wet leaf smell; cabbagey, often of big Italian red wines.

Violets Floral red Burgundies and Chiantis can smell intensely of violets.

Volatile In an unstable – volatile – wine, acids evaporate from the surface giving vinegary, sometimes 'greasy' smells.

Yeast Like newly baked bread; smell found in Champagne, Muscadet *sur lie* and some nuttily rich white wines.

COOKING WITH WINE

'Go on – slosh in a bit more wine. Can't do any harm.' Or can it? All sorts of nonsense has been spoken and written about cooking with wine. On the one hand, there are those wonderful old cookery books that recommend that you use a £50 bottle of Chambertin for your *coq au vin* or *boeuf bourguignonne,* because that's what the Duke of Burgundy's cook would have

A magnificent display of cheeses in Beaune, in Burgundy

used 600 years ago. On the other, there are the people who maintain that any wine that's too caustic to drink will be fine to put in a sauce they want to serve with a fillet steak.

Neither attitude makes sense. A few years ago, Prue Leith, the admirably level-headed cook, caterer and food writer, carried out an experiment at her cookery school in which a panel of tasters was served a dish accompanied by several versions of the same red wine sauce. Each sauce had been made in the same way, but with different wines. The result, which shocked all of the finely-honed palates present, was not only that the greatest wine did not make the best sauce, but that one of the most successful efforts was the one which had been prepared using a can of concentrated 'cooking wine', about which several illustrious food experts had been very sniffy.

But don't run away with the idea that this means you can cook with any old wine, any more than you can get away with casseroling any tough old chicken. The least-liked sauce at Leith's was the one made with the cheapest, nastiest wine. First, ask yourself a very basic question: why (and how) are you going to use wine to prepare this dish? The answer is not as straightforward as you might imagine. There are some dishes in which the wine's essential role is as part of a marinade that will make tough meat tender; in others, such as coq au vin, it will be the liquid in which the food is cooked. Very often the wine will be added at the last minute to turn the juices and fats at the bottom of a roasting pan into a sauce; in a few cases, as in sherry trifle, it will simply taste of itself.

Give a thought, too, to the bottle you are going to serve with the meal. French traditionalists recommend that the two should be the same, or at least come from the same region; a more pragmatic aproach would be to aim for wines of a similar style.

Rules such as these are worth knowing about, but they are also made to be broken – for the simple reason that, very often, one country's or region's rules can contradict those of another. Few traditionally English-trained cooks would dream of letting red wine anywhere near fish, but give a Burgundian housewife a trout and a bottle of Bourgogne Rouge and she'll make you one of the most delicious dishes you have ever tasted. And if there's no trout to be had in Burgundy, they'll simply – and equally deliciously – poach a few eggs in that very same wine.

Rules and hints

* Try to choose a style of wine that suits the particular dish you are cooking with as much care as you chose the food. A chicken does not taste like a duckling; a Beaujolais will not make the same kind of sauce as a Barolo.
* Don't cook with any wine you could not imagine drinking.
* Unless you are making a dish such as sherry trifle, in which you want the flavour of the alcohol to be apparent, don't pour in the wine right at the end of the cooking; cook the liquid for long enough for the alcohol to evaporate.
* Don't overdo it; adding another glassful of wine 'for luck' can be too much of a good thing.
* You can make use of left-over wine and ensure that you always have some cooking wine to hand by preparing for yourself the kind of 'wine concentrate' that did so well in Prue Leith's tasting. All you have to do is simmer the wine (white or red) in a pan until its volume has been reduced by half. Prepared in this way, and stored in sterilised jam jars, the concentrate should keep almost indefinitely.

In Alsace, wines and recipes show French and German influence

The Right Wine For The Right Dish

Champagne

When making dishes whose recipes call for Champagne (such as Champagne sorbet), don't make the mistake of substituting a cheap, basic sparkling wine; it wasn't the fizz that the original cook was after, but the nutty, yeasty flavour of wine that has gone through the *méthode champenoise* process. If you are not going to use Champagne, go for either a better quality fizz that has those two words on the label (although in Europe they are being phased out); any French *appellation contrôlée* sparkling wine (they all have to be made in this way); or, perversely, you could try a high-quality Muscadet de Sèvre-et-Maine *sur lie* – these two words indicate that the wine has enjoyed the same yeasty contact as Champagne.

Dry White Wine

Muscadet, Gros Plant and good dry, fairly neutral wines, such as French *vins de pays* and modern-style white Rioja, can be ideal for sauces to accompany shellfish. Richer wines, such as young white Burgundy and Bordeaux, Australian Semillon (though only the lighter examples) and Alsace Pinot Blanc, can be better suited to white meat dishes such as veal and pork. Sauvignon Blanc from New Zealand or the Loire can be used for these dishes or for poultry, as can dry Rieslings from Alsace or Germany and dry English wines. Another original idea is to sprinkle fruit salad with dry Riesling or Sauvignon just before serving.

Madeira

The sweeter styles of Madeira – Bual and Malmsey – are the ones to use for the classic *sauce Madère*, while the drier Sercial and Verdelho can be added to consommé. Sweet Madeira can also be poured over sorbet, substituted for Marsala in *zabaglione* or added to an apricot sauce for a fruit pie.

Marsala

When Marsala is specified in a recipe, as for example in zabaglione, it is almost always the sweet *Dolce* style that is meant.

Medium White Wine

Any recipe that simply calls for 'medium white wine' is being very unhelpful; there is a huge difference in flavour between a Liebfraumilch and a demi-sec Vouvray, though both can fairly be described as 'medium white'. As a rule, go for the grapier (German *Spätlese* and *QbA*) styles with any dish that includes grapes, and use *demi-sec* Loire Chenin Blancs and most examples of that grape from California for dishes with apple.

Muscat

Any recipe that simply lists Muscat probably means a sweet, fortified version, such as Muscat de Frontignan or Beaumes de Venise.

Port

When French recipes require port, they can mean either cheap, basic tawny, or ruby – the two styles with which Gallic wine drinkers are most familiar. Both can be used in variations of zabaglione.

Red Wine

If the wine is going to be used as a marinade, choose one that has plenty of colour, flavour and tannin. Red Burgundy (with a few exceptions, such as Fixin) or Rioja are far less ideal for this purpose than more hard-edged, full-bodied wines, such as Barbera from Italy, Shiraz from Australia, Zinfandel from California, Douro from Portugal, or Corbières, Minervois or Cahors from France.

Similar styles of wine can be used when you are making sauces from the fat and juices that remain in the pan after you have roasted or sautéed almost any kind of meat. On the other hand, finer-flavoured wines such as Burgundies and Bordeaux are perfect for dishes that require the meat to be gently cooked in the wine.

Don't limit yourself to meat dishes with red wine; it can also be used with fruit to make all sorts of simple puddings. Fruit juice, sugar and wine can make a delicious sweet sauce, and various kinds of fruit can be poached in wine (pears in red wine is perhaps the best-known combination). If you find that you have a little faded (but not vinegary) Bordeaux or Burgundy, you could follow the example of cooks in both these regions by pouring the wine over fresh strawberries.

Riesling

As a general rule, Riesling can be used for almost any recipe that calls for white wine and grapes. It can also make a tasty difference to fresh fruit salad. Sweeter (*Kabinett* and *Spätlese*) Rieslings are widely used in Germany when cooking the veal and pork dishes that are so popular in that country, and chicken in a Riesling sauce is a delicious speciality of Alsace.

Sauternes

Like Champagne, Sauternes is often wrongly thought by cooks to be a catch-all term – in this case covering almost any kind of sweet white wine. In fact, however, the flavour you are looking for here is that of botrytis, the 'noble rot' that gives almost any wine a peachy, dried-apricotty flavour that, once tasted, is instantly recognisable.

Unfortunately, this is one area where you may find that you do have to spend a little extra on buying the right kind of wine because, unless it's a good example of Sauternes from a good

WHITE WINE SAUCE FOR FISH

SERVES 6
1 medium onion, peeled and finely chopped
5 fl oz/150 ml dry white wine
2 tsp lemon juice
6 oz/175 g butter
White pepper

In a small stainless steel or enamel saucepan, bring the onion, wine and lemon juice to the boil, then reduce the heat and simmer the liquid until it has reduced to about 3 tablespoonfuls. Over a low heat, whisk in the butter, a piece at a time, until the sauce has the consistency of cream. Add white pepper to taste.

LOTTE PROVENCALE

Monkfish in a white wine and tomato sauce

SERVES 6
3 lb/1.5 kg monkfish (or any firm-fleshed white fish), cut into chunks
8 tbsp flour seasoned with salt and freshly ground black pepper
8 tbsp olive or vegetable oil
2 medium onions, peeled and chopped
1 pt/600 ml dry white wine
2 lb/1 kg tomatoes, skinned, seeded and chopped, or drained tinned tomatoes, chopped
2 garlic cloves, peeled and minced
2 tbsp parsley, minced

Dredge the fish pieces in the flour and shake off any excess flour. In a large flameproof pan, heat the oil until it is hot but not smoking. Brown the fish and remove with a slotted spoon or slice to a dish. Sauté the onions in the pan until transparent, then add the wine, tomatoes and garlic and cook until the liquid has reduced to a thickish sauce. Add the fish and parsley and cook over a gentle heat for another 5 minutes. Serve with rice or triangles of bread sautéed in butter, and peas.

ONIONS IN WHITE WINE SAUCE

SERVES 6
6 tbsp olive or vegetable oil
2 lb/1 kg pickling onions or any small onion, peeled, whole
2 garlic cloves, peeled and halved
$1/_2$ tsp dried thyme
1 bay leaf
1 tsp black peppercorns
Juice of 2 lemons
5 fl oz/150 ml dry white wine
2 tbsp water
$1/_2$ tsp salt

In a stainless steel or enamel saucepan, combine all the ingredients and bring to the boil. Reduce to a simmer until the onions are cooked but not mushy. With a slotted spoon, remove the onions to a serving dish. Bring the liquid in the pan back to the boil and continue to boil, stirring regularly, until it has reduced to a thickish sauce. Strain out the solids and pour the sauce over the onions. Either serve cold as a first course or hot as an accompaniment to meat or poultry.

RISOTTO CHAMPENOISE

1 medium onion, peeled and minced
2 oz/50 g butter
8 oz/225 g long grain rice
$1/_4$ tsp salt
10 fl oz/300 ml Champagne or dry sparkling wine
15 fl oz/450 ml chicken stock
4 tbsp double cream
4 tbsp grated Gruyère or Parmesan cheese
2 tbsp parsley, minced

In a heavy saucepan, sauté the onions in the butter until they are soft. Add the rice and salt, stir and cook for 1 minute. Add half the wine and cook, stirring occasionally, until the wine has been absorbed. Add the stock and cook until it has been absorbed. Add the remaining wine and cook until it has been absorbed and the rice is cooked, but not mushy. Remove the pan from the heat and stir in the cream, parsley and cheese. Serve as a first course for four or as a main course for two with a watercress salad.

vintage, it may very well not have any of that flavour. You would do better to substitute a French alternative from Monbazillac, Loupiac or Ste-Croix-du-Mont or, more reliably, a German or Austrian *Beerenauslese*, an Alsatian *Sélection de Grains Nobles* or a 'late-harvest' wine from Australia or California. Any such wine could be used to pour over peaches – or, inventively, to make a *Sauce Sauternes* to serve with chicken, which gives it a wonderfully rich flavour.

SALTIMBOCCA ALLA ROMANA

Veal, ham and sage with a white wine sauce

SERVES 4
8 small veal escalopes
8 slices of thin-sliced smoked ham (preferably proscuitto crudo)
Salt
8 fresh sage leaves (or a pinch of dried sage for each escalope)
2 oz/50 g butter
6 tbsp dry white wine

Flatten the escalopes and trim the slices of ham to the size of each escalope. Sprinkle the escalopes with a pinch of salt and a sage leaf (or dried sage). Top with a slice of ham and roll up, securing the roll with a wooden toothpick. In a large frying pan, heat the butter until it foams and sauté the escalopes until they are cooked through and browned. Remove the escalopes to a serving dish and keep warm. Add the wine to the frying pan and bring to the boil, scraping up any solids with a wooden spoon. Boil, stirring, for about 4 minutes and then pour the sauce over the escalopes. Serve with noodles and broccoli or courgettes.

GIGOT PERIGOURDIN

Braised leg of lamb with whole garlic cloves and white wine sauce

SERVES 6-8
4 lb/2 kg leg of lamb
2 oz/50 g butter
30 garlic cloves, peeled, whole
2 tbsp brandy
10 fl oz/300 ml sweet white wine (preferably Sauternes or Monbazillac)
Salt and freshly ground black pepper

Melt the butter in a large flameproof casserole. When it foams, brown the lamb all over. Put the garlic cloves round the lamb and pour over the brandy and set it alight. When the flame has died down, add the wine and salt and pepper to taste. Cover the casserole first with foil and then with the lid. Cook over a low heat for 5 hours, turning the meat every hour. Serve the lamb with the cooking juices and the garlic (which will now have a mild and nutty flavour) as a vegetable. Roast potatoes and a purée of carrot also go well with this dish.

Sherry

Some of the most unhelpful recipes of all are the ones that simply tell you to add sherry, without indicating what kind of sherry they mean. Sherry can be bone-dry, almost savoury wine – or richly, even Christmas-puddingy sweet. Bristol Cream will do your consommé no good at all, while the salty tang of manzanilla is not a flavour most people associate with sherry trifle. Swap the two styles and both dishes will be delicious.

BOEUF BOURGUIGNONNE

A rich beef and wine casserole

SERVES 6
3 lb/1.4 kg stewing steak, cut into 1 ½ in/4 cm chunks
MARINADE
1 ¼ pt/750 ml red wine, preferably Burgundy
4 tbsp brandy
1 large onion, peeled and chopped
Bouquet garni sachet, or bundle made of 1 sprig of rosemary, 2 sprigs of parsley and 1 bay leaf, tied together with cotton
8 whole peppercorns
3 whole juniper berries
1 tsp salt

CASSEROLE
4 tbsp olive or vegetable oil
6 rashers rindless streaky bacon, chopped
3 medium onions, peeled and chopped
3 garlic cloves, peeled, crushed
1 tbsp flour
3 carrots, scraped and diced
1 ½ lb/750 g small or pickling onions, peeled, whole
Bouquet garni sachet, or bundle made of 1 sprig of rosemary, 2 sprigs of parsley and 1 bay leaf, tied together with cotton
Salt and freshly ground black pepper
12 oz/350 g button mushrooms, cleaned, whole if small, halved if large

Stage 1: marinade
In a large ceramic or glass bowl, mix all the ingredients for the marinade and let it stand for an hour. Add the meat and cover the bowl with clingfilm. Refrigerate for at least 4 hours and preferably overnight.

Stage 2: casserole
Remove the meat from the marinade and blot up excess moisture with kitchen paper. Strain the marinade and reserve the juices (discard the solids). In a large frying pan, heat the oil and sauté the bacon until the fat is transparent but not crisp. Remove the bacon with a slotted spoon or slice to a large flameproof casserole. In the frying pan, sauté the onion and garlic over a moderate heat and when the onion is soft, remove it and the garlic with a slotted spoon or slice to the casserole. Raise the heat under the frying pan and add the meat in batches, removing them to the casserole when they have browned. Add the flour to the juices in the frying pan, lower the heat to moderate and stir the flour into the juices, scraping up any solids, for about 2 minutes. Gradually add the marinade liquid, stirring, until a smooth sauce is produced. Pour the sauce into the casserole. Add the carrots and onions, bouquet garni and salt and pepper to taste. Either simmer, covered, on top of the stove for 2 hours or bake in an oven preheated to 350°F/180°C/Gas mark 4 for 2 ½ hours. When the meat is tender, add the mushrooms and cook for another 5 minutes. The mushrooms should be firm. Serve with crusty French bread or plain boiled potatoes rolled in minced parsley.

RABBIT MARINATED IN SWEET WHITE WINE

SERVES 4
MARINADE
10 fl oz/300 ml sweet white wine
3 tbsp white wine vinegar
6 oz/175 g sultanas
6 oz/175 g dried apricots
1 tsp ground ginger
4 cloves
6 juniper berries

RECIPE
8 rabbit portions (make sure each person gets at least 1 meaty back portion)
6 tbsp flour, seasoned with salt and pepper and a good pinch of cayenne (optional)
4 tbsp olive or vegetable oil
2 oz/50 g butter

In a ceramic or glass bowl, mix all the ingredients for the marinade. Let it stand for an hour or so and then put in the rabbit, ensuring that each piece is well coated with the marinade. Cover the bowl with clingfilm and refrigerate for at least 4 hours and preferably overnight. Remove the rabbit and blot up excess moisture with kitchen paper. Dredge the rabbit pieces in the seasoned flour. In a large flameproof casserole, heat the oil and butter until it is very hot but not smoking. Sauté the rabbit pieces until they are golden. Strain the marinade over a bowl. Discard the solids and pour the liquid over the rabbit. Cover and simmer for 45 minutes or until the rabbit is tender. Remove the rabbit pieces with a slotted spoon or slice to a serving dish and keep warm. Bring the liquid to a boil and reduce it until it thickens. Pour it over the rabbit. Serve with potato croquettes and a purée of celery.

CALVES' LIVER GLAZED IN SHERRY

SERVES 4
2 oz/50 g butter
3 medium onions, peeled and finely sliced
1 slice of calves' liver (about 4 oz/100 g) per person
3 tbsp flour
Salt and freshly ground black pepper
2 tbsp olive or vegetable oil
5 fl oz/150 ml sweet or medium sherry (not dry) or tawny port
5 tbsp water
4 tbsp parsley, minced

In a large frying pan, sauté the onions in the butter until they have browned. Transfer to a dish. In a large bowl, mix the flour, salt and pepper. Dredge the liver slices in the flour, shaking off excess flour. Heat the oil until it is hot but not smoking. Sauté the liver slices, turning occasionally, until they are just pink inside (about 5 minutes in all). Add the onions, sherry (or port) and water and cook over a moderate heat until the liquid thickens. Stir in the parsley and season with salt and pepper to taste. Serve with shoe-string sautéed potatoes and steamed broccoli.

SAUCE BORDELAISE

A red wine-based sauce particularly good with beef or pork.

SERVES 4-6
1/2 medium onion, peeled and minced
5 fl oz/150 ml dry red wine (preferably Bordeaux)
5 fl oz/150 ml beef stock
1 tsp cornflour
1 1/2 tsp water
1/4 tsp dried tarragon, or 1 tsp fresh tarragon, minced

In a stainless steel or enamel saucepan, cook the onion in the wine over fairly high heat until the wine is reduced to a quarter of its original amount. In another saucepan, bring the stock to the boil and simmer for 15 minutes. In a bowl, mix the cornflour and water to a smooth paste and add it to the stock, stirring, until the stock thickens. Add the stock, with the tarragon, to the wine and onions. Simmer gently for about 15 minutes.

ONION, RED WINE & PORT CHUTNEY

SERVES 4
2 garlic cloves, peeled and crushed
1 tbsp olive or vegetable oil
1 oz/25 g butter
3 medium onions, peeled and finely sliced
10 fl oz/300 ml port
15 fl oz/450 ml dry red wine
Salt and freshly ground black pepper

In a large flameproof pan, cook the garlic in the oil and butter over a medium heat for 3-4 minutes (do not let it brown). Add the onion and cook, stirring occasionally, until soft. Add the port and red wine and bring to the boil, stirring regularly, for about 5 minutes or until the mixture thickens. Season with salt and pepper. Serve warm with pork, ham, sausages, turkey or game.

WINE JELLY DESSERT

SERVES 6
2 tbsp gelatine powder
4 tbsp warm water
Peel of half a lemon (rind only, no pith)
1 pt/600 ml dry red wine
6 tbsp Madeira or port
6 tbsp sugar

In a stainless steel or enamel pan, dissolve the gelatine in the warm water. Add the lemon peel and wines and place over a low heat. Add the sugar and stir until it is dissolved. Remove the lemon peel. Allow the liquid to cool and pour it into individual glasses. Refrigerate until firm. Serve with whipped cream.

FIGS POACHED IN RED WINE

Serves 6
15 fl oz/450 ml dry red wine
3 tbsp sugar
Cinnamon stick, about 1 ¹/₂ in/4 cm long
1 lb/500 g dried figs
Juice of 1 lemon
4 oz/100 g cream cheese, softened
1 tbsp brown sugar
5 fl oz/150 ml sour cream

In a large stainless steel or enamel saucepan, combine the wine, sugar and cinnamon stick. Bring to the boil, then reduce the heat and simmer, stirring, until the sugar has dissolved. Add the figs and continue to simmer for about 30 minutes or until the figs are soft. Add the lemon juice. With a slotted spoon, remove the figs to a bowl and discard the cinnamon. Boil the liquid until it becomes syrupy in texture. Pour the liquid over the figs and allow to cool. In a bowl, beat the cheese and brown sugar until it is fluffy. Whisk in the sour cream. Serve the figs with the cheese and cream mixture.

CHAMPAGNE SORBET

Serves 6
12 oz/350 g granulated sugar
10 fl oz/300 ml water
15 fl oz/450 ml Champagne or dry sparkling wine
Juice of 1 lemon
Juice of 1 orange
5 fl oz/150 ml double cream

In a heavy saucepan, boil the sugar in the water for 5 minutes, stirring occasionally. Allow it to cool completely and then add the wine and fruit juices. Pour into a freezer container and put in the freezer. When it is at the point of freezing but still soft enough to stir, fold in the cream. Freeze.

ZABAGLIONE

Serves 4
4 egg yolks
5 tbsp sugar
8 tbsp sweet white wine or Marsala

Put all the ingredients in the top compartment of a bain-marie (double boiler) or in a bowl set over a saucepan of boiling water. Make sure the bowl is not in the water, but about 1 in/2 cm above it. Once the water boils, whisk the ingredients until they form a light, hot custard-like mixture. Serve immediately.

REDCURRANT FOOL

Serves 6-8
Cinnamon stick, about 1 ¹/₂ in/4 cm long
5 fl oz/150 ml sweet red wine or port
1 ¹/₂ lb/700 g redcurrants, washed and stemmed
3 tbsp sugar
10 fl oz/300 ml double cream

In a stainless steel or enamel saucepan, add the cinnamon stick to the wine and bring to the boil. Reduce the heat to a simmer and add the redcurrants. Cook until the currants are soft. With a slotted spoon, remove the currants and mash them to a pulp. Add the sugar to the liquid and bring it back to the boil. Boil, stirring occasionally, until it has been reduced to a syrupy consistency. Pour the syrup into the currant pulp and allow it to cool. Whip the cream until it stiffens and fold it into the pulp. Fill individual bowls or glasses and chill.

COOKING WITH WINE – UNTIL THE BITTER END

Of course, there is another way in which wine, or a liquid that began its days as wine, ends up being used in cooking.

The simplest definition of vinegar – literally *vin aigre*, or bitter wine – is that it is wine that has 'gone to the bad'. Any wine that has been attacked by acetic bacteria – possibly through being left for a while in an uncorked bottle – will taste vinegary.

But the 'real' wine vinegar we use for cooking is a rather more sophisticated product, depending for its flavour on the acetic fermentation of the wine by a specific fungus, *Mycoderma aceti*, which coats its surface in a thick, scummy skin.

This fungus, whose action is rather like that of the bacillus with which yoghurt is made, is known as a *mère de vinaigre* – vinegar mother – by cooks who zealously guard and nurture both it and the vinegar it produces in special pots. Which explains why these enthusiasts are sometimes worryingly overheard to offer each other 'a piece of my mother', and seen to exchange items that look like nothing so much as small unappetising pieces of liver.

The value of a good vinegar mother was appreciated by the Greeks and Romans, who not only made vinegar, but even went so far as to have special *oxybathon* and *acetabulum* vinegar bowls on their tables into which guests could dunk their bread.

However you are going to use it, though, any vinegar should taste recognisably of the kind of wine from which it has been made; one from Burgundy would be distinctively different to one from Bordeaux. Unfortunately, but understandably, most winemakers do not like having vinegar mothers anywhere near their wineries, so very few sell 'Bordeaux vinegar' or 'Burgundy vinegar' alongside their wines. The only wine region that is known for the quality of its vinegar is Jerez, where several bodegas make sherry vinegar that is valued by cooks throughout the world.

Over the centuries, vinegar, like salt, was recognised to provide a means of preserving meat and vegetables that would otherwise have perished. But, as the French had already realised over 700 years ago, vinegar could also be used to impart a wide variety of other tastes to foods. Parisian street vendors in the 13th century offered their customers vinegar *'de moutarde i ail'* – flavoured with mustard and garlic. If you want to make your own flavoured vinegar, all you have to do is add generous quantities of the fruit or herb – tarragon and raspberries are both very successful – to a stoneware jar of vinegar and leave it to macerate for a week or so before filtering and re-bottling it. And, for really adventurous cooks, the *Larousse Gastronomique* suggests rose vinegar. To make it, immerse 4oz of rose petals in about two pints (approximately a litre) of vinegar and leave to steep for 10 days.

Although there is this natural connection between wine and vinegar, they do not complement each other very well at all. If for example, you accompany a salad which has been dressed with vinaigrette with a glass of wine, you will find that it alters the taste of the wine, giving it a sharp edge and an almost metallic unpleasantness. Red wine will be more affected than white, but both are wasted on any dish with a vinegary dressing.

WINE AND FOOD

If you were to believe the more traditional French gastronomes and the 'helpful' back labels that feature on some Californian wine bottles, you might be forgiven for thinking that foods and wines have to be matched with the same sort of care as you might apply to volatile chemicals in a laboratory. 'With lamb,' declare Gallic experts, 'you must serve Bordeaux from the commune of Pauillac.' And the Californians can be just as dictatorial, not to mention humourless: 'This wine,' an earnest copywriter informs us via a label in my possession, 'was specifically designed to accompany clams.'

Nonsense. People have enjoyed lamb with all kinds of red wines for centuries, and that Californian wine might have tasted just as delicious with roast chicken – or a plate of baked beans on toast.

But there is nonetheless a great deal to be said for trying to choose flavours that go well together. Discovering a perfect food-and-wine marriage can be just as worthwhile as selecting clothes or furnishing fabrics that look, in that clichéed but useful expression, as if 'they were made for each other'.

And just as personal taste plays a part in putting both a meal and an outfit together, so there are traditional food-and-wine guidelines of the 'blue and green should never be seen' variety. The link between Pauillac and lamb is not purely arbitrary; that

Although most people imagine that white wine is the only possible accompaniment for fish and shellfish, in Portugal, red wine is just as traditional — and just as delicious

part of Bordeaux was always good sheep-farming land . Indeed, until this century, the winemakers that produced the wine would often also have had to have been farmers simply in order to have survived. They would have eaten their meat with their wine and, inevitably, the style of the latter would have been influenced by the flavour of the former. And winemakers would tailor their wines to complement not only the flavours of their local cuisine, but also its style. These are associations well worth bearing in mind when trying to pick out a bottle to go with a particular dish. A wine like Barolo, for example, was never made to be drunk with a plateful (or rather half-full) of dainty *nouvelle cuisine* morsels – any more than Sauternes was intended to be served with grilled sole.

But today, people, dishes and wines travel far more widely than ever before. A London dinner party might easily include dishes from three different countries – and wines from three more. And some unexpected partnerships of flavour and style can be the most successful of all.

There are three kinds of relationship between food and

wine. There are the personality clashes, in which each brings out the worst in the other. Try drinking red Burgundy with a plateful of oily sardines, or with a grapefruit, and you will know exactly what I mean; the combined experience can be so nasty that you don't want another mouthful. At the other end of the scale, there is the love-at-first-sight relationship which, like a bowlful of strawberries and cream, tastes magically better and somehow quite different to either ingredient taken by itself.

And, between the two, there is the great mass of food and wine pairings in which the two rub along well enough, never actively clashing, but not doing an awful lot for each other either.

The key to discovering partnerships that work lies in an understanding of the *weight* as well as the type of flavours you are dealing with – and with a dash of courage. Brave were the souls who first discovered how delicious game with chocolate, or a little pepper sprinkled over fresh strawberries, could be.

Matching Wine with Food

Wine For Fish
To avoid the nasty metallic taste that you get when you drink red wine with fish, the trick is to choose the right wine for the right fish. Oily ones like sardines need crisp dry whites – such as Vinho Verde or Muscadet.

Salmon
Subtle poached salmon needs white wine without too much acidity. Lighter-bodied Chardonnay such as Mâcon-Villages can be ideal – as can good Soave, Frascati or white Châteauneuf-du-Pape. Smoked salmon is said to go well with Alsace Gewürztraminer; I prefer another Alsace – Tokay-Pinot Gris – or white Hermitage.

Seafood
Oysters call for bone-dry whites – Muscadet, Sancerre, Chablis or Verdicchio. For scallops, try slightly richer wines such as lighter Italian Chardonnays or Pinot Bianco – and lobster can be perfect with, again, Tokay– Pinot Gris from Alsace.

Grilled Fish
Sea bass and river fish such as trout go well with Chardonnay – particularly southern Burgundies such as St-Véran, as well as oaky white Rioja (particularly Marqués de Murrieta) or top-class Soave (try Pieropan's version). Dry German Riesling is perfect with turbot.

Wine For Poultry & Game
Chicken and Turkey
Avoid too strong or too subtle a wine with these; simply-cooked dishes go well with light reds (Beaujolais or red Loire, for example). For a white to accompany plainly roasted poultry, try a Chardonnay or an Alsace or German Riesling. Creamy chicken dishes need the acid bite of dry, fruity Sauvignon, good Vouvray or Alsace Riesling.

Duck
Roast duck can be as delicious with fruity wines as with fruity sauces. Try Beaujolais, blackcurranty Cabernet Sauvignon from Chile, a red Loire or a light claret.

Game birds
The gamier the meat, the spicier the wine must be. So, for subtler game birds, try Bordeaux from St Emilion and Pomerol or a red Burgundy. For stronger-flavoured meat go for northern Rhône reds such as Crozes Hermitage, St Joseph, Hermitage or Côte Rôtie, Australian Shiraz or Californian Zinfandel.

Venison and Rabbit
The strong flavours of venison are best matched by spicy French wines such as Cahors, Madiran, Hermitage and Châteauneuf, Barolo from Italy, Australian Shiraz-Cabernet and Californian Zinfandel and Cabernet. With rabbit or hare, serve old-fashioned country-style wines such as Italian Barbera and Chianti, or Bairrada and Douro from Portugal.

Wine For Meat
Tradition dictates that red meat calls for red wine, but the kind of red wine depends on the type of meat and the sauce in which it has been prepared. If the sauce has been made with a wine from a particular region, there is an argument for serving it with a wine from the same region. A creamy sauce, however, needs a soft wine with plenty of fresh, fruity acidity to cut through the richness – say, a good Beaujolais or a Bardolino from Italy. A rich, meaty casserole requires heartier wines such as Châteauneuf-du-Pape, Barolo, a rich Burgundy such as Gevrey Chambertin or a Bordeaux from St Emilion.

Roast beef and steaks prepared without sauce go well with full-flavoured but not overly spicy Bordeaux, Burgundy, Rioja, richer *cru* Beaujolais, Chianti, Douro or lighter Zinfandels from California. Lamb teams well with a rich Rioja or a red wine from Provence. Pork can be paired equally well with red or white wines. For white, try a rich Chardonnay, a traditional Rioja, a Tokay-Pinot Gris or a Pinot Blanc from Alsace, or a drier Riesling from Germany. If you prefer red, then go for a medium-bodied wine such as a Dolcetto, a Valpolicella or Chianti, a red Loire or a Beaujolais.

Foreign Flavours
In some parts of the world, such as India and China, wine has no traditional place at all. Consequently, their cuisine can offer something of a challenge when it comes to selecting wine.

Some curries are so dominated by the flavour of peppers and spice that it is certainly not worth choosing a top-quality wine. But if you must have wine, try freshly fruity or warmly spicy styles, such as chilled Beaujolais Nouveau, red Loires, young Rhônes or Australian Shiraz, dry German Rieslings – or a light, off-dry rosé such as Mateus. For milder curries try Dolcetto, Valpolicella or Bairrada, while creamy dishes are well-matched with Sauvignons.

Creole, Chinese and Thai food often combine so many sweet, sour and savoury flavours that it is best to go for a very tasty wine. My favourite is New Zealand Sauvignon Blanc, but Alsace Gewürztraminer and southern French rosés are lovely – as is chilled Asti Spumante. The same rules apply to Japanese food, though *sake* – rice wine, which is usually drunk warm – is more traditional.

Dessert Wines
According to some rule books all desserts deserve Sauternes – except those which involve chocolate or ginger, both of which are believed to be incompatible with any wine. But while at its most spicy, ginger overpowers almost any other flavour, at its mildest, it can match late-harvest Gewürztraminer.

Chocolate can be lovely with Australian or Californian Orange Muscats or, surprisingly, with rich, fruity Cabernet Sauvignon from California. Fresh fruit tarts and mousses need fruity wines. A sweet Riesling (such as German *Auslese*) or Muscat (a late-harvest Alsace, a Beaumes de Venise from the Rhône, or a Moscatel de Setúbal from Portugal) can be perfect.

Creamy desserts such as syllabub and crème brûlée are better served by sweet wines from the Loire, or by Sauternes.

Very sweet desserts such as baked or steamed sponge puddings will overpower all but the most intense of wines. You could try Hungarian Tokay, Malmsey or Bual Madeira, or my favourites: Liqueur Muscat or Tokay from Australia.

Wine For Cheese
Red wine is not as perfect a partner for cheese as most people imagine; in fact, white wine can be far better – especially with high-fat cheeses.

Dutch cheeses and goat's cheese are delicious with Sancerre or Pouilly Blanc Fumé, though New Zealand Sauvignon Blanc and Chablis can be successful too.

One of the great wine-and-cheese partnerships is Roquefort and Sauternes. The combination of honeyed sweetness and salty tang is perfect, but you can swap the Roquefort for any similar blue cheese and replace the Sauternes with a late-harvest Riesling or even a *moelleux* wine from the Loire.

Soft French cheeses are made for gentle, fruity red Burgundy. Cheddar can go with Bordeaux, provided it comes from St Emilion or Pomerol, both of which use the rich-flavoured Merlot grape. But my own choice for Cheddar would be port (Vintage or Tawny) or Madeira. And don't forget Stilton and port.

WINE IN RESTAURANTS

As recently as a decade ago, the cellars of better restaurants were piled high with well-chosen bottles of wine, laid down over the years so as to be precisely ready to drink on the evening when you or I ordered them from the list. Today, all that has changed; stocks of ready-to-drink old wine have evaporated under the heat of the accountants' and bankers' scrutiny. Some restaurateurs still cellar their wines, or buy at auction, but far too few bother – which explains why, while claret drinkers would ideally like to be drinking such vintages as 1966, 1970, 1976, and 1978, even supposedly classy restaurant lists offer them 1982s, 1983s and 1985s.

Wine waiters, too, rarely seem these days to be the fine, mature specimens they once were. Far too many persevere in trying to make the customer feel uncomfortable, perhaps as a defensive measure when faced with today's wine-literate diners, who have only to browse through the shelves of any good supermarket in order to know as much – and maybe more – than their waiter about sparkling wines from the Penedés in Spain, Pinot Grigios from north-east Italy, the Rieslings of Washington State, Chardonnay from Australia's Hunter Valley, Cabernets from California and Sauvignons from New Zealand.

So, if you want to stay one step ahead of a sniffy sommelier, here's how to avoid the pitfalls of the restaurant wine list.

The Choice

If your eye is immediately caught by wines of the kind listed above, you're off to a good start. A restaurateur with the confidence to choose and offer something a little different from the 'standard' styles obviously takes an interest in what his customers are drinking, and may well ensure that his staff are informed and ready to offer advice on unfamiliar wines. If you're still not quite confident about his powers of discrimination, order a glass of house red or white as an aperitif. If that's good, you can be pretty confident that somebody, somewhere cares about the contents of the cellar; buying the kind of wine that is served by the glass calls for far more skill than listing a well-known claret from a good vintage.

The Vintage

Any wine list that neglects to mention the vintages of the wines it lists clearly doesn't care about them or the drinker – but ones that print '1983/4' are no better. After all, they'd never dream of trying to sell you 'Beef/Pork Casserole'. Even when a vintage is named, beware of the switch 'twixt list and table. You order the 1986 and the stuff that is poured for you to taste is the 1987: be as firm as you would be if your avocado came with prawns when you ordered vinaigrette.

The Producer

Any list that does not include the name of the producer alongside or beneath that of every wine doesn't necessarily guarantee that there will be no good wines on offer – just that their presence will be something of a fluke. And, like vintages, producers get switched too. You order the Sancerre produced by M. Dupont; the one with which you are presented is made by M. Chevalier, who might be a perfectly delightful man – but an inferior winemaker compared to his neighbour Dupont.

The Price

The price you pay for your meal and wine is up to the restaurateur and yourself; just remember, your readiness to hand over three or even four times what he or she paid for an indifferent young Chablis merely helps to perpetuate a scandal. As a general rule, anything beyond twice the retail price is completely out of court. A restaurateur's mark-up is generally between 100-200% on the price he paid, which – to put this in perspective – is usually around 25% less than the by-the-bottle price you would have to pay in most wine merchants.

The Serving

If you don't want to appear pretentious and silly, keep the sniffing and tasting ritual to a minimum. Some wine buffs seem to imagine that a protracted session of examining the cork, inhaling the wine and gargling with it are all some form of essential foreplay that mark the expert from the novice.

Not a bit of it. The real expert rarely pays much attention to the cork – provided that he or she has seen it being drawn from the bottle – but will usually satisfy him or herself with giving the wine the briefest of sniffs (just like the one you might give a carton of milk that's been in the fridge for a few days). If the wine smells fresh, clean and fruity, don't bother to taste it – just ask the waiter to serve.

The Taste

If you are not certain about the smell, take a sip. So what if you then don't like it? Well, first things first. What don't you like? If it's just a matter of the wine being too sweet or too dry for your taste, your right to send the wine back may be no greater than your right to complain that you don't like the tarragon in the sauce on the chicken. On the other hand, just as you would have every justification in returning a *crème brûlée* served with cream that had gone sour, you have every reason to send back a wine that has something wrong with it.

'It's corked' is the most frequent, yet most frequently mistaken complaint. A wine with bits of cork floating on its surface is *not* corked; all that has happened is that the cork has crumbled slightly as it has been pulled from the bottle. A corked wine is one whose cork has been infected by a penicillin mould; its 'corkiness' is evident from a mouldy, dank-cellar-and-stale-dried-mushroom smell that almost invariably gets worse the longer the wine is open. Although the smell is the most recognisable sign of corkiness, a corked wine will also smell mouldy and seem to catch in the back of your throat as, if you've got that far, you swallow it.

White crystals at the bottom of a bottle (or glass) of white wine are perfectly innocuous; they are simply naturally-formed tartrate crystals often encountered in wines that have not been chilled heavily and filtered before bottling. (The Germans, in a rare mood of romanticism, call these 'wine diamonds'.)

If a wine genuinely does taste vinegary – as opposed to merely aggressively dry – the chances are that it has been carelessly stored or, possibly, kept too long. And if it tastes 'dirty' – like damp dish cloths – it may have been badly made and/or matured in casks or tanks that have been poorly maintained. In these cases, the bottle should go straight back.

The Temperature

If your wine is too warm, ask for an ice bucket. Your wine waiter will no doubt look down his nose when he realises it's for the light red Loire or Beaujolais that he zealously parked in hot water in the kitchen for ten minutes to bring it to the tepid state you find so unappealing, but don't be deterred – at least you will be able to drink and enjoy the wine in the way its maker intended. While it's chilling, sip slowly at a mean portion until the rest of the wine has cooled down – don't let the waiter hover

The attitude of the owners and staff can make or mar the enjoyment of wine with a special meal. Here at Restaurant St Quentin in London, the atmosphere is formal yet certainly not intimidating

over you carefully refilling your glass after every mouthful.

If the temperature is too low, simply deter the waiter from replacing the bottle in the bucket. Let him top up your glass to his heart's content, cupping it meanwhile in your hands to warm the wine within.

The Second Bottle

Half-way through the meal you absent-mindedly order another bottle of the Sancerre. What arrives could well be of a different vintage or by a different producer – or it could be a duff bottle of the same wine. So, make sure you get a look at the label and a taste of the wine before it's served – otherwise several half-full glasses of good wine from the first bottle could be spoiled by bad wine from the second.

The Tip

I've constructed some rather depressing – but sadly too often encountered – scenarios here. With luck, though, you'll enjoy not only a delicious meal, but also some delicious wines, which have been knowledgeably and courteously served. This is to be encouraged; so don't neglect to praise both wine and waiter should the manager float over to enquire whether 'everything's all right'.

Bear in mind, too, that very few wine waiters get the chance to taste very many of the wines they serve. If you have ordered one of the more interesting wines from the list and the person who has served you has seemed enthusiastic and interested, invite him or her to taste it – or leave a little in the bottle.

WHAT TO ORDER

There are thousands of wines from which a restaurateur might choose for his list, but some do crop up frequently. I myself would confidently order wines from the following producers.

* **Red and White Bordeaux** Château d'Angludet; Château Chasse-Spleen; Château La Gurgue; Château Haut-Bailly; Château La Louvière; Château La Rivière; Château Potensac.
* **Red and White Burgundy** Joseph Drouhin; Louis Jadot; Olivier Leflaive; Chartron et Trebuchet; Leroy; Vallet Frères.
* **Beaujolais** Georges Duboeuf; Joseph Drouhin; Loron.
* **Alsace** Kuentz-Bas; Trimbach; Hugel; Zind-Humbrecht.
* **Loire** Vacheron; de Ladoucette; Dézat; Huet.
* **Rhône** Guigal; Delas; Jaboulet Aîné.
* **Chianti** Castello di Volpaia; Antinori; Badia a Coltibuono.
* **Barolo** Aldo Conterno; Fontanafredda; Borgogno.
* **Barbaresco** Gaja
* **Other Italian** Lungarotti; Tignanello; Tiefenbrunner; Avignonesi; Pomino; Sassicaia.
* **Rioja** Marqués de Murrieta; La Rioja Alta; CVNE; Montecillo; Faustino; López de Heredia; Contino; Remelluri.
* **Catalonia** Torres; Jean León; Raimat.
* **Germany** Deinhard; Lingenfelder; Sichel; Egon Müller; F W Gymnasium; J J Prum; Bassermann-Jordan; Bürklin-Wolf.
* **California** Mondavi; Fetzer; Simi; Ridge; Trefethen; Firestone; Chateau St Jean; Iron Horse.
* **Australia** Petaluma; Penfolds; Lindemans; Hardy's; Rothbury; Rosemount; Brown Brothers.
* **New Zealand** Montana; Cooks; Selaks; Nobilos; Hunters.

WINE AND HEALTH

There is a growing band of individuals at large in the world who know, apparently, precisely how you and I ought to live our lives. One of their particular interests lies in specifying what we should, and shouldn't, be eating and drinking. Inevitably, alongside tobacco, one of their main targets has been alcohol. Unfortunately, such is their lack of discrimination that the target is alcohol in its every form. Such is the evangelical zeal of the more extreme anti-alcohol campaigners that they lump the lightest of wines together with the hardest of spirits, not to mention sundry other legal and illegal drugs.

Wine, like every other kind of alcohol, is of course a potentially dangerous substance – if it is abused and taken in excess. But this is no reason to treat it as a poison. After all, an overdose of nutmeg can be deadly, and no one has so far advocated posting health warnings on spice racks.

Besides, wine does have an extraordinarily honourable heritage in the annals of western civilisation – as any book of quotations makes immediately clear. Excise it from the works of Chaucer, Shakespeare or Dickens – or the Bible for that matter – and you have to rewrite a large chunk of great literature. The anti-lobby would argue that art and literature contain as many references to the damaging effects of drink; where these occur, however, wine is rarely the culprit; what is more, the alcoholic drinks we consume today are very different to those of the past. The 'gin' of Gin Lane was a rough, almost industrial spirit; Bill Sykes's violent outbursts were not the result of an excess of Beaujolais Nouveau.

And there is some evidence to suggest that, far from being harmful, sensible levels of wine drinking may actually contribute to good health. When a certain Dr Klatsky carried out a study of 85,000 subjects in California between 1978 and 1982 he discovered that the ones who drank moderate amounts of alcohol were actually healthier than both the heavier drinkers *and* the teetotallers. Other studies have indicated that moderate drinking (a glass or two of wine per day) may reduce the likelihood of coronary heart disease.

Wine and other kinds of alcohol

There have been various research projects devoted to the question of whether wine is a healthier form of alcohol than beer or spirits. None has reached a satisfactory conclusion, so it is probably wisest to treat a glass of wine – around a sixth of a bottle – as between one and two units of alcohol (one unit has roughly the same strength as half a pint of beer, lager or cider, a single measure of gin or whisky or a glass of sherry or port).

Wine strength

Wines can vary in strength from the non-alcohol and low-alcohol styles that range from zero to 5%, to fortified wines that can weigh in at as much as 27% (nearly three-quarters the strength of whisky, and usually served in rather larger measures). In general, however, most table wines and fizz have strengths of between 9% and 13%, and most fortified wines – such as sherry or port – average 15-20%.

To help people to drink sensibly, the system of 'units' used in the following table illustrates how strengths can vary. A 12.5cl glass of German wine at 8% is most convenient, containing just one unit of alcohol. But if you fancy a change – a big Châteauneuf, for example – that figure could virtually double.

It is generally considered that the maximum advisable number of units of alcohol for any man to consume in a week is 21. For women the figure is 14, which may seem unfair, but in fact there is a wealth of evidence to prove that, because of their lower body mass but relatively higher proportion of body fat, women metabolise alcohol less efficiently than men. Doctors also recommend an alcohol-free day or two per week.

WINE STRENGTH BY UNITS OF ALCOHOL

% Alcohol	75cl BOTTLE	1 LITRE BOTTLE	glass	% Alcohol	75cl BOTTLE	1 LITRE BOTTLE	glass	% Alcohol	75cl BOTTLE	1 LITRE BOTTLE	glass
0.05	0.04	0.05	0.01	7.0	5.3	7.0	0.9	15.0	11.3	15	1.1
0.5	0.33	0.5	0.07	7.5	5.7	7.5	1.0	15.5	11.7	15.5	1.1
0.9	0.68	0.9	0.12	8.0	6.0	8.0	1.0	16.0	12.0	16	1.2
1.0	0.8	1.0	0.2	8.5	6.4	8.5	1.1	16.5	12.4	16.5	1.2
1.2	0.9	1.2	0.2	9.0	6.8	9.0	1.2	17.0	12.8	17.0	1.2
1.5	1.2	1.5	0.2	9.5	7.2	9.5	1.2	17.5	13.2	17.5	1.3
2.0	1.5	2.0	0.3	10.0	7.5	10.0	1.3	18.0	13.5	18.0	1.3
2.5	1.9	2.5	0.4	10.5	7.9	10.5	1.4	18.5	13.9	18.5	1.3
3.0	2.3	3.0	0.4	11.0	8.3	11.0	1.4	19.0	14.3	19.0	1.3
3.5	2.7	3.5	0.5	11.5	8.7	11.5	1.5	19.5	14.7	19.5	1.4
4.0	3.0	4.0	0.5	12.0	9.0	12.0	1.5	20.0	15.0	20.0	1.4
4.5	3.4	4.5	0.6	12.5	9.4	12.5	1.6	21	15.8	21.0	1.5
5.0	3.8	5.0	0.7	13.0	9.8	13.0	1.7	21.5	16.2	21.5	1.6
5.5	4.2	5.5	0.7	13.5	10.2	13.5	1.7	22	16.6	22.0	1.6
6.0	4.5	6.0	0.8	14.0	10.5	14.0	1.8	22.5	16.9	22.5	1.6
6.5	4.9	6.5	0.9	14.5	10.9	14.5	1.9	23	17.3	23.0	1.7
								23.5	17.7	23.5	1.7
								24	18.0	24	1.7
								24.5	18.4	24.5	1.8
								25.0	18.8	25	1.8
								25.5	19.2	25.5	1.8
								26	19.5	26	1.9
								26.5	19.9	26.5	1.9
								27	20.3	27	1.9

standard glass 12.5 cl

sherry glass 7 cl

0.05–3%	Typical low-alcohol wines
3%–6.5%	Low-strength whites e.g. Moscato
7%–13%	Typical white wines
11%–14.5%	Typical red wines (stronger reds do exist, but are rare)
15%–27%	Typical fortified wines

Wine and weight

Wine is fattening. But then, so is almost everything else. However, despite the frequent endorsement of a 'glass of dry white wine' by the writers of diet books, some dry wines will set you back by considerably more calories than some sweet ones. Alcohol is more fattening than sugar; a strong sweet wine is bad news, but a strong dry wine will be more fattening than a lighter sweet one, as the chart below (based on figures from Pollock & Poole, one of Britain's leading laboratories) confirms.

CALORIES IN WINE BY STRENGTH AND SWEETNESS

This chart shows the variation in calorie content between different styles of wine – and whether the calories (kcal) come from the alcohol or the sugar. Figures are per 12.5cl glass (approx six measures per bottle) for table wines, and per 7cl glass (16 measures per bottle) for fortified wines. 1 gm/litre sugar provides 3.75 kcal; 1 gm/litre alcohol (= 1% strength) provides 7 kcal.

TABLE WINE	Strength	kcal	Sweetness	kcal	Total kcal
Low Alcohol	3.0%	26	40 gm/ltre	2	28
Trocken (dry)	9.0%	79	0 gm/ltre	0	79
Kabinett	9.0%	79	10 gm/ltre	5	84
Asti Spumante	6.5%	57.5	57 gm/ltre	25.5	84
Vinho Verde	9.0%	79	10 gm/ltre	5	84
Liebfraumilch	9.0%	79	15 gm/ltre	7	86
Muscadet	11.5%	100	0 gm/ltre	0	100
Claret	12.0%	105	0 gm/ltre	0	105
Australian Chardonnay	13.0%	114	5 gm/ltre	2	116
Châteauneuf du Pape/ Australian Red	14.0%	122.5	0 gm/ltre	0	122.5
FORTIFIED WINE					
Dry Sherry	17.0%	82.5	0 gm/ltre	0	83.5
Sweet Sherry	19.0%	94	130 gm/ltre	33.5	127.5
Port	22.0%	108	100 gm/ltre	26.5	134.5

This photograph of a small boy was taken by Cartier Bresson in the Rue Mouffetard in Paris in 1954. Today, were that boy's 20-year-old son to visit the USA, he would not be allowed to buy himself so much as a glass of beer

Wine and pregnancy

Most doctors advise mothers-to-be to stop drinking alcohol completely, and there is some evidence to suggest that women who want to have a baby should also abstain from drinking prior to conception. In European wine-producing countries pregnant women often do continue drinking during pregnancy – but in far greater moderation.

Wine and driving

Sorry, but if you want to drive safely – never mind legally – there are no get-out clauses or loopholes. Tests have proved that even the smallest amount of alcohol in the bloodstream can impair judgement – especially in people who are tired or in any other way under the weather. To be safe at the wheel, the only answer is to drink no wine at all – or, for those extraordinarily self-conscious individuals who claim to 'feel silly' holding an orange juice, one that has been de-alcoholised.

Wine and food

To most southern Europeans, food and wine are two halves of a whole; they rarely consume one without the other. Just as their lunch or dinner almost always includes wine, the glass of red they order in a pavement cafe is usually accompanied by savoury titbits. It's a habit worth adopting.

Wine and time

The average human body takes around an hour to deal with a single glass of wine. Heavily-built men may find that they can cope with slightly more than this; lighter men and most women, however, may equally discover this to be too rapid a rate of input for their bodies.

Although it is advisable to accompany any alcohol with food, and to punctuate it with the occasional glass of water or other non-alcoholic drink (to counteract the alcohol's dehydrating effects), it has to be said that there is no effective way to speed up the process of metabolising the alcohol. The capacity of black coffee to achieve this is a myth. Similarly, excessive drinking with dinner can leave you with alcohol in your bloodstream the following morning.

Hangovers

Sensible drinkers will rarely, if ever, suffer from these, but there are occasions – and celebrations – that are followed by mornings when the body feels less than at its best. As a preventative, the consumption of a pint of water (more if you can manage it) between the last glass of wine and going to sleep can perform wonders.

If it's too late for prevention, is there a cure? Ignore any advice to indulge in the hair of any species of dog, and stick to easily-digestible protein, and plenty of liquids with which to rehydrate the body. Substantial quantities of orange or tomato juice can be remarkably effective. As a final hint, beware particularly of over-indulging in vintage port, whose reputation as hangover-fare is wholly earned.

ORGANIC WINE

In 1984, the news broke that samples of Austrian wine had been found to contain substantial doses of DEG – diethylene glycol – a chemical most easily described as first cousin to anti-freeze, and quite deadly if drunk in any quantity. As laboratories in several countries analysed thousands of samples of wine, it was discovered that wines from Germany and Italy contained the chemical too – though in far smaller proportions.

Despite initial claims that DEG was just another of the naturally-occurring chemicals found in all food and drink, it rapidly became apparent that the only way that the chemical could have got into the wine was for someone to have put it there – to 'enrich' its flavour. The reason the German and Italian wines contained such small amounts was that their producers had almost certainly not added it to their vats themselves, but had beefed up their wine with bought-in wine or grape concentrate which had – unknown to them – been adulterated.

What became known as the 'Anti-Freeze Scandal' was followed by a far more serious – indeed fatal – case of fakery in Italy, in which, it was said, only Italian bureaucracy saved those responsible for adding a dangerous industrial alcohol to wine from standing trial for manslaughter.

The only beneficial effect of these damaging incidents was to tighten up controls on wine production internationally, and to focus attention on what could, and could not, legally go into wine. In the longer term, though, the scandals gave a boost to a small group of winemakers around the world who are determinedly trying to make wine on 'organic' principles – not only free from illegal additives, but free from some legal ones as well.

In theory, it is quite possible to produce wine simply by crushing grapes, allowing them to ferment and bottling the resulting liquid. Unfortunately, as most home winemakers will have discovered, wines made in this way often stop tasting good within a very, very short while.

Vines and grapes are subject to all kinds of pests, fungi and diseases that can either prevent growers from making any wine at all, or leave them with a drink that has the unpleasant musty smell and taste of rotten grapes. Once it has been made, wine is similarly subject to the attentions of various kinds of bacteria that are eager to convert it into vinegar.

In the vineyard, there are are a number of chemical sprays that can be used to protect the vines from rot and insects; in the winery, producers almost always have to use sulphur dioxide

ABOVE: *Sulphur compounds are an essential antiseptic in winemaking, killing unwanted bacteria. Here, sulphur has been sprinkled on newly-picked grapes*

BELOW: *A new vineyard in Zimbabwe, where the climatic conditions are such that the baby vines need careful treatment against a battery of pests and diseases*

as an antiseptic to ward off bacterial infection. In addition, winegrowers can, for example, use fertilisers to increase the yields of their vines.

When fining their wine they can, (though rarely, and under supervision) if in Europe, legally use potassium ferrocyanide instead of such traditional agents as powdered clay, milk protein, beaten egg white, fish scales or even ox blood. In principle, the fining agent does not combine with the wine, merely passing through it – dragging, as it sinks, any solid matter with it - but very few conscientious producers, organic or otherwise, believe this sufficiently to use potassium ferrocyanide. Indeed, the substance is banned from use in this way in the USA.

Organic winemakers aim to avoid all unnecessary use of chemicals, encouraging 'good' insects to eat the 'bad' ones, and accepting the lower yields of non-fertilised vines. (In warm, dry climates, this involves rather fewer sacrifices than in the cooler, wetter regions of northern Europe, where growers who do not spray their vines can sometimes lose an entire crop.) In the winery, organic producers use as little sulphur dioxide as possible, and fine with natural materials such as egg white.

So far, so good – and very laudable too. Unfortunately, the problem for anyone who would rather drink wine made by these producers is that it is often difficult to know how to differentiate it from other, less 'organic' wines. Some labels carry the symbols of various associations – but some top-class organic winemakers neglect to pin their colours to the mast.

The avowedly organic winemakers form an incredibly loose-knit band of separate associations around the world, each of which has its own insignia and rules and – in some cases – petty jealousies. To compound the confusion, at least one such organic association in France is actually funded by the manufacturers of organic products for use by the growers: use our products, and you're a member of the club.

Today, as people become increasingly aware of 'green' issues in general and organic foods in particular, the EC is stepping in with rules of its own which will hopefully make the situation clearer. For the moment, however, look out for those retailers who are taking the trouble to indicate which of the wines they stock conform to the organic code.

CRIME AND PUNISHMENT

The bad news for would-be wine adulterators is that their chances of getting away with the crime are smaller today than they have ever been. The Austrian and Italian scandals of the 1980s have made the authorities throughout the world so sensitive to how wine ought and ought not to be made that, in 1990, a number of Chilean wines were removed from the shelves in Britain because they had been found to contain sorbitol, a harmless and natural ingredient that is legitimately added to in the making of all sorts of foods and drinks, yet is illegal in wine.

The wine drinkers of the past were far less well protected, for wine has been faked and adulterated in one way or another for almost as long as it has been drunk. Virgil, predicting that '*The ripening grape shall hang on every thorn*', had no doubt that crooks in cold countries where vines could not be grown would pass off as 'wine' the fermented juice of whatever fruit they found in the hedgerow.

In the 19th century, the French author Stendhal recorded visiting a factory in France where '*Out of wine, sugar, iron filings, and some flower essences, they make the wines of every country.*' Far more often, though, wine merchants merely blended in wines from other regions. Pale burgundy would be enriched with a dollop of thick, dark wine from North Africa; claret was quite openly 'improved' by the addition of a little wine from Hermitage, on the other side of France.

Today, adulteration is still occasionally uncovered. The best insurance against this kind of fraud is to buy your wine from a company that cares about the quality and authenticity of what it is selling. Britain's major retail chains and reputable merchants were untainted by the 'anti-freeze' scandal of 1984; almost all of the adulterated wines discovered were found to have been sold by smaller, non-specialist retailers and by such door-to-door sales companies as Pieroth.

FACTS AND FALLACIES

There are all kinds of misconceptions about wine – many of them wilfully promoted by the people who make the stuff, and by lazy wine writers who merely copy what they have read elsewhere. Which is why I thought it might be a good idea to dispel some of these illusions. And to reveal a few hard-to-believe facts about wine that are guaranteed to be 100% authentic.

Sherry lasts indefinitely

The sweeter styles will keep but, even *before* you pull the cork, dry fino and manzanilla sherries may have lost their original, tangy freshness. So avoid leaving the bottle hanging around before you open it – and drink it up within the week. If you are likely to take longer than that, either pour half the sherry into a half-bottle when you first open it – or, wiser still, buy it in a half-bottle in the first place.

Sherry, port and Champagne can be made anywhere

In Australia and the USA, all sorts of cheap fizzy wine can call itself Champagne. In Europe, however, reasonable EC regulations forbid the sale of 'Champagne' made anywhere outside the French region of that name. Likewise, genuine sherry only comes from Spain and port from the Douro in Portugal.

British wine is made from grapes grown in Britain

'British' wine is actually produced by diluting and fermenting grape concentrate (usually imported in jelly form from warmer countries such as Cyprus). In fact, under European law, it is not even legally defined as 'wine' which, by the EC definition, has to be made from freshly-picked grapes. English wine is the real stuff – though even this is allowed to contain a little sweetening juice from Germany.

Red Bordeaux is made from the Cabernet Sauvignon

Well, quite a lot of it is – but actually, the Merlot is the most widely planted grape in Bordeaux – and in the communes of St Emilion and Pomerol, the blend is often just Merlot and Cabernet Franc.

All wines improve with age

This is a belief still common in the countries of southern and Eastern Europe and South America, where older wines are thought to be better by definition and people have become used to drinking wine with the taste of oxidation – the sherry-like character of wines that are past their best. Most modern wine drinkers now prefer wines with fresher, fruitier flavours. Almost all inexpensive white wines should be drunk within a couple of years (at most) of the harvest, and even some higher class wines such as Bordeaux may need drinking young in some – less good – vintages.

Cheap wines don't travel

Some don't – but then again, nor do some frail old expensive ones. In the case of young, cheap wine, everything depends on the way it has been produced. Well-made wine, whatever its price, should have no difficulty in being carried from one side of the world to the other. When a wine you enjoyed on holiday and brought back with you doesn't taste quite the same at home, it's very likely to be because the circumstances have changed, not the wine.

The word 'château' indicates quality

It certainly does no such thing – however smart the label. Any wine estate in France can call its building a château (even if it is little smarter than a garden hut) and, in Bordeaux, almost every estate will do so. To complicate matters still further, some cooperatives use a loophole in the rules to put 'château' labels on wines they make.

'Legs' in a wine indicate quality

What the French call the 'legs' – and what the Germans call 'cathedral windows' – are the streams that flow down the glass once you have swirled the wine around. These are often thought to mean that the wine is especially good. All they really indicate is that the wine is rich in glycerine and was thus made from ripe grapes. Even ripe grapes can be turned into bad wine.

All Rieslings are basically the same grape

The grape of this name grown in Germany and Alsace is the only one of any real quality. When it's grown elsewhere, it is often called the Johannisberg Riesling or the Rhine Riesling to avoid confusion with the completely unrelated and inferior Laski, Welsch and Italico Rizlings. And the grape the Australians call the 'Hunter Valley Riesling' is actually the Sémillon.

Great wine can never be made in stainless steel tanks

Some of the best châteaux in Bordeaux ferment their wine in stainless steel nowadays – and make better wine than ever.

Beaujolais Nouveau has to be drunk by Christmas

There is technically no difference between Beaujolais Nouveau and the kind of Beaujolais we all drink during the rest of the year – except that it is sold earlier. It is usually best drunk quite young, but good Nouveau from one of the region's better producers and vintages can be delicious – and sometimes even better – a year after the harvest.

Screw-tops are not as 'good' as corks

They are certainly less romantic, but tests have proved that they are just as effective (possibly more so) – and eliminate the risk of corkiness.

You can always tell a corked wine by smelling the cork

Sometimes a musty-smelling cork will warn you that a wine is faulty; quite often, however, the cork may show no signs of deterioration at all. The sure way to tell a corked wine from a dirty or otherwise faulty one is that it will actually smell and taste worse the longer it is in the glass.

All red wines improve with decanting

Some do benefit from the airing they get by being poured from a bottle into a decanter, but less full-bodied wines – such as red Burgundy – can lose some of their fruit by being manhandled in this way. As a general rule, the only wines that need to be decanted are the ones that have a heavy deposit – all vintage port, most mature red Bordeaux, old Rhônes, Barolos, Australian and Californian reds, for example.

Extra Dry (or Extra Sec) Champagne is drier than Brut

Actually, it's slightly sweeter.

Brut Champagne is bone-dry

It tastes dry; in fact, all Brut Champagnes are slightly sweetened. If you want a bone-dry fizz, go for *Brut Zéro* or *Brut Sauvage,* which have 'zero dosage' – no sweetening at all. But I'll lay money that you'll probably prefer the Brut.

Gewürztraminer is the perfect partner for smoked salmon

All the books say so. But try it for yourself; I reckon that the richness and oiliness of the fish actually competes with the rich, fat spiciness of the wine. I much prefer a Riesling from Alsace or Germany.

Red wine doesn't go with fish – or chocolate

In Portugal, the tradition is to drink young acidic red wine with cod; in Burgundy, there is a classic dish that involves poaching fish in a red wine from the region. Some fish-and-red-wine combinations are unsuccessful (sardines can make most red wine taste metallic, for example) and chocolate usually spoils the flavour of red wine. But there are some very tasty exceptions.

'Crémant' means 'less fizzy'

It does in Champagne. But elsewhere in France, it is just the name for sparkling wines that are every bit as fizzy as regular Champagne.

A hot summer always means a good vintage

A cold, rainy summer and autumn will usually make for a bad year, but a hot month of August will not necessarily indicate a good one. Vintages depend on the weather being 'right' at various phases of a grape's development, from the spring to the autumn. A late storm at the end of September can spoil what, at the beginning of that month, seemed set to be a great vintage.

Qualitätswein, Appellation Contrôlée, DO, DOC or DOCG on a label are a guarantee of quality

They should be; unfortunately all these expressions only legally indicate that the producer has made sure his wine conforms to a set of controls governing grape varieties, their origin and methods of production – not that he has to be a good wine-maker. Hence they can only really serve as a guide – albeit a useful one – to what the wine is going to be like.

A good vintage in Bordeaux is also good in Burgundy

These two regions are separated by a substantial mountain range – the Massif Central – and enjoy completely different climates. In 1982, Bordeaux had a historic vintage for its red wines; Burgundy's reds were pleasant but far from great. Beware too of assuming that vintages are of consistent quality for all the styles produced in a single region. Burgundy's white wines were far better in 1982 than its reds; 1967 Sauternes were wonderful; the red Bordeaux of that year were often little short of appalling.

Mouton Cadet is made from grapes harvested at Château Mouton Rothschild

The idea of Mouton Cadet being the 'younger brother', or second label, of the *grand vin* is a nice one, but one which doesn't survive even the briefest comparison of the annual production figures of the wine produced at the château – 20-30,000 cases – and that sold with the Mouton Cadet label – closer to a million. The only connections between the two wines is that both come from Bordeaux and are made and sold by the same company.

INCREDIBLE – BUT TRUE

According to the Guinness Book of Records, the longest distance a cork has flown from an untreated, unheated Champagne bottle is 54.18 metres. The previous record was beaten at Woodbury Winery and Cellars in New York State on 15 June 1988 by Professor Emeritus Heinrich Medicus.

A wine whose label declares its vintage to be 1989 could have been made from grapes which were picked in 1990. 'Eiswein' is a German and Austrian style made from grapes that have been left to freeze on the vine. Sometimes, the winegrowers have to wait so long for the necessary severe frost that they do not harvest the grapes until January, three or four months after the grapes for more conventional wines have been picked.

A teaspoon suspended in an opened bottle of Champagne will help it to keep its fizz. Even the experts at Moët & Chandon admit that they are foxed as to why this works – but it does.

Argentina and Hungary are, respectively, the fourth and fifth biggest wine producers in the world (after France, Italy and Spain).

One American wine company – E & J Gallo – produces more wine each year than the whole of Australia.

White grapes have to be used in red Chianti. Not because they improve its flavour, but because this bit of Tuscany has a surplus of white grape vines. In the Rhône, incidentally, winegrowers in Hermitage voluntarily choose to put some white grapes in their red wine.

A copper coin can remove an unpleasant smell from a wine. If the wine smells like rotten eggs, the chances are that some of the sulphur dioxide used in its preparation has turned into hydrogen sulphide. The copper coin will convert it into copper sulphate, leaving the wine smelling fine.

Salt and white wine can both stop red wine from staining. Even a deeply coloured wine such as Barolo should leave no stain if you dollop on a generous pile of salt, or a splash of white wine, as soon as the wine is spilled.

A peach immersed in Champagne (actually, in any sparkling wine) will soon begin to spin round and round of its own accord. The trick requires rather a large glass – but a smaller downy or hairy fruit (the hairs trap the bubbles), such as a kiwi or gooseberry, will perform to equally entertaining effect. Similarly, a raisin will 'swim' up and down the bubble stream of sparkling wine.

FRANCE

Try listing the world's ten best-known wine regions – without including Champagne, Bordeaux, Burgundy, Châteauneuf-du-Pape, Muscadet, Beaujolais, Sancerre, Sauternes, Chablis and Côtes du Rhône.

Yes, I know that Rioja, Chianti and the Mosel would be fighting pretty hard to get on that list too, along with Barolo, Australia's Hunter Valley and Portugal's Vinho Verde – but so would Pouilly Fumé, Hermitage and Alsace. In other words, France is rather like one of the Hollywood studios of the 1930s and '40s that had somehow managed to sign up Garbo, Gable and Grable, cornering the market in the stars most people wanted to see. France is the one country that no-one interested in wine can possibly ignore.

Of course, despite the chauvinism of most French winemakers, France doesn't produce all of the world's great wines, but it does produce the widest range of the traditionally best-known, from the palate-cleansingly dry whites of the Loire and Chablis to the intensely honeyed dessert wines of Sauternes and Muscat de Beaumes de Venise; from the simple boiled-sweet 'n' fruit-juice gulpability of Beaujolais to the toughly tannic I-defy-you-not-to-take-me-seriously character of wines from St Estèphe in Bordeaux.

And, as if it needed it, France's confidence has also been boosted by the sincerest of all forms of flattery. What kinds of grapes do the winemakers in California, Australia and New Zealand – and even such long-established winemaking countries as Spain, Italy and Greece – want to plant? The Chardonnay and Cabernet Sauvignon, the Pinot Noir, the Syrah and the Merlot – varieties historically most closely associated with France. And what styles of wine do they want to make? Those of Champagne, Bordeaux and Burgundy, the Loire and the Rhône.

But the difference which today separates French winemakers from many of the producers in the countries that have adopted their grapes is the way in which they have planted them. In California and Australia, the Cabernet Sauvignon, Riesling and Chardonnay are all grown almost cheek-by-jowl in the same vineyards. In France, there have been centuries of natural selection to sort out what grows best where; today, the Pinot Noir is cultivated in only five regions, all of which are in the northern, cooler half of the country; the Merlot is more or less restricted to Bordeaux; the Viognier is exclusively at home in a tiny region in the northern Rhône; the Riesling and the Gewürztraminer are grown nowhere outside Alsace.

And that's another of France's great advantages – having all those different places. It is the only country that can make wine in both northern and southern Europe. The vineyards of Champagne, the Loire, Burgundy and Alsace are more or less as close to the North Pole as you can be and still make quality wine; those on the southern coast may overlook some of the sunniest beaches on the Continent.

Climate, Soils and Traditions

Similarly, while the climates of regions such as Muscadet and Bordeaux benefit from the moderating effect of the Atlantic ocean, those further east, such as Burgundy and Alsace, are subject to the more continental heat-chill conditions associated with areas surrounded by a mass of land.

Soil types vary, too, from the sands of the Mediterranean in which Listel's *vin de sable* vines are grown, to the 'pudding stone' pebbles of Châteauneuf-du-Pape, the gravel of the Graves in Bordeaux and the chalk of Champagne. The vineyards in some regions – the Médoc, for example – are boringly

1 CHAMPAGNE
Champagne
Coteaux Champenois
Rosé de Riceys
Bouzy Rouge
1a Marne
1b Aube

2 ALSACE
Alsace Chasselas
Alsace Edelzwicker
Alsace Gewürztraminer
Alsace Grand Cru
Alsace Muscat
Alsace Pinot Noir
Alsace Pinot Blanc
Alsace Riesling
Alsace Sylvaner
Alsace Tokay/Pinot Gris
Crémant d'Alsace

3 BURGUNDY
Bourgogne
Bourgogne Passetoutgrains
Crémant de Bourgogne
3a Chablis
Chablis
Chablis Grand Cru
Chablis Premier Cru
Coulanges-les-Vineuses
Epineuil
Irancy
Petit Chablis
Sauvignon de St Bris

3b Côte d'Or
Aloxe-Corton
Auxey-Duresses
Bâtard-Montrachet/
Chevalier Montrachet /
  Montrachet
Beaune
Blagny
Chambertin
Chambertin Clos de Bèze
Chambolle-Musigny
Chassagne-Montrachet
Chorey-lès-Beaune
Clos de Vougeot
Corton / Corton-Charlemagne
Côte de Beaune
Côte de Beaune-Villages
Côte de Nuits-Villages
Echézeaux / Grands Echézeaux/
  Richebourg
Fixin
Gevrey-Chambertin
Hautes-Côtes de Beaune
Hautes-Côtes de Nuits
Ladoix
Marsannay
Meursault
Montrachet
Monthélie
Morey-St-Denis
Nuits-St-Georges
Pernand-Vergelesses
Pommard
Puligny-Montrachet
St-Aubin
St-Romain
Santenay
Savigny-lès-Beaune
Volnay
Vosne-Romanée

3c Côte Chalonnaise
Bourgogne Aligoté de Bouzeron
Givry
Mercurey
Montagny
Rully

3d Mâconnais
Mâcon
Mâcon-Clessé
Mâcon-Lugny
Mâcon-Prissé
Mâcon Supérieur
Mâcon-Uchizy
Mâcon-Villages
Mâcon-Viré
Pouilly-Fuissé
Pouilly-Loché
Pouilly-Vinzelles
St-Véran

3e Beaujolais
Beaujolais
Beaujolais Supérieur
Beaujolais-Villages
Brouilly
Chénas
Chiroubles
Coteaux du Lyonnais
Côte de Brouilly
Fleurie
Juliénas
Morgon
Moulin-à-Vent
Regnié
St-Amour

4 JURA
Arbois
Château-Chalon
Côtes du Jura
Etoile
Vin Jaune
Vin de Paille

5 SAVOIE
Apremont
Crépy
Roussette de Bugey
Seyssel
Vin de Bugey
Vin de Savoie

6 RHONE
6a Northern Rhône
Château Grillet
Clairette de Die (Tradition)
Châtillon-en-Diois
Condrieu
Cornas
Côte Rôtie
Côtes du Rhône
Crozes-Hermitage
Hermitage
St-Joseph
St-Péray

6b Ardèche
Coteaux de l'Ardèche

6c Southern Rhône
Beaumes de Venise
Cairanne
Châteauneuf-du-Pape
Côtes du Lubéron
Coteaux du Tricastin
Côtes du Rhône
Côtes du Rhône-Villages
Côtes du Ventoux
Gigondas
Lirac
Muscat de Beaumes de Venise
Rasteau
Tavel
Vacqueyras

7 PROVENCE, VAUCLUSE, GARD, BOUCHES DU RHONE
Bandol
Bellet
Cassis
Coteaux d'Aix-en-Provence (les Baux)
Coteaux Varois
Côtes de Provence
Palette

8 CORSICA
Ajaccio
Patrimonio
Vin de Corse

9 LANGUEDOC-ROUSSILLON / HERAULT / AUBE
Banyuls
Blanquette de Limoux
Clairette de Languedoc
Clairette de Bellegarde
Collioure
Corbières
Costières du Gard
Coteaux du Languedoc
Côtes du Roussillon
Faugères
Fitou
Limoux
Maury
Minervois

Muscat de Frontignan
Muscat de Lunel
Muscat de Mireval
Muscat de Rivesaltes
Muscat de St-Jean-de-Minervois
Rivesaltes
St Chinian

10 SOUTH-WEST
Béarn
Bergerac
Cahors
Côtes du Brulhois
Côtes de Buzet
Côtes de Duras
Côtes du Marmandais
Côtes de Montravel
Côtes de St Mont
Côtes du Frontonnais
Gaillac
Irouléguy
Jurançon
Madiran
Monbazillac
Montravel
Pacherenc du Vic-Bilh
Pécharmant
Vin de Lavilledieu
Vin de Pays des Côtes de Gascogne

11 BORDEAUX
Barsac
Blaye
Bordeaux
Bordeaux Supérieur
Cadillac
Canon-Fronsac
Cérons
Côtes de Blaye
Côtes de Bourg
Côtes de Francs
Entre-deux-Mers
Fronsac
Graves
Haut-Médoc

Lalande de Pomerol
Listrac
Loupiac
Lussac-St-Emilion
Margaux
Médoc
Montagne-St-Emilion
Moulis
Pauillac
Pessac-Léognan
Pomerol
Premières Côtes de Blaye
Premières Côtes de Bordeaux
Puisseguin-St-Emilion
Ste-Croix-de-Mont
St Emilion
St-Estèphe
St-Georges-St-Emilion
St-Julien
Sauternes

12 CHARENTES
Vin de pays du Charentais

13 LOIRE
13a Muscadet
Coteaux d'Ancenis
Fiefs Vendéens
Gros Plant du Pays Nantais
Muscadet
Muscadet des Coteaux de la Loire
Muscadet de Sèvre-et-Maine

13b Central: Anjou/Touraine
Anjou
Bonnezeaux
Bourgueil
Cabernet d'Anjou
Cabernet de Saumur
Cheverny

Coteaux de l'Aubance
Coteaux du Layon
Coteaux du Layon Villages
Coteaux du Vendômois
Crémant de Loire
Jasnières
Montlouis
Quarts-de-Chaume
Quincy
Rosé de Loire
St-Nicolas-de-Bourgueil
Saumur
Saumur-Champigny
Savennières
Savennières Coulée-de-Serrant
Savennières la Roche-aux-Moines
Touraine (Mesland, Amboise, Azay-le-Rideau)
Valençay
Vins du Haut Poitou
Vins de l'Orléanais
Vins du Thouarsais
Vouvray

13c Upper Loire
Châteaumeillant
Côtes d'Auvergne
Côtes du Forez
Coteaux du Giennois
Côtes Roannaises
Ménétou-Salon
Pouilly-Fumé
Quincy
Reuilly
St-Pourçain
Sancerre

Given these variables and the fact that French, until very recently, have rarely had anything to do with wines produced in regions other than their own, and have consequently developed winemaking traditions unique to themselves, the range and diversity of France's wines is perhaps hardly surprising.

Rules and Regulations

But, if the French have defined most of what are now accepted to be the 'classic' styles, they have also created a quality hierarchy – the *Appellation Contrôlée* system – that is the envy of winemakers in other countries. The system – usually referred to as AOC – is based on the discovery, made well over a thousand years ago, that certain pieces of land always seem to produce better wine – and that particular climates and types of soil better suit some grapes than others.

In Burgundy, laws covering the way in which vines could be planted and tended were laid down as early as the sixth century. Philip the Bold, duke of the region, issued an ordinance in 1395 banning the planting, in the part of Burgundy we now know as the Côte d'Or, of the heavy-cropping, easy-to-grow Gamay in

place of the traditional Pinot Noir. The former variety makes great Beaujolais, but dull wine in Beaune and Nuits-St-Georges.

Despite these early efforts, the vinous legislation that now governs Burgundy and all of France was not established until 1936, during a period when wine sales were slow and honest producers resented the unfair competition they suffered from people who were either adulterating their wines or simply over-cropping – producing huge quantities of dilute wine per acre.

Stated simply, the system is a quality pyramid. The better the specific vineyard, the stricter the rules and thus the more elevated the designation. The base of the pyramid, which includes the bulk of France's most basic wine, is described as *vin de table*. These wines may be made from more or less any grape, or blend of grapes, grown more or less anywhere in France. The stuff you see in French supermarkets in litre bottles is *vin de table*. (So is Piat d'Or.) Over ten per cent of all France's wine is distilled for brandy or into industrial alcohol, but of what is sold as wine, around half is *vin de table*.

Wines with a definable regional character, but few aspirations to be anything more than simple daily-drinking fare, are allowed to call themselves *vins de pays* – country wines –

FAR LEFT: One of the most impressive châteaux in Bordeaux, Pichon Baron has recently been taken over by a new winemaker after a long period when it was thought to be under-performing; today it is right back on form

LEFT: France has one of the widest ranges of foods and wines in the world. This restaurant in the south-west offers specialities of the region, including pâté de foie gras

ABOVE: Sancerre is not only the place to look for great wine; it also produces first-class goats' cheeses

provided that they comply with rules governing the grapes from which they are made and the regions in which they were grown. A *vin de pays* from Corsica should be of a similar quality to, but recognisably different from, say, a *vin de pays* from the Loire.

Next up the scale is VDQS – *Vin Délimité de Qualité Supérieure* – which is really little more than a waiting room for *vins de pays* that believe they deserve to be counted among the top quarter of France's wines, the ones that can use the magic words *Appellation Contrôlée* on their labels. Around 1.5 per cent of the annual harvest qualifies for VDQS status; these are wines that come from tightly specified regions – often as small as a village – and comply with fairly strict rules covering the grapes from which they can be made and the yields per acre.

Some VDQS wines are among France's best value for money because their producers can rarely ask very high prices for them. But not, perhaps, for long because every year or so the French authorities talk about doing away with the designation altogether. Then the current VDQS will presumably be booted out of the waiting room and into the *Appellations Contrôlées*. The fact that a French wine qualifies for *Appellation Contrôlée* status provides no guarantee that it is of particularly great

quality – a badly-made AOC Muscadet can be a lot less pleasant than a well-produced *vin de pays* – but it should indicate that its producer has complied with a tight set of regulations. His Muscadet can only be made from one grape variety, the Melon de Bourgogne, grown within a strictly defined region. Yields are also regulated, controlling the amount produced per acre.

Beyond *Appellation Contrôlée* there are, in many regions of France, further layers of the pyramid in the shape of local mini-hierarchies. In the Loire, Muscadet *sur lie* (wine matured traditionally in contact with its lees, or yeasts) can command a higher price than Muscadet that is not made in this way.

Muscadet, however, has nothing as grand as the *Grands Crus* and *Premiers Crus* of Burgundy – terms used to describe the region's finest wines. Bordeaux, too, has several hierarchies of its own; the Médoc alone, for instance, has a five-tier set of *Crus Classés*, and its more humble designation *Cru Bourgeois* is also a half-way house, between basic AOC and *Cru Classé* status.

Once you have got to grips with it, the system serves as a useful stair rail from one style and quality level to another. Interestingly, previously sceptical Californians and Australians, are now embracing appellation systems with fervour.

THE LANGUAGE OF FRANCE

Appellation d'Origine Contrôlée (AOC/AC) Designation governing such factors as area of production, grape varieties, levels of alcohol, maximum yield etc. The key French 'quality' label.

Assemblage A blending of base wines that creates the desired *cuvée*.

Ban de Vendange Officially declared regional date for start of grape-picking.

Barrique Wooden barrel holding 225 litres. Traditional in Bordeaux.

Baumé Measuring scale for the amount of sugar in grape must.

Blanc de Blancs White wine made from white grapes.

Blanc de Noirs White wine made from black grapes.

Brut Dry.

Cave Cellar.

Cépage Grape variety.

Chai Cellar/winery

Chaptalisation Addition of sugar to grape must to increase level of alcohol.

Clairet A pale red wine.

Climat Plot within a vineyard.

Clos A plot of land that is, or once was, enclosed by a wall.

Collage The fining of a wine.

Commune An administrative district within a *département*.

Confrérie A 'brotherhood' or association.

Côte/Coteaux Hillside(s)

Courtier A broker who liaises between winemakers and merchants.

Crémant Sparkling wine – in Champagne, traditionally indicates a less fizzy, more 'frothy' style but this usage is now being phased out following the granting of ACs

to the fully-sparkling Crémant d'Alsace, de Loire and de Bourgogne.

Cru Literally a growth; refers to an individual vineyard.

Cru Classé An officially classified growth, or vineyard, in Bordeaux. Also an anachronistic designation in Provence.

Cuvaison/macération Period of time a red wine spends in contact with its skins.

Cuve (de fermentation) Vat.

Cuve close Bulk production method for sparkling wine also called after its inventor, Charmat, whereby second fermentation takes place in a tank.

Cuvée A special batch of wine or the contents of a vat.

Débourbage The period during which the solids are allowed to settle from the must (*moût*) during fermentation.

Dégorgement Stage in sparkling wine production when sediment is removed.

Demi-sec Half dry/half sweet.

Département Administrative region, similar to English county or US state.

Doux Sweet.

Elevage Maturation, rearing of a wine, often including racking and blending, before bottling – the job of the *négociant*.

Egrappoir A machine which removes stalks from grapes before they are pressed.

Encépagement Varietal blend.

En Primeur To offer classic wines (particularly clarets) for sale before they have been finally blended and bottled.

Foudre A large wooden cask.

Fouloir A long, revolving tube which is used to remove the juice in grapes.

Fût Barrel.

Goût de Terroir Literally 'taste of earth' but often meaning that a wine has flavours

typically imparted by the soil of its vineyard.

Grand Cru A top-quality vineyard site: literally, 'great growth'. The meaning has been debased due to lack of legislative control. It has specific status in Burgundy, Bordeaux, Champagne and Alsace.

INAO The Institut Nationale des Appellations d'Origine, the body governing the *appellation contrôlée* system.

Jeunes Vignes Young vines.

Lie Lees, or dead yeasts left over from fermentation. Wine may be bottled '*sur lie*'.

Liquoreux Rich and sweet.

Macération Carbonique Carbonic maceration – see *How Wine is Made*.

Marc The detritus left after pressing grape skins – or the brandy distilled from it.

Méthode champenoise See *How Wine is Made*.

Méthode Rurale/Gaillacoise/Dioise Variations on the *méthode champenoise*.

Mistelle Fresh grape juice which has had alcohol added prior to fermentation. Not technically a wine as it never ferments.

Millésime Vintage date.

Mis en bouteilles (au château, domaine) Bottled at the estate.

Moelleux Semi-sweet.

Mousseux Sparkling, but not a *méthode champenoise* wine.

Moût Must

Mutage The addition of alcohol to must to stop it from fermenting.

Négociant Trader or merchant.

Négociant-Eleveur Merchant who buys wine post-fermentation and blends and bottles it for sale under his own label.

Nouveau Wine intended to be consumed in the months following harvest.

UP FROM THE COUNTRY

If you were to follow the advice of many traditional wine writers, you might well restrict your drinking of French wines to ones whose labels bear the magic words 'Appellation Contrôlée'. A decade or so ago, you'd often have been wise to do just that, because to buy any of the 'lesser' quality wines would have required a readiness to take a gamble; today, however, you would be denying yourself some of the most exciting flavours and best value that France can produce. As the price of wines from, for example, Bordeaux and Burgundy, has risen, and will continue to rise, more and more discerning buyers are looking to areas that have improved their winemaking significantly and, although not yet eligible for VDQS or Appellation Contrôlée status, strive towards that goal. You may not be getting wine of the very highest quality, but you can certainly get quality. The place to look, more than ever before, is among the Vins de Pays, the 'country wines'.

There are over 125 of these; some encompass huge swathes of land that seem to stretch from one end of France to the other, while others are tucked away in small, obscure corners you only ever find your way to by accident. Whatever the relative sizes of the Vin de Pays areas, however, they all tend to have two things in common: their rules allow far greater experimentation with grape types than those governing Appellation Contrôlée wines, and the quality of their wine depends largely on the attitude of the cooperatives and individual growers who produce most of the wine. With few exceptions, it has rarely been the négociants – the merchants – who have led the way in developing the Vins de Pays.

The larger regions such as the prettily named Vin du Pays du Jardin de la France, tend to offer something of a lucky dip: some of the Sauvignon Blancs and Chardonnays can be first class examples of these varieties, while others – and most of the wines made here from the Chenin Blanc, for example – can be either dull or downright poor.

The motor that potentially drives all of the Vins de Pays, to improve the standard of their wines though, is the knowledge that they might one day climb the ladder to become a VDQS and even, ultimately, a fully-fledged Appellation Contrôlée.

There are a few Vin de Pays estates, however, that have become able to ask high prices for their wines because there is a queue of eager customers who want to buy them. Bottles of the red and white from Mas de Daumas Gassac, for example, though 'only' eligible to bear the label of Vin de Pays de l'Hérault, cost as much as some pretty classy Burgundies and Bordeaux.

Although there are Vins de Pays throughout France, the ones I find most reliable are the ones from Catalan, Coteaux du Quercy (in its tough, 'old fashioned' way), Côtes de Gascogne (from Yves Grassa's various domaines, and from the Plaimont cooperative) Côtes de Thongue, Drôme, Gard, Hérault, Ile de Beauté, Principauté d'Orange, Vaucluse, Collines Rhodaniennes, Mont Caume (especially the Cabernet Sauvignon from the Bunan estate), Sables du Golfe du Lion, Uzège, Mont Bouquet, Coteaux de Peyriac, and Vallée du Paradis. The whites of the Loire-Atlantique, Charentais, Loir-et-Cher and Maine-et-Loire can be good – if acidic – alternatives to Muscadet.

There are some first-class, spicy, Rhône-like wines from the Coteaux de l'Ardèche and Bouches du Rhône that easily compete with good Côtes du Rhône, but neither region could be described as reliable. I've never had a memorable bottle of wine from the Côtes du Brian, but I love its name so much that I can never resist buying it. Sadly, importers shy away from importing it into English-speaking countries, so it has to be sold under its alternative name of Coteaux de Peyriac.

LEFT: Winemaking is still a family affair, as this happy band make clear at the end of a long week's picking in Champagne.

BELOW: Signs proclaiming that wine is for sale punctuate the roadside throughout the wine-producing regions of France.

Passerillage The process of allowing grapes to overripen and shrivel.
Pelure d'Oignon 'Onion skin' – used to describe the colour of some rosés.
Perlant Very slightly sparkling.
Pétillant Slightly sparkling.
Pièce Cask.
Pourriture Noble 'Noble rot' – *Botrytis cinerea*.
Premier Cru The highest level of the 1855 Bordeaux classification; the second level in Burgundy.
Primeur New wine.
Pressoir Grape press.
Pupitre Rack used for tilting sparkling wine bottles so that sediment falls on to the cork ready for *dégorgement*.
Rancio A taste created by controlled oxidation by heat of a wine in cask.
Ratafia Liqueur made from *marc* and grape juice in Champagne.
Récolte Harvest.
Remontage The pumping of the must over its skins to extract colour and flavour.
Remuage The manipulation of sparkling wine bottles by turning so as to deposit the sediment in the neck of the bottle.
Rendement The allowed yield of wine from a given area.
Rosé d'une Nuit A rosé created by macerating red grape juice briefly – overnight – with the skins.
Saignée Literally, 'bleeding' – creating a rosé by drawing off lightly-tinted surplus juice from a fermenting vat of red wine.
Sous-marque Secondary brand-name often used for wine not good enough for the producer's main label.
Sec Dry, or low in sugar.
Sélection de Grains Nobles See *Alsace*.

Soutirage Racking.
Stage Apprenticeship in wine.
Sur lie Aged on its lees.
Supérieur/e A term which indicates a higher degree of alcohol.
Surmaturité Over-ripeness.
Tastevin A shallow dimpled metal cup used primarily in Burgundy for tasting.
Terroir 'Earth', but meaning the factors that affect a vine, e.g. soil, slope, climate.
Tête de Cuvée The first and the finest flow of juice from the newly-crushed grapes.
VDN See *vin doux naturel*.
VDQS *Vin Délimité de Qualité Supérieure*, quality level below AOC but above *vin de pays*.
Vendange Harvest

Vendange Tardive Late harvest.
Vieilles Vignes The oldest and best vines.
Vigne Vine.
Vigneron Vineyard worker.
Vignoble Vineyard.
Vin de garde Classic wine capable of improvement if allowed to age.
Vin de pays 'Country wine' with some regional character. Quality level above the basic *vin de table* and below *VDQS*.
Vin de presse Press wine.
Vin doux naturel A wine which has been fortified before all the sugar has been fermented out.
Vin gris A very pale rosé.
Vin de table/Vin ordinaire Basic, everyday wine, from no particular area.

BORDEAUX

If you were to ask a panel of international experts to devise a wine region, I've a sneaky feeling they might come up with one that was very like Bordeaux. The conditions for wine grape-growing are ideal – the vines have to work hard, but not too hard. The climate, not too warm and dry, makes for more interesting flavours in the wine, and a variation in vintage styles helps to maintain interest. The area is large – it's the biggest quality region in France, with nearly a quarter of a million acres of vineyards – so it can produce enough to satisfy international demand, and its wines are sufficiently varied in style to accommodate nearly every taste.

It's at this point that the marketing men in the team would outline their masterstroke. The region would produce a tiny number of top-quality wines which, like the top-of-the-line models from a car manufacturer, would serve as flagships to promote the rest. Thus, out of some 4,000 estates, only around 100 would achieve international prestige. Their wines would be snapped up within months of the harvest – before they were even bottled – and would spend their, on average, 30 or 40-year lifespans changing hands at auction for fantastic, yet eagerly paid sums. And for every one of the really big-name wines – the Latours, Lafites and Yquems – there would be perhaps a thousand others, produced in the same region from the same grape varieties, but in a descending order of price, from the aristocrats down through the crus bourgeois – 'middle-class wines' – to humble Bordeaux Rouge and Blanc, providing an easily-grasped ladder up which to tempt aspiring drinkers.

The History

In a way, Bordeaux *has* been created by a team of experts – the vinegrowers and winemakers working in successive centuries over the 2,000 years that this region has been producing wine, aided and abetted by a fair deal of outside influence and expertise. It is thought to be the Romans who first began or developed winegrowing here, and there were certainly vineyards being

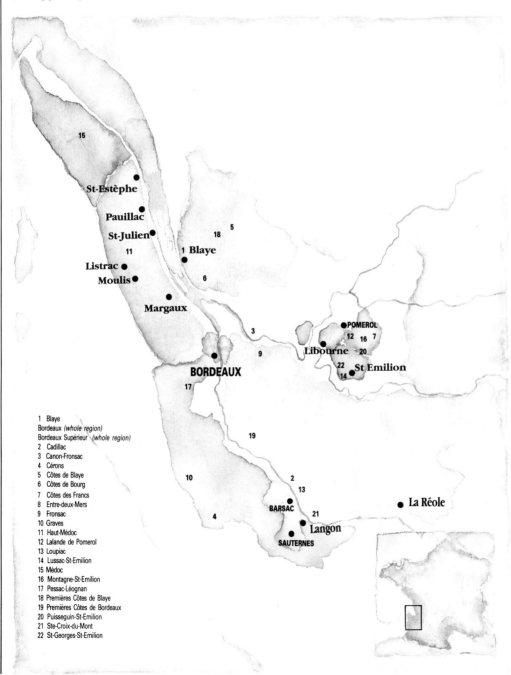

1 Blaye
Bordeaux *(whole region)*
Bordeaux Supérieur *(whole region)*
2 Cadillac
3 Canon-Fronsac
4 Cérons
5 Côtes de Blaye
6 Côtes de Bourg
7 Côtes des Francs
8 Entre-deux-Mers
9 Fronsac
10 Graves
11 Haut-Médoc
12 Lalande de Pomerol
13 Loupiac
14 Lussac-St-Emilion
15 Médoc
16 Montagne-St-Emilion
17 Pessac-Léognan
18 Premières Côtes de Blaye
19 Premières Côtes de Bordeaux
20 Puisseguin-St-Emilion
21 Ste-Croix-du-Mont
22 St-Georges-St-Emilion

BORDEAUX MAP

tended at the time when the centurions first arrived in England. Precisely what happened to the wines made in Bordeaux during the period between the days of the Roman occupation and the early 12th century is unclear, but there are stories of 8th and 9th-century exports to Ireland and the west of Britain.

Everything changed, however, when Henry II of England married Eleanor of Aquitaine, and Bordeaux became for 300 years what it sometimes still seems to be – a part of England. Richard *Coeur de Lion* regularly drank wine from Bordeaux and, under King John, the region's merchants were encouraged to send their wine to England by an exemption from export tax. During the 13th and 14th centuries, thousands of barrels of 'Gascon wine' regularly crossed the Channel – six bottles per year for every English man, woman and child, so contemporary records suggest.

Much of the wine those early English Bordeaux drinkers would have enjoyed drinking in pubs and in their homes was of the style the French called *clairet*, a pale red made by leaving the skins in contact with the fermenting juice for only a day or so. It was from this name that the English took the term they still use for all red Bordeaux – 'Claret'.

But not all of the wine exported as Bordeaux was actually produced close to that city. At that time, Bordeaux was principally a port; any wine shipped from its docks would almost certainly have been described as Bordeaux for the sake of convenience. It would be several centuries before a number of Englishmen, Dutchmen and Irishmen were to help establish the great estates and the merchants that would bring Bordeaux to its present-day pre-eminence. The Bordelais like to play down the part played by these 17th and 18th-century foreigners; top Bordeaux château names such as Cantenac-Brown, Smith Haut-Lafitte, Léoville-Barton and Lynch-Bages give them the lie.

Bordeaux Today

The last two decades have been traumatic ones for Bordeaux. Until the 1970s, to the châteaux owners and to many of their customers, the claret they made was not merely a kind of red wine, it *was* red wine. As they saw it, there were no real alternatives or, hence, competitors. At a pinch they might have

BELOW: Bordeaux's historic role as one of France's major ports did much to spread the renown of the wines made nearby

WHAT IS A CRU?

One of the initially daunting aspects of Bordeaux is the way in which wines are described as *Crus Bourgeois, Crus Classés, Grands Crus Classés, Premiers Grands Crus Classés* and so on. These terms refer to the local classifications established for the Médoc, Graves, Sauternes, Barsac and St Emiiion. The term 'cru' literally means 'growth' and refers to an estate which may consist of a single vineyard or (more often) set of vineyards. Some of these classifications have been virtually unchanged for around 150 years; others, such as the one in St Emilion, have been recently updated. Confusingly, there is little coordination between regions. So, St Emilion has no *Crus Bourgeois* and the Médoc has five levels of *Grands Crus Classés* but none known as *Premiers Grands Crus*.

---

conceded that the far smaller region of Burgundy, somewhere way up on the other side of the country, might be producing some reasonable reds; the chances of a Bordelais ever having voluntarily drunk a wine from California or Australia would have been very close to zero.

Then the early 1970s saw not only a series of poor vintages, but also a widely trumpeted scandal in which one of the region's best-known merchants was found to have been mislabelling large quantities of wine. And if this wasn't bad enough, there was a crash in the Bordeaux investment market and, most influentially of all in the long term, the shattering results of a blind tasting competition between wines from Bordeaux and California that proved that the château owners were no longer the only people in the world who knew how to make great red wine from the Cabernet Sauvignon grape.

But the Bordelais learned their lesson. They knew that their soil, their grape varieties and their experience had to give them the edge over the New World newcomers. All they needed to do was to apply some of the latters' new winemaking techniques and technology. You may not be able to teach an old dog new tricks, but this one was certainly capable of refining some of his old ones.

Money was invested in cleaning up the *cuveries* which, even in some of the better-known châteaux, still looked as though they had last been modernised at some time during the 19th century. Cooling equipment was brought in for the fermentation vats in order to avoid the problems of overheating in hot years, and to allow the production of crisp, dry white wines. Throughout the region, dirty old casks were replaced, either by cleanable tanks or, in the best properties, by a greater number of 225-litre barrels, a proportion of which would be replaced every year, giving the wine a touch of spicy vanilla.

Beyond all this, the château owners disciplined themselves to sell only their best wine under the label of their château. Wine

---

WHAT IS A CHATEAU?

One of Bordeaux's more incidental gifts to the world has been the notion of the château. Visitors to Burgundy and the Rhône expect all the winemakers in those, and every other wine region of France to be based in châteaux. In fact, while there are wine-producing châteaux in other regions, the concept is still very Bordelais – and suprisingly recent. When the brokers of the region were drawing up classifications of the best wines of the region in the 19th century, around half the estates they listed had no mention of 'château' before their name. Gradually, however, the success of such grand properties as Château Margaux drove almost everyone to rename their estates; today, although there is no rule that a Bordeaux estate has to call itself Château anything, there are very, very few Bordeaux domaines that do not do so.

Some 'châteaux' do not materially exist at all. According to the rules, the only necessary condition is that the name proposed for use is 'linked to...a specific vineyard that has been known for a very long time by the name in question'.

---

from younger vines, for example, that lacks the richness of the fruit of older plants, would now go into good, but lesser 'second label' wines.

Today, thanks to these developments, to a growing interest in its wines around the world and to a series of good vintages in the 1980s, Bordeaux has reasserted its position securely atop the wine world. And it does so both as France's largest quality wine region and as a collection of related appellations, each of which has its own style.

What Gives Bordeaux Its Flavour?

Most New World winemakers would give the greatest credit to the grape varieties that are grown here. For the red wines, these consist of the blackcurranty, sun-loving Cabernet Sauvignon; its easier-to-please, lighter-bodied 'kid brother' the Cabernet Franc; the plummier Merlot, which ripens a little earlier and is an invaluable softening ingredient in any Bordeaux blend; the sturdy Malbec and the Petit Verdot, which only ripens in the best vintages but imparts a wonderfully spicy note, even when it only makes up two or three per cent of the wine.

For the whites, the two key grapes are the rich, honeyed Sémillon, which can make great dry and sweet wines, and the tangier, more gooseberryish Sauvignon Blanc – better known as the variety used to make Sancerre in the Loire. The white counterpart to the Petit Verdot is the similarly spicy Muscadelle, which is almost always used fractionally in blends; and almost never by itself.

However, the Bordelais themselves would stress that it is not so much the grapes *per se* as the soil in which they grow – the well-drained gravel which covers clay or sand in the Médoc and Graves; the limestone and chalk of Sauternes and Barsac; and the clay and limestone in St Emilion and Pomerol – and the way in which it nurtures the grape varieties that makes Bordeaux special.

The third factor is one of crucial importance, and one which is only now being understood by would-be Bordeaux mimics in other countries – the way in which grape varieties are blended together. With very, very few exceptions, there is no such thing as a 100% Bordeaux Cabernet Sauvignon or 100% Bordeaux Merlot; almost every top-quality claret you are ever likely to drink will be a blend of at least two grape varieties. It is this marriage of complementary characteristics – a union strengthened by long and careful maturation – that helps to give Bordeaux the complexity (the wonderful mixture of flavours and smells that can be found in a single glass) that sets its best wines above even some of their most delicious counterparts from other regions. And it is the variations on each of these three themes – grapes, soil and blending – that gives each of the Bordeaux appellations its distinctive style.

Styles and Appellations

The British traditionally like the wines of the Médoc, made principally from the Cabernet Sauvignon, which tend to be fairly tough and tannic when they are young. In the United States, on the other hand, the softer, more immediately approachable wines of Pomerol and St Emilion are often more popular. Each appellation has its 'satellites': nearby areas whose wines echo its style but at less cost. British wine drinkers looking for a bargain might, for example, go for a wine from a château in the less well-known appellation of Listrac, while the Americans might prefer one from Fronsac.

The Vintage

But even within these regional appellations, winemaking styles – and skills – vary. When buying Bordeaux, you need to look for the commune – or region, in the case, for instance, of the Médoc, Haut-Médoc and Graves – and the château (and

Above: Château Margaux, one of the most impressive buildings – and wines – in Bordeaux

Left: The other face of Bordeaux, in the form of a sign advertising basic wine 'in bulk' at 14 francs a litre

possibly château owner – the owner of one good estate may also have others). And, of course, the vintage.

Because of the size of the region and the range of soils and grapes, some vintages are more successful for some appellations than they are for others. In 1964, for example, the pickers of St Emilion and Pomerol had already harvested their grapes when many of their neighbours in the Médoc (where the Cabernet Sauvignon ripens rather later) saw their crop washed out by torrential storms. Years that are good for red wines are often disappointing for sweet whites – and vice versa. The reputation of Bordeaux vintages is often greatly affected by their investment – in other words, long-term potential. Years such as 1987, which produced wines which were generally light-bodied and for early drinking, are often underestimated by the experts. When fairly priced, these can be well worth buying, particularly by those waiting for wines from 'better' vintages to reach their peak – or by those who would like a taste of great Bordeaux style at a more affordable price.

THE LANGUAGE OF BORDEAUX

Bordeaux Basic quality. 10% for red and 10.5% for white.

Bordeaux Supérieur One level above basic bordeaux with reds at 10.5% and whites at 11.5%.

Cru Bourgeois the middle class. Ranked below *cru classé*.

Cru Classé A classed property or growth. Refers to one of the 5 quality levels classified in 1855.

Cru Grand Bourgeois Official rank above *cru bourgeois*.

Cru Grand Bourgeois Exceptionnel Above *bourgeois supérieur*. The *exceptionnel* is unofficial but when stated may indicate wine not far off the lower *crus classés*.

Grand Cru Classé Top classification.

Premier Grand Cru Classé Top-classed Médoc growths from the 1855 classification.

THE MEDOC

While the Graves, St Emilion and Pomerol regions all produce great wine – including some of the greatest Bordeaux of all – there is no question that the Médoc is first division red (there are almost no whites) territory. This is the region that can boast Châteaux Lafite, Latour, Mouton Rothschild and Margaux, and in their wake a small fleet of other illustrious estates. When most people think of Bordeaux this is the part most of them, consciously or unconsciously, have in mind.

In some ways, the international fame of the Médoc and its wines is rather surprising. To look at, it's one of the least prepossessing, flattest bits of winegrowing land in the world – far less impressive than the best parts of Burgundy or the northern Rhône. What makes the vineyards special, though, is less the lie of the land than the land itself. As any Bordelais will tell you, Bordeaux's success has always been that of the character of each piece of soil. While the Californian is striving

to express the flavour of the grape, the Bordeaux grower's aim is to convey the character of the *terroir* – the vineyard.

For around 1,300 years, while the Burgundians were busily growing vines and making wine in the Côte d'Or, most of the Médoc was no more than wild and lonely marshland. Even such now-illustrious estates as Margaux and Lafite were largely devoted to the growing of wheat. There wasn't even very much in the way of roads between the villages, landowners travelled to their châteaux from Bordeaux by boat along the Garonne.

But, at the end of the 16th century, the winegrowing potential of the Médoc was finally realised by the ingenuity of a team of Dutchmen, who drained the marshes and then introduced the novel idea of planting vines in rows instead of in the higgledy-piggledy way the Bordelais had been using.

The following two centuries were Bordeaux's – and the Médoc's – heyday as virtually the world's only source of great wine, and much of this success was directly attributable to the Irish, English and Scots families – the Johnstons, Lynches, Bartons, Smiths and the rest – who settled here and produced and sold wine to the rest of Europe.

The key date for the Médoc, however, was 1855, the year of the Great Exhibition in Paris, and the year which saw the publication of an official classification which divided the red wines of the Médoc into first, second, third, fourth and fifth growths – the *Crus Classés*. The red and white wines of the Graves and the white wines of Sauternes and Barsac also received their own classifications with just two levels – *Premier* and *Deuxième Cru*. It is often supposed that these league tables were specially produced for the exhibition; in fact, they were merely official versions of lists the brokers of Bordeaux had long been using among themselves to establish the prices for which wine might be sold to local customers and to such distinguished foreigners as Thomas Jefferson. Even in the previous century Médoc first growths such as Latour and Lafite had been worth twice as much

as second growths, three times as much as the thirds and so on.

The accuracy of the classification was remarkable. Over the years, countless blind tastings have resulted in sufficiently consistent results for no full-scale revision of the 1855 list to have taken place – despite the attempts by various wine writers to come up with hierarchies of their own. So, nearly a century and a half later, the wine world continues to treat the 1855 classification as if it had been carved in tablets of stone. Which is not always a very good idea.

The brokers took no account of the specific size and location of each château's vineyards. In other words, Château Margaux could sell off almost all of its best land and replace it with less good vineyards in the same commune, and still sell its wine with its First Growth label. Château Margaux wouldn't do that, but some other classed growths certainly have.

And because the basis of the classification was the price for which the wines were sold in the 18th and 19th centuries, a well-sited château which had at that time employed a succession of bad winemakers could have been less well classified than it now deserves.

The Communes of the Médoc

Driving north from Bordeaux, you have barely left the outskirts of the city before you find yourself in the gravelly soil of the Haut-Médoc. This appellation – literally 'High Médoc' – confusingly comprises the lower part of the overall region and includes the six higher quality communal appellations of Margaux, St-Julien, Pauillac, St-Estèphe, Moulis and Listrac, while the Médoc appellation itself covers a lesser-quality area mostly further north.

Haut-Médoc wines from land that falls outside those six communes can offer some of the best value in Bordeaux. Only five are classed – the delicious La Lagune and Cantemerle, de Camensac, La Tour-Carnet and Belgrave – but some unclassed châteaux, like Larose-Trintaudon, Caronne-Ste-Gemme, Beaumont, Lanessan and Sénéjac are easily better than some fifth and even fourth growth wines.

THE ESSENTIALS — THE MEDOC

Location Along the left bank of the Gironde, north-west of the city of Bordeaux.

Quality AOCs are: Bordeaux; Bordeaux Supérieur; Haut-Médoc; Médoc; Moulis; Listrac; St Estèphe; Pauillac; St Julien and Margaux. Superimposed on these are the *Cru Bourgeois* and *Cru Classé* hierarchies, the latter in a strictly-ranked league. No VDQS or *vin de pays* wines are produced.

Style All appellations bar the first are for red wine; the tiny amount of white made qualifies only as Bordeaux Blanc. Reds are blackcurrant/cedary and more or less tannic depending on the region and in proportion to the amount of Cabernet Sauvignon used. Styles are very site-specific, varying with each communal appellation and with the care given to winemaking.

Climate Basically maritime, though the position, between two masses of water (the Atlantic and the estuary of the Gironde), moderates extremes of temperatures, creating a unique micro-climate. The Gulf Stream gives mild winters, warm summers and long autumns. The area is also fortunate in being shielded from westerly winds by the pine forest seaboard strip that runs parallel to the Gironde.

Cultivation Vineyards are planted on flattish land, with occasional low, rolling hills. Soils are variable but principally composed of gravel over limestone and clay.

Grape Varieties *Reds*: Cabernet Sauvignon, Cabernet Franc, Merlot, Malbec, Petit Verdot. *Whites*: Sauvignon, Sémillon.

Production/Maturation Style of winemaking is very influential, the best wines being the most complex and concentrated, and those which have received the most new oak ageing though use of new oak is dependent on the wine having sufficient concentration to handle it: Old oak is being gradually replaced, and stainless steel is now commonly used for fermentation.

Longevity Bordeaux Supérieur, Médoc and Haut-Médoc: 1 to 6 years; *Crus Bourgeois*, Moulis and Listrac: 4 to 10 years (though good wines in good years can last longer); *Crus Classés*: anything up to 25 years and sometimes more.

Vintage Guide 78, 79, 82, 83, 85, 86, 88, 89

Top Producers The league of *Crus Classés*, unchanged since 1855, is still reliable but not infallible. Some 'second label' wines made by classed châteaux from grapes that aren't quite good enough for the "Grand Vin' can be as good as other châteaux's best wines. A growing list of good unclassified estates include: Châteaux Reysson, St Bonnet, Sénéjac, Siran, Sociando-Mallet, Potensac, d'Angludet, Chasse-Spleen, Caronne Ste-Gemme, Beaumont, Labégorce-Zédé, Maucaillou, de Pez, La Tour-de-Mons, La Tour-St-Bonnet, La Tour du Haut Moulin, La Tour de By, Belgrave, Citran, Le Crock, Dutruch Grand Poujeaux, Fonbadet, Fonréaud, Gloria, Haut Marbuzet, Clos du Marquis, La Gurgue, Monbrison, Poujeaux.

ABOVE LEFT: High-Tech vineyard mobility at Château d'Angludet, an unclassed Médoc estate whose wines are made by Peter Sichel of Château Palmer. The wooden cases are more usually employed to safeguard wine on its way from the château to the consumer.

FAR LEFT: The British-owned Chateau Rausan Segla, one of the smartest châteaux in Margaux.

LEFT: Not all Bordeaux châteaux are this smart however; Terrey Gros Caillou's buildings may lack the cachet of some of its neighbours in Margaux, but it still produces good wine.

The key words to look for on Haut-Médoc labels are, in descending order of quality, *Cru Grand Bourgeois Exceptionnel*, *Cru Grand Bourgeois* or *Cru Bourgeois*, all of which ought to indicate that the wine is a cut above the average. But a word of warning: there are two lists of *Crus Bourgeois* – one a 1932 classification, and the other a 1978 membership list of the *Syndicat des Crus Bourgeois*. According to the Syndicat, there are just 127 wines that can describe themselves as any kind of *Cru Bourgeois*; a significant number of the better wines from the 1932 list, such as Labégorce Zédé and Siran in Margaux were excluded. In addition, some châteaux which could call themselves *Cru Bourgeois* prefer not to be included among the 'middle class', perhaps fearing that to do so might jeopardise their chances of ever being considered for inclusion in a revised classification of the classed growths.

Margaux

The first 'classy' appellation you reach after leaving Bordeaux is Margaux. The only one that shares its name with its best château, this as countless hopelessly lost visitors have discovered to their exhasperation, is actually more of a collection of villages than a single commune; wines from Arsac, Cantenac, Labarde, Soussans and Margaux itself can all call themselves Margaux. This occasionally raises a wry smile in the cafés of Labarde, Arsac and Cantenac – these quiet villages to the south of Margaux boast some of the juicier wines of the appellation. Châteaux such as Giscours, Siran, d'Angludet, du Tertre, d'Issan, Prieuré Lichine, Kirwan and Brane-Cantenac can, and do, legitimately describe themselves as Margaux .

But it would be dangerous to overstate that juiciness; Margaux has a reputation for making the most delicate and perfumed wines of the Médoc, with a scent of violets and flavour of blackberries, rather than the more usual Bordeaux blackcurrant. The vines have to work hard for their nourishment, fighting their way through the gravelly soil, but, as the locals say, the plants never get their feet as wet here as they do in the clayey soil of more northerly St-Estèphe.

Margaux is (relatively) big – the largest communal appellation in the Médoc, and the most blessed with classed growths and top-quality *crus bourgeois*. Sadly though, as some of its more forthright producers would admit, the quality of Mar-

The vineyards of the St Julien second growth Château Léoville-Las Cases and the Pauillac first growth, Château Latour are adjoining; the former estate's lion overlooks the latter's tower insignia.

gaux's land is often let down by some pretty poor winemaking,

Apart from the glorious Château Margaux itself, and Château Palmer, its closest rival, the best classed wines are d'Issan, Lascombes, Rausan-Ségla, Malescot-St-Exupéry (the last two most particularly in recent vintages) and du Tertre. Prieuré-Lichine, which belonged to the great Russian-American wine writer Alexis Lichine, is fairly priced and good value can also be found in Château Notton and Pavillon Rouge du Château Margaux (the second wines of Châteaux Brane Cantenac and Margaux).

Among non-classed wines, seek out Château d'Angludet (made by Peter Sichel, who is also responsible for Château Palmer), La Gurgue, Labégorce-Zédé, Monbrison and Siran, all of which make wine of at least fourth growth quality at far lower prices than most actual fourth growths cost.

Before leaving Margaux, I have to mention the exception that proves the rule. The Médoc is emphatically not white wine territory – but then there's Pavillon Blanc du Château Margaux, an extraordinary oaky, honeyed, tangy Sauvignon Blanc.

Moulis and Listrac

From Margaux the obvious next stop, quite a drive north, is St-Julien. Worth a diversion on the way, though, by turning off to the west into the forest, are two communes rarely mentioned in the old wine books – for the simple reason that neither includes any classed growths. But the villages of Moulis and Listrac well repay a visit, because they both produce some of the best-value wines in the region.

Moulis and the village with which it shares its small appellation, Grand Poujeaux, lie on gravelly soil, are bang next door to Margaux and have everything it takes to make wine of classed quality. Château Chasse-Spleen and, to a slightly lesser extent,

---

A PINCH OF SALT WITH YOUR MARGAUX

Margaux provides two perfect examples of the danger of treating the 1855 classification as though it were gospel. In 1811, an English Major General called Charles Palmer bought Chateau de Gasq from an attractive young widow he met on a train. Palmer renamed the château and, following the Prince Regent's misplaced advice, changed the vines and the winemaking style – and went bankrupt.

Today, Château Palmer is a third growth next-door-neighbour of Château Margaux that makes wines of first-growth quality. I wonder how it would have been classed if the good General had never boarded that train...

Château Margaux itself provides a similar object lesson. Until the mid 1960s this first growth estate which had so impressed Thomas Jefferson consistently produced one of very best wines in Bordeaux; its 1953 was – and is – one of the most perfect wines ever made anywhere. However, in the 1960s and 1970s, things started to go wrong; neither the vineyards nor the winery were getting the care, attention and money they needed, and it showed in the wine. It was like a great restaurant with a tired chef and a broken-down range. Then, in 1978, the château was bought for a small fortune by the Mentzelopoulos family which then went on to spend another small fortune on putting everything to rights and employing the Bordeaux guru Professor Emile Peynaud as a consultant. The medicine worked instantly. Critics who had been calling for Margaux's demotion were, and still are, rightly declaring it second to none.

Château Maucaillou prove what can be done here every year and Poujeaux and Gressier-Grand-Poujeaux are both good too. All these wines 'come round' rather more quickly than Margaux, but good examples can last at least 15 years.

If Moulis wines can be enjoyed young, Listrac's demand greater patience; they're much tougher, and much more closely related to those of St-Estèphe, a little further to the north. The Merlot grows well in the gravelly soil here, but isn't used as much as it ought to be. Château Clarke, which belongs to Edmond Rothschild, who is not one of the Rothschilds of Lafite and Mouton Rothschild, has recently been rebuilt and replanted and is now distinctly up-and-coming. Both Fourcas-Hosten and Fourcas-Dupré can be good in ripe vintages.

St-Julien

You know that you've got to St Julien when you round the bend in the road and see the smart gates and gardens of Château Beychevelle. Before continuing north, turn right just beyond the château and drive down to enjoy the peaceful view from the river bank. This is where it is said that passing boats obeyed the command to lower their sails ('*Basse-les-Voiles*') issued by the then owner of the château, the Duc d'Eperon, one of France's best known admirals. Sadly, neither the story that this command gave the château its name, nor the one that the sailors occasionally dropped their trousers instead of the sails, is true.

Château Beychevelle is as good an introduction to the commune as you are likely to need. This is a place for grand, big châteaux though, surprisingly, no first growth wines. But, if there are no firsts, there are certainly two famous 'super-seconds' – second growths that make wine as good as the firsts – in the shape of Léoville-Lascases and Ducru-Beaucaillou; the almost as impressive Gruaud-Larose; and a clutch of other richly wonderful wines in recent vintages, particularly Beychevelle, Branaire-Ducru, Talbot and (in recent vintages) Lagrange.

This is Bordeaux the way the British have always like it: blackcurrant, but cedary too, with the unmistakable sweet scent traditionally described as 'cigar-box'. Interestingly, it is an Englishman, Anthony Barton, who makes another of the best wines here, Léoville-Barton – and its slightly lighter-weight stable-mate, Langoa-Barton.

Both Barton's wines are fairly priced (particularly considering their quality); for other affordable St-Juliens try the unclassed Lalande-Borie or Terrey-Gros-Caillou, or Clos du Marquis, the second wine of ChÈateau Léoville-Lascases.

Pauillac

The town of Pauillac is disconcertingly like a sleepy seaside resort, with café terraces and fish merchants lining the bank of the Gironde. This looks far more like the kind of place that couples run away to for illicit weekends in French films than the town whose name appears on the names of some of the world's greatest red wine.

It's not easy to know that you've arrived in Pauillac's vineyards; they run into those of St-Julien almost seamlessly. Léoville-Lascases is right next door to Latour; indeed, according to some old maps, the latter estate really ought to be situated in St-Julien. But it was Pauillac that drew the better hand.

It *is* easy to understand why these wines have made so many friends for themselves; they are magnificent in the way that they manage to combine the intense flavour of blackcurrant with those of cedar and honey. Taste these against the best Cabernet-Sauvignon from California and you will understand just how brilliantly this variety shines here – and how far Pauillac goes beyond the simple Cabernet flavour of most of those New World wonders. According to French experts, Pauillac's pre-eminence is explained by the quality of its soil. In fact, Margaux has a greater proportion of top quality land but Pauillac has the better winemakers.

ABOVE: The lions on the gate guard the impressive entrance of the Cos d'Estournel.
RIGHT: Smoke from the burning of vine trimmings drifts across the autumn landscape of the Médoc.

THE EXTRAORDINARY BARON PHILIPPE

Until 1973, Pauillac had only two first growths: Châteaux Lafite and Latour. Mouton Rothschild, though almost unanimously ranked alongside the firsts, was only a second growth. In that year, however, Baron Philippe de Rothschild achieved what had been thought to be the impossible – he persuaded the powers-that-be and his Rothschild cousins at Lafite to right the injustice of 1855. The elevation of Mouton Rothschild is the only change to the 1855 classification since it was first drawn up. While the argument still rages over which (if any) of the other second growths deserve a similar dispensation, no one who has tasted Mouton's wines in recent years has ever denied that it is as great a first growth as its neighbours.

But Philippe de Rothschild was a pioneer in all kinds of ways. So many of the things everyone else has done since – both here in Bordeaux and throughout the winemaking world – he did first. He was the first to make a point of bottling all his estate's wines at the château rather than sell in barrel for other people to bottle – and possibly mistreat or adulterate – themselves. He was the first to create a wholly new kind of wine label, inviting well-known and frequently unconventional artists such as Salvador Dali, Pablo Picasso and Andy Warhol each to illustrate the label of a single vintage of Mouton Rothschild.

He was the first (and still the only truly successful) person to create a branded Bordeaux. Mouton Cadet was born in 1934 when Rothschild blended the previous three (poor) vintages together to make a single, non-vintage wine. Today, Mouton Cadet is still the biggest-selling branded red Bordeaux. But don't expect it to taste anything like Mouton Rothschild – there isn't enough of that flavour to go round.

Apart from Latour, Lafite and Mouton Rothschild, there is a second row of wines that are chasing hard on their heels: Pichon Longueville-Comtesse-de-Lalande (usually referred to as Pichon-Lalande) is Pauillac's best-established 'super-second', now rivalled by its neighbour Pichon-Longueville-Baron, which has recently been restored to its former prestige by Jean-Michel Cazes. Cazes' own Château Lynch-Bages, though on paper only a fourth growth, can also perform as well as a first, while fine wines can be found at Clerc-Milon, Grand-Puy-Ducasses, Grand-Puy-Lacoste, Haut-Bages-Libéral, Haut-Batailley, Mouton-Baronne-Philippe and Pontet-Canet. For a relatively affordable taste of Pauillac, try Réserve de la Comtesse, Haut-Bages-Averous and Les Forts de Latour, the second wines respectively of Châteaux Pichon-Lalande, Lynch-Bages and Latour.

St-Estèphe

St-Estèphe is the most attractive town in the Médoc, but it feels like a distant outpost. And the wine is like that too – distant and forbidding stuff that tempts me to use expressions like 'austere' and 'masculine' that I would normally avoid like the plague.

It is distinctly cooler here and this, coupled with the less gravelly, more clayey soil, makes for wines that can take forever to soften and become more friendly.

The finest wines here used to be Châteaux Montrose and Calon-Ségur – particularly if you were prepared to wait half your life for the former to soften – but their place has more recently been usurped by another rather extraordinary estate. Château Cos d'Estournel is a folly; a mock-Oriental palace built

by its owner to remind him of his travels in the East. Its oak door was imported from Zanzibar

In a way, it's a shame that so many Bordeaux lovers know what the château looks like, it would be easy to think that their descriptions of the wine as 'spicy' were influenced by thoughts of the exotic building.

In fact Cos (as it is known by its aficionados, who pronounce it like the lettuce) benefits from its gravelly soil to make wines that are rather closer to Pauillac in style than they are to those of most of its neighbours. But their wonderful, spicy flavour is all their own.

Strangely, the majority of St-Estèphe's other best wines are unclassed: Marbuzet, Haut-Marbuzet, Andron-Blanquet, Beau-Site, Le Boscq, Meyney, Les Ormes-de-Pez, de Pez and Lafon-Rochet.

Beyond St-Estèphe, where the gravel gives way to clay and the Cabernet is supplanted by the Merlot, the wines can only be sold as Médoc; in theory, this northern counterpart to the Haut-Médoc really ought to be called the Bas (low) Médoc; it is where much of the wine that is sold as 'Médoc' and 'House Claret' is made.

There is very little of real class here, though there are occasional flashes of brilliance such as Château Potensac (made by the owner of Château Léoville-Lascases), Castéra, Patache d'Aux, La Tour-St-Bonnet and Les Ormes-Sorbet. Most can be drunk young (thanks to their high Merlot content) but when well made they can be kept for a decade or longer. One that seems built to last is the St-Estèphe-like Château Cissac, but it has never given me much pleasure, young or old.

ST EMILION AND POMEROL

Although they would hate to admit it, most of the château owners of St Emilion and Pomerol have, until recently, been the poor relations of their neighbours on the other, left, bank of the Gironde. Both are popular in France and the USA, but have received relatively short shrift from the brokers of Bordeaux and the wine merchants of Great Britain.

Neither region was included in the 1855 classification of the Médoc and Graves, so even the best St Emilion châteaux, such as Cheval Blanc, Ausone and Figeac, and Château Pétrus in Pomerol, were never directly ranked alongside Latour, Lafite, Margaux and Haut- Brion.

All· of which seems rather unfair when one considers that good winemaking has been going on here for rather longer than

softer, and more approachable than it had been, but riper and easier than the wines of the Médoc.

One of the most instructive tasting exercises of all is to compare a set of Bordeaux 'blind' and to try to guess which side of the Gironde they come from. If it's tannic and tastes of blackcurrant and cedar it's probably a Médoc; if its flavours make you think of ripe plums, honey and toffee, my money would be on the wine in your glass coming from St Emilion or Pomerol.

The next task is to decide in which of the two communes it was made. This is a great deal trickier - indeed, it can flummox many experienced tasters. But, with practice, this too is an art you could master.

LEFT: The vineyards of St Emilion surround the tiled buildings of the old town, making for abstract views from its walls

RIGHT: The town of St Emilion itself, a popular tourist spot little changed since the Romans made wine here

it has in the Médoc. One of the best châteaux, Ausone, owes its name to the Roman poet Ausonius, who was born near here; ownership of the vineyards of another top château, Figeac, can be traced back to the same era. And the wines of the region were already known abroad as early as the 12th century.

There are several possible reasons for this region's more recent second-class status, which prevailed until some years after World War II. First, in the days when merchants travelled by horseback, this whole area seemed a long way from Bordeaux. Secondly, there was the fact that, for a long time, the church was a major vineyard owner. Thirdly, in the 18th century the producers here chose to concentrate on selling to France and Belgium rather than England or Holland, the traditional markets for wines of the Médoc. Fourthly, there was the small size of the estates; the average château in Pomerol produces less than half as much wine as its Médoc equivalent and the annual harvest at Château Pétrus yields just 25,000 bottles, a tenth of the quantity Château Margaux usually makes. With this small a production, it was rarely easy for an estate to make an international reputation for itself. Lastly, there was the style of the wines.

The clay soil that covers most of the region does not suit the Cabernet Sauvignon; it simply doesn't ripen properly. Despite this, it was this variety and the uninspiring Malbec that were used to make much of the wine. It was hardly suprising that the St Emilions and Pomerols of the last century, and even of the first half of this one, were often lean, unripe, rangy beasts.

The fortunes of the producers changed dramatically and unexpectedly in 1956, when vicious frosts wiped out large sections of the vineyards and obliged the growers to replant. Suddenly, the Merlot and Cabernet Franc were introduced, and with them came a new style of wine, one that was not only

St Emilion

This is one of the few parts of Bordeaux that looks the way most people want wine regions to look. The land has some contours to it and the vines run up and down slopes; the town itself is set right amongst the vineyards.

The vine-covered hillsides form one long south-facing slope, the Côtes, that contributes towards the quality of some of St Emilion's best, most long-lived wines: Ausone, Belair, Canon, Pavie, Pavie-Décesse and Magdelaine all include grapes grown on the Côtes. L'Arrosée is one of the very few châteaux to make good wine exclusively from the hillside.

Much of the rest of St Emilion's vineyard area is planted in sandy soil – the *sables* – that always results in lighter, young-drinking wine. In theory, young-drinking Merlot should be delicious; unfortunately, sometimes, the Merlot's toffee can take over from the plum and make for wine that's a bit dull.

But there are two top-class St Emilion châteaux that aren't on the Côtes. Cheval Blanc and Figeac both sit on the same long outcrop of gravel, and both compete with Ausone for the commune's crown. It's an unfair fight, really, because Cheval Blanc always wins; its big, sumptuous flavours simply eclipse the other wines. But give Figeac time, taste it beyond Cheval Blanc's shadow, and its gentler, more perfumed character could well seduce one into calling the whole thing a draw.

However, both these wines are atypical St Emilions; neither is predominantly Merlot-based, and Cheval Blanc is a true rarity in being largely made from the Cabernet Franc.

Other good St Emilions grown on gravelly soil include La Tour Figeac, Dominique, Soutard and de Grand Corbin, all of which can be rather less costly than Figeac or Cheval Blanc.

The St Emilion Satellites

Until 1936, this set of villages could sell their wine as St Emilion but now have to prefix it with their own names, and are generally known as St Emilion's 'satellites'. The best of these more affordable appellations is St Georges-St Emilion, where Château St Georges makes wine of soft, classed St Emilion quality. Montagne-St Emilion partly overlaps this appellation and some châteaux have the choice of which label they prefer to use. Of the wines labelled as Montagne-St Emilion, I'd go for Vieux-Château-St-André, made by the oenologist at Château Pétrus. Lussac-St Emilion can produce attractively plummy wine too (try Château Cap de Merle), but I've never been able to become very excited about any of the wines I've tasted from Puisseguin-St Emilion.

Pomerol

If the Médoc has a small fleet of flagships, Pomerol – a fraction of its size at just 2,000 acres – has just one: Château Pétrus, the world's most expensive red wine. But even as recently as 50 years ago, the name Pétrus would have aroused very little response among even some of the keenest British wine drinkers; after all, its name doesn't feature in the 1855 classification, and nor does Pomerol have any 'quality signposts', in the form of a Medoc, St Emilion, Graves or Sauternes style *cru* system, to call its own.

It was America that discovered Pétrus – and wine buffs there fell head-over-heels for its extraordinary spicy-fruity-gamey intensity. Of course, they couldn't all actually drink it – the château makes only 25,000 bottles in a good year – but they fell

---

THE ESSENTIALS — ST EMILION & POMEROL

Location The right bank of the Dordogne, 50km east of Bordeaux. The district known as the Libournais encompasses all of the best properties. Pomerol is close to the village of that name and while St Emilion surrounds its town, it also stretches down to the Dordogne. The 'satellites' of St Emilion and Pomerol surround these appellations. The Côtes de Francs and de Castillon overlap to the east, while Fronsac and Canon-Fronsac lie north-west towards Bourg and Blaye.

Quality AOCs are: St Emilion, Pomerol, Montagne-St Emilion, Lussac-St Emilion, St Georges-St Emilion, Puisseguin-St Emilion, Fronsac, Canon-Fronsac, Côtes de Castillon, Bordeaux Côte-de-Francs and Lalande de Pomerol. There are no VDQS or *vin de pays* wines.

Style Red, almost all Merlot-based, softer than a Médoc with a plummy, spicy, toffeeish richness. Pomerol is a juicier, more voluptuous, though sometimes 'slatier' style. Wines of the satellites are similar, but generally with less finesse, though some Montagne-St Emilion properties can make far better wine than poorly-sited châteaux in St Emilion itself.

Climate More continental than the Médoc: slightly warmer and drier.

Cultivation Soils vary, from the Côtes (slopes) composed of limestone or clay, through sandy gravel and large stretches of sand and clay to the *sables* (sands).

Grape Varieties Merlot and Cabernet Franc predominate.

Production/Maturation Stainless steel for fermentation with a mixture of new and old small oak for maturation.

Longevity 3 to 20 years for St Emilion and Pomerol; wines from the satellites drink well between 3 and, in good years and from good producers, 15 years.

Vintage Guide 82, 83, 85, 86, 88, 89

Top Producers *St Emilion*: Châteaux Figeac, Cheval Blanc, Pavie, Ausone, L'Arrosée, Bel Air, Canon, Cadet Piola, l'Angélus, Larmande, Magdelaine, Fonroque, Clos Fourtet, Ferrand, La Grave Figeac, Troplong Mondot. *Pomerol* : Châteaux Le Gay, Le Bon Pasteur, Petit Village, Clos du Clocher, Certan de May, Vieux-Château-Certan, Pétrus, Trotanoy, Lafleur, L'Evangile, Le Pin, La Conseillante, Clinet, L'Eglise Clinet. *Satellites:* Durand Laplagne, Bel-Air, Maison Blanche. *Fronsac/Canon-Fronsac/Côtes de Castillon/Francs:* Châteaux Canon-de-Brem, Canon, La Rivière, Pitray, Mazeris, Villars.

in love with the idea of it, and with the rich, plummy, chocolatey, berryish Merlot flavour of the other Pomerols they proceeded to seek out.

None of the rest quite matches Pétrus, partly because of the careful way in which it is made, but more essentially because of the magic piece of clay soil in which its vines are planted. To look at, there doesn't appear to be anything special about Pétrus's soil – nor about the château itself, which could easily be a modestly successful Bordeaux merchant's weekend re-treat. But that's Pomerol's style. The land here is flatter and less picturesque than St Emilion, but its very flatness helpfully allows you to see just how small the estates are – you could pack at least half a dozen into the vineyards of the average Médoc château.

The soil is far less variable here than it is in St Emilion, but there are parts of the commune where the clay does contain all kinds of minerals that help to give the best Pomerols an extra dimension, a minerally edge which balances what could all too easily be jammy sweet fruit.

As there is no Pomerol classification, the commune's estates can all compete for the role of prince to Pétrus's king. Among a strong field, I favour Vieux-Château-Certan, Certan-de-May, La Conseillante, La Fleur-Pétrus, L'Evangile, Le Pin, Trotanoy, Bon-Pasteur, Petit-Village, Clos-René, Lafleur, Feytit-Clinet, Clos du Clocher, Franc-Maillet, l'Eglise-Clinet and Clinet, La-tour-à-Pomerol and La Grave Trigant de Boisset.

Lalande-de-Pomerol

What's in a name? Well, in this case, there's the recognisable name of Pomerol which, particularly in the USA, has helped to boost prices of this once-inexpensive appellation. Even so, the wines of Lalande-de-Pomerol can still be delicious, plummily ripe buys. There are lots of good examples, but I'd particularly recommend Châteaux Tournefeuille, Bel-Air and Siaurac.

Fronsac

In the 18th century Fronsac was one of the classiest wines of Bordeaux and sold for a higher price than Pomerol. All that changed with the Revolution. From being scarce and good, Fronsac suddenly became plentiful and mediocre.

Today these wines, at their best, can still rival supposedly better wines from St Emilion. Try a bottle from Château la Rivière; better still, go and taste the wine at the château – it's straight out of one of Polanski's more Gothic films. Other Fron-sacs to look out for include Villars, Mayne-Vieil and La Valade.

Canon-Fronsac

This is a patch of hillside country within Fronsac itself. The style of the wines is somewhat similar to that of Pomerol, but rather more rustic, particularly when the wines are young. Give them time, though; they can be worth it. The best wine here comes from one of Bordeaux's`several estates called Château Canon. It provides an inexpensive opportunity to sample the winemak-ing skills of Christian Moueix, best known for Chateau Pétrus.

Bordeaux-Côtes-de-Castillon

Castillon, almost hidden between St Emilion and the Dordogne river at Bergerac, seems such a sleepy little place that it is hard

LEFT: *Château Cheval Blanc, one of the greatest châteaux in St Emilion*

ABOVE: *Michel Roland, owner of the excellent Château Le Bon Pasteur in Pomerol, and advisor to many of that commune's best producers – as well as to a number of wineries abroad*

Filet de Porc farci aux Pruneaux et Noix

Pork fillets stuffed with prunes and walnuts

In an area that was once occupied by invading Arab armies it is not surprising that prunes — a favourite in North African cooking — should be found in one of the most delicious summertime dishes of this region.

SERVES 8-10
*2 pork fillets, about 1 lb/500 g each
10 fl oz/300 ml cold tea
10 prunes, stones removed
Salt and freshly ground black pepper
1 lb/500 g pork sausage meat
2 garlic cloves, peeled and minced
4 crushed juniper berries
2 tbsp fresh parsley, chopped, or 1 tsp dried parsley
2 oz/50 g shelled walnut halves (approx. 50)
1 tsp dried thyme
2 tbsp dry white wine*

Dry the fillets with kitchen paper. Soak the prunes in the cold tea for 2-3 hours, drain and coarsely chop. Beat the fillets flat, to about 2 tbsp dry white wine ½ in/1 cm thick, and season with salt and pepper. In a bowl mix the sausage meat, garlic, juniper berries, parsley, walnuts, thyme and wine and season with salt and pepper. Leave the mixture to stand, covered, in the refrigerator for about an hour. Take a third of the prunes and layer them on one fillet. Put half of the stuffing mixture on the prunes, then another layer of prunes, a layer of stuffing and then the remainder of the prunes. Top with the second fillet and tie the whole bundle with string. Roast in a preheated oven at 375˚F/190˚C/Gas mark 5 for about 50 minutes or until it has cooked through. When the meat is completely cold, chill before serving in slices.

to imagine that, in 1453, this was the site of one of the most important battles in which English soldiers were ever involved; it was here that Aquitaine and the vineyards of Bordeaux were snatched back by the French after 300 years of English ownership. Today the town, or rather its hills, are known for Merlot-based, good value reds from such châteaux as Robin, Belcier and Pitray.

Bordeaux-Côtes-des-Francs

A name that even the best-informed Bordelais would rarely have known – until recently. Today, as vineyard and wine prices in the rest of Bordeaux climb steadily higher, this warm, dry farmland area that was once part of St Emilion has suddenly attracted new interest – from some very keen and skilful young winemakers. The first wines are already impressive and surprisingly inexpensive; look out for Châteaux de France, Puygueraud and La Claverie.

THE ST EMILION RULES

Unlike the Médoc, St Emilion's classification is occasionally revised – but in a way that has failed to satisfy the critics of the standards of some of the 'Grands Crus' châteaux here.

The fact that St Emilion classed growths can bob up and down the league like erratic football teams is confusing enough. Worse still is the fact that, apart from the official classification, there is another designation – *St Emilion Grand Cru* – which can be used by *any* château whose wines pass an annual tasting test. To be a little surer of what you are getting, look for *St Emilion Grand Cru Classé* rather than *St Emilion Grand Cru*.

THE 1985 CLASSIFICATION OF ST EMILION

Premiers Grands Crus Classés (Class A)
Ausone; Cheval Blanc

Premiers Grands Crus Classés (Class B)
Beauséjour (Duffau-Lagarrosse); Canon; Belair; Clos Fourtet; Figeac; la Gaffelière; Magdelaine; Pavie; Trottevieille

Grands Crus Classés
L'Angélus; l'Arrosée; Balestard la Tonnelle; Beau-Séjour-Bécot; Bellevue; Bergat; Berliquet; Cadet-Piola; Canon-la-Gaffelière; Cap de Mourlin; le Châtelet; Chauvin; Clos des Jacobins; Clos la Madeleine; Clos de l'Oratoire; Clos Saint Martin; la Clotte; la Clusière; Corbin; Corbin-Michotte; Couvent des Jacobins; Croque-Michotte; Curé-Bon la Madeleine; Dassault; la Dominique; Faurie de Souchard; Fonplégade; Fonroque; Franc-Mayne; Grand-Barrail-Lamarzelle-Figeac; Grand-Corbin-Despagne; Grand-Corbin; Grand-Mayne; Grand-Pontet; Guadet-St-Julien; Haut Corbin; Haut Sarpe; Laniote; Larcis-Ducasse; Lamarzelle; Laroze; Matras; Mauvezin; Moulin-du-Cadet; l'Oratoire; Pavie-Décesse; Pavie-Macquin; Pavillon-Cadet; Petit-Faurie de Soutard; le Prieuré; Ripeau; Sansonnet; St-Georges-Côte-Pavie; la Serre; Soutard; Tertre-Daugay; la Tour-du-Pin-Figeac (Giraud-Belivier); la Tour-du-Pin-Figeac (Moueix); Trimoulet; Troplong-Mondot; Villemaurine; Yon-Figeac

GRAVES

The French have a wonderful wine expression: *'le goût de terroir'* – 'the flavour of the soil'. For those of us who have never even kissed the dirt, let alone chewed a mouthful of it, this kind of language seems either fanciful or downright unhelpful. Until, that is, you get to this part of Bordeaux – and discover just how important the gravel is to the winegrowers here; important enough for them to name their region after it. Except that they got its boundaries slightly wrong: the southern part of the Graves isn't very gravelly at all, but sandy and clayey. Which is why, in 1987, the owners of the best châteaux of the north of

the region declared independence and created their own appellation, named after two of Bordeaux's duller suburbs: Pessac-Léognan. So, paradoxically, if you want to find the wines of the gravel, the Graves is no longer the place to look.

The Graves is the oldest of the regions around Bordeaux, the one that, in the 13th century, produced all the best wine. Today it is still recognised as being the only bit of Bordeaux to make quality red and white. At least, that's the theory. In fact, until quite recently, what the Graves produced was delicious red wine and, with a very few glorious exceptions, a huge quantity of awful white that either smelled and possibly even tasted of damp, dirty dishcloths, or was simply an unripe travesty of Sauvignon Blanc. Only three well-known properties made good white wine: Château Haut-Brion, La Mission-Haut-Brion (whose white is called Laville-Haut-Brion) and Domaine de Chevalier.

Then, in the early '80s, there was a revolution. Faced with the prospect of a major revision of the Classification of the Graves (due in 1984 but in the event postponed until the 1990s), and influenced by three men – Peter Vinding-Diers, a Dane who'd worked in Australia; Pierre Coste, a wine merchant; and Denis Dubordieu, an oenologist at Bordeaux University – a small but growing band of producers introduced a number of changes to the way in which they made their wine.

First, they gave up the practice of picking too early – and instantly did away with those raw flavours. Secondly, they cooled down their fermentation tanks – and increased the flavour of their wine. Thirdly, in some cases they left the juice in contact with its skins (following Dubordieu's advice), fermented it with specially cultured yeasts (that was Vinding-Diers' idea) and even in oak barrels (in the same way as the Burgundians). And fourthly, they cut down on the amount of sulphur dioxide they used, simultaneously casting out all those dirty dishrags.

THE ESSENTIALS — GRAVES

Location On the left bank of the Garonne, stretching south-east from the suburbs of Bordeaux.
Quality AOC Graves, Graves Supérieur, Pessac-Léognan and Cérons, with a *cru* classification for red and white Graves.
Style Reds are very much a cross between Médoc and Pomerol, with soft, blackcurranty fruit and raspberry and even floral notes. Dry whites vary in style depending on the grape varieties used and winemaking style (with or without new oak). Graves Supérieur and Cérons can be a little like a light Sauternes, though of lesser quality.
Climate Slightly warmer than the Médoc.
Cultivation The terrain is more undulating than the Médoc; soil varies from classic gravel in the north (the area recently granted its own AOC, Pessac-Léognan) to a more sandy gravel in the south.
Grape Varieties As in the Médoc, Cabernet Sauvignon, Cabernet Franc, Merlot, Malbec and Petit Verdot are used for reds; Sémillon, Sauvignon Blanc and Muscadelle for whites.
Production/Maturation New oak is increasingly used for fermenting white Graves by good châteaux, while mixtures of old and new small oak remain the preferred method of maturation for reds.
Longevity *Reds*: 6 to 25 years; *whites*: 3 to 10 years.
Vintage Guide 78, 79, 81, 83, 85, 86, 88, 89
Top Producers Châteaux Haut-Brion, Haut Bailly, La Louvière, Fieuzal, Couhins-Lurton (white), La Tour Haut-Brion, La Mission Haut-Brion, Smith Haut-Lafitte (white), Pape-Clément and Domaine de Chevalier.

Left: Château Haut-Brion, the only Graves estate to be included in the 1855 classification of the Médoc.

The results were startling. Suddenly the Graves began to make wines that tasted ripe, buttery and peachy, with all the fascinating flavours of ripe Sémillon that had already dazzled visitors to Australia in the examples made there.

Today, as an increasing number of châteaux follow the revolutionaries' example, and as even Château Carbonnieux, the last of the old guard and the region's largest property, turns to make good wine, the only real debate concerns the choice of white grape. For some people, the Sémillon should be king; for others, including André Lurton, who makes great wine at several châteaux including La Louvière and Couhins-Lurton (which, like Malartic-Lagravière and the fast-improving Smith-Haut-Lafitte, is 100% Sauvignon), the Sauvignon Blanc is essential. The authorities seem to have agreed with him, insisting that Pessac-Léognan whites contain at least 25% Sauvignon Blanc.

But if the whites have been undergoing a revolution, the traditional focus of attention has remained on the reds. And the best place to discover how they should taste is more or less in the middle of a housing estate at Pessac, not far from Bordeaux's Mérignac airport. Château Haut-Brion is the Graves' finest property, and one of the oldest and greatest in Bordeaux.

On April 10, 1663, Samuel Pepys tasted 'A sort of French wine, called Ho Bryan' and thought its flavour 'good and most particular'. Two centuries later, in 1855 it was the only Graves château to be ranked alongside Lafite, Latour and Margaux. Today, it is still quintessential Graves, combining the blackcurranty Cabernet fruit of the Médoc with the richer, softer approachability of Pomerol. This is wine that is dangerously easy to drink in its youth, before it has had time to develop a whole host of more mature, more complex flavours.

Haut-Brion is an easy wine to underestimate because its style is so understated; its next-door neighbour, La Mission-Haut-Brion, is tougher, as is Pape-Clément. All three develop flavours reminiscent of top-class wines from Margaux, but with a honeyed, slightly minerally flavour of their own.

Down the road, in the commune of Léognan, there lies my favourite Graves estate, Domaine de Chevalier, a small property that produces wonderfully subtle, raspberryish red and rich, peachy white wine almost every year. Domaine de Chevalier's neighbour, Château Fieuzal, though classified for its red, was never recognised for its whites. Today they are among the region's oaky superstars. Château Haut-Bailly makes a deliciously soft, approachable red wine, but no white.

Further south, once you have left the new appellation of Pessac-Léognan and moved into the Graves, you are heading towards affordability. This is the place to look for early-drinking reds that are packed with ripe, easy fruit, and some of the most innovative whites. It was in this area, after all, that Peter Vinding-Diers first showed the region how good well-made, carefully oaked Sémillon could be, at Château Rahoul. Vinding-Diers has moved on to make wine at Domaine de la Grave and Château Landiras.

Other wines from the south that are certainly worth looking out for include the reds from Châteaux Ferrande and Cardaillan; both reds and whites from Pierre Coste's châteaux, Montalivet and l'Etoile; Domaine de Gaillat; and Châteaux Chicane and Chantegrive.

Cérons

Tucked away in the Graves, on the border with Barsac, Cérons is a sweet white appellation that has switched its attention to making dry wine. In a way, it's a pity, because Cérons' sweet whites, which have to be made in the same way as Sauternes, can be a good cheap alternative to that wine; on the other hand, it's quite understandable because, unlike the Sauternais who can only call their dry white Bordeaux Blanc, the Cérons pro-

Brochette de Lotte Citron et Thym
Kebabs of monkfish with lemon and thyme

Much of the Graves region is covered in woodland with an abundance of game, particularly pigeon, and wonderful wild mushrooms. The drier white wines of the northern Graves also go well with fish from the nearby Atlantic, such as the firm-fleshed *lotte*, or monkfish. Other firm white fish, such as haddock or cod, will do just as well.

SERVES 4
1 lb/500g boned monkfish, haddock or cod
3 tbsp olive oil
Juice of 1 lemon
1 tsp dried thyme or 1¹/₂ tsp fresh thyme, minced
Salt and freshly ground black pepper
¹/₂ green pepper, seeded and cut into squares
¹/₂ red pepper, seeded and cut into squares
4 oz/100 g cleaned button mushrooms

Remove any skin from the fish and cut into 1 in/2.5 cm cubes. Mix the olive oil, lemon juice, thyme, salt and pepper in a shallow dish. Put fish in this marinade, coating well, and chill, covered, for about an hour. Thread skewers with fish followed by red pepper, mushroom and green peppers. Brush the remaining marinade over the kebabs. Preheat the grill and cook — turning every 3 or 4 minutes — for about 15 minutes or until nicely browned. Serve with crusty French bread and salad.

ducers can call theirs Graves – and charge a higher price. The best wines here are Château d'Archambeau (made by a nephew of Denis Dubordieu), Grand Enclos du Château de Cérons, Château de Cérons and Mayne-Binet.

As for Graves Supérieur, this is a white wine appellation that most wine drinkers overlook - despite the fact that it applies to one in every five bottles of wine produced in this region. There are some reasonable dry examples made, but the best ones are are sweet. Occasionally they can compete with Barsac.

THE CRUS CLASSES OF THE GRAVES

The Graves is the only Bordeaux region to award the *cru classé* distinction to both red and white wines; thus, certain châteaux appear in both lists. Haut-Brion is the most notable, though its fame has largely been achieved through its annexation, in 1855, into the *Premiers Crus Classés* of the Médoc. Most authorities agree that the long-awaited revision of the league table is well overdue – especially following the recent improvements in white winemaking. The name of each château is followed by that of its commune.

Red Wines
Bouscaut, *Cadaujac*; Carbonnieux, *Léognan*; Domaine de Chevalier, *Léognan*; de Fieuzal, *Léognan*; Haut-Bailly, *Léognan*; Haut-Brion, *Pessac*; La Mission-Haut-Brion, *Pessac*; La Tour-Haut-Brion, *Talence*; La Tour-Martillac, *Martillac*; Malartic-Lagravière, *Léognan*; Olivier, *Léognan*; Pape-Clément, *Pessac*; Smith-Haut-Lafitte, *Martillac*

White Wines
Bouscaut, *Cadaujac*; Carbonnieux, *Léognan*; Domaine de Chevalier, *Léognan*; Couhins-Lurton, *Villenave d'Ornan*; Haut-Brion, *Pessac*; La Tour-Martillac, *Martillac*; Laville-Haut-Brion, *Talence*; Malartic-Lagravière, *Léognan*; Olivier, *Léognan*

SAUTERNES AND BARSAC

LEFT: The view from Château Rieussec in Sauternes, one of the calmest regions in Bordeaux. BELOW: The ugly 'noble rot', or Botrytis cinerea, that is responsible for the unique flavour of great Sauternes and Barsac.

A liquid calling itself Sauternes almost put me off the whole idea of wine drinking. On my 12th birthday, I was thought old enough to be treated to a glass of 'Spanish Sauternes'; the mixture of sugary sweetness, sulphur and decaying meat was as effective a form of aversion therapy as even the most fiendish psychologist could have devised.

My dislike of what I thought of as Sauternes was only vanquished years later when I was introduced to 'real' quality Sauternes – in the form of 1967 Château d'Yquem. Suddenly I realised what great sweet wine was all about – and, far more crucially, what it was not about. The differences lie in naturally ripe grapes, cleanness of flavour (no nastily obvious, meaty sulphur dioxide), balance (the harmony between refreshing acidity and honeyed sweetness) and complexity (the combination of several different flavours and smells).

The people who make real Sauternes, the stuff that only comes from a hilly corner of Bordeaux, are a dedicated and masochistic bunch. If their main aim in life was to make wine for profit, they'd have switched their attention to red or dry white ages ago, either of which would have enabled them to produce at least a bottle of wine per vine instead of just a glass or two of Sauternes.

The History

Sauternes has been making wine since the Roman occupation – but the wine we know today is a recent innovation. The winemakers of 400 years ago had to add alcohol to their light, dryish white wine to stabilize it for the journey to Holland, where much of it was drunk. With or without the alcohol, the stuff they were making must have tasted pretty good because, in 1787, Thomas Jefferson described Sauternes as one of the three best white wines in France – with Hermitage and Champagne – and bought some for his cellar.

The switch from the style Jefferson enjoyed to the Yquem that converted me came some time in the 1800s, though no-one is quite certain of precisely how or when. According to one story, it was a German called Focke who, in 1836, recognising noble rot in the vineyards, tried to recreate a German-style botrytised wine in France. The Sauternais don't like giving credit to a foreigner; they prefer to fix the date of the first 'modern' Sauternes vintage to 1847, when a delay in the harvest at Château d'Yquem allowed the rot to develop in the vineyards. It was the combination of that rot and the skill they developed

THE ESSENTIALS — SAUTERNES

Location South-east of Bordeaux, on the left bank of the Garonne near Langon.
Quality AOC Sauternes and Barsac, which also share their own *cru* classification, drawn up in 1855 at the same time as that for the Médoc.
Style Very sweet, luscious whites, with tropical or marmalade aromas. The lusciousness and complexity depend upon the degree to which *Botrytis cinerea* has affected the vintage and the care taken to restrict picking to nobly-rotten grapes. Barsac is perhaps lighter but can be of as high a quality as Sauternes. Barsac may be sold as Sauternes, but not vice versa. The little dry white produced may be sold only as Bordeaux Blanc, though it can be of high quality in its distinctive, nutty way.
Climate A warmer micro-climate within Bordeaux; the region is also peculiarly susceptible to morning mists rising from the Cérons river which, combined with warm afternoons, provide ideal conditions for the development and proliferation of botrytis.
Grape Varieties Sémillon, plus Sauvignon Blanc and Muscadelle.
Cultivation Soil is of clay limestone to sandy gravel. The most experienced pickers are needed for the vintage here as, to make fine Sauternes, only the overripe and, when appropriate, botrytised grapes must be plucked from each bunch. Several sorties into the vineyard are made — at the greatest châteaux, as many as ten — until all the grapes are harvested; these successive selective pickings are known as *tries*. In some years, though, noble rot never appears; when this happens, Château d'Yquem makes no vintage wine.
Production/Maturation Grapes are whole-pressed and wood fermented and matured (new oak is used only in the very best châteaux).
Longevity Anything between 5 and 30 years.
Vintage Guide 70, 75, 76, 78, 80, 81, 83, 85, 86, 88, 89
Top Producers Châteaux d'Yquem, Rieussec, Lafaurie-Peyraguey, Suduiraut, Coutet, Climens, Guiraud, Doisy-Daëne, Doisy-Védrines, D'Arche, de Malle, Nairac, Broustet, Raymond-Lafon, Gilette, Bastor-Lamontagne', Rabaud-Promis, Sigalas Rabaud, Caillou, Filhot, Rayne-Vigneau.

at handling sulphur dioxide, an essential protection against bacteria, that allowed the Sauternais to establish their tradition of sweet, unfortified wine.

Unfortunately, that skill with the sulphor dioxide has still not been mastered as widely and consistently as most modern wine drinkers might wish. In the past, when wines were left to age for decades in their owners' cellars, the sulphor overdose from which even some of the biggest names suffered would have been less apparent; today, with younger bottles being opened, it can remove a large amount of the pleasure from the wine, quite obscuring the fascinating, spicy flavour of grapes that have been subject to noble rot.

But the capricious *Botrytis cinerea* will not appear to order. Everything depends on the weather – and on the winemaker's preparedness to wait for a warm, humid fog from the river Ciron that will encourage *pourriture noble* to grow on the grapes.

In some years, when the weather has been perfect for red wines, the crucial blanket of mist does not show up. I remember visiting the region in 1985, a vintage which produced wonderful, rich, ripe red wines, and finding the château owners complaining at the clear blue skies and warm, dry weather, wondering whether to give up waiting and start to pick – or to summon up just a little more patience.

(At Yquem, they *were* harvesting – but only the grapes that were covered by the rot. That day's picking was just one of eight sorties into the vineyard, the combined crop of which would finally go into the new oak barrels in which all Yquem slowly matures, adding a marvellous vanilla note to its wine – at a substantial cost per bottle.)

But if you are going to wait, Sauternes is a very pleasant place in which to do it. This a far easier region to fall in love with than the flatlands of the Médoc or Pomerol. Even today, Sauternes itself is still extremely small and makes no great effort to flaunt its fame: there are just 600 inhabitants, the odd church and a town hall – and the *Maison du Sauternes*, which looks as though it only opens once a year. The meandering tourist might well pass it by in favour of the comparatively bustling village of Barsac down the road.

Barsac

Barsac can produce wine under its own name which, when of the likes of Châteaux Coutet and Climens, can compete with the finest Sauternes, though with a slightly drier, less unctuos style. Other Barsac properties, however, often prefer to take advantage of the permission given to them and their winemaking neighbours, Fargues, Preignac and Bommes, to give their wines the better-known label. Which is perhaps a pity; Barsac certainly shouldn't be thought of as second-class Sauternes.

It is, of course, quite possible to make Sauternes from grapes with very little, or even no noble rot, and this is precisely the way in which cheaper commercial Sauternes is made in even the best vintages. Though it cannot compare with the nobly-rotten stuff, well-made rot-free Sauternes can be delicious. But beware the very cheapest basic Sauternes. It can be very disappointing; sugary and over-sulphured. Only consider buying it from shops that choose their wine very carefully.

But do treat yourself – even just once – to a finer example, that's redolent of honey and peaches, the hallmarks of the Sémillon, the deep, dried-apricot taste of the noble rot, the balancing tangy gooseberryish fruit of the Sauvignon Blanc and the spiciness of the Muscadelle. Taste these in a young wine – or, if you're lucky, one that's 20, 30 or 40 years old – and you will enjoy a sweet wine that is quite unlike those produced anywhere else on earth. And, if ever you get the chance, look out for a bottle from Chateau Gilette, the extraordinary property whose wines are left to age for decades in large tanks. Old bottles (and that is all anybody ever sees; in the late 1980s, the 1955 was still available), taste extraordinarily fresh. They are fascinating to compare with other Sauternes of a similar age.

Foie de Volailles avec Raisins
Chicken livers with grapes

Sauternes goes particularly well with rich liver pâtés. The famous version from this area — *pâté de foie gras* — is usually made from goose or duck livers, but chicken livers can also be made into a good accompaniment for wines with a sweeter accent. This recipe makes a tasty starter.

FOR EACH PERSON
Small knob of butter
4 chicken livers, defrosted if frozen
1 triangle of bread, without crusts and lightly toasted
8 white grapes, peeled and seeded if necessary
1 tsp brandy
Salt and freshly ground black pepper

Heat the butter in a frying pan without letting it brown. Fry the chicken livers until they are browned on the outside but still pink inside. Put the livers on the toast and keep warm. Add the grapes to the pan and heat them gently. When they are hot, place them on top of the livers. Add the brandy to the frying pan juices, bring to the boil and scrape the pan with a wooden spoon or spatula. After one minute reduce the heat to a gentle simmer and add salt and pepper to taste. Pour the sauce over the livers and grapes.

DRY WINES FOR A RAINY DAY

Under appellation law, dry wine made in Sauternes can only be sold as Bordeaux Blanc. It is, however, almost always identifiable by its smell and flavour, which combine – sometimes disconcertingly – the honey of the sweet wine with a dry nuttiness. The first and most famous of these dry wines was Yquem's 'Y' (ask for it as 'Ygrec'); Château Rieussec now has its 'R', Guiraud 'G' and so on. Other châteaux simply label their dry wine with 'Le Vin Sec de' tacked on to their names.

THE 1855 CLASSIFICATION OF SAUTERNES

As in the Médoc, the original classification of 1855 has been modified o accommodate changes of name (for example, Guiraud was then called Château Bayle) and divisions of estates. Thus the original Château Doisy is now three châteaux, Doisy-Daëne, Doisy-Dubroca and Doisy-Védrines. The name of each château is followed by its commune.

Grand Premier Cru Classé
D'Yquem, *Sauternes*

Premiers Crus Classés
La Tour Blanche, *Bommes*; Lafaurie-Peyraguey, *Bommes*; Clos Haut-Peyraguey, *Bommes*; Rayne-Vigneau, *Bommes*; Suduiraut, *Preignac*; Coutet, *Barsac*; Climens, *Barsac*; Guiraud, *Sauternes*; Rieussec, *Fargues*; Rabaud-Promis, *Bommes*; Sigalas-Rabaud, *Bommes*

Deuxièmes Crus Classés
Myrat, *Barsac*; Doisy-Daëne, *Barsac*; Doisy-Dubroca, *Barsac*; Doisy-Védrines, *Barsac*; d'Arche, *Sauternes*; Filhot, *Sauternes*; Broustet, *Barsac*; Nairac, *Barsac*; Caillou, *Barsac*; Suau, *Barsac*; de Malle, *Preignac*; Romer, *Fargues*; Romer du Hayot, *Fargues*; Lamothe, *Sauternes*; Lamothe-Guignard, *Sauternes*

OTHER WINES OF BORDEAUX

THE ESSENTIALS — THE OTHER WINES OF BORDEAUX

Location The Entre-deux-Mers region lies between the Dordogne and Garonne, east of Bordeaux; Bourg and Blaye surround the confluence of these two rivers.

Quality AOCs are: Bourg; Côtes de Bourg; Blaye; Premières Côtes de Blaye; Côtes de Blaye; Blayais; Entre-deux-Mers; Loupiac; Ste-Croix-du-Mont; Cadillac. Reds from Entre-deux-Mers are sold as Bordeaux Rouge. Premières Côtes de Bordeaux can be red, pink or white.

Style Bourg and Blaye produce less refined versions of the Médoc style, rarely as supple, and lacking in complexity; Premières Côtes de Bordeaux are better than basic Bordeaux. Whites are principally from Entre-deux-Mers, predominantly dry and light bodied, and though rarely exciting can, when well-made, be fresh and lively. Loupiac and Ste-Croix-du-Mont produce Sauternes-style wines, though rarely botrytised. Cadillac can produce unusually successful honeyed demi-sec wines, but these are rarely seen.

Climate Bourg and Blaye have a similar climate to the northern Médoc, while Entre-deux-Mers is quite cool. Loupiac, Ste-Croix-du-Mont and Premières Côtes de Bordeaux enjoy a mild, dry climate.

Cultivation Rolling to steep hills with rich fertile soils.

Grape varieties *Red*: Cabernet Sauvignon, Cabernet Franc, Merlot, Malbec and Petit Verdot. *White*: Sémillon, Sauvignon Blanc, Muscadelle, Colombard and Merlot Blanc.

Production/Maturation Stainless steel is increasingly used for fermentation: cool fermentation temperatures and early bottling are helping to improve the freshness of the whites. For reds, old oak for maturation; very little new wood is as yet seen.

Longevity Dry whites: between 1 and 3 years. Sweet whites and reds: generally 5-6 years though the producer is important. Wines from a good château may keep for 10 years.

Vintage Guide Red 82, 83, 85, 86, 87, 88, 89
White 79, 80, 81, 83, 85, 86, 88, 89

Top Producers *Bourg and Blaye*: Châteaux de Barbe, de Haut Sociando and le Chay. *Entre-Deux-Mers*: Château du Barrail, Château Bonnet, Château La Tour Martines. *Loupiac and Ste-Croix-du-Mont*: Châteaux Ricaud, Rondillon, Lousteau Vieil, Mazarin, Clos Jean. *Cadillac*: Château Fayau. *Premières Côtes de Bordeaux*: Châteaux Fayau, Grand-Moueys and Barreyres.

Below: Well-tended vineyards in the Premières Côtes de Blaye.
Right: Promotional harvesting paniers in Entre-Deux-Mers.

While the spotlight of attention inevitably tends to play on the 'classic' regions of the Medoc, St Emilion, Pomerol and Graves, keen bargain hunters are usually to be found following their nose to a number of other parts of Bordeaux where, every year, a growing number of so-called 'petits châteaux' are making some truly impressive wine.

Premières Côtes de Blaye

Blaye is one of the longest established wine regions of Bordeaux, a large area mostly covered with forest and with fields of asparagus, which seems to like the black, sandy soil here. In the last century, white grapes were grown and the acidic wine they produced was sent away to be distilled. From 1909, brandy grapes have been outlawed and, more recently, there has been a switch to growing Merlot. Unfortunately, the soil that the asparagus finds so congenial is often less than ideal for this or any other grape variety, and there are no really classy producers to raise the image of the appellations here, of which there are no less than four: Blaye, Blayais, Côtes de Blaye and Premières Côtes de Blaye. The first two are used for white wines; most of the reds are sold as Premières Côtes de Blaye. The best property in this part of Bordeaux at present is probably Château le Chay.

Bourg

The winemakers of Bourg are an enterprising lot; they did what many other regions ought to consider doing and employed a team of market researchers to find out what people thought of their wine. The answer came back that Bourg, which has been making wine since Roman times, was thought now to be producing 'rustic', 'country' wine that lacked the finesse most people look for in red Bordeaux. The solution, it seemed, was

to learn a few lessons from their neighbours in Margaux, on the other side of the Gironde.

Today, the wines are decidedly classier in style than they used to be – and considerably more so than those of the Blayais, which are produced all around them. Both the Cabernet and Merlot grow well here and styles vary depending on which of the two is used. The Tauriac cooperative is spearheading the move towards quality, and Château de Barbe is a model for the region as a whole. Most of the wines is red and is sold as Côtes de Bourg, but the Bourg and Bourgeais appellations also exist and there is a tiny amount of white Bourg made.

Premières Côtes de Bordeaux
Like the Graves, this is a region where land tends to be valued in two ways – as vineyards and, for rather higher sums, as building plots. As the city of Bordeaux expands, there seems little hope for the vines – particularly because this 30-mile-long strip of riverside land has no great reputation for its wines. However, the Premières Côtes have tremendous potential; not for the sorts of wines it has traditionally made – sweet and semi-sweet whites – but for its blackcurranty reds and *clairet* rosés. Among the best châteaux at present are Lamothe, Barreyres, Grand-Moueys, Tanesse, Fayau and de Bouteilley.

Cadillac
Within the region of the Premières Côtes, Cadillac sits on the Garonne facing Sauternes. All the wine made here is sweet and semi-sweet white, and most is dull stuff – sales are difficult and there is little incentive for quality winemaking. One estate that is trying hard, though, is Château Fayau, which backs up its Yquem-style label with some pretty luscious wine – despite the evident absence of the botrytis that makes Sauternes special.

Loupiac
Making sweet white wine often referred to as 'poor man's Sauternes', this island in the Premières Côtes tries hard, despite public indifference and the unwillingness of botrytis to visit its vineyards as often as it does Sauternes and Barsac. As those more famous sweet wines return to favour, hopefully the overall quality of Loupiac will rise too. Wines worth looking for now are the ones made by Château Loupiac-Gaudiet and de Ricaud.

Ste-Croix-du-Mont
The third and best of the Premières Côtes appellations, producing sweet and very sweet white wines. There is a little more botrytis here, and even when the rot doesn't appear, the wines can be well-made and well-balanced. The top château is Louhens; la Rame and des Tastes are good too.

Entre-Deux-Mers
The name is misleading; there are no seas, only the rivers Garonne and Dordogne. In fact, it would make rather more sense to call this large region 'Entre-Deux-Vins' in recognition of the way in which it separates the Graves from St Emilion and Pomerol. Once a name that was synonymous with the most awful cheap, sweet white wines, the Entre-Deux-Mers has recently gone through a between-two-sea-change to become a region that now produces perfectly decent dry white and a surprising amount of good red and pink Bordeaux.

This is attractively varied country, where farmland competes with woods and vineyards and a growing number of small estates have to combat not only the frequent unwillingness of the grapes to ripen properly but also the readiness of some big customers to buy on price rather than quality. But quality is possible, as the Lurton family have proved at Château Bonnet, a property whose oaked white puts some famous Graves wines to shame

Although it has been the whites that have put Entre-Deux-Mers back on the map, my own suspicion is that the future stars of this region will be red. Just taste the wines of Châteaux La Tour Martines, Thieuley and Toutigeac, and you'll see what I mean. Unfortunately for the area, these, like all of the other reds made here can only be sold as Bordeaux Rouge and Bordeaux Supérieur, names that can be used for red wine made anywhere in Bordeaux. Perhaps one day soon, the authorities will allow them to call themselves Entre-Deux-Mers Rouge.

BURGUNDY

You can always spot the true Burgundy lover in a wine shop. The claret fan relaxedly strolls across to pick up a bottle of Château This or That, pausing only to check the vintage. Back among the Burgundies, the enthusiast has pulled out his magnifying glass and his pocket guide, reading the small print on every label like a nervous householder examining an insurance certificate.

Every now and then, he probably glances across at the Bordeaux buyer, envying him the simplicity of his choice – but, until he's got to the last bottle on the shelf, he'll go on searching. He knows that, if he can find precisely the bottle he's looking for, it will give him far more pleasure and excitement than even the greatest Bordeaux. But if he gets it wrong, he'll end up with a few glasses of very expensive disappointment.

And that's it in a nutshell, really. Buying Bordeaux is a pretty simple process; all you have to do is remember the names of a few châteaux that make wine you enjoy and follow them faithfully from year to year. Château Lynch-Bages, Château La Louvière, Château Rieussec... apart from vintage variations (and they're less severe in temperate Bordeaux than they are in inland Burgundy), the wines from any of these or a few hundred other estates will always taste recognisably the same.

At first glance, Burgundy should be just as simple; except that instead of the names of châteaux, it's villages you're looking for;

RIGHT: The entrance to a grower's piece of the Grand Cru Clos de la Roche. In Burgundy, famous vineyards like this are almost always divided amongst a number of individual producers.

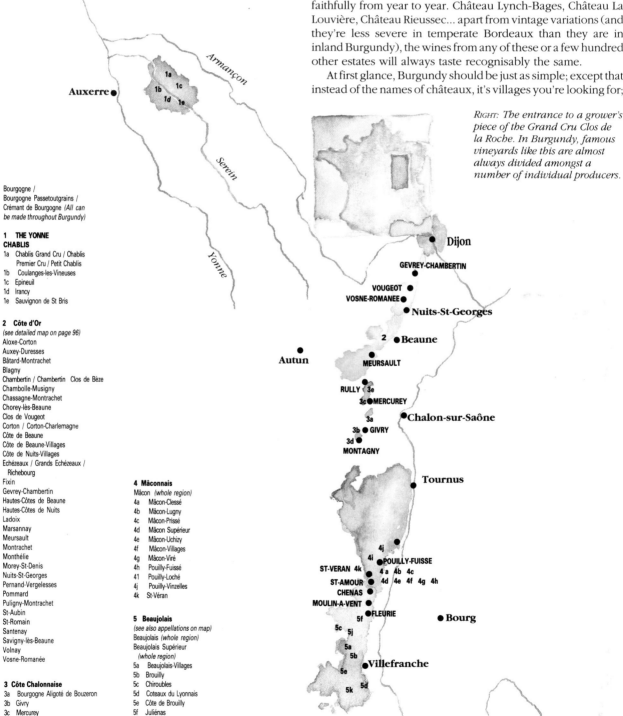

Bourgogne /
Bourgogne Passetoutgrains /
Crémant de Bourgogne *(All can be made throughout Burgundy)*

1   THE YONNE
CHABLIS
1a   Chablis Grand Cru / Chablis
        Premier Cru / Petit Chablis
1b   Coulanges-les-Vineuses
1c   Epineuil
1d   Irancy
1e   Sauvignon de St Bris

2   Côte d'Or
(see detailed map on page 96)
Aloxe-Corton
Auxey-Duresses
Bâtard-Montrachet
Blagny
Chambertin / Chambertin Clos de Bèze
Chambolle-Musigny
Chassagne-Montrachet
Chorey-lès-Beaune
Clos de Vougeot
Corton / Corton-Charlemagne
Côte de Beaune
Côte de Beaune-Villages
Côte de Nuits-Villages
Echézeaux / Grands Echézeaux /
    Richebourg
Fixin
Gevrey-Chambertin
Hautes-Côtes de Beaune
Hautes-Côtes de Nuits
Ladoix
Marsannay
Meursault
Montrachet
Monthélie
Morey-St-Denis
Nuits-St-Georges
Pernand-Vergelesses
Pommard
Puligny-Montrachet
St-Aubin
St-Romain
Santenay
Savigny-lès-Beaune
Volnay
Vosne-Romanée

3   Côte Chalonnaise
3a   Bourgogne Aligoté de Bouzeron
3b   Givry
3c   Mercurey
3d   Montagny
3e   Rully

4   Mâconnais
Mâcon *(whole region)*
4a   Mâcon-Clessé
4b   Mâcon-Lugny
4c   Mâcon-Prissé
4d   Mâcon Supérieur
4e   Mâcon-Uchizy
4f   Mâcon-Villages
4g   Mâcon-Viré
4h   Pouilly-Fuissé
4l   Pouilly-Loché
4j   Pouilly-Vinzelles
4k   St-Véran

5   Beaujolais
(see also appellations on map)
Beaujolais *(whole region)*
Beaujolais Supérieur
    (whole region)
5a   Beaujolais-Villages
5b   Brouilly
5c   Chiroubles
5d   Coteaux du Lyonnais
5e   Côte de Brouilly
5f   Juliénas
5j   Morgon
5k   Regnié

villages like Nuits-St-Georges, Meursault and Gevrey-Chambertin. Unfortunately, it doesn't work like that. Every bottle of Château Lynch-Bages will taste the same for the simple reason that it was all made and bottled at the same place by the same person; a bottle labelled Gevrey-Chambertin could have been produced by any one of several hundred individual winegrowers, all of whom own their own little slices of land here.

Sometimes those growers bottle their own wine; sometimes they sell it to one of the region's *négociants,* or merchants, who may blend it with other growers' wines from the same village in order to have enough wine to sell around the world.

Burgundy is a small-scale place. If you include Beaujolais, it produces around half as much wine as Bordeaux; if you exclude that sea of fruity young red, the figure drops to 25%. And if you focus in on the tiny strip of the Côte d'Or, two dozen villages together produce less wine than only four – Margaux, Pauillac, St-Julien and St-Estèphe – do in the Médoc.

Visiting Burgundy cellars is very different to visiting ones in Bordeaux. And it takes longer. Even the tiniest estate probably makes at least five wines every year; some will produce a dozen – but in tiny quantities. In an average vintage, a Bordeaux château could easily produce 25,000 12-bottle cases of the same wine; a Burgundy estate might make just 250 cases each of 10 different ones. The difference is all to do with 18th-century politics. Most Bordeaux estates escaped the wrath of the Revolutionaries because they often belonged to anti-papist merchants with whom the new order had no quarrel. Burgundy, on the other hand, was Church territory through and through.

The small plots into which the vineyards were divided among the gleeful villagers were made smaller still in subsequent generations, thanks to the new inheritance laws that guaranteed equal shares to all of a landowner's sons and daughters. The death of a man with 10 acres and 10 children could have resulted in 10 winemakers, each with just an acre.

The only reason, apart from the ability of heirs to come to common-sense agreements among themselves, that estates did not shrink to the size of postage stamps was the propensity for sons of winegrowers to marry winegrowers' daughters from the next village, combining names and vineyards to create new estates with new ranges of wines. This process (which continues to this day) not only explains the diverse ranges of wines but also the confusing plethora of neighbouring domaines with confusingly similar double-barrelled names, such as Coche-Debord and Coche-Dury.

The diversity of wines would be rather less broad if the Burgundians had not discovered over the centuries that the differences in quality and character between vineyards could be so significant that each of the best plots, or *climats* (microclimates), deserved to be known by its own *lieu-dit* – placename. By the 1330s, when the Cistercians were building the stone walls to enclose their Clos de Vougeot vineyard, they had already identified most of the *climats* that are best known today, including Clos de Tart, Clos de Bèze, the Chambertin (Bertin's field) and Montrachet. When these vineyards were taken back from the Church and split up and distributed among the villagers, the new owners were often more than happy to perpetuate their fame.

Indeed, the vineyards were often so much more famous than the villages in which they were sited that the villagers eventually decided to reflect a little glory on to their other wines by adopting the best plots' names; the little-known village of Gevrey became the well-known village of Gevrey-Chambertin; Nuits became Nuits-St-Georges and both Chassagne and Puligny added the name of the Montrachet to their own.

After the Revolution, marriages and inheritances, a grower might have ended up with small patches in three different *climats* of Gevrey, two in Morey-St-Denis, four in Vosne-Romanée and one in land that could only be called Bourgogne.

The problem with only making ten barrels (3,000 bottles) each of ten different wines is that it is hard not to frustrate one's customers – so the brighter growers began to buy in wine from the same village and to blend it with their own to produce a larger, more saleable amount. The *négociant-éleveur*, the merchant who literally *'élevé'* or 'brought up' the wine, was born.

For the following 200 years, the *négociants* more or less ran things, buying in barrel, blending and bottling. Some did the job shoddily, some did it well and honestly and some, caught between the frequent unwillingness of the Pinot Noir and Gamay to ripen and customers' demands for rich, alcoholic red, 'helped' pallid wines along with judicious additions of beefier wine from further south.

Then, in the 1970s, a new generation of wine drinkers decided that it was more *sympathique* to buy wine made by an individual in a little cellar rather than by a big company in a factory – only to discover that some of those little cellars were full of filthy barrels and filthier wine, and that some of the 'factories' were producing the best wine in the region.

Today, there are rather fewer people who would want to categorically declare themselves for or against either growers, *négociants* or cooperatives; most would acknowledge the need to seek out the best in each category.

The Quality

So what makes one producer and his or her Burgundy better than the next one on the shelf? If there were no vines planted in France, and if a team of Californian experts were to visit on a mission to decide where to plant them, one thing is pretty certain; they wouldn't linger for long in Burgundy. Almost the entire region would be dismissed as being too cold, too damp, too frost-prone, too hail-prone, too variable... You can't grow the Cabernet Sauvignon here and even the Pinot Noir and Chardonnay almost never ripen sufficiently, so winegrowers have to unload sacks of sugar into their vats to boost the alcohol to an adequate level. The Californians would be just as dismissive of Burgundy as many of them have been of the similarly cool, damp north-western state of Oregon where (just by coincidence?) the Pinot Noir is beginning to achieve a little of the success it has in Burgundy.

The climatic conditions shared by Burgundy and Oregon are officially described as 'marginal'; in other words, both regions are right on the northernmost boundary that defines where great red wine can be made. This closeness to the edge coupled, in the case of Burgundy, with the character of the Pinot Noir and Chardonnay and the region's extraordinary range of soil types, can make for sharply-defined fruity flavours and complexity rarely achieved in warmer, easier climates where the Pinot Noir, at least, tends to produce duller, jammier wine.

But a marginal climate is no place for a lazy, greedy or even unlucky winegrower. Even when the vines escape the attentions of frost, rot and hail, they have to be pruned tightly. If they are allowed to overproduce, both red and white wine will be

ABOVE: Newly-made burgundy in the brandy glass traditionally used by the growers here to taste their wine. At this stage – as later – the wine is lighter in colour and less tannic than Bordeaux

RIGHT: Traditional baskets are still used in Côte d'Or villages such as Aloxe Corton, where this harvester has just picked a load of valuable Pinot Noir

thin, flavourless and low in natural sugar. To rectify this, the producers who are now (in theory at least) denied the possibility of adding stronger wine from the Rhône or North Africa, resort to the sugar bag. They are allowed to use cane sugar to raise the strength of a wine – to *chaptalise* it – by 2% – for example, from a natural 10.5% to 12.5%. What they are not allowed to do is jack up a 9% wine to 13%. A lot of nonsense is talked about chaptalisation, particularly by Californians who pat themselves on the back for not having to add sugar to their ripe grapes (they usually have to add acidity instead); the only sensible thing to be said is that, while with rare exceptions most good and even great Burgundy is chaptalised to a certain extent, there are still too many thin wines whose mouth-burning alcohol reveals a very heavy hand with the sugar bag.

Then there is the question of new barrels – to oak or not to oak. The flavour of new oak, like that of alcohol, can be overdone. On the other hand, top class red and white Burgundy can, like top class Bordeaux, broaden its range of flavours extraordinarily if enough of the wine spends just enough time in new enough wood.

The Regions

Burgundy is a very disparate region, strung out like a series of lakes, beginning in Chablis, around 100 miles (160km) south of Paris, and stretching down through the Côte d'Or (the heart and the greatest part of the region), the under-appreciated Côte Chalonnaise, the Mâconnais and Beaujolais, almost at the outskirts of Lyon and well within the southern half of France.

Today, it can be hard to imagine what Chablis has in common with Beaujolais. The answer in part is politics; both fall within the boundaries of what was once one of the most powerful states in the then developed world. At its heyday in the 14th and 15th centuries, the Duchy of Burgundy extended all the way up to the coast of Flanders and the Duke of Burgundy was a major political player, who negotiated with the king of England and delivered him Joan of Arc.

But the style, the diminutive size of the estates and the varieties of grapes grown are common themes that run through all of Burgundy's regions. This is essentially a land of just four grape varieties; two greats – the Pinot Noir and Chardonnay – that are shared with Champagne and a growing number of wine regions throughout the world, and two – the red Gamay and the white Aligoté – that are allocated very specific roles. The former is used to make Beaujolais, a lot of red Mâcon and, in a two-thirds, one-third blend with the Pinot Noir, Bourgogne Passetoutgrains, traditionally most Burgundians' daily red in the

---

BURGUNDY'S HUMBLER WINES

Bourgogne Passetoutgrains and *Bourgogne Aligoté* are respectively the region's daily red and white. The former wine is a blend of two-thirds Gamay and one-third Pinot Noir (though the proportions do vary) that, when well made can taste not suprisingly like a cross between a classy Beaujolais and a Bourgogne Rouge; the latter is made from the Aligoté grape. Good Aligoté can be like lemony-limey white Burgundy; some can be aggressively acidic and only really useful when blended with *cassis* – blackcurrant liqueur – in the region's *Kir* cocktail.

Crémant de Bourgogne is Burgundy's answer to Champagne Blanc de Blancs; often rich, appley-creamy *Méthode Champenoise* Chardonnay.

days when they could afford to drink their own wines. The Aligoté produces good, basic white that, at its rare ripest and best, can have a creaminess not unlike that of Chardonnay; more usually, its wines are light and acidic, and best drunk mixed with locally made *cassis* – blackcurrant – liqueur in a cocktail known as 'Kir'. Apart from these four, there are a few Pinot Blanc and Pinot Gris vines around, as well as a few oddities such as the César and Tressot, grown in northern Burgundy, but wines made from these are very rare.

The Styles

Avoid anything labelled Bourgogne Grand Ordinaire; the odds are 250-to-one against it being any good and the only relevant part of its name is the 'Ordinaire'. Thankfully this catch-all, Gamay-dominated appellation is rarely seen nowadays.

Bourgogne Rouge and Bourgogne Blanc, on the other hand, can range from basic to brilliant, depending on where it was made, how and by whom. Wine made anywhere from the chilly hills of Chablis to the warm vineyard of the Mâconnais can bear these labels, provided that, in the case of the white, it has been made from the Chardonnay (or, in very rare instances, the Pinot Blanc or Pinot Gris, here called the 'Pinot Beurot'), and in the case of the red that it has been produced from the Pinot Noir (or in the even rarer instances in the Chablis region, from the Tressot or César). There is one other exception; wines made in the Beaujolais *cru* villages, where only the Gamay is grown, may be declassified to Bourgogne Rouge.

The vineyards in which this basic red and white Burgundy are produced range from the flat land of the Côte d'Or to the hills of the Côte Chalonnaise. And then there are the 'almost' wines made by top-class producers in the top-class villages of the Côte d'Or from grapes grown on vines that are just outside the legal limits of those villages. Occasionally, these producers may also decide to declassify some of their potentially higher-class wine that doesn't quite come up to scratch.

More tightly defined than Bourgogne are the *Villages* appellations for areas within the overall region. These include Beaujolais-Villages as well as smaller appellations such as the Côte de Beaune-Villages and Côte de Nuits-Villages in the Côte d'Or.

Next come the appellations centred around villages and towns, such Chablis, Fleurie, Beaune and Pouilly-Fuissé, and, in some cases, the best vineyards within those appellations. Some villages – like Pouilly-Fuissé, St-Romain and Fleurie – have no official recognition for their best *climats,* but may include a vineyard name – such as Morgon 'Le Py' – on their labels.

Other, more fortunate communes – including Beaune, Meursault and Nuits-St-Georges – have sets of *Premier Cru* vineyards, whose names also feature on labels, usually, but not always, with the additional words 'Premier Cru' – such as Beaune Grèves Premier Cru or Meursault Charmes. Some producers whose *Premiers Crus* have little-known names, or who blend wine from two or more *Premiers Crus* vineyards together, may simply choose to label a wine Beaune Premier Cru.

A very few communes – Aloxe-Corton, Gevrey-Chambertin and Chassagne-Montrachet for example – have *Premiers Crus* and *Grands Crus. Grands Crus* are considered to be so important that their labels don't need to mention the name of the village in which the wine was made. So Le Corton labels say nothing about Aloxe-Corton, and Richebourg labels don't say that the wine is made in Vosne-Romanée.

These *Grands Crus* are all situated in the grand vineyards of the Côte d'Or. Chablis has *Premier* and *Grand Crus* plots of its own – but helpfully tacks them on to the region's name – 'Chablis Grand Cru Grenouilles', for example. In theory, if they were all lined up in the same cellar, the *Grand Cru* will have more complex flavours and greater potential longevity than the *Premier Cru* from the next-door vineyard; the *Premier Cru* will be a notch above the wine made from a humbler piece of land in the same village and the village wine will have a more characterful flavour than one simply labelled Bourgogne.

Life gets trickier when you compare wines made by different producers; one man's carefully-made Bourgogne Rouge could be better than his careless cousin's Vosne-Romanée – and even his Richebourg.

CHABLIS

During the summer months, the owner of the only decent café in the village of Chablis gets rather bored by the stream of tourists – even French tourists – who ask for 'a glass of red Chablis'. American visitors are more likely to order 'blush Chablis'. Neither exists. Chablis comes in one style: dry and white. And wine sold in Europe as 'Chablis' must, moreover, be made only from Chardonnay grapes grown on some 4,000 acres of vineyards on the sloping banks of the Serein river.

Until just a few years ago, Chablis, to British merchants and restaurateurs, was no more than a convenient, easy to pronounce (and remember) name for any old white wine. The lazy attitude of pre-EC Britain still prevails in the New World, where US and Australian winemakers can make 'Chablis' out of any old grapes, any old where, any old how. And so they trade – quite legally – on the prestige of one of France's most famous wine names. And, ironically, the more this abuse is practised, the more famous Chablis becomes. And the price of the real thing rockets, leaving its aficionados to bemoan the fact that their favourite tipple does not hail from a Burgundian village with a less approachable name – like Auxey-Duresses.

The unique quality of good, typical, authentic Chablis isn't easy to describe. It is absolutely dry, but with a suppleness and a fatty fulness that you seldom find in the dry wines of Sancerre and Pouilly-Fumé, neither of which are far away. But there's also a flinty flavour to Chablis, particularly when it is young, and the wine still has its characteristic green-tinged colour.

The region of Chablis lies almost midway between Paris and Beaune, the heart of Burgundy. You'll recognise the village, because you've already been there – every time you've watched one of those old French films; black and white even when they're in colour; brightly-lit cafés in empty, rainswept streets; and quiet country folk of the kind who murder each other in Simenon novels.

But look up, and you'll see the reason for its fame – in the shape of the vineyard-covered hill that overlooks the town, home to the *Grand Cru* vineyards with their mysterious and evocative names: Vaudésir, Valmur, Grenouilles, Blanchot, Les Clos, Bougros and Les Preuses. These are the epitome of what Chablis can be, the 'big wines', the ones most worth keeping. Beneath them on the scale of excellence, there are the *Premiers Crus*; beneath these, plain Chablis and, most humble of all, Petit Chablis. And all must be made from the grapes of this 4,000-acre Burgundian oasis.

THE OTHER WINES OF CHABLIS

Though none is allowed to be called Chablis, there are red and rosé wines made in this region. The best-known red is Bourgogne Irancy, a fruity, raspberryish wine that is usually made from the Pinot Noir, though it may include a generous dose of the duller local varieties Tressot and César. The village of Coulanges-La-Vineuse produces a similar red, while Epineuil makes red, white and *gris* (dustily pale pink) wines, all AOCs, though the leanness of their style in cool years could leave you wondering why.

Ironically, the dry white produced in the village of St Bris, which really deserves an AOC, has been denied one – probably because it is made from the 'wrong' grape. The Sauvignon, prized and pricy not so far away in Sancerre, is underrated here...

A little over a century ago, the Chablis vineyard was perhaps ten times that size. The ravages of the phylloxera louse in the 1880s, then the depredations of two world wars, took a heavy toll on the region's vines and vinegrowers. By the early 1960s, when thirsty Americans were already gulping back their version by the gallon, the area of Chablis vines had shrunk to less than 1,500 acres – less than the size of a modest Texan farm.

In those days, few men could rely on making a living simply from their vines. One of their biggest problems was frost, which could – and can – destroy a whole year's crop in a single night. The reason why Chablis is so subject to frost – as late as May in some years – is because of the way that the sheltered valley of the Serein traps and holds cold air.

At the end of rows of vines one can still see the archaic oil burners which are lit as soon as the temperature falls below zero. Now, however, many growers prefer to rely on sprinklers that protect the vines from frost by, paradoxically allowing a thin layer of ice to form on them.

The flavour of Chablis has changed in the last decade. The steely style has gradually given way to a softer, less demanding one, thanks to over-production, to a succession of ripe vintages, and to the decision of some winemakers to allow their wine to

LEFT: Bougros, one of Chablis' Grand Cru vineyards, provides perfect chalky clay for the Chardonnay

ABOVE: A young Chablis vine growing in the controversial Kimmeridgian soil

undergo malolactic fermentation and, in a few cases, to ferment and age it in new oak barrels. To Chablisien purists, both ought to be outlawed; in their view, producers who use them are merely trying to make Meursault-style wines 150 kilometres north of Meursault.

Also contributing to the change in style is the recent authorisation to expand the vineyards that make Chablis and Chablis Premier Cru into land where previously only Petit Chablis could be produced. The crucial difference between the 'new' land and the area from which the original, most typical Chablis comes, lies in the soil. Or, more precisely, beneath it.

The limestone bedrock on which Chablis rests has been the subject of a violent squabble between two groups of Chablisien winegrowers. The traditionalists claim, with the vehemence of real ale campaigners, that 'real' Chablis can only be grown on the small area of Kimmeridgian limestone which takes its name from the village in Dorset where it is also found. The modernists, like keen urban planners, argue that the Portland limestone that sits beneath the rest of the region can produce wine that is just as good. Tasting the wines side by side, I tend to agree with the traditional line – but then again, the Portland faction are making wines that are certainly of good, if not great, quality. And, given the way that demand for this, the most famous white wine in the world, has forced its price through the roof, it's very tempting to allow the Chablisiens to expand their vineyards as much as they'd like.

Saumon aux Herbes
Raw salmon marinated in herbs, olive oil and lemon juice

The flinty crispness of the wines of Chablis makes them very good with this marinated salmon dish which, although traditional in this region, has an almost Scandinavian character.

SERVES 6 AS A STARTER
1 lb/500 g salmon fillet, skinned and boned
5 tbsp olive oil
2 tsp tinned green peppercorns, drained and crushed
2 tsp whole black peppercorns, coarsely crushed
Juice of 1 lemon
3 tbsp fennel leaves, finely chopped, or 1 tbsp dried fennel seeds

Dry the salmon with kitchen paper and coat it with olive oil. Rub in the green and black pepper, the lemon juice and fennel. Put the salmon in a glass or ceramic dish, covered, and refrigerate for at least four hours, turning occasionally. Serve thinly sliced as a starter with brown bread and butter or toast triangles.

THE ESSENTIALS — CHABLIS

Location Centred on the town of Chablis, half-way between Paris and Beaune.
Quality AOC Chablis, with a further hierarchy of *Grands* and *Premiers Crus (see below)*. Also AOC Petit Chablis, Irancy, Epineuil, and Crémant de Bourgogne, and VDQS Sauvignon de St Bris.
Style Flavours range from steely and austere to pineappley and rounded, usually with either no or clearly detectable oak. *Premier Cru* wines are finer, the choicer soil contributing a minerally acidity and the capacity to develop with age. *Grands Crus* are the biggest, richest, most complex wines, yet are lean and restrained compared with white Burgundy from farther south. Sauvignon de St Bris is gooseberryish and Sancerre-like; Irancy and Epineuil are light reds.
Climate Continental.
Cultivation Soils are of calcareous clay. Rivalry exists over the benefits of the classic Kimmeridgian versus the more recently allowed Portland-ian limestone. All the *Grands Crus* are on one south-west-facing slope.
Grape varieties Chardonnay for Chablis; Sauvignon Blanc in St Bris; Pinot Noir, Tressot and César for reds; Sacy for Crémant de Bourgogne.
Production/Maturation Stainless steel has largely replaced oak for both, but new oak still has some fervent and successful supporters, notably William Fèvre.
Longevity Petit Chablis, Sauvignon de St Bris and red wines are intended to be drunk young. Chablis drinks from 1 to 8 years; *Premiers Crus* for up to 15; *Grands Crus* should be kept for five years, and can be drunk for a further 15.
Vintage Guide 81, 83, 85, 86, 88, 89
Top Producers Raveneau, William Fèvre, René Dauvissat, Domaine Laroche.

The difference in potential quality between Premier and Grand Cru Chablis can be very significant because, while the Grands Crus have remained unchanged, some of the Premier Cru vineyard sites have recently been expanded to include previously less well-thought-of land.

THE GRANDS CRUS OF CHABLIS
Bougros; Blanchot; Les Clos; Grenouilles; Les Preuses; Valmur and Vaudésir. One vineyard within the Grands Crus, La Moutonne, is not classified as such but, because of its status and position, is tacitly allowed to describe itself as 'Grand Cru La Moutonne'.

THE PREMIERS CRUS OF CHABLIS
Beauroy; Côte de Léchet; Fourchaume; Les Fourneaux; Melinots; Montée de Tonnerre; Montmains; Mont de Milieu; Vaillons; Vaucoupin; Vaudevey and Vosgros.

THE CÔTE D'OR

The best description I ever heard of travelling in the Côte d'Or was that it was just like driving down a wine list. And it's true. Just set out from Dijon on the *route nationale* heading south, with the east-facing vine-covered hills on your right and the humbler, flatter land on your left and read the village signs as you pass. Even if you stick rigorously to the speed limit, there they are, one every two or three minutes – Gevrey-Chambertin, Morey-St-Denis, Chambolle-Musigny, Clos de Vougeot, Flagey-Echézeaux, Vosne-Romanée and Nuits-St-Georges...

But for more than signposts to some of the world's greatest wines, take one of the narrow tracks to your right and follow the *Route des Vins* that links these villages together. Look at the stone archways that occasionally indicate the name of the vineyard – or of the man or company that owns a corner of it. If you've arrived in the autumn, bask in the different shades of colour, from green to bronze via the gold after which these hills were named. At the end of the day, you may even sense the fractional variations in temperature between vineyards – and, by picking up a handful of soil, you may be able to see how the way the earth was folded here aeons ago, leaving one tiny piece of land far richer in fossil material than the next.

The Côte d'Or is divided into two parts; the 3,500 acres (1,400 ha) of the more northerly Côte de Nuits, in which most of Burgundy's greatest reds are made, and where there is scarcely a drop of white; and the 7,500 acres (3,000ha) of the Côte de Beaune, where the Pinot Noir still covers 75% of the land, but a handful of villages produce the white wine that turns owners of Chardonnay vineyards in other countries green with envy.

Both Côtes produce simpler wine labelled as Bourgogne Rouge, Bourgogne Blanc, Bourgogne Passetoutgrains and Aligoté, from land that cannot legally produce wine of a grander appellation; some of these can be delicious, especially when made by a grower who also makes loftier wines.

The Côte de Nuits

Apart from the wines produced in the 'big-name' villages and the Bourgogne Rouge (often very well) made from grapes grown in the less well-situated flat land on the wrong – eastern – side of the *route nationale,* the Côte de Nuits has two other appellations. Côte de Nuits-Villages can come from the villages of Fixin and Brochon just north of Gevrey-Chambertin, and from the marble-quarrying country around Comblanchien, Corgoloin and Prissy, immediately to the south of Nuits-St-Georges. Little of the wine does actually come from Fixin, which has an appellation of its own, but Brochon and the more southerly communes can produce good-quality, blackcurranty, plummy wine with a recogniseable family resemblance to the wines of the better-known villages along the Côte. These are the country cousins, dressed up for a day in the town.

Rather more rustic wines are also produced high in the hills behind the Côte in the Hautes Côtes de Nuits. These definitely can sometimes have wisps of straw poking out of their hats, but they can also be one of the nearest things to a bargain Burgundy has to offer. Stick to warm years; it can get quite chilly up here and lesser vintages tend to produce unripe-tasting wine. Almost all of the wine made here is red; the occasional white can make you wonder why they don't make more.

What was once called the Côte Dijonnaise is now largely full of the tyre-fitting operations and *hypermarchés* that fill Dijon's southern suburbs, so the Côte d'Or now officially begins with Marsannay, a village which is still celebrating its recent elevation to join its *appellation contrôlée* neighbours.

Marsannay's traditional reputation was for rosé, and that's still arguably the one style it can claim as its own (pink Pinot Noir is a rarity). Its reds are still rather closer in quality to decent Bourgogne Rouge (the label they used to bear) than to the kind of stuff one might expect from Gevrey-Chambertin. One label to look out for (you're sure to notice it) is that of wine from the 'Montre Cul' vineyard, whose name – literally 'show-arse' – refers to the steepness of the slope and the view male pickers got of their female companions' bloomers.

As one might gather, Marsannay's a fairly jolly place and wine, so Fixin comes as a bit of a shock. Wine merchants have a description for the wines of this village: 'Hard to say (it's pronounced *Fissan*), harder to drink and almost impossible to sell.' This is a good a place as any to learn about the effects of Burgundian microclimates – Fixin harvests its grapes a week later than the next-door village; they still haven't ripened. Even when they have, they produce tough, uncompromising wine that seems to taste the way it must have done when the Cistercian monks first made it in the early 12th century. Give it a decade or so and it can soften – a bit – but it's still Burgundy's answer to old-fashioned St-Estèphe.

Gevrey-Chambertin's much more fun. Or it ought to be. Sadly this, like Nuits-St-Georges, Beaujolais and Châteauneuf-du-Pape, has suffered from the fame syndrome. There are brilliant vineyards here – the *Grands Crus,* including the Chambertin itself, the more immediately appealing Charmes-Chambertin, the Chambertin-Clos de Bèze, Mazis-Chambertin and the Griotte-Chambertin (named after and tasting of bitter cherries), and the slightly lighter-weight but sometimes equally impressive *Premiers Crus* such as the Clos St Jacques and Cazetiers – but

Dijon

2d
2c

GEVREY-CHAMBERTIN
2a

MOREY-ST-DENIS
CHAMBOLLE-MUSIGNY
CLOS DE VOUGEOT
2e
2b
VOSNE-ROMANEE

NUITS-ST-GEORGES
1

Prémeaux

4g
4e
4d **ALOXE-CORTON**
4k
4c

POMMARD
BEAUNE
VOLNAY
Rhoin
4f
4j
4i
MEURSAULT
AUXEY-DURESSES
3
4b
4a
4h
PULIGNY-MONTRACHET
CHASSAGNE-MONTRACHET
4j
Chagny

Canal de Bourgogne

1 Hautes Côtes de Nuits
2 Côte de Nuits
(See also appellations on map)
2a Chambertin / Chambertin
    Clos de Bèze
Côte de Nuits-Villages *(Appellation for red and white from the region south of Nuits St Georges and north of - and including - Fixin)*
  2b Echézeaux / Grands Echézeaux /
      Richebourg
2c Fixin
2d Marsannay
2e Romanée-Conti

3 Hautes Côtes de Beaune
4 Côte de Beaune
(See also appellations on map)
4a Bâtard-Montrachet /
    Chevalier Montrachet /
    Montrachet
4b Blagny
4c Chorey-lès-Beaune

4d Corton / Corton-Charlemagne
Côte de Beaune *(small set of vineyards around Beaune)*
Côte de Beaune-Villages *(Appellation for red wine from the white wine producing communes of this Côte)*

4e Ladoix
4f Monthélie
4g Pernand-Vergelesses
4h St-Aubin
4l St-Romain
4j Santenay
4k Savigny-lès-Beaune

Top: Harvesters in one of Vosne Romanée's best vineyards

ABOVE: *This basket will contain some of the most prized grapes in the world – the Pinot Noir that will become Romanée-Conti*

Beaune than Côte de Nuits, with that area's more delicate style. Bonnes Mares is the other top *Grand Cru.*

Clos de Vougeot is Burgundy's nearest to a Bordeaux-style château – or that's what it used to be in the days when the Cistercian monks owned this 125 acre (50ha) walled vineyard and made wine here, carefully separating the less good grapes grown on the flatland from the best ones grown on the slopes. The French Revolution and inheritance laws changed all that; today there are 85 individual owners and 85 different wines, ranging from the poor (badly made and/or from the flattest parts) to the sublime (well made, from the slopes). But every drop is *Grand Cru.* Confusingly, there is also an appellation for Vougeot for wine made outside the walls, 90% of which is classified as *Premier Cru.* Good Clos de Vougeot ought to be soft and velvety with the flavours of ripe raspberries and plum. The château itself, which looks just like a ship sinking in a sea of vines, is worth visiting too, either by day to see its old presses, or by night when the local order of wine enthusiasts, the Chevaliers de Tastevin, dress up for one of their banquets.

There isn't a lot of village at Flagey-Echézeaux – a few houses, a great café/restaurant and a church – and it's in the wrong place, down on the flat land, a fair distance from its *Grand Cru* Echézeaux and Grands Echézeaux vineyards up on the slopes. Both produce tiny amounts of gloriously rich, raspberryish, plum-flavoured wine with more than a hint of spice. They can be among the more affordable *Premiers Crus,* except when they are made by the Domaine de la Romanée-Conti, Burgundy's equivalent of Château Pétrus. Hidden away in a modest building in the heart of Vosne-Romanée, this is the shrine to which well-heeled Burgundy lovers flock to worship – and buy. Less well-off enthusiasts merely stand and stare at the domaine's minuscule *Grand Cru* Romanée-Conti vineyard. If you want to taste that wine, you have to buy it from the domaine, where a bottle would cost you at least a week's wages. You can, however discover the juicy, blackberryish flavour of Vosne-Romanée's wines a little less pricily by going for a village wine, or one of the *Premier Crus.* My favourites are Beaux Monts, Suchots and Chaumes.

this is one of the region's biggest villages and its appellation includes a huge tract of flat land, including some which is on the other side of the *route nationale,* the side that usually only makes Bourgogne Rouge. Dull winemaking and over-production don't help either. Gevrey-Chambertin *should* be a rich cocktail of dark cherries and really ripe plums.

Morey-St-Denis is not a name that rings many bells with Burgundy fans, and nor is Clos-St-Denis, the *Grand Cru* that gave it its name. This is a village with lovely village wines vying for attention with poorly-made *Grands* and *Premiers Crus.* The best stuff from the Clos de la Roche *Grand Cru* can be majestic, deep wine – better than most Clos-St-Denis. The Clos Sorbès and Clos des Ormes are the best *Premiers Crus.*

Chambolle-Musigny provides your first chance to taste classy white Burgundy – of which a very few bottles are made in the primarily red *Grand Cru* Musigny vineyard – and a red from one of the most romantically named *Premiers Crus,* Les Amoureuses. Chambolle Musigny's wines should taste more like Côte de

If you find yourself enjoying a glass of young Nuits-St-Georges, beware – it is unlikely to be a really good one. This is like Fixin with class; tough, broody wine that needs at least five years to soften. But when they do, the mulberry-and-plum wines of Nuits itself, or the ones made at Prémeaux just down the Côte, are among the best buys in Burgundy. Nuits has no *Grands Crus*. This is an injustice; Les St Georges, Les Vaucrains and Les Pruliers could all make a case for themselves.

As you leave Prémeaux, you leave the big name villages of the Côte de Nuits and pass through a tract of Côte de Nuits-Villages before imperceptibly crossing the border into the Côte de Beaune, just south of the village of Corgoloin.

The Côte de Beaune

Like its Côte de Nuits counterpart, Côte de Beaune-Villages is a rag-bag appellation for wine produced almost throughout this half of the Côte d'Or. Unlike the Côte de Nuits, however, it only covers red wines, despite the fact that this bit of Burgundy is where all of the best whites are made; white wines that ought to be sold as Côte de Beaune-Villages are stuck with plain Bourgogne Blanc. The hillside appellation, Hautes-Côtes de Beaune,

does include wines of both colours – or rather all three, because a little light, raspberryish *clairet* and rosé is made here. All are pleasant in warm years, and lean in cool ones.

The first Côte de Beaune village is Ladoix-Serrigny, whose little-known wines are usually sold as Ladoix. They actually *taste* as though they are made on the border; they combine some of the gentle, raspberryish flavours of Beaune with the toughness of Nuits-St-Georges, but in rather a rustic way. With time, they can, however, sometimes outclass some of the less impressive wines from its neighbour Aloxe-Corton.

A village that is quite literally in the shadow of its *Grands Crus,* grown on the hillsides here, Aloxe-Corton makes red wines that, like those of Nuits-St-Georges, can take forever to 'come round'. Some examples of the *Grand Crus* Corton, Corton-Vergennes, Corton Bressandes et al (there are 21 different bits of the Corton vineyard) do eventually develop glorious richness of flavour; others remain perpetually comatose. The more reliably exciting wine is the white Corton-Charlemagne, made in vineyards that belonged to the emperor and were named after him, it is implausibly said, following his conversion from red to white wine by his wife who complained at the red stains on his snowy imperial beard.

THE ESSENTIALS — THE COTE d'OR

Location In Burgundy, a narrow strip of land from Dijon in the north to Cheilly-les-Maranges 30km south of Beaune.
Quality *Overall Côte d'Or AOCs*: Bourgogne; Bourgogne Aligoté; Crémant de Bourgogne; Bourgogne Passetoutgrains. *Principal Côte de Nuits AOCs*: Chambertin*; Chambertin Clos de Bèze*; Charmes Chambertin*; Chambolle-Musigny; Clos de la Roche*; Clos de Vougeot*; Côte de Nuits-Villages; Echézeaux*; Fixin, Gevrey Chambertin; Grands-Echezeaux*; Hautes-Côtes de Nuits; Marsannay; Morey St Denis; Nuits St Georges; Richebourg*; Romanée*; Vosne Romanée. *Principal Côte de Beaune AOCs:* Ladoix; Aloxe-Corton; Auxey-Duresses; Bâtard-Montrachet*; Beaune; Blagny; Chassagne Montrachet; Chorey-lès-Beaune; Corton*; Corton-Charlemagne*; Côte de Beaune; Côte de Beaune-Villages; Hautes Côtes de Beaune; Meursault; Monthélie; Montrachet*; Pernand-Vergelesses; Pommard; Puligny Montrachet; St Aubin, St Romain; Santenay; Savigny-lès-Beaune; Volnay. Superimposed on most of the appellations is a complex structure of named vineyards: the *Grands* and *Premiers Crus*. The AOCs marked (*) are in themselves *Grands Crus.*
Style Whites, at their best, have a dazzling array of enticing flavours, with rich, buttery fruit, a creamy/nutty texture and splendid overtones of honey, vanilla and toasty oak. The reds are more varied in quality but should have delicate strawberry/raspberry fruit in the Côte de Beaune and a finer character, with greater depth and a sumptuous silky texture, in the Côte de Nuits. With bottle age, the reds develop a gamey flavour. Because of the myriad of small-plot owners, the producer's name is all important and the best guide to quality. A general rule is that the wines are reasonably straightforward at village level, with greater complexity and depth of flavour to be expected from *Premier* and *Grand Cru* wines. Tiny quantities of dry rosé, packed with soft currant and berry fruit flavours, are also made.
Climate Temperate continental climate with hot, sunny summers and long, cold winters. Hail and heavy rain can cause rot and dilute wines.
Cultivation Subtly varying marl, clay and calcareous soils overlay a limestone subsoil which underpins the east-facing slopes of the region. Vines generally grow at 200-400m above sea level and vineyards generally face north-east or south-east. Vines are trained low to maximise heat reflected from the soil during the day.
Grape Varieties The dominant red is the Pinot Noir, though the Gamay is also grown. Principal white is the Chardonnay; secondary white the Aligoté.
Production/Maturation Traditional methods are used. For red wines the grapes are at least partially de-stemmed and the juice receives 8–14 days' skin contact. Top whites are cask-fermented although stainless steel is used for lesser wines. Both reds and whites are matured in oak.
Longevity *Reds*: Village wines and basic Bourgogne: 4 to 17 years; Premiers Crus: 8 to 25 years; Grands Crus:10 to 30+ years. *Whites*: Village wines: 3 to 11 years; Premiers Crus: 6 to 15 years; Grands Crus: 10 to 30+ years. *Rosés*: up to 4 years.
Vintage Guide Reds 71, 76, 78, 79, 83, 85, 88, 89
　　　　　　　　　Whites 78, 79, 81, 83, 85, 86, 88, 89
Top Producers *Côte de Nuits:* Jayer, Jayer-Gilles, Ponsot, Dujac, Rion, Mongeard-Mugneret, Domaine de la Romanée-Conti, Jean Grivot, Alain Michelot, Joseph Drouhin, Leroy, Faiveley. *Côte de Beaune:* Bonneau du Martray, Leflaive, Sauzet, Pothier Rieusset, Domaine de la Pousse d'Or, Domaine Bachelet, Ramonet, Comtes Lafon, Joseph Drouhin, Leroy, Chartron & Trébuchet, Michelot-Buisson, Louis Jadot.

If Aloxe-Corton makes tough wine, the little-known appellation of Chorey-lès-Beaune, (*lès*, by the way, is an ancient word meaning 'near') produced from grapes grown on the flat land on the east of the *nationale*, is a place to look for lovely, soft, raspberryish Pinot Noir which, drunk young, is one of the region's classiest bargains.

Back in the hills, Pernand-Vergelesses also produces soft, approachable reds, some of which can be so soft that they taste a bit too like damson jam and make you wonder if their makers are not over-compensating for the tough Cortons most of them produce from the part of that *Grand Cru* vineyard that strays into their village. The best wine here is the white, which can be very distinguished – hazelnutty and buttery, sometimes with a hint of the quality of the Corton Charlemagne many of its producers make too. Les Vergelesses and Ile des Vergelesses are the best *Premier Crus*. The village of Savigny-lès-Beaune is just beneath Pernand-Vergelesses and has a good *Premier Cru*, Les Basses Vergelesses. Red Savigny can be – and often is – like a classier version of Chorey-lès-Beaune (several estates make both), with lovely, ripe, blackberryish, mulberryish sweetness. There is very little white wine made here, but it's tastily worth looking out for – and unusual in being made from the Pinot

Blanc, a variety usually associated with Alsace.

Standing in Savigny-lès-Beaune, you can see the old walled town of Beaune, its church and its most famous building, the Hospices at which, every November, wines of the most recent vintage from various Côte de Beaune vineyards (and one Côte de Nuits plot) are auctioned in aid of the town's hospital.

Like Nuits-St-Georges, Beaune has no *Grands Crus*; like that appellation, it has at least three contenders in Theurons, Grèves and Bressandes. None really fits the mould of *Grand Cru* Côte de Nuits wines, however, because these are far less 'big' wines; they whisper rather than roar. My classic tasting note for a mature Beaune is of the smell of faded roses and the flavour of wild raspberries and honey.

Perhaps because most of Burgundy's best-known merchants have their cellars in a rabbit warren beneath the town, and more crucially because they almost all have large vineyard holdings here and so are often making wine from their own grapes, Beaune remains one of the most reliable labels in Burgundy. A tiny amount of white Beaune is made too; it tastes a little like a leaner version of Meursault.

Apart from the appellation of Beaune itself, there is the tiny anomaly of one called simply Côte de Beaune that includes a

LEFT: Nicolas Rolin, the tax collector who founded the Hospices de Beaune for the Duke of Burgundy, stands – as a statue – against the backdrop of the Hospices roof, one of the most recognisable symbols of the region

TOP: Tastevins, the traditional tasting cups used by Burgundian winegrowers, can now be bought as tourist souvenirs

ABOVE: Burgundians love banquets, where traditional drinking songs are de rigueur

A BURGUNDY BUYER'S GUIDE

The process of choosing Burgundy can be frustrating and, often, very disappointing. If you follow the advice below, I cannot guarantee that you will always end up with a good and, more importantly, a good value, bottle of Burgundy (I've wasted my money on far too many bad ones ever to believe that there is any foolproof route through the maze) but it should improve the odds in your favour.

Vintages
These are crucially important in Burgundy where the climate can be unfriendly to grapes. Good producers can make tasty wine in 'poor' vintages such as 1984, but careless ones often end up over-compensating for a lack of natural sugar by pouring in too much cane sugar, and thus giving their wines an intrusively alvcoholic 'burn'. Similarly, in potentially good years such as 1982, there is often the phenomenon of over-production – of pink wines being sold as red. In all but the greatest vintages (for reds: 1978, 1985, 1988; for whites: 1973, 1979, 1982, 1986) when almost everybody made wine of at least reasonable quality, it is doubly essential to buy from good producers (see the recommendations in *The Essentials - Burgundy* box on page 99).

It is also worth bearing in mind that, in the coolest vintages, the least well-sited vineyards fare worst. So wines from the hillside vineyards of the Hautes Côtes de Nuits and Beaune were good buys in the ripe years of 1985 and 1988 and often riskier ones in the cooler vintage of 1986. By the same token, it is most worth buying Premiers and Grands Crus in those 'lesser' vintages – provided that they are fairly priced and from a reliable producer.

Good Value Villages
Some villages do offer better value than others; seek reds and whites from St-Aubin, Savigny-lès-Beaune, Monthélie, Auxey-Duresses, Mercurey, Rully, Givry, Ladoix; reds from Fixin, Chassagne Montrachet, Chorey lès Beaune and Meursault; whites from Pernand Vergelesses and Montagny.

Vignerons Versus Négociants
Once upon a time, almost all of Burgundy's wines were sold by the region's merchants - the *négociants*. More recently, the trend has been towards buying from individual growers - the *vignerons*. Neither group has any kind of monopoly over good Burgundy; each has its superstars – and its knaves, fools and people who simply don't care very much about the quality of what they are selling.

Who's Who?
If the price is high, you've never heard of the grower or merchant and you have no reason to trust the buying skills of the restaurant or shop, just say no thank you. The chances of a random bottle of Gevrey-Chambertin being worth its money are very slim. Unfamiliar *négociants* should be treated with suspicion. Most Burgundy merchants have sets of fictitious names they can legally stick on labels for their customers.

Beware too, of apparently familiar labels. Most growers use the same few printers and many are happy to use the same basic label (complete with heraldry, grapes, parchment or whatever) as their neighbours.

The town of Meursault, home of some 300 individual winegrowers — and source of some of the greatest white wine in the world

small set of vineyards in the hills overlooking the town. Often quite understandably confused with Côte de Beaune-Villages, Côte de Beaune can be good value.

Pommard is a little like Gevrey-Chambertin, a well-known village too much of whose wine comes from the wrong side of the *nationale,* except that here, any grapes that cross the road do so illegally. Good Pommard, like Aloxe-Corton, is quite sturdy stuff. Like Aloxe-Corton, they need time and sensitive winemaking to bring out the plummy fruit that's hiding behind all that muscle. The best *Premiers Crus* are Les Epenots, Les Rugiens and Les Arvelets.

Many of Pommard's growers make prettier wine a few yards further south in Volnay, a village that can make some of the greatest red Burgundy of all. The *Premier Cru* Les Santenots – which, confusingly, is actually in Meursault – should be a *Grand*

Cru, but it rarely dazzles as most Côte de Nuits *Grands Crus* are expected to, because of a lightness of touch, attributable to its very, very shallow topsoil and deep limestone. The best Volnay combines ripe plums and violets; the Côte de Beaune's counterpart to Vosne-Romanée, the Côte de Nuits almost-namesake with which it is often confused.

On the same hillside, you next arrive in the village of Monthélie, which makes little-known wines that used to be sold as Volnay. Tasting them you can see why the rules excluded these more rustic wines, but they still often offer good value. The whites can be tasty too, but they are very, very rare.

Auxey Duresses is a victim of its – to foreigners – hard-to-pronounce name. Prices are often lower for well-made whites here than they are for fairly basic Meursault, but the quality is more variable, sometimes, I suspect, because of the care taken (or not taken) by the winegrowers, or because of the poor siting of some of the vineyards. The reds, which make up 25% of the wine made here can be good and juicy, but rarely delicate.

Further up in the hills, among the Hautes-Côtes de Beaune, St-Romain is a glorious place to picnic and watch hungry birds circling over the vines. The reds can be fruitily appealing, but only in warm years; in cool ones, the grapes don't ripen well. The whites are better, in their lean way – provided they aren't overexposed to the new oak barrels made by the village success-story, Jean Francois, most of whose casks end up being used for the big Californian Chardonnays that can handle them.

Ragoût de Canard aux Navets
Fricassee of duck with turnips

Some have called this region of the Burgundy the heart of French gastronomy, so rich is the tradition of great wines matched with sumptuous food. The richness of this duck recipe will do justice to the deep wines of Beaune and the Côte de Nuits.

SERVES 4

8 oz/225 g unsmoked bacon, diced
1 medium onion, peeled and sliced
3 garlic cloves, peeled and minced
1 tbsp olive oil
1 oz/25 g butter
2 lb/1 kg duck, cut into pieces
4 tbsp plain flour
4 tbsp fresh parsley, chopped
1 bay leaf
2 juniper berries, crushed
Salt and freshly ground black pepper
3 wine glasses of dry white wine
1½ lb/750 g small whole turnips, peeled, or larger turnips
peeled and cut into quarters

In a large pan, sauté the bacon, onion and garlic in the olive oil until the onion is lightly browned. Remove from the pan with a slotted slice or spoon. Dredge the duck pieces in flour and brown in the pan. Pour off excess fat if necessary. Return the bacon, onion and garlic to the pan and add the parsley, bay leaf, juniper berries, salt and pepper and wine and cook, uncovered, for about 45 minutes. Add the turnips, cover the pan and cook at a bare simmer for about an hour.

The wine many of those Californians really want to make is Meursault; they just love the fat, buttery, hazelnutty style of those wines, but sometimes miss the point that Meursault shouldn't just be buttered toast and oak; it should also be about subtlety and complexity. For these qualities, sidestep the obvious appeal of village Meursault and the immediately seductive Charmes (these names *do* mean something) and try the *Premiers Crus* Genevrières, Goutte d'Or and Perrières, all of which could be *Grands Crus* if Meursault had any. Incidentally, if Meursault's *Premiers Crus* are undervalued, so are some of its village wines, many of which proudly print their non-*premier cru* names on their labels. Red Meursault is a rare oddity, but try some if you get the chance – it can be like drinking liquidised wild raspberries; pure Pinot Noir.

Puligny-Montrachet and Chassagne-Montrachet *do* have *Grands Crus* of their own – but they have to share the small plot of land that gave them their name. The 18.5 acre (7.5ha) Le Montrachet vineyard makes what is quite simply the greatest dry white wine in the world. Its flavour is almost impossible to describe, an explosive marriage of ripe, peachy, appley, peary fruit, butter, roasted nuts and digestive biscuits and honey. Drink it when it's at least 10 years old.

The Montrachet has a decidedly odd set of neighbours: Bâtard (bastard) Montrachet; Bienvenue Bâtard (welcome bastard) Montrachet; Criots Bâtard (cries of the bastard) Montrachet and Chevalier (Knight) Montrachet, all of which transcend the village appellations in which they are situated.

Tasting village or *Premier Cru* wine from either village alongside one of the *Grands Crus* is a little like looking at a black-and-white photograph next to a colour one. Knowing which is the Puligny-Montrachet and which is the Chassagne-Montrachet can be tricky but, as a rule, the latter is toastier in style and the former is slightly more floral. Both tend to be ferociously priced, but Chassagne can be a touch cheaper.

Red Chassagne-Montrachet (over half the production) can be good, if rarely delicate Pinot Noir, but beware disappointing examples forced on to merchants by producers who refuse to offer their white to anyone who won't take the red too.

Slightly off the beaten track, close to the village of Gamay, said to be the birthplace of the Beaujolais grape, St Aubin is one white wine-producing village I wasn't going to mention. Because I'm not certain if I want the secret of this commune's nutty, buttery wines to spread too far. When well made, they can show up a Meursault, Chassagne or Puligny – for a far lower price. The reds (of which there are far more) are a little less impressive, but can still be good value.

Santenay is the last important commune on the Côte, and a less than distinguished note on which to leave. The reds here from the *Premiers Crus* Clos Tavannes, Gravières and Commes can be good, straight-down-the-line Pinot Noir, but too many Santenays are a bit dull and earthy. The whites are, if anything, less impressive, but Santenay is worth a visit – by anyone who fancies a flutter at the casino or a dip in the spa.

Beyond Santenay, Dézize-les-Maranges, Sampigny-les-Maranges and Cheilly-les-Maranges unaccountably have their own appellations and even some *Premiers Crus*. Sensible producers, however, sell their often rather basic wine as Côte de Beaune-Villages.

SOUTHERN BURGUNDY

As you drive away from the Côte d'Or and into the Côte Cha-lonnaise, you cross the invisible border that separates 'smart' Burgundy from the rest. The names of the villages around here are less well known than the ones in the Côte d'Or; Givry has none of the lustre of Gevrey-Chambertin and Mercurey features more rarely on restaurant lists than Meursault.

But 'twas not ever thus. This is a region of might-have-been places. Tourists flock to the magnificent medieval abbey of Cluny – but it's a ruin; the town of Autun was intended, Brasilia-like, by the Romans to be a 'Rome of the West'; today, all that remains is the Forum and bits of an amphitheatre. As for Châlon-sur-Sâone itself, its industrial heyday is long past and the visitors who used to stop in on their way southward on the N7 now zoom past on the *autoroute.*

The wines here are forgotten too, though to an 18th-century Frenchman names like Mercurey, Rully and Givry would have rung louder bells than some of today's superstar villages of the Côte d'Or. Henri IV, the French king who made the name of Sancerre's wines, was a particular fan of Givry; his mistress lived there. The *négociants* of Beaune, Nuits-St-Georges and Mâcon have always treated the Côte Chalonnaise rather as though it were their mistress; a region to be taken advantage of and not referred to in public. And their attitude was understandable. This area has always been a good minor source (20% of the crop) of Chardonnay and Aligoté and more plentiful red Burgundy, almost all of which (even the humblest Bourgogne Rouge) is grown on hillsides in temperatures that are surprisingly a little lower than those of more northerly villages.

Today, there is a keen local *Chanteflûtage* tasting to compete with the Côte d'Or's *Tastevinage,* and talk of a 'Côte Cha-lonnaise' appellation for the humbler wines with no village to their name. For the moment, this is still bargain territory.

The Côte Chalonnaise begins just outside the small town of Chagny, where well-heeled gastronomes can enjoy one of the best meals in France at the three-star Lameloise restaurant. Among the wines on offer there is a selection from the village of Bouzeron, a few windy miles further south.

The Aligoté, Burgundy's second white grape, isn't allowed to go into any wine sold under a village appellation except here, because, since 1979, thanks to the quality of the climate or soil, growers in Bouzeron can sell Bourgogne Aligoté de Bouzeron. It's a perfect place to discover how good this light, lemony variety can be – particularly when vinified by Aubert de Villaine who, when not making this and good, plain Bour-gogne Rouge and Blanc at his home in Bouzeron, is busily overseeing his 50% share of the Domaine de la Romanée- Conti.

Rully is not so much little-known as almost unknown outside the region. Which is a pity, because this village – whose vines were planted by the Romans – makes Chablis-like Chardonnay, pleasantly plummy and rather 'pretty' Pinot Noir and a large quantity of good Crémant de Bourgogne sparkling wine that all sells for – by Burgundian standards – low prices.

Rully's wines used to be sold under the name of the far larger, more southerly commune of Mercurey. The historic cre-dentials of this quiet town are confirmed by the presence of a Roman temple dedicated to the messenger of the gods from whom it took its name.

It was traditionally said that there were three types of Mer-curey: for masters, for servants and for washing horses' hooves – and until recently, the masters took little interest in it. Today, however, it is increasingly acknowledged that the tiny quantity of this buttery white can compete with Meursault, while the beefier red can put some Pommard to shame.

Givry used to be thought the equal of wines from the Côte d'Or. Well, perhaps... Its jammy, easy-drinking reds *can* match some of the less exciting stuff from Pernand-Vergelesses, but

it's a far cry from Beaune or Volnay – but then again, so's the price. There is a tiny amount of white wine made; for the most part, nutty, up-market Bourgogne Blanc

For good white, travel a little further to Montagny where they make nothing else. Of at least basic Chablis quality, though with a slightly nuttier, more buttery richness, this is another good buy. But don't get taken in by the words 'Premier Cru' on the label; they only indicate a higher natural alcohol level.

Montagny is the southernmost appellation of the Côte Cha-lonnaise, but in the unrecognised village of Buxy, the coopera-tive produces large quantities of good Bourgogne Rouge, in-cluding some that has been matured in new oak.

The Mâconnais

The region of Mâcon has one of the longest-established wine traditions in Burgundy – Ausonius, the Roman poet who was born in Bordeaux, wrote about it in the 4th century and, in 1660, a grower called Claude Brosse travelled to Versailles and introduced it to the court. Brosse, it is said, was a giant who was noticed by the king when, because of his height, he appeared not to be kneeling during a church service.

In Brosse's day – and even in the last century – the region was thrice as big as it is today. Now, it's very varied in its agriculture; the savage hill of Solutré over which primitive man chased hundreds of horses in religious ritual are now inhabited by goats and creamy-white Charolais cattle. The main style here used to be dull red, made from the Gamay, but without using the *macération carbonique* technique. Today, however, two-

thirds of the vineyards have been given over to Chardonnay. Mâcon Blanc and the rather better Mâcon-Villages are many people's idea of affordable white Burgundy. Both these wines can be perfectly pleasant but, made in large quantities by 15 cooperatives, they are rarely exciting – and they still cost Burgundian prices.

The best bet round here is to look for Mâcons from communes such as Clessé, Lugny, Prissé and Viré and Chardonnay (the last thought to be the grape's birthplace), which can tack their names onto the Mâcon appellation.

The wines of St-Véran *should* be a cut above these Mâcon villages, but I wouldn't bet on it. A new appellation, created as an alternative for wines otherwise eligible to call themselves Beaujolais Blanc, this is often seen as a cheaper alternative to Pouilly-Fuissé. It *can* outclass poor Pouilly-Fuissé, but can't compete with one that's half-way good.

Pouilly-Fuissé's problem (the inhabitants wouldn't call it a problem) is its inexplicable ease of pronunciation by Anglo-Saxons. At its best, made and oak-aged at the Château Fuissé or Domaine Ferret, its wines do deserve their international fame and Meursault-level prices; they can be wonderfully ripe, at once peachy and nuttily spicy – and quite 'serious'. Far too much is, however, made in bulk to be sold to people who don't notice that they are paying through the nose for stuff that tastes no better than Mâcon-Villages.

Bargain hunters are often pointed towards the wines of Pouilly-Vinzelles and Pouilly-Loché, but the harvest of both appellations is unambitiously vinified by the Loché cooperative and sold as Pouilly-Vinzelles whichever commune the grapes come from. The style and quality is like that of St-Véran.

BELOW: The village of Fuissé, surrounded by the vineyards of Pouilly-Fuissé, the finest wine of the Mâconnais

Suprèmes de Volaille a l'Epinard et au Fromage

Chicken breasts stuffed with spinach and cheese

The lighter meats that go so well with Beaujolais are also suitable for the wines of the Mâconnais. Ham, veal and chicken are equally good with either the whites or the reds.

SERVES 4

*8 oz/225 g fresh spinach, washed and stemmed, or an equal
weight of frozen leaf spinach
2 tbsp double cream
Salt and freshly ground black pepper
4 chicken breasts, beaten flat to an even
thickness of about ¼ in/5 mm
4 slices of Gruyère or Emmenthal cheese, cut to the size of the
flattened chicken breasts
1 oz/25 g butter*

In a large saucepan, steam the fresh spinach with only the water remaining on its leaves from washing until it is just wilted (if using frozen, heat thoroughly until most of the moisture is evaporated). Squeeze it as dry as possible and chop. Combine it with the cream and season with salt and pepper. Divide the spinach mixture equally between the chicken breasts and spread in an even layer. Place a slice of cheese on top and roll up the breasts, securing each one with a wooden toothpick. In a frying pan, heat the butter until the foam subsides and cook the breasts, turning occasionally, for about 12 minutes, or until they are browned and cooked through. Serve with whole baked tomatoes, first coated with olive oil and rolled in dried thyme.

THE ESSENTIALS — SOUTHERN BURGUNDY

Location Between Beaune and Lyon.

Quality AOCs· Crémant de Bourgogne, Bourgogne Passetoutgrains; Bourgogne Aligoté de Bouzeron; Givry; Mercurey; Montagny; Mâcon; Mâcon-Villages; Mâcon + village name (may be used by 42 specified villages, e.g. Mâcon-Viré, Mâcon-Lugny, Mâcon-Clessé); Pouilly-Fuissé; Pouilly-Loché; Pouilly-Vinzelles; St-Véran; Rully.

Style Dry whites are soft, but with good acidity, and can achieve a fair degree of richness in good years or in the hands of the right producer. For example, the intense, richly-flavoured Château Fuissé Vieilles Vignes, with its delicious creamy-vanilla and honey aromas, can match many whites from the Côte d'Or. Virtually no sweet white is produced, though Jean Thevenet has made small quantities of a botrytised white at Mâcon in hot years. Reds are – at best – generally light-bodied with soft raspberry fruit; white Mâcons from named villages have greater depth and complexity and should, but often do not, offer excellent value.

Climate Drier than the Côte d'Or, these more southerly regions enjoy some Mediterranean influences.

Cultivation Gentle rolling hills with clay, alluvial and iron deposits covering a limestone subsoil. All the red vines of the Côte Chalonnaise are planted on hillsides.

Grape Varieties Pinot Noir, Gamay, Aligoté and Chardonnay.

Production/Maturation Similar to the Côte de Beaune in that the very top whites are barrel-fermented. Most, though, are fermented in stainless steel and bottled early to retain acidity and freshness. Reds are vinified using the *macération carbonique* technique.

Longevity *Whites:* Mâcon-Villages and lesser wines: up to 4 years. Montagny, Mercurey, Rully, Pouilly Fuissé: 4 to 12 years. *Reds:* Mâcon-Villages and lesser wines: up to 6 years. Mercurey, Rully, Mercurey *premiers crus:* 5 to 15 years.

Vintage Guide Reds 78, 80, 82, 83, 85, 88
Whites 78, 79, 81, 83, 85, 86, 88

Top Producers *Mercurey:* Faiveley. *Aligoté de Bouzeron:* A & P Villaine. *Mâconnais/Côte Chalonnaise:* Jean Thevenet, Andre Bonhomme, Henri Goyard, Château de Viré, Marcel Vincent, Domaine Ferret.

BEAUJOLAIS

There's one sure-fire way of telling whether a person is a wine snob – just ask them what they think of Beaujolais. If their nose turns up by as much as a millimetre, you know that you're talking to a label-lover, to someone who cares more about what the wine is called than about the way it tastes. Because that's what Beaujolais – and most especially Beaujolais Nouveau, the target of some of the sniffiest disdain – is all about: taste. It's quite simply the tastiest, fruitiest red wine of them all, wine for gulping back by the chilled glassful and enjoying without snobbery or inhibitions.

But Beaujolais has been misunderstood for a long time. For over 200 years, from the time vines were first planted on the gentle hills of this region in the 17th century, this was a wine that rarely saw a bottle; it was driven up to Lyon in a cart and shipped up to Paris by river and canal, to be drawn directly from the barrel and served from jugs over the zinc-topped bars of cafés in both cities.

It was when it reached other countries that Beaujolais was found wanting; this purple-red cherry juice was nothing like what British, Belgian and Dutch wine drinkers thought of as 'real' wine. It wasn't alcoholic enough, it was too vibrantly fruity, and its colour was wrong.

So, they – or the merchants from whom they were buying the Beaujolais – turned it into 'real' wine, quite simply by dosing it up with a good dollop of red from North Africa or the Rhône. Served at room temperature, from a bottle with a label, Beaujolais became just another soft, anonymous red.

Its producers, proud of their wine, quite naturally took exception to this 'everyday' image. In the 1960s, the drum-beats of revolution were heard when the winemakers, cooperatives and merchants of the region, led by pioneers like Georges Duboeuf, began to take control of their wine – and their destiny.

For many people, it took some time to get used to the new style, and to the idea that it was, and still is, best drunk young and chilled. It is quite possible that the flavour would never have really caught on, but for the invention of a marvellous marketing gimmick: Beaujolais Nouveau.

Taking advantage of an old rule that banned the sale of Beaujolais before midnight on the 14th November following the harvest, one of Beaune's top merchants, a British newspaper and a huge number of keen enthusiasts created an annual race to get the new wine back to London.

The race no longer exists in its original hell-for-leather, no-holds-barred form and the wine is now released at midnight on the third Wednesday of November (thus saving customs officers paperwork at weekends), but Beaujolais Nouveau has become the most successful trend of all. More than one bottle in two of the wine labelled as Beaujolais is now sold as Nouveau and drunk by New Year's Eve.

The Styles

Beaujolais is the basic stuff, well over half of which is sold within weeks of the harvest as Beaujolais Nouveau or Primeur, which is exactly the same as any other kind of Beaujolais but made to be ready to drink early. After New Year's Eve, wine merchants and producers can legally relabel any unsold Nouveau or Primeur as plain Beaujolais. Wines labelled Beaujolais-Villages come from vineyards surrounding a select group of better-sited communes; they are usually worth their slightly higher price. Some Beaujolais-Villages Nouveau is also made and this, too, is usually a cut above plain Nouveau.

Beaujolais Blanc is very rare – for the simple reason that most is quite legally sold as St-Véran. Whatever the label, this is pleasant Chardonnay; a tad better than most Mâcon-Villages.

The Cru Villages

These ten communes make better wine than the Beaujolais villages further north. There are no *premiers crus* within these communes, but there are quite certainly vineyards with their own characteristics; just compare a Fleurie La Madone with one from the Pointe du Jour.

Similarly, winemaking styles vary, from wines that are light, fruity and made for immediate consumption, to fuller-bodied, longer-vatted, traditionally-fermented wines which seem to want to be taken as seriously as Burgundy.

Chiroubles is the classically the lightest Beaujolais *cru* and the one to offer at any blind tasting as the best example of what young Beaujolais is supposed to be. But drink it young. Wonderfully named, Fleurie really can smell and taste the way

Top: The La Madone vineyard is one of the best in the village of Fleurie. Below: Georges Duboeuf, the 'king of the Beaujolais' and his son Franck watch over a vat of busily fermenting grapes

you'd imagine a wine made from a bowlful of flowers immersed in plenty of cherry juice.

Another glorious name – taken from that of a Roman centurion is St Amour, as romantic as it sounds, though it's a suprisingly little known *cru*.

Brouilly's a little less exciting – up-market Beaujolais Villages sold at Beaujolais *cru* prices. The vineyards are too big, too flat and too far south to compete with the best. Better spend a (usually very) little more on Côte de Brouilly, produced on the volcanic hillside in the middle of the Brouilly vines; it's just as fruity, but richer and longer lasting.

Regnié is controversial because it was only recently promoted to *cru* status. Some examples do support its case for promotion; more taste like good Beaujolais-Villages, the label under which it was previously sold. Chénas has never been an easy sale – indeed much of the small amount of wine made here has, in the past, legally been sold by Beaune merchants as Bourgogne Rouge. Its style is – for a Beaujolais – rather tough, particularly when young.

Juliénas isn't immediately seductive but, like Chénas, can be an ugly duckling that needs three years or so to develop into a splendid swan.

There isn't a village of Moulin à Vent, but there is still a windmill. The vineyards make some of the richest, most 'serious' wines in the region. Drink a bottle at two or three years old and you'll enjoy its cherryish, chocolatey flavour.

Another 'big' Beaujolais, Morgon, has even given its name to a verb – *morgonner* – which describes the way the wine develops a cherryish flavour that, with time, really does vaguely resemble wine from the Côte de Nuits.

Just to the south of the Beaujolais, there are the Coteaux du Lyonnais, which produce lightweight versions of that region's wines and some pleasant, fruity rosé.

Jambon à la Crème de Bourgogne

Ham in a cream and mushroom sauce

The fruity tang of a chilled glass of young Beaujolais goes particularly well with the ham and cream combination of this simple and absolutely delicious Burgundian dish.

SERVES 4
4 good thick slices of cooked ham
SAUCE
1 medium onion, minced
2 juniper berries, crushed
6 tbsp white wine vinegar
2 tbsp butter
2 tbsp plain flour
10 fl oz/275 ml chicken stock, heated
8 tbsp dry white wine
2 oz/50 g mushrooms, thinly sliced
Salt and freshly ground black pepper
10 fl oz/275 ml double cream
2 tbsp dried breadcrumbs
Knob of butter

Put the ham slices into a shallow ovenproof dish. In a saucepan, simmer the onions and juniper berries in the wine vinegar until the liquid has evaporated. Remove from the heat. In another pan, melt the butter and stir in the flour, cooking gently and stirring until the mixture just begins to brown. Gradually pour in the stock, little by little, stirring constantly. Add the wine, the onion and juniper berries and the mushrooms and cook over a low heat, stirring occasionally, for 30 minutes. In a small saucepan, bring the cream to the boil and remove from heat. Add the knob of butter and stir. Add the cream to the sauce, stir and pour over the ham. Sprinkle with breadcrumbs and grill until golden brown. Serve with boiled new potatoes and young peas.

THE ESSENTIALS — BEAUJOLAIS

Location The most southerly part of Burgundy, Beaujolais is in fact in the Rhône *département*.
Quality AOCs: Beaujolais; Beaujolais Supérieur; Beaujolais-Villages; Coteaux du Lyonnais. There are 10 named *cru* villages — Brouilly; Chénas; Chiroubles; Côte de Brouilly; Fleurie; Juliénas; Morgon; Moulin-à-Vent; Regnié; St Amour.
Style Reds are soft, full of attractive, juicy raspberry fruit with smooth, supple character and fresh acidity. Generic Beaujolais, made by the *macération carbonique* method, has a characteristic 'pear-drop' aroma. *Cru* wines are firmer, more complex and compact. White Beaujolais is rare; the best — often sold as St-Véran — is dry and peachy.
Climate A temperate continental climate with temperatures and rainfall that are ideal for winegrowing, although the influence of the Mediterranean leads to the occasional storm and problematic hail.
Cultivation Traditional, on rolling hills of granite-based soils. Vines are 'spur-trained' (following a single main branch) for plain Beaujolais; Villages and *cru* vines follow the 'gobelet' (bush) pattern and the fruit is generally hand-harvested.
Grape Varieties The dominant red grape is the Gamay; Pinot Noir may be used in *cru* wines. Whites are from the Chardonnay.
Production/Maturation The *macération carbonique* method is widely used although *cru* Beaujolais producers frequently employ traditional vinification methods. New oak is rarely used except for the best wines.
Longevity Generic Beaujolais — including Nouveau — is intended for early consumption (within 2 years). *Crus* are capable of ageing for up to 10 years — up to 20 years in great vintages like 1983 and 1985 — and with age, these wines become more Burgundian in style.
Vintage Guide 83, 85, 88, 89
Top Producers Georges Duboeuf, Loron, Louis Tête, Château des Jacques, Jacques Depagneux, Chanut, Ferraud, Sylvain Fessy, Eventail, André Large, Jean Garlon.

MUSCADET

If someone were handing out prizes for Most Half-Understood Region in France, the Loire would get my nomination. How many diners in smart London restaurants, ordering an obligatory Sancerre to go with their monkfish, know that they could have had the pigeon instead – and washed it down with a *red* Sancerre, made from the same grape as Nuits-St-Georges? How many Nouveau fans realise that there are winemakers in the Loire using the Gamay to make red wines that could make some Beaujolais blush? How many restaurateurs offer sweet white Loires as comparable alternatives to their Sauternes.

The best way to explore the Loire is to get in a car at Nantes in Muscadet country, and to head along the river towards Sancerre. At the end of a long and somewhat tortuous journey, you'd have tasted wines made from the Chardonnay, the improbably-named Melon de Bourgogne, the Chenin Blanc, the Sauvignon Blanc, the Pinot Noir, the Gamay, the Cabernet Franc and the Malbec. In other words, you'd have discovered wines that are directly related to Champagne, to red and white Burgundy, to Bordeaux and Cahors, but all with their own distinctive styles. Some, like most of the Muscadet produced

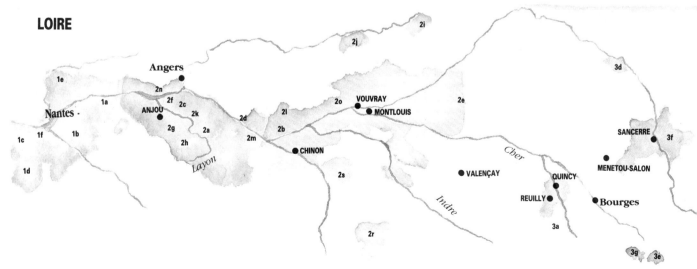

LOIRE

nowadays, are wines to be taken more or less for granted; others, like Savennières and dry Vouvray can be among the most exciting – and demanding – in the world.

Muscadet

If Muscadet has a red cousin, it has to be Beaujolais. Both are light, easy-going and perfect to drink within a few months of the harvest, and they've both come a long way from where they started out. A hundred years ago neither wine would have found its way into a bottle; Muscadet's the stuff Brittany fishermen and poor Montmartre artists would have been given by the jugful as basic 'house white'.

Since then, like Beaujolais, Muscadet has become an international star. Sometimes it's difficult to understand why. New Beaujolais tastes of a bowlful of fresh fruit, while Muscadet tastes of... well, it's rather difficult to define precisely what it does taste of. Eventually, it is all too easy to fall back on the description of it as prototypical 'dry white wine'.

But Muscadet matured in a certain way can have its own, distinctive flavour. Most newly-fermented white wine is removed from its lees – solid yeasts – as quickly as possible; good, typical Muscadet is left to sit for several months on this yeast, picking up a nutty, biscuity flavour and a slight fizz in the process. Unfortunately, there are rather more bottles of Muscadet which claim to have been *mis en bouteilles sur lie* – bottled on their lees – than have the biscuity flavour those words theoretically ought to promise.

Like Beaujolais, there are a few key villages that make better, more characterful wine than the surrounding area. Unlike Beaujolais, they don't feature helpfully on the labels. So, as elsewhere in France, it is essential to look for the name of the producer. And if you're just looking for a pleasant, dry white to wash down your seafood, you could always save a few francs by buying the Nantes region's lesser white, Gros Plant. This bone-dry VDQS, made from the Folle Blanche, is generally even less fruity than the Muscadet. When well made *sur lie*, however it can give some Muscadets a run for their money.

Other regional VDQS wines include the light red, rosé and white Coteaux d'Ancenis, often made from the Gamay, the Pinot Gris (here called the Malvoisie) and the Chenin Blanc (or Pineau de la Loire), and the Fiefs Vendéens, with its attractive dry rosé, Cabernet-influenced red and less dazzling dry white.

LEFT: The secret of Muscadet 'sur lie' revealed by a special barrel in which one can see the yeasts at the bottom of the cask. Many Muscadet properties mount this kind of display for interested visitors

1 Western Loire			
1a	Coteaux d'Ancenis	2l	St-Nicolas-de-Bourgueil
1b	Fiefs Vendéens	2m	Saumur-Champigny
1c	Gros Plant du Pays Nantais	2n	Savennières / Savennières
1d	Muscadet		Coulée-de-Serrant / Savennières
1e	Muscadet des Coteaux de la Loire		la Roche-aux-Moines
1f	Muscadet de Sèvre-et-Maine	2o	Touraine (Mesland, Amboise,
			Azay-le-Rideau)
2 Central: Anjou/Touraine		2p	Vins du Haut Poitou
(See also appellations on map)		2r	Vins de l'Orléanais
2a	Bonnezeaux	2s	Vins du Thouarsais
2b	Bourgueil		
2c	Cabernet d'Anjou	**3 Upper Loire**	
2d	Cabernet de Saumur	*(See also appellations on map)*	
2e	Cheverny	3a	Châteaumeillant
2f	Coteaux de l'Aubance	3b	Côtes d'Auvergne
2g	Coteaux du Layon	3c	Côtes du Forez
2h	Coteaux du Layon Villages	3d	Côteaux du Giennois
2i	Coteaux du Vendômois	3e	Côtes Roannaises
Crémant de Loire *(throughout the region)*		3f	Pouilly-Fumé
2j	Jasnières	3g	St-Pourçain
2k	Quarts-de-Chaume		
Rosé de Loire *(throughout the region)*			

Mussels a l'Armoricaine
Mussels in an onion and tomato sauce

The wine grown here, around the estuary of the Loire as it enters the Atlantic, was made for shellfish, especially oysters. But if you cannot get oysters, this recipe for mussels complements these crisp white wines beautifully.

SERVES 4 AS A MAIN COURSE
6½ lb/3 kg mussels
2 oz/50 g butter
1 medium onion, coarsely chopped
3 large tomatoes, seeded, peeled and chopped or a 16 oz/500 g
tin of tomatoes, drained and chopped
Freshly ground black pepper

Scrub the mussels and remove the small blackish tassle (the 'beard'). Soak in frequent changes of clean cold water for several hours, discarding any which have opened or are cracked or broken. Melt the butter in a large heavy-bottomed pan. Sauté the onion until it is transparent. Add the tomatoes and the mussels. Cook covered, shaking the pan occasionally, until the mussels have opened (discard any that do not open). Season with pepper and serve, perhaps with crusty French bread and a green salad.

OAKED MUSCADET

At the Château de Chasseloir, the domaine Cherau-Carré has proved that good Muscadet can taste even better with a little ageing in oak. Other producers complain that Muscadet and oak don't mix. The debate between the two camps is fierce.

THE ESSENTIALS — MUSCADET

Location The Pays Nantais; a 40km sweep around Nantes encompassing the Loire estuary.
Quality AOCs are: Muscadet; Muscadet de Sèvre et Maine; Muscadet des Coteaux de la Loire. All may be bottled, and bear the designation, *sur lie*. VDQSs are: Gros Plant du Pays Nantais, Coteaux d'Ancenis and Fiefs Vendéens.
Style Whites are crisp and dry, light-bodied and modestly fruity, occasionally slightly *pétillant*. The best are bone-dry (but not tart), lemony and fresh. *Sur lie* wines have a yeasty, more complex character and are generally better; Muscadet de Sèvre et Maine should be better than straight Muscadet. Coteaux d'Ancenis and Fiefs Vendéens reds and rosés are dry, light-to-medium-bodied, lively and often grassy.
Climate Maritime.
Cultivation On the flat land around Nantes mechanical harvesting has been introduced with ease. The vineyard area stretches away to the gentle Sèvre-et-Maine hills; soils are mainly sandy overlying schist and volcanic subsoils.
Grape Varieties Primarily the white Muscadet (Melon de Bourgogne) and Folle Blanche (Gros Plant). Coteaux d'Ancenis and the Fiefs Vendéens use a mix of Loire and classic Bordeaux and Burgundian varieties for reds, rosés and whites.
Production/Maturation Stainless steel is increasingly used for fermentation. *Sur lie* wines are aged on their lees – yeasts – until, traditionally, the February 15 following the harvest; the process by which the yeasts affect the wine's character is known as *autolysis*. Bottling is direct from the tank; new oak is very occasionally found.
Longevity Most of these wines are best young or in their first two years. A very few producers make Muscadet in good years which can age very well for up to 10 years, more to show that they can do it than from commercial motives.
Vintage Guide 88, 89
Top producers Sauvion et Fils, Donatien Bahuaud, Luneau, Chéreau-Carré, Louis Métaireau, Marquis de Goulaine.

THE MIDDLE LOIRE

Anjou

Following the river Loire eastwards through a vinous no-man's-land surrounding the village of Ancenis, within a few miles you will be deep in the heart of one of the most abused wine appellations in France – Anjou, the area that helped to give the colour pink such a bad name that the Californians had to try selling their rosé as 'blush'.

In fact, Anjou Rosé is also a relatively modern invention, created earlier this century by winemakers who found they were unable to sell their dry red wines.

In the Loire, though, the change of style must have come as a shock to those used to the red and white wines Anjou had been producing for nearly 2,000 years. In the 16th and 17th century the Dutch had developed a taste for the region's sweet whites. As buyers, they were evidently more quality-conscious than some of today's customers for Anjou Rosé; in those days, the region's wines were divided into *vins pour la mer* (the stuff that was considered good enough for foreigners) and *vins pour Paris* (the dregs, kept back for the easy-going domestic market). Some examples of Anjou Rosé can be decent, but even these are handicapped by being largely – and often poorly – made from the intrinsically dull Groslot grape. Pay a few pennies more for a Rosé de Loire, which has to contain at least 30% of Bordeaux's Cabernet Franc and (to a far lesser extent) Cabernet Sauvignon, the pure Cabernet d'Anjou, or the slightly lighter Cabernet de Saumur from just along the river. At their best, these pink wines are crunchily blackcurranty, as is Anjou Rouge when it is made from the Cabernet varieties. When Anjou Rouge is made from the Gamay, however, and by the same method as Beaujolais, the effort to match that more southerly wine rarely quite works – because neither climate nor soil suit the grape so well here.

When well made by *domaines* like Richou and caught young, they can, however, be fruitily enjoyable, with flavours of raspberries and ripe redcurrants. For the best examples of all, look for Anjou-Villages, which can only be made from the Cabernets and can taste like good summer-picnic claret.

From Pink To White

Anjou Blanc, by contrast, provides a good introduction to the often difficult character of the Chenin Blanc, a grape that fails to ripen in any but the warmest years and best sites and which, even then, can produce wines with either tooth-scaling acidity or a dull nuttiness that is the opposite of refreshing. Throughout the region, modern winemakers are learning to work with the Chenin, allowing the skins to remain in contact with the juice before fermentation or, in Anjou, adding a proportion of Chardonnay or Sauvignon Blanc to the blend. These wines range from bone-dry to lusciously sweet; they can be inexpen-

---

HONEY, NUTS AND APPLE

If the Chenin Blanc were only used to make dry wine, it would probably have been relegated to the ranks of 'potentially good but difficult' varieties, along with such other non-household names as the Marsanne and Arneis. It certainly wouldn't feature among the world's greats. The trouble with it lies in its peculiar combination of nuts and honey and the biting acidity of unripe apples that can either strip the teeth of their enamel or, paradoxically, be just plain dull.

In good examples, however, the balance of these conflicting flavours can produce some of the most extraordinary sweet wines in the world. Everything depends on the ripeness of the vintage and the skill of the winemaker.

LEFT: The inhabitants of Vouvray – or some at least – still live in 'caves' burrowed into the chalky cliffs here. More energetic tunnelling has traditionally provided the winemakers with ideally cool cellars in which to store their maturing bottles

RIGHT: A great deal of Vouvray is still made by small, individual producers

sive, fresh and clean tasting and a good showcase for the Chenin hallmarks of apple and honey. Pure Chenin Blancs of slightly higher quality are labelled Anjou Coteaux de la Loire; these can be good, cheaper alternatives to Vouvray. Most need drinking young, but exceptions like the ones made (in suprisingly large quantities) by Moulin Touchais should be left until they are at least 10 years old – the age at which they are sold.

For top-class sweet wines, though, turn your back on the Loire and visit a set of villages that face each other across the river Layon, surrounded by vineyards that produce rich, honeyed, semi-sweet-to-luscious Chenin appropriately called Coteaux du Layon. The best of these villages, Rochefort-sur-Loire, has a micro-climate that allows the grapes to ripen almost every year, and sometimes to develop noble rot, thus producing a pair of more intense wines: Coteaux du Layon Chaume and Quarts de Chaume, which latter owes its name to the local lord who used to extort a quarter of the tiny harvests.

At their best, these wines are at once apricotty, rich and floral, with a suprisingly attractive hint of zesty bitterness; they can keep for at least 10 – more like 20 – years. Bonnezeaux, though often as well thought of, is rarely quite as good. The few great examples, however, are extraordinary honey-and-spice cocktails that last for decades.

For a lower price than any of these, and built on a lighter scale, Coteaux de l'Aubance provides good, cellarable demi-sec Chenin Blanc – but in small and diminishing quantities.

The sweet style of these wines was once shared by Savennières which is now made dry or demi-sec. It's 'difficult' wine that can often taste bitterly like unripe limes until it has been given a decade or so to soften; of 15 producers, only five survive by making and selling wine alone. One of these, Madame Joly, proves what can be done here with her fruit-and-flower, dry-Sauternes-like Grand Cru Coulée de Serrant, which slightly outclasses Savennières' other Grand Cru, La Roche aux Moines.

Saumur

Saumur once enjoyed the same prestige as Vouvray, but today neither the white nor the red produced under this appellation is inspiring, and sparkling wine has become the focus of attention. Links with Champagne go back to 1811, when a winemaker called Jean Ackerman, who had worked there, decided to use its techniques on grapes grown in the similarly

---

THE ESSENTIALS — THE MIDDLE LOIRE

Location Surrounding the Loire river and its tributaries, particularly the Cher, largely between Angers and Tours.
Quality AOCs: Anjou; Anjou Coteaux de la Loire; Anjou Gamay; Anjou Mousseux; Cabernet d'Anjou and Cabernet d'Anjou-Val-de-Loire; Rosé d'Anjou and Rosé d'Anjou Pétillant; Bonnezeaux; Bourgueil; Chinon; Coteaux de l'Aubance; Coteaux du Loir; Coteaux du Layon and Coteaux du Layon-Chaume; Crémant de Loire; Jasnières; Montlouis; sparkling Montlouis; Quarts de Chaume; Rosé de Loire; Saumur; Saumur Champigny; sparkling Saumur; Cabernet de Saumur; Coteaux de Saumur; Savennières; Savennières-Coulée-de-Serrant and Savennières-Roche-aux-Moines; St-Nicolas-de-Bourgueil; Touraine; Touraine-Amboise; Touraine-Azay-le-Rideau; Touraine-Mesland; sparkling Touraine; Vouvray; sparkling Vouvray. VDQSs are: Cheverny; Coteaux du Vendômois; Valençay; Vins du Haut Poitou; Vin du Thouarsais. *Vin de pays*: du Jardin de la France.
Style The Cabernet Franc produces cool reds which have clean, blackcurrant fruit and an appealing herbaceous freshness. The best are undoubtedly Chinon, Bourgueil and Saumur-Champigny. Though pleasant when young, these tend to need ageing to lose their early earthiness. The dry and medium white wines are generally light, fresh and for early consumption. Savennières and Jasnières have a stark acidity in youth but open out with age into rich and honeyed, yet still dry wines; Vouvray, Quarts de Chaume and Bonnezeaux are the best sweet styles, and again need ageing, often lasting for decades. Rosés, both dry and medium, can be appealing and very fruity, though many are over-sweetened and dull. The best sparkling wines — Saumur, Vouvray and Crémant de Loire — are soft and approachable but with good acidity.
Climate Influenced by the Atlantic, though less maritime than Muscadet. Warm summers and autumns and little rain.
Cultivation Crammed between fields full of other crops in this agricultural region, the best sites are south-facing on gentle slopes or terraced on steeper slopes, as in the schist soils of the Layon valley. Elsewhere, soils vary from chalk to clay overlying sand and gravel.
Grape Varieties Arbois, Aligoté, Cabernet Franc, Cabernet Sauvignon, Chambourcin, Chenin Blanc (Pineau de la Loire), Chardonnay, Gamay, Grolleau/Groslot, Gros Plant, Malbec, Meslier, Pineau d'Aunis, Pinot Blanc, Pinot Gris, Pinot Meunier, Pinot Noir, Plantet, Romorantin, Sauvignon Blanc.
Production/Maturation Though old wood is still used for fermentation and maturation, stainless steel and new oak are becoming more common. To make Bonnezeaux and Quarts de Chaume, Chenin grapes are left on the vines until late October to await noble rot. Fermentation takes at least 3 months and the wines are bottled the following October.
Longevity Lesser reds, dry and medium whites and rosés should be drunk within 3 years. Chinon, Bourgueil and St-Nicolas-de-Bourgueil will last at least 5 years. Sweet Bonnezeaux, Chaume and Layon and the dry Savennières and Jasnières will develop over a decade and beyond.
Vintage Guide 83, 85, 86, 88, 89.
Top Producers Clos de la Coulée-de-Serrant, Château Chamboreau, Château de la Roulerie, Ammeux Taluau, Raffault, Château de Bellerive, Moulin-Touchais, Couly, Richou.

The modest and little-known VDQS, Vin du Thouarsais, similar in style to basic Anjou, but slightly cheaper, certainly deserves a backward glance as one crosses the frontier into the next of the Loire's major regions.

Touraine

If Touraine had no other claim to vinous fame, it would have been sure of a place in the history books because it was here that, according to local legend, St Martin invented vine-pruning, after discovering that he made better wine from vines that had been partially nibbled away by his donkey.

Today, the region owes much of the success of its blanket appellation to the Oisly et Thesée cooperative whose *directeur*, Jacques Choquet, took the rare and brave step of enforcing a quality test for his member-growers' grapes. His audacity was all the more impressive given the ever-present financial temptations to the producers to uproot their vines and replace them with other crops. Oisly et Thesee Sauvignon and Chenin (here called Pineau de la Loire) are among the most reliably affordable whites in the region, and the blended reds are also worthwhile, thanks to the way in which the Cabernet is allowed to make up for the failings of the Malbec (here known as the Cot) and the Gamay. Experiments with Pinot Noir andsparkling wine are interesting too.

The Touraine vineyards cover around a tenth of the land they would have occupied a century or so ago. It is a striking polyculture, with easy-to-grow, easy-to-sell strawberries, sunflowers, asparagus and wheat all competing for space on level terms with vines. From a distance, the layers of gold, yellow and

The red wine vineyards of Chinon surround the ruins of the old castle; these belong to Couly, one of the best producers in the appellation

BELOW: The castle of Langlois–Château, one of the best sparkling producers in Saumur. OPPOSITE: Modern marketing methods in Bourgueil.

chalky soil of his native Saumur. His wine was sold as Champagne; today the rules are stricter, yet Champagne houses like Bollinger, Taittinger and Alfred Gratien all own sparkling Saumur houses here, making fizz labelled until very recently with the now-banned words 'Méthode Champenoise'.

Even at its best, sparkling Saumur never really matches even the most modestly successful of Champagnes, largely because the Chenin Blanc and the red Cabernet grapes simply aren't as good at the job as the Chardonnay and Pinots. On the other hand, the quality is rarely less than adequate, thanks to the combination of the Chenin, the chalky soil and the cool(ish) climate. Coteaux de Saumur, Saumur's appellation for its sweet wines, was once the priciest in the Loire, partly thanks to the enthusiasm of Edward VII, a loyal customer, and partly to the reputation of the curious Clos des Murs, a set of 11 100-metre-long walls along which vines were trained to obtain as much sheltered sunshine as possible. Today, sadly, examples are very, very rare, but the vineyard is still worth a visit.

Apart from its sparkling and still whites and pinks, Saumur also produces two reds, Saumur Rouge and Saumur Champigny. The former is rarely impressive Cabernet Franc-dominated stuff. Champigny, however, is much classier – either young, or after five years or so (though not between the two) this can be gorgeously crunchy blackcurrant wine. To taste Saumur Champigny at its best, look out for Filliatreau's Vieilles Vignes, made from old vines.

South of Saumur, in stark contrast to the small scale of some of the region's estates, there stands the Loire's biggest modern cooperative, the Cave du Haut Poitou. The success here has been the Sauvignon Blanc, a wine that has on occasion shown the potential to fight its corner against classier and pricier examples from Sancerre and New Zealand. The Chardonnay is less impressive, but there is a reliable *méthode champenoise* sparkling wine.

green crops make the countryside here look like nothing so much as a slice of vegetable terrine. The Touraine appellation – and its three village appellations, Azay-Le-Rideau, Amboise and Mesland – can produce fair to excellent dry and demi-sec Chenin Blanc and, in the case of Amboise, good, fruity Cabernet Franc.

Non-wine-buff visitors to the region are often unknowingly led by their guide books to the source of the Loire's best reds, Chinon. The castle here was, as some readers may remember from the play or film of 'The Lion in Winter'. Almost all of Chinon's wines are red, combining – in ripe years – rich flavours of mulberry, blackberry and blackcurrant, with just a hint of earthiness. There is a little rosé and white, the latter made in a floral-spicy style said to have been popular with Rabelais.

Like Chinon, red Bourgueil is built to last and can take as long as a decade to soften. But in good vintages it's worth waiting for, delivering a real mouthful of wonderfully jammy damson and blackcurrant fruit. St-Nicolas-de-Bourgeuil is usually less impressive, less intense and less long-lived but can be more approachable than Bourgueil when young.

Vouvray

Before my first visit to Vouvray, I had never quite believed in the tales I had heard of the town's community of cave dwellers. But there they were – modern Frenchmen and women who not only make and store wine but live in homes burrowed deep into the sides of cliffs. Of course, these are 20th century troglodytes, with video recorders, shiny new Citroëns and central heating flues channelled up through the chalk, but there is still something deeply traditional about their wines.

Vouvray comes in just about every white style you could want – and several you wouldn't. But whatever they are like – dry (Sec), semi-sweet (Demi-Sec), sweet (Moelleux) or sparkling (Crémant)   they provide an invaluable insight into what the Chenin Blanc is really like. And how difficult it is to get right. The dry style can have all the mean, cooking-apple character of the grape while the Demi-Sec and Moelleux can be respectively honeyed and dull, and sweetly honeyed and dull. At its least successful, semi-sweet Vouvray can make you long for a glass of fairly basic Liebfraumilch.

Then, just as you decide to drive further west to Sancerre, you stop and have lunch at a little roadside restaurant, order a last bottle – and discover what the mayor of the village, Gaston Huet (pronounced 'wet') can do with the Chenin Blanc. Suddenly both wine and grape make sense. His Vouvray Sec has the rich, creamy texture of Chardonnay and the appley bite of the Chenin. His Demi-Sec is beautifully well balanced – sweet but not cloyingly so – and his Moelleux has the luscious intensity of noble rot. All of these, but particularly the Moelleux, are made to last – 'for 50 years or so', as his neighbours in Vouvray say. Huet also makes great sparkling wine. Bubbles are very saleable around here – as the producers of nearby Montlouis have discovered to their delight. Turning their back on the still wines they used to make lighter, less acidic, less long-lived versions of Vouvray – they have switched to sparkling wine, so successfully that of the 4.2 million bottles of Montlouis made every year, only 700,000 come without bubbles.

Having come to terms with dry Chenin Blanc in Vouvray, you could put yourself to a further test in Jasnières, a wine that can be so bitingly acidic in cool years that only a masochist or a drinker with a palate lined with elephant hide could enjoy it. But, in warmer vintages and – this is essential – given a decade or so in the bottle, Jasnières can be one of the most exciting, dry yet honeyed, wines of all.

Of the region's other wines, VDQS Chéverny can be good, lightly floral still and sparkling white, despite the presence in the blend of the 'characterful' Romarantin, which seems to work against the fresh appeal of the Sauvignon, Chenin and Chardonnay with which it shares the vat. Sales are growing fast, though this owes much to buyers' confusing it with Chardonnay.

Rillettes
Potted pork pâté

This land of châteaux and tranquil rivers has often been called the garden of France. Pike, bream, salmon and carp abound in the Loire river and its tributaries. *Andouillette* (a tripe sausage), *boudin de volaille* (a sausage made of chicken breast, truffles and mushrooms) and *rillettes* (a delicious and easily-made country pâté) are just some typical dishes of this beautiful region.

SERVES 8-10 AS A STARTER
2 lb/1 kg belly pork, cut into thick strips
2 juniper berries, crushed
2 garlic cloves, peeled and halved
Bouquet garni sachet, or a bundle made of 1 sprig of rosemary, 2 sprigs parsley and 1 bay leaf tied
together with cotton
Salt and freshly ground black pepper

Put at least ¼ in/5 mm of water into a heavy-bottomed casserole dish. Add the pork, juniper berries, garlic and bouquet garni. Cook, covered, in an oven at 300°F/150°C/Gas mark 2 for 4-5 hours until the meat is very soft. Allow to cool slightly and pour the contents into a sieve over a large bowl. When drained, shred the lean meat off with two forks. Season the meat well with salt and pepper and put into small bowls (individual ramekins are useful). Pour over the reserved juices until the meat is completely covered. Cover each bowl with foil and refrigerate when cool enough. Serve with crusty French bread and gherkins, or as a more substantial lunch dish with crisp green salad and new potatoes.

THE UPPER LOIRE

Leopards do change their spots. For most wine buffs, Sancerre is almost synonymous with the extraordinarily gooseberryish, blackcurranty, asparagussy Sauvignon Blanc. Winemakers from around the world come to this easternmost part of the Loire to look at the chalky soil – or the variety of chalky soils – of Sancerre itself, and of the 14 villages that surround it. And to marvel at the perfect marriage of site, climate and grape.

One hundred years ago they wouldn't have found any Sauvignon at all; what they would have found growing here instead was the dull Chasselas. Taste the old-fashioned Pouilly-sur-Loire, which is still made from this variety, before moving on to the more modern Pouilly-Fumé, which will bring you back to the fruitiness of the Sauvignon.

It is easy to understand how both these communes came to achieve their historic prominence. Sancerre overlooks the whole region, and Pouilly is on the Loire itself. Sancerre is usually thought of as a single appellation; in fact, it's more a collection of 14 villages with slightly differing versions of the same chalky soil, on varying slopes that surround the little hill-top town of Sancerre itself. If Sancerre were Beaujolais, and if the inhabitants of these villages had their way, at least a few if them would be promoted to *cru* status. The strongest contenders for any such promotion are the village of Bué and a cluster of houses called Chavignol, locally famous for its little round goat's cheeses, *crottins de Chavignol,* and for wines which would, it was said by the wine-loving King Henri IV, if drunk by the entire populace, put an instant stop to religious wars. Chavignol's best wines come from its Les Monts Damnés, Clos Beaujeu and Clos du Paradis vineyards; Bué's finest vineyards are the Clos du Chêne Marchand and Le Grand Chemarin. Other villages worth looking out for include Champtin, Sury-en-Vaux, Reigny, Ménétréol and Verdigny.

The wines from any of these should be packed with the same kind of zappy gooseberry fruit as the Sauvignons from New Zealand – but in a less obvious way. The steely backbone to Sancerre should make it easier to drink time after time; some of the simple flavours of those New Zealanders can get a bit boring after a while. But beware. The tangy flavour of the Sauvignon Blanc is not an easy taste for people from warmer climates to acquire; often, they dismiss it as 'vegetal'. Their influence, and a series of warmer vintages, have encouraged Sancerre producers to make softer, fatter versions of their wine. You may like them; I miss the mouth-cleansers.

Sancerre also makes red and rosé wines from the Pinot Noir. The former are pleasant, raspberryish versions of the grape, but woefully overpriced; the latter have much of the style of good, basic Bourgogne Rouge, but with less stuffing.

Down on the Loire itself, the featureless town of Pouilly-sur-Loire has over the years confused countless wine drinkers who can never quite remember that the Pouilly-Fumé it makes from the Sauvignon Blanc has nothing to do with the Pouilly-Fuissé made from the Chardonnay in the quite different village of Pouilly in southern Burgundy. And if this were not confusing enough, the Loire Pouilly also gives its name to dull Chasselas, which still occupies the substantial chunk of the area's vineyards where the soil is unsuitable for the Sauvignon.

The 'Fumé' in Pouilly-Fumé is said to come from the smoky dust from the grapes that hangs over the vineyards during the harvest or, more popularly, from the smoky flavour of the wine. The first explanation is said to be the correct one, but I prefer the latter; these wines really *can* taste as though they have spent a while in a salmon smokery. Some descriptions also refer to

BELOW: The vineyards of Sancerre during the harvest of 1985, beneath a layer of early morning mist

gun-flint and, even without having tasted any, I know what they mean; this character is reckoned to come from the flintier, lighter clay content of some of Pouilly's best slopes. To taste the mixture of smoke and flint at its best, look for wines whose labels mention *silex*, the term for this kind of soil.

Pouilly-Fumé is said to be the Loire Sauvignon with the best potential for ageing – which really means that the wines here develop their flavours of asparagus rather more slowly. Apart from rare exceptions, I prefer to drink this wine, like Sancerre, within three or four years of the harvest.

The best of Pouilly's communes, and the ones you are most likely to see mentioned on labels, are Les Berthiers and Les Loges. For the quintesssence of Pouilly-Fumé, splash out on a bottle of 'Baron de L' from the Baron de Ladoucette's Château de Nozet. And remember that taste the next time you taste a Blanc-Fumé from California or Australia; warm-climate Sauvignon Blanc plus new oak does not equal the sheer complexity of this variety grown in the cooler conditions and the best soil of the Loire.

Reuilly needs your support: its growers have to be encouraged to stop growing vegetables and to turn their attention back to the vines that used to cover this commune. Reuilly's soil is very similar to that of Sancerre or Pouilly-Fumé, and most of the vines are the same variety – the Sauvignon Blanc – so there seems little reason why its wines shouldn't be every bit as fine.

In fact, the slightly greater limestone content here makes for lighter, leaner wines that rarely have the richness of its more famous neighbours. What Reuilly can make, however, is that most unfashionable style, rosé, produced not (as in Sancerre) exclusively from the Pinot Noir, but with a generous dose of the pink-skinned grape known here as the Pinot Beurot and more readily found in Alsace, where it's called the Tokay-Pinot Gris. The small (250 acre/100ha) appellation of Menetou-Salon has the same *terre blanche* soil as Reuilly, and an even longer history; its growers proudly yet wrily point out that Menetou-Salon had its appellation before any of its neighbours. Its best whites are comparable to good – but not great – Sancerre and cost less than that wine; its Pinot Noir reds are disappointing.

Quincy should be inexpensive, ultra-gooseberryish Sauvignon Blanc, grown on the gravelly soil of vineyards overlooking the river Cher. Unfortunately, too few examples are well-enough made; too many taste raw and green, or earthy and dull.

Leaving Pouilly and heading up the river towards Orléans, you pass through the VDQS vineyards of Coteaux du Giennois and Côtes de Gien on either side of the Loire. The pink produced from these grapes can be light and pleasant; the white usually tastes raw and uninteresting. Châteaumeillant's red and pink Gamay is better and the *vin gris* rosé is worth looking out for.

The wines of Orléans itself – the Vins de l'Orléanais – were once thought equal to those of Beaune. Today they are less exhalted but the pale pink Pinot Meunier is a rare treat; the white Auvernat Blanc, however, is unimpressive; this is the local alias for the Chardonnay, though from tasting the wine you'd never guess.

Among the other lesser-known wines in this part of the Loire, the Côtes Roannaises and Côtes du Forez both make easy-going wines from the Gamay. St Pourçain Blanc is a weird blend of Chardonnay, Sauvignon and the oddly smoky Tressalier. It's very dry, and very much an acquired taste. Minuscule quantities of Gamay-Pinot Noir rosé are made too.

Even more obscure, high among the ski slopes of the Massif Central in the Côtes d'Auvergne UDQs, the villages of Châteaugay, Chanturgues, Mandargues and Corent – make fresh white wine from the Chardonnay and light raspberryish rosé from the Gamay. There are two *vins de pays* made nearby: the Coteaux du Cher et l'Arnon, producing Sauvignon Blanc whites and red and pink wines from the Gamay; further east is the exclusively white wine region of the Coteaux Charitois. Quality is rising steadily, but there are yet to be reports of any superstars.

Saumon Roti en Sauce Sancerre
Sautéed salmon steaks in a white wine sauce

Wines from the the eastern limit of the Loire region, especially Sancerre and Pouilly Fumé, go particularly well with the fish from the many tributaries which fan out from the Loire and Cher rivers.

SERVES 4
SAUCE
1 medium onion, finely minced
1½ wine glasses of dry white wine, preferably Sancerre
2 tbsp crème fraîche
4 oz/100 g cold butter, cut into pieces
Salt and freshly ground black pepper

In a small saucepan combine the onion and wine. Bring to the boil then immediately reduce the heat to a simmer until almost all the wine has evaporated. Stir in the crème fraîche and bring to the boil, whisking. Whisk in the butter piece by piece (occasionally lifting the pan off the heat to prevent the sauce líquefying). When all the butter has been used, reduce the heat to warm and season with salt and pepper.

SALMON
4 salmon steaks (about 4 oz/100 g each)
¼ tsp dried thyme
Salt and freshly ground black pepper
2 oz/50 g butter
Parsley sprigs to garnish

Rub the salmon steaks on both sides with the thyme, salt and pepper. Melt the butter in a frying pan and sauté the steaks for about 3 minutes on each side, or until the flesh has just started to flake. Put the steaks on to a warmed serving dish or individual plates and pour over the sauce. Garnish with fresh parsley. Delicious served with boiled potatoes, steamed courgettes and a purée of celery.

THE ESSENTIALS — THE UPPER LOIRE

Location At the eastern end of the Loire Valley towards Burgundy: Sancerre and Pouilly Fumé face each other across the river.
Quality AOCs: Ménétou-Salon; Pouilly Fumé; Pouilly-sur-Loire; Quincy; Reuilly and Sancerre. VDQSs are: Châteaumeillant; Coteaux du Giennois; Côte Roannaise; Côtes d'Auvergne; Côtes du Forez; St-Pourçain-sur-Sioule; Vins d'Orléanais. *Vins de pays*: Coteaux du Cher et l'Arnon; Coteaux Charitois.
Style Classic Sancerre and Pouilly Fumé rank among the most exciting Sauvignons in the world, with a smoky aroma and full of gooseberry and asparagus flavours. Though there are no *grands crus*, certain villages – e.g. Bué, Chavignol, Les Loges, Tracy, Les Berthiers – are noted for quality. Lesser whites may capture a little of this style and are generally crisp, herbaceous and appealing. Pouilly-sur-Loire, a rather ordinary white wine made mostly from the Chasselas grape, is not to be confused with the infinitely better Pouilly Fumé, from the Sauvignon Blanc. Red and rosé wines, from Sancerre in particular, are delicate and cool with rich strawberry fruit.
Climate Continental, with short, hot summers.
Cultivation Soils are mainly chalk and clay with a lot of limestone. The vineyards are on mainly south-facing, often steep slopes, with other crops being grown on the opposite side of the valley. Picking is usually done by hand.
Grape Varieties Aligoté, Cabernet Franc, Chardonnay, Chasselas, Chenin Blanc, Gamay Noir à Jus Blanc, Gamay, Pinot Gris, Pinot Meunier, Pinot Noir, Sauvignon Blanc, Tresallier.
Production/Maturation Stainless steel is widely used although some of the red wines spend up to 18 months in oak.
Longevity Most wines are at their best within 3 years. Although the top wines will continue to develop, they may lose their initial freshness.
Vintage Guide 86, 88
Top Producers Vacheron, Château de Nozet (Ladoucette), Pinard, Jean Vatan, Henri Natter, Domaine H Pelle.

THE RHONE

They always say that the French are a Latin people but, talking to some of the starchily-mannered gentlemen of Bordeaux and Champagne, it's an idea I sometimes find very difficult to accept. And then I arrive back in the Rhône, to the land of terracotta roof tiles, of fresh herbs growing at the roadside, of olive oil and garlic and ripe, tasty tomatoes, and I know I'm in the land of the sun – savage country that must look almost exactly the way it did when the Romans arrived.

The vineyards of the Rhône valley begin in Lyon's southern backyard, and follow the river south almost as far as the Mediterranean. But to talk of the Rhône as though it were a single region is misleading. Like the Loire, the river is more of a link between two very different winemaking areas: the northern and southern Rhône.

The essential differences between the two lie in the grape varieties, and the land in which they are planted. The north, like Burgundy, is a region in which winegrowers use just one kind of black grape – in this case, the smoky, brooding Syrah. With it they produce their long-lived red wines such as Côte-Rôtie, Hermitage and Cornas, and their more approachable but still muscular neighbours, Crozes-Hermitage and St-Joseph.

If the wines are tough, so is making them; the vineyards are some of the most spectacular in the world, rivalling those of the Rhine and Douro in the way they cling to the perilously steep slopes that overlook the river as it snakes its way southwards.

Down south, in the Côtes du Rhône-Villages (the more select area within the broad Côtes du Rhône appellation), Gigondas and Châteauneuf-du-Pape, it is another grape, the peppery, berryish Grenache, that holds sway, but as the captain of a team

that also includes such dazzling players as the Mourvèdre, the Cinsault and, of course, the Syrah.

Here, as in Bordeaux, winemakers have to be as skilled at the art of blending as they are at growing grapes. In some cases, for example in many Côtes du Rhônes, the Grenache is allowed to trumpet its presence in juicy-fruity reds that are almost indecently easy to drink. In Châteauneuf-du-Pape, on the other hand, the blender's art can be taken to absurd lengths, with a total of 13 permitted grapes to choose from. Very few producers use even half this number but, even with three or four to play with, they can make wonderful wine that takes one straight to the spice bazaar.

The flat vineyards of the south are different too, and they're a revelation. Until you see them, you would never believe that vines – or any plants for that matter – could grow in what looks just like the uncomfortable pebbles that cover Britain's least hospitable beaches.

But if the Rhône is best known for characterful reds (and for its readiness, in times gone by, to supply them to winegrowers in Burgundy and Bordeaux whose own wines lacked enough body and needed a little body-building and 'beefing-up'), it's also the place to find an extraordinary range of other styles. Muscat de Beaumes de Venise, now a favourite inexpensive alternative to Sauternes, comes from a village that makes great red Côtes du Rhône-Villages; Clairette de Die Tradition, a less pungently perfumed counterpart to Asti Spumante, comes from here too. So do the strange and wonderful creamy-spicy dry whites of Condrieu and Château-Grillet, and the dry, peppery rosés of Tavel and Lirac.

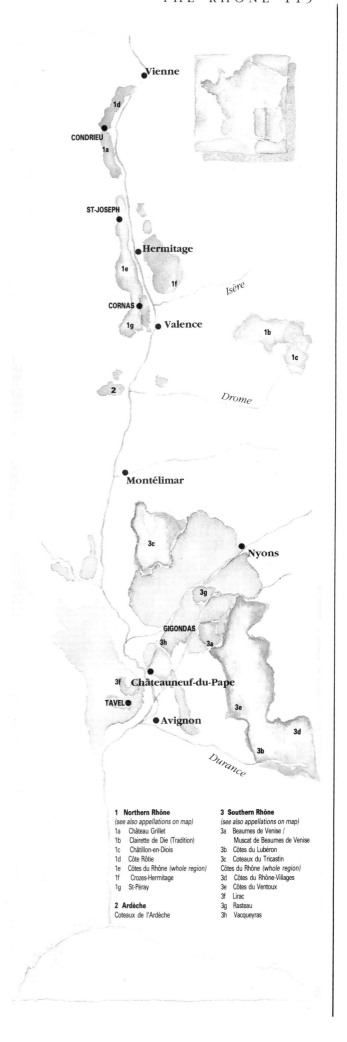

LEFT: *Harvesters in Côte Rôtie, one of the great red wine appellations of the Northern Rhône*

ABOVE: *The 'pudding-stones' of Châteauneuf-du-Pape reflect the sun's warmth on to the grapes, giving this wine its rich, spicy intensity of flavour*

But ultimately the reds have always been the Rhône's strong suit. Unfortunately, in the past, too much of the wine was dull and disappointing; Châteauneuf-du-Pape, for example, once rivalled Beaujolais for the prize for best-known, worst-made red. The problem was that no one paid these wines much respect. Old-timers recalled the days when Hermitage sold for a higher price than the best Bordeaux, and when a dollop of their wine could raise the value of a barrel of Lafite – and shrugged their shoulders.

Today, though, the Rhône is back in fashion. The region's growers, merchants and cooperatives are tidying themselves up and despite the size of the area – it's nearly 150 miles (240 km) long – the amount it makes (over 200 *million* bottles of Côtes du Rhône each year) this has quietly become one of the world's most reliable, good value wine regions. And people are beginning to notice.

America's wine guru Robert Parker, is the author of what has been described as the 'definitive' guide to Bordeaux. What would you find if you looked in his cellars – loads of claret? Not a bit of it; they're packed wall-to-wall with Rhônes, red *and* white. And what kinds of grape varieties are California's most pioneering wineries all falling over each other to plant? Yes, you guessed – Syrah, Viognier, Mourvèdre and Cinsault.

For the moment at least, the prices of the best wines of the northern Rhône don't reflect this growing success and popularity, but they're already rising fast. Buy now before everyone else gets the taste for them. And stock up on a few dozen cheap bottles of Côtes du Rhône to enjoy while you wait for your brooding monsters to soften.

1	**Northern Rhône**	3	**Southern Rhône**
	(see also appellations on map)		(see also appellations on map)
1a	Château Grillet	3a	Beaumes de Venise /
1b	Clairette de Die (Tradition)		Muscat de Beaumes de Venise
1c	Châtillon-en-Diois	3b	Côtes du Lubèron
1d	Côte Rôtie	3c	Coteaux du Tricastin
1e	Côtes du Rhône (whole region)		Côtes du Rhône (whole region)
1f	Crozes-Hermitage	3d	Côtes du Rhône-Villages
1g	St-Péray	3e	Côtes du Ventoux
		3f	Lirac
2	**Ardèche**	3g	Rasteau
	Coteaux de l'Ardèche	3h	Vacqueyras

THE NORTHERN RHONE

Just to the south of the quiet, riverside town of Vienne you have the choice of whether to travel to the coast on the *autoroute* or the *route nationale*. On the motorway, the trip would probably take four or five hours; on the old road, I defy you to do it in less than couple of days – not because of the slow speed at which you'll be driving, but because, if there's any romance in your soul, you won't be able to resist heading off the road and up into the vineyards at almost every bend in the river.

The first temptation will strike on the west bank of the river, on the sheer 'roasted hillside' of Côte Rôtie. Only a masochist would ever have wanted to plant vines up here – but what else could anyone have done with this land?

The men and women who prune the Syrah vines here and harvest their grapes deserve every penny they can get for their wine, and not just for their talents as mountaineers. The 250 acres (100ha) of vineyards here are very, very exposed. In the summer, as the sun blazes down, you soon learn how the Côte got its name – and then there's the 90mph *mistral* wind and the winter frosts... But their efforts pay off. The flavour of the Syrah, tempered slightly by the addition of up to 20% of white Viognier grapes, is a cocktail of ripe, dark berries and wild flowers, with just a hint of woodsmoke.

The Viognier's role in red Côte Rôtie is generally unrecognised, but this curious variety gets and deserves all the credit for the two white wines that are made, on similarly steep slopes, a little further down the river at Condrieu and Château-Grillet. The former appellation is small at just 25 acres (10ha), but the latter is tiny, with just six and a half acres (2.5ha) of terraced vineyards. This diminutive size only partly explains Château-Grillet's astronomical price; the fact that there is only one producer (Château-Grillet) has some bearing too.

My advice would be to save some money and go for a Condrieu (particularly from Georges Vernay), which will give you almost as perfect a taste of the Viognier's weird aromatic perfume and peach, apple and cream cheese flavours. Try it, and you'll see just why all those Chardonnay-sated Californians are turning to it in their droves.

The appellation of St-Joseph overlaps that of Condrieu or, to be more precise, runs along beneath it on the flat land by the river. Elsewhere, close to Tournon and Mauves, between Hermitage and Valence, it runs up into the hills on its way to Valence. It is in these hills that the best wines are made: spicy, peachy whites from Marsanne and Roussanne, and intensely blackcurranty, spicy (it's all spicy round here) reds from the Syrah. Most examples of St-Joseph are good; some are much more chunky and long-lived than others.

Hermitage

As the St-Joseph vineyards continue down the west bank of the Rhône, this part of the river's finest terraces stare imperiously across at them at Hermitage. From here, either at the level of the town or up in the hills standing beside a huge statue of the Madonna, you can see steep terraces dotted with long signs proclaiming the names of the region's biggest merchants: Jaboulet-Aîné, Chapoutier, Guigal... The tiny chapel you can see high on the hill stands in the middle of Hermitage's most famous plot.

Jaboulet-Aîné's 'La Chapelle' vineyard produces one of the very best Hermitages. And the view from here at dusk is one of the most unforgettable sights in the vinous world.

Red Hermitage is usually made exclusively from the Syrah, though growers are allowed to add a little Marsanne and Roussanne grapes, the ones from which the appellation's white wine is made. Good red Hermitage is simply one of the most astonishing wines of all – classy, but raunchy too. The flavours should be very, very concentrated and they should combine just

about every berry and spice you can imagine. There's tannin, but also a sweet ripeness; in all but the lightest years, you should allow these wines 10 or 15 years for flavours to develop.

By comparison, white Hermitage is rarely as exciting an experience but, like the red, it too can need time. When young, it can taste dull and earthy but, given 10 years or so, the earthiness can miraculously turn into all kinds of floral, herby, peachy smells and flavours.

The easiest way to describe Crozes-Hermitage is to say that it is scaled-down Hermitage. The winemaking rules are the same, and so is the region, more or less, except that the Crozes appellation covers a lot more ground, extending eastwards behind Hermitage and away from the river. The wine still has those flavours of berries and spice, but you can get at them earlier, and they don't last as long. The whites are definitely for early drinking.

Steak Diane

Steak in a brandy sauce

The dark, robust wines of the region need to be accompanied by a dish with a character rich enough to do them justice.

SERVES 4
5 fl oz/150 ml beef stock
4 tsp Worcestershire sauce
2 tsp lemon juice
2 tsp Dijon mustard
3 tsp brandy
3 tsp sherry (preferably amontillado)
1 tsp cornflour
1 oz/25 g butter
1 tbsp olive oil
Four 6oz/175 g sirloin or entrecôte steaks, flattened
to about ¼ in/5 mm thick
1 medium onion, peeled and finely sliced
1 tbsp fresh parsley, minced

In a bowl, mix the stock, Worcestershire sauce, lemon juice, mustard, brandy, sherry and cornflour. In a large frying pan heat the butter until the foam subsides and sauté the steaks for about 25 seconds on each side (for medium-rare) and transfer them to a heated serving dish or individual plates. In the pan juices, cook the onion over moderate heat until it is softened and add to it the mixture from the bowl. Bring to the boil, stirring, until it thickens and then pour it over the steaks. Garnish with the parsley and serve with sautéed potatoes and a purée of fennel or celery.

ABOVE: The vines around this chapel produce Hermitage La Chapelle, the Rhône wine that can rival the best of Bordeaux. LEFT: The steep hillside of Côte Rôtie, where signs like these are commonly seen.

Cornas

As outsiders discover Hermitage and Côte Rôtie, the last remaining semi-secret red of the northern Rhône is the tiny (165 acre/ 67ha) region of Cornas. Critics complain that the wines here are more 'rustic' in style than their northern neighbours, and that they take even longer to come round. (Those critics obviously haven't tasted the smoky, blackberryish wines made by Auguste Clape, Guy de Barjac and Alain Voge.) Even if these wines don't ever *quite* match up to the very best of Hermitage, they're still terrific value for money.

South of Cornas, the interesting red wines of the northern Rhône dry up and it's time to move on to sparkling whites. St-Péray, whose vineyards rub shoulders with the suburbs of Valence, makes dull still wine and fizz from the Marsanne and Roussanne, so it's hard to blame the growers for selling their vineyards to house builders.

More interesting stuff is produced down to the south-west, along the Drôme river, in Clairette de Die and Châtillon-en-Diois, close to the village of Bourdeaux. The wine to avoid is Clairette de Die itself; made from at least 75% of the neutral-tasting Clairette grape, it's fresher than St-Péray, but hardly more interesting. The one to look for is Clairette de Die Tradition. Made primarily from Muscat grapes, though with a little Clairette, this can be first-class, emphatically grapey wine. It is produced by the traditional *méthode dioise*, in which the wine is bottled before its first fermentation is complete.

THE ESSENTIALS — NORTHERN RHONE

Location From Vienne, just below Lyons, to Valence in the south.
Quality AOCs: Châtillon-en-Diois; Château Grillet; Clairette de Die and Clairette de Die Tradition; Condrieu; Cornas; Côtes du Rhône; Côtes du Rhone-Villages; Coteaux du Tricastin; Crozes Hermitage; Hermitage; St Joseph; St-Péray and St-Péray Mousseux. Côtes du Vivarais is the VDQS, while *vins de pays* include Coteaux de l'Ardèche.
Style Reds vary from the cheap and cheerful to the mighty – Hermitage and Côte Rôtie are two of France's greatest wines. Immensely tannic in youth, Hermitage matures into an approachable but serious wine, with a cocktail of rich fruit flavours and characteristic smokiness. Côte Rôtie is slightly softer but even smokier. More affordable, but still showing good Syrah character are St Joseph and Crozes Hermitage. The white wines are dry and quite full in style. Condrieu, in particular, produces rich yet dry wines with an inviting tropical fruit aroma. Sweet, grapey sparkling Clairette de Die Tradition is infinitely superior to plain Clairette de Die.
Climate Continental, with hot summers and cold winters.
Cultivation Varied soil, but mainly granite. The vineyards are set into the steep slopes of the rocky hillsides.
Grape Varieties Aligoté, Bourboulenc, Calitor, Camarèse, Carignan, Chardonnay, Cinsault, Clairette, Counoise, Gamay, Grenache, Marsanne, Mauzac, Mourvèdre, Muscardin, Muscat Blanc à Petits Grains, Pascal Blanc, Picardan, Picpoul, Pinot Blanc, Pinot Noir, Roussanne, Syrah, Terier Noir, Ugni Blanc, Vacarèse, Viognier.
Production/Maturation Traditional methods prevail, with less emphasis on new oak than elsewhere.
Longevity Lesser whites should be drunk as young as possible and even the better white wines tend to peak before 5 years. Côtes du Rhône, Crozes Hermitage and St Joseph will be drinkable at 3 years but as the quality of the wine increases so does its ageing potential.
Vintage Guide 76, 78, 82, 83, 85, 88
Top Producers *Hermitage:* Jaboulet Aîné, Chapoutier, Guigal, Chave, Grippat, Delas, Sorrel. *Côte Rôtie:* Jasmin, Jamet & Barge, Vidal-Fleury, Jaboulet Aîné, Guigal. *Condrieu:* Georges Vernay, Guigal. *St Joseph:* Chave, Coursodin, Grippat, Jaboulet Aîné, Co-op St-Désirat-Champagne. *Crozes-Hermitage:* Guigal, Desmeure, Tardy & Ange, Delas, Fayolle, Jaboulet Aîné. *Cornas:* Clape, Guy de Barjac, Alain Voge.

THE SOUTHERN RHONE

According to the *Appellation Contrôleé* maps, the area between the northern and southern Rhône is a grapeless no-vine's-land. In fact, although there is no AOC wine made here, there are two *vins de pays*: the Collines Rhodaniennes (easy red from the Gamay and Syrah) and the Coteaux de l'Ardèche which, apart from the reds it makes from the Gamay and from Rhône and Bordeaux varieties, has now become an unofficial outpost of the Côte d'Or, following the decision of that region's Louis Latour to produce pleasant but overpriced Chardonnay there. A litle further south, there is the up-and-coming new *Appellation Contrôlée* of the Coteaux du Tricastin, source of some first-class, pure, smoky Syrah.

Wines labelled Côtes du Rhône can legally be made anywhere along the Rhône valley; in practice most come from the flat land on either side of the river south of Montélimar. This is a huge area, and quality and styles can vary enormously. The same appellation can be used to label a Syrah that tastes just like Hermitage's kid brother and a blend of the Grenache, Cinsault and Carignan that's first cousin to Beaujolais Nouveau.

The key to knowing what you are going to find in the bottle is to look for wines from individual estates, or to pay a little extra for a Côtes du Rhône Villages, which legally has to come from one of 17 named villages, be made from grapes that come from lower-yielding vines and be a blend that includes at least 25% of Syrah, Mourvèdre and Cinsault.

The winemakers of the 17 villages are nothing if not individualists, and are active promoters of the wines of their communes, driven on by the example of Gigondas which, in 1971, was promoted from Côtes du Rhône Villages and now has its own appellation. It is easy to understand why Gigondas got its appellation first; its red wines *do* taste a bit more 'serious' than those of its less honoured neighbours, and its (rare) rosés are first-class. Good examples are a much better buy than many a wine sold under the label of Châteauneuf-du-Pape. So far, no other commune has followed in Gigondas's footsteps, but most take advantage of the rules that let them print their commune's name on the labels of their wines.

Best known of these villages and the hottest tip for promotion is Vacqueyras, but Visan, Cairanne, Valréas and Séguret could all make a case for the quality of their reds. Chusclan deserves an appellation for the rosé made by its cooperative (better than a great deal of Tavel), and Laudun merits one for its white. Ironically, Beaumes de Venise and Rasteau, which make decent reds, have had appellations of their own for nearly 50 years, but not for their unfortified wines; both make *vins doux naturels,* fortified wines made by adding pure grape spirit to partly fermented juice. Muscat de Beaumes de Venise is a world-famous success story; Rasteau's fortified Grenache is less immediately appealing but has a plummy, port-like charm.

Châteauneuf-du-Pape

Châteauneuf-du-Pape is one of the world's famous wine names – but, until quite recently, despite their embossed keys, and their price, the wines here were often a little like the Pope's castle itself; impressive from a distance and a hollow ruin when viewed at close range.

Châteauneuf *should* be brilliant stuff. The 'pudding stones' covering the vineyards, which release heat during the night, invariably ensure perfectly ripe grapes. The local appellation laws, the first to be drawn up in France, further guarantee the quality of the fruit (in a way unique to Châteauneuf) by obliging producers to use the least-ripe 5-20% of the crop to make *vin*

THE ESSENTIALS — SOUTHERN RHONE

Location In south-eastern France, north of Avignon.
Quality AOCs: Châteauneuf-du-Pape; Côtes du Rhône; Côtes du Rhône-Villages (named villages include Cairanne, Vacqueyras, Séguret, Visan, Valréas, Chusclan and Laudun) Côtes du Lubéron; Côtes du Ventoux; Gigondas; Lirac; Tavel. *Vins de pays* include: Vaucluse, Collines Rhodaniennes and Bouches-du-Rhône.
Style Ripe, full-bodied red wines are produced, warmer and softer than their northern Rhône neighbours, simple in style though with more depth and complexity in Gigondas, Châteauneuf-du-Pape and some of the better Côtes du Rhône villages, such as Cairanne and Séguret. There are also some soft, fresh and fragrant whites, most notably in Châteauneuf-du-Pape and Lirac. The most famous rosé is Tavel, though neighbouring Lirac can be better. The now-famous sweet white Muscat de Beaumes de Venise is arguably the best and classiest of France's *vins doux naturels,* luscious yet elegant, while the area's other VDN, Rasteau, can be almost port-like.
Climate Mediterranean with very long, hot summers.
Cultivation Arid chalk and clay soils covered with large, round 'pudding-stone' pebbles reflect and intensify the heat. As the river widens the vineyard slopes become less steep.
Grape Varieties As for northern Rhône; 13 varieties are designated for use in Châteauneuf-du-Pape, chiefly Carignan, Cinsault, Grenache, Mourvèdre and Syrah. Whites are principally from Muscat, Clairette, Picpoul and Bourboulenc.
Production/Maturation Increasing use of stainless steel with old wood being used for maturation.
Longevity Reds, apart from the best village appellations and Châteauneuf-du-Pape, peak after about three years. Good village wines will last beyond 5 years, and the best Châteauneuf-du-Pape beyond a decade. White and rosé wines are generally for early consumption.
Vintage Guide 81, 83, 85, 86, 88
Top Producers Vidal-Fleury, Château de Beaucastel, Jaboulet, Guigal, Delas, Domaines de Durban and du Vieux Télégraphe. Château Rayas.

de table. The rules also strictly control yields and restrict the use of grape varieties to eight reds and five whites.

The fact that these rules had to be drawn up as early as 1923 illustrates the well-established tradition of abusing the reputation of what has long been a household name. Today, fortunately, the merchants who were largely guilty of that abuse are prevented from doing so by the keenness of the individual estates to make and bottle their own wine. This has made for a huge improvement in quality, but today's Châteauneuf is still rather two-faced; some are big, packed with pizza herbs, bitter chocolate and oriental spice; others, made by the *macération carbonique* method, taste rather like peppered Beaujolais. There's nothing wrong with these lighter versions, but they don't really do justice to Châteauneuf. The biggest examples from the best estates are worth keeping for a decade or so but, unlike their counterparts from the northern Rhône, they can all be broached by the time they are five years old.

White Châteauneuf-du-Pape is very rare – maybe two or three bottles in a hundred – but it's worth looking for.

Tavel

The traditional claims for Tavel are, first, that it is one of the world's only rosés that can age, and secondly that it is a cut above its neighbour Lirac. As far as I'm concerned, both claims fail the taste test. Old Tavel tastes duller than young Tavel, and young Tavel tastes duller than young Lirac. The trouble is that the producers at Tavel now try too hard to make 'serious' pink wine. Sadly, the winemakers at Lirac, which *does* produce good rosé, are increasingly turning their attention to red instead.

Other Wines

There are several 'lesser' appellations and VDQSs in the region for which bargain-hunters ought to keep their eyes open. The Côtes du Ventoux benefit from limestone soil to make light, but still quite spicy red. The Côtes du Lubéron, between Avignon and Aix-en-Provence, got their brand new AOC largely through the efforts of vegetable oil millionaire Jean-Louis Chancel of Château Val Joanis, where he makes lovely, early-drinking red and rosé. Still a VDQS, the Côtes du Vivarais behave like an AOC by having a set of *crus* – Orgnac, St Montant and St Remèze – which produce attractive lightweight reds and rosés. Finally, up in the mountains, in the VDQS of the Coteaux de Pierrevert could serve you a jugful of refreshing rosé.

ABOVE: *The ruins of the original Papal palace at Châteauneuf in the southern Rhône overlook both the town and the vineyards of the commune. It was the presence here of the Papacy that first established the reputation of the wines of this region.* BELOW: *The beach-like Châteauneuf-du-Pape vineyards are some of the most dramatic in the world.*

Crème aux Fruits

A light cream with summer fruits and brandy

One of the great stars among the wines of the southern Rhône — in fact, one of the greatest dessert wines — is Muscat de Beaumes de Venise. To say it is merely sweet is like saying Champagne is merely sparkling. This dessert has a lightness which complements the wine deliciously.

SERVES 4

12 oz/350 g raspberries or strawberries, fresh or thawed from frozen, mashed and sieved
10 fl oz/275 ml double cream
1 egg white
2 oz caster sugar
1 tsp orange liqueur (e.g. Cointreau or Triple Sec)
12 sponge fingers

Whisk cream until it thickens. Fold in the egg white, sieved fruit pulp, caster sugar and liqueur. Arrange sponge fingers in a serving dish or on individual plates and pile mixture on top.

ALSACE

As winemakers throughout the world have seemingly given up naming their wines after places and begun to call them after the grape varieties from which they are made, the Alsatians smile knowingly to themselves. They invented 'varietal' labels long before the Californians and Australians; indeed, in Alsace, more or less the only way wine is sold is by its grape variety, be it the Riesling, the Pinots Gris, Blanc and Noir, the Muscat, the Gewürztraminer or, to a decreasing extent, the Sylvaner.

Talk to the Alsatians about their German neighbours' recent conversion to dry wines and again they will smile; round here, dry Riesling is no novelty and, as they will point out, in Alsace's warm climate the grapes actually ripen much more easily than they do on the other side of the Rhine.

The History

The Alsatians have a way with knowing, if wry, smiles, and when you consider their history, it's hard to blame them. Over

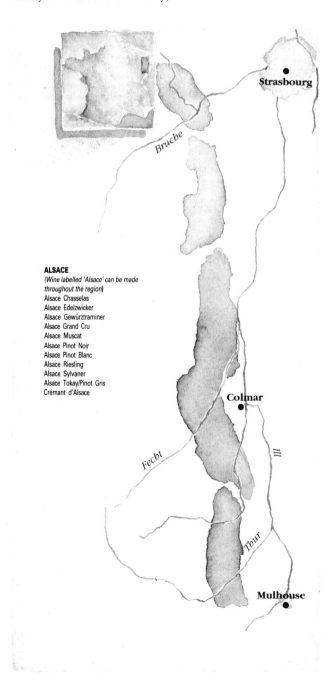

ALSACE
(Wine labelled 'Alsace' can be made throughout the region)
Alsace Chasselas
Alsace Edelzwicker
Alsace Gewürztraminer
Alsace Grand Cru
Alsace Muscat
Alsace Pinot Noir
Alsace Pinot Blanc
Alsace Riesling
Alsace Sylvaner
Alsace Tokay/Pinot Gris
Crémant d'Alsace

the years their region has been a territorial ping-pong ball; they've seen it all. As early as the 14th and 15th centuries, Strasbourg was at the heart of a thriving wine-producing area that included vineyards on both sides of the Rhine, exporting 100 million litres a year from its river docks.

But this early prosperity did not last. When the French took control in 1648 at the end of the Thirty Years War, Alsace was no prize acquisition. The war had so devastated the region that immigrants from neighbouring lands were offered free land to encourage them to cultivate it once more.

However hard these times were, they did not deter some from starting wine businesses; among the family firms that are still in operation today, Hugel, Dopff, Trimbach, Zind-Humbrecht and Kuen had all opened their doors by 1700. Over the following century, they learned to work with another immigrant – the Riesling grape, from the Rheingau on the other side of the river. The end of the Franco-Prussian war in 1871 brought a return to German rule. Less than 50 years later, at the end of the First World War, Alsace became French again – only to fall back into German hands in 1940. The Second World War brought some of the worst times Alsace has ever known; villages were fought for house by house. In Bennwihr, precious wine literally boiled in the cellars as the buildings were burned to the ground.

Today, some of the people speak French; others retain a Germanic dialect – but, whatever the language, they are all quick to stress that they are, above all, Alsatian. And perhaps that's the best image for Alsace wines, too: German spoken with a French accent. Or vice versa.

The Best of Both Worlds

This dual nationality is just as apparent in the villages; both in their names and their appearance. This is one of the few parts of the world in which holiday brochure expressions like 'fairy tale' and 'picturesque' actually do ring true; the narrow streets, the crooked, half-timbered houses, often painted pink, yellow or blue, with their gilded signs are straight out of an illustrated volume of stories by the Brothers Grimm. And overlooking all of the villages, there are vineyards, basking in the sun that, thanks to the shelter of the Vosges mountains, gives the vines one of the driest, warmest environments they could want.

In the autumn, these vineyards are packed with families

ABOVE LEFT: The old towns of Alsace are almost too pictur-esque to be true. Some producers and merchants, like Hugel, have been making wine here for more than three centuries

ABOVE: One of Alsace's Grand Cru vineyards proclaims its identity to passers-by

sharing the task of picking. The slopes are too steep for mechanical harvesters; besides, most of the plots are too small for their owners to afford a machine. Although the soils of particular villages can suit particular varieties (for example, the Muscat does particularly well in both Mittelwihr and Gueber-schwihr) most growers produce wines from several different grapes.

But here, there is another contrast with Germany. Whereas the liberal German wine laws have allowed winegrowers in even the best parts of the Rhine and Mosel to replace their Ries-ling with a range of new, easy-to-grow varieties, in Alsace, the trend has been towards the Pinot Blanc and region's four tra-ditionally best white grapes, the Riesling, Pinot Gris, Muscat and Gewürztraminer. There are no new varieties here, and indeed even traditional ones such as the dull Sylvaner and Chasselas are now treated as second-class citizens; neither can be used to make Alsace's recently established *Grands Crus.*

With these *Grand Cru* vineyards, first introduced in 1983 and fast growing in number, the Alsatians have characteristically put together an appellation system that's half-French, half-German too. Although it is often imagined that each of the region's grape varieties has an appellation of its own, in fact it is the region of Alsace as a whole to which the appellation applies. The names of individual villages have no importance, but those of the 50 *Grand Cru* vineyards around those villages do – provided that the wines made there are produced from one of the four permitted varieties.

So much for the French-style part of the rules; the Germanic

THE ESSENTIALS — ALSACE

Location North-eastern France, on the border with Germany, along the Vosges mountains.
Quality AOC Alsace, usually followed by the name of the wine's grape variety. Crémant d'Alsace is the region's sparkling AOC. Around fifty vineyard sites are currently entitled to use an additional *Grand Cru* appellation, adding their name to that of the grape variety. Although the growers of Alsace would like this designation extended to cover yet more sites, outside observers feel that even the current figure is too high, thus devaluing the appellation. There is nothing to prevent winemakers printing their vineyard name on a wine's label, be it *Grand Cru* or not, and, in view of the fact that cru status has in some cases been granted somewhat arbitrarily, this seems excusable. However, it does confuse matters for the average winedrinker, who might in turn be forgiven for not committing to memory all 50 (and rising) *Grand Cru* names. In similar vein, *Réserve* or *Cuvée Personelle/Spéciale/Particu-lière* are commonly seen, indicating the producer's favourite wines but having no official significance. Ironically, while these anomalies would be cause for concern almost anywhere else, Alsace as a region has one of the best reputations for honest and reliable winemaking in France.
Style Rich, spicy, dry still whites, usually from a single grape variety (Edelzwicker, a blend, is losing favour); usually sweet Vendange Tardive; always sweet Sélection de Grains Nobles. Light-bodied Pinot Noir reds. Crémant d'Alsace is a *méthode champenoise* sparkling wine, dry and often quite full-bodied. Though little seen, it can be good value.
Climate Continental: sheltered by the Vosges mountains, this area is warmer and drier than the surrounding countryside.
Cultivation Middle and lower hillside vineyards, usually south or south-easterly in aspect. Soils are diverse and complex.
Grape Varieties Predominantly *white*: Riesling, Gewürztraminer, Muscat, Pinot Blanc, Tokay-Pinot Gris (Tokay d'Alsace), Auxerrois, Knipperlé, Sylvaner, Chasselas and a little Chardonnay. *Red*: Pinot Noir.
Production/Maturation Traditionalists prefer old oak for fermentation and maturation while modernists use stainless steel. The jury is still out over which is better. Some new oak is being used for Pinot Noir.
Longevity Riesling: 5 to 20 years; Gewürztraminer: 3 to 15; Pinot Gris: 5 to 10. Most Muscat, Sylvaner and Pinot Blanc are best drunk young, though the last can keep for up to 4 or 5 years, as can the reds.
Vintage Guide 83, 85, 86, 88, 89
Top Producers Zind Humbrecht, Hugel, Trimbach, Faller, Muré, Rolly Gassmann, Kreidenweiss, Schlumberger, Dopff au Moulin. The coopera-tive at Turckheim produces always reliable, sometimes excellent wine.

part is all to do with the ripeness of the grapes – in other words, their natural sweetness. Although Alsace is almost exclusively a dry wine region, the Alsatians love to prove that they can make sweet wine that's every bit as luscious as the stuff produced across the Rhine.

Sweet Alsace

These sweet Alsace wines have two designations, Vendange Tardive – literally 'late harvest', the equivalent of Germany's *Spätlese*, and Séléction de Grains Nobles – 'selection of noble/ nobly rotten grapes', similar in style to a German *Beerenauslese* or *Trockenbeerenauslese*. Beyond just two more terms – the increasingly rare Edelzwicker (used for a basic blend of various varieties) and Crémant d'Alsace (the region's often excellent *méthode champenoise* sparkling wine), there is almost nothing else to learn. Expressions such as the commonly seen Réserve Personelle and Cuvée Spéciale have no legal significance, but they should indicate that the producer believes the wine to be a cut above the rest of his production.

Comparing Alsace's dry and sweet white wines with their German counterparts is a fascinating experience, and one that sends writers scurrying in search of similes. One somewhat pretentious analogy that nevertheless makes sense to me likens the wines of the Mosel and Rhine to Mozart quartets, and those of Alsace to Beethoven symphonies.

The difference is all to do with volume and richness. The peculiar warm, dry microclimate created by the Vosges mountains allows the grapes to develop those few extra grammes of sugar almost every year and that, in turn, makes for a higher level of alcohol and a richness rarely attained in northern Germany; if a wine seems Germanic, yet exotically spicy and tangibly oily in texture, there's a strong chance that it comes from Alsace. And if you are looking for a wine to go with food, you've come to the right place.

ABOVE: Most of Alsace's small estate wineries are still situated in the towns. Blanck is one of the region's best

BELOW: Harvest-time at a family estate in Alsace. The people here take mealtimes very seriously

The Grapes

Riesling

Is this the greatest of Alsace's varieties – or should that honour go to the Pinot Gris? I'm not certain, but I've a pretty clear idea what the Riesling thinks. Tasted young, Alsace Rieslings can be forbidding, hiding their richness behind their acidity. Leave them to sulk for a few years and you'll be rewarded with an extraordinary appley, spicy glassful that can smell – not unpleasantly – just like petrol. Weinbach, Blanck, Sick-Dreyer, Trimbach and Kientzler make good examples.

Tokay-Pinot Gris/Tokay d'Alsace

Until recently confusingly known as the Tokay, this is no relation of the Hungarian wine of that name (which is made from the Furmint, another variety altogether). Some stories say that the Pinot Gris was imported from Hungary to Alsace; others that the reverse is true. Whichever is correct (and it is grown in Hungary – where it is called the 'Greyfriar') this pale-pink-skinned grape produces some of the spiciest, smokiest wine in Alsace. Like the Riesling, it's worth waiting for, but far easier to drink when young. Ostertag, Kreydenweiss, Schlumberger and Muré make good examples.

Gewürztraminer

I remember tasting Gewürztraminer with a Burgundian who had never encountered it before. 'Bizarre!' he said. 'Is this wine or is it perfume?' I know what he meant, and I know why a fair number of people are put off by the sweet-yet-dry, pungent smell and taste of wines made from this dark-pink-skinned grape. It *is* over-the-top, but unashamedly so – like the most cleverly designed low-cut dress. The words that often appear on tasters' notes are 'grapy', 'lychees', 'Parma violets', 'rose water' and, above all, 'spice'. And that's how it's supposed to taste; the word 'Gewürz' in German means 'spice', and thus one can deduce that this is the spicy version of the Traminer grape. If it didn't taste this way, it simply wouldn't be living up to its name. For a taste of Gewürztraminer at its best, try it made by Schlumberger, Zind-Humbrecht, Schleret, Trimbach or Faller.

Muscat

The Muscat has all the Gewürztraminer's grapiness – and then some – but far, far less of its spice. Tasting Alsatian Muscat alongside a Muscat de Beaumes de Venise is like seeing a great actor in two very different roles. Here, unless it is late-picked, the style will be dry and wonderfully refreshing. But there is not a lot made, so you may have to search a little to find a bottle. Names to look for include Kuentz-Bas, Dopff & Irion and Zind-Humbrecht.

Pinot Blanc

The least characterful, and thus the most immediately approachable of Alsace grapes, this cousin of the Pinot Noir is the same variety that the Italians often misleadingly label as Chardonnay (here, confusingly, producers can legally do the reverse). Alsace Pinot Blanc always reminds me of the fatty, hard-to-define flavour of Brazil nuts and offers an affordable introduction to Alsace for people who are deterred by the spice and perfume of some of the region's more characterful varieties.

Among my favourites are examples from the Cave de Turckheim, Gisselbrecht, Hugel and Kreydenweiss.

Sylvaner

This rather earthy-flavoured grape used to be one of the most widely-grown here, but is rapidly going out of favour. Good examples can have a rich style of their own but they are rarely exciting. Rolly Gassmann makes a good one.

Chasselas

Another, and rather duller, traditional resident that has been chased out by more attractive newcomers.

Pinot Noir

The one style that seems to unite Germany and France in Alsace is red wine; on both sides of the Rhine, the Pinot Noir produces wines that, in warm years and when yields are kept low, can be very raspberryish and attractively like a light-to-middleweight Burgundy. Good examples benefit from being matured in new oak too – provided that they have enough guts to carry the woody flavour. Look out for examples from Hugel, Rolly Gassmann and the Turckheim cooperative.

Other Wines of the Region

There are two VDQS regions close to Alsace. Côtes de Toul, in what was once the huge winegrowing region of Lorraine, can produce pleasant light red and rosé (*vin gris*). And in Lorraine the Mosel crosses the border into France to become the Moselle – but the wine of this name, made on the banks of the river is very dull.

THE GRANDS CRUS OF ALSACE

Altenberg de Bergbieten; Altenberg de Bergheim; Altenberg de Wolxheim; Brand; Br{rotated}Bruderthal; Eichberg; Engelberg; Florimont; Frankstein; Froehn; Furstentum; Geisberg; Gloeckelberg; Goldert; Hatschbourg; Hengst; Kanzlerberg; Kastelberg; Kessler; Kirchberg de Barr; Kirchberg de Ribeauvillé; Kitterlé; Mambourg; Mandelberg; Markrain; Moenchberg; Muenchberg; Ollwiller; Osterberg; Pfersigberg; Pfingstberg; Praeletenberg; Rangen; Rosacker; Saering; Schlossberg; Schoenenbourg; Sommerberg; Sonnenglanz; Spiegel; Sporen; Steinert; Steingrubler; Steinklotz; Vorbourg; Wiebelsberg; Wineck-Schlossberg; Winzerberg; Zinnkoepflé; Zotzenberg.

CHAMPAGNE

Everybody has their own image of Champagne. The word itself, with its connotations of luxury, the sound of the cork popping out of the bottle, the stream of foam fired at the crowds by victorious racing drivers, the glass raised to toast a bride and groom... All of these take Champagne out of the wine rack and turn it into something that really is rather magical.

Everybody wants to drink it, too – and winemakers in just about every winemaking region in the world, from England to India, want to copy it. Somehow, though, however hard they have tried, however often they have turned out wine that outclasses poor-quality Champagne, none of the would-be sparkling wine makers – including overseas subsidiaries of the Champenois themselves – has produced anything that quite compares with Champagne at its best.

So what is it that gives the Champenois their edge? Well, the one thing it is most emphatically *not* is the way in which the wine is made. The Champagne method – the *méthode Champenoise* – is used all over the place, often by those subsidiaries. No, the answer lies in a peculiar combination of climate, soil and grape varieties which are particular to the region of Champagne itself.

The climate in this northern part of France is ideal for making sparkling wine, simply because it's not much good for any other kind of wine; it's just too cold and damp for the grapes to ripen properly. But acidic grapes that have partially ripened in a cool climate are just what you want for sparkling wine – far better than the juicier sweet ones grown in warmer climes.

Then there is the soil – the deep chalk that gives the wines their lightness and delicacy – and lastly, there are the grape varieties: Burgundy's Pinot Noir and Chardonnay, and the Pinot Noir's paler-skinned cousin, the Pinot Meunier.

Put all, or even some, of these elements together somewhere else and you might begin to make a wine that is a little like Champagne. But you'd still have to learn one of the Champenois' other tricks: the art of blending that they call *assemblage*. The closest parallel to this is to be found in Bordeaux, where winemakers marry together varying proportions of Cabernet Sauvignon, Cabernet Franc, Merlot and Petit Verdot from a

number of vineyards within the same commune. The difference in Champagne is that here, the blend is often of wines from villages several miles apart and, in the case of non-vintage Champagne (the vast majority of the region's production), from different years. The winemakers of Champagne and the port producers of the Douro share a peculiar habit of not making vintage wine every year, but of only 'declaring' a vintage when they think its wine is good enough.

Of course, every Champagne producer is delighted to be able to declare a vintage and to bottle a batch of wine from a single harvest, but the greatest compliment you can pay him is to say that the most recent glass of his non-vintage wine tasted exactly the same as the one you had a year ago.

What every Champagne house is selling is a combination of a recognisable style and consistency. (The Krug brothers, who run one of the greatest Champagne houses of all, believe this so strongly that they price their non-vintage wine as highly – and it *is* highly – as their vintage.) Most producers believe that the best way to achieve that consistency is to blend wines made from two or three of the region's grape varieties, produced in several vintages, and in vineyards throughout the region.

BELOW: Pinot Noir and Chardonnay grapes, freshly picked from the chalky-soiled hillsides close to Epernay. Both types of grape will be used to make white sparkling wine

CHAMPAGNE
Champagne
(throughout the region)
Coteaux Champenois
(throughout the region)
1a Rosé de Riceys
1b Bouzy Rouge

THE LANGUAGE OF CHAMPAGNE

Assemblage Mixing of base wines to create the desired blend, or cuvée.
Atmosphere 1 atmosphere = 15 pounds per square inch. The average Champagne is under 6 atmospheres of pressure.
Autolysis The flavour-imparting process of ageing wines on their lees.
Bead The size of the bubbles.
Blanc de blancs Champagne made purely from the Chardonnay grape.
Blanc de noirs Champagne made purely from the black grapes Pinot Meunier and/or Pinot Noir. The wine itself is white.
Brut Very common sparkling wine term – literally 'dry' but in practice not bone-dry.
B.O.B. 'Buyer's own brand' wine.
Crémant A Champagne with less effervescence. This style traditionally contains 3.6 atmospheres, less than two-thirds of the usual pressure, and so the wines have a softer feel to them.
Cuvée The assembled or blended wine.
Cuvée de prestige/Deluxe The flagships of the Champagne houses. Supposed to be the finest cuvées. Sometimes very great (Roederer Cristal and Dom Pérignon) and always very expensive.
Dégorgement Removal of the yeast lees created during the second fermentation.

Dosage Wine added to top up Champagne after disgorging, setting sweetness level.
Giropalette Remuage machine.
Grande Marque Literally 'great brand', a grouping of recognized producers whose names should be a guarantee of quality. Usually the name of the house or grower, but it may be a brand name.
Liqueur de tirage Mixture of sugar, yeast and wine added to still Champagne to create the sparkle.
Matriculation number This number, mandatory on all Champagne labels, reveals, by the two letters preceding it, the origins of the contents of a bottle of Champagne. **NM** = *négociant-manipulant;* wine from all over the region was bought and blended by a commercial house.
CM = *coopérative-manipulant;* a group of growers 'pool' their grapes/wine to produce a blend. **RM** = *récoltant-manipulant;* a grower/producer who grows, vinifies and sells his own wine.
MA = *marque auxiliare;* a brand name owned by the producer or purchaser.
Microbilles See *pille.*
Mousse The effervescence of Champagne.
Non-dosage A term for wines without sugar added at dosage – also called *Brut Zéro* or *Brut Sauvage.*
Non-vintage The objective of these blends

is to keep to a uniform 'house' style. A blend will be based on one vintage, normally the last, plus wine from older vintage(s). 'NV' accounts for over 80% of the region's production.
Pille A membrane-coated yeast capsule under experimentation in Champagne.
Pupitre The racks which hold Champagne bottles on end while *remuage* takes place.
Ratafia Liqueur made in Champagne by blending grape must and marc.
Récemment dégorgée Recently disgorged. Bollinger has registered the abbreviation 'RD' as a trademark.
Remuage The 'riddling' – twiddling – of bottles of Champagne undergoing its secondary fermentation to move the yeast deposit on to the corks. A laborious task by hand, it is today increasingly done by *giropalettes.*
Rosé Pink champagne. Uniquely in EC wine law, may be made in this region by blending white and red wines. To some, however, the best method is to use only black grapes, as with Blanc de Noirs, but allowing minimal maceration.
Vintage Wine from a single 'declared' vintage. Must have more bottle-age than non-vintage, with strict quality control of the cuvée. No more than 80% of the harvest can be sold as Vintage.

THE ESSENTIALS — CHAMPAGNE

Location Centred on Epernay and Reims, 90 miles north-east of Paris.
Quality Within the Champagne AOC, villages may be further classified as *Grands or Premiers Crus.* Practically, this is less important than elsewhere because of the blending of wines from different areas. AOCs for still wines are Coteaux Champenois, Bouzy Rouge and Rosé de Riceys.
Style Champagne varies from the very dry Brut Zéro, which has no *dosage,* through Brut — the most common — to the dessert styles Demi-Sec and Doux. It varies greatly in quality but, from the better non-vintage Champagnes upwards, should be biscuity with soft, ripe fruit (particularly if from the Chardonnay grape) and clean balancing acidity. Côteaux Champenois is white, bone-dry and fiercely acidic; Rosé de Riceys and Bouzy Rouge can be fair to good examples of Pinot Noir, but are usually wildly overpriced.
Climate Similar to that of southern England with long, often cool summers and cold, wet winters. Frost may be a problem at times.
Cultivation Because of the inhospitable climate, vines need careful placing and vineyards are normally on south or south-east facing slopes. Soil is mainly of chalk with occasionally sandy topsoil. To combat the effects of frost, growers now employ sprinklers. AOC Champagne regulations forbid mechanical harvesting.
Grape Varieties Chardonnay, Pinot Noir and Pinot Meunier.
Production/Maturation Champagne production is an exact science. The grapes are quickly and carefully pressed. Fermentation is mainly in stainless steel and lasts approximately 10 days. The still wines are then blended to make a particular style of *cuvée.* A sugar, yeast and wine solution, the *liqueur de tirage,* is then added to make the bottled wine undergo a second fermentation. The bottles are stacked on special racks in the cellars during which time *remuage* takes place. This involves turning and tapping each bottle of wine, while gradually inverting it so the sludge containing the dead yeast cells from the second fermentation falls on to the cap. Traditionally this was done by hand; now machines called *giropalettes* are more common. Then the bottle neck is placed in freezing brine to freeze the sludge; the bottle is turned upright and the cap, and with it the sludge plug, is removed. This is called *dégorgement.* Finally, the *dosage* is added to the wine.
Longevity In basic terms, the better the base wine, the longer the finished Champagne will last. Most Champagne, including non-vintage, will benefit from up to three years' ageing before drinking.
Vintage Guide 75, 76, 79, 81, 82, 83, 85, 88
Top Producers Krug, Bollinger, Louis Roederer, Gosset, Jacquesson, Pol Roger, Ayala, Laurent Perrier, Alfred Gratien, Boizel, Deutz. The *Syndicat des Grandes Marques de Champagne* was established in 1964. Basically a historical 'club', it is a grouping of the best-known producers. Its members are: Ayala & Montebello, Billecart-Salmon, Bollinger, Canard Duchêne, Deutz & Geldermann, Charles Heidsieck, Heidsieck Monopole, Henriot, Krug, Lanson, Laurent Perrier, Massé, Mercier, Moët & Chandon, Mumm, Joseph Perrier, Perrier-Jouët, Piper Heidsieck, Pol Roger, Pommery & Greno, Ch & A Prieur, Louis Roederer, Ruinart, Salon, Taittinger & Irroy, Veuve Clicquot-Ponsardin.

The Regions

For white grapes, they might well look to the Côte des Blancs, the Chardonnay-covered slopes south of Epernay where, in villages like Cramant and Le Mesnil-sur-Oger, the best *blanc de blancs* – white wine made from white grapes – is made.

For the Pinot Noir, they'd probably head north to the Montagne de Reims where, in villages like Bouzy, Verzenay and Mailly, this hard-to-ripen grape can surprisingly – though only occasionally – produce red wines with almost as much depth as some Burgundy. Most of the Pinot Noir goes into blends, but occasionally you can find a *blanc de noirs* or a rosé that will give you a taste of what the grape can do here.

West of Epernay, following the Marne river towards Château-Thierry, there is the essential, but unsung, region of the Vallée de la Marne, where huge quantities of Pinot Meunier are grown. The Champenois rarely say much about the Pinot Meunier, a grape grown in England as the 'Dusty Miller' because of the fine white powder that covers its skin (*meunier* means 'miller' too), and they certainly don't mention the fact that it is the most widely-planted grape in Champagne.

The advantage of the Pinot Meunier is that it ripens well in clayey soil that the Chardonnay and Pinot Noir disdain. It can give a soft fullness to any blend; its disadvantage is that, in itself, it doesn't have much to offer in the way of fruity flavour. Most cheap Champagnes contain a fair whack of Pinot Meunier; but Rémy Krug acknowledges the essential rôle it plays in his wine.

If most of Rémy Krug's fellow producers refrain from mentioning the Pinot Meunier, they are just as reticent about the Aube region, way to the south of Epernay. If pressed, they might mumble something about the vineyards there being quite good for the Pinot Noir (because they are a little warmer) but imply in the same breath that Aube wines lack delicacy. A glance at some of their annual shopping lists will reveal, however, that most of them are very happy to put Aube Pinot Noir in their blend. The proportion may vary from year to year, but few Champagne houses own enough land to supply the grapes for more than a fraction of their production; most like to buy in the same varieties from the same regions every year.

The quality of each vineyard and the price of its grapes is officially designated on a percentage scale, known as the *échelle*. Those of Champagne's 18,500 growers lucky enough to own a

---

THE MONK AND THE WIDOW

Despite what some wine writers have said, Dom Pierre Pérignon did *not* invent fizz; more or less sparkling wine of one kind or another was already being made in various parts of France and Spain before he arrived to take up responsibilty as treasurer at the Abbey of Hautvilliers in 1668. On the other hand, Dom Pérignon did accidentally invent a wine that was very similar to to the Champagne we know today.

Ironically, the last thing the monk was aiming to make was fizzy wine; what he wanted to do was produce a white wine that was as good as the best red Burgundy. Discovering that white grapes made stuff that turned yellow, he restricted himself to the black-skinned Pinot Noir grapes, devising grape presses that crushed them gently enough for the skins not to tint the wine. Tasting the grapes that were picked, he discovered that the best wine could be produced from a blend of wines from different parts of the region. And lastly, most crucially, he bottled the wine as quickly as possible, knowing that the old barrels in which it was stored had a tiring effect on its flavour.

This early bottling, soon after the harvest, usually meant that the wine still contained a little yeast and had not quite finished fermenting; this was not apparent in the autumn and winter but was very much so in the warmer weather of the spring when the stuff in the bottle began to fizz.

Despite Dom Pérignon's initial dismay, his wine proved popular and fetched a higher price than any other in the region. However, in these early days its fizziness would have been far less vigorous than that of today's Champagne – largely because the French bottles of the time weren't tough enough to withstand much pressure. In England, however, thanks to the development of of a new glassmaking process, bottles were far stronger and heavier – and far better suited to withstand the carbon dioxide in the 'Champaign' that was shipped to England in barrels. And it was thus in London that modern Champagne was first tasted and appreciated.

During the 18th century producers, including such now-familiar names as Ruinart, Roederer, Heidsieck and Moët, had begun to include white grapes in their blends because they made fizzier wine (which was one of the reasons why Dom Pérignon had excluded them), and to age the wine in bottle-shaped quarries left beneath Reims by the Romans.

The only drawback to the Champagne of this time was its variability of style and the residue of dead yeast whose presence required the wine to be decanted, thus losing some of its precious bubbles. However popular the wine had become, its production was still very much a cottage industry. Then, in 1805, a little-known producer called Ponsardin died, leaving his 27-year-old wife in charge of the firm. Nicole-Barbe Clicquot-Ponsardin, soon to become internationally renowned as 'the widow', devoted herself to her firm and its wines for over 60 years, during which time, with the help of

her winemaker, Antoine de Muller, she created the first efficient Champagne production line and certainly the first that guaranteed clean wine.

De Muller discovered that standing the bottles on their corks – *cul en air*, literally 'bottoms up' – allowed the yeast to settle in the neck. Even so, some stuck stubbornly to the sides of the bottles, so he experimented withstanding the bottles neck-downwards in holes drilled in the top of a kitchen table. Lifting them out daily for a few weeks, shaking them and letting them drop heavily back into the holes shifted the dead yeasts down to the cork, whence they could easily be *dégorgé* – 'disgorged' – from the bottles.

The kitchen table was replaced by more sophisticated A-shaped wooden racks called *pupitres* in which the bottles could be turned as well as shaken in a process known as *remuage*. Pupitres are still used in Champagne today, but in recent years they have more often that not been replaced by machines called *giropalettes*.

But, whether the task is done manually or mechanically, the principal of shaking the yeast out of the wine remains unchanged. And unless and until new experimental techniques using yeast capsules called *microbilles* are put into practice, Champagne and *méthode champenoise* bottles will go on being shaken for the foreseeable future.

Despite this innovation – a Clicquot trade-secret until 1821 – Champagne making remained a hit-or-miss affair because there was no way of being certain of the strength of the bottle and the pressure in the wine; in 1828, 80% of the bottles exploded in the cellars. 40 years later, the failure rate had dropped to 15 or 20% but sensible visitors to Champagne cellars in the spring still wore protective face masks.

During the 19th century, however, the Champagne producers gradually sophisticated their art. A method was devised – by one Armand Walfart – of freezing the liquid and yeast in the necks of the bottles, thus simplifying *dégorgement*. Winemakers learned how to start with dry wine to which was added a precisely blended mixture of Champagne, sugar and yeast called the *liqueur de tirage*. And they perfected the essential trick of *dosage*, of topping up the bottles after *dégorgement* with a *liqueur d'expédition*, made from older wine, cane sugar and (then but seldom nowadays) brandy, thus sweetening and softening what can be aggressively dry wine.

In the early 1800s, most Champagne would have seemed astonishingly sweet to modern tastes; indeed, served almost frozen, it would have tasted like a cross between a sorbet and Asti Spumante. It was the Russians who were responsible for encouraging the production of sweet fizz – and the British who popularised their own taste for dry Champagne, though even today most examples contain at least a little sugar.

vineyard in one of the 17 villages, including Bouzy, Cramant, Le Mesnil-sur-Oger and Ay, that are rated as *Grands Crus* receive 100% of the annually agreed price per kilo of grapes. Their neighbours in the 140 *Premier Cru* villages, whose land is rated at 90-99%, get proportionately less money per kilo while those unfortunates in the rest of Champagne's vineyards – including most of those in the Aube – are rated at 80-89%.

The Styles

Brut
This is the most common dry Champagne style but, however dry they may taste to some people (and there are examples that can scrape your teeth cleaner than any dentist) all Brut Champagnes are slightly sweetened.

Extra Dry, Brut Zéro, Brut Sauvage
They sound similar, but for a taste of bone-dry champagne, don't try Extra Dry – which is, in fact, slightly *sweeter,* than Brut. Look for Brut Zéro or Brut Sauvage. These wines are sugar-free and are thus sometimes recommended to diabetics; for most people, however, they are too dry to be enjoyable.

Demi-sec, Doux, Rich
For the sweeter-toothed, Demi-Sec is, as its name suggests, semi-sweet while the rarer Doux and Rich are really very sweet indeed. Good examples of these styles are rare.

Blanc de Blancs and Blanc de Noirs
The words Blanc de Blancs feature on so many white wines nowadays that it is worth remembering that the expression is only relevant to sparkling white wines – for the simple reason

BELOW: The cellars of Pommery reveal the long-standing international popularity of Champagne; each tunnel is named after a different city

RIGHT: The chalky soil of Champagne makes parts of the region reminiscent of the southern coast of England — and allows its grapes to develop the characteristic flavour of Champagne

that these are almost the only ones that can ever be made from anything other than white grapes.

A Blanc de Blancs Champagne will be made exclusively from the Chardonnay, while the rarer Blanc de Noirs can be made from a blend of Pinot Noir and Pinot Meunier.

Crémant

If you are one of those people who find most sparkling wines too gassy, the producers of Champagne helpfully produce a softer, creamier, less aggressively fizzy version they call *crémant*. The Chardonnay grape lends itself particularly well to this style; thus a *crémant* Champagne will often be a *blanc de blancs* too.

Rosé

While other pink wines – or at least the ones that haven't renamed themselves 'blush' – have gone out of style, rosé Champagne has caught the public fancy in a way that has surprised even the Champenois, who don't really approve of the style, possibly because of the effort they take to keep the pink colour *out* of their wine. Rosé Champagne can be made in two ways. You either crush the grapes as if you were going to make white Champagne, but leave the skins in the juice for just long enough to tint the wine, thus producing what the Champenois call Rosé de Noir; or you simply blend a little of the region's red wine into the white fizz.

Vintage

Vintage Champagne can be made by any producer in any year thought to be up to the mark. Small domaines may produce a vintage fizz every year simply because they lack the old stock with which to blend a good non-vintage. Thus there is no guarantee that a vintage Champagne will be better than a good non-vintage, but it should have been made from the best available grapes harvested in a ripe year. Just as crucially, it must have been aged on its lees – or yeasts – for at least 36 months, which should give it a richer, yeastier, nuttier flavour than non-vintage, which enjoys a legal minimum of just 12 months' yeast contact (though good Champagne houses will aim to give their non-vintage fizz three years or so too).

Prestige Cuvée

The first 'Prestige Cuvée', or super-Champagne, was Dom Pérignon, the 1921 vintage of which was launched, after much hesitation, by Moët & Chandon in 1937. After the Second World War, Roederer entered the competition with its Cristal, a wine originally created for the Tsar of Russia and, over the last 50 years, almost every Champagne house has felt constrained to have a vintage or non-vintage prestige cuvée.

Some of these wines can be sublime: Dom Pérignon, despite its image of being every newly-famous pop star's first choice, *is* a great Champagne, as are Taittinger's Comtes de Champagne, Roederer's Cristal and Bollinger's Grande Année Rare.

The non-sparkling wines of Champagne

Coteaux Champenois Blanc.
At its best, Coteaux Champenois Blanc can be a little like Chablis, but rarely like top-class Chablis. In cooler vintages, a glass could save you from having to visit the dentist; do-it-yourself teeth-scaler. Laurent Perrier's version comes in a pretty bottle; Saran and Ruinart are usually better.

Coteaux Champenois Rouge.
If the white grapes find it hard to ripen, the Pinot Noir and Pinot Meunier have very little chance of doing so. In some ripe years, however, Coteaux Champenois Rouge can be made, which has some of the character of basic red Burgundy – but at a much higher price. Bouzy Rouge is the one to look for, if only because of its delicious name, but several other villages – for example, Ay and Ambonnay – proudly put their name to their own reds.

Rosé de Riceys.
Rosé de Riceys is a more interesting wine, if only because Pinot Noir rosé is quite rare. It is produced in the Aube, a region which is not generally thought to make the best Champagne. Like its still red and white neighbours, it can be lean stuff – and expensive – but good examples are juicily raspberryish.

The larger Champagne bottles are named after Old Testament patriarchs. Jeroboams, Rehoboams and Methusalehs contain four, six and eight bottles respectively

Filets de Sole Champagne

Sole fillets in a Champagne, cream and mushroom sauce

Although its wine is distinctive, the Champagne region does not have a cuisine that is quite as individual. This is not to say that the countryside is not well endowed. Pork dishes are prominent, as is game, such as wild boar and venison, and there is plenty of fish — pike and trout in particular — from its rivers. The following recipe need not be made with Champagne, but is certainly delicious if it is accompanied by a glass or two.

SERVES 6
12 unskinned sole fillets
Salt and freshly ground black pepper
8 oz/225 g mushrooms, minced (include the left-over stems)
2 small onions, finely diced
2 oz/50 g butter
18 button mushroom caps
Juice of half a lemon
3 wine glasses of dry Champagne or a good dry white wine
10 fl oz/275 ml double cream
2 tbsp brandy
2 egg yolks
Chopped fresh parsley to garnish

Season the fillets with salt and pepper. Mix the chopped mushrooms with the onion in a bowl. Melt half the butter in a small frying pan. Add the mushroom caps and sauté gently. Remove the pan from the heat after about 4 minutes and keep warm. With the remaining butter, grease a shallow flameproof dish and spread the onion and mushroom mixture in it evenly. Sprinkle with lemon juice and arrange the fillets on top. Pour in the wine and bring to the boil, then immediately reduce to a simmer. Cook gently for about 4 minutes or until the fish is just cooked through. Remove the fillets with a slotted slice and place on a warmed serving dish. In a small saucepan mix the cream, brandy and egg yolks and, while cooking gently, stirring all the time, gradually add the juices from the pan in which the fish was cooked. Simmer and stir until the sauce thickens. Pour over the fillets, add the mushrooms and garnish with the parsley. Serve with boiled potatoes and a carrot purée.

SPARKLING SERVICE

Cool but not *too* cool is the rule, particularly for vintage Champagne; an hour or so in the fridge or 10 minutes in a bucket full of ice and water should do the trick. A half-hour in the freezer may be similarly effective, but potentially very dangerous; if you allow it to freeze, it could explode.

When opening Champagne bottles, treat them with as much care as you would a firework. From the moment you remove the wire *capsule*, the cork could fly out at any moment, forced out with the same amount of pressure as you'd find in the tyre of a London bus. So don't leave it unattended. Point the bottle away from people and valuables and, holding it at an angle of 45 degrees, gently turn it while keeping a firm grip on the cork (there are special plier-like grips to help this part of the operation).

Unless you are a racing driver, avoid spraying anyone with wine. So let the cork out gently. Keeping the bottle at that 45-degree angle should reduce its keenness to froth over.

All Champagne, vintage and non-vintage, is sold ready to drink. Most will benefit from a further year or so in your rack at home – provided (and this is crucial) that you buy it from a supplier who has a swift turnover.

Top: The Pommery vineyards in winter. Frost is a major hazard here, particularly in the spring. Above: Presses like this one at Bollinger and its more modern equivalents are crucially important to Champagne because of the gentle way in which they crush the grapes without allowing too much of their skin colour to dye the juice.

EASTERN FRANCE

1 Arbois
2 Château-Chalon
3 Côtes du Jura
4 Etoile
5 Vin Jaune
6 Vin de Paille

7 Apremont
8 Crépy
9 Roussette de Bugey
10 Seyssel
11 Vin de Bugey
12 Vin de Savoie

Isolated, geographically, from the rest of wine-producing France, the modest appellations of the east have never enjoyed export success. As a result, they have never tailored their wines to suit the palates of foreign customers, and thus some unique, deeply traditional styles have been preserved almost intact.

The Jura is caught in a time warp, making eccentric, old-fashioned wine in precisely the same way it has done for centuries. But the Jura has a place in wine history because it was in this region of vineyards and dairy cattle that Louis Pasteur was born, and it was here that he carried out his first experiments on ways to prevent milk from going bad, and wine from oxidising.

The wines that fascinated Pasteur were the dry, but curranty-raisiny *vin de paille* still produced (though rarely now), like some of Italy's most traditional wines, from grapes laid out to dry on straw mats beneath the autumn sun and, more particularly, *vin jaune* which, like fino sherry, is allowed to oxidise in its barrels beneath a film of scum-like yeasts that the Spanish call *flor*.

Vin jaune is an exception that proves the rule. Leave almost any other red or white wine in a cask that hasn't been topped up properly and you will end up with vinegar; *vin jaune* is protected from harmful bacteria by its blanket of yeast during the 18 months it can take to ferment and the six years that it has to be matured. The flavour of vin jaune is inevitably more like that of sherry than any other white wine, but it's lighter in alcohol (not having been fortified) and packed with more of a punch of flavour because, unlike the neutral Palomino used for fino, the French wine is made from the assertive Savagnin grape. Some people hate it; others revel in its extraordinary nutty, salty, woody, flower-and-leaf flavours.

The best *vin jaune* is made (in tiny quantities) at Château-Chalon and l'Etoile, but examples from the small market town of Arbois and the regional Côtes du Jura are slightly less rare. All *vin jaune* comes in the eccentric *clavelin* bottle, which only contains 62cl because, the Juraciens claim, six years' evaporation from the barrels 'costs' them 13cl a time. The EC would love to oblige them to fall into line, and switch to 75cl like everyone else – but as President Mitterand is the local *deputé*, the clavelin seems safe for the moment at least.

Of the Jura's other wines, the whites, even when they are made from the Chardonnay, seem to have unwanted vin jaune character – and get sent back in restaurants for being oxidised. L'Etoile is, again, the one appellation that gets it richly right, often by blending the Savagnin with Chardonnay and even a little of the red-wine Poulsard grape.

There is no red l'Etoile, but Arbois makes red and rosé wines from the Pinot Noir, sometimes blended with the Pinot Gris, both of which taste a little like middle-weight Pinot Noir from Alsace and rarely repay ageing. Arbois reds made from the Trousseau and Poulsard vary in style, depending on the blend; the former makes heavy, tannic wines with little discernible flavour, while the latter can be delicate and floral, but with a hint of woodsmoke; a marriage of the two is decidedly characterful.

Savoie

Far less bizarre, but even less well known beyond this region, are the wines of Savoie. Of course, every year, there are a whole lot of people who discover these wines for the first time – because this is winter sports country, and if you ask for a bottle of something white as an après-ski refresher in Val d'Isère, this tangy, floral and often slightly sparkling wine is what you'll probably be given. But, as the skiers pack up their goggles, their boots and their recipe for Glüwein, they tend to forget the wines they drank on holiday. Even in Paris, bottles labelled Crépy and

THE ESSENTIALS — EASTERN FRANCE

Location To the east of, and running parallel to, Burgundy: Savoie comprises a series of small wine-producing areas from Lac Léman (Lake Geneva) south to Grenoble; Arbois lies within the Côtes du Jura to the north of Savoie, on the slopes of the Jura mountain range.
Quality AOCs: Arbois and Arbois Mousseux; Arbois Pupillin; Côtes du Jura and Côtes du Jura Mousseux; L'Etoile; Château-Chalon (*vin jaune*); Crépy; Roussette de Savoie (and *Cru*); Seyssel; Seyssel Mousseux; Vin de Savoie (of which the most widely seen *cru* is Apremont) and Vin de Savoie Mousseux. The best-known VDQS is Bugey (and Cru); Bugey Mousseux is also made.
Style Still and sparkling white wines are very fresh, floral and light, reminiscent of the wines of nearby Switzerland; more traditional wood-aged Jura whites are slightly fuller. Jura reds and rosés are light and vaguely Burgundian, while Savoie reds can sometimes be quite robust. *Vin jaune* and *vin de paille* are the Jura's speciality styles; the former, though unfortified, has been called France's answer to fino sherry, while the latter is extremely sweet with an appealing nuttiness.
Climate The area is affected by the proximity of the Alps and while the summers are warm, it can be very damp, cold and frosty during the winter and spring.
Cultivation The vineyards are found on gentle lower slopes. The soil is predominantly clay, with some limestone and marl.
Grape Varieties Cacabboué, Chardonnay, Chasselas, Gringet, Jacquère, Molette, Mondeuse, Mondeuse Blanche, Pinot Blanc, Pinot Noir, Poulsard, Roussanne, Roussette (Altesse), Savagnin, Tressot, Trousseau.
Production/Maturation Stainless steel and, in the Jura, large wood is used for fermentation. Sparkling wines are made by the *méthode champenoise*. Côtes du Jura Mousseux is the best sparkling wine appellation here. *Vin jaune* must be matured for at least 6 years in oak with no topping up so that a yeast flor develops, as in fino sherry; *vin de paille* is made from bunches of grapes that have been laid out to dry for up to 6 months while the sugar concentration intensifies. *Vin jaune* is made entirely from the Savagnin grape, while *vin de paille* is generally made from a blend of grapes, but always including the Savagnin. Labour-intensive to produce, these are fairly rare, expensive wines.
Longevity All Savoie whites should be drunk as young as possible, as should rosés. Red wines will last for between 3 and 6 years, while *vin jaune* and *vin de paille* appear to last almost indefinitely.
Vintage Guide 85, 86, 87, 88.
Top Producers *Arbois:* Château d'Arlay, Jean Bourdy, Château de l'Etoile, Henri Maire. *Savoie:* Pierre Boniface.

Left: Arbois is a great way off the beaten track of most of the rest of France's wines. Signs like this one (Above) reveal how firmly this region is rooted in the traditions of the past

Chignin-Bergeron are rare.

It would be easier for the Savoyards if those vineyards were all in a single area, but instead they're scattered around the valleys and on the slopes like patches of melting snow left over from what was once a far larger area; in the 18th century, there were around 22,500 acres (9,000ha) of vines; today the figure is just over 2,500 acres (1,000ha).

The local grapes are a curious bunch too: the Jacquère, Roussanne, Roussette, Cacabboué, Gringet, Mondeuse and Persan and the Petite-Sainte-Marie. This last may sound like the most obscure of them all, but actually, the Little-Saint-Mary is one of the only two that are grown anywhere else; it's the local name for the Chardonnay. And the other one? The usually dull Chasselas.

There's something about the cool climate of Savoie, as in nearby Switzerland, that lets this variety shine. Here, it's used as an ingredient in a wide range of tangily floral whites; but it's not the one that gives them their distinctive spicy character that comes from the obscure Roussette (also known as the Altesse) and Jacquère, and in some cases, the Pinot Gris.

The blanket regional appellation of Vin de Savoie includes some good, lightweight but emphatically refreshing *méthode champenoise pétillant and mousseux* whites made from blends of local grapes; and reds and rosés that combine the Gamay and Pinot Noir with local red and even (up to 20%) white varieties. There are a number of individual villages whose names can appear on labels. Of these, the best are Ayze (which makes good sparkling wine) Apremont, Abymes and Chignin-Bergeron (whose white offers a rare chance to experience pure Roussanne).

Best-known of Savoie's other appellations is Crépy, which, like Muscadet, is bottled *sur lie* and is thus very slightly sparkling. But it's got bags more flowery freshness than most Muscadet. For the flavour of pure Roussette, try the dry, flowery Seyssel; the *mousseux* made here can be good but slightly less distinctive, probably because of its high Chasselas content. Roussette de Savoie and Roussette de Bugey can both (with the exception of a few specified villages) include Chardonnay,

which tends to make for a creamier, less tangy flavour. The Vins du Bugey are often single-varietals, including some first-class pure Chardonnay, but the label also appears on some refreshingly fruity Gamay/Pinot Noir/Poulsard/Mondeuse blends.

Heading south, there are also the Vin de Pays de la Haute-Sâone, du Franche-Comté, du Jura, de l'Ain, de la Haute Savoie, de Savoie, de l'Allobrogie, des Balmes Dauphinoises, and des Coteaux du Grésivadan. The majority of these wines (red, pink and white) are fairly lightweight, the whites being made from the same local grapes as the region's appellations, and the reds and rosés being mostly Pinot Noir and Gamay.

Gratin aux Cèpes

Baked sliced potatoes in a mushroom and cream sauce

The crisp, white wines of the region go splendidly with trout, crayfish and char from the lakes and mountain streams. They also complement the region's dairy produce, which is often teamed up with the area's particularly good potatoes.

SERVES 6

2 lb/1 kg peeled and thinly sliced potatoes
1 ¹/₂1b/750 g mushrooms, sliced (cultivated will do if cèpes are unobtainable)
4 tbsp finely chopped onion
6 tbsp grated Gruyère or Emmenthal cheese
1 garlic clove, peeled and minced
Salt and freshly ground black pepper
1 pt/575 ml double cream
2 tbsp milk
¹/₂ tsp grated nutmeg
1 oz/25 g butter
4 tbsp chopped parsley

Butter a shallow ovenproof dish. Layer potatoes with mushroom sprinkled with onion, cheese, garlic, salt and pepper. Mix the cream and milk in a saucepan and bring almost to the boil. Pour over the dish. Sprinkle on the nutmeg. Dot with butter and bake in a preheated oven at 350˚F/180˚C/Gas mark 4 for about 1 ¹/₄ hours. Remove from oven and sprinkle with parsley. Serve either as a lunch dish with salad or as an accompaniment to roast lamb or beef.

PROVENCE AND CORSICA

Somewhere, close to the village of Cassis, so the locals say, there's a staircase to heaven built by God to facilitate deliveries of His favourite wine. Sitting at a café on the sea front here, watching the fishing boats bobbing away, with a plateful of olives on the table and a glass of chilled, fresh peppery Côtes de Provence pink in your hand, it's extremely easy to imagine that they are right.

For most people, thoughts of Provence's wines are all too

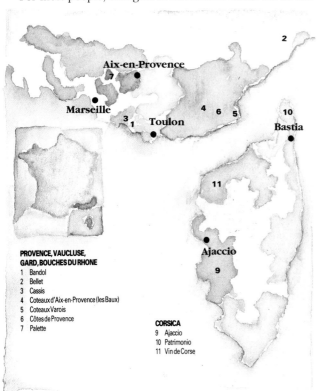

PROVENCE, VAUCLUSE, GARD, BOUCHES DU RHONE
1 Bandol
2 Bellet
3 Cassis
4 Coteaux d'Aix-en-Provence (les Baux)
5 Coteaux Varois
6 Côtes de Provence
7 Palette

CORSICA
9 Ajaccio
10 Patrimonio
11 Vin de Corse

The primitive landscape of Les Baux in Provence, source of some of the most exciting new red wines of southern France

often wrapped-up in memories or conjured-up images of sun-baked holidays. When they actually *taste* the same wines on a chilly day in London or Paris doubts begin to creep in. Is it the wine that's changed, or is it me? It's probably a bit of both – but no matter which, the wines never taste as good without the accompaniment of olives and sunshine.

This is far too easy a region in which to be lazy. And then, there are all the traditional ways that no one wants to cast off – such as allowing dull local white grapes to ferment at high temperatures, or of leaving the reds for too long in old casks. And we have willingly paid over the odds for wines whose faults we have overlooked for the sake of that 'holiday spirit'.

Over the last decade, thank goodness, the Provencaux have realised that to prosper, they must export good wine and have begun to get their act together, making consistently better, fruitier wines from fruitier grapes. Cotes de Provence is not all rosé; a fifth of the wine made here is red and a tenth, white. Too much of the red and pink is still made from the Carignan, but growers are busily planting Cabernet Sauvignon, Syrah and Mourvèdre, and taking more care of their Grenache. Cool fermentation has arrived for the whites too, giving hope for the workhorses, Ugni Blanc and Clairette.

Within this area, close to Aix-en-Provence itself, there are two recent AOC promotions, one of which – the Coteaux des Baux-de-Provence – is actually within Coteaux d'Aix-en-Provence. Both already made adequate-to-good white wines from the Ugni Blanc, and cool fermentation and the introduction of Sémillon and Sauvignon Blanc is bringing improvements. The rosés are fruitily soft, but the focus is on reds – modern reds, made from blends of Grenache, Syrah, Mourvèdre, Cinsault and Cabernet Sauvignon, and tasting like the best kinds of blends of fruit and spice.

Needless to say, this process has not been unimpeded.

THE ESSENTIALS — PROVENCE AND CORSICA

Location The Provence region covers the south-east corner of France, bounded by the Rhône and the Italian border. The Mediterranean island of Corsica lies 110km off the coast, south-east of Provence.

Quality *Provence* AOCs: Bandol; Bellet; Cassis; Côtes de Provence; Coteaux d'Aix-en-Provence; Coteaux d'Aix-en-Provence les Baux; Palette. The best known VDQSs are Coteaux de Pierrevert and Coteaux Varois. *Vins de pays* include: Bouches-du-Rhône, Mont Caume, Oc, Var and Maures. *Corsican* AOCs: Vin de Corse (with a number of suffixes), Ajaccio and Patrimonio are the best-known; the *vins de pays* de l'Ile de Beauté and of Pieves, however, include some of Corsica's more interesting wines, from Cabernet Sauvignon, Syrah, Chardonnay and Sauvignon Blanc. *Vins doux naturels* are from Patrimonio and at Cap Corse.

Style The red wines of Corsica and Provence are generally deep, dense and ripe, varying in style from Bandol, which must contain at least 50% Mourvèdre, to the excellent Château Vignelaure, made from Cabernet Sauvignon. Provence rosés tend to be dry, often with an evocative herby character while the white wines, although rarely exciting, are pleasantly aromatic.

Climate The Mediterranean influence ensures mild winters and springs and long, hot summers and autumns. The vines are planted on both hillside and plain sites. The soil is mainly composed of sand and granite, plus some limestone.

Grape Varieties Aramon, Aramon Gris, Barbarossa, Barbaroux, Barbaroux Rosé, Bourboulenc, Braquet, Brun-Fourcat, Cabernet Sauvignon, Calitor, Carignan, Chardonnay, Cinsault, Clairette, Clairette à Gros Grains, Clairette à Petits Grains, Clairette de Trans, Colombard, Counoise, Doucillon, Durif, Folle Noir, Fuella, Grenache, Grenache Blanc, Marsanne, Mayorquin, Mourvèdre, Muscat d'Aubagne, Muscat Blanc à Petits Grains, Muscat de Frontignan, Muscat de Die, Muscat de Hamburg, Muscat de Marseille, Muscat Noir de Provence, Muscat Rosé à Petits Grains, Nielluccio, Panse Muscado, Pascal Blanc, Petit Brun, Picardan, Picpoul, Pignol, Rolle (Vermentino), Roussanne, Sauvignon Blanc, Sémillon, Sciacarello, Syrah, Teoulier, Terret Blanc, Terret Gris, Terret Noir, Tener Ramenée, Tibouren, Ugni Blanc, Ugni Rosé.

Production/Maturation New-tech applied to traditional grapes and styles is producing some exciting reds. Provence rosés are benefiting from the introduction of cool-vinification methods although large old wood is still widely used for fermentation and maturation of other wines. Red Bandol must be matured in cask for a minimum of 18 months.

Longevity White and rosé wines should be drunk within 3 years; red wines generally within 5, although Bandol and the wines of the producers starred (*) below will last a decade.

Vintage Guide 82, 85, 87, 88.

Top Producers Domaine Ott, Château Simone*, Domaine de Trevallon*, Château Vignelaure*, Domaine Tempier*.

Rouget à la Nicoise

Sautéed red mullet in a tomato and herb sauce

The heat of the south of France gives the region's classic ingredients — garlic, tomatoes, olives and herbs — such an intensity of taste that Provençale dishes seem to be soaked in the sun.

SERVES 6

12 small whole red mullet or 12 fillets, scaled and cleaned
Salt and freshly ground black pepper
Plain flour
Olive oil, enough to cover a frying pan to a
depth of $\frac{1}{2}$ in/1 cm
2 lb/1 kg tomatoes, peeled, seeded and chopped, or tinned
tomatoes, drained and chopped
Dried thyme
12 anchovy fillets
36 black olives, pitted
6 tsp capers
Juice of 1 lemon
Chopped fresh parsley to garnish

Season fish with salt and pepper and then dust lightly with flour. In a frying pan heat the oil until it is almost smoking. Put in a batch of fish, turning until they are browned on both sides. Remove with a slotted slice and drain on kitchen paper. Repeat until all the fish are cooked. Put them in a shallow ovenproof dish. Pour over the tomato and sprinkle a pinch of thyme on each piece of fish, then place on each an anchovy fillet, 3 olives and $\frac{1}{2}$ tsp capers. Sprinkle with the lemon juice. Bake, uncovered, in a preheated oven at 325°F/170°C/Gas mark 3 for about 20 minutes, until the flesh of the fish parts easily from the bone or, if filleted, is just flaking. Serve with boiled rice.

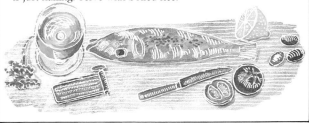

Traditionalists are scared that the Cabernet Sauvignon may take over their regions – so they are reducing the amount that can be used (to 40% in the reds now, and 30% after 1995) and expelling one of the best estates of the Coteaux des Baux de Provence, Domaine de Trévallon, from the appellation because it oversteps the Cabernet mark.

Palette is curious stuff, and very characterful. Its best wine is the rosé which, like the white, is exclusively made and aged in oak by Château Simone. Both these wines are very herby in flavour, but pleasantly so; the red is simply herby and dry.

Relax in this pleasure-port with a glass of Cassis's spicy rosé, or of its fresh, floral Ugni-Blanc/Sauvignon Blanc white. But skip the red; it's far too heavy and dull.

Bandol proudly claims the best climate of the Côte d'Azur. Californian winemakers hasten from one cellar to another. What brings them here is the chance to sample a grape that they've heard a lot about in the Rhône. Red Bandol has to include at least 50% Mourvèdre (the rest is made up by Grenache, Cinsault and Syrah) and should reveal that variety's spicy, herby flavour and, in good examples, its ability to age. The rosé, made from the same grapes is similarly good (but expensive).

On the maps of wine regions, Bellet looks huge, covering 17,500 acres (700 ha) of steep slopes around Nice. And there's the rub; the land here is worth too much as gardens for millionaires' villas. A mere two dozen producers farm just 125 acres (50ha) to make these crisp whites and rosés, using the local Rolle, Roussanne, Pignerol and Mayorquin for the former and Braquet and Folle Noire for the latter. Prices, like those for almost everything else in Nice, are very high.

Lastly, there are the country wines here at the mouth of the Rhône and heading eastwards and westwards along the coast:

the variable Vins de Pays des Bouches du Rhône, excellent de Mont Caume and Vin de Pays des Sables du Golfe du Lion in which is situated the go-ahead Listel winery.

Corsica

Corsica is part of Italy. I know that's not what they believe in Paris, and I know the Corsicans would probably (just) prefer to be French than Italian, but the winemakers of this glorious island have far more in common with their neighbours in Campania than their counterparts on the French mainland.

The names of the producers: Torraccia, Peraldi, Gentile – and of the grape varieties: Nielluccio, Sciacarello, Vermentino – and the styles of most of the wines – dull, oxidised whites and rosés and big, alcoholic reds – all support Corsica's case as a long lost cousin of Sardinia and Sicily.

And so does the extraordinary generosity with which the Appellation Contrôlée authorities have dished out no less than eight inadequate appellations, deftly avoiding giving one to the one style that actually deserves it, the raisiny Muscat produced in various parts of the island.

What Corsica has needed is modernisation. Unfortunately neither Corsicans nor the North African immigrant winemakers seem too keen on ideas like that.

The wines are improving fast though. For the best examples, and the best value, apart from the Muscat, go for the wonderfully-named Vins de Pays de l'Ile de Beauté, made by the UVAL cooperatives and now featuring Chardonnay, Syrah and Cabernet alongside the local varieties. And if you're there and want a Corsican classic with your dinner, try the good but overpriced very old-fashioned reds from the Domaine Comte Peraldi.

THE SOUTH

THE ESSENTIALS — SOUTHERN FRANCE

Location A large area stretching inland from the Mediterranean coast between the Pyrenees and the Rhône delta.
Quality AOCs: Banyuls (VDN — *vin doux naturel*)**;** Blanquette de Limoux; Clairette de Bellegarde; Clairette du Languedoc; Collioure; Corbières; Costières de Nîmes; Coteaux du Languedoc; Côtes du Roussillon; Côtes du Roussillon-Villages; Faugères; Fitou; Limoux; Maury (VDN); Minervois; Muscat de Frontignan (VDN); Muscat de Lunel (VDN); Muscat de Mireval (VDN); Muscat de St-Jean-de-Minervois (VDN); Muscat de Rivesaltes (VDN); St Chinian; Vin Noble du Minervois.
VDQSs include: Costières du Gard; Côtes de la Malepère; Cabardès.
Vins de pays include: Gard; Coteaux Flaviens; Hérault; Coteaux de Murviel; Côtes de Thongue; Aude; Vallée de Paradis; Oc; Pyrenées Orientales; des Sables du Golfe de Lion.
Style The majority of wines produced are red. At their best, for example a good Corbières or Côtes du Roussillon-Villages, they are firm, rounded, deeply-coloured and packed full of spicy, peppered fruit. White and rosé wines may be dry or medium-dry but are rarely distinguished. Sparkling Blanquette de Limoux is produced using a local (and ancient) variation on the *méthode champenoise*; appley-lemony, sometimes quite full and earthy, it can more resemble Spanish *cava* than more northerly French sparkling wines. Some of the region's most interesting — if rather over-powering — wines are its *vins doux naturels* from Banyuls, Maury and Rivesaltes; deep, dark and raisiny-sweet. Muscat de Frontignan is lighter but just as intensely sweet. Bordeaux grapes are increasingly being planted in the Midi and more modern vinification techniques are being incorporated into the wineries. The resulting wines are cleaner, fresher and more forward in their fruit, though perhaps at the expense of some of the better traditional styles of wines. These southern French wines are some of the best value-for-money wines to be found anywhere.
Climate Influenced by the Mediterranean and also the savage *marin* and *mistral* winds.
Cultivation Vineyards are found on the alluvial soils of the plains and on slopes above valleys such as the Aude.
Grape Varieties Alicante-Bouschet, Aspiran Gris, Aspiran Noir, Auban, Bourboulenc, Cabernet Franc, Cabernet Sauvignon, Carignan, Carignan Blanc, Cinsault, Clairette, Couderc, Grenache Blanc, Grenache Rosé, Fer, Lladoner Pelut, Malbec, Malvoisie, Maccabeo, Marsanne, Mauzac Blanc, Merlot, Mourvèdre, Muscat d'Alexandre, Muscat Blanc à Petits Grains, Muscat Doux de Frontignan, Muscat Rosé à Petits Grains, Négrette, Oeillade, Palomino, Picpoul, Picpoul Noir, Roussanne, Syrah, Terret, Terret Noir, Tourbat, Ugni Blanc, Villard Blanc.
Production/Maturation While oak is still used for fermentation, stainless steel is becoming more common. *Macération carbonique* is increasingly used for red wines. VDN is half-fermented, then a very strong spirit is added to stun the yeasts and raise the alcohol level.
Longevity Most wines are made to drink within 3 years, although some of the better reds may last beyond 5. If a VDN is non-vintage it should be ready to drink but vintage VDNs can continue to develop in bottle for decades.
Vintage Guide 83, 85, 86, 88.
Top Producers Cazes Frères, Château de Jau, Mas de Daumas Gassac, Château de Lastours.

Welcome to the wine lake. Yes, this area, in what a local producer indelicately described as the armpit of France, is the one that has traditionally produced huge quantities of wine that might just as well have been taken straight to the distillery to be turned into industrial alcohol.

But, over the last few years, the level of the lake has begun to go down, as an increasing number of farmers have switched their attention from growing unwanted wine grapes to planting orchards. And, while the bulk-wine producers give up, some of their younger, keener neighbours have begun to think quality. They've studied modern winemaking at the nearby University of Montpellier, and they've tasted wines grown in other warm parts of the world like California and Australia, compared their region to the Napa Valley and thought 'Why not?'

LANGUEDOC-ROUSSILLON / HÉRAULT / AUBE

Hidden Strengths

But before considering those reds, there is one set of wines that deserve to be considered together: the *vins doux naturels* Ironically, while France's best known sweet, fortified Muscat comes from Beaumes de Venise in the Rhône, the far wider range of sometimes richer Muscats here go almost unnoticed.

Or not quite – because one of these, the Muscat de Frontignan was once well enough known to have given its name to the finer kind of Muscat, the Muscat à Petits Grains. As in Beaumes de Venise, the cooperative makes almost all of the wine, but an independent jury tastes each year's production to ensure regularity of quality which is generally good, but not quite as zingy as the wine from the Rhône. The rather bigger, richer Muscat de Mireval owes its style to the way in which it is matured at the often very warm outdoor temperature for two years before bottling but, like the delicate Muscat de St Jean de Minervois, it's produced in very small quantities.

There are two other Muscats which claim to be the best in France: the light Muscat de Lunel and beefier Muscat de Rivesaltes. Both come in white and pink styles and are usually of at least good quality – and often rather better than wine that is just labelled Rivesaltes which is made in red, white, pink and tawny styles from a rag-bag of local varieties and accounts for half of France's *vins doux naturels*. The mixture of Grenache and Muscat used for the red and pink tends to make for emphatically old-fashioned flavours that seem reminiscent of stewed fruits, while the Maccabeu white can taste fascinatingly like currants and spice. Rivesaltes is also a good place to discover the style the French call *rancio*, produced by ageing *vin doux naturel* in barrel and intentionally allowing it to oxidise. This sweet sherry-like style is an acquired taste, but good examples can have bags of spicy, plummy flavour.

The village of Minervois is one of the most savage and least changed sites in France. Like the wines to which it gives its name, it is a rugged, no-compromise place

ABOVE: This old chapel in Corbières is dedicated to St Martin, the man who is credited as having invented vine pruning
RIGHT: The old walled city of Carcassonne, one of the most popular tourist attractions of Languedoc and the site of much of the region's tumultuous history

Banyuls, the appellation that's usually described as France's answer to port, also makes a *rancio* style. The interesting style here, though, is the red which, made primarily from the Grenache, tastes the way ruby port would taste if that wine were better made. Sadly, really good examples are rare, but look for the words 'Grand Cru' on the label; they indicate that there's no Carignan in there. They use the Grenache to make the fortified red and rosé at Maury too – and some *rancio*. All three are curiously spicy; they have their fans.

From Dull to Divine

Grapes for Banyuls are picked late; earlier picked fruit from the same vineyards can be sold as Collioure, taking their name from the tiniest and least spoiled fishing village of this region. There's very little made, but what is produced is wonderfully intense red wine. Clairette du Languedoc, is made from the dull Clairette grape in three styles: dull table wine; dull fortified and dull *rancio*. All are, however, more impressive than the unfortified wine made from the same grape at Clairette de Bellegarde.

The Clairette was once used in the sparkling wines of Blanquette de Limoux which are made mostly from the local Mauzac; its banning in 1978 led to an instant improvement in the appellation which claims to be the oldest sparkling wine of all, though styles and quality vary depending on how much Chenin Blanc or Chardonnay feature in the blend. Widely touted as a good alternative to Champagne, Blanquette de Li-

moux can, at best, be light and appley and not unlike a basic Blanc de Blancs from that region. Most sparkling Vin de Blanquette and non-fizzy Limoux Nature are dull and fruitless.

Back towards the coast, in the mountainous region around Perpignan, you know you're close to the Spanish border; some of the villagers speak Catalan; some speak heavily accented French – but it makes little difference; both are almost equally unintelligible even to some visiting Parisians. The Côtes du Roussillon is the place to find some of the most delicious, good-value, juicy-fruity reds and rosés - and some aniseedy whites that need drinking straight from the cooperative vat before they lose their freshness. The Côtes du Roussillon Villages, especially from the communes of Caramany and Latour de France, produce the appellation's best wines but these too need drinking as young possible.

Fitou has a reputation for flavour and value too, which seems slightly suprising, given the fact that this appellation's reds have to be made from 70% of the usually derided Carignan, aged for 18 months in (usually old) wood. Fitou isn't specifically fruity, but it is big-bodied and rich, and everyone's idea of how good, southern red should taste.

Up in the hills, Faugères and St Chinian compete in making fruity, plummy-cherryish reds, using traditional blends of Carignan and Rhône varieties. The former is the more impressive,

Cassoulet

Hearty bean and meat casserole

Like its wines, the cooking of Languedoc is robust and no-nonsense. Cassoulet, a rich bean and meat stew, traditionally contains preserved duck; this is a simpler version and a tasty complement to the red wines that come from this region.

SERVES 8-10

1 ½ lb/750 g dried white haricot beans
1 tbsp olive oil
1 lb/500 g unsmoked bacon, cut into pieces
10 chicken pieces
1¼ pt/1 l chicken stock
1 large onion, peeled and pierced with 3 cloves
1 carrot, peeled and cut into chunks
4 garlic cloves, peeled and coarsely chopped
1 lb/500 g pork spare ribs, cut into bite-sized pieces
1 lb/500 g breast of lamb cut into bite-sized pieces
1 lb/500 g garlic sausage (Spanish chorizo is
good) cut into chunks
1½ lb/750 g tomatoes, skinned, seeded and
chopped, or drained and chopped tinned tomatoes
Salt and freshly ground black pepper
Fresh breadcrumbs
Butter

Wash the beans under cold running water. In a frying pan brown the chicken pieces and bacon in the olive oil. In a large casserole put the beans, onion, carrot and garlic and pour in the stock, topping up with water if necessary until the contents are covered. Add the lamb and spare ribs and cook gently on top of the stove for about an hour, adding water if it seems to be drying out. Turn off the heat and add the chicken, bacon and sausage, tomato, salt and pepper. Sprinkle enough breadcrumbs over the surface to give a ½ in/1 cm crust. Dot with butter and cook, uncovered, in a pre heated oven at 350°F/180°C/Gas mark 4 for about 1½ hours. The crust should be golden. Serve with crusty French bread and a watercress salad.

and fuller-bodied, but both are worth looking for; good flavour; good value.

Corbières got its appellation after Fitou, but the wines made in this savage region are also Carignan-dominated and have a similar style. Except that here, lighter, fruitier wines are being made. For real class, though, go to the Château de Lastours (a home for the mentally handicapped) one of whose reds beat the world at the 1989 *WINE Magazine International Challenge*.

Similar changes are visible nearby in the Minervois, thanks to a number of innovative producers, including the Châteaux de Gourgazaud, de Blomac and Ste Eulalie, that are producing reds with all kinds of rich flavours.

On the coast, the Coteaux du Languedoc is a region – and a collection of villages including the commune of La Clape which, in the Middle Ages, was actually an island, connected to the mainland by a bridge. Malvasia and Terret Blanc are used to make distinctively grapey whites that can last. The reds and rosés lean heavily on the Carignan but include Cinsault and Grenache. La Clape is the region's only white wine; of the other villages, the best are St Saturnin that makes a good, light, *Vin d'une nuit* rosé by leaving the juice with the skins overnight, St Drézéry, with a 24-hour rosé, St-Christol (a favourite of the Tsar Nicholas II of Russia) Quatourze, Coteaux de Verargues and Cabrières, famous in the 14th century for its 'bronze' rosé, and still the place to sample the local Oeillade grape.

Of the region's VDQSs, the best are the Costières du Gard that can be perfectly pleasant, if sometimes dull, reds, whites and pinks from mixed asortments of local grapes. The wines of the Côtes de la Malepère can be more impressive - and in the case of the red, a bit more Bordeaux-like – as can the Rhône-like Cabardès

Throughout these regions, and in the *vin de pays* areas such as the Hérault, there is an ever-growing number of ambitious producers, spurred on by the international acclaim given to the wines of Mas de Daumas Gassac which, although 'only' supposedly of *vin de pays* status, sells for *Appellation Contrôlée* Bordeaux prices.

The men and women of Languedoc and Roussillon are stubborn folk; it has taken a very long time to persuade them to join the winemaking revolution and many of the old-timers have yet to be seduced by the appeal of fresh, light, fruity wines.

But every year's new set of wine school graduates and the interest of every rich Parisian would-be winery owner, drags the region into the future. And it's not only the French who are investing. Big money is arriving from as far away as Australia and it can't be long before some of the people who have been considering vineyards in the Napa Valley at $40,000 an acre, see the sense in buying land for a fifth of that price here...

THE SOUTH-WEST

THE ESSENTIALS — SOUTH-WEST FRANCE

Location This large and varied wine-producing region is bordered by the Atlantic, Bordeaux, the Pyrenees and Languedoc-Roussillon.

Quality AOCs: Béarn; Bergerac; Cahors; Côtes de Bergerac; Côtes de Saussignac; Côtes de Buzet; Côtes de Duras; Montravel; Côtes du Frontonnais; Gaillac; Irouléguy; Jurançon; Madiran; Monbazillac; Pacherenc du Vic Bihl; Pécharmant; Rosette. VDQSs: Côtes du Brulhois; Côtes de St Mont; Côtes du Marmandais; Tursan; Vins d'Entraygues et du Fel; Vins d'Estaing; Vins de Lavilledieu; Marcillac. The best-known *vins de pays* are Côtes de Gascogne, Charentais and Tarn.

Style Dry white wines are generally fresh, crisp and Bordeaux-like, the exception being dry Jurançon which has a spicy, honeyed quality. Sweet Jurançon is rich and raisiny while the best examples of Monbazillac resemble Sauternes. Red wines vary from the rustic to Bordeaux style; from good producers, these can be good-value alternatives to *Bordeaux petit château* or *cru bourgeois* wines. The wines of Cahors, made primarily from the Malbec grape, tend now to be lighter in style. In Irouléguy, it is again the reds to look out for; rather earthy, spicy wines made from the Tannat grape. Gaillac can produce good Gamay.

Climate Atlantic-influenced, with warm and long summers but wet winters and springs.

Cultivation Soils are varied. Vineyard sites facing east or south-east offer protection from the Atlantic.

Grape Varieties Abouriou, Arrufiac, Baroque, Cabernet Franc, Cabernet Sauvignon, Camaralet, Chardonnay, Chenin Blanc, Cinsault, Clairette, Caret des Gens, Claverie, Colombard, Courbu Blanc, Courbu Noir, Crachiner, Duras, Fer, Folle Blanche, Fuella, Gamay, Grapput, Gros Manseng, Jurançon Noir, Lauzet, L'En de L'Elh, Malbec, Manseng Noir, Mauzac, Mauzac Rosé, Merille, Merlot, Milgranet, Mouyssaguès, Muscadelle, Négrette, Ondenc, Petit Manseng, Picpoul, Pinot Noir, Raffiat, Roussellou, Sauvignon Blanc, Sémillon, Syrah, Tannat, Ugni Blanc, Valdiguié, Villard Noir.

Production/Maturation White wines and some red wines are produced by modern methods as in Bordeaux. Sparkling wines are made by the *méthode champenoise*.

Longevity Most red wines are at their best between 3 and 5 years although some of the heavier wines, notably Cahors and Madiran, can last beyond 10. The dry white wines should be drunk within three years. Good Monbazillac and sweet Jurançon will last for at least a decade.

Vintage Guide 83, 85, 86, 88, 89.

Top Producers *Bergerac:* Château la Jaubertie. *Jurançon:* Domaine Cauhapé. *Gaillac:* Domaine Jean Cros. *Monbazillac:* Château de Monbazillac. *Vin de Pays des Côtes de Gascogne:* Grassa, Plaimont.

The South West of France is rather like one of those disaster movies in which as disparate a group of people as might ever be found in the same ship, airplane or skyscraper are all gathered together in order to add interest to the plot.

Apart from finding themselves within this area of France, wines like Cahors, Vins de Pays des Côtes de Gascogne and Monbazillac have almost nothing in common except that, like the people in the movie, they all have readily defined characters of their own. Until now, few of the wines have been known outside their own patch, but with Bordeaux prices rising sharply and the quality of wine-making in the South-West improving all

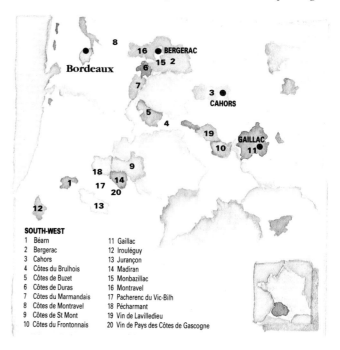

SOUTH-WEST

1 Béarn	11 Gaillac
2 Bergerac	12 Irouléguy
3 Cahors	13 Jurançon
4 Côtes du Brulhois	14 Madiran
5 Côtes de Buzet	15 Monbazillac
6 Côtes de Duras	16 Montravel
7 Côtes du Marmandais	17 Pacherenc du Vic-Bilh
8 Côtes de Montravel	18 Pécharmant
9 Côtes de St Mont	19 Vin de Lavilledieu
10 Côtes du Frontonnais	20 Vin de Pays des Côtes de Gascogne

LEFT: The Château de Monbazil-
lac, source of what can be one of
the best, most affordable
alternatives to Sauternes

ABOVE: The wine of Cahors – like
this door knocker in one of the
town's side streets — can be
initially forbidding stuff

the time, it all adds up to make this one of France's most interesting up-and-coming regions and one that will particularly repay a little study.

Perhaps the easiest way of dealing with the south-west is to separate its wines into two groups: ancient and modern. Among the 'ancient', I would include the appellations with names like Pacherenc du Vic-Bilh, made from local grapes such as the Gros Manseng and the Petit Manseng. The 'modern' group principally includes wines made from Bordeaux-style varieties and / or by up-to-date methods.

Cahors was until recently one of the most ancient styles of all. The 'great black' wine, drunk by the Romans has been sold as Bordeaux and used to beef up Bordeaux. Made from the Tannat and the Malbec (Bordeaux's unwanted red variety) Cahors has always had the reputation of being extremely old-fashioned: tannic, tough, and sweetly tobacco-spicy – more Italian in style than French. In fact, however, this old-timer has had a partial face-lift; some of its wines taste the way they used to and some taste light, fruity and very agreeable. They're more approachable – and less interesting.

For light, fruity reds, I'd rather go to Gaillac, another ancient appellation whose name means 'fertile place' in Gallic. All sorts of odd grapes are used, from the wonderfully-named, tangy L'En de l'El ('far from the eye') to the rather dull Mauzac. Of white Gaillacs, the best are probably the slightly sparkling Perlé, the semi-sweet *méthode rurale* fizz (made by allowing the wine to finish fermenting in the bottle), and some good attempts at wines with low alcohol. The sweeter versions are rarely exciting. Of the reds, the best are the Beaujolais-style *macération carbonique* wines, made from the local Duras, the Gamay, Syrah and Cabernets.

Sweet Pacherenc du Vic-Bilh sounds more like Normandy cider than wine. Its name refers to the fact that this was one of the first places to plant vines in rows – 'piquets en rangs') and rather more memorable than 'Madiran Blanc' which is what it really is. It is made from the Gros and Petit Manseng and the local Arrufiat, often '*sur lie*' and, when young, has soft peachy-peary flavours.

Côtes de St Mont is mostly (and well) made by a large cooperative according to the same rules as Pacherenc but makes more use of the less outlandish grape varieties such as the Sémillon and Sauvignon. The red which can be similarly good, is made from a blend of the local Tannat and Fer grapes, with Bordeaux varieties.

Madiran is now making a comeback after almost disappearing in the late 1940s. Today, it's still resolutely tough stuff, thanks to the presence of the Tannat and Fer grapes, but the Cabernet Franc is making inroads, softening the style and adding a touch of blackcurranty fruit.

Béarn reds contain more Tannat, are lighter in weight, but even tougher; its rosés are pleasant though, as are its Gros and Petit Manseng whites. Tursan has a similar style.

Jurançon

Jurançon is Manseng country too, and an appellation that has survived by changing from sweet to dry. Good examples of both can be oddly spicy with flavours of tropical fruits and a refreshing whack of acidity that allow the sweet versions to last for aeons. But beware; it is easy to buy sweet Jurançon when you want the (less interesting) dry. Unless the label says 'Sec', the wine isn't. Up in the Pyrénées, Irouléguy makes earthy-but-spicy reds and rosés and dull whites. Côtes du Frontonnais reds are much more fun; lovely juicy, rich wine, made from the unusual Negrette.

There are four VDQSs here, the basic Vins d'Entraygues et

du Fel, Vins d'Estaing, and Vins de Marcillac, and the rather better Negrette-dominated Vins de Lavilledieu.

The Shadow of Bordeaux

Cyrano de Bergerac's home town of Bergerac has, like Cyrano, himself, always been kept out of the limelight in which Bordeaux, made on the other side of the Dordogne from the same grape varieties' so happily basked. King Edward III, the English King who ruled this part of France during the Middle Ages banned the passage of wine, fruit, men, women and children (in other words, just about everything) across the river. In the 17th century, in a similar mood, the local authorities obliged Bergerac's wine makers to use smaller casks than the Bordelais because tax was levied per barrel and this was a pretty effective way of levying an extra tax on their rivals.

Despite these handicaps, Bergerac, which now grows one in six of France's strawberries and a fair amount of tobacco (it even has a tobacco museum!), made a market for its wines in Holland, where the sweet wines we now know as Monbazillac became very popular. In post-war years it fell out of favour and its unimpressive dry successor didn't make much impact and made few new friends.

Ironically, Bergerac owes its current renaissance to the enthusiasm of an Englishman, Nick Ryman, his son Hugh, and a visiting young winemaker from Australia who, between them proved that Ryman's Château de la Jaubertie Bergerac Blanc could compete with all but the best Graves, and that his juicy, blackcurranty red could beat many a bottle labelled Haut-Médoc. Others are following Ryman's lead with Bergerac Sec – which explains why the local, slightly sweeter alternative appellation of Saussignac is fast disappearing. Still surviving here though, is Pécharmant, which really is of Médoc petit château standard.

Sadly, Ryman's influence, nor yet the growing popularity of Sauternes, have touched Monbazillac. Too little care is taken over the winemaking here, and too little patience by pickers who cannot wait for botrytis to develop.

Nearby Rosette, makes tiny (and shrinking) quantities of pleasant, delicate, Cadillac-like demi-sec rather more successfully than the various sweet wines made at Montravel which, when compared to most modern white Bordeaux, taste quaintly old-fashioned. And dull.

Côtes de Duras is good basic red and white-Bordeaux-by-any-other-name, produced from the same kinds of grapes grown in the same kind of soil; only the fact that it's just over the border in the next département denies it the appellation. Buy it and try to tell the difference. The same advice applies to the generally excellent Côtes du Marmandais, and the Côtes de Buzet, produced within the region of Armagnac (but only for the Buzet reds and rosés; the whites are dull). The Côtes du Brulhois makes no white, but its rosé is pleasantly light and Cabernet-ish and rather better than the rustic red made here from the same varieties.

Of the south-west *vins de pays*, there is the region-wide Vin de Pays du Comte Tolosan and a white superstar in the shape of the Vin de Pays des Côtes de Gascogne where, led by the Domaine Grassa, good, fresh Colombard and Ugni Blanc whites have revolutionised their region. Vins de Pays d'Agenais can be either Bordeaux-style or old-fashioned, depending on the grapes that are used. Vin de Pays de Dordogne is similar in style to Bergerac; Coteaux de Quercy and tiny Coteaux de Glanes are good Gamay – and Merlot – influenced reds; Bigorre is like mini Madiran; Côtes Condomois are old–fashioned Tannat reds and dull Ugni-Blanc whites, and Côtes de Montestruc include unusual, beefy reds made partly from the dark-fleshed Alicanté-Bouschet. Close to Toulouse, the Côtes du Tam combines local and Bordeaux varieties with, for some reason, the Portugais Bleu, Saint-Sardos produces traditional reds, whites and rosés from local varieties.

Poule au Pot Le Roi Henri IV

King Henry's chicken casserole

It was Henri IV, King of France in the 16th century, who vowed to his subjects that he would put 'a chicken in every pot'. The king came from Béarn in the south-west, and this dish will go very well with the good robust reds of the region.

SERVES 6
1 large chicken, 4-5 lb/2-2.5 kg
Salt and freshly ground black pepper
6 pt/3.5 l chicken stock

STUFFING
4 slices ham (Bayonne is traditional but not
essential), chopped
8 oz/225 g veal, minced
8 oz/225 g pork, minced
2 chicken livers, chopped
1 oz/25 g butter
2 medium onions, chopped
2 garlic cloves, crushed
4 oz/100 g dried breadcrumbs
1 tsp dried tarragon
1 tsp crumbled dried sage
1 tbsp single cream
2 tbsp brandy (Armagnac is traditional but not essential)
½ tsp grated nutmeg
2 egg yolks
Salt and freshly ground black pepper

Season the bird inside and out with salt and pepper. In a large bowl combine all the ingredients for the stuffing. Mix well and leave to stand, covered, for at least 30 minutes. Stuff the bird and put it in a large flameproof casserole. Close the opening through which the bird was stuffed by pulling the flap of skin across the opening and tucking it under the bird. Pour over the stock. Bring to a boil and then reduce to a moderate simmer and cook, covered, for 2-2 ½ hours. Remove the chicken to a serving plate (keep the stock for soup) and serve with creamed potatoes and steamed cabbage.

ABOVE: Bergerac is great farming country - for sunflowers like these as well as for vines

LEFT: Gascony, the source of Armagnac and an increasing amount of fresh, light, wine is still one of the most traditional regions of France

RIGHT: Englishman Nick Ryman's Château la Jaubertie has become one of the best-known – and the best – wines in Bergerac

ITALY

Italy is the most gloriously and infuriatingly confusing country on earth – except that, like Germany, it is not so much a country as a collection of disparate regions, seemingly stuck together with a rather unreliable experimental glue. What realistic link could there be between the German-speaking producers of Lagrèin Dunkel in the mountains of the South Tyrol on the Austrian border, the Franco-Italian winemakers of Valle d'Aosta who make Enfer d'Arvier, the Sardinians who use the Spanish Garnacha grape for their Cannonau and the peasants of Sicily, who farm grape varieties such as the Frappato and Perricone, that have never been seen on the mainland of Italy?

Latin Labyrinth

The more closely you look at Italy's wines and wine regions, the more confusing it all becomes. You could start by learning the names of the regions – but the ones listed in wine books rarely feature on labels. Bordeaux comes from Bordeaux, Champagne comes from Champagne; Barolo comes from Piedmont and Chianti comes from Tuscany.

Of course, you could bone up on Italy's 1,000 or so different grapes, but you'd still end up banging your head against the wall in frustration. The Montepulciano grape is used to make Montepulciano d'Abruzzo, but it's *not* used for Vino Nobile di Montepulciano which is made from another variety altogether; the same grape can be called the Nebbiolo in one Piedmont vineyard and Spanna in the one next door.

Holes in the DOC Net

In France, at least you can rely on the list of *Appellations Contrôlées* to include almost all of the country's best wines. Italy's equivalent – the DOC, or *Denominazione di Origine Controllata* – excludes a growing number of some of the country's best, most highly priced and highly praised wines. They can only call themselves *vino da tavola* – 'table wine', precisely the designation that applies to the cheapest plonk on the market.

The Italians have, until very recently, made matters much worse by encouraging foreigners to concentrate their attention on their lowest common denominators in food and wine. So, when most people think of Italian cooking, their minds go little

1 VALLE D'AOSTA
Donnaz
Enfer d'Arvier

2 PIEDMONT
Arneis di Langhe (whole region)
Arneis dei Roeri
Asti Spumante (whole region)
Barbaresco
Barbera d'Asti / Dolcetto /
   d'Asti / Moscato d'Asti
   Nebbiolo d'Asti / Grignolino
   d'Asti
Barbera d'Alba / Dolcetto d'Alba
Barbera del Monferrato
Barolo
Brachetto d'Acqui / Dolcetto
   d'Acqui
Bricco Manzoni
Carema
Cortese di Gavi / Gavi di
   Gavi
Erbaluce di Caluso
Freisa
Gattinara
Ghemme
Greco
Spanna

3 LIGURIA
Cinqueterre
Riviera Ligure di Ponente
Rossese di Dolceacqua

4 LOMBARDY
Franciacorta
Lugana
Oltrepò Pavese
Valtellina

5 TRENTINO-ALTO ADIGE
Alto-Adige (Süd-Tirol)
Bozner Leiten
Caldaro
Casteller
Etschtaler (Valdadige)
Goldenmuskateller (Moscato Giallo)
Kalterersee (Lago di Caldaro)
Marzemino di Isera
Rosenmuskateller
Somi
St Magdalener (Santa Maddelena)
Terlano
Teroldego Rotaliano
Trentino

6 FRIULI-VENEZIA GIULIA
Aquilea
Carso
Colli Goriziano
Colli Orientali
Grave del Friuli
Isonzo
Latisana
Picolit
Vintage Tunina

7 VENETO
Bardolino
Bianco di Custoza
Colli Berici
Lison-Pramaggiore
Piave
Prosecco di Conegliano

Raboso
Soave / Recioto di Soave
Tocai di Lison
Torcolato
Valpolicella / Recioto della
   Valpolicella (Amarone)
Venegazzú della Casa

8 EMILIA-ROMAGNA
Albana di Romagna
Colli Bolognesi
Colli di Parma
Lambrusco
Pagadebit
Rosso Armentano
Sangiovese di Romagna
Terre Rosse Chardonnay
Trebbiano di Romagna

9 TUSCANY
Bolgheri
Brunello di Montalcino
Carmignano
Castello della Sala
Cetinaia
Chianti Classico
Coltassala
Elba
Galestro
Ghiaie della Furba
Sodi di San Niccolo
Le Pergole Torte
Montecarlo
Pomino
Rosso di Montalcino
Sassicaia
Solaia
Tignanello
Vernaccia di San Gimignano
Vinattieri Rosso
Vino Nobile di Montepulciano
Vin Santo

10 MARCHES
Rosso Conero
Rosso Piceno
Sangiovese dei Colli Pesaresi
Verdicchio dei Castelli di Jesi

11 UMBRIA
Colli Altotiberini
Colli del Trasimeno
Colli Perugini
Grechetto/Greco
Montefalco
Orvieto
Torgiano
Vin Santo

12 LATIUM
Aprilia
Cerveteri
Est!Est!!Est!!!
Falerno
Fiorano
Frascati
Marino
Torre Ercolana

13 ABRUZZI-MOLISE
Biferno
Montepulciano d'Abruzzo
Montepulciano del Molise
Ramitello
Rubino
Trebbiano d'Abruzzo

14 CAMPANIA
Fiano di Avellino
Greco di Tufa
Lacryma Christi del Vesuvio
Ravello
Taurasi

15 APULIA
Castel del Monte
Copertino
Primitivo di Manduria
Rosa del Golfo
Squinzano
Torre Quarto
Il Falcone

16 BASILICATA
Aglianico del Vulture

17 CALABRIA
Cirò
Greco di Bianco

18 SICILY
Cerasuolo di Vittoria
Corvo
Etna
Marsala
Regaleali

19 SARDINIA
Anghelu Ruju
Cannonau di Sardegna
Giro di Cagliari
Malvasia di Planargia
Vermentino

further than spaghetti Bolognese and pizza (which is rather like limiting French cuisine to quiche and pâté); when they think of Italian wines, they imagine two-litre bottles of Soave, Lambrusco and Valpolicella.

The Burden of Tradition

The trouble is that great Italian wines do still seem to be the exceptions to the rule. One of this country's greatest handicaps has been its readiness to allow tradition and local politics rather than quality and common sense to dictate the way Italian wines are made.

In Chianti, for example, winemakers are legally obliged to put white grapes in their red wine. Now, odd though it may seem, this blend of black and white grapes is a perfectly respectable tradition in other regions of the world; in the northern Rhône, the producers of Hermitage have always been

LEFT: Until recently, Italians often revered old wine for its age rather than its quality

ABOVE: In the Tuscan town of San Gimignano, trattorias are the perfect place to enjoy the local wine and food

---

LANGUAGE OF ITALY

Abboccato Semi-sweet.
Amabile Semi-sweet, but usually sweeter than *abboccato*.
Amarone Bitter.
Annato Year.
Asciutto Bone-dry.
Azienda/Azienda Agricola Estate/winery.
Azienda Vitivinicola Specialist wine estate.
Bianco White.
Cantina Cellar, winery.
Cantina Sociale Co-operative winery.
Cascina Farm or estate (northern Italy).
Cerasuolo Cherry-red.
Chiaretto Somewhere between rosé and very light red.
Classico Wine from a restricted area within a DOC. Usually the central area and often the source of the best wines.
Colli Hilly area.
Consorzio Group of producers who control and promote the wines in their particular region.
Denominazione di Origine Controllata (DOC) Controlled wine region. The DOC system has been recognised as having many faults, notably that it patently fails to recognise some of the best wines in Italy and that it has been granted to some areas more for their wine tradition than for their present quality. The best guarantee of quality is the name of the producer.
Denominazione di Origine Controlla e Garantita (DOCG) Theoretically a superior classification to DOC but this was cast into doubt when the first white DOCG

was granted to Albana di Romagna, a rather undistinguished wine. Nevertheless it does recognise some of the best Italian reds, for example, Barolo, Barbaresco and Brunello di Montalcino.
Dolce Very sweet.
Enoteca Literally a 'wine library' – most commonly a wine shop but sometimes a local wine 'institute' or regulatory body.
Fattoria Farm.
Fermentazione Naturale Natural fermentation, but can be in bottle or tank.
Fiore Literally 'flower', refers to the first pressing of grapes.
Frizzante Semi-sparkling.
Frizzantino Very lightly sparkling.
Gradi Percentage of alcohol by volume.
Imbottigliato Bottled.
Liquoroso Sweet and fortified, or a dry white wine high in alcohol.
Localita (Also **Ronco** and **Vigneto**) Single vineyard.
Metodo Classico The *méthode champenoise*.
Passito Strong, sweet wine made from semi-dried (*passito*) grapes.
Pastoso Medium-sweet.
Podere Small farm or estate.
Ramato Copper-coloured wines made from Pinot Grigio grapes briefly macerated on their skins.
Recioto (della Valpolicella, di Soave) Speciality styles of the Veneto made from semi-dried grapes. Can be dry and bitter (*amarone*), sweet (*amabile*) or an intermediate style (*amandorlato*). All are characterised by strong, concentrated flavours and high alcohol levels.

Ripasso Wine fermented on the lees of a *recioto.*
Riserva/Riserva Speciale DOC wine matured for a statutory number of years in a barrel.
Rosato Rosé.
Rosso Red.
Secco Dry.
Semi-Secco Medium-dry.
Spumante Fully sparkling wine.
Stravecchio Very old.
Superiore DOC wines meeting certain additional conditions, such as higher alcohol content.
Uvaggio Wine blended from a number of grape varieties.
Uvas Grapes.
Vecchio Old.
Vendemmia Vintage.
Vin Santo/Vino Santo Traditionally sweet – although can be dry – white from *passito* grapes stored in sealed casks that have not been topped up for several years. Literally means 'holy wine', as was traditionally racked during Holy Week.
Vini Tipici Equivalent of French *vins de pays* – 'country wines' with some regional character. A new designation which may or may not catch on.
Vino novello New, 'nouveau-style' wine.
Vino da arrosto A robust red that is a 'wine for roast meat'.
Vino da pasta Ordinary 'mealtime' wine.
Vino da tavola Literally means 'table wine' but includes some of Italy's finest wines since the DOC laws place onerous restrictions on the use of non-traditional grape varieties and innovative methods.

LEFT: One of Italy's most traditional wines is the sherry-like Vin Santo, the flavour of which is derived from the drying of the grapes in lofts and barns before fermentation is allowed to begin

BELOW: Alba in Piedmont is one of the world's shrines for food lovers – especially during the truffle festival that takes over the whole town

RIGHT: A classical – and unchanging – still life at the Avignonesi cellars in Tuscany

allowed to chuck a few Marsanne grapes in their red wine. But there is one essential difference: in Hermitage, the white grapes are optional; growers who want to restrict themselves to using the Syrah grape can do so. In Chianti, quality-conscious wine-makers who want to make *their* wine solely from the region's classic Sangiovese grape may not call it Chianti, but have to label it *vino da tavola*.

Old Habits Die Hard

As elsewhere in southern Europe, Italy has also suffered from the old belief that all wines benefit from a prolonged stay in barrel. So, a wine bottled within a few months of the harvest is simply labelled Bardolino; a Bardolino Superiore is not necessarily (as one might expect) better wine, but will merely, for better or worse, have been aged for at least a year in barrel. Bardolino's role in life is to compete with Beaujolais; it should hit the streets as young as possible; so in this case Superiore is a contradiction in terms; that extra year usually makes for wine that is distinctly *inferiore*.

Unlike those of Germany and France, Italy's wine laws do not officially acknowledge the identity of specific vineyard sites. The closest they come to reçognising that some parts of a DOC make better wines than others is the set of *Classico* sub-regions – such as Chianti Classico, Soave Classico and Valpolicella Classico – whose French equivalent is the 'Villages' (Beaujolais Villages, Côtes du Rhône Villages) appellation.

What there is not, however, is the overlying system of prestigious Grand Cru and Premier Cru vineyards with which the French have built their vinous reputation. Burgundy's vineyards are divided into good, better and best; those of Barolo are all considered equal.

In Germany, a similar lack of official recognition is treated with a Germanic respect for the rules. In Italy, winemakers just go right ahead and print the names of particular vineyards on their labels. Unfortunately, and inevitably, this has allowed all sorts of fudging to go on, and all sorts of meaningless and misleading references to non-existent or no-better-than-ordinary-quality pieces of land. So while one Barolo Cannubi, from a good part of the Cannubi hill, could be the equivalent of a Premier Cru Burgundy, another, from a less well-exposed section of the same hill, might be no better than an an ordinary Barolo. As it happens, the winegrowers of Barolo and nearby Barbaresco are trying to establish their own official set of top-

class vineyards – but the battles they will probably fight among themselves are likely to be very tough. The prospects of their counterparts in other regions categorizing *their* vineyards seem highley unlikely.

Quantity v. Quality

Italian wines are still suffering from the mistakes that were made during the years after the Second World War. Almost throughout the country, the call was for productivity; for vines and vine varieties that would yield plenty of wine. In some regions – Soave, for example – winegrowers took over land previously used to grow maize; in others, such as Chianti, anaemic red wines were beefed up with heady stuff from the southern parts

of the country. The more wine people made, the more problems they had; space was short, and so was the money to pay for the bottles, so a single vintage would often be bottled in several sessions spread over two, three and even four years – during which time the quality of the wine in the barrels could change and deteriorate. So, three bottles of Chianti, of the same vintage, with identical labels, could taste completely different.

The Italian Renaissance

During the 1980s, however, a new generation of Italian winemakers followed the example of a few pioneers and turned their attention to quality rather than quantity. Cooling equipment was installed into wineries, allowing producers to make fresh, clean white wines rather than fat, flabby ones. Old barrels were thrown out and replaced by clean new ones. Throughout Italy, winemakers planted Chardonnay and Cabernet Sauvignon and started to make wines that competed with white burgundy, red Bordeaux and the best varietals of California.

Traditionalists began to complain that this sudden rush to make 'international'-style wine was undermining Italy's own vinous heritage. Almost as if anticipating this, the pioneers turned their attention back to the indigenous grapes that had for so long been under-exploited – and revealed some extraordinary unsuspected potential. Thus it is that, at the beginning of the 1990s, Italy has quietly become the most exciting of the established wine countries, quite simply because no one knows what its producers are going to do next. Sidestepping the rules where they seem to be silly, bending them wherever possible, this new breed of Italian winemaker is probably experimenting on a wider range of wine flavours than his or her counterparts anywhere else in the world.

Quality Designations

In 1415, long before Christopher Columbus sailed for America, Chianti became the first wine region in the world whose boundaries and production were controlled by law. Five centuries later, in 1924, Italy began to lay the ground rules for regional designations that finally led to the allocation in 1966 of the first *DOC – Denominazione di Origine Controllata* – to the Tuscan white wine of Vernaccia di San Gimignano.

Over the last 25 years, around 250 other wines have been given DOCs of their own, and half a dozen of those have been awarded the higher designation of *DOCG – Denominazione di Origine Controllata e Garantita* – which is expected to be given to another batch in the early 1990s.

It is generally acknowledged that the DOCs were doled out too generously (a lot of Soave and Lambrusco certainly doesn't deserve this distinction); now questions are being asked about the way in which the DOCGs are awarded.

The 1980 list of the first DOCGs – Barolo, Barbaresco, Brunello di Montalcino and Vino Nobile di Montepulciano – aroused little controversy, though eyebrows were raised at the delay in including Chianti Classico until 1984. It was the news that, in 1988, Albana di Romagna would become the first white DOCG in 1988 that sent those eyebrows up to the hairline; the few Italian wine experts who had ever tasted more than a handful of wines made here checked their calendars to be sure that it wasn't April 1. As Dario Lanzoni, director of the DOCG Chianti Classico producers' association, wrily explains: 'Albana di Romagna got the DOCG because they asked for it.' Now Torgiano, Gattinara, Carmignano, Frascati, Vernaccia di San Gimignano, Inferno, Valtellina, Sassella, Bardolino Classico and parts of Collio have all asked too – and all look set to receive their DOCGs. In short, this seems to have become a club almost anyone can join.

The Unofficial Elite

In response to the often lax regulations, growers in some regions have formed *consorzios* – associations – that are supposedly devoted both to improving quality and promoting their local wines. The best known of these is the Chianti Classico Gallo Nero Consorzio, membership of which is proclaimed by the presence of a bottle-neck collar depicting a black cockerel. Unfortunately, even the best consorzios rarely include all the producers of their region (Antinori, probably the biggest name in Chianti Classico, is not a member) and some seem to be all promotion and little quality.

One much more reliable national alternative to the consorzios is the VIDE association, whose 30 members' wines have to be tasted and analysed before they are allowed to carry the VIDE symbol on their labels.

Wines that, however good they are, fail to comply with DOC and DOCG rules may only be labelled as *vino da tavola*. In Tuscany, a group of quality-conscious producers of these wines have launched an alternative, unofficial designation, *vino con predicato*, based on the kinds of criteria (vineyard site, yields per acre etc) that dictate Premier Cru status in France. There are some signs that winemakers in other regions may well follow the Tuscan example by launching Predicato classifications of their own.

Indications of Change

After much hesitation, the authorities have riposted with the official tag *Vino da Tavola con Indicazione Geografica* – literally, table wine that tells you where it comes from (*vino da tavola* cannot disclose its vintage, grape variety or even the region where it was made). Unfortunately, although the new designation was supposed to be limited to quality wines its allocation has been very generous, not to say indiscriminating; at best it could be seen as a poor shot at mimicking France's *vin de pays* – a designation which hardly trumpets a wine's quality. Launched in 1989 after a decade of head-scratching and negociation, *vino tipico* is supposed to be slightly stricter in its criteria; sadly, the key word is 'slightly'.

Further changes and confusion are reportedly to be expected with the creation of a three-level pyramid for Italy's better wines. At the top of the ladder there will (still) be DOCG; beneath that there will be DOC, followed by VQPRD (quality wine from determined regions, a basic EC concept).

There are many who doubt that Italy's basically unsound quality structure can take another round of cosmetic repairwork: Burton Anderson, the American wine writer and leading authority on Italian wines, has advocated renovating its foundations with his simple proposal that DOCs should be allocated to entire regions such as Tuscany and Piedmont, in much the same way that they are allocated to Burgundy and Bordeaux.

THE NORTH-EAST

The north-eastern corner of Italy is a crazy, mixed-up part of the world, full of people who refuse to speak Italian, call their wines by all sorts of confusing names and, in the Veneto at least, apparently do their best to ensure that the wines anyone is likely to have heard of, such as Valpolicella and Soave, are often the ones that taste worst. And yet this is a great region for vinous explorers – for people who are ready to brave the labyrinth of language for the sake of excitingly different flavours.

5   TRENTINO-ALTO ADIGE
5a Alto-Adige (Süd-Tirol)
5b Caldaro
5c Kalterersee
5d St Magdalener (Santa Maddelena)
5e Terlano
5f Teroldego Rotaliano
5g Trentino

Goldenmuskateller (Moscato Giallo)
Marzemino di Isera
Rosenmuskateller (whole region)

6   FRIULI-VENEZIA GIULIA
6a Aquilea
6b Colli Orientali
6c Grave del Friuli
6d Isonzo
6e Latisana
Picolit (whole region)

7   VENETO
7a Bardolino
7b Bianco di Custoza
7c Colli Berici
7d Lison-Pramaggiore
7e Piave
7f Soave / Recioto di Soave
7g Tocai di Lison
7h Torcolato
7i Valpolicella / Recioto della
     Valpolicella (Amarone)
7j Venegazzu della Casa

THE ESSENTIALS — FRIULI-VENEZIA GIULIA

Location North-east Italy, on the Yugoslavian border.
Quality One third of production is from 7 DOC areas — Grave del Friuli, Carso, Collio, Colli Orientali, Latisana, Isonzo and Aquilea.
Style Whites are crisp and dry at best, with tangy lemon fruit. There is also a fine pair of new-wave *vino da tavola* whites; Ronco delle Acacie, which combines this appealing fresh fruit with understated new oak, and Vintage Tunina, which has the added weight and richness of Chardonnay. Some dessert wines, notably the very pricy Picolit and Verduzzo di Ramandolo, are also produced. Reds are generally light, refreshing and slightly grassy, but the local Schioppettino produces a big, spicy wine with rich fruit flavours which can mature extremely well. Friuli produces some of Italy's best varietal Cabernets and Merlots.
Climate Cool European climate with warm summers and cold winters. Extremes are moderated by the Adriatic sea. Lack of sun may be a problem for reds in some years.
Cultivation Flat, alluvial plains with the better vineyards in the hills.
Grape Varieties *Red:* Merlot, Cabernet Franc, Cabernet Sauvignon, Pinot Noir, Refosco, Schioppettino. *White:* Chardonnay, Sauvignon, Tocai, Pinot Grigio, Malvasia, Pinot Bianco, Picolit, Ribolla, Traminer, Müller-Thurgau, Verduzzo.
Production/Maturation Stainless steel and cold-fermentation have been widely adopted to the detriment, in some cases, of the personalities of the grape varieties. More recently there has been some experimentation with oak in order to add complexity to the fruit flavours.
Longevity Reds may last for 8 years — Schioppettino can be kept for 5-15 years — although most are best drunk within 3-5 years. Whites are at their best within 1-3 years of the vintage. The 'super-deluxe' *vino da tavola* whites can benefit from up to 8 years' ageing.
Vintage Guide Reds 82, 83, 85, 86,88
Whites 83, 85, 86, 88
Top Producers Jermann, Schiopetto, Marco Felluga, Collavini, Gravner, Dri, Puiatti.

Alto Adige

In deference to the official maps, I shall call this former Austrian region the Alto Adige, but it is known by the majority of its inhabitants as the Südtirol, and many of the wines they make bear the names Vernatsch, Müller-Thurgau and Lagrein Dunkel.

Thankfully, those labelled Pinot Grigio, Chardonnay, Cabernet Sauvignon and Franc, Traminer, Sauvignon and Müller-Thurgau are reasonably straightforward. But then there is the oddly and deliciously smoke-and-cherry-flavoured Schiava, or Vernatsch, grape which makes wine most outsiders would describe as deep rosé but the locals insist is red. Some of the best examples come from St Magdalener (or Santa Maddalena), and from the region around the Kalterersee (Lago di Caldaro).

The wild-berry-flavoured Lagrein makes light, raspberryish rosé (Kretzer or Rosato) and beefy reds (Dunkel or Scuro) and can do wonders for Schiava. It might also be beneficial blended with some of the region's Cabernet Sauvignons and Cabernet Francs, some of which can taste a little raw. A few of these can be quite impressive though, as, in their light, raspberryish way, can the Pinot Noirs.

Betwixt red and white there is an extraordinary wine that is made almost nowhere else. Rosenmuskateller is the nearest I have ever found to a liquid rose garden. My favourites are the dry example made by Tiefenbrunner and Graf Kuenbeg's sweeter versions, which can last for a decade or more, developing all kinds of fascinating rose-petal flavours (yes, flavours) and smells.

Of Alto Adige whites, the ones that have received the greatest media attention have been the oaked and unoaked Chardonnays. I am less convinced than some of the enthusiasts; the unwooded versions taste light, pineappley and hard to discern from the Pinot Biancos made by the same producers in the same region. A few of the better examples, such as those from Tiefenbrunner and Lageder, can handle ageing in oak, but most seem to be overpowered by the experience. No, the wines that excite me more are those made from more aromatic varieties, such as the Muscat, the Pinot Gris, the Gewürztraminer (the grape that is supposed to have its origins here in the town of Tramin), the Riesling and, believe it or not, the Müller-Thurgau. Anyone who doubts that this variety can make special wine should try the one made by Herbert Tiefenbrunner from grapes grown in his mountain-top Feldmarshall vineyard.

Unfortunately, fine, concentrated wines such as this are not as common in the Alto Adige as the region's apologists like to claim; far too many of them show all the dilute signs of vines that have been allowed to produce far too much juice. Apart from Tiefenbrunner, Lageder is a name to look out for; try his Terlano, a tasty blend of classic and non-classic white varieties.

Trentino

South of the Alto Adige, Trentino is a warm, productive area where huge amounts of anonymous fizz are made, usually from a blend of Chardonnay, Pinot Bianco and Pinot Grigio. The climate and the terrain make Trentino an easy place to grow grapes; unfortunately, most of the farmers here prefer to leave the winemaking to the huge Cavit cooperative, which processes around three-quarters of the region's crop. There is very little wrong with any of the wines Cavit makes, but most have the typical Trentino characteristic of tasting pleasantly bland. Good whites made here – such as those from Pojer e Sandri – are the exceptions to the successful commercial rule.

The reds have more to offer, provided that you sidestep such 'French' varieties as the Cabernets, Merlot and Pinot Noir and turn to the characterful local grapes. The Teroldego, used to make Teroldego Rotaliano, and grown almost nowhere else, is one of Italy's underrated varieties. Its wines are rich and fairly spicy, as are those from the almost mentholly Marzemino.

Facing Page: Herbert Tiefenbrunner, one of the greatest winemakers of the Alto Adige, prunes the vines of his mountainous vineyard

Above: While 'commercial' Valpolicella is made in huge quantities, Recioto is still a cottage industry. Signora Quintarelli, wife of one of Veneto's best producers, still bottles the estate's wines by hand

---

THE WINE OF MEDITATION

The term *Recioto* is used to describe the strong and naturally sweet wines produced from grapes taken from the ears (*recie* comes from *orecchie*) of the bunches. These upper parts of the bunch receive the most sun, and have much higher sugar levels than the others. When picked, the grapes are hung indoors in lofts or barns to allow them partially to dry and to concentrate the sugars. The semi-dried grapes - the passito - are then pressed and fermented very slowly to produce the strongest natural wine possible (up to 17° alcohol).

Reciotos are a specialty of the Veneto region and can be made from either red or white grapes. Classic, creamy, honeyed, Recioto de Soave dei Capitelli is made by Anselmi, while Maculan produces the rather finer Torcolato. The red Recioto della Valpolicella from producers such as Quintarelli, Masi and Tedeschi rank among the greatest and most unusual wines of Italy. If all the sugar is fermented out of the wine it is known as Amarone and combines fascinating smells and flavours of bitter chocolate, plums, raisins, cherries and smoky charcoal. Wines that do not undergo a second fermentation remain sweet and are termed Amabile. An intermediate bitter-sweet, sweet and sour version is Amandorlato Neither style is an ideal accompaniment to food, but both are ideal *Vini di Meditazione* for sipping at by the fireside.

Valpolicella Ripasso is produced by pumping young Valpolicella over the lees of a Recioto to precipitate a second fermentation. Such wines have a higher alcohol content and take on some Recioto character but can only be sold as Vino da Tavola.

THE ESSENTIALS — THE VENETO

Location North-east Italy, bordered by the Adriatic, Trentino-Alto Adige, Friuli, Austria and the river Po in the south.
Quality Soave is Italy's largest white DOC which, together with red Valpolicella and Bardolino, accounts for well over half of the region's output. Other DOCs: Breganze, Colli Berici, Gambellara, Piave Raboso, Recioto di Soave/della Valpolicella/della Valpolicella Amarone.
Style Soave, Valpolicella and Bardolino are, because of the size of their output, often cheap, dull, commercial, even rather nasty wines but one can get much higher quality at only a slightly higher price. Soave at its best is dry and nutty with a pleasant creamy texture, and Recioto di Soave can be lusciously delicious. Bardolino is soft and light with some cherry-stone bitterness. It needs to be drunk young. Valpolicella is a richer, heavier version of Bardolino, and single vineyard wines reveal a much greater depth of plummy fruit. The rich, alcoholic, port-like Recioto della Valpolicella can be dry (Amarone) or sweet (Amabile). Fine Cabernet Sauvignons are made by Maculan (Breganze) and Conte Loredan-Gasparini (Venegazzù della Casa), and some excellent value wines with soft, plummy fruit are made from the indigenous Raboso grape. The Prosecco grape is capable of producing some decent sparkling wines at Conegliano.
Climate Hot summers and warm autumns. Winters are cold and can be foggy.
Cultivation Alluvial plains in the coastal region provide very fertile soil for vine growing.
Grape Varieties *Red:* Cabernet Sauvignon, Cabernet Franc, Merlot, Corvina, Rondinella, Molinara, Negrara, Raboso, Pinot Nero. *White:* Garganega, Trebbiano, Prosecco, Pinot Grigio, Pinot Bianco, Tocai, Riesling, Verduzzo.
Production/Maturation Veneto is dominated by cooperatives and in-dustrial concerns which mass-produce cheap commercial wines. A Bordeaux influence can be detected in the production of some of the Cabernets and Merlots. Reciotos are produced from *passito* grapes, slowly fermented to give their characteristic alcoholic strength and richness.
Longevity Reds: Most basic reds should be drunk within 5 years. Re-ciotos can be left for some 15 years, good Cabernets for 10 years. Whites: Basic whites — within 1 year; good Soave Classico — 2 to 4 years; Recioto di Soave, Torcolato — up to 10 years
Vintage Guide Reds 77, 78, 79, 81, 83, 85, 86, 88
Whites 82, 83, 85, 86, 87, 88
Top Producers Quintarelli, Masi, Tedeschi, Santa Sofia, Allegrini, Anselmi, Maculan, Conte Loredan Gasparini.

RIGHT: Verona is not only the vinous capital of the Veneto, it is also one of the most beautiful towns in Italy

BELOW: These grapes are being allowed to dry naturally before they are fermented into raisiny Recioto

Veneto

The greatest red wine of the Veneto has one of the most abused wine names in Italy. If your only experience of Valpolicella is of dull, flavourless stuff from a two-litre bottle, you'd be forgiven for finding it hard to believe that this wine is capable of any kind of real drinkability, let alone greatness.

Back in the 1960s, the authorities generously extended the name Valpolicella to a huge area of undistinguished land, effectively undermining the reputation of the good producers with individual vineyards within the original Valpolicella Clas-sico zone. Today, those producers, such as Masi and Allegrini-Boscaini, are still making serious Valpolicella with lots of plummy, cherryish flavour and a fascinating bitter, almondy twist, but they sensibly focus wine drinkers' attention on the names of their vineyards rather than that of the region; some labels barely seem to mention Valpolicella at all.

For really great Valpolicella, seek out the rather rarer Recioto della Valpolicella, made from grapes dried in barns and slowly fermented. Wines bearing this label are sweet and raisiny; ones also labelled Amarone are dry. Both can be as alcoholic and intense as some fortified wines, amply deserving their local name of vini da meditazione; wines to sip at thoughtfully.

Bardolino is a lighter-weight red – and pink, known as Chiaretto – cousin of Valpolicella, made from the same grape varieties a few miles to the west of that region. Good examples can be packed with cherry fruit and compete easily with Beaujolais, though without ever quite losing the characteristic bitter twist of the region. Buy young vintages labelled Classico, but avoid Superiore wines, which legally have had to spend a year in barrel losing their flavour. The only exceptions are the single-vineyard wines from a few quality-conscious producers, such as Masi, Boscaini, Portalupi and Guerrieri-Rizzardi. Even these need drinking long before their fifth birthday.

If Valpolicella is a debased name, Soave has been dragged through the dirt. Sadly, until recently, almost no one except Leonaldo Pieropan was making anything other than the poor-est, dullest wine the Garganega and Trebbiano di Soave grapes can produce. Today a few other producers have come to Soave's rescue, producing rich-yet-fresh wines with lovely lemony flavours. Look for young examples of Soave Classico from individual vineyards made by producers such as Anselmi, Allegrini, Masi and Boscaini. And look too for the rare, honeyed, curranty Recioto di Soave, the white version of Recioto della Valpolicella. For better alternatives to basic Soave, try the Garganega-based Gambellara and Bianco di Custoza.

One producer – Maculan – has almost single handedly put the region of Breganze on the map. My own favourite of the range of wines made here is the gorgeous, raisiny-honeyed Torcolato, made from a blend of this region's native Vespaiola and Tocai grapes that have been left to dry before fermentation and maturation in new oak. But the Maculan Cabernet reds are just as impressive, and the oak-aged white Prato di Canzio shows what the Tocai can do in a blend if it is given the chance.

Piave's interesting grape is the Raboso, which can pack a real punch of rustic fruity flavour. The white Verduzzo is locally just as well thought of, but its naturally low acidity tends to make for soft, dull wine; if you want a white from Piave, stick to the Pinot Bianco or Grigio, or the Tocai.

Lison-Pramaggiore is in the Veneto, but only just. The atti-tudes here – and the styles of wine – are far more akin to those of Friuli; varietals are the order of the day, with a firm emphasis being placed on Cabernet, Merlot and Tocai.

Friuli-Venezia Giulia

If the Alto Adige is overtly Austrian in style, parts of this easterly region – usually referred to simply as Friuli – are Yugoslavian in all but name. But who cares about nationalities when there's a glassful of flavour to be drunk? And Friuli is all about flavour and tip-top winemaking. While wine writers have taken a growing interest in this region's wines its unwieldly name has yet to make its mark with most wine drinkers. The reason for this is that Friuli has no identifiable regional style; all you really have to know is the name of the grape variety you enjoy drinking, and take your pick. No one quite knows precisely how large a number you can choose from, but it's certainly over 70. Unlike the Alto Adige though, Friuli doesn't complicate matters by swapping around the names of its grapes and names, but it

Fegato alla Veneziana

Sautéed liver and onion, Venetian style

In this classic dish of the Veneto, use the very best calves' liver available. The thinner it is sliced, the quicker it cooks and the sweeter it tastes. It is a simple dish, the success of which depends on the quality of its ingredients.

SERVES 4
5 tbsp olive oil
2 lb/1 kg medium onions, peeled and thinly sliced
¹/₂ tsp dried sage, crumbled
1 ¹/₂ lb/750 g calves' liver, thinly sliced

In a shallow flameproof pan (large enough to take the liver slices in one layer) heat 3 tbsp of olive oil and sauté the onions over a low heat until they are soft (about 3 minutes). Remove them with a slotted slice or spoon and keep warm. Add the remaining oil to the pan and turn up the heat until the oil is very hot. Add the liver slices in one layer. As soon as the bottom of the liver turns grey, turn it over. The total cooking time will be about 1 minute if the slices are less than ¹/₄ in/5 mm thick. Serve immediately with the onions and risotto rice.

does confuse newcomers with its major white variety, the Tocai, which isn't the Tokay of Hungary, the Tokay-Pinot Gris of Alsace, or the Liqueur Tokay-Muscadelle of Australia. No, this is another variety altogether. Grown here and in the Veneto, it can make dull wine, but it can also produce unusual, rich, figgy, pear-flavoured stuff.

Of Friuli's seven regional zones, the one to start with is the large, flattish area of Grave del Friuli, where the red varieties of Bordeaux produce refreshing, unpretentious wines with plenty of crunchy berry fruit; there's some pleasant, similarly undemanding Chardonnay here too, that can be every bit as good as, and rather cheaper than, examples from the Alto Adige.

The black grape the locals would prefer you to concentrate on though, is the tough, spicy Refosco dal Peduncolo Rosso (its friends just call it Refosco), which is indigenous to the region. There are some good examples of this variety produced in Grave de Friuli, but, like all of the region's best wines, the ones to write home about here are the intensely fruity examples made up in the hills of Collio and the Colli Orientali (the eastern hills) on the Yugoslavian border.

There are all sorts of familiar flavours to be found here, ranging from crunchy blackcurranty Cabernets and plummy Merlots to creamy Pinot Bianco and spicy Pinot Grigio. But the unfamiliar ones are worth looking at too. Try the Refosco, the tangy white Ribolla, the berryish Schippettino and the limeylemony sweet or dry Verduzzo di Ramandolo. If you aren't paying, take a sip or two of Picolit and try to imagine why this grape's wine has been compared not just to any old Sauternes, but to Château d'Yquem. But be warned – you'll need a really vivid imagination.

Finally, a word or two about Silvio Jermann and Francesco Gravner, two of Italy's best, and least-vaunted, producers, who have arguably made their greatest wines by blending various grapes together, Jermann's unoaked Vintage Tunina and Gravner's Vino Gradberg are among the most deliciously intriguing white wines in the world.

THE NORTH-WEST

If you listen to the winemakers of Tuscany, and to the majority of the wine writers in the rest of the world, the most exciting part of Italy is the region to the south of Florence. The revolution may have started there, but today the place to be is way up in the north-west of the country.

Piedmont

If you want to grab a taste of what's going on here, fly into the industrial city of Turin, rent a car and prepare your palate for a ride through one of the broadest range of vinous flavours in the world. But you must leave all of your prejudices at home. For too long, I thought that Piedmont offered very little apart from the wonderfully grapey fizz of Asti Spumanti. I had been pretty effectively deterred by the tough, tannic character of most of the Barolo and Barbaresco I somehow inevitably ended up drinking in Italian restaurants. Then a kind Italophile friend introduced me to 'modern' wines in the shape of a range of wines from different producers and communes surrounding the village of Barolo. And I discovered the Nebbiolo grape, one of the most exciting and most frustrating varieties of them all.

Suddenly I was back in Burgundy, where the similarly pernickety Pinot Noir is just as difficult to grow, just as easy to get wrong, just as influenced by the precise character of the piece of soil in which it is planted and, when everything goes right, just as fascinating in the variety of its flavours. The links between Barolo and red Burgundy are actually remarkably close. Both are wines made from a single grape and both have long suffered by being adulterated with beefier wines from further south. Like Burgundy, Barolo used to be a far lighter wine – indeed until the early 20th century the wines bearing this name would have been sweet and slightly fizzy. Then in the 1930s Barolo slid into the phase of trying to be too big for its boots. The grapes were over-pressed to extract every possible ounce of tannin and the wines were left to age for far too long in barrel. That was the way people liked them – until Professor Emile Peynaud arrived from Bordeaux and declared some of the most illustrious wines to be oxidised.

Since the French guru's visit there have been all manner of discussions about the way Barolo ought to be made. Should it be fermented for a long time with the grape skins to extract as much tannin as possible, and aged for several years in large *botti* casks to be softened by oxidation? Or should it be handled in much the same way as Bordeaux, and matured less lengthily in small oak barrels? The local jury is still out on all these questions, but outsiders are rapidly coming to their verdict; what they like is wines with personality and fruit. In practice these are usually from single vineyards, and made by young go-ahead producers who do their best to prevent the wine from oxidising as it ages. (But there are exceptions to the rule. The ultra-traditional wines of Borgogno and Pira need to be kept.)

Under present law all Barolos are equal. Until, that is, you begin to read the labels of Barolo bottles and find yourself immersed in such names as Cannubi and La Morra. But hold on, say some of the traditionalists, 'real' Barolo shouldn't come from a single vineyard it ought, like Champagne, to be a blend of wines grown in various plots. That argument is still raging; as always, both sides can make a convincing case for themselves, the blenders claiming that some of the vineyard names appearing on labels are far from special, while the plotters talk keenly about the differences in flavours between vineyards.

The traditional view of Barbaresco is that it is a more approachable, lighter-weight version of Barolo. But if good examples of Barolo have been hard to come by, good Barbaresco has been rarer still. One man who has done more than any to stake a claim for Barbaresco is Angelo Gaja, who makes a range

of extraordinarily pricy single-vineyard wines here. At their best, these are excitingly spicy, intense wines.

Those who question Barbaresco's potential for greatness point out that Gaja has committed the sacrilege of planting Chardonnay here, and that he has 'disloyally' begun to make Barolo. Gaja's supporters fairly reply that it is traditional for producers in Piedmont to make several styles of wine and that his Chardonnay is one of Italy's most successful white wines.

1 DONNAZ
1a Enfer d'Arvier

2 PIEDMONT
Arneis di Langhe *(whole region)*
2a Arneis dei Roeri
Asti Spumante *(whole region)*
2b Barbaresco
Barbera d'Asti / Dolcetto /
   d'Asti / Moscato d'Asti
   Nebbiolo d'Asti / Grignolino
   d'Asti
2c Barbera d'Alba / Dolcetto d'Alba
2d Barbera del Monferrato
2e Barolo
2f Brachetto d'Acqui / Dolcetto
   d'Acqui
2g Bricco Manzoni

2h Carema
2i Cortese di Gavi / Gavi di]
   Gavi
2j Erbaluce di Caluso
Freisa *(whole region)*
2k Gattinara
2l Ghemme
Greco *(whole region)*
Spanna *(whole region)*

3 LIGURIA
3a Cinqueterre
3b Riviera Ligure di Ponente
3c Rossese di Dolceacqua

4 LOMBARDY
4a Franciacorta
4b Lugana
4c Oltrepò Pavese
4d Valtellina

Left: Monforte d'Alba is typical of the small towns of Piedmont, where winemaking is still one of the major forms of agriculture

Above: These calm vineyards produce Asti Spumante, one of the most joyous, most light-hearted wines in the world

If Barolo and Barbaresco are the potentially daunting Everest and K2 of wine here, there are some wonderfully individual, far less demanding smaller peaks among the region's reds that are just as worth exploring. You can find various versions of less-matured wines sold with a DOC as Nebbiolo d'Alba, or as *Vini da Tavola* as Nebbiolo delle Langhe.

Up in the north of the region, Carema, Gattinara, Ghemme, Bramaterra and Fara all make floral, delicate wines based on the Nebbiolos, but that also include Bonarda and, in a few instances, Vespolina. *Vini da Tavola* wines made here from this kind of blend (with a fair dollop of the Aglianico) tends to be sold as Spanna and can be of very variable quality.

Even the lightest Nebbiolo can be a bit of a mouthful though, which makes the Barbera such a very welcome alternative. But Barberas vary too, depending on where and how they are made. Some versions are best classified as basic table wine to be drunk by the jugful; some are really quite serious. Look out for Barbera d'Asti, Barbera d'Alba and Barbera del Monferrato from producers such as Vitticoltori dell'Acquese and Bava.

Five other varieties make wine for easy drinking. The Dolcetto sounds as though its wines ought to be sweet. They're not, but when well made, they are so perfumed and so packed with plummy, chocolatey, raspberryish flavours that they taste as though they can't be 100% dry. Look for Dolcetto d'Alba, Dolcetto di Dogliani and Dolcetto delle Langhe Monregalesi.

To anyone who speaks Spanish or French, the Freisa sounds as though it ought to produce wines that taste of strawberries; actually, I reckon raspberries or mulberries are closer to the mark, but whichever fruit it is, Freisa wines are more tightly packed with it than most pots of jam. Like many of the wines in this region, Freisa used to be be sweet and fizzy; sadly, few producers make it that way now, but whatever the style, good Freisa should have a lovely, refreshing acid bite of not-quite-ripe fruit. Try examples from Bava, Voerzio and Vajra.

THE ESSENTIALS — PIEDMONT

Location North-west Italy, in the foothills of the Alps around Turin.
Quality Barolo and Barbaresco are two of only five Italian reds with the top–level DOCG designation. Around 25% of production is DOC, notably Asti Spumante, Barbera, Gavi, Gattinara, Ghemme, Moscato d'Asti, Dolcetto, Arneis and Freisa.
Style Some dry, lemony whites are produced at Gavi, while a rich and full-flavoured wine is made from the Arneis, an ancient grape variety grown in the foothills of the Alps, north of Alba. The region around Asti is renowned for its light, refreshing, grapey *spumante* wines. Equally famous are the massive, chewy reds of Barolo and Barbaresco, wines that can take many years to reveal all of their complexities. Rich in tannins and high in acidity, both have a variety of fruit flavours — raisins, plums, prunes, blackberries — together with liquorice, chocolate and a whiff of smoke.
  Also from the Nebbiolo grape, but more readily approachable, are Gattinara, Ghemme, Nebbiolo d'Alba and Spanna, the local name for Nebbiolo. Barbera from Alba, Asti and Monferrato can produce a rich, raisiny wine with good underlying acidity. The Dolcetto makes soft, juicy wines which at their best combine succulent cherry fruit with bitter chocolate.
Climate Severe winters with plenty of fog — the '*nebbio*' of Nebbiolo, which enjoys relatively hot summers and long autumns, although lack of sunshine can cause problems.
Cultivation The best vineyards, in Barolo, are situated on free-draining, south-facing hillsides. Around Asti the hills are much gentler. Soils are varied, but calcareous marl mixed with sand and clay predominates.
Grape Varieties *Red:* Nebbiolo (Spanna), Barbera, Dolcetto, Bonarda, Vespolina. *White:* Moscato, Arneis, Cortese, Chardonnay, Pinot Bianco.
Production/Maturation Traditionally, Barolo spent a long ageing period in wooden vats; today, ordinary Barolo is released at 3 years old, *riservas* at 4 years old and *riserva speciales* at 5 years old, and there has been a move away from oak to bottle age. Barberesco must be aged for a minimum of 2 years, one of which must be in oak. Asti Spumante is produced using the *cuve close* method.
Longevity *Reds*: drink Dolcetto within 3 years, but most other reds (Barbera, Ghemme, Gattinara, good Spanna) require 4 to 12 years. Barbaresco can be kept for 5 to 20 years while Barolos are capable of ageing for between 8 and 25 years. *Whites*: Asti Spumante and Moscato d'Asti should be drunk within a year. Gavi requires 2-3 years.
Vintage Guide Reds 78, 82, 83, 85, 86, 88, 89
                 Whites 83, 85, 86
Top Producers *Barolo*: Giacosa, Ceretto, Ratti, Fontanafredda, Pira, Borgogno, Altare, Clerico, Poggio, G Mascarello, Vietti, Conterno, Prunotto. *Barbaresco*: Gaja, Ceretto, Giacosa, Castello di Neive, Pio Cesare. *Other reds*: Vallana, Brugo, Dessilani. *Asti/Moscato*: Fontana-fredda, Duca d'Asti, Cantina Sociale Canelli, Bava.

Ruche is a variety that very few of the books ever bothered to mention, for the simple reason that it was so rarely grown. According to some local producers, it was brought to the region from Burgundy, and I believe them; Bava's example tastes like one of the best, most creamy and floral Beaujolais.

Grignolino has always been a name that seemed to promise juicy-fruity flavours, but most of the ones I have tasted have seemed disappointingly unripe. Try one from Vietti though, with a plate of antipasto prepared with good olive oil, and you might just develop a taste for it. I prefer Brachetto, both in its dry and wonderfully grapey-floral sweet styles. Blended with the black Muscat, this is one of the best arguments for sweet red wine. Low alcohol (5.5%) versions compete on level terms with Moscato d'Asti and Asti Spumanti.

Both these wines provide one of my favourite means of testing for wine snobbery; the moment you see the nose begin to lift at the mention of sweet fizz, you know that you are in the presence of a label drinker. Great Asti is quite simply one of the most unpretentious, fun drinks I know; served chilled on a warm summer's afternoon it's the nearest thing to drinking ripe grapes. And that's hardly suprising because the Muscat grape from which both wines are made is quite simply the grapiest grape of them all.

Apart from Asti Spumanti and Moscato d'Asti, Piedmont is not usually thought of as white wine country. There are, however, two characterful whites that are worth looking out for. Gavi's gain – and most wine drinkers' loss – was to be likened to white Burgundy. This meant that this perfectly pleasant, dry, creamy, appley wine made from the local Cortese grape rapidly became a 'smart', over-priced, pleasant, creamy, appley wine. Some bottles are labelled Gavi, some as Gavi di Gavi, which is a sort of Chianti Classico-style designation for wines from the village itself. The latter are rarely worth their extra price.

I'd rather opt for the far more distinctive Arneis di Roero made in small quantities from the Arneis grape, whose name in local dialect actually means 'little difficult one'. It may be difficult to grow, but I've always found it remarkably easy to drink – and one of the freshest, most spicy mouthfuls in the world. Try the ones from Gianni Voerzio or Deltetto.

Lombardy

Lombardy is to Milan what Chianti is to Florence and Barolo is to Turin – the city's vinous backyard. Surprisingly, given the thirst of the Milanese, their historic mercantile fortune, and the tourist attraction of the lakes, none of the region's wines have achieved as much fame as their counterparts in other parts of the country. The problem is perhaps one of definition; too many of the wines of Lombardy are often like, and frequently better than, those produced elsewhere. So Lugana, in the east, is fairly described as up-market Soave (good Trebbiano in other words); Valltelina in the north makes Piedmont-like Nebbiolos, and in the Oltrepo Pavese hills there is a mass of varietals – Riesling, Pinot Grigio, Moscato et al – producing pleasant wines that could be made almost anywhere in Italy.

Lombardy does have some very characterful wines of its own, though even here, they often owe their individuality to the fact that they are blends of grapes that elsewhere rarely share a blending vat. The reds made in Oltrepo Pavese, for example, are produced from blends of the Barbera and the Bonarda, a variety normally only found in the Veneto. And then there is the fact that many of these wines are slightly sparkling. Judged on their own terms, like real Lambrusco, they can be refreshingly fruity wines with just enough of an acid bite to balance their juicy plummy fruit. The whites often fizz here too.

Finally there's Valltelina, produced up in the mountains, close to Switzerland, in a quartet of villages called Grumello, Inferno, Sassella and Valgella. Labelled as Valtellina, these wines are at once delicate, floral and fruity – like a water-colour version of Barolo. Bottles labelled Valtellina Sfursat can command a higher price because of their beefier flavour and alcohol.

THE ESSENTIALS — LOMBARDY/LIGURIA/VALLE D'AOSTA

Location North-west Italy. Lombardy is in the foothills of the Alps around Turin while Valle d'Aosta is very much in the Alps. Liguria is in the Appennine country of the coastal strip around Genoa.

Quality Mostly *vino da tavola* with a few DOCs in each region, notably Lombardy with Franciacorta, Lugana, Oltrepò Pavese and Valtellina. Liguria has 3 DOCs, Cinque Terre, Riviera Ligure di Ponente and Dolceacqua.

Style Valle d'Aosta makes fresh, tart white wines and light, fruity reds for local consumption. Donnaz, from Nebbiolo grapes, is sturdier stuff and is one of only two DOCs in this region, the other being the softer Enfer d'Arvier. Some good dessert wines are made. Liguria, again, produces a lot of wine for local consumption from over 100 grape varieties but few of these wines are seen outside Italy. Lombardy produces some very good *méthode champenoise* wines at Franciacorta, dry with a fine biscuity character. Franciacorta also produces some rich bittersweet reds and smooth, fruity whites.

Oltrepò Pavese produces many styles of red and white, the best being red Barberas. Valtellina produces rich reds from the Nebbiolo, which take several years to mellow into elegance. Some pleasant whites are made at Lugana.

Climate Winters are severe but the growing season is hot and long.

Cultivation A wide range of soils is found in these varied regions, although calcareous marl is common. Relief ranges from the Alpine scenery of Valle d'Aosta to the alluvial plains of the river Po.

Grape Varieties *Red:* Nebbiolo, Barbera, Cabernet Sauvignon, Merlot, Bonarda, Cabernet Franc, Rossola, Brugnola, Pinot Nero. *White*: Trebbiano, Pinot Bianco, Pinot Grigio, Uva, Chardonnay, Riesling.

Production/Maturation Sparkling wines are generally made by the *méthode champenoise*.

Longevity Most *whites* are for early drinking. The sparkling wines may be fruitfully kept for 2-3 years. *Reds*: the reds of Valle d'Aosta are best drunk young. Oltrepò Pavese: 2 to 5 years; Franciacorta: 3 to 8 years; Valtellina: 5 to 15 years; other reds: 2 to 8 years

Vintage Guide Reds 82, 83, 85, 86
Whites 85, 86

Top Producers Berlucchi, Ca' del Bosco, Longhi de Carli.

Liguria

The crescent-shaped region of the coast around Genoa is arguably the least well-known of all the winemaking areas of northern Italy. The most characterful wines here are the fragrant, floral red Rossese (reputedly the wine Napoleon drank when he wasn't sipping at his watered-down Chambertin) and two whites: the light, lemony Vermentino (no relation of the Sardininan grape of the same name) and the rather heavier Pigato. All three need to be drunk with rich Genovese cooking.

ABOVE: The steeply terraced vineyards of Val d'Aosta, source of some of Italy's least internationally familiar wines

BELOW: Mauro Mascarello's vineyards produce tiny quantities of great Piedmontese wine, from Barolo to Dolcetto

Carbonata di Manzo

Hearty beef casserole with wine and vegetables

White truffles, gnocchi (tiny potato dumplings), risotto and polenta (a savoury cornmeal cake) as well as beef, venison and poultry, are characteristic of an area renowned for its hearty, no-nonsense eating, with wines to match.

SERVES 4-6
6 tbsp olive oil
2 lb/1 kg stewing beef, cut into chunks
10 fl oz/275 ml red wine (Barbera is traditional though not essential, but use a wine with body)
1 lb/500 g pickling or other small onions, peeled and whole
2 oz/50 g butter
4 medium carrots, scraped and cut into thick rings
4 celery stalks, cut in chunks (remove strings if necessary)
1 lb/500 g fresh or frozen peas
Salt and freshly ground black pepper

Put 4 tbsp of olive oil into a frying pan and heat until hot but not smoking. Brown the meat in batches and transfer it to a plate. Pour off the fat and add half the wine to the pan. Bring it to the boil and scrape up any solids. Turn off the heat. In a large flameproof casserole, mix the remaining olive oil, the browned meat, the juices from the frying pan, onions, butter, carrots and the remaining wine. Cover and cook over a low heat for 20 minutes. Add the celery and cook, covered, for 45 minutes. When the meat is tender, add the peas and cook for 5 minutes. Season to taste with salt and pepper. Serve with rice or noodles.

Valle d'Aosta

This is such a tiny region, with less than 2,500 acres (1000 hectares) of steeply sloping vineyards, that it is hardly surprising that a single DOC bearing its name is used for all of the various wines produced here. Unfortunately, the range is so wide that the DOC is really rather meaningless. Linguistically this is tricky country too; Valle d'Aosta is as French as it's Italian.

Unfortunately, too, this is another of those regions where vinegrowing is an endangered occupation. Tucked away among the eminently skiable mountains, Valle d'Aosta is a far from easy place in which to grow grapes. Trained monkeys might be happy working these terraces and slopes that overlook the Dora Baltea river, and they might even enjoy leaping between the pergolas on which the vines are trained; the young men of the 1990s tend to prefer a monthly pay-packet from Fiat.

There is, as I say, no such thing as a typical Valle d'Aosta wine, but you could start your exploration of the region by trying the Donnaz or an Arnad-Montjovet, both of which give a different accent to the Nebbiolo, allowing it to display a pungently distinctive violetty perfume. From those semi-familiar flavours you could progress to Chambave Rosso, Torrette and Enfer d'Arvier (all of which are made from the local Petit Rouge), the Nus Rosso (made from the Vien de Nus) and thence to such obscure whites as Blanc de Morgex (from the grape of the same name) and Nus, which will bring you back to the familiar territory of the Pinot Grigio. (See what I mean about it being varied!) And then, of course, there's the Pinot Nero (used to make red, pink and white - yes, white), the Gamay and even the Müller-Thurgau.

CENTRAL ITALY

Heading south, one comes to the heart of the country, the part that includes the regions of Emilia-Romagna, Latium and Tuscany, and produces such traditionally famous – and in some cases infamous – wines as Chianti, Frascati and Lambrusco. But this is also the area where you will find the majority of Italy's most exciting new wines, the 'super-Tuscans'.

Tuscany

Tuscany is Renaissance country – in every way. The towns, the villages, the terracotta-roofed houses and the absurdly hummocky hills have changed little since the days when Leonardo da Vinci painted them, but this is also the heart of the renaissance of Italian wine. During the years when Italy seemed to be sliding down the same slope of mediocrity as Germany, fans of the best French wines lamented the paucity of Italian wines that could be realistically compared to the best of Bordeaux and Burgundy. And the region that attracted most of the flak was Tuscany.

Chianti's shortcomings had been less evident in the old days when most of the wine was sold cheaply in straw-covered *fiasco* bottles. But when the region's producers became pretentious enough to introduce Bordeaux-style bottles and to spend money promoting the black cockerel emblem of the supposedly quality-oriented Chianti Classico consortium, the general reaction among outsiders was that they were simply dressing their mutton as lamb.

The late 1970s saw a reassessment of what Chianti could and should be. The definition of where Chianti might legally be produced had been more or less established for nearly 700

8 EMILIA-ROMAGNA
8a Albana di Romagna
8b Colli Bolognesi
8c Colli di Parma
8d Lambrusco
8e Pagadebit
8f Rosso Armentano
Sangiovese di Romagna *(whole region)*
8g Terre Rosse Chardonnay
8h Trebbiano di Romagna

9 TUSCANY
9a Bolgheri
9b Brunello di Montalcino
9c Carmignano
9d Castello della Sala
9e Cetinaia
9f Chianti Classico
9g Coltassala
9h Elba
9i Galestro
9j Ghiaie della Furba
9k Sodi di San Niccolo
9l Le Pergole Torte
9m Montecarlo
9n Pomino
9o Rosso di Montalcino
9r Sassicaia
9s Solaia
9t Tignanello
9u Vernaccia di San Gimignano
9v Vinattieri Rosso
9x Vino Nobile di Montepulciano
Vin Santo *(whole region)*

10 MARCHES
10a Rosso Conero
10b Rosso Piceno
10c Sangiovese dei Colli Pesaresi
10d Verdicchio dei Castelli di Jesi

11 UMBRIA
11a Colli Altotiberini
11b Colli del Trasimeno
11c Colli Perugini
Grechetto/Greco *(whole region)*
11d Montefalco
11e Orvieto
11f Torgiano
Vin Santo *(whole region)*

12 LATIUM
12a Aprilia
12b Cerveteri
12c Est!Est!!Est!!!
12d Falerno
12e Fiorano
12f Frascati
12g Marino
12h Torre Ercolana

13 ABRUZZI-MOLISE
13a Biferno
13b Montepulciano d'Abruzzo
13c Montepulciano del Molise
13d Ramitello
13e Rubino
13f Trebbiano d'Abruzzo

THE ESSENTIALS — TUSCANY

Location Central west Italy, on the Tyrrhenian coast.

Quality Possesses 3 of the 6 DOCGs in Brunello di Montalcino, Chianti Classico and Vino Nobile di Montepulciano. Notable DOCs are Carmignano, Pomino and Vernaccia di San Gimignano. There are also some fabulous red *vini da tavola* (the 'super-Tuscans') such as Sassicaia, Solaia and Tignanello.

Style Vernaccia di San Gimignano is the most famous local white. Smooth and nutty, with lots of fresh fruit and a hint of honey, it should be drunk within 2-3 years. Galestro and Pomino, a blend of Trebbiano, Pinot Bianco and Chardonnay, are both good. Chianti is by far the most important Italian red but as a consequence of its large production quality varies considerably. However, single estate and *riserva* wines show good depth of raspberry and cherry fruit, gentle oak and a whiff of tobacco. Produced nearby, Carmignano gains chocolatey richness from around 10% Cabernet Sauvignon, while Vino Nobile di Montepulciano has a richer, generous fruit character in its finest wines. Mature Brunello di Montalcino, at its best, is rich, heady and complex, full of concentrated dried fruit, plum and tobacco flavours. Some of the best wines of Tuscany, though, are the new-wave barrique-aged wines from a handful of producers using Sangiovese, Cabernet Sauvignon or a blend of the two. The sherry-like Vin Santo, a red or white *passito* wine, can be dry, semi-sweet or sweet and, at its best, has a fine concentrated richness.

Climate Summers are long and fairly dry, winters are cold.

Cultivation The best vineyards are on free-draining exposed hillsides where altitude moderates the long, hot growing season. Soils are complex; *galestro*, a crystalline rocky soil, dominates the best vineyards.

Grape Varieties *Red:* Sangiovese, Cabernet Sauvignon, Brunello, Canaiolo Nero, Colorino, Mammolo. *White:* Trebbiano, Malvasia, Vernaccia, Grechetto, Chardonnay, Pinot Grigio, Pinot Bianco, Sauvignon Blanc.

Production/Maturation Barrique-ageing has become much more common. Vin Santo is still very traditional, with grapes being dried indoors and the wine being aged for up to 6 years in sealed casks.

Longevity *Reds:* Chianti: 3 to 6 years for ordinary Chianti, but up to 20 for the best. Brunello di Montalcino: 10 to 25 years; Vino Nobile 6 to 25 years; barrique-aged reds: 5 to 25 years; other reds: 3 to 10 years *Whites:* up to 5 years although Vin Santo can last far longer.

Vintage Guide 78, 82, 83, 85, 88

Top Producers Antinori, Avignonesi, Castello di Volpaia, Marchese Incisa della Rochetta, Isole e Olena, Villa di Capezzana, Castello di Rampolla, Il Poggio, Vinattieri, Altesino, Badia a Coltibuono.

LEFT: *New oak barrels like these are used by Antinori and a growing number of other pioneers in Tuscany to age their 'super-Tuscan' Cabernet Sauvignon and Sangiovese reds*

Below: *The typically Tuscan vineyards of Altesino, one of the best producers of Brunello di Montalcino*

ABOVE RIGHT: *The instantly recognisable black cockerel insignia of the Chianti Classico producers' consortium appears at almost every turn in the heart of Chianti*

Petti di Pollo alla Fiorentina

Chicken breasts sautéed with spinach

Olive oil, beef from the Val di Chiana, chicken, herbs and game from the wooded hills are the hallmarks of Tuscan food. This recipe comes from the capital of the region — Florence — where the use of spinach, a local speciality, is often signalled by the phrase 'alla Fiorentino'.

SERVES 4
*2 lb/1 kg fresh spinach, washed and destalked, or equal weight of frozen leaf spinach
4 tbsp olive oil
1 clove garlic, peeled and minced
3 tbsp single cream
Salt and freshly ground black pepper
1 oz/25 g butter
4 skinless chicken breasts, slightly flattened*

If fresh spinach is used, cook it in a covered saucepan over a low heat with only the water left on the leaves from washing. Toss to prevent scorching and cook until wilted and most of the moisture has evaporated. If frozen spinach is used, heat until most of the water has evaporated. In a frying pan, heat 2 tbsp of olive oil until it is hot but not smoking. Sauté the garlic for 2-3 minutes (without burning) and reduce the heat. Add the spinach and cook for 3-4 minutes. Stir in the cream, seasoning with salt and pepper to taste. Cook for 2-3 minutes. Remove contents with a slotted spoon or slice to a bowl and keep warm. Add the remaining oil and butter to the pan and heat. When the butter foam has subsided add the chicken and cook over a high heat for about 3-4 minutes on each side or until browned. Cover the pan, reduce the heat to moderate and cook for a further 10 minutes or until the chicken is cooked through. Remove to a serving dish and dress with the spinach. Serve with sautéed potatoes.

years; the region had, however, grown in that time and split into segments including the central Chianti Classico and the Chianti Rufina zones. What remained questionable was the grape varieties from which this region's wines ought to be made. The principal and traditional variety, the Sangiovese, seemed unwilling to provide much in the way of flavour, which explains why some of the producers began to think about adding Cabernet Sauvignon to their vats. The only problem was that to do so in any bottle labelled as Chianti would have involved breaking the law.

But the Cabernet campaigners, a forthright bunch, conceded that even if their wines could only be sold as *vini da tavola*, they could still gain a reputation of their own and sell for a higher price than most Chianti.Thus were born the super-Tuscans, the growing range of vini da tavola that have catapulted Italy's wines back onto the world stage.

During the 1970s a long list of other winemakers turned to making Bordeaux-style vini da tavola; most famous among them was Piero Antinori, whose ancestor was using Cabernet in his Chianti at the beginning of the century. Antinori's Sangiovese-Cabernet Sauvignon blend, Tignanello, was instantly acknowledged to be one of Italy's finest reds. And for those producers who felt their wines needed the letters DOC on their labels, the authorities finally granted a DOC to the Chianti Montabano region of Carmignano for wines made from a blend of Sangiovese and Cabernet.

Just as it began to seem as though Chianti would become Cabernet country, in which all the best wines would owe at least some of their flavour to the Bordeaux variety, Antinori and a number of his fellow producers began to experiment with different clones, including old Sangioveto (Sangiovese Toscano) vines and to make pure Sangioveto wines, which they aged in small, new oak barrels.

Tuscany is now an anarchic mess; Chianti Classico has been promoted to a DOCG, producers are now allowed to add 10% of Cabernet to their vats, and a blind eye is turned to those who

neglect to put in the obligatory white grapes. These developments have finally encouraged a move towards higher quality Chianti – both in the Chianti Classico region and in other parts of the area – but they haven't deterred anyone from making vino da tavola. In fact, today few ambitious wineries in Tuscany have not produced one, using Bordeaux or Sangioveto grapes, or a blend of both. At their best, these wines are some of the tastiest reds in the world with a distinctly 'Italian' flavour of blackcurrants, oak and fresh herbs.

Ask most well-read wine drinkers to name Italy's greatest wine and some, at least, are sure to come up with the estate of Biondi-Santi in Brunello di Montalcino. Then ask them when they last tasted a bottle of its wine. Biondi-Santi and Brunello (as the DOCG is known) have lived on their reputations for a very long time, relying on the sheer muscle of their wines and the requirement that they be aged for four years in wood to convince people that they were the best in the region. What used to make Brunello special was the fine character of the grape, the brown-skinned clone of the Sangiovese.

Today, as other Tuscans pay greater heed to their clones, Brunello's producers have to work hard to compete. Some of those long-aged wines can shed their tannic husks to develop glorious herby, spicy, dried-fruit flavours; some never make it. If you are impatient, or not much of a gambler, try the less woody, more immediately approachable Rosso di Montalcino instead. Old Biondi-Santi wines are worth tasting if you are offered the chance, if only because they provide an insight into the way wines used to taste here. For current pleasure, I'd recommend ones made by Altesino or Tenuta Caparzo.

Until quite recently, the least noble thing about the wonderful hilltop town of Montepulciano was its Vino Nobile di Montepulciano. In blind tastings, few people could tell the difference between Vino Nobile and fairly basic Chianti; both were both dull, over-aged and often oxidised. Becoming a DOCG (the first in Italy) has changed things here, however, just as it did in Chianti. Spurred on by the quality of Avignonesi's wines, Montepulciano's producers have begun to make finer, spicier, more intense wines. Some are still left for too long in barrel, but a new DOC – Rosso di Montepulciano – now gives an incentive for all but the very best wine to be bottled earlier.

There is no longer any such wine as white Chianti, but that's

Umbria

Umbria has never quite had the magic of Tuscany; Perugia has yet to gain the cachet of Siena and Florence. But, as the more northerly region increasingly deserves John Mortimer's witty description of it as 'Chiantishire', the focus of attention is bound to shift downwards. And when it does, hopefully Orvieto, one of Italy's most ancient wines, will be taken more seriously. Sadly, most modern Orvieto lacks the honeyed, nutty character that earned this town's wines their reputation. The occasional sweet, nobly rotten examples can be good, but the more usual medium-dry Abboccato or dry examples are unmemorable. Antinori's is pleasant, but uninspiring; for a more special experience, try the Terre Vinati from Palazone.

But it isn't Orvieto that is attracting the attention these days, it is Torgiano, a region that owes its reputation almost exclusively to the efforts of Dr Giorgio Lungarotti, whose extraordinarily successful wines – notably the Rubesco reds – have become so established that he has single-handedly won Torgiano its own DOCG.

Latium

Rome's backyard is a surprisingly barren source of good wine. The one DOC almost everyone has heard of, Frascati, has, like Soave, sadly become 'just one of those cheap Italian whites,' produced and drunk in bulk by people who care little about quality. Actually, Frascati is, if anything, often an even worse buy than Soave, because, while the latter wine is rarely worse than dull, the former can be just the other side of likeable because of its odd sour-cream character. And don't imagine that paying a little extra for Frascati Superiore will buy you anything better; it won't – just a wine that's a little more alcoholic.

The problem, as so often in Italy, is silly local laws; if you make wine in this region exclusively from the local Malvasia del Lazio, it can be terrific – but it's illegal as Frascati, because the rules limit its proportion to 30%. To produce a wine that can call itself Frascati, you have to use the lesser quality Malvasia di Candia or, worse still, the Trebbiano. In other words, the less palatable it tastes, the more likely it is to be genuine.

Fortunately, there are Frascati makers who get their Malvasias mixed up and sidestep the law by using the good Malvasia del Lazio instead of the di Candia. And, as in Soave, there is a move towards wines from individual vineyards, such as Fontana Candida's Santa Teresa. Even so, it does not bode well for the Frascati's image that Colle Gaio, the best wine to come out of the region recently, makes almost no mention of Frascati.

Marino and Montecompatri can both be better buys – providing that they are caught young. Traditional writers like to pretend that Est! Est!! Est!!! di Montefiascone is one of the region's finest wines, recounting the old story that it owes its name to the enthusiasm of a visitor who shouted, with growing enthusiasm 'It is! It is!! It is!!!'. For most of the examples on offer today, the words 'Boring! Boring!! Boring!!!' would be rather more appropriate.

There is so little Aleatico di Gradoli produced that it is hardly worth mentioning, but for the fact that this is one of Italy's more unusual grapes, and the fortified and unfortified sweet whites it produces close to Rome boast a perfumey, grapey character.

Up in the Castelli Romani hills, Velletri's is a name that deserves to be better known. The Wine Research Institute of Latium has experimental vineyards here and makes tasty reds

what Galestro is in all but name. Light, slightly Muscadet-like (though with even less character than the best examples of that wine), Galestro is the commercial brainchild of a group of Chianti producers who sought a way to dispose of a surplus of white grapes.

For the moment it has no DOC, but is controlled by an association of its makers. Its quality rarely rises above, nor descends below, a basic level of adequacy. Vernaccia di San Gimignano (from the extraordinary town of that name whose medieval towers dominate the landscape like so many ancient skyscrapers) on the other hand, is a white wine that has both a DOC and the delicious, tangy flavour of the Vernaccia grape.

Before leaving Tuscany, don't miss the chance to taste the local examples of the sweet or (less impressive) dry Vin Santo. These wines' sherry-like flavour comes partly from intentional slight oxidation, and partly from the fact that good producers use a type of solera system, adding a little 'madre' (mother) of the previous year's wine to the new cask. Dunk a *cantuccini* almond biscuit in a top-quality Vin Santo (Avignonesi makes an especially good one) and you will wonder why this wine is so little known. Taste the cheap, syrupy versions served in most restaurants and you'll wonder why anyone drinks it at all.

The Barbera vineyards of the Colli Piacentini in Emilia-Romagna, and town Ziano Piacentini from which they take their name. The Barbera is Italy's most widely planted red grape variety, and it can be used to make wines that range from light, easily-quaffable, cafe fare put out by some of theproducers of this region, to the rich, intense reds made by quality-conscious estates in Piedmont in the north-west.

THE ESSENTIALS — EMILIA–ROMAGNA

Location The region surrounding Bologna in central east Italy.
Quality Contains the first white DOCG, Albana di Romagna, and a number of DOCs but the bulk of the production is *vino da tavola*. DOCs you may come across are Colli Bolognesi and Sangiovese di Romagna.
Style Straightforward commercial wines of all types, including sparkling and semi-sparkling. The generally dull Albana di Romagna typifies much of the white wine production. It comes in either a dry or semi-sweet version that may be *spumante*. Fortunately there are a few outstanding wines, such as the buttery Terre Rosse Chardonnay or Baldi's rich, balanced Sangiovese reds. Lambrusco is by far the most well-known wine produced in the region and may be dry, semi-sweet or sweet, red, white or *rosato*, barely *frizzantino* or virtually sparkling. Traditional red Lambrusco is low in alcohol, off-dry and full of ripe cherry-flavoured fruit. 'Commercial' Lambrusco, recognisable by its screw-cap, is more like fizzy pop.
Climate Hot, dry Mediterranean summers, the effects of which are alleviated by altitude and aspect. Winters are cool.
Cultivation Flat plains of rich alluvial soil, notably in the valley of the river Po, result in abundant yields. The best vineyards are, however, located in the well-drained foothills of the Appennines.
Grape Varieties *Red:* Sangiovese, Barbera, Bonarda, Cabernet Sauvignon, Pinot Nero, Cabernet Franc. *White:* Trebbiano, Lambrusco, Albana, Malvasia, Chardonnay, Sauvignon, Pinot Bianco, Pinot Grigio, Müller-Thurgau.
Production/Maturation Viticultural practices and vinification techniques are as varied as the quality of the reds. Bulk-blending is used for the commercial wines but elsewhere traditional practices are maintained with the adoption of modern methods where necessary.
Longevity Most wines – red, white or *rosato* – are best drunk young, although the quality reds of producers like Baldi, Vallania and Vallunga may need up to 15 years to be at their best. Terre Rosse Chardonnay requires 2 to 5 years.
Vintage Guide Vintages have little effect on the majority of commercial or blended wines from this fertile area. For the better quality reds and whites: 82, 83, 85, 86, 88
Top Producers Baldi, Vallania, Vallunga.

---

from a blend of Cesanese, Sangiovese and Montepulciano, and a rich white from the Malvasia and Trebbiano that is immeasurably better than all but the very best Frascati. The Cesanese is also used to make a number of other reds, such as Cesanese di Olevano Romano, Cesanese di Affile, Cesanese del Piglio and, with a little help from the Montepulciano and the Nero Buono di Cori, Cori Rosso.

Emilia-Romagna

Think of Parma ham, of Parmesan, of Spaghetti Bolognese... Emilia-Romagna is the home of all of these, and of the barrel-aged intense Balsamic Vinegar of Modena, and of one of the world's most commercially successful wines: Lambrusco, the sweet, frothy red, white or pink stuff drunk directly from its screw-top bottle by countless thirsty drunks in Britain and the USA. But the stuff those drunks enjoy would be unrecognisable to an Italian; his version of Lambrusco has a DOC, comes in a bottle with a cork and is bone dry, with a bite of unripe-plum acidity that takes a lot of getting used to.

Beyond Lambrusco, Emilia-Romagna – a hot, flat swathe of land – has some worthwhile wines to offer. The place not to look for good wine is, paradoxically, Italy's first white DOCG, Albana di Romagna, which is rarely other than pleasantly boring. Much the same (though without the 'pleasantly') could be said for Trebbiano di Romagna. The red Sangiovese di Romagna is better, but don't go expecting it to taste like Chianti; the clone is different and the style lighter; Fattoria Paradiso make one of the few decent ones.

Down in the south-west of the region, Bianco di Scandiano proves that the Sauvignon can make good wine in the warmer parts of Italy, but it is up in the Colli (the hills) that most of the region's tastiest wines are to be found. Close to Umbria, Colli Piacenti produces dry and *amabile*, (slighty fizzy) whites, in which the aromatic qualities of grapes such as the Malvasia and Moscato are sometimes smothered by the ubiquitous Trebbiano. The reds – particularly Gutturnio, a tobaccoey-fruity blend of the Bonarda and local varieties – are more interesting.

There is some first-class red too, made by Terre Rosse and Tenuta Bissera from the Cabernet Sauvignon in Bologna's hills – the Colli Bolognesi, a DOC that confusingly encompasses the DOCs of Monte San Pietro and Castelli Medioevali. Other varieties, including the Malvasia and (unofficially, because it is not allowed by the DOC) Chardonnay, are similarly well handled, but it is the Sauvignon that is the real star, both here and in nearby Colli di Parma, provided you aren't looking for wines with the bite of good Sancerre.

The Marches

For some reason Verdicchio has achieved greater fame and popularity in the USA than it has in Britain or even in Italy itself. Outsiders imagine that the shape of the recognisable bottle is traditional, and based on that of ancient amphora; older Italians wink knowingly; they refer to it as the 'Gina Lollobrigida', after the spectacularly proportioned Italian actress, and recall its introduction back in the 1950s.

There are actually several kinds of Verdicchio, all made in this hilly region from the Verdicchio grape, a high-acid variety that needs careful handling. Used carelessly, its wines taste the way they sound – green, or 'verde'. The fact that a wine comes from the castles of Jesus – Castelli di Jesi – or from the lesser known DOC of Verdicchio di Matelica, means little too. Everything depends on the producer; Umani Ronchi has proved that Verdicchio from a good single vineyard, such as his Casal di·Serra, can handle new oak and can even age quite well; others are taking advantage of the variety's acidity to use it for sparkling wine. Another local grape, the Bianchello, also produces pleasant, if unexciting, light white wines that are labelled as Bianchello del Metauro.

The Marches' reds are blends of the Montepulciano and the Sangiovese, and vary depending on which of the two grape varieties has been allowed to take charge. Rosso Conero has bags of rich depth, thanks to the 85% of Montepulciano that it has to contain; Rosso Piceno is more common, lighter and less emphatically fruity because of its higher Sangiovese content. It is also worth looking out for Cumaro, Umani Ronchi's answer to the super-Tuscans, and the pure Montepulciano Vellutato from Villa Pigna. This last winery is also breaking new ground in a very Tuscan style with a Cabernet/Sangiovese/Montepulciano blend called Tenuta di Pongelli. Watch these two wineries; I've a hunch that they may be the fore-runners of a wave of interesting Marches wines.

Abruzzi

One day soon – when it catches up with the last decade of winemaking progress in Tuscany and Piedmont – this empty, mountainous region on the Adriatic coast is going to be worth knowing about. There are two main grape varieties grown here, the red Montepulciano, used for Montepulciano d'Abruzzo, and the local clone of the Trebbiano, from which the white Trebbiano d'Abruzzo is made. The former wine can be rich, peppery and chocolatey (from producers such as Valentini and Barone Cornacchia), but the latter is rarely better than dull.

Molise

This tiny region is better known for its pasta and honey than for the two DOCs – Pentro and Biferno – that it received years after every other part of Italy had been allotted its quota. Pentro certainly deserved to remain unknown, but Biferno is of greater interest, partly because of the proximity of its vines to the sea and partly because one estate, Masseria di Majo Norante, is using Montepulciano and Sangiovese to make a first-class red called Ramitello. The spicy white made here from Trebbiano, Malvasia and Falanghina, is good too, but has no DOC because of the presence of the Falanghina. Such are the rules.

THE ESSENTIALS — THE MARCHES/ABRUZZI–MOLISE

Location Central east Italy.
Quality The majority of wines are *vini da tavola* but around 12% are DOC, notably Montepulciano d'Abruzzo, Rosso Conero, Rosso Piceno, Verdicchio dei Castelli di Jesi and Biferno.
Style Verdicchio dei Castelli di Jesi is the most famous wine of the Marches which, at its best, has a full appley flavour with hints of honey and nut. Rosso Piceno produces firm, fruity, sometimes herby reds with good acidity. Those from Rosso Conero are richer, more complex, combining under-ripe plums, dried fruit and herbs with a pinch of spice. Montepulciano d'Abruzzo ought to be the only wine of real quality from the Abruzzi region; at its best it can be full of ripe, plummy fruit with a velvety texture and fine balancing acidity. The *rosato* is called Cerasuolo. Molise produces tannic reds and dry *rosatos* that as yet have proved unexciting.
Climate Typical Mediterranean climate with dry, hot summers and cool winters. Cooler micro-climates occur at higher altitudes.
Cultivation Limestone and granite outcrops occur often in these hilly regions, although alluvial soils dominate in the coastal plains.
Grape varieties *Red:* Montepulciano, Sangiovese, Ciliegiolo, Merlot. *White:* Trebbiano, Malvasia, Verdicchio, Pinot Grigio, Riesling Italico.
Production/Maturation Still a traditional area, although modern methods are beginning to creep in. Barrique-ageing is employed for Rosso Conero, Rosso Piceno and for some whites. Molise in particular requires considerable investment to improve its poorly-equipped wine industry.
Longevity *Reds:* Rosso Conero and Rosso Piceno: 5 to15 years; Montepulciano d'Abruzzo: 4 to 20 years, depending on the style and the producer; other reds: up to 8 years. *Whites:* Verdicchio: 2 to 3 years; other whites: within 4 years of the vintage, though most are best drunk young.
Vintage guide 81, 82, 83, 85, 86, 88
Top Producers Mecvini, Umani Ronchi, Marchetti, Tatta, Tenuta S. Agnese, Valentini, Pepe, Illuminati.

THE SOUTH

The warm south of Italy has been handicapped by its hot climate, a lack of equipment and modern winemaking know-how, the poverty of its populace and, most crucially, an absence of the will to produce better wine. And why should the winegrowers here bother? For far too long, they have had a ready market for their thick, alcoholic The pity of this is that they have ranges of characterful grape varieties that are grown nowhere else, and the potential to use them to make some interesting wines.

Campania

The region overlooked by Mount Vesuvius is one of the cradles of Italian winemaking and the home of the ancient Falerno del Massico, whose three styles provide the opportunity to taste the local grape varieties. The old-fashioned, woody reds and rosés are made from the Aglianico, the Piedirosso and the Primivito; the dull white is 100% Falanghina. Far more interesting than these, though, is the pure Aglianico Taurasi, which can display all sorts of plummy, spicy flavours. Mastroberardino, who makes most of the Taurasi, also produces the white Fiano di Avellino and the spicily attractive Greco di Tufo.

Calabria

This poor, windy and mountainous region deserves to be better known for its success with one grape, the Greco. With the help of equipment to cool the fermentation tanks, producers are now using this variety to make creamy-peachy dry wines in the shape of Melissa and the rather more intense Ciro Bianco, and glorious sweet and fairly alcoholic Bianco in Greco di Bianco. (Look for examples from Umberto Ceratti.) Calabria's reds are mostly made from the local Gaglioppo grape. Best of these potentially chocolatey wines are Ciro Rosso and Savuto.

14 CAMPANIA
14a Fiano di Avellino
14b Greco di Tufa
14c Lacryma Christi del Vesuvio
14d Taurasi

15 APULIA
15a Castel del Monte
15b Copertino
15c Primitivo di Manduria
15d Rosa del Golfo
15e Squinzano

16 BASILICATA
16a Aglianico del Vulture

17 CALABRIA
17a Cirò
17b Greco di Bianco

18 SICILY
Cerasuolo di Vittoria
Corvo
Etna
Marsala
Regaleali

19 SARDINIA
Anghelu Ruju
Cannonau di Sardegna
Giro di Cagliari
Malvasia di Planargia
Vermentino

Basilicata

If Calabria appears poor, this scrubby region seems positively poverty stricken. It's not a good place to farm anything really;

some areas are parched by the sun and drought; others, on the hills, are astonishingly cool. But it is on the extinct volcano of Mount Vulture here that the Aglianico can make its most impressive wine. Donato d'Angelo makes long-lived, deep spicy, chocolatey Aglianico del Vulture here and a vino da tavola called Cannetto, which is probably the south's most exciting 'modern' wine.

Puglia

The heel of the Italian boot has long been considered to be the source of blending wine for the north, but modern winemaking techniques are beginning to pay off. Castel del Monte is a good DOC for red (mostly Montepulciano), rosé (made from the Uva di Troia) and, to a lesser extent, white. Look for the Il Falcone made by Rivera, this region's best producer. Brindisi is very characterful stuff, largely made from the Negroamaro. The best example is probably Taurino's Patriglione, in which the bitterness is toned down with a little Malvasia Nera.

Sicily

Like most winemaking islands, Sicily has its own vines, such as the Nero Mascalese, the Frappato and the Perricone, and its own winemaking traditions. The best known stuff here is, of course, the fortified wine of Marsala. A potentially great fortified wine, its name has been debased by the limited aspirations of its producers and consumers and by wrapping itself up in silly and lax laws (you can use almost any old grape variety, make almost any style and bottle it at almost any age.) Apart from the wines made by a tiny band of quality-conscious producers led by Marco de Bartoli there is little hope for the DOC.

De Bartoli also makes great fortified Moscato Passito on the island of Pantelleria. To the north east of Sicily, producers on the volcanic Lipari islands produce various sweet wines using the Malvasia under the DOC of Malvasia delle Lipari. One producer, Carlo Hauner, makes one of the fruitiest, best-balanced examples in the world and his range of vini da tavola wines have become so well marketed internationally that the company name is widely thought to be a DOC. None of the wines is bad – but they're pricy. The red and white Vini da Tavola of Regaleali, probably the island's most consistent non-fortified winemaker are cheaper and worth trying.

FACING PAGE: Ancient and modern often meet in Italy, and nowhere more evidently than here at the Regaleali winery in Sicily, where this statue of the Madonna keeps a watchful eye on stainless steel tanks

Sardinia

Until recently this was a better place for a holiday than for wine. Today thankfully, a growing number of producers are exploring new ways to use some of the island's grapes, many of which are better known on the mainland. Arguably the best wine being made in Sardinia today is Sella & Mosca's Anghelu Ruju, an extraordinary port-like wine made from the Cannonau (the Spanish Garnacha and the French Grenache). Sella & Mosca also use this variety to make good, light-bodied, easy-drinking red. Nuragus di Cagliari, the best known of Sardinia's whites, is cleaner, lighter and fresher than in the past, but is still pretty anonymous. Instead, try the sherry-like Vernaccia di Oristano and the Malvasia and Moscati.

Pasta Siciliana

Anchovy, garlic, hot pepper, tomato and olive sauce

This dish combines ingredients which are particularly characteristic of Sicily — anchovies, tomatoes, garlic, olives and capers. They combine to make a tasty pasta sauce which does justice to the robust red wines of the region.

SERVES 4-6
16 tinned anchovy fillets, chopped, with their oil
¹/₂ tbsp olive oil
2 cloves garlic, peeled and minced
1 tbsp capers, chopped
1 lb/500 g tomatoes, skinned, seeded and chopped, or
drained and chopped tinned tomatoes
12 black olives, stoned and chopped
1 fresh chili pepper, seeded and chopped, or ¹/₄ tsp dried
red pepper flakes
2 tbsp parsley, minced
1 wine glass of dry white wine

Drain the oil from the anchovies into a flameproof pan. Add the olive oil and heat. Add the anchovies and garlic. Cook and stir for 2-3 minutes. Add the capers, tomatoes, olives, chili pepper (or pepper flakes), parsley and white wine. Cook uncovered until the mixture is quite thick. Serve over spaghetti or pasta shells.

GERMANY

German wine: sweet, cheap, unsophisticated and invariably white. Or is it? What if it were dry, or rich and complex; what if it were red? The very idea of a wine from Germany that doesn't conform to the Liebfraumilch/Niersteiner/Piesporter style most of us have firmly fixed in our minds is faintly disconcerting – rather like the thought that the term 'claret' might also be used to describe sparkling white wines, or that Champagne could suddenly become a term for full, oaky reds.

And, of course, over the last 50 years the vast mass of Germany's wine has increasingly and shamefully lived down to its basic image – cheap, sugary plonk. But that's not what Germany's wines ought to be about and, ironically, it's neither the style of wine the Germans like to drink themselves, nor the style Germany is best suited to produce. It's as though Marlon Brando and Robert de Niro had accepted major roles in afternoon-television soap opera, to the exclusion of all else.

The Quality Compromise

Trying to ripen grapes in Germany can sometimes be a little like trying to grill a steak over a candle. Which might seem to be a pretty good reason for not making wine here at all – except that, like the Loire and Burgundy, Germany enjoys the benefits of a 'marginal' climate. Like a racing driver whose skills come to the fore when his car is closest to its top speed, grapes tend to produce their most impressive feats of flavour in the testing conditions provided by regions where they cannot ripen too easily.

Before the Second World War, Germany used to produce two kinds of wine: dry and often rather raw-tasting stuff in the frequent cool years, and sweeter, sometimes gloriously sweet wines in the rare years when the sun shone sufficiently to ripen the grapes and, more especially, when noble rot (here called *Edelfäule*) appeared in the autumn to give the wines its char-

acteristic rich intensity of flavour.

Unfortunately, those rare years came far too rarely to guarantee grape growers a decent livelihood and, after the War, the rest of the world was not overly eager to buy German wines of any description. It was hardly surprising, therefore, that the growers embraced any new idea that promised to make their lives easier. First came the simple but radical decision to begin replacing the Riesling, which had made Germany's reputation, with a range of easier-to-grow, easier-to-ripen varieties such as the Müller-Thurgau, Optima and Reichensteiner, all of which were specially developed to be reliable producers of large quantities of fruit even in the least hospitable climates. None of these grapes makes wine that is quite as good as Riesling, but they make up in quantity what they lack in quality.

Then, the winemakers developed ways of countering the quality problem. Following Mary Poppins' advice, they added a spoonful of sugar – or, to be more precise, two spoonfuls. The first was of granulated sugar, to raise the alcohol level (the same legitimate process of chaptalisation that has long been used in such northern French regions as Burgundy), while the second was in the form of sweet grape juice, or *süssreserve* which, 'backblended' with the wine, gave it an appealing grapiness that would either make a good but not-quite-ripe wine taste better, or turn a dull unripe dry wine into an equally dull sweet one. It was this combination of the new grape varieties with the widespread adoption of backblending, and thus sweeter flavours, that revolutionized the style of German wine.

The German Wine Laws

None of this would, however, have been possible without Germany's rather eccentric set of wine laws. One of the best ways to understand these laws is to compare them with those of Ger-

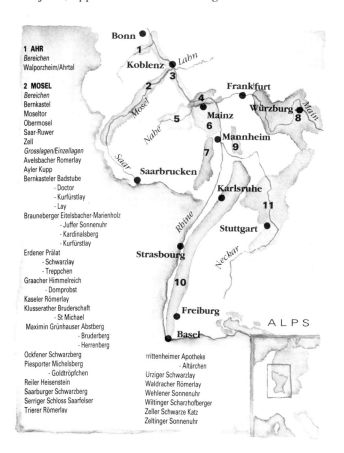

1 AHR
Bereichen
Walporzheim/Ahrtal

2 MOSEL
Bereichen
Bernkastel
Moseltor
Obermosel
Saar-Ruwer
Zell
Grosslagen/Einzellagen
Avelsbacher Romerlay
Ayler Kupp
Bernkasteler Badstube
  - Doctor
  - Kurfürstlay
  - Lay
Brauneberger Eitelsbacher-Marienholz
  - Juffer Sonnenuhr
  - Kardinalsberg
  - Kurfürstlay
Erdener Prälat
  - Schwarzlay
  - Treppchen
Graacher Himmelreich
  - Domprobst
Kaseler Römerlay
Klusserather Bruderschaft
  - St Michael
Maximin Grünhauser Abstsberg
    - Bruderberg
    - Herrenberg
Ockfener Schwarzberg
Piesporter Michelsberg
  - Goldtröpfchen
Reiler Heisenstein
Saarburger Schwarzberg
Serriger Schloss Saarfelser
Trierer Römerlay

Trittenheimer Apotheke
  - Altärchen
Urziger Schwarzlay
Waldracher Römerlay
Wehlener Sonnenuhr
Wiltinger Scharzhofberger
Zeller Schwarze Katz
Zeltinger Sonnenuhr

3 MITTELRHEIN
Bereichen
Bacharach
Rheinburgengau
Siebengebirge
Einzellage
Bopparder Hamm Ohlenberg

4 RHEINGAU
Bereich
Johannisberg
Grosslagen/Einzellagen
Eltviller Sonnenberg
Erbacher Deutelsberg
Geisenheimer Erntebringer
  - Klauserweg
Hallgartener Jungfer
Hattenheimer Nussbrunnen
Hochheimer Kirchenstück
Johannisberger Erntebringer
  - Klaus
  - Schloss Johannisberg
Kiedricher Sandgrub
Oestricher Lenchen
Rauenthaler Baiken
Rudesheimer Bischofsberg
Steinberger
Winkeler Jesuitengarten
  - Schloss Vollrads

5 NAHE
Bereichen
Kreuznach
Schloss Böckelheim
Grosslagen/Einzellagen
Kreuznacher Brückes
  - Kronenberg
Rüdesheimer Rosengarten
Schlossböckelheimer Kupfergrube

6 RHEINHESSEN
Bereichen
Bingen
Nierstein
Wohnegau
Grosslagen/Einzellagen
Binger St Rochuskapelle
  - Scharlachberg
Niersteiner Auflangen
  - Gutes Domtal
  - Hipping
  - Hölle
  - Rehbach
  - Spiegelberg
  - Kreuz
  - Krötenbrunnen

7 RHEINPFALZ
Bereichen
Südliche Weinstrasse
Mittelhaardt/Deutsche Weinstrasse
Grosslagen/Einzellagen
Deidesheimer Herrgottsacker
  - Hofstück
  - Leinhöle
  - Mariengarten
Durkheimer Hochmess
Forster Jesuitgarten
  - Mariengarten
Freinsheimer Annaberg
Kallstadter Steinacker
Neustadter Kapellenberg
Ungsteiner Herrenberg
Wachenheimer Mariengarten

8 FRANKEN
Bereichen
Maindreieck
Mainviereck

Steigerwald
Einzellagen
Iphofener Kronsberg
Randersacker Sonnenstuhl
Würzburger Stein

9 HESSISCHE-BERGSTRASSE
Bereichen
Starkenburg
Umstadt

10 BADEN
Bereichen
Badische Bergstrasse
Badisches Frankenland
Bayerische Bodensee
Bodensee
Breisgau
Kaiserstuhl-Tuniberg
Markgraflerland
Ortenau

11 WURTTEMBERG
Bereichen
Kocher-Jagst-Tauber
Remstal-Stuttgart
Württembergisch Unterland

Harvesting in the Rhine. Mechanical harvesters have largely taken over for commercial, inexpensive wines but quality-conscious producers and those making late-picked styles, particularly on hillside vineyards, still pick by hand

many's neighbour on the other side of the Rhine. France's vinous legislation is unashamedly class-conscious; if you are Château Latour, or a slice of a Burgundy Grand Cru vineyard such as Le Corton or Le Montrachet, your wine will be classed among the French wine nobility because, for hundreds of years, these particular vineyards have consistently made the best wine. But if you are a parcel of land on the other, the middle-class, side of the tracks, then however well your vines are tended and your wine is made it will never earn you the respect paid to a true aristocrat.

In Germany, almost all vineyards are created equal. Although, as in France, there are inevitably slopes and parts of slopes that have a centuries-old reputation for making the best wines in their regions, German legislation, unlike French law, recognises no such inherent superiority. In other words, a piece of poorly-situated flat land could theoretically produce a wine of the same legally designated 'quality' as one on the finest hillside in the country.

Ripeness is All

Why? Because the only criterion is ripeness. The more natural sugar the grapes contain, the higher the quality designation the wine can claim. So, a wine labelled as *Auslese*, for example, will have been made from riper, sweeter grapes than one labelled as *Spätlese*, which would, in turn, have been produced from

riper ones than a *Kabinett.*

All three of these designations, along with the still riper *Beerenauslese*, *Trockenbeerenauslese* and *Eiswein*, fall into Germany's top, QmP – *Qualitatswein mit Prädikat* (literally, 'quality wine with distinction') – category and are subject to (somewhat) stricter regulation than wines that are simply labelled QbA – *Qualitätswein bestimmter Anbaugebiete* ('quality wine from a given area').

A Lack of Definition

'Quality wine from a given area'? Isn't that the equivalent of France's AOC? No – for the simple reason that the 'given area' in question encompasses all of Germany's recognised vine-growing land. It is the 'quality' (ripeness) factor that earns the wine its designation. In all but the very best or very worst vintages, around 80% of Germany's wine – including every drop of Liebfraumilch – is legally sold as QbA, with the finer QmP wines and the two most basic, least ripe categories, *Landwein* and *Tafelwein*, making up the remaining 20%. In a great, warm year like 1985, for instance, nearly half of Germany's production could be sold as QmP and not a drop had to languish as Landwein or Tafelwein. In France, by comparison, much less than a third of the national annual harvest can ever be sold as *Appellation Contrôlée*, and there is in France no national 'super-AOC' equivalent of QmP.

Supporters of the way the German laws have been drawn up claim, quite reasonably, that the ripeness rules themselves help to sort out the good, well-sited, hillside vineyards (which get a lot of sun) from those on poor flat land (which don't). This may

The Riesling, the variety that ought to be used to make more of the wines from Germany's best vineyards. FACING PAGE: High-tech equipment is used throughout Germany in modern, large-scale wineries

well be true for the Riesling, but it conveniently ignores the readiness of those newer varieties to ripen in cooler places.

For the egalitarianism of German wine law also extends to the kinds of grapes that are grown. In the regions of France, there exists what could be called viticultural apartheid. If you want to make Gevrey Chambertin, you have to use the Pinot Noir; if your label says Sauternes, there are only four grape varieties you can legally grow. In Germany it's almost a free-for-all. All of which makes buying German wine pretty complicated, as anyone who has wondered what on earth all those words on the label mean, will testify.

Gothic Horror

Apart from the vintage and producer, there is the region (one of a possible 11), the district and/or village and/or vineyard (of which there are over 2,500, most of which have dauntingly long and complicated names by themselves, let alone in combination), the grape variety, the quality level (in other words, the ripeness) and, quite possibly, an indication of the wine's sweetness or dryness in the form of such terms as Kabinett, Spätlese and Auslese, Trocken and Halbtrocken.

And this is where it all gets more complicated still. Most wine books equate the ripeness 'quality ladder' with an ascending order of sweetness – hence an Auslese will be sweeter than a Spätlese, which will, in turn, be sweeter than a Kabinett. Except that the amount of natural sugar in the grape may not have any bearing on the sweetness of the finished wine; the super-ripe grapes of the sunny Rhône, after all, make wines that are *more alcoholic* – not 'sweeter' – than those of cooler Burgundy.

Is it any wonder that the average wine drinker just feels too confused to dare to buy a bottle of finer German wine? (If it's to accompany a meal, knowing how sweet a wine is in advance can be crucial.) The German authorities have handicapped their

producers still further by interpreting EC wine laws so literally that they forbid a German winemaker (or his British or other European importer) from describing his wines in the same way as, say, the Australians or Californians do. So a producer in the Mosel cannot print a back-label telling potential customers that his wine is 'dry and appley' – because, the authorities claim, he might mislead consumers into thinking that it was made from apples rather than grapes. Hardly surprisingly, by the late 1980s the outlook for Germany's quality winemakers was bleak. The combination of complex and pedantic legislation and customers' confusion – and hence unwillingness to buy – had driven many to cut their losses and join those making huge amounts of wine which they would sell at knock-down prices.

Producers Take the Lead

Fortunately, a growing number of producers have begun to fight back, to disassociate themselves from the Liebfraumilch lobby, to create new styles and to reiterate traditional ones, to devise clearer labels and, above all, to rehabilitate Germany's reputation as a producer of some of the most uniquely exciting wines in the world.

Thanks to demand for new styles from German wine drinkers themselves, to the enthusiasm of importers in other countries – particularly Britain – and to a series of good and very good vintages, the range and quality of German wines is improving by the year. Today, wine drinkers can find dry German whites that compete for quality and price with Muscadet; Chardonnays, and more particularly Pinot Noirs, to worry quite a few producers in Burgundy; juicy reds made from such varieties as the Dornfelder and Lemberger; and versions of the Pinot Gris and Gewürztraminer that are excitingly different from the Alsatian examples most people have encountered.

The New Wines

And then, of course, there are the Rieslings, the wines that still set Germany apart and that now come in almost any style you could desire: dry (Trocken), off-dry (Halbtrocken), with or without the vanilla of new oak barrels... you name it, somebody is probably trying to make it from the Riesling somewhere in Germany, extracting all the nuances of flavour they can find in what, in the right hands, can be the most aristocratic white grape of them all.

The good guys who are making these wines get precious little help from their government – which has been more interested in keeping the votes of the rather more numerous and vociferous bulk wine brigade – so they have set up their own self-help, self-regulating associations. Dismayed by the fact that an official revision, in 1989, of 1971 German wine law did almost nothing to encourage quality, they are now beginning to create, albeit unofficially, a French-style hierarchy for the best vineyards, with tighter controls on the kinds of grapes grown in them and the quantity of wine they can produce every year.

The day on which their efforts are granted official recognition will be a red-letter one for those people bored with the prospect of a world in which there are only two kinds of white wine – Liebfraumilch and Chardonnay.

THE AP NUMBER
Of all the confusing verbiage that you may encounter on a German wine label, there is a set of numbers that can be genuinely helpful. Every wine that is bottled in Germany has to have an Amtliche Prüfungsnummer – AP – number which, for anyone has the code books to decipher it, reveals the identity of the producers as well as the date and place it was bottled.

In order to recieve its AP number, every wine has to undergo what is officially described as a 'strict' blind tasting, though quite how strict outsiders would consider the required pass mark of 1.5 out of five to be is another question.

THE LANGUAGE OF GERMANY

Amtliche Prüfungsnummer Literally means 'official proof number' – refers to the unique code given to batches of wine that have passed statutory tests for the area of origin. Usually referred to as the AP number.

Anbaugebiet Wine region, e.g. the Rheingau or Baden.

Auslese Third step on the QmP quality ladder: wine made from grapes with a high natural sugar content. The wines are usually rich and concentrated.

Beerenauslese Fourth step on the QmP quality ladder: wine made from individually selected overripe grapes with up to 16° potential alcohol. Such wines are rich and very sweet.

Bereich Grouping of villages or district within an *Anbaugebiet*, e.g. Bernkastel.

Bundesweinprämierung German state wine award.

Charta Organisation of Rheingau estates whose members make drier (*halbtrocken*) styles, observing (far) higher standards than the legal minimum.

Deutscher Sekt Sparkling wine made from 100% German grapes.

Deutscher Tafelwein Lowest grade of German wine.

Deutsches Weinsiegel Quality seal around the neck of a bottle for wines that have passed certain tasting tests.

Domäne Domaine or estate.

Edelfäule Noble rot – *Botrytis cinerea*

Einzellage 'Single site' or individual vineyard, usually following name of a specific town or village : e.g. Graacher *Himmelreich*.

Eiswein Literally, 'ice wine', made from grapes of at least *Beerenauslese* ripeness, picked while the water content is frozen thus leaving the concentrated sugar, acids and flavour. Eiswein is rare and expensive.

Erzeugerabfüllung Estate-bottled.

Flurbereinigung Government-assisted replanting of slopes to up-and-down rows instead of terracing.

Gemeinde Commune or parish.

Grosslage A group of neighbouring *Einzellagen* producing wines of similar style and character – a group site, e.g. Piesporter *Michelsberg*.

Halbtrocken Half-dry.

Herb German equivalent of Brut.

Hock English term for a wine from the Rhine, derived from Hochheim.

Kabinett First step on the QmP quality ladder. The equivalent of reserve wines, Kabinetts are the lightest and driest of the naturally unsugared QmP wines.

Kellerei Winery.

Landwein German equivalent of French *vin de pays*: *trocken* or *halbtrocken* wines of a higher quality than *Tafelwein* and produced in a specific region.

Lieblich Wine of medium sweetness, equivalent to the French *moelleux*.

Oechsle German measure of the ripeness of grapes used as the basis for determining the quality level of individual wines.

Perlwein Semi-sparkling wine.

Qualitätswein bestimmter Anbaugebiete (QbA) Quality level below QmP for wines that satisfy certain controls, such as area of origin, but which have had sugar added for extra alcohol.

Qualitätswein mit Prädikat (QmP) Wines made from grapes that are ripe enough not to require any additional sugar. Meaning 'a quality wine predicated by ripeness', these top wines are further classified into the categories *Kabinett* to *Trockenbeerenauslese*.

Rotling Rosé.

Rotwein Red wine.

Schaumwein Sparkling wine.

Sekt Sparkling wine, usually made by the *cuve close* method, which, if not prefixed by 'Deutscher', can be produced from grapes grown outside Germany. Little of it is any good.

Spätlese The second step on the QmP ladder; literally means 'late-picked'. Sweet or dry and full-flavoured, these wines are balanced with fine acidity.

Spritz/Spritzig Light sparkle.

Süss Sweet.

Süssreserve Pure unfermented grape juice used to sweeten basic German wines. Also used by English winemakers.

Tafelwein Table wine that, even if bottled in Germany, may be a blend of wines from different EC countries. *Deutscher Tafelwein* must be 100% German.

Trocken Dry.

Trockenbeerenauslese Fifth and highest step on the QmP quality ladder. Made from 'shrivelled single overripe berries' affected by botrytis, these intense, complex wines are extremely rare and expensive. With a potential alcohol of at least 21.5° although only 5.5° need be actual alcohol. The high level of residual sugar produces rich wine with wonderfully intense honey, raisin and caramel flavours.

Weingut Wine estate. Can only be used on labels where all the grapes are grown on that estate.

Weinkellerei Wine cellar or winery.

Weissherbst Rosé of QbA standard or above produced from a single variety of black grape.

Weisswein White wine.

Winzergenossenschaft Wine growers' cooperative.

THE MOSEL

If the Rhine is the most famous wine river in Germany, it is the Mosel that is the most exciting, and the most dramatic. Rivers all over the world are so often said to curve like snakes that the description has become a cliché, which is a pity, because the Mosel genuinely is just about the nearest thing to a liquid boa constrictor you would ever want to see. From Perl, the meeting point of Luxembourg, France and Germany, it turns back and forth, carving its way sinuously for 145 miles (233km) north-eastwards to meet the Rhine at Koblenz. On its way it passes forests, castles, tiny, precariously perched villages, and sheer slopes covered with vineyards facing in every direction.

These slopes and the Riesling grape grown on them are the Mosel's greatest gifts and its greatest curse. Even when it is planted on flattish, easy land, the Riesling is not the easiest of grapes to grow, and far from the most productive; when it is grown on slopes that rise almost vertically from the river, the challenge is well nigh impossible.

At its very best, the Mosel is precisely what the Riesling is all about: a glorious mixture of crisp apples, of flowers and honey, coupled with the 'slatey' character derived from the soil in which the Riesling is grown. And, it is here that most of Germany's most impressive wines are now being made.

2 **MOSEL**
Bereichen
Bernkastel
Moseltor
Obermosel
Saar-Ruwer
Zell
Grosslagen/Einzellagen
Avelsbacher Romerlay
Ayler Kupp
Bernkasteler Badstube
 - Doctor
 - Kurfürstlay
 - Lay
Brauneberger Eitelsbacher-Marienholz
 - Juffer Sonnenuhr
 - Kardinalsberg
 - Kurfürstlay

Erdener Prälat
 - Schwarzlay
 - Treppchen
Graacher Himmelreich
 - Domprobst
Kaseler Römerlay
Klusserather Bruderschaft
 - St Michael
Maximin Grünhauser Abstberg
 - Bruderberg
 - Herrenberg
Ockfener Schwarzberg
Piesporter Michelsberg
 - Goldtropfchen
Reiler Heisenstein
Saarburger Schwarzberg
Serriger Schloss Saarfelser
Trierer Römerlay
Trittenheimer Apotheke
 - Altärchen
Urziger Schwarzlay
Waldracher Römerlay
Wehlener Sonnenuhr
Wiltinger Scharzhofberger
Zeller Schwarze Katz
Zeltinger Sonnenuhr

One essential key to these wines is their acidity; the Mosel is not the region to go looking for rich, fleshily ripe wines, or for Germany's best dry or red wines; most of these come from the warmer vineyards further south. No, the words most applicable to the Mosel's wines are those such as 'racy', 'elegant' and 'finesse' – terms that I normally struggle to avoid. Another word that springs to mind when trying to describe these wines is 'perfume', because of their floral style. Interestingly, when perfumiers talk about the precious liquids in *their* bottles, they traditionally divide them between daytime perfumes, such as Nina Ricci's *l'Air du Temps*, most of which they call 'green', and evening scents, such as *Chanel No. 5* or *Poison*, which they generally term 'brown'. If you apply the perfumiers' rules to wine, it seems highly apropriate that while the riper, more richly spicy wines of the Rhine are bottled in brown glass, those of the Mosel always come in green bottles. These are the 'daytime' wines – the ones I most crave on warm summer afternoons.

All of these descriptive terms are worth remembering when you are tasting Mosel wines, because all too often they will seem entirely out of place, for the simple reason that far too many wines from the Mosel are pale shadows of what they ought to be. In many cases they are handicapped by being made from the Müller-Thurgau rather than the Riesling; all too often the vines will have been so overburdened with flavourless fruit that the wine tastes like heavily diluted apple juice.

The slopes of the Mosel should be covered with Riesling vines that are physically incapable of this kind of over-production, but in the 'good old days', when the growers here did tend Riesling vines on their hillsides, they got precious few thanks for doing so. Most years the wretched grapes never ripened sufficiently to make wine of even *Kabinett* level, and even when the climate did allow good, naturally sweet wines to be produced, no one was rushing to pay a price for them that even began to repay the work, struggle and risk their production had entailed. So when it was suggested that the growers replace their old Riesling with some new Müller-Thurgau (as recommended by Professor Helmut Becker at the Geisenheim wine school), who could blame them for saying yes?

The change in the make-up of the region was dramatic. The Riesling used to cover so much of the Mosel that producers didn't even bother to mention its presence on their labels any more than a grower in Burgundy might tell people that his Nuits St Georges is made from the Pinot Noir. Today less than half of the Mosel's vineyards, and far less than half of its wines, are Riesling. Any label that doesn't name a grape variety is almost certainly hiding the fact that the wine is at least partly made from the Müller-Thurgau.

So the first lesson when buying Mosel is 'Look for the Riesling'. This is not to say that good wines are not being made from other varieties – some of that Müller-Thurgau can be refreshingly drinkable if it has been treated with care – just that if you want to taste that peculiar Mosel cocktail of apple, flowers, honey and slate, pure Riesling is what you need.

Fortunately, the chances of your finding it are slightly brighter than they appeared a few years ago, when the onward march of the Müller-Thurgau seemed almost unstoppable. Today, the advent of *Trocken* and *Halbtrocken* wines has made producers stop and think; these dry styles suit the Riesling far better than the newcomer. The decision to replant with Riesling has been made a little easier, too, by the development of new easier-to-work and more productive vineyards that run vertically rather than horizontally – and by generous local government grants towards the costs of replanting. Well over three-quarters of the region's vineyards have been transformed in this way and the success of the scheme has been great enough to ensure that terraced vineyards will disappear from all but the

The Bernkasteler Doctor, greatest vineyard in the Mosel — and arguably the whole of Germany

very steepest (and thus untransformable) slopes. This modernisation of the way vines are grown was the first dramatic change in the vineyards since winegrowing was introduced to the Mosel by the Romans 2,000 years ago. It was the Romans who invented the system of using individual stakes rather than wire trellises to support the vines that is still used here – and almost nowhere else in the world.

Among the other aspects of life in the Mosel that have barely changed over the centuries has been the ownership of the vineyards. There are cooperatives here, but they are less powerful than they are elsewhere and account for just one bottle in every five that are produced. Winemaking here remains in the hands of the Church, the state, old families (some of which can prove ownership of over 12 generations) and merchants, including, most notably, the innovative and quality-conscious Deinhard in Koblenz. Between them, this disparate band produce one of the most diverse collections of wines of any of Europe's wine regions. To be painfully blunt, it is far easier to describe the flavours you might hope to find in a bottle of Mosel than the one you are really likely to encounter.

The Regions

Moseltor and Obermosel

These two *Bereichen* in the southernmost part of the Mosel both produce basic, light, acidic wine, most of which, thankfully, ends up having bubbles put into it by the producers of *Sekt*. The only interest here lies in the continued presence in the Obermosel of the Elbling, the grape variety the Romans grew here; if you ever wonder what Roman wine may have tasted like, try a modern example from this region – it'll make you believe in progress.

THE ESSENTIALS — MOSEL-SAAR-RUWER

Location Western Germany, from Koblenz south to the French border.
Quality Mostly QbA, although there are some exceptional QmP wines in the best years.
Style White wine only: Rieslings from the northerly vineyards of the Mosel-Saar-Ruwer are pale and light-bodied, with racy acidity and surprisingly intense flavours of crisp apples, steel and slate with a hint of honey. In hotter years some superb wines of *Auslese* quality or above are produced which retain vitality and freshness amidst the luscious, honeyed flavour of the overripe grapes. Mosel-Saar-Ruwer wines, never fat and overblown, age extremely well and can be superb. The Doctor vineyard in Bernkastel produces Germany's most famous and most expensive wine. Müller-Thurgau, only introduced in the 19th century, is now almost as predominant as the Riesling but its rather angular mixture of thick grapiness, flowery overtones and an unnerving sharpness does not produce very exciting wines.
Climate Temperate, with modest rainfall. The steep valley sides provide protection for the vines and also allow rapid warming during the day.
Cultivation Soils are varied with sandstone, limestone and marl in the upper Mosel giving way to slate and clay soils in the lower reaches. There are, in addition, alluvial and gravel soils. The best sites for Riesling are the slatey slopes of the Saar-Ruwer and Bernkastel *bereichen*. The valley has very steep sides (at Bernkastel rising 700ft above the river as a virtually sheer face), giving altitudes of 100-350m (330-1150ft) and making cultivation laborious, in some places, tractors have to be winched up the vineyards.
Grape Varieties Riesling, Müller-Thurgau, Bacchus, Kerner, Optima, Elbling, Auxerrois, Ortega.
Production/Maturation Cool fermentation results naturally from the early onset of winter. Individual growers — most with long family traditions of wine-making — predominate although cooperatives flourish and play an important role. There are some important merchants with the best, like Deinhard, being amongst the leading producers.
Longevity Mosel-Saar-Ruwer wines generally age better than their counterparts in the Rhine because of their higher acidity. *Deutscher Tafelwein* and *Landwein* should be drunk immediately; QbA wines: within 1 to 3 years; *Kabinetts*: 2 to 10 years; *Spätlesen*: 3 to 15 years; *Auslesen*: 5 to 20 years; *Beerenauslesen*: 10 to 35 years; *Trockenbeerenauslesen, Eiswein*: 10 to 50 years.
Vintage Guide 71, 76, 79, 83, 85, 86, 88, 89
Top Producers Deinhard, Dr H Thanisch, J J Prum, Friedrich-Wilhelm Gymnasium, Schubert, Dr Loosen, Bischöfliches Priesterseminar, Lauerburg, Max Ferd Richter.

Above: Sundials (Sonnenuhren) like this are a common sight on the river slopes – as is the vineyard name Sonnenuhr

Facing Page: The Deinhard estate in Bernkastel. Deinhard is one of the best estates and merchants in this part of Germany

Saar-Ruwer

This *bereich* is the one part of the region that involves rivers other than the Mosel. Both the Saar and the Ruwer deserve to stand alongside the Mosel as part of a great region because they produce some of the best, least-well-known wines here.

The Ruwer would be worth visiting, if only to spend an hour or so in the Roman town of Trier. There are vines around the town itself, but these produce fairly run-of-the-mill wine; for the good stuff you have to head down to the water. The Ruwer has one *Grosslage* – Romerlay – within which are situated the Maximin Grünhaus, Karthaushofberg (notable for its bottles that wear nothing but a neck label) and Marienholtz vineyards, all of which can, in the right hands, make sublime, steely wines. The 'right hands' here, as elsewhere in Germany, are generally the state domaines, the old family estates and the Church. Names to look out for include Von Schubert, Bert Simon, Bischofliches Konvikt Trier and Eitelsbacher Karthauserhof.

Very few producers market their wine under the *Grosslage* name – as they do in Bernkastel for example – because they make so little; by the same token, they have no need to sell much to merchants, and the cooperatives have little role to play here. For all these reasons, the odds on getting a good wine from the Ruwer are among the best in Germany.

The same cannot quite be said of the Saar, partly because producers do offload fair quantities of unimpressive wine under the *Grosslage* name of Wiltingen Scharzberg, and partly because the climate tends to be cooler, so, in all but the ripest years, the wines can taste a bit raw. But when the sun hangs around for long enough at the end of the year, the Saar can produce some of Germany's most intense, longest-lived wines.

As elsewhere, the best vines are grown on the slopes, a fact that is emphasised by the vineyards that are named Kupp after the round-topped hillsides. Among these, the best are Ayler Kupp, Wiltingen Scharzhofberger, Wiltingen Braune Kupp, Filzener Herrenberg, Serriger Herrenberg and Schloss Saarfelser, Saarburger Rausch and Ockfener Bockstein. Look for wines made by Egon Müller, Hohe Domkirche-Trier, Reichsgraf von Kesselstatt and Staatl. Weinbaudomäne.

Bernkastel

This name, which must be the most famous *Bereich* in the Mosel, covers the whole region of the Mittelmosel, the central stretch of the river's course from the frontier to Koblenz. In the confusing jungle of German wine, few words are more misunderstood than the name of this small town. On the one hand there is the great Bernkasteler Doctor vineyard that overlooks the town and river and makes one of Germany's finest wines, and on the other, there are the oceans of dull wine legally labelled as Bereich Bernkastel produced in vineyards nowhere near the the town of Bernkastel at all – which ought to bear the regional name of Mittelmosel they were allowed in the 1960s.

There are two *Grosslagen* here: Kurfürstlay and Badstube. The former contains the least interesting of Bernkasteler's vineyards and the best of those of Brauneberg; the great Doctor vineyard and Bernkasteler Lay are both in the *Grosslage* Badstube. Named after the supposedly healing qualities of its wine, this sheer, slate-soiled, 3.5-acre (1.4-ha) vineyard is the German equivalent of Burgundy's Romanée-Conti. In ripe years its wines are everything that the Mosel should be: rich, honeyed and as 'slatey' as the roofs the vines overlook, but with a balancing acidity that makes this a wine to keep for decades.

In that same sensible world, the Bernkasteler Doctor would long ago, like the Romanée-Conti, have been recognised as some kind of Grand Cru or First Growth to distinguish it from its neighbours. Instead, it found itself at the centre of a ludicrous court case begun because the German authorities decreed in 1971 that no vineyard could be smaller than 12.5 acres (5 ha).

Instead of changing the rules to fit the tiny size of this particular plot, the authorities sought to justify expanding it. Hardly surprisingly, they were supported in this by the 13 owners of the neighbouring vines, who were keen to sell their wine as Bernkasteler Doctor. Ultimately – it took 13 years and considerable effort on the part of the three original owners of the Doctor vineyard – a compromise was agreed, whereby the size of the plot was increased to eight acres (3.24 ha). The story says a great deal about everything that has been wrong with the German wine industry since the war. The official prestige of a piece of vinegrowing soil should be judged by the quality of the wine it produces, not by its ability to fit legal criteria drawn up by those for whom numbers and neatness are all important.

There is a very similar problem at Piesport, another wine-producing village within the *Bereich* of Bernkastel. Look at the bottles on the shelf: on the left, there's Piesporter Michelsberg, on the right there's Piesporter Goldtropfchen. Both seem to come from Piesport, so which should you buy? The answer is that the Goldtropfchen ('golden droplets') is a single, hillside vineyard that produces wine that should taste distinctive and wonderful, while the Michelsberg is a huge, flatland *Grosslage*, most of whose wines are produced in enormous quantities and rarely have much more flavour than tap water. Unfortunately the international fame of Piesporter Michelsberg has not only debased the wine of that name; bottles of Piesporter Goldtropfchen don't always come up to scratch either.

Brauneberg is less well known than either Bernkastel or Piesport and consequently often a better buy. The best vineyard here is the Juffer, which overlooks the village of Brauneberg itself from the other side of the river and produces delicate wines that once sold for higher prices than those of the Berkasteler Doctor. It still competes at the equivalent of First Growth level with that vineyard, but at a (relatively) lower price.

The *Grosslage* of Munzlay boasts some of the region's best

estates and three riverside villages – Graach, Wehlen and Zeltingen – all of which can produce some of the finest, gentlest wines in the Mosel. Graach's best vineyards are the Domprobst, Josephshofer and Himmelreich. Zeltinger Himmelreich is worth looking out for too, as is Wehlener Sonnenuhr, named after the vineyard clock that ensures the pickers are never late for lunch.

Collectors of bizarre wine labels will appreciate the *Grosslage* Nacktarsch, which, literally translated, means 'naked arse' and whose label depicts a small boy having that particular part of his anatomy spanked. Unfortunately, the wine made here is far less exceptional than either the name or the label.

Zell

The village of Zell used to be better known outside Germany than it is today, thanks to the success of one of its wines, the Zeller Schwarze Katz. Recognisable by the black cat on its label, this wine is supposed to owe its name to an occasion when three merchants could not make up their minds over which of three barrels to buy. As they asked for another sample from one of the casks, the grower's cat sprang onto it, hissed, arched its back and generally treated the merchants as though they were dobermans intent on stealing a kitten. This, the men decided, must be the best wine in the cellar.

Until quite recently, the producers of Zell adopted a slightly more scientific method of selecting the wine that could call itself Schwarze Katz – by holding a blind tasting. The region of Zell has now been expanded by the addition of the villages of Merl and Kaimt and, sadly, the tasting is no longer held. The cat can now grace the labels of any wine from this *Grosslage* and today you would be far better advised to opt for a bottle of Zeller Domherrenberg. Elsewhere within the *Bereich* of Zell, the best wine probably comes from the village of Neef, whose Neefer Frauenberg can be great Riesling.

A Liebfraumilch-equivalent called *Moselblumchen* can be found throughout the Mosel. It should be treated with the same suspicion as Liebfraumilch. However, bottles bearing this label will probably be no worse, and cheaper, than many that abuse the name of the Bereich Bernkastel and Piesporter Michelsberg.

Salm in Saurer Sahne

Salmon in a sour cream sauce

The valley of the Mosel is close to the French regions of Alsace and Lorraine, and the cooking of this part of Germany has a lightness perfectly in tune with the wines that are produced here.

SERVES 6
6 salmon steaks
Salt and freshly ground black pepper
Juice of 1 lemon
1 oz/25 g solid butter
2 tbsp mixed grated Parmesan and Gruyère cheese
2 tbsp dried breadcrumbs
3 oz/75 g melted butter
5 fl oz/150 ml sour cream
1 tbsp plain flour
5 fl oz/150 ml dry white wine
Chopped parsley to garnish

Season the steaks on both sides with salt and pepper, and sprinkle them with lemon juice. With the solid butter, grease a shallow ovenproof dish, into which you place the fish. Sprinkle with the grated cheese and breadcrumbs. Dribble the melted butter over and pour the sour cream between the steaks. Bake uncovered in an oven preheated to 350°F/180°C/Gas mark 4 for about 25 minutes, until the fish just begins to flake but is still firm. Remove the steaks with a slotted slice to a warm serving dish. In a saucepan mix the wine and flour to a smooth sauce. Add what remains in the baking dish. Bring to the boil and immediately reduce to a simmer, stirring, until the sauce begins to thicken. Remove from heat and stir in the parsley. Pour over the fish. Serve with new potatoes and steamed courgettes.

THE RHINE

First, forget Liebfraumilch. Okay, so it's all made here, but to associate the wine for which the vineyards of the Rhine are best known outside Germany with the kind of glorious, unique wines produced by the regions of the Rheingau and Rheinpfalz – and, to a lesser extent, the Rheinhessen – is like imagining there to be some kind of link between Piat d'Or and top-class Bordeaux or Burgundy. There is nothing actually *wrong* with well-made Liebfraumilch – provided that you treat it as what it is: white plonk developed almost exclusively for foreigners.

In a sense though, the success of Liebfraumilch has probably done less damage to the image of the rest of the Rhine's wines than the generally mediocre quality of the contents of bottles bearing such apparently 'classier' names as Niersteiner Gutes Domtal and Bereich Johannisberg – and the widely held belief by non-Germans that there is a single identifiable region called the Rhine that produces a sweet wine called 'hock'. In fact, when they can take their minds off the job of making anonymous-tasting Liebfraumilch, the three main regions of the Rhine – the Rheingau, the Rheinhessen and the Rheinpfalz – should each produce identifiably different styles of wine like those of nowhere else in the world.

4 RHEINGAU
Bereich
Johannisberg
Grosslagen/Einzellagen
Eltviller Sonnenberg
Erbacher Deutelsberg
Geisenheimer Erntebringer
　　- Klauserweg
Hallgartener Jungfer
Hattenheimer Nussbrunnen
Hochheimer Kirchenstück
Johannisberger Erntebringer
　　- Klaus
　　- Schloss Johannisberg
Kiedricher Sandgrub
Oestricher Lenchen
Rauenthaler Baiken
Rudesheimer Bischofsberg
Steinberger
Winkeler Jesuitengarten
　　- Schloss Vollrads

5 NAHE
Bereichen
Kreuznach
Schloss Böckelheim
Grosslagen/Einzellagen
Kreuznacher Brückes
　　- Kronenberg
Rüdesheimer Rosengarten
Schlossböckelheimer Kupfergrube

6 RHEINHESSEN
Bereichen
Bingen
Nierstein
Wohnegau
Grosslagen/Einzellagen

Binger St Rochuskapelle
　- Scharlachberg
Niersteiner Auflangen
　- Gutes Domtal
　- Hipping
　- Hölle
　- Rehbach
　- Spiegelberg
　- Kreuz
　- Krötenbrunnen

7 RHEINPFALZ
Bereichen
Südliche Weinstrasse
Mittelhaardt/Deutsche Weinstrasse
Grosslagen/Einzellagen
Deidesheimer Herrgottsacker
　- Hofstück
　- Leinhöle
　- Mariengarten
Durkheimer Hochmess
Forster Jesuitgarten
　- Mariengarten
Freinsheimer Annaberg
Kallstadter Steinacker
Neustadter Kapellenberg
Ungsteiner Herrenberg
Wachenheimer
　Mariengarten

The Regions

The Rheingau

This *ought* to be the 'best bit' of the Rhine. It was the village of Hockheim that gave the English that term 'hock' in the first place, and the village of Johannisberg after which the Californians have named the wines they make from the Riesling. In the eighth century the Emperor Charlemagne recognised the potential of the land and decreed that vines be planted on it forthwith. They have been there ever since.

The Rheingau distinguishes itself from other parts of the Rhine in several ways. It is far smaller than its neighbours, with only a little over 10% of the vineyard area of either the Rheinhessen or Rheinpfalz; and the Riesling is still the major grape variety, producing yields of around 350 cases per acre (140 per hectare), compared to around 430 and 500 (174 and 200) respectively for the other Rhine regions. Thanks to these factors, and to the individualism of the Rheingau's 500 estates and 2,500 growers, the cooperatives have not achieved the stranglehold on production and marketing here that they have elsewhere, so quality has every reason to be higher than almost anywhere else in Germany. And so, occasionally, it is. The mark of a typical Rheingau will be the same appley-grapey flavour that the Riesling produces in the Mosel, but with more honeyed richness, and less of that region's acid bite. At their best, particularly at *Spätlese* and *Auslese* levels of sweetness, these can be the most exquisitely well-balanced and refreshing wines.

Unfortunately, sales of such wines are less than brisk – which helps to explain why a group of Rheingau producers decided to switch their emphasis from sweet to dry, anouncing their decision to the world with the establishment in 1983 of the Association of Charta Estates, whose recognisable seal appears on members' *Trocken* and *Halbtrocken* wines.

The first thing to be said about the Charta wines is that, apart from being dry, they will always be produced from the Riesling (this is obligatory), and are likely to be more carefully made than many of the Rhine's other wines. The second thing to be said about them, though, is that their dryness all too often makes them far less enjoyable to drink when they are young than slightly sweeter wines made from similar grapes – or than dry French wines that achieve a higher natural level of ripeness.

Dry wines of equal or greater quality than *Spätlese* can compete with their counterparts from Alsace, and in good vintages they genuinely do achieve their object of being a good accompaniment to food. As QbAs, too, they can be softened up sufficiently to make them drinkable. Even so, to most non-Germans, these still tend to be rather like Japanese films – to be admired and talked about rather than enjoyed. If you have ever thought a Chablis or a Sancerre dry and acidic, you would find it hard to imagine the meanness of some of these wines.

The Charta members counter any such comments from visitors with the argument that these wines need time to soften and that, in any case, they are being ordered by the cellarful by German restaurants, whose customers seem ready to pay high prices for these wines, patriotically drinking them instead of a French import. Today the dry Rheingaus are indeed selling so well that most of the people making them have cut their production of sweeter wine to just 30 or 40% of the total. The Rheingau is now, quite literally, going dry; tragically, its producers seem resolute in their desire to rewrite history by claiming that their region's wines were traditionally made without any remaining sweetness. Well maybe in cool, unripe, years this was the case; in warmer ones, however, as anyone

RIGHT: Vineyards in the Rheingau, following replanting — Flurbereinigung — to improve the quality of the wine (and the quantity produced) by allowing the use of tractors

who has been lucky enough to pull the cork on a glorious, petrolly, 30- or 40-year-old *Auslese* or *Spätlese* knows, they were still producing the kind of sweet, part-fermented wines that had so enchanted the Romans 2,000 years earlier.

When buying Rheingau wines, beware of wines labelled as *Bereich* Johannisberg; although some are good, they could come from literally anywhere in the region – this is the Rheingau's only *Bereich*. Look out instead for wines from individual villages – but not necessarily villages such as Lorch and Lorchhausen, both of which are close to the border with the Mittelrhein and produce good but unexceptional Riesling.

Assmannshausen has a local reputation for the quality of its Pinot Noir reds, few of which stand comparison with good examples from the Rheinpfalz, let alone those from across the French border. As you round the elbow of the river, however, you come to the tourist town of Rudesheim, with its street of wine bars and its steep Berg vineyard, source of some of the biggest-tasting wines of the region.

Next stop on the river is Geisenheim, site of Germany's top wine school and research institute, and the place where vine experts labour to create new kinds of easy-to-grow grapes that are ideally adapted to these northerly conditions. The best vineyard here is probably the Mauerchen.

Beyond Geisenheim, one arrives at Winkel and its Hasensprung vineyard, and two German oddities: Schloss Johannisberg and Schloss Vollrads, old-established estates that are allowed to print their own names rather than that of an individual vineyard on their labels. Both are in the forefront of the dry-wine movement. Today the Steinberg vineyard planted by the monks houses the German Wine Academy and a wine museum, but it still produces full-flavoured, honeyed wine with a dash of slate and flowery acidity that is sold as Steinberger.

The nearby riverside villages of Oestrich and Hattenheim make similar, if less intense wines. Hattenheim is also the place to come in June for its annual Erdbeerfest – strawberry and wine fair. The Nussbrunnen and Wisselbrunnen are the top vineyards here. The little hillside villages of Hallgarten and Kiedrich make great, if slightly more spicy and floral, less honeyed Riesling, especially good examples of which come from the Sandgrub and

Gebäckenes Schweinsfilet im Broselteig
Tenderloin of roast pork baked in a herb crust

The sandy soils of some parts of the Rhine valley are perfect not only for vines but also for that other great Rhineland delicacy — asparagus, which accompanies this dish to perfection.

SERVES 4-6
3 lb/1.5 kg pork tenderloin or fillet
Olive oil
Salt and freshly ground black pepper
1 onion, peeled and halved
1 bay leaf
2 egg yolks
½ tsp dried sage
½ tsp dried marjoram
2 oz/50 g dried breadcrumbs
1 glass dry white wine

Rub the meat all over with olive oil and season with salt and pepper. Place in a roasting tin with the onion and bay leaf and put into an oven preheated to 425°F/220°C/Gas mark 7 for about 1½ hours. Remove and allow to cool a little. In a large bowl mix all the other ingredients except the wine until it forms a spreadable paste (if too wet, add more breadcrumbs; if too dry, a little water). Season this mixture with salt and pepper and spread over the meat. Return the joint to an oven preheated to 450°F/230°C/Gas mark 8 for 15 minutes, basting regularly. Remove the meat to a heated serving dish. Add the wine to the roasting tin. Bring to the boil and scrape up any solids. Strain the juices over the meat. Serve with steamed young asparagus and noodles.

Left: The Liebfrauenkirche in Worms, the church after which billions of bottles of often very ordinary Liebfraumilch from throughout the Rhine have been named. Ironically, this vineyard still produces fine wine

Below: Müller-Thurgau grapes arriving at a winery in the Rheinhessen, from which they will soon emerge as Liebfraumilch

Right: The Wagnerian Schloss Ehrenfels in the Rheingau is typical of some of the forbidding castles in Germany. It also gave its name to the Ehrenfelser grape

Grafenberg vineyards, while Erbach has the Rheingau's greatest plot of vines, the Marcobrunn, as well as Schloss Rheinhausen, one of its oldest (eighth-century) and best estates. The Rieslings and dry Chardonnays here are impressive .

Eltville's claim to fame includes the fact that it was the home of Johannes Gutenberg; it is also the place to find one of Germany's best state-owned estates, the Staatsweinguter, which makes a wide range of top-class wines, including, when possible, extraordinary Eiswein.

Back in the hills, Rauenthal makes small quantities of intensely flavoured wines that need longer to soften than those made closer to the river – but they're worth the wait. Nearby, Walluf boasts two of the oldest vineyards in the region, while Martinsthal's has the Wildsau vineyard .

Finally, on the River Main close to Wiesbaden, is Hochheim, the town that gave the English 'hock' – their easy-to-remember term for the wines of the Rhine. Like all the vineyards on the Main, Hochheim makes 'earthier' wine than the rest of the Rheingau, but the flavours can be rich and tangily refreshing.

Rheinhessen

The biggest wine region in Germany – with some 165 vine-growing villages, 11,000 growers and around a quarter of the annual production – this is also one of the oldest. Historically at least, the Rheinhessen could be called the heartland of the Rhine. Fifty percent of all Liebfraumilch is made here, and millions more bottles of undistinguished wine are labelled Bereich Nierstein or Niersteiner Gutes Domtal.

The weather here is comparatively mild, with neither the frosts suffered in the Mosel, nor the greater warmth enjoyed by the Rheinpfalz. The Riesling can fare well; unfortunately, this is lazy winemaking country in which bulk-oriented merchants and cooperatives hold sway and the Müller-Thurgau and its fellow recently developed varieties have taken over in the largely flat, featureless vineyards. Just one vine in 20 is now a Riesling and most of these are grouped around a set of nine riverside towns and villages now called the Rhein Terrasse. These include Auflangen Bodenheim, Nackenheim, Oppenheim and Nierstein, the lovely old town whose 150 growers more or less lost their birthright when their neighbours stole the name of Nierstein and that of one of its least distinguished vineyards, the Gutes Domtal and doled them out like confetti to an enormous amount of mediocre Müller-Thurgau produced throughout a large chunk of the Rheinhessen. Nierstein's real wines are worth seeking out, as are those of Oppenheim and nearby Ingleheim, where the speciality is Spätburgunder.

Rheinpfalz

Though the winegrowers of neither region would readily admit it, there are some pretty solid links between the vineyards of the Rheinpfalz and Alsace, which is just across the southern border and in the same rain shadow provided by the range the French call the Vosges and the Germans know as the Haardt Mountains. The Rheinpfalz is warmer country; grapes ripen better here, taking on the richer, spicier character often found in Alsace. Picking out a wine from the 'Pfalz 'blind' can be one of the easiest of tasting party-tricks; if there seems to be more body to the wine and more spice the odds of it being from the Rheinpfalz are pretty good.

You have to pick and choose though – that ripeness can mean a lack of fresh acidity; much of the wine here is soft, dull Müller-Thurgau – basic Liebfraumilch in name or nature. This is not only Germany's second largest wine region, but also, on occasion, its most productive, thanks to the combination of the sun and those generous Müller-Thurgau vines. It is also cooperative country – as you might expect from any region whose 25,000 winegrowers have less than two and a half acres (one hectare) of vines each. But the winemakers here know that their grapes are likely to ripen most years, that theirs is a climatically

privileged part of Germany and, they would argue, the pre-eminence of their region was recognised 2,000 years ago by the Romans and more recently, by Napoleon.

Just as the Mosel has its best part in the Mittelmosel, the Pfalz's finest vineyards are to be found around a set of half a dozen villages in the Bereich Mittelhaardt-Deutsche Wein-strasse to the north of Neustadt. Inevitably, however, the allocation of *bereichen* was as mishandled here as it was elsewhere, and this one takes in the whole of the northern half of the Rheinpfalz, leaving the south to the Bereich Südliche Weinstrasse. The most northerly vineyards of the Bereich Mittelhaardt-Deutsche Weinstrasse are an undistinguished bunch, and the first village of any interest is Kallstadt, whose Annaberg vineyard produces great Riesling. Unusually, the labels of the wines made in the Annaberg, like those of a Burgundian Grand Cru, such as the Corton, do not need to include the name of a village. Which is just as well, because while most of the rest of Kallstadt's vineyards are in the Grosslage Kobnert, the Annaberg confusingly falls into the Grosslage Freurberg, along with Bad Dürckheim, another source of potentially great wine.

It is in the next most southern Grosslage, the Mariebgarten (Forst an der Weinstrasse), and in Wachenheim, Forst and Deidesheim, most specifically, that the winemaking fireworks really begin. Other wines produced in the Rheinpfalz may equal the best made here; none beats them. The secret of these vineyards lies in their exposure to the sun, to the black basalt of Forst's vineyards – especially in the Forster Jesuitengarten – that helps to give the grapes a little extra ripeness, and to the quality of the producers. The names of the estates with vines here – Bassermann-Jordan, Reichsrat von Buhl, Burklin-Wolf – reads like a roll-call of Germany's vinous aristocracy.

This southern region is actually relatively new to the game of bottling its own wine; until as recently as 20 years ago a large proportion of its crop was shipped in bulk to be blended and bottled elsewhere. Since then, however, the vineyards have been modernised, and a set of younger vinegrowers have addressed themselves to the task of making better wine. So far they have been handicapped in that ambition by the prevalence of cooperatives intent on producing good rather than great wine, but this remains a part of Germany to watch.

THE ESSENTIALS — THE RHINE

Location Western Germany, bordering Switzerland. Includes 3 of the 11 German wine growing regions — the *Anbaugebiete* of the Rheingau, Rheinhessen and Rheinpfalz.

Quality Plenty of *Deutscher Tafelwein* and QbA but also the full range of QmP styles.

Style As elsewhere in Germany, almost all wine produced is white. The Rheinpfalz and Rheinhessen produce virtually all of Germany's Liebfraumilch, whose dull sweetness or, if they are more fortunate, mild, flowery grapiness is the first introduction to wine-drinking for many people. From the Rheinhessen, too, comes Niersteiner Gutes Domtal, produced in dull and dubiously large quantities, a wine that has debased the good name of the Nierstein vineyards as bulk Liebfraumilch has the original Liebfrauenstift wines. Further up the quality scale, around 16% of production is Riesling of *Kabinett* and *Spätlese* standard, full of soft, honeyed floral fruit in Rheinhessen, riper and spicier in the Rheinpfalz, more delicate in the Rheingau, with underlying acidity and steeliness to balance the richness of the fruit. Intensely rich, honeyed and unctuous wines of *Auslese* quality and above are produced in small quantities (around 5 % of total production and only in the very best years) in the Rhine from famous vineyards such as Schloss Vollrads and Schloss Johannisberg in the Rheingau, and Forster Jesuitengarten in the Rheinpfalz. A tiny quantity of light red wine is produced, and an increasing amount of *trocken* and *halbtrocken* (dry and semi-dry) white is made, with a steelier, mineral character to it.

Climate Temperate, due to the moderating effects of the river, the protection of the Taunus mountains to the north and local forests.

Cultivation Soils are varied, with quartzite and slate at higher levels and loams, clay loess and sandy gravel below. Vineyards are located on the flat hinterlands and gentle slopes of the Rhine, the best sites being the south-facing river banks. New crosses of grapes such as Kerner and Scheurebe have been introduced since the 1960s.

Grape Varieties *White*: Riesling, Müller-Thurgau, Silvaner, Kerner, Bacchus, Huxelrebe, Morio-Muskat, Scheurebe, Muskateller, Gewürztraminer. *Reds* are from the Spätburgunder and Portugieser.

Production/Maturation The finest quality wines are produced in minute quantities, allowing for great attention to detail. Many of the independent producers market their own wines as well. At the other extreme, a great deal of bulk-blended generic wine, such as Liebfraumilch and Niersteiner, is produced.

Longevity *Deutscher Tafelwein* and *Landwein*: drink immediately. QbA: 1 to 3 years; *Kabinetts*: within 2 and 8 years; *Spätlesen*: within 3 and 12 years; *Auslesen*: between 5 and 18 years; *Beerenauslesen:* between 10 and 30 years: *Trockenbeerenauslesen, Eiswein*: between 10 and 50 years.

Vintage Guide 71, 76, 79, 83, 85, 86, 88, 89

Top Producers *Rheingau*: Balthasar Ress, Deinhard. *Rheinhessen*: Louis Guntrum, Carl Koch, Carl Sittman. *Rheinpfalz*: Bürklin-Wolf, Von Buhl, Bassermann-Jordan, Spindler.

OTHER WINES OF GERMANY

If the winemakers of the Rhine and Mosel went on strike, would-be German wine drinkers would still have a surprisingly wide range of bottles from which to choose – a far wider range, in fact, than either of those regions could ever begin to offer.

Nahe

The wines of the Nahe don't really have a style of their own; the region is a meeting point of the Mosel and the Rhine, and elements of both regions are found in the wines, some of which taste like basic Rheinhessen, while others combine the depth of fruit of the Rheingau with the acid bite of the Mosel. The Riesling is a newcomer here, but at its best – in villages such as Bad Münster and Münster Sarmsheim – it can be richly intense. Another speciality of the region is it's grapefruity Scheurebe.

Good wine is, however, the exception to the Nahe rule. A lot of the wine is fairly basic – particularly when it bears such convincing-sounding labels as Rudesheimer Rosengarten (which is sold on the reputation of the great Rudesheim of the Rheingau) and Schloss Böckelheim. Look for Rieslings from the cellars of Hans Crusius (especially from the Traiser Rotenfels and Raiser Bastei vineyards) and von Plettenberg (from Schlossböckelheimer Kupfergrube and Bad Kreuznacher Narrenkappe).

Mittelrhein

From its name, one might expect this region to be as important a part of the Rhine as the Mittelmosel is of the Mosel. But in fact, the Mittelrhein is best described as tourist country, the Germany on which Hollywood based its Grimms Fairy Tales.

Its riverside villages are almost to well kept, but so, thankfully, are the sheerly sloping vineyards in which the Riesling still holds sway. Unfortunately, the wines produced here are rather less spectacular. The best – from villages such as Braubach, Bacharach, Boppard and Oberwesel – can be quite intensely, if often rather acidically, reminiscent of the Mosel, but very little is made, and very few bottles escape the grasp of the region's landlords, who have no difficulty in selling them.

ABOVE: The Schlossbockelheim vineyards overlook the Nahe river and produce some of the best wine of this anbaugebiet. In the last century, there was a copper mine here. BELOW: Schloss Pfalz Kaub in the Mittelrhein

Franken

Poor old Franken. Very, very few people know its wines and at least some of those who do imagine that this region stole its *Bocksbeutel* bottle design from Mateus Rosé rather than vice versa. The earthy Silvaner grape still occupies much of the land, producing similarly earthy wine; but, like the Chasselas in Switzerland, the Silvaner does its very best here, producing dry wines that go well with the region's heavy Bavarian dishes.

Württemberg

When German wine drinkers want a red wine produced by their countrymen, this is the region to which they look. The only problem, to an outside observer, is that while they accept the stuff they are given as red, most non-Germans would call it sweet and pink. The handicaps here are the heavy-handed influence of the cooperatives (half the growers have vineyards of less than half an acre) and the range of grapes that are used. The main varieties are the Trollinger, the Pinot Meunier (here known as the Schwarzriesling) and the Lemberger, all of which make better rosé than red. Some decent Pinot Noir is made, and some better Riesling – particularly in the *Grosslage* of Heuchelberg and in the Stuttgart suburb Einzellagen of Berg, Goldberg, Hinterer Berg, Steinhalde, Wetzstein and Zuckerle – but these wines are rarely seen outside the region.

Ahr

The wines from this area rarely leave German soil either, partly because Ahr is so tiny – under 1,000 acres (400 ha) of vines are divided among nearly a 1,000 growers – and partly because over two-thirds of its wine is red (pink) *Weissherbst*, made either from the Portuguiser or Spätburgunder (Pinot Noir).

Making red wines this far north, even in the favourable microclimate provided by the valley slopes of the river after which the region is named, is impracticable. The producers might do better to concentrate a little more on their pleasant Riesling and Müller-Thurgau whites.

Hessische Bergstrasse

'The spring garden of Germany', this is orchard country where, the 1,000 acres (400 ha) of grapes have to compete with a wide range of fruits and vegetables. The Riesling can ripen well enough, but its wines (most of which are made by two cooperatives) are rarely better than middle-of-the-road Rhines.

Baden

For decades now, under the guidance of its huge ZBW cooperative, Baden has gone its own way. While other regions were busily planting Müller-Thurgau with which to make semi-sweet plonk, Baden has been increasing its acreage of Riesling, and concentrating its attention on making dry and off-dry wines. Today, of course, growers throughout the rest of Germany have followed Baden's example; unfortunately for them, few enjoy the warm climate of this region.

It would be wrong to paint too rosy a picture – many of the cooperative's 500 different wines are neutral, dry, Müller-Thurgau, Gutedel, or unexciting red or pink *Weissherbst* – but both the Riesling and Rulander can make really tasty wine here. Look out for slightly sparkling *spritzig* examples.

Sekt

What producers of *Sekt* are loathe to admit is that the very worst Spanish *Cava* is a million times more drinkable than most German sparkling wine. At its finest, *flaschengarung* – champagne-method – Riesling can be both delicious and refreshingly different, but unfortunately, such examples are very, very rare; most *Sekt* is made by the *cuve close* method from dull, unripe Müller-Thurgau or Elbling. And, unless the label says *Deutscher Sekt*, the mass of the wine in the bottle won't even be German. Try the ones made by Deinhard and Schloss Rheinhartshausen or stick to *Cava*.

Konigsberger Klopse
Meatballs in a creamy caper sauce

Berlin, cosmopolitan crossroads of East and West, first adopted this dish (originally brought by East Prussian immigrants) as its own, but today variants on this tasty recipe with its piquant sauce are served throughout Germany.

SERVES 6
8 oz/225 g minced beef
8 oz/225 g minced pork
8 oz/225 g minced veal
2 slices stale white bread, crust removed, soaked
in water and squeezed dry
4 tbsp dried breadcrumbs
2 medium onions, finely minced
2 eggs
3 anchovy fillets, finely chopped
2 tbsp melted butter
Salt and freshly ground black pepper
25 fl oz/700 ml beef stock
2 egg yolks
2 tbsp capers
Lemon juice

In a large bowl, mix the meats, the bread, 1 tbsp breadcrumbs, onion, eggs, anchovy and melted butter. Season with salt and pepper and shape into balls. In a large saucepan bring the stock to the boil and lower in the meatballs with a spoon or ladle. Cook for about 20 minutes and then lift them out with a slotted spoon and keep warm. Stir the remaining breadcrumbs into the stock and simmer and stir until the sauce begins to thicken. Remove from the heat. Beat the egg yolks well and add a spoonful of the stock and mix well. Add this mixture to the stock and simmer gently, stirring constantly, until it just begins to thicken. Do not let it boil. Add the capers and a few drops of lemon juice. Add the meatballs to the sauce. Serve with noodles and broccoli.

THE ESSENTIALS — OTHER GERMAN REGIONS

The Ahr, Franken, Württemberg, Baden, Nahe, Mittelrhein and Hessische Bergstrasse.
Quality Overwhelmingly QbA, although Kabinett wines are made in reasonable quantities in hot years. Very little *Auslese* or above.
Style The northerly Ahr is the best area for reds. They are very pale, light, with gentle cherry fruit. The Mittelrhein and Nahe make good, slatey, refreshing Riesling. Württemberg produces a light, grapey red from the Trollinger grape and a characterful soft summer fruit Schillerwein. These regions also produce classic racy Riesling, aromatic with piercing green apple fruit, in contrast to the richer Riesling made in Hessische Bergstrasse, which is full of soft, almost tropical fruit flavours. Baden's wide range is rarely seen outside the region. Franken produces full, earthy, dry wines. Riesling from warm years can be excellent.
Climate These regions are characterized by sheltered, temperate climates although the climate of Franken is more continental.
Cultivation Most vineyards are located on gentle slopes or south-facing hillsides of river valleys.
Grape Varieties *Ahr and Württemberg*: Riesling, Müller-Thurgau, Kerner, Silvaner, Scheurebe, Ruländer, Blauer Portugieser, Spätburgunder. *Ahr*: Domina, Dornfelder. *Hessische Bergstrasse*: Ehrenfelser, Gewürztraminer. *Franken*: Bacchus, Silvaner, Ortega, Perle, Riesling, Rieslaner. *Württemberg*: Trollinger, Mullerrebe, Lemberger, Pinot Meunier. *Baden*: Gutedel, Sylvaner, Riesling, Nobling.
Production/Maturation Much of the wine in these regions is produced by technically proficient co-operatives from grapes grown by small growers who use labour-intensive methods.
Longevity Varies enormously, depending on the style of the wine. Most reds and whites made from 'new' varieties should be drunk young.
Vintage Guide 71, 76, 83, 85, 88, 89
Top Producers *Ahr*: Winzergenossenshaft Heimersheim. *Franken*: Ernst Popp, Hans Wirsching, Juliusspital. *Württemberg*: Staatliche Weinbau Lehrund Versuchsanstadt Weinsberg. *Baden*: Bezirkskellerei Markgräflerland. *Mittelrhein*: Heinrich Weiler. *Nahe*: Staatliche Weinbaudomane/Graf Von Plettenberg.

SPAIN

Spain's red wines have been the seducers of the wine world, the wines that gently led countless white wine drinkers down the path towards more 'sophisticated' claret and Chianti. The point was that while, to many novice drinkers, those French and Italian wines were dauntingly tannic, Spain's reds were soft, sweet and, to use a term cherished by the hacks who write the descriptive labels on the backs of bottles, 'mellow'. They were, above all, very, very approachable. The trouble was that once all those novice drinkers (of whom I was one) had been introduced to wine, where did they go next? Straight to claret.

And it wasn't as if the Spanish had much in the way of white and pink wine to fall back on. The traditional image of wines sold as 'Spanish Sauternes' and 'Spanish Chablis', should have been buried long ago when European law took these wines off the market. Sadly, it lives on because there have been too few modern success stories to take its place.

Rioja and Navarra can make lovely dry *rosado* rosés, but they have never really caught the public eye. With the exception of a tiny number of great, traditional, oaky white Riojas, a handful of expensive Albariño wines from Galicia, a larger number of new style, pleasant, but wholly anonymous dry whites and the wines of Miguel Torres in the Penedés, there have been no strong Spanish contenders to join the white wine bandwagon of the last few years. Many of the wines for which Spain has been traditionally famous have gone out of fashion, and the only really current success story is the *cava* sparkling wines.

Over the last 25 years, Spain's wines have been a little like an athlete who starts well, but runs out of steam somewhere a few feet before the last hurdle. Throughout that time, they have always been on the brink of taking the world by storm – and that's where they've stayed, while wines from California and Australia, Eastern Europe and even New Zealand have all

1 Rias Baixas	22 Priorato
2 Ribeiro	23 Terra Alta
3 Valdeorras	24 Valencia
4 El Bierzo	25 Utiel-Requeña
5 Valle de Monterrey	26 Almansa
6 Toro	27 Jumilla
7 Rueda	28 Yecla
8 Cigales	29 Alicante
9 Ribera del Duero	30 Bullas
10 Rioja	31 Cebreros
11 Navarra	32 Mentrida
12 Campo de Borja	33 Madrid
13 Calatayud	34 La Mancha
14 Cariñena	35 Valdepeñas
15 Somontano	36 Tierra de Barros
16 Ampurdán-Costa Brava	37 Montilla-Moriles
17 Costers del Segre	38 Malaga
18 Alella	39 Jerez
19 Conca de Barbera	40 Condado de Huelva
20 Penedés Cava	41 Binisalem
21 Tarragona	42 Tacoronte-Acentejo

ABOVE: Quintessential, unchanging Spain – the 'sombra' (shade) entrance to the bullring in Jerez

RIGHT: The harvest festival – the joyous crushing of the first grapes – in the seaside town of Sitges in the Penedés is one of the most important dates in the region's calendar

overtaken them and leaped into the limelight. With the exception of the red wines of one region – Rioja – the sparkling wines of another – the Penedés – and the fortified wines of a third – Jerez – Spain remains almost as undiscovered as it was in 1965.

So, what's the problem? The Spaniards' greatest handicap is their raw material – Spain's indigenous grape varieties, of which there are over 600. This may sound like a wealth of choice, until you go on to discover that just 20 of these cover 80% of the vineyards. And the trouble is that these 20 produce wine as monotonous and undemanding as the contents of an average Top Twenty pop chart. The Airen, for example, the most widely planted grape in the world, covers nearly a third of the country's vineyards – and makes dreadfully dull white wine.

The second most widely planted variety, the Garnacha – the grape the growers of the Rhône know as the Grenache – covers around 10% of the vineyards and here produces mostly easy, young-drinking reds, but few of any great distinction. And none, apart from Priorato, built to last. The only red grape of note, the Tempranillo, covers around a fifth as much land as the Garnacha and only achieves real recognition for its essential contribution to the flavour of Rioja and Ribera del Duero. Of course, Italy's winemakers use grape varieties not grown elsewhere – but their odd grapes are a far more interesting lot. Spain does have interesting grapes, to be sure – but Graciano, Loureira and Albariño, for example, never make the top 20.

But it's not as if they *have* to grow these grapes. The wines of Miguel Torres, Penedés superstar, first demonstrated what could be done with foreign varieties such as Bordeaux's Cabernet Sauvignon, as do such other Cabernet and Chardonnay producers as Raimat, Jean León and Marqués de Griñon.

Age to Age

Another Spanish self-inflicted handicap is an obsession with age and ageing. To most Spaniards, an old wine is, by definition, better than a young wine. And a wine that has been matured for a long time in oak barrels is best of all. Spain's *Denominación de Origen* system – its equivalent of France's Appellation Contrôlée – has age as one of its central tenets, officially designating wines that have undergone the required period of maturation with the words *Con Crianza, Reserva* or *Gran Reserva*.

When applied to the wines from best bodegas of Rioja, all three terms should indicate higher-than-usual quality – especially because the bodegas only produce Reservas and Gran Reservas in the best vintages, and because Rioja is one of the few wines in Spain that can benefit by being kept. Elsewhere, however, the same terms and rules are applied even when the wines are made from grapes that have no natural propensity for

ABOVE: *The town of Cenicero in the Rioja Alta is the address of some of the region's best-known bodegas*

RIGHT: *Grape picking can be thirsty work — especially in the heat of Spain in September*

ageing. Visitors from other countries often leave the tasting rooms of *bodegas* – wineries – shaking their heads in dismay that the winemakers insist on keeping ready-to-drink young wine to flatten out in cask. But it's hard to blame the winemakers; the oak-aged wine will not only sell for a higher price, but will probably do so very easily on the local market.

In the past, this local keenness on ageing was catered for by displaying on the labels of wine bottles not a vintage, but that the wine was a '2nd', '3rd' or '4th' *Año*, or 'year', meaning that it had been matured for two, three or four years. When vintages did appear, they were often used in what one might call rather a 'relaxed' fashion, with a single batch of labels being used on

a succession of vintages. But what did it matter? After all, the wines were almost always ready to drink when they were sold and all but the best producers liked to promote the erroneous idea that there was little variation in wines of different vintages. Indeed, one quite go-ahead winemaker freely admitted having blended together wines of two or three years so as to maintain a commercially successful flavour. As he said, people liked the 1982 so we made the '83 taste as similar to it as we could.

THE LANGUAGE OF SPAIN

Abocado Medium-sweet.
Añejado Por Aged by.
Año Year
Blanco White.
Bodega Wine shop, firm or cellar.
Cepa Vine.
Clarete Very light red.
Consejo Regulador Official organisation controlling each region's system of *Denominación de Origen*.
Cosecha Harvest, vintage.
Criada Por Matured by.
Crianza A red wine with a minimum of two years in the barrel (six months for whites).
Denominación de Origen (DO) Controlled quality wine region, equivalent to France's AOC. Every such region possesses its own quality stamp. A superior quality level, *Denominación de Origen Calificada* (DOC), was set out in a Royal Decree of February 1988 but this has not been

adopted in practice at present.
Doble Pasta A wine macerated with twice the normal proportion of grape skins to juice during fermentation.
Dulce Sweet.
Embotellado Bottled.
Espumoso Sparkling.
Elaborado Por Made by.
Flor Wine yeast peculiar to sherry that is vital to the development of the fino style.
Garantia de Origen Simple wines that have received little or no oak ageing.
Generoso Fortified.
Gran Reserva The top quality level for wines. Reds must have spent two years in oak and three years in bottle, or vice versa. Whites must have been aged for four years with at least six months in cask.
Granvas Sparkling wine made by the *cuve close* method.
Nuevo 'Nouveau-style' red.
Reserva Reds matured for a minimum of three years, of which at least one was spent in cask. Whites and *rosados* receive

two years ageing with at least six months in cask.
Rosado Rosé.
Seco Dry.
Semi-Seco Medium dry.
Sin Crianza Without wood ageing.
Solera Traditional system of producing consistent style of sherry or Malaga whereby increasingly mature barrels are topped up – refreshed – with slightly younger wine.
Tintillo Light red (like *clarete*).
Tinto Red.
Vendimia Harvest, vintage.
Viejo Old.
Viña/Viñedo Vineyard.
Vino de aguja Wine enlivened with a slight sparkle.
Vino de mesa Table wine.
Vino de pasta Ordinary, inexpensive wine, usually light in style.
Vino de la Tierra Equivalent of France's *vin de pays*; 'country wine' with some regional character.

Tiny Production

The winemaker who would like to break out of this stultifying mentality faces two other barriers, one connived at and one wholly created by the DO system. The conditions they impose are utterly conflicting. First, yields in Spain are very low – on average only 25hl/ha – half those of Burgundy, for example. It is these low yields that explain why, although Spain has more vineyards than any other country in Europe and nearly half as many again as France, its annual production is far smaller than it ought to be. This limited production is directly attributable to the lack of rain. But irrigation is still against the law in the denominated regions.

However, the authorities not only favour large bodegas, but also make life very difficult for small ones. Ageing bodegas in Rioja, for example, are legally obliged to stock a minimum of 2,250 hectolitres – or around 1,000 225-litre barrels. Even spread over several vintages, 1,000 barrels could hold the production of four or five estates in Burgundy or St Emilion. And without a legally recognised ageing bodega, you can't use those magic 'Con Crianza', 'Reserva' and 'Gran Reserva' labels that guarantee a valuable extra few pesetas per bottle. The inevitable consequence of this is that Spain still has far too few small, maverick wineries to pioneer new developments; compared with Italy, for example, it has a pitifully small band – less than a dozen strong – of internationally recognised superstars.

During the 1990s, a complete review of Spanish wine law is planned, which should hopefully remove some of the anomalies that currently exist. But as it stands now, to put it bluntly, the DO system makes more sense politically than it does in terms of winemaking. The existence of a local DO helps to satisfy the growing desire apparent throughout Spain to establish regional identity. Outside the regions, however, the names

of the DOs – with a handful of exceptions – are almost unknown. This is hardly surprising, when one can taste wines from two or three such *denominaciónes* side by side and discover no discernible difference of the kind that distinguishes say, Barolo from Chianti or Bordeaux from Burgundy.

Following the lead of Miguel Torres Jr in Penedés, most go-ahead producers just shrug their shoulders and sidestep the system altogether. If nobody's heard of Méntrida or Conca de Barberá, why print its name on your label? Particularly if doing so means having to obey local rules that oblige you to use dull-flavoured grapes. If you can persuade your region to accommodate your ways (as Torres has done in Penedés), so much the better. If not, well it's just too bad. Bottles of Marqués de Griñon cannot use the name of the La Mancha DO in which they are produced (because they are made from the non-approved Cabernet Sauvignon and – heavens! – from irrigated vineyards) but, even without a DO, these wines sell better and at a higher price than almost any others in the region.

But their producers are famous as winemakers, not as makers of Spanish wine. And when the introduction of new grape varieties upsets old-timers who cannnot see what's wrong with the old ones, you can almost see their point. Does Spain really want to end up making precisely the same kinds of wines as California, Australia and just about every other warm country in the world? What Spain needs now is men and women who want to make great wine from the few Spanish grape varieties that do have individual flavours of their own, and who want, for example, to revive the traditions of good old-fashioned white winemaking of Rioja wineries like the Marqués de Murrieta. The 'revolutionary reactionaries' of the Italian wine industry are impressing the world with wines that combine the best of old and new worlds; winemaking of this calibre could enable Spain to clear that hurdle with ease.

RIOJA AND NAVARRA

As recently as the 1960s, Rioja had little of the fresh vanilla flavour with which it is now associated – for the simple reason that it only comes naturally from new oak barrels which were thought neither necessary nor affordable. You simply bought them when the old ones fell apart. Then came the 1970s and a boom time for the region. New bodegas needed new barrels, and modern winemaking equipment was introduced, including temperature control for the fermentation vats.

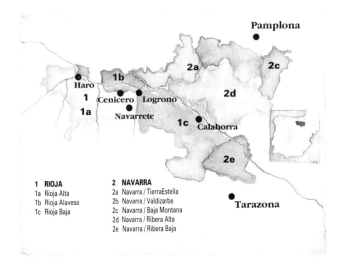

1 RIOJA
1a Rioja Alta
1b Rioja Alavesa
1c Rioja Baja

2 NAVARRA
2a Navarra / TierraEstella
2b Navarra / Valdizarbe
2c Navarra / Baja Montana
2d Navarra / Ribera Alta
2e Navarra / Ribera Baja

THE ESSENTIALS — RIOJA/NAVARRA

Location Northern Spain, following the river Ebro from Haro to Zaragoza.
Quality Rioja and Navarra are classified as *Denominación de Origen* (DO) but Rioja is by far the best region in terms of quality. It in turn is divided into 3 subregions, the Rioja Baja, Alavesa and Alta, in ascending order of quality.
Style Red Rioja should have soft strawberry and raspberry fruit with rich vanilla overtones from ageing in American oak barriques. There are two very different styles of white Rioja. One is the very clean, cool-fermented, anonymous new-wave style exemplified by Marqués de Cacerés. The other is the traditional *reserva* style with a very deep golden colour and intense vanilla flavour resulting from slow maturation – and oxidation – in oak, such as Marqués de Murrieta. Some wines, such as CVNE'S Monopole, successfully combine the two styles, producing fruity wines that have an attractive creamy vanilla character. The wines of Navarra tend to be lighter, lesser versions of those of Rioja, at their best when oak is used to produce a similar vanilla taste and style.
Climate The Pyrenees and the Cantabrian mountains moderate the climate, offering protection from the Atlantic winds and the excessive heat of the Mediterranean. The climate does become hotter and drier as one moves towards the coast.
Cultivation Relief in the region ranges widely, from the foothills of the Pyrenees to the flatter, hotter Rioja Baja. The best vineyards are in the central hill country of Rioja Alta and Alavesa. Limestone is the dominant component of the soils with additional sand and clays in Alta and Alavesa and silty alluvium deposits in Baja and Navarra.
Grape Varieties *Red*: Tempranillo, Garnacha Tinta, Graciano, Mazuelo, Cabernet Sauvignon. *White*: Viura, Malvasia, Garnacha Blanca, Muscat Blanc à Petit Grains.
Production/Maturation Ageing in Bordeaux-style barriques imparts the characteristic vanilla flavour to the wines of Rioja, where the new-style whites are cold-fermented. A lowering of minimum ageing periods in cask and bottle has, some say, resulted in a lessening of quality and character in red Riojas, many of which are now sold much younger than previously.
Longevity Red Rioja Crianza: 3 to 8 years; Reserva: 5 to 30 years; Gran Reserva: 8 to 30 years. New-wave white Rioja is for drinking young (within 3 years); the traditional white can be kept for 15 years but good examples are rare.
Navarra reds: 3 to 10 years; whites: 1 to 3 years.
 Vintage Guide Red Rioja 78, 81, 82, 83, 85, 86, 87
Red Navarra 81, 82, 85, 86
Top Producers *Rioja*: Lopez de Heredia, La Rioja Alta, CVNE, Remelluri, Contino, Marqués de Cacerés, Marqués de Murrieta, Muga, Riojanas, Martínez Buianda. *Navarra*: Chivite, Señorio de Sarria, Ochoa.

A century before, a number of winemakers had crossed the Pyrénées from their native Bordeaux, where their vineyards had been devastated by the phylloxera louse. These Bordelais, who set up as merchants rather than estate-owners, found their new region very different from the one to which they were used, and hardly suprisingly, they brought ideas and styles of winemaking that were just as new to the Riojanos. The most innovative were prolonged ageing in small (50-gallon/225-litre) casks and the practice of crushing the grapes rather than fermenting them whole. Rioja became a wine worth keeping rather than the tavern quaffer it had been previously.

Today the region is split into three parts, the Rioja Alta, the lower Rioja Baja and the Rioja Alavesa. The Riojanos maintain that the best Rioja is a blend of wines from two or three of the regions. The Rioja Alta's calcium-rich soil is well suited to the Tempranillo and produces fine, long-lived red wines, while the Alavesa, shaded by mountains, has less extremes of temperature and makes the plummiest, best early-drinking wines. Which leaves the Baja, which, some unfairly say, lives down to its 'low' name by making the region's most basic wine.

The region has gone through enormous changes in the last 20 years. The oaky days of the 1970s were followed by the less oaky vintages of the following decade, when the *bodegas* were busily consolidating after the boom. Today oak is back with a vengeance, as producers have finally caught onto the idea that the flavour of vanilla is the 'Unique Selling Point' of their wine. Around 40% of Rioja is now matured in wood, ranging from the wine sold *con crianza* ('with ageing'),which must spend at least 12 months in barrel, to Gran Reserva wines (usually only made in better vintages), which have to be aged for two or three years in wood and be at least five years old when they are sold. Reserva wines can be bottled after a year in cask, but must be kept for at least another three years in bottle.

The oaky flavour associated with red Rioja was once also the mark of the region's whites. For these, the ageing requirements are slightly less stringent; sadly, only a handful of *bodegas* now make good oaky, traditional wine that conforms to these rules.

Far more important than the oak is the choice of grape variety used to make the white wine; the only interesting variety here is the Malvasia; sadly, this is the least used. Most white Rioja is made from the dull Viura and Garnacha Blanca. Once there were around 40 red Rioja varieties here; today, although sensible rationalisation has increased the proportion of the (good, strawberryish) Tempranillo, and reduced the role of the (dull, slightly peppery) Garnacha, the tannic, Mazuelo and the perfumed, interesting Graciano have both almost disappeared.

Changes are taking place, but slowly, handicapped as the region is by the structure of its wine industry. Almost 90% of the wine is still sold by *bodegas,* which only actually produce a quarter of it themselves, half from their own fruit and half from bought-in grapes farmed by some of the region's 14,000 growers. The rest of the wine is made by 30 cooperatives and by individual growers. The number of small estate wineries is restricted by the unfortunate rule that obliges any *bodega* that is going to mature wine that will sell as Crianza, Reserva or Gran Reserva to hold at least 1000 barrels of wine in stock at any given time. Today a growing number of producers question the relevance of such rules and smaller wineries are increasingly jolting the region out of its Big-is-Beautiful complacency.

Navarra

Navarra's wines have traditionally had a second-class reputation and sell for lower prices than those of its neighbour. And yet part of Rioja is actually on Navarra territory. So, shouldn't someone be asking why Navarra's wines taste so recognisably

Top: *The contrasting landscape of the Rioja Alavesa, source of some of the finest Riojas of all*

Above: *The Olite experimental bodega in Navarra has quietly helped to revolutionise the winemaking of its region.*

different to – and less impressive than – the wines of Rioja? This is what the local government did in 1980, and it didn't take long to discover the answer; almost all of the region's grapes were Garnacha and 90% of its wine was made by ill-equipped and old-fashioned cooperatives.

Further planting of the Garnacha was banned and growers were given financial incentives to plant better varieties, including the Tempranillo, Cabernet Sauvignon and Graciano. The local government even invested money in the new Cenalsa blending and bottling *bodega* that sells 20% of all the Navarra wine sold in Spain. As recently as 1984 none of the cooperatives had any kind of cooling equipment; today, however, they almost all have some.

Navarra's fresh, fruity and emphatically 'modern' whites and rosés now often compete on level terms with their much more famous counterparts from Rioja, and a growing number of its its young, unoaked reds are among the most plummily refreshing in Spain. The *Crianza*, *Reserva* and *Gran Reserva* reds will take a little longer to get right – and my guess is that, certainly within five years at the most, some of the big bodegas of Rioja will have to look to their laurels.

Lomo de Cerdo con Pimentos

Pork chops with a tomato, olive and red pepper sauce

The Rioja region of Spain is not only blessed with luscious, oaky wines but also fruit and vegetables, particularly peppers, which add a subtle sweetness to this traditional recipe.

SERVES 6
6 pork loin chops
Salt and freshly ground black pepper
2 oz/50 g plain flour
3 tbsp olive oil
2 medium onions, minced
2 cloves garlic, peeled and minced
2 tomatoes, peeled, seeded and chopped or 2 tinned tomatoes, drained and chopped
1 1/2 lb/750 g red peppers, seeded and chopped
6 tbsp dry white wine
10 fl oz/275 ml water
1 bay leaf
1 hard-boiled egg, finely chopped
2 tbsp parsley, chopped
12 black olives, pitted and halved

Season the chops with salt and pepper. Dredge them in the flour and shake to remove any excess. In a flameproof casserole, heat the oil until it is hot but not smoking. Brown the chops, turning regularly. Transfer the chops to a plate. To the casserole dish, add the onions and garlic and cook until the onions are soft but not brown. Add the tomatoes and peppers and cook over a moderate heat for about 5 minutes. Stir in the wine, water, bay leaf, egg, parsley and olives and bring to the boil. Immediately reduce to a simmer and add the chops (ensuring they are well-basted with the sauce). Cook gently for 30-40 minutes or until the chops are tender. Serve with rice and steamed courgettes.

CATALONIA

Twenty years after first stunning French tasters with his Cabernet Sauvignon, Miguel Torres Junior is still Spain's best known wine-maker — and the driving force behind the Penedés

---

THE ESSENTIALS — CATALONIA

Location The north-east corner of Spain, around Barcelona.
Quality Penedés, Alella, Terra Alta and Priorato are notable areas with DO status.
Style Both red and white wines are varied, ranging from light and fruity to full, oak-matured to oak-free, dry to juicy-sweet.
Although renowned as being Spain's most innovative wine-making region, most wines tend to be little more than sound and commercial. A significant difference can be seen in those wines from producers such as Torres and Jean Leòn who use 'foreign' grape varieties, oak-ageing and the latest techniques. Cava is the largest source of fine-quality sparkling wine outside Champagne. Most are dry although there are sweet and *rosado* versions. Once recognisable by a characteristic earthy flavour, cava has improved remarkably in recent years. The area around Tarragona is the source for much of the world's sacramental wine. Similarly rich and dark reds are produced at Terra Alta and Priorato.
Climate A relatively mild Mediterranean climate on the coast, becoming more continental further inland, with frost an increasing hazard.
Cultivation A wide variety of soils ranging from the granite of Alella to the limestone chalk and clay of Penedés and Tarragona, where there are, in addition, alluvial deposits. There is a similar variety of relief, ranging from the highest vineyards of Alto Penedés, which benefit from cooler temperatures, to the flat plains of Campo de Tarragona.
Grape Varieties *Red*: Cabernet Sauvignon, Merlot, Tempranillo, Garnacha, Monastrell, Pinot Noir, Cabernet Franc. *White*: the Parellada predominates, with some Chardonnay, Sauvignon, Gewürztraminer, Muscat, Riesling, Garnacha Blanca, Macabeo, Malvasia and Xarel-lo.
Production/Maturation With the exception of the very traditional Priorato, techniques are modern. Torres introduced cool-fermentation to Spain while the cava companies have invented their own apparatus and methods besides adopting those – for example, the *méthode champenoise* – from outside. The Raimat estate at Lerida exemplifies the good use of ultra-modern vinification techniques.
Longevity Reds: up to 5 years for most, but top-class Penedés wines can last for 15. Whites are best drunk early, but between 3 and 8 years for fine whites such as Jean Leòn's Chardonnay. Cava: within 1 to 3 years for non-vintage; vintage wines can be kept for up to 8 years.
Vintage Guide *Penedés*: Reds 80, 82, 85, 86
  Whites 81, 82, 84, 85
Top Producers *Penedés*: Torres, Jean Leòn. *Alella*: Raimat. *Cava*: Masia Bach, Codorníu, Freixenet, Castellblanch.

Catalonia is the home of the biggest Champagne-style winery in the world, and the region that produces some of the best Chardonnays and most successful Bordeaux-style reds of the whole of Iberia. According to the Catalonians themselves, their region is Europe's answer to California, but this is an absurd exaggeration; to be blunt, the only way to make Catalonia look impressive is to compare it with the rest of Spain.

There are nine Catalonian DOs, ranging from the tiny Costers del Segre and Conca de Barbera to the huge Penedés, but ask most sophisticated non Catalan Spaniards to name as many as three and you'll be very lucky to get much of a reply.

The Regions

Penedés

This is the most successful part of Catalonia, thanks almost exclusively to the efforts of its *cava* – sparkling wine – producers and to a single *bodega* called Torres. There are two famous Catalonians called Miguel Torres – Miguel Junior, who makes the wine and Miguel Senior, who sells it. Miguel Torres Junior has been a true revolutionary in Spain; he it was who persuaded his neighbours of the benefits of clean, temperature-controlled fermentation; who proved that the Cabernet Sauvignon could make top-class wine in the Penedés by winning international tastings against the best of Bordeaux with his Gran Coronas Black Label and who, following a spell in France, took a fresh look at the local varieties and found ways of using them in blends with French grapes to make good, commercial wines. A few small estates, such as Jean León, have followed in Torres' footsteps towards the Cabernet Sauvignon and Chardonnay, but none of the big bodegas – with the exception of Codorníu's Raimat winery – has even begun to compete on any kind of major scale. And yet there are few regions in the Old World in which an adventurous winemaker would have greater scope to experiment; between them, the Upper, Middle and Lower Penedés really do offer an extraordinarily broad range of climates. Down near the coast in the Lower Penedés, it's hot,

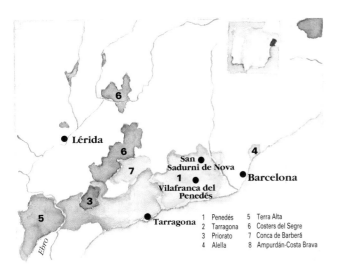

1	Penedés	5	Terra Alta
2	Tarragona	6	Costers del Segre
3	Priorato	7	Conca de Barberá
4	Alella	8	Ampurdán-Costa Brava

ripe country – ideal for Muscat, but less suited to even medium-bodied reds and whites. For better examples of either of these styles, you have to cross the hills to the white wine country where the grapes for *cava* are grown, and where Torres has produced his prize-winning Cabernet Sauvignon. Even here the temperature is still a bit high for really fine whites; these are to be found in the Upper Penedés at 2,000-2,600ft (600-800m).

Surprisingly, given its importance to the region, the one style Torres has never marketed has been *cava*, the Penedés' *méthode champenoise* sparkling wine. *Cava's* early success merely served to confirm to a few cynical critics, who maintained that these wines tasted earthy, dull and unrefreshing, how easy it is to sell bubbles. Old-fashioned wineries (including cooperatives) do little to maintain the wine's freshness and flavour and the climate where the grapes are grown is also less than ideal, but the main problem is the grape varieties – the Parellada, the Macabeu and the dull, alcoholic Xarel-lo.

When the Raimat winery introduced its Chardonnay Brut Nature, few who tasted it blind recognised it as a *cava* and non-Spaniards, used to Champagne, declared it a winner. Today, Chardonnay is rapidly appearing in all sorts of *cavas*, but even so, far too many producers are still busily promoting traditionally made vintage *cavas* and 'special reserves'. Save your money and stick to young non-vintage examples from companies such as Raimat, Codorníu, Freixenet and Segura Viudas.

Conca de Barberá

Some day the name of this almond-growing region ought to be as well known as that of the Penedés to its north-east. After all, this is the cool area from which Torres gets the grapes to make Milmanda, its top-of-the-range Chardonnay.

Costers del Segre

This one-estate *denominación* to the west of the Penedés owes its growing reputation to the success of the wines made at Raimat. The Raventos family of Codorníu, who own this ultra-modern *bodega*, today have over 2,500 acres (1,000ha) of vineyards, soon to be doubled, and make red wines (from Cabernet Sauvignon and Tempranillo) that are among Spain's best. Its most impressive wine is the pure Chardonnay *cava*, but the non-sparkling Chardonnay is improving fast.

Tarragona and Terra Alta

Despite their dusty, hot, summer climate, two of Tarragona's three regions specialise in white wine. Little of it is worth going out of your way to find, however, and much the same can be

Merluzza Marinara

Fish poached in a tomato and almond sauce

The capital of Catalonia, Barcelona is one of the most exciting cities in Europe and, as a port, famous for its seafood dishes. Hake is traditional, but any firm-fleshed white fish will do.

SERVES 4
3 tbsp olive oil
1 medium onion, minced
2 cloves garlic, peeled and minced
2 oz/50 g blanched and ground almonds
1 lb/500 g tomatoes, skinned, seeded and chopped, or tinned tomatoes, drained and chopped
12 black olives, pitted and chopped
Salt and freshly ground black pepper
2 ¹/₂ pts/1.25 l water
Juice of 1 lemon
1 tsp salt
2 lb/1 kg fillets of firm-fleshed white fish such as cod, turbot, haddock or hake
2 tbsp parsley, minced

In a frying pan, heat the olive oil until it is hot but not smoking. Add the onions and garlic and cook until the onions are soft. Add the almonds, stirring for a minute. Add the tomatoes and olives. Season with salt and pepper. In a large pan, boil the water with the lemon juice and a teaspoon of salt. Reduce to a simmer and add the fish. Cook until the flesh just begins to flake. Remove the fish to a heated serving dish with a slotted slice. Add 5 tbsp of the water in which the fish was cooked to the tomato mixture and stir thoroughly. Simmer until the sauce just begins to thicken. Pour the sauce over the fish and garnish with parsley. Serve with triangles of bread sautéed in butter and steamed green beans.

said for the Cariñena and Garnacha based reds. For good examples look for the dry, grapey Moscatel Seco from De Muller and the Viña Montalt Blanco Seco from Pedro Rovira.

Though technically within Tarragona, the hot dry region of Terra Alta has its own DO for the fairly hefty whites and dullish reds it produces. The *denominación* is more deserved by its organically produced, sweet, lightly fortified altar wines.

Priorato

Primitive wine from a primitive region, in which olive trees, men and vines struggle to survive on steep, rocky slopes. Lack of rainfall, an intensely hot climate and slatey soil mean tiny yields, mostly of Garnacha and Cariñena, which are used to make wines that are highly alcoholic – often up to 18%.

Alella and Ampurdán-Costa Brava

Alella has become a doomed wine region; over the last 25 years over half of its vineyards have been stolen to extend Barcelona. True, the world can live without the sort of dull, wood-aged semi-sweet wine made by the Alella cooperative (producer of around two-thirds of the wine here), but the Marqués de Alella makes a range of dry whites, including promising Chardonnay, and good *cava* from its sister company Parxet.

If the name of Ampurdán-Costa Brava puts you in mind of seaside summer holidays, think again; it is a parched inland region whose cooperatives make big, alcoholic rosé, big, dull whites and big, unsubtle fortified wine.

OTHER WINES OF SPAIN

Travelling through the rest of Spain's wine regions can be a very patchy experience. Although great wines are being made throughout Spain, they seem to be the exceptions to the regional rule. And the fact that a given region is labelled as a *Denominación de Origen* or a *vino de tierra* is often of very little qualitative importance.

The North-West

Rias Baixas
Up in Galicia far too many of this cool, damp region's wines are made from European hybrid grapes left over from the days following the ravages of the phylloxera. For a taste of the real thing, seek out the Albariño made by Bodegas Cardallal and the 'Martin Codax' from Bodegas de Vilariño-Cambados.

Ribeiro
This warm, dry region has high aspirations. The reds here – made from the Brencellão, Caino and Souson – can be light and herby, but the trend is towards white wines. Those made from the spicy Albariño, the Godello, the Treixadura and the Muscat-like Torrentés are promising, but the Palominos are as dull as almost every other non-fortified example of this variety.

Valdeorras
The Palomino is just as prevalent in the mountainous vineyards here, along with the dark-fleshed Garnacha Tintorera. Sadly, while the growers of Ribeiro are experimenting with new varieties and more modern winemaking techniques, the producers up here are handicapped by low yields, low prices and land that's almost too difficult to tend.

El Bierzo
The Bodegas Palacio de Arganza, the best *bodega* here, is most widely respected for its skills at blending, ageing and bottling wines from various other regions. The red wines produced from the local Mencia grapes are pleasantly light and grassy but hardly distinguished enough to justify El Bierzo's promotion from *vino de la tierra* to *Denominación de Origen*.

Toro
This is another 'new' region (it received its DO in 1987) that hopes to benefit from the success of its eastern neighbour Ribera del Duero (see below). The grape used here, known as the Tinto de Toro, is that region's Tinto Fino – and indeed the Tempranillo of just about everywhere else – but the lower altitude and rainfall, and the use of up to 25% Garnacha, tend to give Toro's wines a softer, more beefily alcoholic style. Wines made by Bodegas Fariña, including the oaky Gran Colegiata, show that this is a region to watch.

León
The unhappy acronym VILE – standing for Vinos de León – appears on every bottle of wine from this region's modern cooperative. The reds, mostly made from the Prieto Picudo, are soft, woody and comparable to some mid-range Rioja.

Rueda
Once exclusively the source for unimpressive sherry-like fortified wine, Rueda has pinned its colours to the mast of modern white winemaking. In this the region's producers have a great advantage over their neighbours in the Penedés; their Verdejo grape (not to be confused with Portugal's Verdelho) has far more character than the latter region's Parellada and Xarel-lo. Even so, many producers still choose to take advantage of regulations that allow tangy Sauvignon Blanc to be added to the blend. Marqués de Griñon is one of the best examples of young, pure Verdejo, while Marqués de Riscal has proved with its Reserva Limousin that this aromatic grape can handle ageing in new oak.

Cigales

Like Toro, this name ought to be one to remember; it's close to Ribera del Duero and grows the same grape varieties (reds have to contain at least 75% Tempranillo), but so far has no *bodegas* that make wine of better than basic quality.

Ribera del Duero

Almost unknown to many Rioja drinkers, Ribera del Duero is famous among Spanish wine buffs as the region that produces Spain's most historically illustrious and most expensive wine – Vega Sicilia. Until recently, however, Vega Sicilia's success has somewhat confused outsiders because it is actually rather atypical of its region, due to the fact that 40% of its blend is made up of such interlopers from Bordeaux as the Cabernet Sauvignon, Merlot and Malbec.

The traditional grape variety here is the Tempranillo (locally known as the Tinto Fino) and that's what's used, for example, in Protos, the over-praised wine made by the Bodega Ribera Duero. Vega Sicilia's position as the region's top *bodega* has been undermined by the sudden stardom of Pesquera, a wine made by another *bodega* from local varieties, but with much less ageing in oak. The description of Pesquera by American wine guru Robert Parker as 'the Château Pétrus of Spain' ensured that bottles of this wine would be grabbed from the shelves despite a sudden hike in price. For a more affordable taste of this region's wine, try the wines of Balbas and Pedrosa.

The North-East

Campo de Borja

This is red and pink territory where alcohol levels are often too high and the Garnacha makes wines that often have little flavour. Even so, there are hopes that good winemaking – especially Beaujolais-style fermentation – will make for a wider range of lighter, fresher styles.

Cariñena

This hot, dry region was where the Carignan grape apparently got its name, but the red wine varieties used here are the (unrelated) Cariñena, the Tempranillo and, more particularly, the Garnacha. Few wines are better than basic table fare, though the softly fruity Don Mendo red and pink from Bodegas San Valero show what can be done. Nearby Calatayud has no such flagships, but it makes plain, acceptable wines.

Somontano

Cool, green Somontano is Aragón's most exciting region, though its potential is only beginning to become apparent. Winemaking techniques are still pretty old fashioned, and too much of the production remains in the hands of the cooperative. Even so, the Tempranillo, Moristel and Macabeo are being used to make decent wines and encouraging experiments are being made with foreign grapes such as the Chardonnay.

The Centre

Madrid

Despite their *vino de la tierra* status, these wines have more in common with the most backward village in the country than with the restless modernity of Madrid. Nearby Cebreros is primitive country that makes primitive wines.

Mentrida

I can't imagine many people getting too ecstatic about pink wine that, at a strength of 18-24%, packs more of a punch than some vermouth, but the wine drinkers here seem keen enough on the style. They also make a similarly strong red, often adding tannic bite to the alcohol by drawing off half the juice at the beginning of fermentation and thus doubling the proportion of skins to juice.

FACING PAGE: Holidaymakers on the beaches of Majorca rarely explore the vinegrowing regions of the island, where winemakers like Jose Ferrer are celebrating the award of a regional denomination for wines from their Binisalem vineyards

ABOVE: Mariano Garcia of Vega Sicilia in Ribera del Duero has no such problems of obscurity. His wines have been described as the 'Chateau Lâtour of Spain'

La Mancha

La Mancha's indigenous Airén grape is, incredibly, the world's most widely planted variety and the region itself is the largest appellation in Europe. But it's far from the most productive; the lack of water, the high summer and low winter temperatures make for tiny yields. In addition, the authorities have decided that irrigation is forbidden.

The area as a whole is woefully under exploited. Only one in ten of the bottles made in La Mancha can carry the distinctive Don Quixote logo of the *Consejo Regulador de la Denominación de Origen*, for the simple reason that most of the wine has been made in apparently medieval *bodegas*, where the juice of over-ripe, intrinsically flavourless Airén grapes was still fermented in *tinajas* (amphoras), with only the most rudimentary attempts at cooling.

These methods of winemaking can, when carefully employed, produce creditable reds, but are less well suited to the production of dry white wine. If you like young wine with the colour of ochre, the flavour of nuts that have been left to mature for a few years in a dusty loft and the alcoholic kick of a lethargic mule, traditional La Mancha whites are for you. But not for long.

For the moment, at least, even the best wines are light, commercial and inexpensive. La Mancha has yet to produce a 'Premium' wine, but it was here, at the Vinicola de Castilla, that the Beaujolais-like Castillo de Alhambra was made that won the 1988 *WINE Magazine/Sunday Telegraph Good Wine Guide* award as Red Wine of the Year.

Valdepeñas

The 'Valley of Stones' is white, Airén, country too, but its reputation was won by the red and pink wines made from the Cencibel. The Bodegas Félix Solís and Los Llanos provide the best chance to try this variety's red wines in their *Reserva* and *Gran Reserva* form, but most Valdepeñas reds should be caught as young as possible and bought with care, because the use of Airén white grapes in their production makes many of them taste flat and earthy. Avoid the *clarete* pink wine too; it's often only Airén dyed with a little Cencibel.

The South-West

Condado de Huelva

Interesting sherry-like versions of fino and oloroso are produced here, as well as some promising whites that display a triumph of modern winemaking over dull local grapes and hot summers. Ignore the Extramedura, close to the Portuguese border; its wines are boring bruisers.

The South-East

Valencia

If any of Spain's regions stand to benefit from Spain's membership of the European Community, it will be this, the most quietly dynamic part of the country. This is the region into which Swiss investors have pumped enormous amounts of money, and the one in which the Swiss and Spanish exporters have combined forces to discover the kinds of wine they should be selling to the USA. The Valencians are more interested in producing wines that sell than in styles that have a specifically identifiable regional character.

Utiel-Requena

The good red and *rosado* wines of this neighbouring region are often sold under the better-known name of Valencia, despite its right to bear its own DO. The high altitude is ideal for crisp winemaking and the Bobal, the variety from which the wines are made, is one of Spain's few underrated grapes.

Almansa

This is the place to go for a real taste of the Garnacha Tintorera; this variety is widely planted here and used, along with the Monastrell and Cencibel, to make beefy, unsubtle red wines. Bodegas Piqueras prove themselves to be the exception to the local rule by making lighter-bodied, oak-aged reds.

Jumilla

It says much about Jumilla's isolation from the rest of winemaking Europe that it was by-passed by the phylloxera louse when it munched its way through the rest of the continent. But, now it's arrived at this dry (there was almost no rain at all between 1982 and 1986), old-fashioned region, it is making up for lost time; whole vineyards are being wiped out. New vines are being grafted onto the same kinds of resistant rootstock that are being used elsewhere, and the opportunity has been taken to introduce experimental plantings of foreign grape varieties.

Yecla

Another recent DO, Yecla is, however, still at risk of extinction. The altitude is high (at 2,000ft/650m above sea level) and the soil stony, so yields are uneconomical. The hope for the area lies in the modern Bodegas Ochoa, which makes and exports large quantities of soft reds, and the huge Cooperative La Purisima, which, despite a tendency to over-age its wines, can produce fairly rich red wine.

Alicante

This is not only the name of a region, but also that of a grape that was traditionally prized by winemakers in Burgundy and

Bordeaux. The variety, which is also known as the Garnacha Tintorera, is still grown here, though it is the Monastrell that is more frequently used to make the region's big, dark, alcoholic reds. The most interesting drink made from grapes in Alicante, though, is Fundillon, a cask-aged liqueur.

The Islands

Majorca

What most tourists miss is a range of ripe reds and fresh, young *vino joven* wines, produced in the hot, windmill-bestrewn land around Binasalem on a plateau nearly 500ft (150m) above sea level. Most are made from the good-quality, local Manto Negro and Callet grapes and the dull Fogoneu, though both the Jaume Mesquida and José Ferrer wineries are experimenting quite successfully with Cabernet Sauvignon. Whites are mostly less inspiring.

Canary Isles

Some of the most interesting-looking vineyards are to be found here – because of the black volcanic soil in which Lanzarote's vines are planted – and some of the least interesting-tasting wines. The problem in the Tacoronte-Acentejo region to the north east of Tenerife is partly the Listán Blanco and Negro and the Negramoll grapes, and partly the way they are vinified. This is holiday wine, to be drunk very cold – if at all. Lanzarote's Malvasias can be appealingly nutty, dry and rich; but these too are usually spoilt by bad winemaking.

Tortilla con Chorizo

Potato 'omelette' with spicy sausage

This wonderfully versatile dish is found all over Spain. It can have innumerable additions, such as shrimp or ham (here we have used the traditional spicy sausage of Spain — chorizo). It can be eaten cold as a starter or hot as a main course and it has the advantage of going well with lighter reds, whites or rosados.

SERVES 4-6
*8 tbsp olive oil
1 medium onion, peeled and finely chopped
2 garlic cloves, peeled and minced
3 oz/75 g spicy sausage (Spanish chorizo is
traditional but not essential)
2 lb/1 kg large potatoes, peeled, thinly sliced, washed and
dried on kitchen paper
5 eggs
Salt and freshly ground black pepper*

In a frying pan, heat 5 tbsp of olive oil and sauté the garlic, onion and sausage for 5 minutes. Add the potato and cook until browned. Remove the contents of the pan to a colander and drain off excess oil. In a large bowl, beat the eggs well and add the potato mixture. Stir well and season with salt and pepper. Heat the remaining oil in the frying pan until it is very hot (but not smoking). Pour in the mixture, shaking the pan to prevent sticking. Cook until the bottom is browned. Slide the tortilla on to a large plate. Invert another plate on top of the tortilla and turn them over. The uncooked side is now on the bottom and the tortilla can be slid back into the pan and cooked until the bottom browns. Serve with a large green salad.

Castles in Spain... This one is at Peñafiel in the Ribera del Duero

THE ESSENTIALS — CENTRAL SPAIN

Quality La Mancha, Valdepeñas, Galicia, Valencia, Tierra de Barros, Utiel-Requena, Alicante, Yecla and Jumilla have their own DOs although La Mancha produces a large quantity of non-DO wine of mostly fairly basic quality.
Style Reds, whites and *rosados* are generally dull and flabby with a lack of balancing acidity. However, Valdepeñas can, with the help of oak-ageing, produce well-balanced wines that can be good value. Valencia is now producing light-bodied, fruity wines that can give immediate pleasure, besides the richer Moscatels for which it is more famous. Similarly, Utiel-Requena is producing some lighter wines but Alicante still makes old-style Spanish reds, full-bodied and high in alcohol and of very little interest.
Climate Very hot and arid in most regions, though there are some cooler, damper microclimates in areas such as Rias Baixas.
Cultivation Efforts are being made to counter the effects of the climate on the grapes; harvesting earlier to retain acidity and freshness, for example. There has also been investment in replanting particularly in Valencia.
Grape Varieties *Red :* Garnacha Tinta, Bobal, Monastrel, Cencibel. Airen, Macabeo. *White*: Airén, Garnacha Blanco, Jaén, Muscatel, Malvasia, and Cirial.
Top Producers *Valdepeñas:* Señorio de los Llanos, *La Mancha* Felix Solis, Castillo de Alhambra.

THE ESSENTIALS — OTHER SPANISH DOs

Quality Ribera del Duero, Toro, Rueda, Ribeiro and Rias Baixas are the notable DO areas.
Style Some of these areas are producing good quality, even exciting, wines. Good Ribera del Duero reds are packed with rich plummy fruit and have a velvety texture which, when combined with generous oaking, has resulted in a wine – Pesquera – which has been compared to Pétrus by a famous American wine-writer . Toro is capable of producing similarly generous wines, which are often oak-aged, while neighbouring Rueda makes good-quality whites from classic and local grape varieties. Ribeiro and Valdeorras are both located in Galicia, producing fresh, aromatic and slightly sparkling whites, resembling the *vinhos verdes* of Portugal, and attractively fresh and fruity reds. Few of these wines are exported but as boredom and disatisfaction grows with Rioja, hopefully, they will attract greater attention..
Climate Ribera del Duero, Toro and Rueda have typical continental climates – hot summers and cold winters. Ribeiro and Rias Baixas in the far north-western tip of Spain, influenced by the Atlantic, have a warm wet climate.
Cultivation Ribera del Duero and Rueda compare favourably to Penedés in terms of innovative use of foreign grape varieties.
Grape Varieties *Ribera del Duero*: Albillo, Cabernet Sauvignon, Garnacha, Malbec, Merlot, Tinto del Pais. *Toro:* Albillo, Garnacha, Malvasía, Palomino, Tinto de Toro (Tempranillo), Verdejo. *Rueda*: Cabernet Sauvignon, Chardonnay, Palomino, Sauvignon, Verdejo, Viura. *Galicia:* Albariño, Albilla, Caiño, Garnacha, Godello, Mencia, Merenzão, Palomino, Sousão, Tempranillo, Treixadura, Valenciano.
Production/Maturation These areas show what can be achieved in Spain by the adoption of modern vinification methods and the use of the latest knowledge, combined, in some cases, with the best of local wine-making tradition. The wines of Bodegas Alejandro Fernandez, sold as Tinto Pesquera, are the result of both old and new techniques; Vega Sicilia Unico is produced combining an age-old formula requiring 10 years' oak-aging with the local Tinto Fino and French grape varieties.
Longevity *Red* Ribera del Duero: 3 to 25 years; *Toro:* 3 to 8 years. *White* Rueda: 1 to 3 years; *red* Galicia: up to 5 years; *white* Galicia: within 2 years.
Vintage Guide *Reds:* Ribera del Duero 82, 83, 85, 86
Toro 82, 85, 86
Rueda 82, 83, 84, 85, 86 Galicia 85, 86
Top Producers Vega Sicilia, Alejandro Fernandez, Victor Balbas, Bodegas Fariña, Marqués de Griñon, Bodega Jesus Nazavero, Marqués de Riscal.

SHERRY

Let's play a word association game. I'll say 'sherry', and you reply with the first word that comes into your head. If you were born in Britain, it's almost even odds that you said 'vicar', 'maiden aunt', 'Bristol Cream' or 'trifle'. If, on the other hand, you were brought up on the other side of the Atlantic, I'll bet that your mind shot straight to Bowery bums drinking locally-produced headache-juice straight from a brown paper bag.

The word that would have been the long shot, unless you happen to be Spanish, was 'wine'. It's precisely the one most Spaniards – but no-one else – would have come up with; they not only think of sherry as wine, they drink it that way – bone-dry, with food, and out of glasses that hold a proper mouthful of liquid, not the thimbles that it usually brims from in Britain.

So put all those Anglo-American prejudices out of your mind and try to look at sherry through Spanish eyes. Which means accepting right away that, just as one small corner of north-eastern France is the only place in the world that makes genuine Champagne, the only source of *real* sherry is a similarly small area around Cadiz, near the southernmost point of Spain. And, like Champagne, the best sherries (particularly the *finos*, the region's main style) have traditionally been dry.

Nor does either region make table wine of any great quality; while Champagne's grape varieties produce thin, acidic stuff in

FAR LEFT: Sherry is a style of wine whose name and whose quality need protection. Without this white albariza soil and the climate of this part of Spain, it is impossible to make wine that compares with sherry

LEFT: The Barbadillo bodega; source of some of the best and most reliable of manzanillas

ABOVE: A special barrel at the Lustau bodega reveals the scum of 'flor' yeast that protects sherry from unwelcome bacteria

THE ESSENTIALS — SOUTHERN SPAIN

Location Spain's south-west corner, from Condado de Huelva near the Portuguese border south-west to Málaga and inland to Montilla-Moriles.
Quality DOs are Jerez , Manzanilla, Condado de Huelva, Málaga, Montilla-Moriles.
Style Sherry is one of the world's greatest and, in England at least, most misunderstood fortified wines. Its style varies enormously (*see box*); in general, dry Manzanilla sherries are thought to be lighter and more delicate than their Jerezano counterparts. Montilla-Moriles, to the north-east of Jerez, produces a similar range of wines, but they are generally softer and lower in alcohol — they may or may not be fortified. Málaga makes wonderful sweet wines with a strong raisiny flavour which are still underrated.
Climate The Mediterranean climate makes southern Spain the hottest wine region in the country, although the climate is moderated by the Atlantic towards Portugal. The Atlantic *poñete* wind is wet and encourages the flor yeast that produces fino sherry to grow on the surface of the wines. The easterly *levante* wind is hotter and drier and partially dries the grapes on the vines while they ripen, concentrating their sugars.
Cultivation The land of southern Spain is generally flat but ranges in altitude from the low-lying coastal plains near Sanlúcar de Barrameda to the plateau of Málaga at some 500 metres. The unique *albariza* soil of Andalusia is a lime-rich marl that is able to soak up and retain moisture, while its brilliant white colour reflects the sun on to the lower parts of the vines, helping the grapes to ripen.
Grape Varieties Principally the white Palomino (Listan), plus Moscatel Fino, Pedro Ximénez, Baladi, Garrido Fino, Lairén, Mantuo, Torrontés, Zalerna.
Production/Maturation Sherry making invoolves the aart of mastering wine and naturally occurring yeast. The *solera* system, coupled with skilful blending, ensures that a consistent style of sherry is produced over a number of years, though *almacenista* wines, from a single, unblended solera, are worth seeking out for their charactered individuality, particularly if shipped by Lustau. Sweetening and colouring agents — usually thick, concentrated wines from grapes such as Pedro Ximénez or Moscatel — may also be added.
Longevity Fino sherries should ideally be drunk soon after they are bottled. An opened bottle should be consumed within a very few days. Sweeter, more alcoholic, traditionally made styles can be kept indefinitely but will not normally improve in the bottle.
Top Producers *Sherry:* Lustau, Garvey, Gonzalez Byass, Valdespino, Diez Merito, Domecq, Caballero, Barbadillo. *Málaga:* Scholtz Hermanos.

their cold-climate region, sherry's dull Palomino makes even duller wine in the near-drought conditions of vineyards where there are only ten weeks of the year when the sun doesn't shine. Both wines owe their natural lightness of touch to the fact that they are made from grapes that have been grown on some of the chalkiest soils in the world – in sherry's case, on the brilliantly white *albariza* that covers much of the vineyards. Both are made in a peculiar way that depends on prolonged contact with yeast, and both are essentially non-vintage wines that call for great expertise in blending different vintages – usually by merchants with huge stocks of wine. And if you agree that not only is Champagne a wine, but a great and historic one, then you're half-way to being convinced that so, too, is sherry.

The History

Sherry is one of the oldest wines of all. The town of Cadiz had been founded by the Phoenicians before 1200 BC, and a thousand years later, a wine called Ceretanum which almost certainly came from Ceret – Jerez – was being exported to Rome to be praised by the Roman poet Martial.

In the 14th century, the naturally high alcohol levels of wine from this hot region made it travel well, and sherry had become a firm favourite in Britain. Chaucer wrote of the wine of Lepe (a village near Jerez) *'of which there riseth such fumositee'* that three draughts were enough to confuse a drinker as to whether he was in La Rochelle, Bordeaux or home in bed.

In 1587, a short-term supply was assured when Sir Francis Drake took Cadiz and captured 2,900 butts of what was by then known as 'sherris' or 'sack' after the Spanish word for export, '*saca*'. Ten years later, it was given its first testimonial under its new name when Shakespeare's Sir John Falstaff declared, in Henry IV, Part 2: 'If I had a thousand sons, the first humane principle I would teach them would be to foreswear thin potations and addict themselves to sack.' In Shakespeare's day, this naturally dry wine was already being sweetened for the English palate; at the Boar's Head Tavern in Eastcheap, where Falstaff supposedly lived, sugar was sometimes added, as were pieces of toast and even egg (vividly described by Sir John as 'pullet-sperm').

During the 18th century, the English and Irish moved into Jerez in much the same way as they moved into Bordeaux; soon, the bodegas of Thomas Osborne, William Garvey, Sir James Duff and James Gordon were shipping wine to England where, in the port of Bristol, firms like Harvey's and Averys had established their own blending and ageing cellars.

Styles

It was in these cellars in both countries that the styles of sherry we know today gradually evolved. Some barrels developed an unpleasant-looking white scum on their surface that was later discovered to be a kind of yeast which, unlike the other kinds of bacteria that attack wine, actually kept it fresh and fragrant.

In honour of this quality, the Jerezanos dubbed the scum *flor*, or 'flower'. The wine it made was thought the finest in the cellars, and so, quite naturally, was called *fino*, though the slightly lighter version made and aged a little further up the coast at Sanlúcar, became known for some reason as 'the little apple', *manzanilla*, a word still used elsewhere in Spain for camomile tea. These wines were said to be saltier because of the sea air; this character and the lightness may, however, be attributable to the fact that the yeast grows more thickly here.

Usually, the inhabitants of Jerez drank the wine soon after it was made; when they left it in its barrel for a few years, the wine darkened and took on a nutty flavour. By topping up last year's fino barrels with this year's flor-affected wine, however, they found that the freshness could be maintained. Soon, they developed the *solera* system, keeping back a number of casks every year from which to refresh the wine of the preceding vintage, and from there to the vintage before that, and so on.

Today, the oldest barrels are never emptied – indeed, no more than a third is ever removed from them – and the transfer is always made from one year's casks to that of the year before. Somehow, and no one is quite certain precisely why, provided the quality of the initial wines is carefully chosen and the chain of ever-older barrels – the solera – is well maintained, this relay-race gives the oldest casks the vinous equivalent of immortality, allowing bodegas to sell a consistent style every year.

The blending of flor-affected wines of different ages remains the basis of fino sherry production today, but a great many of

RIGHT: In some regions, the presence of donkeys in the vineyards would be a publicity stunt. In Jerez, such traditions still survive

RIGHT, BELOW: Sherry remains as reliant on the image of the big bodegas as Champagne is on its Grandes Marques. Here, the instantly recognisable Sandeman caped figure is being stencilled onto one of the bodega's barrels

the barrels did – and do – not develop flor; these are protected from oxidation by the addition of brandy. These, stronger, darker, wines were called *oloroso*, or 'fragrant', but they were never as well considered by the Jerezanos as their fino and manzanilla. A third style, a cross between fino and oloroso, was invented too. *Amontillado*, literally 'in the fashion of Montilla' (*see below*) was made by leaving fino unrefreshed by younger wine to develop a deeper colour and a rich, nutty flavour.

Neither fino nor manzanilla, with a natural strength of around 15% alcohol, were sturdy enough to ship overseas; without the protection of their flor, they oxidised very quickly. So, the Jerezanos developed a tradition of fortifying them and of sweetening them up with cooked grape juice. This not only created a number of new styles, but had the useful side-effect of masking any defects in taste or style.

Today, the British still expect sherry to be sweet, and many firms in Jerez and England still obligingly sweeten all of their styles for the British palate. It can be infuriating, when one expects the bone-dry nutty tang of a good fino, to find a sweetened version. Only trial and error will tell you which producers are exporting the kind of sherry they drink themselves.

However, there's nothing wrong with those sherry styles intended to be medium-sweet or sweet – some can have a delicious Christmas pudding flavour – but they are rarely great wine, and it is only exceptions like Gonzalez Byass's Matusalem compare with the world's other sweet fortified wines.

Which is just as well, because they are going out of fashion fast. Unfortunately, their place has been taken by an odd aberration called Pale Cream, developed to suit people who like the taste of traditional sweet, Cream sherry but want to be seen to be drinking fashionable wine the colour of Muscadet. Pale Cream is basically failed fino sherry sweetened up with grape juice concentrate or even sugar syrup. Drink them by all means if you like their simple sugary flavour – but don't offer them to a Spaniard.

THE BUSINESS OF SHERRY

Most sherry is produced by big sherry houses, some of which have soleras that were begun in the last century. The size of the companies is partly dictated by rules that require any bodega to store a minimum of 100,000 litres of wine. There are, however, around 50 smaller *Almacenistas*, small maturers that buy wine from cooperatives or small producers and age it, selling most for blending by the bigger bodegas, but bottling a little themselves. These Almacenista wines, because of their small-scale production, can be some of the most exciting sherries on the market.

Montilla-Moriles

Montilla-Moriles – or plain Montilla, as it is more generally known – is the region and the style that gave its name to *amontillado*. The wines produced here are often quite reasonably considered to be 'poor man's sherry', because they tend to be low-priced and of fairly basic quality. But they can be not only good, but indeed better and more delicate than poorly-made sherry. Montilla's producers use grapes grown in chalky soil to make a range of styles that are just like those of Jerez – from flor-affected fino to rich dry oloroso.

There are, though, two differences. First, the Pedro Ximénez grape, used almost exclusively here, ripens so well that Montilla can often achieve the same strengths as sherry without fortification. And secondly, there's the continuing tradition of fermenting Montilla in large terracotta *tinajas*, which are nothing more nor less than the same kind of amphorae the Greeks and Romans would have used to ferment their wine, over 2,000 years ago. But despite this evidence of tradition the Jerezanos had until very recently managed to prevent the Montilla producers from using the term 'amontillado', which was a little like the parfumiers of France barring their counterparts in Cologne from selling eau de cologne.

What Montilla needs most urgently is to be taken seriously. Sales of the most illustrious wines of Jerez and Sanlucar are far from brisk, and the need for cheap alternatives reduces every year. Watch out for wines labelled Moriles. Produced in the village of that name, they can be more delicate than ones from the town of Montilla – and lighter and more evidently wine-like than many sherries.

Malaga

Malaga was being shipped from the port of the same name as early as 1500 and was first sold in Britain as 'sack', then as 'Mountain'. In the 18th century, when sherry fell out of favour and the British turned to port, the harbour town of Malaga lowered its export duties and effectively stole the London 'sack' market from Jerez. But everything went wrong late in the following century, when the phylloxera beetle made Malaga its first Spanish port of call. The vineyards were never properly replanted; today, they cover just 3,000 hectares, compared with 112,000 before the arrival of the louse.

The wine has gone out of fashion too, and standards of winemaking have often dropped to accommodate a small, undemanding market. Unlike their counterparts in Jerez, the Malaga bodegas have mostly turned their backs on tradition, and make little effort to attract the attention of tourists. But when Malaga is good – as in the case of the examples made by Scholtz Hermanos – it can be wonderful, molasses-rich wine. The solera system is used here, on wine that is often a mixture of dry wine and grape juice, part of which has been boiled until it has turned into sweet treacle *(Arrope)*, and part *(the Vino Maestro)* fortified in a very similar way to sherry.

Malaga can vary enormously both in colour, which ranges from white *(Blanco)* to black *(Negro)*, rough golden *(Dorado)*, tawny *(Rojo-Dorado)* and dark *(Oscuro)*, and sweetness (from *Seco* to *Dulce)*. Bottles labelled *Dulce Color* are pretty simple in their syrupy style; ones that describe themselves as *Lágrima* ought to be of far higher quality, and are made without recourse to a press, from free-run juice. The difference in flavour between a good example of Lagrima and a basic Malaga is as great as that between a top class Bordeaux and a house claret. The finest Malagas have an intensity of flavour and a balancing acidity which combine to prevent the sweetness being in any way cloying.

'Solera' wines are common too; examples like the excellent Scholtz Hermanos Solera 1855 proudly proclaim the year in which their particular solera was founded. Unfortunately, few of the other Solera Malagas are of anything like as high a quality as the Scholtz Hermanos, and many simply borrow the term to give their wine an image of venerability that cannot be detected from its flavour.

Tapas

The word 'tapa' originally referred to the piece of bread placed over a glass of wine in order to keep flies out, but tapas are now the appetizers of Spain — little mouthfuls of delightful tastes. They are designed to be eaten with a glass of chilled manzanilla or fino sherry or a glass of wine (they make the perfect cocktail party snacks). These are some of the classics.

CHAMPINONES RELLENOS
Mushroom caps filled with slices of spicy chorizo sausage, which are then grilled.

ALBONDIGAS
Garlicky little balls of minced beef, fried and served with a home-made tomato sauce.

POLLO AL AJILLO
Small chunks of chicken sautéed in olive oil and garlic and coated in chopped parsley.

JAMON SERRANO
Cured raw ham, grilled in pieces and served with a garlic mayonnaise.

BOQUERONES
Fresh anchovies (or whitebait) dipped in batter and deep-fried.

CHORIZO
Spicy Spanish pork sausage cut into slices and grilled.

GAMBAS AL AJILLO
Unshelled prawns sautéed in olive oil and garlic.

SHERRY STYLES

FINO
A fino should be light, dry and delicate. It develops beneath the light-coloured film of the flor which gives the fino its yeast character and absorbs any residual sugar. Fino is generally made from 100% Palomino grapes; finos range in alcoholic strength from 15.5° to 18°; it is at its fragrant best when first bottled. Finos do not keep.

MANZANILLA
The two main styles of wines from the port of Sanlucar de Barrameda are fino and pasada (fino-amontillado), although there are intermediate styles.
  The fino is pale and light in body with a bitter, salty flavour. They tend to be between 15.5° and 17° in alcohol. Manzanilla finos are also distinguished from traditional Jerez finos by the more vigorous nature of the flor and the greater amount used per cask. Manzanilla sherries are said to have a salty tang, purportedly from the sea air of the town.

AMONTILLADO
An amontillado is a fino which, as a result of ageing for over 8 years 'without refreshment' (the flor having died after 2-3 years, and fallen to the bottom of the cask) has developed an amber colour and a dry nutty flavour. Amontillados are fuller-bodied at a strength of between 16-18%. There is an intermediate fino-amontillado stage characterised by amber colour but not the nutty character or body.

OLOROSO
Oloroso is the darkest, richest and most full-bodied of the natural sherry styles. Literally meaning 'fragrant', it is completely dry but with an appealing soft richness from the higher fortification and glycerine content. These are wines that grow very little or no flor and, as a result, are fortified with a higher spirit strength (up to 18°). The wines are allowed to oxidise and to take on the characteristic nutty, raisin and caramel flavours of traditionally-made oloroso, while also evaporating and becoming even stronger.

CREAM SHERRIES
Originally developed for the UK market but now popular in other countries, such as the USA, cream sherries are made in 2 ways. Pale creams are poor quality finos sweetened artificially. Dark creams are a far superior sherry being made from olorosos sweetened with Pedro Ximenez.

PEDRO XIMENEZ
Pedro Ximenez is the traditional sweetening agent for sherry but occasionally a pure Pedro Ximenez is released. Such wines are a luscious blend of dried fruit flavours and Muscovado brown sugar and are a fine accompaniment to Christmas pudding.

PALO CORTADO
This is a sherry that cannot be deliberately made and is, theoretically, very rare, since only one butt in a thousand is said to turn into a true palo cortado.

PORTUGAL

LEFT: The slow pace of life in the villages of the Douro has changed very little over the centuries

RIGHT: Portugal is one of the more self-sufficient wine-making countries, because it is the largest cork-producing country in the world. These cork oak barks are the raw material

FAR RIGHT: The traditional style of Portugal – at the JM da Fonseca winery, near Lisbon

1 Vinho Verde
2 Douro
2a Port
3 Bairrada
4 Dão
5 Estremadura
6 Colares
7 Bucelas
8 Carcavelos
9 Setúbal
10 Algarve
11 Madeira
12 Ribatejo
13 Alentejo

'You see, Senhor, we are a calm, conservative people. Even when we have a revolution we avoid making too much fuss and noise'. The Portuguese winemaker raised the subject of the almost violence-free 1974 revolution to illustrate the fundamental quality of his countrymen's character: they are people who aren't terribly fond of change. Winemakers in other countries may have been importing tons of cooling equipment and thousands of new oak barrels for decades; the Portuguese have, until recently, preferred to go on drinking the kind of wine they've always drunk. And doing so in some quantity; this is the seventh-largest wine-producing country in the world and its small population has always done a pretty good job of making sure that none of its produce goes to waste.

The Portuguese divide their wine into two very different styles: the stuff they sell to foreigners, and the stuff they drink themselves. The off-dry, slightly sparkling rosé and white wines that most people associate with Portugal are treated very sniffily by the Portuguese themselves. The wine they enjoy most is still either the mouth-scouringly dry, red Vinho Verde (traditionally made in far greater quantities than the white, but unsaleable anywhere outside Portugal and its former colonies), or tough, inky dark, venerable reds from Dão, Bairrada or the Douro.

To understand the Portuguese taste for these wines you have to have experienced Portuguese cooking. Until you have ploughed your way through a deep bowl or three of *caldo verde* vegetable soup, a platter piled high with *bacalhâo*, (the national dish of salt-cod), half a suckling pig and a pudding that can best be described as half-cooked cream caramel, you can never imagine the essential role those tannic, high-acid reds manfully perform. But just try drinking a delicate white Burgundy or even a claret with one of these meals and you'll experience the taste sensation of a lightweight boxer trying his luck against a fighter of the calibre of Mike Tyson.

Of course, few people outside Portugal live on a diet of salt-cod and suckling pig, which explains why, in the middle of this century, a few Portuguese producers cleverly created the export styles of light, sweetish pink and white wine, with which most foreigners have become familiar. Mind you, this wasn't the first time the Portuguese had sent sweet wine abroad and kept the dry stuff for themselves. Mention the Douro to a British wine merchant and he'll instantly think of it as the part of Portugal that produces port; mention it to even the most sophisticated of

Lisbon restaurant diners and his mind will turn to the unfortified beefy reds made there. Port has never been a popular drink in its home country.

Today, as wine drinkers around the world increasingly turn away from off-dry pink and white wine, and as the increasingly health-conscious Portuguese themselves cut back on the suckling pig, Portugal's winemakers are beginning to take a fresh look at the kind of stuff they are making. They know that they have one tremendous advantage over their Spanish neighbours; theirs is a far more interesting arsenal of grape varieties. Admittedly, names like the Roupeiro, the João de Santarém and the Loureiro ring few bells in the tasting rooms of London or Los Angeles but, properly used, these are just the kinds of grapes that will enable the Portuguese to make some of the most characterful wines in the world.

To exploit these varieties, however, the Portuguese are going to need another 'calm revolution' – in the vineyards and wineries. Firstly, they are going to have to sort out the system of regional appellations, the *regiões demarcadas*. Portugal more or less invented the idea of *appellation contrôlée* years before the French got around to it. Until now, however, the whole country has had just 11 such regions; of these, four – Bucelas, Carcavelos, Colares and Moscatel de Setúbal – produce tiny amounts of wine, while another – the Algarve – makes appalling wine and owes its legal recognition solely to its importance as a tourist region. Many of Portugal's best wines have no regional denomination at all, and the label of Barca Velha, Portugal's top red, doesn't trouble to mention that it comes from the demarcated region of the Douro.

The second problem lies in the way in which the industry has been largely held in a stranglehold by a small number of giant cooperatives that buy in most of the grapes and make most of the wine, selling it to an even smaller number of merchants, whose creative input has often been restricted to the way in which they have aged and bottled it. Inevitably, this has encouraged the Iberian tradition of keeping wine for a long time before bottling. Quite often this is far more appropriate here than in Spain, because a lengthy period in tank will generally allow a tough red to shed some of its impenetrable tannic husk. In some cases the final result is a wine with fascinating, mature, tobaccoey flavours . Far too often, though, it makes for dull wines that lost their fruit along with the tannin. Portugal is a great place to buy inexpensive old wine; some of it tastes attractively old, but some tastes of almost nothing at all.

However, over the last few years a growing number of small producers and innovative merchants have begun to wrest back control from the cooperatives and to take a more careful look at their grapes and at the best ways to extract as much fruit as possible from them, however long the wine is going to be aged.

For the first time too, the Portuguese are looking overseas for inspiration. For the moment at least, they are not falling into the trap of copying everybody else with lookalike Chardonnays and Cabernets, but they *are* discovering the lessons of modern winemaking from people such as Peter Bright, who learned to make wine in his native Australia and is now producing some of the most exciting wine in Portugal.

The tough, old-fashioned reds and the semi-sweet pinks and whites are finally making way for fruity young wines that can compete with Beaujolais, for clean, dry whites that have nothing to do with Vinho Verde, and for deep, richly flavoured red wines that stand comparison with the best of Italy. Of course, as you'd expect in a 'calm, conservative' country, the wine revolution is a leisurely, undramatic affair. Given time and encouragement, though, Portugal will become one of the most exciting wine countries of all, with one of the broadest ranges of different flavours. Companies such as Sogrape, JM da Fonseca and João Pires (the winery at which Peter Bright makes his wines) are already proving what can be done – and at prices that are low enough to encourage even the most timid wine drinker to risk buying a bottle.

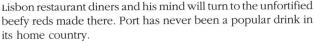

THE LANGUAGE OF PORTUGAL

Adamado Sweet.
Adega Cellar, winery.
Branco White.
Carvalho Oak.
Clarete Light red wine.
Colheita Vintage.
Doce Sweet.
Engarrafado na Origem Estate–bottled.
Espumante Sparkling.
Garrafeira A wine made from one or more areas and matured for 3 years including one in bottle if red, and for one year including 6 months in bottle if white. Wines must bear a vintage date and have 0.5° alcohol above the minimum. Often, the garrafeira is the 'private reserve' of the merchant.
Licoroso Sweet fortified wine.
Maduro Matured (in vat).
Quinta Farm.
Regiões Demarcadas At present there are 11 such demarcated reions (roughly equivalent to the French *appellation contrôllée*) but upto 20 more are planned to be added during the 1990s.
Reserva A wine from one or several areas from an outstanding vintage. It must contain 0.5° alcohol above the minimum.
Rosado Rosé.
Seco Dry.
Tinto Red.
Velho Old. Reds must be over 3 years old, whites over 2 years old before they may use the term on the label.
Verde Young, 'green' (as in Vinho Verde).
Vinho consumo Ordinary wine.
Vinho generoso Fortified aperitif or dessert wine.
Vinho de mesa Table wine.
Vinhos Regionãos A classification of table wines which is roughly equivalent to the French *vins de pays*, and due to be introduced shortly.

Mateus Rosé was my first love. It was that brilliantly stylish bottle and its easy-to-drink contents that turned me onto wine; somehow, between them, they made wine drinking seem almost too easy – rather like discovering you could walk into the Savoy Grill wearing jeans and a T-shirt. But that wine was a Portuguese aberration, invented by a marketing genius called Fernando Guedes, specifically for sale to foreigners. Guedes was one of those rare men who could hold two apparently conflicting ideas in his head at the same time; and few ideas could conflict more vigourously than the acidic, slightly sparkling, red Vinho Verde most Portuguese knew as their daily red, and the Anglo-Saxon taste for sweet, fizzy, non-alcoholic drinks.

If only, Guedes reasoned, he could turn red Vinho Verde into a drink that combined alcohol with the easy appeal of Coca-Cola, a whole new market could be opened almost overnight. Having concocted his sweet, pink wine (with a slight fizz for the British market, without for the USA), Guedes went one stage further. Instead of packaging it in the customary hock-style bottle used for Vinho Verde, he found inspiration further south in Frankonia, Germany, where the growers traditionally use flagon-shaped flasks. It was with his label, however, that he arguably showed the greatest marketing skill of all. While almost every other commercial wine has gone through several major 'packaging' changes over the last few decades, Mateus still proudly bears the image of the palace that happened to be situated nearby the winery in which he made his wine. Very fairly, he offered the palace's owner a choice between a royalty payment on every bottle sold and a small lump sum. The aristocrat, doubting the commercial potential of the new wine, declined the royalty, and turned his back on a fortune.

But, if Mateus and Lancers, its wine-in-an-earthenware-crock competitor, were success stories, Portugal's more traditional wines were less welcomed by non-Portuguese wine drinkers. The problem was, as Guedes had realised, that very few of them were really suited to the foreign palate or diet; the young wines were too acidic and the older ones were generally too tough, tannic and fruitless. And the more foreigners tried to learn about Portugal's wines, the more confused they became; the demarcated regions, such as Dão, that were supposed to make the best wine, often seemed to produce the least impressive stuff, while the rare bottles that really did taste good generally bore labels that revealed no provenance whatsoever, but merely described the contents as *garrafeiras* – reserve wines. Today, 20 years after those Portuguese wines first arrived in Britain, the picture has changed – but not to nearly as great an extent as one might expect.

The North

Vinho Verde

Among the first of Portugal's less commercial wines to be shipped overseas in any quantity was the 'real' Vinho Verde on which Guedes had based Mateus. Surprisingly to foreigners, who rarely encounter it, most Vinho Verde is red (the verde part ·of its name refers to 'green' youth, not colour), though the proportion of white has increased dramatically in recent years. Made in the (relatively) cool Minho region in the north of the

---

THE ESSENTIALS — VINHO VERDE

Location On the banks of the Minho River in north-western Portugal.
Quality *Região demarcado* (RD)
Style Red is forceful, with plummy fruit and swingeing acidity.
White is pale, low in alcohol and commonly slightly sparkling. When good, it has a fresh, lemony fragrance and a surprising richness of fruit. Those available in the UK have usually and unfortunately been lightly sweetened.
Climate Dry, hot summers and mild, wet winters.
Cultivation A combination of flat areas plus smaller vineyards higher up. Granite soil. Vines are often trained high on trellises, to gain more sunshine and ensure air circulation. Other crops are grown underneath.
Grape Varieties *Red:* Azal Tinto, Borraçal, Brancelho, Espadeira, Rabo de Ovelha, Vinhão. *White:* Alvarinho, Avesso, Azal Branco, Perdena, Trajadura.
Production/Maturation Grapes are picked under-ripe and bottled early. This encourages malolactic fermentation in bottle, which gives the wine its sparkle, though most commercial examples are carbonated.
Longevity The wine should be drunk as young as possible.
Vintage Guide Vintages are relatively unimportant but the wines must be drunk as young as possible.
Top Producers Palacio da Brejoeira, Quinta da Aveleda, Gatão, Solar das Bouças.

country, from grapes grown on high trellises and among the trees so as to allow the farmers to plant cabbages and other vegetables at ground level, these wines give an insight into the way wine might have tasted a thousand or so years ago.

All sorts of local grapes were – and still are – used and, if asked, few of the growers (most of whom farm garden-sized plots) could name any of them. The traditional winemaking techniques were pretty basic too, but their peculiarity was the fact that the wine was bottled during, rather than after, the malolactic fermentation, which transforms the natural appley malic into creamier lactic acid.

The flavour, the fizz and the unpredictability from one bottle to the next were often as reminiscent of home-made cider as of wine. Unfortunately, the flavour of unripe apples and plum skins (of the red) and of unripe apple and lime (of the white) took more acquiring than most non-Portuguese drinkers were prepared to allow. Hence the switch to more modern winemaking techniques, the use of CO_2 canisters to provide the bubbles, and the generous dollops of sugar that go into the whites that are to be sent overseas (little of the red is exported).

Vinho Verde seemed destined to become another commercial drink. Fortunately, under the leadership of estates such as the Palacio da Brejoeira and the Solar das Bouças, and of Peter Bright, the Australian winemaker at João Pires, a small band of producers have begun to take Vinho Verde seriously, concentrating on the best varieties – the Alvarinho and Loureiro.

Whichever colour you buy, though, try to ensure that it is of the most recent harvest, which is not always an easy task, given the producers' tendency to print the vintage in tiny figures on the back label or, more frequently, nowhere at all.

LEFT: These terraced vineyards belong to the Quinta do Cotto estate in the Douro and produce both port and table wines

BELOW: Vinho Verde harvesters have to climb ladders to pick grapes that are trained to grow at tree-level

Bolinhos de Bacalhôa

Codballs with parsley, coriander and mint

With one of its borders entirely taken up by the Atlantic, it is not surprising that cod — particularly salt cod — features prominently in Portuguese cooking.

SERVES 6

1 lb/500 g skinned and boned salt cod
2 oz/50 g dried breadcrumbs
3 tbsp fresh coriander leaves, minced, or 1 tsp crushed coriander seeds
2 tbsp parsley, chopped
2 tsp fresh mint, minced, or 1 tsp dried mint
2 cloves garlic, peeled and crushed
Salt and freshly ground black pepper
8 tbsp olive oil

The day before, immerse the salt cod in water for at least 12 hours in a glass, ceramic or stainless steel bowl or pan, changing the water 3 or 4 times. Drain and rinse the cod and place it in a saucepan with enough water to cover. Bring to the boil, then reduce to a simmer and cook for about 20 minutes or until the fish flakes. In a large bowl, mix 4 tbsps of the olive oil and breadcrumbs and leave until the breadcrumbs have absorbed the oil. Drain the cod and flake it into the breadcrumb mixture. Stir in the coriander, parsley, mint and garlic, adding salt and pepper to taste. Form the mixture into balls. In a frying pan, heat the remaining oil until it is hot but not smoking. Sauté the cod balls until they are browned all over. Serve with ratatouille.

Douro

Portugal's top red wine is made here, but you'd never know it from the label. The only hint that Barca Velha comes from the same part of Portugal as Taylors and Dows port lies in the presence on the label of the producer's name Ferreira and their address in the port shipping centre of Vila Nova da Gaia; otherwise it might come from anywhere in Portugal. At their best, Douro reds can be packed with berry flavours and, when young, taste like a cross between ruby port without the sweetness and freshly made Bordeaux. Apart from Ferreira (who only make Barca Velha in good vintages) and the Quinta da Cotto, there are few producers achieving this kind of quality at the moment. None of the whites is worth travelling any distance to find.

The Centre

Bairrada

When Bairrada finally joins the ranks of the world's internationally recognised wine regions, three producers will share the credit for dragging this region into the late 20th century. The winemakers at Caves Alianca and Caves São João have been unusually quality conscious and Luis Pato has seen the wines made at his estate thrown out of local tastings – because the overly conservative judges, many of whose own Bairradas tasted of nothing at all, could not come to terms with the blend of new oak and plummy-herby fruit they found in them. Hopefully, Bairrada's characterful Baga grape will soon be given rather more opportunities to show off these flavours. In the meantime, stick to the reds from these three producers, and explore their lemony whites and often impressive *méthode champenoise* fizz.

ABOVE: A famous vinous landmark, this palace close to the Mateus winery has featured on millions of labels of this popular wine. Its owner refused a royalty payment per label. BELOW: the Quinta da Bacalhôa, one of the most attractive estates in southern Portugal

Dão

Until Portugal joined the EC, local protectionist rules more or less restricted the production of Dão to the region's cooperatives. Almost incredibly, given Dão's reputation as one of Portugal's best appellations, there was only one individual estate, the Conde de Santar; its wines rarely did the region much credit. All of the rest of the wine was made by the cooperatives who then sold it to the merchants, who, in their turn, matured, bottled and sold it. Blind tastings of Dão were so monotonous.

One company, Sogrape, the firm behind Mateus, tried to improve the quality of the wine it was buying by supervising the winemaking at the Tazem co-operative, where its Grão Vasco is made, and managed to transform the region's flabbily nutty whites into fresher, more lemony versions. Finally, in the late 1980s, Portugal's entry into the Common Market, and the banning of that restrictive monopoly, have allowed Sogrape and others to buy grapes and make their own wine. At last, Dão has the chance to show what it can do.

Ribatejo

The temperate climate region of the banks of the Tagus – the Ribatejo – is still little-known for its wines, but one day soon it will get the greater recognition it deserves. For the moment, there are just three names to look out for: the huge cooperative at Almeirim, Caves Velhas (producers of the reliable Romeira red and some good Garrafeiras) and the Herdeiros de Dom Luis de Margaride estate, where the local João de Santarem and Fernão Pires grapes are successfully used alongside such imports as the Cabernet Franc and Merlot.

Colares

Colares's immunity to the phylloxera is explained by the desert sand in which the vines are grown, but these conditions can make it pretty difficult for people too; the sand is up to 16ft (5m) deep and every time an old vine has to be replaced, a hole has to be dug down to the clay beneath. The reds they make are tough and tannic and need at least a decade to soften enough for their intense, plummy fruit to become apparent.

Bucelas

Twenty miles (32km) from Lisbon, this tiny region produces just half a million bottles of exclusively white wine, from around 420 acres (170 ha) of vines. Confusingly, the young wine made here by Caves Velhas, the region's biggest producer, is labelled as Bucellas Velho, combining an archaic spelling of the region's name with a misleading implication that the wine is old. At its best, Bucelas can marry a fatty, almost Chardonnay-like, texture to some fairly biting lemony acidity.

Carcavelos

With just one estate to its name – the Quinta do Barão – and an annual production of generally unimpressive fortified wine, Carcavelos seemed in danger of extinction at the hands of eager local urban developers. Fortunately, Peter Bright of João Pires has just announced that he will be producing wine here.

Sétubal

Made from vines grown almost in Lisbon's backyard, the Moscatel here is one of Portugal's – and the world's – most famous fortified wines, competing directly against Muscat de Beaumes de Venise, but with far greater age on its side. Almost all of the production is in the hands of a single firm: José Maria da Fonseca, whose go-ahead winery also produces a range of table wines from this region, most notably the Periquita, and Camarate reds (and the TE and CO *garrafeira* reserve versions) as well as Pasmados and Quinta de Camarate, both of which are worth looking out for in red and white versions. Also nearby is João Pires, the winery at which Peter Bright makes the excellent Bordeaux-like Quinta da Bacalhôa, the João Pires unfortified white Muscat and some impressive attempts at Chardonnay.

Alentejo

JM da Fonseca's ultra-traditional JS Rosado Fernandes estate is typical of the kind of adega with which this southern region is associated. The grapes are still trodden by foot and fermented in terracotta amphoras that were precisely like the ones that would have been used by the Romans. The only concession to modernity is the careful way in which the amphoras are hosed down to control the temperature of the fermentation, and a concentration on red rather than the white that was more usually produced here. But the old ways clearly work; the high-strength Tinto Velho is, given five years or so in the cellar, one of Portugal's more impressive reds.

In the same region, two other companies use more modern ways to make similarly good wines. The Esporão winery is based on the Torres plant in the Penedés and there are some 40 varieties of grapes planted, and Peter Bright at João Pires buys the grapes here for the woodily plummy Tinto da Anfora.

Buçaco

Lovers of grand hotels, over-the-top architecture and good wine can indulge themselves in all three at the extraordinary Buçaco Palace Hotel, tucked away in the Bucaco forest. The rich red and white wines are made – very traditionally – by the hotel general manager, Senhor José Santos, and they last for ever, taking on an increasingly piney flavour from the mixture of beeswax and resin with which the bottles are sealed. But don't go looking for these wines in the shops; sadly, they are only available at this and three other Portuguese hotels.

Algarve, Arruda and Torres

The kindest way to deal with the wines of the Algarve would be to say nothing about them at all. They owe their demarcation to local politics, are (poorly) made from the Tinta Negra Mole, and are among the least impressive of the entire country. Arruda and Torres, which like so many other Portuguese regions were given their demarcation because the largest cooperative asked for it, both make pleasant, light, 'modern' wines of a style that goes down better abroad than locally.

Caldo Verde

Potato and kale soup

The Douro is one of the most rugged regions of Portugal but one which has produced some of the best dishes. This delicious soup is traditionally made with kale, but spring greens or spinach can successfully be substituted.

SERVES 4-6

4 oz/100 g spicy sausage (linguica is traditional but Spanish chorizo or other garlicky pork sausage can be used), cut into chunks
2 ¹/₂ pts/2 l water
1 tsp salt
1 lb/500 g large potatoes, peeled and sliced fairly thick
6 tbsp olive oil
Freshly ground black pepper
12 oz/375 g kale, spring greens or spinach, washed, trimmed of coarse stalks and shredded

In a frying pan, sauté the sausage first over low heat (to release its fat) and then on a higher heat until browned. Remove and drain on kitchen paper. In a saucepan, bring the water, salt and potatoes to the boil and cook until the potatoes begin to break when pressed with a fork. Remove the potatoes (keeping the water in the pan) to a large bowl and mash with a fork. Return the potatoes to the pan. Add the kale, and stir in the olive oil. Season with pepper and bring to a rolling boil for 5 minutes. Reduce the heat to a simmer and add the sausage. Continue to simmer until the sausage is heated through. Serve with chunks of French bread.

THE ESSENTIALS — BAIRRADA/DAO

Location South of the Douro in central Portugal.
Quality Both are *regiões demarcadas* (RD).
Style Both RDs, for red and white, still produce a great deal of disappointing wine; however, good white Dão has an appealing nuttiness and is crisp and dry, while white Bairrada can have an attractively fresh, lemony tang. There is also some sparkling white Bairrada produced. The better red Dãos, although quite fiery in youth, soften out into deep, rich, easy-drinking wine. Red Bairrada again benefits from bottle ageing and is characterised, at its best, by lovely deep blackcurrant fruit.
Climate Summers are dry but short, and the temperature then falls sharply in the autumn. The area also has relatively high rainfall. Despite its higher altitude, inland Dão is hotter than Bairrada.
Cultivation Clay soil characterises the low-lying coastal vineyards of Bairrada while vines in the Dão area are scattered across an uncompromising landscape of granite outcrops.
Grape Varieties *Red Dão:* Touriga Nacional (20% minimum), Alfrocheiro Preto, Bastardo, Jaen, Tinta Pinheira, Tinta Roriz, Alvarelhão, Tinta Amarela, Tinta Cão. *White Dão:* Encruzado (20% minimum), Assario Branco, Barcelo, Borrado das Moscas, Cercial, Verdelho, Rabu de Ovelha, Terrantez, Uva Cão. *Red Bairrada:* Baga (50% minimum), Alfrocheiro Preto, Agua Santa, Bastardo, Jaen, Preto de Mortagua, Trincadeira; *white Bairrada:* Arinto, Bical, Cerceal, Cercealinho, Chardonnay, Maria Gomez, Rabo de Ovelha.
Production/Maturation In both areas there is a combination of old-style production by small growers and larger cooperatives using modern techniques. Where these have been adopted, the result has been more approachable wines, particularly in Bairrada where there has been a move away from the traditional coarseness caused by leaving the fermenting juice on the skins and stalks.
Longevity Whites should be drunk young. The red wines begin to show their potential after about 5 years. Thereafter their lifespan is dependent on quality, the best being capable of lasting for over 20 years.
Vintage Guide 75, 80, 83, 85
Top Producers São João, Grão Vasco, Alianca, Sogrape, Luis Pato Cava da Insua.

PORT

To understand port, and before taking the slow train up alongside the Douro River to the farms or *quintas* where it is made, it is worth wangling your way into the Oporto Lawn Tennis and Cricket Club down on the coast. Previously known as the English Club, this is a good place to watch the Portuguese play the British at tennis, and to watch the British play each other at cricket. The nuance translates directly to port. The Portuguese drink copious amounts of wine; little of it is port and even less is remotely comparable to the kind of vintage port most British wine drinkers would recognise and enjoy. Port is a drink invented by and for Anglo-Saxons.

The History of Port

Although Portuguese wines from various regions had been shipped to Britain since the days of 'Chaucer, the first Anglo-Saxons to discover the wines of the Douro were 16th-century merchants – or 'factors' – visiting the market town of Viana do Castelo in search of olive oil and fruit. By 1666 there were sufficient of these factors to start a club, called the Factory House, at which their successors still meet every week for lunch and a decanter or three of port.

When the first shipments of 'pipes' – the region's rugby-ball-shaped 115 gallon (522-litre) casks – arrived on British soil, the wine was called Vinho do Porto, after Porto, the harbour town from which it was shipped. It would have tasted similar to the port we know today – but without the fortification.

There are several stories to explain how brandy was first added to the Douro wine. According to one explanation, two British merchants chanced upon a monastry at Pinhao that was making particularly delectable wine. To satisfy the abbot's sweet tooth, some of the sugar and the grapes had been preserved during fermentation by adding spirit before it had all been fermented out. Another more prosaic, but probably more credible, explanation was that the naturally sweet wine continued to ferment while being transported in barrels across the

Atlantic to Newfoundland, where the ships used to stock up on cod, the fish that the Portuguese needed for their national dish of *bacalhau*. The addition of brandy before the wine left Portugal was intended to stop the fermentation and thus to prevent the casks exploding in mid-ocean.

We know that the sweet strong wine had already begun to create a small market for itself in Britain by 1677, when French wines were banned as a move in what could fairly be described as a 17th-century cold war between Britain and France. The ten years of hostilities that followed meant a heyday for the Portuguese winemakers, who, in 1683, despite the poor quality of most of their wine, apparently managed to sell the British some eleven and a half million bottles of the stuff.

The signing of the Methuen Treaty in 1686 more or less gave the Portuguese a monopoly of wine sales to Britain, in return for which the British received a similar concession for the export of woollen textiles to Portugal. (The tax on French wines was set at £55 per tun while importers of Portuguese wines had to pay only £7.) The British (and a few Dutch) merchants were not slow to take advantage of this privilege. During the early years of the 18th century they established offices and warehouses – 'lodges' (*loja* in Portuguese means storehouse) – for themselves in the village of Vila Nova de Gaia on the south bank of the Douro opposite the harbour town.

During the 1750s the market for port grew too quickly and, perhaps inevitably, the lack of scruples of the growers (who adulterated their wine with elderberries) and of the merchants (who paid little attention to the quality of what they bought) led to a slump. The growers blamed the merchants, the merchants blamed the growers, and the already questionable quality of the wine deteriorated still further. The man who rescued port was the Portuguese Chief Minister, the Marqués de Pombal. In 1756 he started the Douro Wine Company and effectively wrested back control of the region's wines from the foreigners, who were allowed to buy and ship port only once it had been tasted by officials of the company.

The late 18th century was a heyday for the port trade, with 50,000 pipes (nearly 36 million bottles) being shipped to Britain – three times as much as is exported today. Port's popularity owed much to the development in 1775 of a new way of blowing bottles. Before that year bottles were squat containers that could only be stored standing up, and thus for a limited period of time. That year, the first port bottle – purpose-designed for laying down – was made, and with it, the first vintage port, and probably the first vintage wine since the Egyptians and Romans indicated years on their amphoras.

How Port is made

Every bottle of wine legally labelled as port comes from grapes grown in vineyards planted along a 45-mile (72km) stretch of the river Douro as it ambles its way towards Spain. On the western, Oporto, side of the town of Regua, the region is known as the Lower Douro; it is this part of the river that produces the more basic styles of ruby and tawny port. To the east of Regua is the Upper Douro, where grapes used for vintage, crusted and top-quality tawny port are grown.

The Upper Duoro is extraordinary, savagely beautiful country, good for nothing but grapegrowing and goats. The banks that were once fought over by the armies of Napolean and Wellington are now covered with terraces of vines, but the lot of the vineyard worker is scarcely more enviable than that of the 18th-century soldier. According to the rules there could actually be 10 times as much vineyard land as there is on the terraces of these sharply sloping banks, but you can see why few people are planting new vines and why, throughout the region, the dry-stone walls are crumbling, allowing the vertical steps to erode under the elements. The terraces cannot be worked by machines, and there are few Portuguese men who fancy the work.

ABOVE LEFT: Vineyard terraces like these at Quinta da Noval are some of the most difficult in the world both to tend and pick

ABOVE: Bruce Guimaraens of Taylors and Fonseca tastes a tawny port, a style drunk chilled during the Douro summer

Walnut and Gorgonzola Grapes

These morsels are particularly delicious when eaten with a glass of port, perhaps at the end of a meal when you want something lighter that can stand in for both dessert and cheese and biscuits.

4 oz/110 g Gorgonzola (or any blue-veined, softish cheese)
3 oz/75 g soft cream cheese
4 oz/110 g seedless grapes, preferably green
3 oz/75 g shelled walnuts, chopped fine
1 tbsp parsley, chopped fine, or 1 tsp dried parsley

In a bowl, cream together the Gorgonzola and cream cheese until smooth. Take a tablespoonful of the mixture and press a grape into it. Mould the mixture round the grape until it is completely covered. When all the grapes have been coated lay them in one layer on a plate and refrigerate for 20 minutes. In a bowl, combine the walnuts and parsley. One by one, roll the cheese-covered grapes in this mixture until they are completely coated. Chill and serve with little savoury cheese biscuits.

The salvation of the region, as in the steeply sloping vineyards of the Rhine, is the reorganisation of the slopes to enable the vineyards to be planted the other way – up and down, rather than along the hills. All this work in the vineyards has inevitably redirected attention to the kinds of grapes that are planted. Any vine planted in the Douro has to be a sturdy plant. Rainfall is about 20 inches (500mm) a year; in the summer, the valley becomes an oven, with temperatures of over 104°F (40°C); in the winter it can be a deep freeze.

No less than 47 different varieties are permitted for the production of port; in older vineyards perhaps a dozen or more different types will be planted side by side on the same hillside, and all will be vinified together. Now, though, the port shippers have begun to concentrate on isolating the best varieties from which to make their wine. Certainly top-class port, like top-class claret, will never be made from a single variety, but most shippers believe that it would be possible to reduce the number significantly. The best varieties are probably the Touriga Nacional, the Roriz, the Mourisco, and the Tinta Francisa, which is rather dubiously said to be related to the Pinot Noir.

The grapes are grown on quite small *quintas* or farms, which belong either to the port houses themselves or to the 28,000 peasant-farmers from whom they buy their wine. Each shipper carefully oversees the yearly cycle and knows precisely when the harvest will begin (generally about 20th September) in each vineyard. Bands of pickers called *rogas,* headed by a *rogador,* bring the grapes into the farm for crushing.

Until 1960, all crushing took place by foot in low, open, concrete or wooden troughs called *lagars.* About 14 men per *lagare* would trample back and forth to the accompaniment of an accordion, four hours on, four hours off, until the grapes were crushed and the juice floated on top of the solids. The must would then start to ferment, and would be stirred continually, bringing the solids to the top. When a sufficiently high alcohol level had been achieved, still leaving a good deal of sugar in the must, the wine would be run off into wooden vats and blended with *aguardente* – grape brandy – at 77% strength to a ratio of 97 gallons (440 litres) of wine to 24 gallons (110 litres) of brandy. The spirit stops the fermentation process, leaving the strong sweet liquid that is port. In an ideal world, each producer would make or choose its own spirit; in practice, they have to buy from the government.

ABOVE: Young port in the Quinta da Noval tasting room in Vila Nova da Gaia

FACING PAGE: Until the Douro was dammed, port was shipped downriver on these barcos ravelhos

Today the *lagares* are only used by the most primitive farms, and by the best port shippers for the wine from their best vineyards. Most of the annual harvest is crushed and fermented mechanically using autovinifiers, whose principle is to build up pressure inside the sealed vat, which forces the wine to spill out on top of the tank. Valves then regulate the pressure, allowing the wine to cascade down again over the blanket formed by continuous fermentation. The right strength and sugar balance is achieved in two or three days, and the wine is then drawn off into vats, where it is married with the *aguardente*, and the fermentation halts.

Following the harvest, the port shippers travel around the *quintas* tasting their new wine and trying to gain an overall impression of the vintage. During the winter the wines are held in vats until the spring, when they are transported down to the lodges in Vila Nova de Gaia, where they will be variously blended, matured and bottled. The pipes of young wine used to be shipped down the Douro on *Barco Rabelo* sailboats, but since the building of roads and railway track, and the slowing of the river by dams, the boats have been relegated to use as mobile advertising hoardings for the producers.

Once in the port lodge, the wine of each pipe is tasted again to decide on its future. Top-quality wines are separated from the others, blended only among themselves, held for 18 months, and retasted to establish whether they are potentially good enough to be sold as vintage port or whether they will be kept in wood for long enough to become tawny. The skill of tasting and judging young port is one of the hardest to attain in the wine trade, because the tannic nature of the wine makes it very tricky to assess. Choosing whether or not to declare a vintage can cost port producers many sleepless nights.

Types of Port

In 1877 a visiting English writer called Henry Vizetelly complained that there were 'almost as many styles of port as shades of ribbon in a haberdasher's shop.' Today, thankfully, the range is narrower, but it still offers ample scope for confusion.

Theoretically, port can be divided into two fundamentally different styles: wood aged – wine that has been matured in barrel – and bottle aged – wine that has been bottled young, with a significant amount of the solid matter that will eventually drop out in the form of a deposit.

Unfortunately, nothing is that simple. There are several types of bottle-aged, and several types of wood-aged, wine – and their producers have traditionally made remarkably little effort to make it clear to prospective customers which are which. Until recently, the producers used to defend their ways with the explanation that 'most port drinkers know what they are buying'. So saying, they shrugged off any criticism of their indiscriminate labelling as tawny of both old, wood-aged wine and young blends of white and ruby – and any complaint that terms such as 'fine old' really ought to mean something. Today labelling is a little clearer, but it's still far from clear cut. So a bottle of Taylor's (and just about everybody else's) Late-Bottled Port will have been filtered to ensure that it needs no decanting, while one bearing the same words from Warre's or Smith Woodhouse will have as much of a deposit as any vintage port – and taste twice as delicious.

Ruby Port

Ruby is yesterday's basic port style – the stuff people used to drink in British pubs as half of that memorable cocktail, the 'port 'n' lemon'. The snootier members of the port trade would naturally never have dreamed of drinking their wine in this way – but it didn't stop them from making vast amounts of a raw, spirity drink that needed a good dose of lemon to help disguise what would otherwise be fairly awful.

White Port

White port is supposed to be a 'smart' drink, to be sipped at by elegant folk at the right kind of cocktail party. I only wish it were. Unfortunately, the most revealing thing to be said about most of this stuff is that it can be pleasantly refreshing on a hot summer's day, provided that it is drunk the way its makers serve it – with a handful of ice cubes and a generous dollop of tonic or soda. In other words white port is a very pricy alternative to vermouth – and one that has the added disadvantages of coming in unpredictable levels of sweetness and losing its freshness on wine merchants' shelves.

Tawny Port

A lot of the stuff traditionally labelled as 'Tawny', 'Fine Old Tawny', 'Superior Old Tawny' and so on, is another of the port men's little jokes. Unlike *real* tawny, which owes its name, its colour and its tangy, nutty flavour to its prolonged sojourn in barrel, this stuff is simply a blend of young white and ruby ports, mixed to look and taste vaguely like the genuine article. Telling the two kinds of tawny apart has never been easy, but a higher price and/or a specific age such as 10 or 20 year old, will ensure that you are getting the real thing. Real tawny is a delicious alternative to vintage, but in the heat of the Douro the shippers often surprise visitors by serving it chilled.

There is another style of Tawny from which British consumers have, so far, been shielded: *Colheita* ports, or Tawny port with a vintage date. To the traditionalists the very idea makes no sense because, in theory at least, the best tawny is always a blend of ports of different ages (according to the rules it only has to have the character of the age it claims) and, in fact, younger tawnies are often tastier than older ones. But that doesn't stop the traditionalist port houses from selling *Colheita* ports in countries such as France and Portugal.

PORT VINTAGES

1985 A great and immediately delicious vintage declared - with rare unanimity – by all of the major shippers. Its wine may be ready to drink before the 1983s. Look out for Fonseca and Grahams.

1983 A vintage to keep, though at seven years old, the wines are still pretty tough. Taylor's was a star.

1982 A bit disappointing (especially when compared to 1983) but a pleasant enough, middleweight vintage.

1980 Initially overpriced and underrated, this vintage has seemed rather tough, but it's worth waiting for.

1977 A rotten vintage in Bordeaux and Burgundy, but a great one for port - provided that you've got the patience they'll need.

1975 A light vintage that most port houses oughtn't to have declared. The wines are pleasant enough but they have little depth and they won't last.

1970 A classic vintage that has taken a long while to 'come round'. Great now and for the future. All the top producers made fine wine.

1966 Not as much of a stayer as 1963, but a pretty good vintage all the same. Drink it while waiting for the '63 and the '70.

1963 The great vintage, this is port's answer to 1961 claret - and similarly pricy. But it's worth every penny; extraordinary, rich, classic port.

1955 A great vintage which proves how this remarkable wine can go on improving for 40 years.

Vintage Port

Vintage ports do not reveal themselves immediately. Even in a very good year no shipper will be foolhardy enough to declare a vintage as soon as the wine is made. Instead he wants to see how the juvenile protégé develops after 18 months, and then, if both he and the *Instituto do Vinho do Porto* agree that the wine of a given year is exceptional enough, a vintage is declared, and the wine of that single year is bottled during the following year. For some reason, although British port houses often disagree over which vintage to declare, none will ever declare in two consecutive years. Vintage ports take considerably longer to mature than wood-aged ports, and their longevity is legendary, though it does vary from one vintage to another. All vintage ports throw a sediment in the bottle and need decanting anything up to a day before drinking.

Late-bottled Vintage Port

This is wine from a single vintage, matured in wood for between four and six years. The result is usually a wine that has been filtered and consequently has less character and weight than vintage port and lacks the fine nuttiness of good tawny. Look out, though, for traditional, earlier-bottled, unfiltered examples made by Warre's and Smith Woodhouse.

Crusted Port

Crusted port is a blend of good wines from different vintages. Bottled young, it retains a lot of body and should be decanted. It offers one of the best alternatives to real vintage port.

Single Quinta Port

Made by a port shipper from wine produced at a single estate (while vintage port is a blend of wines from several), usually in an undeclared year, but in the same way as vintage port. Wines from Taylor's Vargellas, Warre's Cavadinha and Dows Bom Fim *quintas* offer real vintage style for a lower price.

THE ESSENTIALS — THE DOURO

Location The Douro valley traverses northern Portugal.
Quality *Região demarcado* (RD) for port, which is further classified, in descending order of quality, from A to F. Unfortified table wines are *vinhos de mesa* only, but can be good.
Style Red port comes in a variety of styles (*see box*). In most of its forms it is classic after-dinner drinking, full of rich, spicy sweetness. The best old tawnies have faded in wood to a dry yet mellow smoothness. White port can be sweet or dry and is commonly drunk chilled as an aperitif, often mixed with tonic water. A few unfortified Douro reds are of very high quality and all are characterised by weighty berry fruit. The white wines are dry and again can have good fruit.
Climate High summer temperatures and rainfall. Winters can be surprisingly cold.
Cultivation The steeper and more inaccessible vineyards higher up the valley have better quality schist soils which produce the finest ports. Thus production of Douro table wines is concentrated on the granite soil of the lower valley.
Grape Varieties *Port*: of the 45 permitted red port grapes the best are Tinta Amarela, Tinta Barroca, Tinto Cão, Tinta Roriz, Touriga Francesa, Touriga Nacional. *White port* is made from a ragbag of varieties. Little selection is practised. *Red table wines*: as for red port plus Tinta Francisca, Bastardo, Mouriscò Tinto, Alvarelhão, Comifesto, Donzelinho, Donzelinho Tinto, Malvasia, Malvasia Preta, Mourisca de Semente, Periquita, Rufete, Sousão, Tinta Barca, Tinta Carvalha, Touriga Brasileira. *White table wines*: Arinto, Boal, Cercial, Codega, Donzelinho Branco, Esgano Cão, Folgosão, Fernão Pires, Malvasia Corada, Malvasia Fina, Malvasia Parda, Moscatel Galego, Rabigato, Rabo de Ovelha, Verdelho, Viosinho.
Production/Maturation Port grapes are brought back to the central *quinta* where they are in many cases still trodden by foot in stone troughs, or *lagares*. Fermentation takes place at temperatures up to 32°C until the alcohol content reaches 6%. It is at this stage that the wine is fortified with clear grape spirit (*aguardente*). The port is then matured and bottled at Vila Nova de Gaia, a suburb of Oporto.
Longevity The best vintage ports will last at least 20 years and often double that. White port should be drunk young; the unfortified white wines should be drunk within 3 years and the red wines between 2 and 10 years.
Vintage Guide The best of recently declared port vintages are 63, 66, 77 and 85. Red table wine: 80, 83, 84, 85.
Top Producers *Port*: Taylor, Warre, Graham, Dow, Fonseca, Noval, Ramos Pinto. *Table wine*: Quinta do Cotto.

MADEIRA

FACING PAGE: The offices and winery of the Madeira Wine Company, producers – under one name or another – of most of Madeira's best wine.

ABOVE: The rocky, volcanic coastline of Madeira is the ideal place to grow flowers and bananas – and grapevines aplenty.

THE ESSENTIALS — MADEIRA

Location This Atlantic island under Portugese jurisdiction lies 370 miles off the coast of Morocco.

Quality Região demarcado (RD).

Style Table wines rarely leave the island, which is chiefly famous for its classic fortified wines. These vary in style *(see box)* from dry Sercial and Verdelho, for drinking chilled as an aperitif, through to lusciously sweet after-dinner Bual and Malmsey. All have extraordinary ageing potential and good balancing acidity.

Climate Hot summers and mild winters. High rainfall.

Cultivation Terraced vineyards hug the island's cliffs, the best sites being in the south of the island. The soil is fertile, due in part to its volcanic origins and the fire-raising of the island's first settler. Vines are trained on trellises to allow other crops to be grown underneath.

Grape Varieties The four quality grapes are Sercial, Bual, Verdelho and Malmsey. Should a bottle not specify any of these it will probably be produced from the Tinta Negra Mole, either on its own or blended.

Production/Maturation The grapes are fermented and then placed in a heated storeroom — an *estufa* — heated gradually to 45°C and then cooled. Fortification takes place before this *estufagem* ('baking') for dry Madeira and afterwards for the sweeter styles. 18 months after cooling the wine enters a solera system similar to that used in Jerez.

Longevity Madeira, vintage or otherwise, is ready to drink when it is bottled. After this time it will keep almost indefinitely; it is also one of the rare wines that still taste good — sometimes better — even weeks after the bottle has been opened, since air-contact is such a crucial and desirable factor in its style.

Vintage Guide Most Madeiras are a product of the solera system, although there are still a few old single-vintage wines available.

Top Producers Henriques & Henriques, Rutherford & Miles, Harveys, Cossart Gordon, Blandy.

Once the favourite tipple of American and English gentlemen, Madeira would have been the staple of every self-respecting dinner table of the late 18th and 19th centuries. George Washington, for example, a man described by his friend Samuel Stearns as 'very regular, temperate and industrious', used to dine every day at three, drinking 'half a pint to a pint of Madeira wine. This with a small glass of punch, a draught of beer, and two dishes of tea'.

But what would Washington's 'Madeira wine' have tasted like? According to one Edward Vernon Harcourt, whose *A Sketch of Madeira* was published in 1851, it would have been made from a mixture of three grapes: the Verdelho (for 'body'), the Tinta, and the Bual (both for 'flavour'). This use of several different grape varieties in a single blend may surprise anyone who has learned that each of the four principal types of Madeira – Sercial, Verdelho, Bual and Malmsey – is named after, and made from, its own grape. But our ancestors would have known about wines with those names *as well as* one known simply as 'Madeira'; such names were fairly loosely applied .

In the late 19th century there was also a Madeira Burgundy, made from the Tinta Negra Mole, a grape supposedly grown originally in France as the Pinot Noir. Always less well thought of than the quartet of better-known Castas Nobles, the Tinta wine was said by one contemporary author to have 'the astringent property of port', losing some of its fine aroma and delicate flavour 'after its first or second year'. Even further down the quality scale, the colourfully named Bastardo and the Moscatel. Wine simply called 'Madeira' would have been made from a mixture of any or all of these. Casks that had had the benefit of the warm voyage through the tropics, were sold as either 'East' or 'West India Madeira'; Madeira that had not taken either trip was simply styled 'London Particular'.

As the years passed, and as producers discovered that the wine could be 'cooked', Madeira passed from being the preserve of the Anglo-Saxon gentleman to that of the Gallic or German cook. The quality of the wine inevitably fell, and the four difficult-to-grow fine varieties – the Castas Nobles – were gradually replaced by the easier Tinta Negra Mole. After all, so the producers often thought, the wine it produces can be pretty similar, and once it's in the soup, who's going to notice?

For the true Madeira-lover, the more serious wine-lodges continued to produce Madeira of a remarkable quality, using the 'noble' grapes and a solera system, and wines bearing specified vintages were made in good years. Even so, it was not until the late 1970s that the island's winemakers finally decided to take a firm grip on the situation and concentrate on quality – or rather on reminding the rest of the world about the quality they had never really stopped producing. Suddenly, wines such as Blandy's 10-year-old Malmsey began to appear: beautifully packaged, fairly highly priced, but, most essentially of all, with the depth of flavour that Madeira shares with no other fortified wine. Where sherry has its own kind of identifiable savoury woodiness, and port its stemmy, tannic acidity, Madeira has a unique quality – a nutty, old-English marmaladey 'tang' that can be quite adictive.

This concentration on reinstating Madeira in the public mind as a quality product stems partly from the fact that the costs of production of even the most mediocre wine on the island are so high that it can never be sold as cheaply as port or sherry, and partly from the accession of Portugal into the EEC. Among the more meddlesome of European laws, there is one that states that a product must conform to the description that appears on its label. So Sercial, for instance, will have to be made exclusively from the Sercial grape. (Traditionally, the amount of pure Sercial in an average bottle bearing that name might well have been as low as 10% or even less.) Equally, the 'Eurosnoops' have not been as lenient as the Portuguese authorities towards some of the 'vintaged' Madeira that used to fill the shops on the island. Rows of bottles, each proclaiming its vintage as 1884, inevitably inspired suspicion.

The island's future success or failure lies in a relatively small number of hands. The Madeira Wine Company (previously known as the Madeira Wine Association) embraces several of the best-known Madeira names, including Blandy, Cossart Gordon and Rutherford & Miles. Its current head, Richard Blandy, also owns Reids Hotel, a hire-car company and a fairly substantial acreage of the island. A descendant of the first Blandy, the subaltern who started the trade in Madeira to Britain, he is clearly determined to establish a quality image.

Among Portuguese Madeira houses, the best – and best-known – are Barbeito, and Henriques & Henriques. Walking through the Dickensian entrance hall of the latter, with its outmoded desks and typewriters, the atmosphere of an England long gone hangs thickly and pleasantly on the air. Here you can taste run-of-the-mill Madeira sold on price, and bottles of the Solera 1907 Bual, which fill both mouth and memories with their richness and orangey tang. Some people on the island say that such solera wines are a thing of the past, that from here onwards the best commercial wines will be like tawny port and fine whisky in declaring an age (ten years old for instance) rather than a specific solera year. It would be a great pity if they were to disappear, because, like some of the real vintage wines, they can offer delicious proof that, thanks to the way that it is made, Madeira can be the longest-lived drink of them all.

Tasting cheap, 'cooking' Madeira is rather like watching a fine actor play in a soap opera; you know that he's capable of better things, but that doesn't improve the show. Tasting the 'real stuff' is something else again, an experience like sampling the finest table wines in the world. Cooking wine will always have its place – in the saucepan rather than the glass – but fine Madeira has a far more important role to play. Try a bottle of the finest ten-year-old or older and you may be converted for life.

MADEIRA STYLES

Sercial
Made from a grape thought to be related to the Riesling, this is the driest, palest and most perfumed style of Madeira. Ideal as an alternative aperitif to fino sherry - or as an accompaniment to consommé.

Verdelho
Also drinkable as an aperitif, this is slightly sweeter, with a hint of the lime flavour that is the mark of this variety.

Bual/Boal
The second sweetest type of Madeira. Smoky and complex, with a typical marmaladely tang of acidity that sets it distinctly apart from sherries of similar levels of sweetness.

Malmsley
The original and sweetest Madeira style, made from the Malvasia grape. Rich, dark and brown-sugary but, like the Bual, with a tangy vein of balancing acidity that makes it a far easier drink than vintage port.

Rainwater
US name for a dryish blend of Sercial and Verdelho, so named because the casks were stood outside in the rain.

Reserve
At least five years old.

Special Reserve
At least ten years old.

Exceptional Reserve
At least 15 years old.

Vintage
At least 20 years in cask and two in bottle.

NORTH AMERICA

Once upon a time (around 50 years ago to be precise), two young brothers decided to start a winery. Their sense of time and place were impeccable; they were in California, the grapegrowing heart of a nation that had just been freed from 14 years of Prohibition. If they could make the right kind of wine, there was a huge and very thirsty market that was ready to buy it by the gallon.

Today those same, now rather older, brothers own and personally control the world's largest winery. And the second largest. And the third. Every year their company makes more wine than the entire region of Australia; the annual production of New Zealand would barely fill one of their larger vats. And they're still producing – albeit to a far lesser extent – the cheap, fortified port–like wines that made their name among the unsophisticated wine drinkers of the post–war years

A short drive from those giant wineries, there's a small estate whose owner lovingly produces just 1,200 bottles of wine per year – around half the annual output of Château Pétrus, the fabled Château whose scarcity value is beyond peer among the larger, Bordeaux estates.

The big wineries belong to Ernest and Julio Gallo; the tiny one to the Lambourne family. And I'll bet that, unless you live in the USA, until the E&J Gallo marketing men decided to attack Europe in 1989, you'd almost certainly have heard of neither their wines nor the Lambournes'. That's the first crucial thing to remember about the wine industry of North America; it's huge, varied and as challenging to would-be explorers as the continent itself. And, as in so many other industries in that country, it is remarkably self-sufficient.

The second thing to bear in mind is that, while the Gallo and the Lambourne operations are as different as they could possibly be, they share, with every other US winery from the smallest to – in the local expression – the most humungous, that peculiarly American spirit of pioneering possibility, the belief in the key words: 'can-do'.

In some states this kind of confidence is entirely justified; in California, where almost any kind of farmer can grow almost any kind of crop, there is little excuse for not making good wine. Elsewhere, however, the climatic handicaps are often so severe that 'can-do' seems rather reminiscent of the sickly child who stubbornly believes that he is going to grow up to be a champion heavyweight boxer.

But climate has not been the only handicap would-be winemakers have had to overcome. Throughout North America there is a deeply puritanical resistance to alcohol that has, of course, led to its total ban in the past but also, in more recent years, been immeasurably strengthened in recent years by healthy-living and road-safety campaigners who, for the best of motives, have endeavoured to ensure that wine is never treated as casually as it is in the Old World.

North America is riddled with a confusing mass of restrictions that vary from state to state and even from county to county. Some counties have remained 'dry' since Prohibition finally ended in 1933; elsewhere, wine sales are controlled by state monopolies; shops that sell wine are forbidden to sell peanuts or glasses (or vice versa); importers are barred from trading as wholesalers and retailers (and vice versa); and there is almost nowhere that a young man or woman can buy a bottle or glass of wine until they are 21-years-old.

With hurdles like these to be cleared, most European producers and merchants might be forgiven for thanking their lucky stars that they are still allowed to ply their trade in the relative freedon of the Old World.

But the North Americans have their own advantages. Selling

While a huge proportion of the population of the USA has still to fall under the spell of wine, American wine enthusiasts are the most enthusiastic on earth – hence this car registration plate bearing the name of one of the greatest wines in Burgundy.

wine may sometimes be less than straightforward, but there's very little to stop would-be producers from making the stuff in any way they choose. A Bordeaux château would encounter all kinds of problems if it wanted to plant a few acres of Chardonnay, and it certainly couldn't label the wine made from that grape as 'Bordeaux'. A winemaker in North America can take his – or her – pick from all of the varieties on offer in the nursery, and call the wine more or less anything they like; so, if it's got bubbles, label it 'Champagne', if it's sweet and pink, dub it 'Blush Chablis'.

And then there's the Madison Avenue factor. Winemakers in the Old World are often still far more firmly rooted in the era of feudalism than that of 20th–century marketing. If your father, grandfather and great grandfather made Barolo in a particular way from the Nebbiolo grape, and sold it to a local merchant for whatever he was prepared to pay, that's what you would most probably go on doing. And if one of those forebears had taken the brave step of deciding to bottle his wine himself, then you'd more than likely go on using the label he chose from the local printer. The words 'promotional budget' almost certainly wouldn't feature in your vocabulary; your entire marketing effort might well consist of a hand-painted roadside sign to tell passers-by that you have wine to sell and a few printed cards bearing the name of your estate.

In North America, there is a far greater appreciation of the fact that while, winemaking is part of an agricultural tradition, it also inhabits the same, hard-selling business world as the motor, computer or even entertainment industries. So, the 1990 vintage Cabernet Sauvignon from the Mondavi winery will be described as that producer's latest 'release' – just as though it were a pop record or a movie.

And if the success of a feature film can lie in the hands of the ctitics, so can that of a wine. If Robert Parker, author and publisher of an enormously influential newsletter called *The Wine Advocate*, gives a new wine a top mark, it can sell out before the first case reaches the shops. And if he decides that a winery isn't up to scratch, woe betide the unfortunate salesman who's trying to persuade a wine retailer to stock it.

This critical spotlight, coupled with the US enthusiasm for all things fresh and new, has not only led to a wine industry in which scarcely a week goes by without another new winery opening its doors, but one in which winemakers are constantly aware of the style of wine the public wants to buy at any given moment. While his Italian cousin in Barolo remains wedded to the Nebbiolo vines he inherited from his father, the US producer can decide, almost from one vintage to the next, to switch

production from Zinfandel to Chardonnay, or from Chenin Blanc to Cabernet Sauvignon.

In Europe, such an upheaval – literally – would not only be unlikely; it would also be time–consuming, as the land is normally left to rest for three or four years between the pulling-up of the old vines and the planting of new ones which, in their turn, would take another three or four years to begin producing good wine.

In California, particularly, where the vineyards are almost all much younger, the switch is often made far more simply, by a process known as 'T-budding' which simply involves grafting a new variety on to the old one, possibly even for one vintage, producing two kinds of grape on the same rootstock.

This expertise at grafting vines might seem shockingly new–fangled to European traditionalist but, ironically, harks right back to a historical link between European and US vinegrowing – a link which was one of the most significant and perhaps the most significant development in vinous world history.

Vines were growing on North American soil before earliest European settlers arrived. These were of the *Vitis labrusca* species - producing table grapes, rather than the wine-making *Vitis vinifera* traditionally grown in Europe - hardy plants that were tough enough to survive cold winters and sweltering summers. Most particularly, they were resistant to various kinds of disease and pest, most notably the locally prevalent and voracious *Phylloxera vastatrix*, a louse that simply loves to kill vines by chomping away at their roots.

Until the late 19th century, thanks to the ocean separating the two continents, the vineyards of Europe were as untroubled by the phylloxera as British kennels are by rabies. Then disaster struck: the louse was carried over the water and, in the space of a few decades, lived up to the *vastatrix* part of its name by devastating almost all of Europe's traditional vine-growing regions.

All kinds of remedies were tried; ultimately the only avenues left open to the Europeans led back to the source of the problem. If the louse didn't kill the vines in America, why not plant those same kinds of vine and use them to make wine in Europe?

The answer to this was simple. Although the American vines were easy to grow and their grapes pleasant to eat, the wine produced from their grapes really tasted rather awful. But it wasn't the grapes the Europeans were interested in; what they wanted was the rootstock on to which – and this was the clever part – they grafted their good *vinifera* vines. This combination of resistant American rootstock and quality *vinifera* vine was soon adopted by winemakers everywhere. Today, almost every top quality vineyard in the world (with the exception of tiny pockets that escaped the attentions of the louse) is planted in this way.

Initially, this was thought to be a two-way solution, engendering visions among U.S. planters of an America gushing forth quality *vinifera* wine whenever the hardy *labrusca* flourished.Unfortunately, however, there are regions of north America where *vinifera* grapes simply will not grow. In the cold climate of parts of Canada and of the northern states of the USA, the winters can be so cold that the plants simply freeze to death. Elsewhere, perversely, the weather can be too good for them. One of the main reasons why Florida has become such a popular holiday destination also explains why that state has never been able to attract top quality winemakers. The virtual absence of winter denies the vines the essential period of dormancy that protects them against disease. Only one type of vine can survive in this tender trap, and this, a native variety with the wonderful name of Scuppernong, produces less than wonderful wine.

Earlier this century, the USA was broadly divided between those regions that could produce good wine from *vinifera* grapes, and those that could make poor-to-mediocre stuff from

Left: The Ste Chapelle winery in Idaho is a Disney-style copy of the original church in France; throughout the USA, architects can make fortunes designing new wineries. Above: Quality winemaking in the USA is almost wholly obsessed with 'varietal' wines, made from the cream of Europe's grape varieties. These Cabernet Sauvignon vines are in the Mercer Ranch vineyard in Washington State.

labrusca. Expertise in the nursery improved matters considerably by creating hybrid vines with one *labrusca* and one *vinifera* parent whose wines tasted better than those made from the former, but less good that those of the latter.

Similarly, increased knowledge of vinegrowing and of cloning, and improved pesticides and fungicides permitted producers to plant *vinifera* vines in some regions where it had previously been impossible.

Today, there are vineyards in no less than 43 US states and in three regions of Canada. Of these, California remains far and away the most important in terms of both quality and quantity. It not only produces around 95% of all the wine made in North America, but it is also the area in which one of the world's best oenological colleges has been established and where most of the greatest U.S. wines have been made.

The supremacy of California is easily explained. Quite apart from the quality (and the useful diversity) of its climate, winemaking here has benefited from what might be called the Hollywood syndrome. The fact that Hollywood has a successful film industry has encouraged thousands of would-be actors and directors to flock there - which has helped to ensure that Hollywood has continued to have a successful film industry.

The Napa and Sonoma Valleys are the Hollywood of California's wine world, the magnets that have not only attracted winemakers from other parts of the USA, but also such illustrious overseas investors as Baron Philippe de Rothschild of Château Mouton Rothschild and a clutch of some of the best-known producers in Champagne. And, with every new release from every new winery, the 'can-do' confidence grows; it's a brave

man who will tell a top Napa Valley winemaker that he'll never make a wine as good as Château Pétrus or Le Montrachet. Quite often he's half–convinced that he's already made it – and has a quote from a well–known wine critic to prove it.

Over the last few years, however, Californians are beginning to find themselves facing increasingly stiff domestic competition. Up in Oregon, the cool climate suits the Burgundian Pinot Noir rather better than the warmer weather enjoyed by most parts of California. Washington State has concentrated its attention on the Riesling, the Cabernet Sauvignon and the Merlot, varieties that also seem to flourish on the eastern seaboard, on Long Island though not, interestingly, in other, cooler parts of New York State.

Throughout North America, this growing understanding of the varying climatic requirements of different types of grapes and the readiness of producers to explore new regions has led to the creation of *Appellation Contrôlée*-style districts called AVAs – Approved Viticultural Areas – each of which supposed to have its own identifiable characteristics.

In some cases, as in Long Island and Carneros in California, both of which genuinely do have micro-climates of their own, the existence of their AVA designation makes perfect sense. Elsewhere, however, there are all sorts of curious boundary definitions that seem horribly reminiscent of the political way in which DOCs and DOCGs have been doled out in Italy.

In general, the scheme has been well-received. All the same, the prosaic 'Approved Viticultural Area' does not have the same ring to it as, say, 'Premier Grand Cru'. Just as democratic America is fascinated by the class divisions of Europe, so there must be U.S. winemakers who long for a hierarchy with all the social nuances of say, French wine law.

Such a development seems distant at present, but one never knows... The only certainty about North America is that whatever you saw and learned today will have changed by tomorrow. If not before.

CALIFORNIA

According to atlases of North America, California is neither more nor less than one of the 50 states of the union. In reality, as anyone who has come into even the slightest contact with this uniquely privileged part of North America will have discovered, California is far more like a nation within a nation. And a highly successful one at that.

Apart from movies, computers and oranges, Its 160.000 square miles produce sufficient grapes to keep hospital bedsides amply supplied in several countries, while still allowing California's wineries to make this the sixth biggest wine producing nation on earth. Every year, they turn out around two and a half *billion* bottles of wine.

As any Californian will readily tell you, this state has all of the attributes almost any farmer could ask for: an ideal climate - or rather a range of different ideal climates - relatively inexpensive Mexican immigrant labour, the world's most advanced training college and plentiful local investment.

In short, California ought to be making huge numbers of superlative wines that knock the rest of the world right off the shelves; at the moment, it is producing a mass of adequate quality wine and a relatively limited group of dazzling individual success stories. Tasted blind impartial palate, it is surprising how few of California's wines compete in value or quality terms with alternatives from France, Italy, Australia or New Zealand.

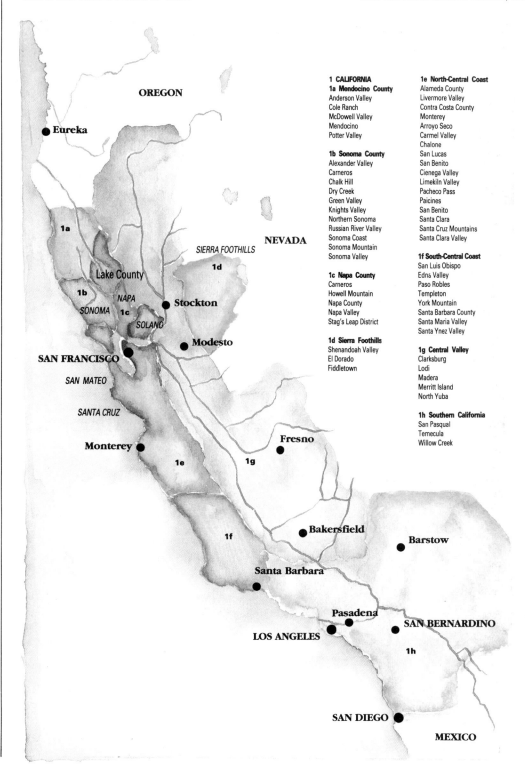

1 CALIFORNIA
1a Mendocino County
Anderson Valley
Cole Ranch
McDowell Valley
Mendocino
Potter Valley

1b Sonoma County
Alexander Valley
Carneros
Chalk Hill
Dry Creek
Green Valley
Knights Valley
Northern Sonoma
Russian River Valley
Sonoma Coast
Sonoma Mountain
Sonoma Valley

1c Napa County
Carneros
Howell Mountain
Napa County
Napa Valley
Stag's Leap District

1d Sierra Foothills
Shenandoah Valley
El Dorado
Fiddletown

1e North-Central Coast
Alameda County
Livermore Valley
Contra Costa County
Monterey
Arroyo Seco
Carmel Valley
Chalone
San Lucas
San Benito
Cienega Valley
Limekiln Valley
Pacheco Pass
Paicines
San Benito
Santa Clara
Santa Cruz Mountains
Santa Clara Valley

1f South-Central Coast
San Luis Obispo
Edna Valley
Paso Robles
Templeton
York Mountain
Santa Barbara County
Santa Maria Valley
Santa Ynez Valley

1g Central Valley
Clarksburg
Lodi
Madera
Merritt Island
North Yuba

1h Southern California
San Pasqual
Temecula
Willow Creek

RIGHT: The Heitz winery is best known for its Martha's Vineyard Cabernet Sauvignon, one of the most famous and most distinctive red wines in California. This sign invites visitors to stop and buy bottles of this - or one of Heitz's other wines

BELOW: The Mondavi Winery at Oakville is situated on the floor of the Napa Valley, on land that is technically described as the Rutherford Bench.

History

Winemaking began in California in the late 18th century, following - or so it is generally believed - the arrival of Franciscan missionaries from Mexico. Initially, the grapes planted were the same Criolla variety that were grown in Mexico (though here they soon became known as the Mission) but in the early 1800s higher quality French varieties were introduced from the east coast by a Bordelais winemaker called Jean-Louis Vignes and an eccentric Hungarian who liked to be known as 'Colonel' or 'Count' Agoston Haraszthy and was reputedly eaten by alligators in Nicaragua.

However he died, Haraszthy's legacy to California's infant wine industry was a 400 acre nursery, stocked with some 300 different types of grape brought back from a three-month expedition to Europe, and the still-functioning Buena Vista Winery in Sonoma County. Surprisingly though, the one grape the Hungarian probably did not introduce to California was the Zinfandel, a variety which is thought to have originated in Italy.

The mid 19th century, were the first heyday of Californian winemaking. Using Haraszthy's cuttings and the widely planted Mission grape, a large number of such familiar names as Paul Masson, Wente and Almaden had arrived. In the 1870s, progress was halted by the devastation of the vineyards by the Phylloxera vastatrix louse which had already begun to put a halt to winemaking in Europe and, 50 years later, by the introduction of full-scale Prohibition in 1920.

The Prohibition years were a time of keen amateur winemaking, and of similarly keen conversion to almost any religion that needed sacramental wine. It was wrily said that there was scarcely an appartment block in Manhattan that didn't have a resident rabbi or priest, and scarcely a household that wasn't experimenting with the do-it-yourself kits which included a block of dried grapes and some powdered yeast, along with the strict injunction not to allow the two to come into contact with each other, 'lest they ferment'.

After Repeal in 1933, although a few of the old-established wineries, such as Inglenook and Beaulieu, continued to make wine from high quality varieties, most preferred table grapes that made poor wine but could be turned into juice or jelly.

It was not until the 1960s and 1970s that a new generation of winemakers began to explore the potential that Vignes and Haraszthy had revealed over a century earlier. The region that attracted most of their interest during those years, was the Napa Valley, despite the fact that some of the most successful pioneering producers, including Haraszthy, had made their wine in neighbouring Sonoma County.

Throughout its early history, the Californian wine industry like those of Australia and New Zealand, unashamedly labelled its wines as 'Champagne', 'Burgundy' and 'Claret'. Although this kind of labelling still goes on today – the giant Gallo winery has no compunction in selling 'Hearty Red Burgundy' and 'Blush Chablis' – the quality-conscious producers of the 1970s began to market their wines in a rather different way.

Faced with the choice of whether to use the names of European styles or of Californian towns and villages of which few people would ever have heard, they did neither. Instead they resorted to printing the names of the grape varieties from which the wines were made. Today, in a wine world awash with Cabernet Sauvignon and Chardonnay, it is worth recalling that Alsace is the only major part of Europe in which the winemakers have traditionally referred to grapes rather than places.

Labels on bottles of red Burgundy never referred to the Pinot Noir; most of the people who drank Château Latour had no reason to know that it was prinicpally made from the Cabernet Sauvignon and Merlot. What the Californians had done was to invent a new concept: 'varietal labelling'. Wines made from particularly popular grapes were dubbed the 'fighting varietals'.

One Track Wines

The varietal labels have, however, become something of a trap. This obsessive drive to 'replicate' or ideally 'out-do' Bordeaux or Burgundy bcomes a little tedious after a while; even the Royal Shakespeare Company feels the occasional need to mount plays by other authors. And so too, does the tendency to play Follow-My-Leader by treating each grape in much the same way as everybody else: Chardonnay has to taste oaky; Sauvignon Blanc has to be slightly sweet...There are some mavericks thank goodness. Like the reactionaries who persist in using California's 'own' variety to make big, dark, Zinfandel with spicy flavours encountered nowhere else, and the small group of individualists like Randy Grahm at Bonny Doone who are exploring such European varieties as the Syrah, the Viognier, the Nebbiolo and the Sangioveto. And, thankfully, there are people like Patrick Campbell at Laurel Glen and David Coleman at Adler Fels, who use the Chardonnay and Cabernet to make wines that do not fit the identikit picture dictated by the market. But they are still the exceptions to the rule.

Ask almost any winemaker with aspirations to quality what styles he sells most easily and it's a dollar to a dime that top of his list will be Chardonnay and Cabernet Sauvignon. Then wander out and look at what's being planted and grafted in the vineyards – that's right, more Cabernet and more Chardonnay.

Now that every winery has a Chardonnay or three, and grape prices regularly go through the roof (most producers buy their fruit from farmers), the variety's name stands in danger of losing its cachet. This became apparent in the late 1980s when the Sebastiani winery unblushingly launched a wine labelled 'Domaine Chardonnay' that contained not a single drop of that variety; the effort was foiled by the authorities, but not without considerable discussion. Today, any wine labelled as Chardonnay or any other grape variety – has to contain at least 75% of that grape. These rules have not prevented at least one successful winery from selling Chardonnay that tastes as though it is made from 100% Muscat.

The Regions

If far too many of California's wines taste alike, the regions where they are made could hardly be more varied. Visitors who drive up from San Francisco to the Napa Valley, wander around the one or two well-known wineries – and imagine that they have 'seen' vinous California. In fact, there are vineyards and producers throughout the state, and even the big-names in the Napa buy grapes from other regions to broaden their range.

The climate varies enormously too. There are vineyards that are as cool as those of northern Germany, while others have everything in common with the oven-like conditions of north Africa. (For a clear picture of these varied climates, see the 'A Matter of Degrees' table on page 213). Elsewhere in the northern hemisphere, one might reasonably expect the temperature to rise as you head south. In California, latitude has far less of a role to play than the situation of the vineyard in relationship to the coast and the range of mountains that run parallel to it. Almost all of the best vineyards of the Napa Valley and Sonoma County benefit from the cooling effect of the fogs. Without them, the viability of most of California as a quality wine region would be very questionable.

Until recently, a majority of winemakers tended to believe that the difference between any two wines lay in the grapes from which they were made, the style of winemaking and the climate. Today, having learned to acknowledge that maybe the Europeans who talked about such things had a point, they are giving greater recognition to the effect of the soil.

So, within each of California's winemaking regions, the authorities are allocating AVAs – 'Approved Viticultural Areas' – in a way that sometimes recalls that of a mediaeval monarch creating dukes and earls. The legitimacy of some of the AVAs, like Stag's Leap in the Napa Valley for example, is unquestionable; that of some of the others, like Lodi in the bulk wine region of the Central Valley, smacks of local politics.

Napa Valley
The essential word here is 'valley'; this is one of the world's wider, flatter, more featureless pieces of vineyard land. The region's defenders counter any charges that this kind of land is less than ideal by pointing to the Médoc, where a lack of hills has not stopped anyone from making great wine. But the Médoc has magic soil, which is more than can be said for much of the Napa. There are some really special vineyards here though,

BELOW: Possibly the smartest small estate in California, the Newton Winery is situated high above St Helena in the Napa Valley. British born owner Peter Newton's Chinese-born wife is as involved in the winemaking as in the design of the gardens.

ABOVE RIGHT: Newcomers to the Napa Valley are not allowed to remain in any doubt about where they are. The quotation from Robert Louis Stevenson helps to remind them that winegrowing in California is no novelty.

Ceviche

Marinated fish salad

With its abundant fish, shellfish, vegetables and fruit, California is the most innovative part of America as far as cookery is concerned. With its emphasis on lightness and freshness, it has pioneered what might be called 'American nouvelle'.

SERVES 6-8 AS A STARTER
1 lb/500 g white fish fillets, skinned and boned (halibut, monkfish, hake or cod are good)
8 oz/225 g scallops
Juice of 4 limes
8 tbsp olive oil
1 garlic clove, peeled and crushed
½ tsp oregano
½ tsp dried thyme
1 tsp ground coriander seeds
½ green pepper, seeded and finely chopped
½ red pepper, seeded and finely chopped
4 spring onions, finely chopped
2 tomatoes, chopped
2 tbsp fresh parsley, finely chopped
Freshly ground black pepper to taste

Cut the fish and scallops into thin slices and place in a large glass or ceramic serving dish. Pour the lime juice over the fish, cover the dish with clingfilm and put in the refrigerator for 2 hours. Mix the remaining ingredients and stir into the marinated fish. Re-cover and refrigerate for at least an hour before serving.

THE ESSENTIALS — NAPA, LAKE AND MENDOCINO COUNTIES

Location 34 miles long, this region follows the Napa Valley in a north-westerly direction from San Francisco Bay, with the Sonoma Valley to the west. Lake and Mendocino are to the north of the Napa.
Quality AVAs are: Carneros; Howell Mountain; Napa Valley; Stag's Leap District; Anderson Valley; Mendocino; Cole Ranch; Clear Lake; Guenoc Valley; McDowell Valley; Potter Valley.
Style Top-quality dry whites and reds, with small quantities of botrytised whites. Some sparkling blush (rosé or white) wines are also made. Wines tend to be rich and powerful with maximum varietal expression. Chardonnays have good fruit character and the best, particularly from the cool Carneros region, have good acidity and balance. At their best the Sauvignons are fresh and grassy with an attractive softness. Some rich, intense botrytised Johannisberg Rieslings can also be found. Napa County produces some of the finest North American reds, particularly Cabernet Sauvignons. Good Pinots are made in the cool Carneros region which is shared by Sonoma.
Cultivation Vines tend to be grown, at altitudes ranging from sea level near the bay to 125m at Calistoga. Soils consist of gravel loams in the north and more fertile silt loams in the south.
Grape Varieties *Red*: Cabernet Sauvignon, Merlot, Pinot Noir, Zinfandel, Alicante Bouschet, Cabernet Franc, Carignan, Gamay Beaujolais, Malbec, Petite Syrah, Grenache. *White*: Chardonnay, Sauvignon Blanc, Chenin Blanc, Johannisberg Riesling, Gewürztraminer, Muscat, Sémillon.
Production/Maturation Methods, like the size of wineries, vary widely, although small 'boutique' wineries tend to employ traditional methods where possible while large firms use the latest high-tech methods.
Longevity *Reds*: Many are approachable when young but the best are capable of ageing for up to 20 years. *Whites*: Again, can be drunk immediately in most cases but the top wines can last for 10 to 20 years.
Vintage Guide Reds 74, 78, 80, 82, 84, 85, 96, 87
Whites 78, 80, 84, 85, 86, 87
Top Producers Caymus, Cuvaison, Dunn, Flora Springs, Heitz, Long, Mayacamas, Robert Mondavi, Joseph Phelps, Silver Oak, Stag's Leap Wine Cellars, Sterling, ZD, Newton, Saintsbury, Vichon, Fetzer, Trefethen, Schramsberg, Grgich Hills, Forman, Franciscan, Beringer, La Jota, Acacia, Duckhorn, Far Niente, Lamborne Family Vineyards, Frog's Leap, Opus One, Girard, Sterling.

THE ESSENTIALS — SONOMA COUNTY

Location North of San Francisco, situated between the Napa Valley and the Pacific Coast.
Quality AVAs: Alexander Valley; Chalk Hill; Dry Creek Valley; Knights Valley; Los Carneros; Northern Sonoma; Russian River Valley; Sonoma Coast; Sonoma County Green Valley; Sonoma Mountain; Sonoma Valley.
Style Very fine dry whites and reds, and good late-harvest, sparkling and blush wines. Wines from Sonoma are generally softer and more approachable than their Napa counterparts. Chardonnays are well struc-tured with good fruit and acidity, which, at their best, are stunning. Good 'fumé'-style Sauvignons are also made. Cabernet Sauvignons tend to be soft and juicy, although denser and more austere styles are made. Excellent Zinfandels, with rich spicy varietal character, and seductively soft Merlots are produced by several wineries. Pinot Noirs can be spectacularly good too.
Climate Like Napa County, the climate ranges from hot in the north to cool in the south, although the areas towards the coast benefit from the cooling effect of the Pacific ocean breezes. Fog can affect the southern areas.
Cultivation Most vines are grown on the floors or the gentle lower slopes of the Sonoma and Russian River Valleys. Soils vary considerably from loams to alluvial deposits; there are also unique local varieties such as Dry Creek Conglomerate.
Grape Varieties *Red*: Cabernet Sauvignon, Merlot, Pinot Noir, Zinfandel, Syrah, Petite Sirah, Alicante-Bouschet, Cabernet Franc, Gamay Beaujolais, Carignan, Grenache, Malbec. *White*: Chardonnay, Chenin Blanc, French Colombard, Sauvignon Blanc, Pinot Blanc, Gewürztraminer, Riesling, Chasselas, Muscat, Sémillon, Sylvaner.
Production/Maturation Plenty of bulk wine-making is carried on in the Russian River Valley but small 'boutique' wineries are growing in number, particularly in remote mountain locations.
Longevity Basic table wines can be drunk immediately. Top *reds* can last for up to 20 years; top *whites* up to 12 years.
Vintage Guide Reds 74, 78, 80, 82, 84, 85, 86, 87
Whites 78, 80, 84, 85, 86, 87
Top Producers Alexander Valley Vineyards, Buena Vista, Carmenet, Chateau St Jean, Clos du Bois, Dry Creek, Jordan, Laurel Glen, Mark West, Matanzas Creek, Ravenswood, Sonoma-Cutrer, De Loach, Kistler, La Crema, Iron Horse, Quivira, Simi.

such as the ones at Rutherford that Mondavi uses for its Cabernets, the extraordinary Martha's Vineyard where Heitz uses that grape to make wines that reek of eucalyptus.

The other most exciting parts of the Napa Valley are situated in the fog-cooled region Carneros that it shares with neighbouring Sonoma County, and the hillside areas such as the Mayacamas, Howell and Spring Mountains.

Sonoma

To get to Sonoma County from Santa Helena in the Napa Valley, the best and most memorable route is across a high wooded ridge called the Petrified Forest. It's fanciful I know, but I've always attributed magic powers to the forest; everything seems so different on the other side. Sonoma is somehow far more relaxed, less hyped and big-time than the Napa. Its varied, mostly farm-covered countryside is far fuller of individualists like Patrick Campbell with his Cabernet-based Laurel Glen reds and David Coleman with his Loire-style Sauvignon Blanc.

Among the parts of the region to remember are Carneros, 'California's Burgundy', Dry Creek where E&J Gallo have traditionally bought large quantities of grapes, but where some great Sauvignon Blancs (from Dry Creek Vineyards and Quivira) and Zinfandels are made and the Alexander Valley. This is the place to come for spectacular Cabernet Sauvignon (from Jordan) and Burgundy-style Chardonnays (from Simi) and the more avowedly 'Californian' ones made by Sonoma Cutrer in the nearby Russian River. Sparkling wines are very successful here too. Iron Horse can make the best in the state from its cool-climate vineyards, but Piper Sonoma's are pretty good too.

Lake County

Taking its name – and a welcoming cooling effect – from the biggest lake in the state, this is one of the most interesting regions of California. The Hollywood actress, Lillie Langtry started winemaking here around a century ago, today a label depicting her face still helps to sell bottles of Cabernet Sauvignon and Chardonnay made at the Guenoc Winery. The Kendall Jackson winery needs no such help to sell its wines; it relies instead on making 'dry' white wines that strike Europeans as tasting positively sweet. Watch out for wines from the hills of Humboldt County.

Mendocino

When the Champagne house of Roederer decided to follow its neighbours to California, it thought long and hard about where it could find the best grapes with which to make sparkling wine. Finally, they chose this schizophrenic region which, through a fluke of geography, can produce rich reds and lean whites. The coastal range protects red wine districts from the cooling fog while a gap in the hills allows it to have its beneficial effect on the heat-sensitive white grapes in the Anderson Valley.

Sierra Foothills

A large region to the east of the Napa Valley, this is old, gold-mining country where, if you hurry, in the Shenandoah Valley of Amador County, you can still find thick, port-like Zinfandels made the way they liked them in the day when real men had never even heard of quiche.

The Bay Area

Some of the roots of California's winemaking are to be found here, in Alameda County, in wineries like Wente and Concannon, both of which were founded in the 1880s. Today, Concannon still produces some really fine, full-flavoured Cabernet; Wente has preferred to concentrate its efforts on more commercial fare. Go to Santa Clara County though, and drive up the mountain track to the Ridge winery, and you'll be surprised to find a wooden shed, vineyards situated almost precisely on the San Andreas fault – and some spectacular Zinfandels.

North Central Coast

Once written off as too cold and dry, the region of Monterey to the south of San Francisco actually has conditions that vary from those of Champagne to those of the Rhône. Look out for juicy Cabernets and clean, fruity Rieslings from Jekel, produced in Aroyo Seco, and at classy Pinot Noirs and Chardonnays from Chalone's 2,000 ft vineyards.

For even better Pinot Noir, though, head for the AVA of San Benito County where Calera makes individual-vineyard examples that really are of Burgundy standard. And don't miss out on Bonny Doon, in mountainous Santa Cruz County, where Randy Grahm is producing his tremendous Rhône-style reds that have finally turned a few people's attention away from the totems of the Cabernet and Chardonnay.

South Central Coast

The counties of Santa Barbara and San Luis Obispo are two old regions that are finally – and very speedily – coming into their own. The cool Santa Maria and Edna Valley AVAs are good for Pinot Noir and Chardonnay, while the warmer Santa Ynez, as Firestone has proved, can produce rich Merlots. Look out too for big reds from Paso Robles.

Central Valley and Southern California

The warm, fertile 'Jug-wine' region of the Central Valley produces around two thirds of California's wines, almost none of it worthy of note. The only name worth remembering is that of Quady, the winery that makes spectacular sweet Essensia Orange Muscat. Southern California is mostly hot and dry, but the Temecula Valley has a cooler microclimate, allowing Callaway to make good, crisp whites.

THE ESSENTIALS — SOUTH-CENTRAL CALIFORNIA

Location San Luis Obispo, Santa Barbara and Southern California.
Quality *South-Central AVAs:* Edna Valley; Paso Robles; Santa Maria Valley; Santa Ynez Valley; York Mountain; San Pasqual Valley; South Coast; Temecula.
Style Good quality dry whites and reds and some sweet wines from the South-Central coast. The warm South-Central coast region produces rich, ripe and powerful wines with plenty of varietal character. Chardonnays are rich and toasty, while Johannisberg Rieslings can be either tangy and grapey yet still dry, or wonderfully luscious and rich when late-harvested. Reds are generally good but unexciting with warm and rounded fruit flavours. Exceptions are the Pinot Noirs and Zinfandels grown in the higher altitude locations of San Luis Obispo, which have intense fruit flavours because of the longer growing season.
Climate The coastal area is generally warm, though cooler at altitude or where fog encroaches inland.
Cultivation Soils are largely fertile sandy or silty loams. Hillside locations, generally south-facing, are favoured in the South-Central Coast area.
Grape Varieties *Red:* Cabernet Sauvignon, Barbera, Pinot Noir, Grenache, Zinfandel. *White:* Chardonnay, Chenin Blanc, French Colombard, Riesling, Sauvignon Blanc, Gewürztraminer.
Production/Maturation The coastal area uses oak for maturation and is a hot-bed of innovation and experimentation with premium grape varieties, notably those from the Rhône.
Longevity *Jug wines:* drink immediately. *Whites:* up to 8 years for the better quality Chardonnays. *Reds:* up to 12 years for the top wines
Vintage Guide Reds 74, 78, 81, 82, 84, 85, 86, 87, 88
Whites 80, 83, 84, 85, 86, 87, 88
Top Producers Edna Valley Vineyard, Firestone, Sanford, Zaca Mesa, Ojai, Calera, Qupé, Au Bon Climat, Vita Nova.

LEFT: Paul Draper of Ridge Vineyards is a rare believer in the importance of soil to wine quality. ABOVE: The Firestone Vineyards in the Santa Ynez Valley in Santa Barbara are cooler than they look.

THE ESSENTIALS — SOUTHERN, AND OTHER PARTS OF CALIFORNIA

Location Alameda, Santa Clara, Santa Cruz, Monterey, San Benito, Sierra Foothills, San Joaquin Valley.

Quality AVAs are: Arroyo Seco; Carmel Valley; Chalone; Cienega Valley; Lime Kiln Valley; Livermore Valley; Monterey; Paicines; San Benito; San Lucas; Santa Cruz Mountains Sierra Foothills; Eldorado; Fiddletown; Shenandoah Valley; Merced; Clarksburg; Lodi; Madera; Merritt Island; Solano-Green Valley; Suisun Valley.

Style Dry whites and rich, fruity reds, both of which can be outstanding. Small amounts of fine dessert wine are also produced. Whites can show good varietal character with plenty of fruit extract and good acidity. The Chardonnays, in particular, are full of flavour and the complex examples from Chalone and Mount Eden rank amongst the best made anywhere in the States. Although some juicy Cabernet Sauvignons are made, the region is better known for its Zinfandels and Pinot Noirs. The former are rich in berry fruit and require ageing while the latter are packed with rich, velvety fruit. The remarkable Bonny Doon vineyard produces some brilliant wines, notably a rich, perfumed 'Vin de Glacière' sweet style and a large range of Rhône varietals including Syrah, Marsanne and Roussanne. The Central Valley produces a lot of sound commercial 'jug' wine but is capable of making some better quality wines in the hands of small conscientious wine-makers.

Climate Generally warm, although the effects of altitude and sea breezes produce cooler micro-climates.

Cultivation Vines are located on the flat and gently sloping lands of the valleys although some producers have chosen the Santa Cruz Mountains. Soils are varieties of gravel loam.

Grape Varieties Red: Cabernet Sauvignon, Pinot Noir, Zinfandel, Syrah, Petite Sirah, Carignan, Gamay. White: Chardonnay, Chenin Blanc, Riesling, Sauvignon Blanc, Gewürztraminer, French Colombard, Semillon.

Production/Maturation The large producers of the Central Valley harvest the irrigated fruit mechanically and ferment the wine in temperature-controlled stainless steel tanks. The smaller, quality-conscious producers of the other regions are very keen on more traditional methods (oak maturation, etc) and experimentation. Bonny Doon is a fine example of innovative wine-making.

Longevity Drink *Jug wines* immediately. *Whites* can be kept for up to 10 years. *Reds* will improve for 15 years (up to 20 for the very best Zinfandels).

Vintage Guide Reds 74, 78, 81, 83, 84, 85, 86, 87, 88
Whites 78, 80, 82, 84, 85, 86, 87, 88

Top Producers Bonny Doon, Chalone, Jekel, Mount Eden, Ridge, Sarah's Vineyard, Quady, Angelo Papagni.

A MATTER OF DEGREES

In the 1920s, a scientist called A.J Winkler at the Davis Campus wine faculty of the University of California, developed a system of 'heat summation' which classified regions by 'degree days'.

Winkler took the northern hemisphere growing period - the 182 days between April 1 to October 31 - and established the average daily temperature for that period for any given region. From that figure he subtracted 50°, the Farenheit temperature at which grapes ripen, and multiplied the result by the 182. So, a cool area where the average temperature was 60 would have a 1,820 heat units (60-50 x 182) while a warmer one where the thermometer registered a steady 70 would have 364.

Armed with this overly simplistic but still useful formula and a slide rule, Winkler was able to divide up the winemaking world - and California - into the following five regions. The flaw to the Winkler scale lies in the fact that it is based on averages and lumps together regions with very different climates. Grapes are as affected by when the weather is warm as by the temperature itself.

Region I (2,000-2,500 degree days) *Champagne, Côte d'Or, Rhine* Anderson Valley, Carneros, Edna Valley, Marin County, Mendocino, Monterey, Napa, Russian River Valley, Santa Clara, Sonoma *Recommended grapes:* Riesling, Chardonnay, Sauvgnon Blanc, Cabernet Sauvignon, Pinot Noir

Region II (2,500-3,000 degree days) *Bordeaux* Alexander Valley, Anderson Valley, Chalk Hill, Edna Valley, Mendocino, Monterey, Napa, Potter Valley, Russian River Valley, Santa Clara, Sonoma. *Recommended grapes:* Chardonnay, Sauvignon Blanc, Cabernet Sauvignon, Pinot Noir, Merlot.

Region III (3,000-3,500 degree days) *Rhône* Alameda, Alexander Valley, Contra Costa, El Dorada, Knight's Valley, Lake, McDowell Valley, Mendocino, Monterey, Napa, Paso Robles, Placer, Redwood Valley, Riverside, San Benito, Santa Clara, Sonoma. *Recommended grapes:* Carignan, Ruby Cabernet, Zinfandel, Syrah, Sauvignon Blanc, Semillon.

Region IV (3,500-4,000 degree days) *South of Spain.* Amador, Calveras, El Dorado, Fresno, Merced, Riverside, Sacramento, San Diego, San Joaquin, Yolo. *Recommended grapes:* port, varieties, Ruby Cabernet, Barbera, Emerald Riesling.

Region V (over 4,000 degree days) *North Africa* Amador, Calveras, Fresno, Kern, Madera, Sacramento, San Bernardino, San Diego, San Joaquin, Stanislaus, Tulare *Recommended grapes:* port and Madeira varieties.

PACIFIC NORTH-WEST

The north-west of the United States is a wonderful antidote to some of the over-hyped regions of California. These three states – Oregon, Washington and Idaho – are full of small wineries, strugggling to survive financially, and against a potentially unfriendly climate. But they're making some really good wines...

Oregon

Oregon is Pinot Noir country, and the red soil of the Dundee hills in this part of the Willamette Valley has produced Pinots that have stood their own in tastings against top-class Burgundies. But as recently as the early 1960s, the only grape thought suited to the cold, damp conditions here was the Riesling, and the potential of even this relatively hardy variety was disputed by the experts at the University of California, who more or less discounted Oregon's chances to make it in the big time of quality wine making.

In 1965, however, a California-trained winemaker called David Lett, recognising similarities between the Oregon climate and that of Burgundy, resolved to prove those experts wrong by establishing the Willamette Valley's first vineyards – and planting them with Pinot Noir vines. Over the following two decades Lett was joined by a succession of fellow pioneers, almost all of whom shared his passion for the elusive wild raspberry flavour. Almost from the beginning, these producers proved successful in replicating Burgundy in a remarkable number of ways. Their estates were small, their vintages were varied (though astonishingly similar to those of Burgundy itself) their prices were high, and they often had little idea of why one wine had turned out to be so much better than the next.

Partly as an attempt to expand their knowledge, and partly as a piece of public relations, the Oregonians launched an annual Pinot Noir celebration in the small town of McMinnville and invited winemakers from throughout the world to participate in seminars covering every aspect of winemaking.

So far, the Oregonians' efforts have only partly paid off.

Apart from a set of promising wineries – David Lett's Eyrie Vineyards, Adelsheim, Amity, Ponzi, Bethel Heights, Cameron and Knusden Erath – most of Oregon's producers are making wine that is lean, light-bodied and short-lived. Uncertainty over clones of both Pinot Noir and Chardonnay might account for the failure of some of these wines to live up to Oregon's potential.

But the Oregonians are great experimenters, and as their experiments begin to bear fruit, as they discover that they can make good wine from other grape varieties (both David Lett and David Adelsheim have produced first-class Pinot Gris), and as they learn from the wines that will be made here by such experienced French Pinot-handlers as Véronique Drouhin from Burgundy and Laurent Perrier from Champagne, theirs will be a region to watch, particularly when it recovers from the overdose of hype to which it was subjected in the late 1980s. Oregon's wines will never be cheap – the cost of land and the often unfriendly climate both keep prices high – but the combination of keenness, soil and climate give them every reason to be world class.

Washington

In the right hands, Washington grapes can produce better wine at a lower price than any but the best wineries in California. The confusing thing about Washington, though, is that when the state boundaries were drawn they took no account of climate. To give a general comment on the weather in Washington is rather like lumping together Scotland and Algeria. In Seattle, the slug is an unofficial local emblem and the semi-tropical rainforest across the bay from the city has become a tourist curiosity. Further south, on the west side of the Cascade Mountains, the climate is very similar to that of Oregon, but worse. The conditions here are cool, damp and attractive only to a small group of masochists led by Joan Wolverton of Salishan Vineyards, who (quite rightly) believe that this kind of 'marginal' weather does wonders for grape varieties such as Pinot

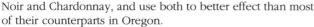

LEFT: The Amity vineyards are situated in the pine-covered, red-soiled hills of Oregon. The cool climate here suits Burgundy's Pinot Noir
ABOVE: Eastern Washington is an almost totally rain-free area; vineyards like these, at Blackwood Canyon in the Yakima Valley, have to be irrigated to survive

Noir and Chardonnay, and use both to better effect than most of their counterparts in Oregon.

It is the area east of the Cascades, however, that ought to be bothering the Californians. At first glance this looks like land in which nothing thirstier than a cactus could ever be farmed. But irrigation here is sophisticated; half-mile long sprinklers pivoting on the centre of the vineyards, feeding them a stready mist of life-preserving moisture.

Vines have been grown in Washington since the mid-19th century, but the potential of the dry land of the Yakima Valley was only explored in the early 20th century, and no good wine was made until 1969 – partly because the farmers had not troubled to plant high-quality grape varieties, and partly because local laws effectively prevented producers from selling their wine anywhere other than in bars. These rules more or less obliged would-be wine drinkers to make their own, and it was these home wine makers who, using grapes grown in the Yakima Valley and Walla Walla, created the Washington wine industry that exists today. Even Columbia, one of the state's biggest wineries, was started by a group of academics who formed themselves a company they named Associated Vintners.

From the beginning, one of the most popular grapes here has been the Riesling, and it is certainly a Washington success, with some wonderful late-harvest versions being made by Kiona, for example. But Washington's winemakers are having just as much success with buttery Chardonnay (try the one from Hogue Cellars), green, gooseberryish Sauvignon Blanc (from Columbia Crest) and, perhaps most particularly, Merlot (from Gordon Brothers, Stewart, Quilceda Creek and Mercer Ranch). At their best these wines are packed with fruit, but have a bite of fresh acidity often lacking in commercial California wines.

Land in Washington is cheap, the weather and irrigation are reliable and the winemakers are – so far at least – unaffected by the hype that has pushed prices up elsewhere, so the future for tasty, affordable wine looks bright.

Idaho

Idaho's wines come mostly from the savagely barren Snake Valley in the east of the state, from vineyards planted at an altitude of 2,300ft (700m). According to the Winkler scale of heat units, which acknowledges only the average amount of heat received by the grapes, this oughtn't to matter. In practice, however, when the temperature drops the fruit simply fail to ripen. So despite the fact that the sun-tanned Idaho residents complain of the highest incidence of skin cancer in the USA, the grapes they grow produce wine that tastes as though it comes from somewhere far cooler.

One way Idaho winemakers have dealt with this is to ship in grapes from Washington and Oregon – in the case of one

winery for a while, forgetting to mention the fact on its label. Today Château Ste Chapelle – the designer winery responsible for that lapse of memory – has a first-class new winemaker with the memorable name of Mini Mook, who uses local fruit to make good sparkling wine and Riesling, and 'Washington Cabernet' now openly and unashamedly graces the labels of its deep, rich reds. The Rose Creek winery has also been spectacularly successful with Washington Cabernet, and Hell's Canyon is doing well with a light Chardonnay many a Californian would have been proud to have made.

THE ESSENTIALS — THE PACIFIC NORTH-WEST

Region The Pacific North-West area encompasses the states of Washington, Oregon and Idaho.

Quality AVAs: Columbia Valley, Umpqua Valley, Walla Walla Valley, Willamette Valley, Yakima Valley.

Style Washington produces soft, ripe Chardonnays, fragrant Rieslings and aromatic Gewürztraminers. Sémillons and Sauvignons showing typical varietal character are also made. The reds are impressive with the soft Merlots and minty Cabernet Sauvignons being the most notable. Oregon is best known for its high quality Pinot Noirs, which are rich in soft, plump fruit, but some good whites are also made. The Chardonnays have a soft yet crisp character, while the Rieslings and Gewürztraminers have a fragrant appeal. Idaho makes some crisp, yet rich and alcoholic Chardonnays and Rieslings that have good fruit. Reds are generally less successful .

Climate Oregon is the coolest Pacific state as a result of sea breezes, otherwise its climate is generally continental. Washington is very variable: over 100in of rain falls on the coast, but vineyards inland rely heavily on irrigation; the Cascade Mountains shield eastern Washington from the rain and sea breezes. Idaho enjoys typical continental climatic conditions with a high altitude and widely varying temperatures. The vintage variations in Washington are far less significant than in Oregon.

Cultivation Vines are mainly located in valleys or on low-lying slopes to escape frosts. Soils are silty, sandy or clay loams.

Grape Varieties *Reds*: Pinot Noir, Merlot, Cabernet Sauvignon, Zinfandel, Pinot Gris. *Whites*: Chardonnay, Riesling, Sauvignon Blanc, Chenin Blanc, Gewürztraminer, Sémillon, Muscat.

Production/Maturation Stainless steel is widely used for fermentation and oak for maturation, although the winemakers are open to experimentation. Washington vines are ungrafted.

Longevity Most wines are bottled ready to drink but *whites* can develop for up to 5 years; Washington, and good Oregon PinotNoir *reds* for up to 8 years.

Vintage Guide (Oregon) Reds 85, 87, 88.
Whites 85, 86, 87.

Top Producers *Idaho*: Ste Chapelle, Hell's Canyon, Rose Creek. *Oregon*: Amity, Adelsheim, Eyrie, Knusden Erath, Cameron, Bethel Heights, Ponzi. *Washington*: Arbor Crest, Hogue, Columbia, Chateau Ste Michelle, Covey Run, Gordon, Woodward Canyon, Kiona, Stewart, Quilceda Creek, Chinook, Salishan.

OTHER WINES OF NORTH AMERICA

The fact that California has been allowed to hog the limelight of North American wine is hardly surprising; after all, it does produce 95% of the nation's wine. The fact that most of the other states do not make large quantities of high-quality wine is not for want of trying, however. The problem is that climatic conditions often offer a choice between feast and famine. Some regions suffer such bitterly cold winters that even the hardiest vines cannot survive. In other, warmer, corners of the country, such as Florida, the problem is the reverse; the absence of winter may be ideal for octagenarian sun-seekers, but it plays havoc with plants such as vines, depriving them of the essential low temperatures that kill off the bugs.

The only vines that can reliably survive in such extreme conditions are the native labrusca, which have been in North America long enough to grow used to them, and the more recently developed hybrids. Vinifera, the kind of grape from which the world's best wines are made, has a tougher time. All of which makes more impressive the determination of a growing number of winemakers in Canada and no less than 43 states of the Union to make good wine from vinifera grapes.

Unfortunately, though, even when they succeed in overcoming the handicaps of climate and pests, producers in many states still often have to deal with the stalwart opposition of local officialdom. The anti-alcohol lobby, which for 13 years succeeded in halting the legal sale of wine and spirits, is still strong enough in some parts of North America to hinder and, in some instances, to prevent its sale.

The North-East

There are two main winemaking regions of New York State: the Finger Lakes in the far north of the state and Long Island just over the bridge from Manhattan. The former area can be very chilly, but it produces good Germanic-style whites and, at the Wagner winery, some wonderfully fruit-salady Chardonnay. Long Island enjoys a Bordeaux-like micro-climate that allows winemakers such as Alex Hargrave to make top-class Merlot and Chardonnay. This is curious country where land is traditionally used either to grow potatoes or for million-dollar holiday homes for weekending New Yorkers. If wineries survive as the meat between this sandwich, this could be one of the most exciting winemaking regions in the USA.

Elsewhere on the north-east coast, Connecticut has lots of hybrids and labrusca and the Crosswoods winery, which makes good Chardonnay, Pinot Noir and Gamay. Massachusetts is the region where, in 1602, Bartholomew found a vine-covered island he called Martha's Vineyard. Today various vinifera are grown and made into wine here by the Chicama winery; their Chardonnay is particularly good.

New Hampshire has little to offer the wine lover, but several wineries in New Jersey are trying hard with vinifera. The best of these are probably Tewksbury, Renault and Alba. William Penn believed that the state to which he gave his name could make wine 'as good as any European countries of the same latitude', but there appeared to be few grounds for that confidence until this century. Today good Pennsylvania Rieslings are made on Lake Erie, while less hardy varieties do better in the south-east of the state. Names to look out for here are Chadds Ford, Allegro, Naylor and Presque Isle.

The South-East

Despite the curious allocation of the first AVA on the East Coast to Mississippi, a state where all of the wine is made from the low-quality local Muscadine, there are few friendly places for quality grapes in the south-east. In Virginia, however, there is still a vineyard and winery at Monticello, the old home of the wine-loving President Jefferson. This state is gearing itself up to compete with Oregon and New York State as a good cool-climate region. Whites are generally better than reds, but wineries such as Meredyth have been successful with Cabernet Sauvignon. Elsewhere, Montbray Wine Cellars have made Riesling Ice Wine in Maryland, while, in Arkansas, where the winters can be cold enough to kill fruit trees, there are warmer micro-climates that allow the Post Winery and Wiederkehr Wine Cellars to perservere with Cabernet Sauvignon.

The Mid-West

Few of the states here have proved successful with vinifera, but cool Michigan has wineries such as Boskydel, Fenn Valley and Tabor Hill, making good Riesling, while Ohio, once the biggest winemaking state of the Union, has Firelands, Grand River and Markko, all of which are making impressive Chardonnay and are progressing with other quality varieties.

THE ESSENTIALS — REST OF THE UNITED STATES AND CANADA

Quality The following are major AVAs: *Arizona*: Sonoita. *Arkansas*: Altus, Arkansas Mountain, Ozark Mountain. *Mississippi*: Mississippi Delta. *Missouri*: Augusta, Hermann, Old Mission Peninsula, Ozark Highlands. *New Mexico*: Middle Rio Grande Valley, Mimbres Valley. *Texas*: Bell Mountain, Fredericksburg, Mesilla Valley. *Canada* is hampered by having no quality-control laws, but archaic liquor laws instead; however, the main wine-producing areas are: Niagara Peninsula, Ontario; Okanagan Valley, British Columbia; Alberta and Nova Scotia.

Style Dry, medium and sweet whites, reds and sparkling wines are all produced. Most wines are made from classic grape varieties with some creamy Chardonnays coming from Texas and decent Cabernet Sauvignons from Arkansas and Texas. Both these states show good potential for the future. In Canada, plenty of *labrusca* wine is produced although some good dry whites and light fruity reds are made in the Niagara region. Chardonnays show good fruit character with a restrained oaky richness. Rieslings can be made dry or rich and honeyed if harvested late as "ice wines". Some good quality sparkling wines are produced from Chardonnay. Light, fruity reds are made from Pinot Noir, Gamay and Cabernet Sauvignon. Imported grape concentrate is also used for a number of wines. *Labrusca* varieties are used for sparkling and sweet wines.

Climate Obviously, varies considerably, with Texas and New Mexico being hot and fairly dry and the other states of the south-east being wetter. In Canada, near European conditions may prevail: The Ontario region enjoys a temperate climate similar to that of Tuscany, with the Niagara Escarpment acting as a wind-break. However, the Okanagan Valley of British Columbia has very hot temperatures during the day and cold nights.

Cultivation Vines are grown on a variety of soils and generally on flatter, lower-lying ground below the snow line. Canadian vines tend to grow on lakeside slopes, where the main soil types are sandy loams and gravel.

Grape Varieties *Red*: Cabernet Sauvignon, Carignan, Grenache, Merlot, Zinfandel. *White*: Chardonnay, Chenin Blanc, Gewürztraminer, Moscato, Riesling, Sauvignon Blanc. Canada also grows the *vinifera* Aligoté, Cabernet Franc, Chasselas, Gamay, Petite Sirah, Pinot Gris and Pinot Noir, as well as the *labrusca* Agawama, Alden, Buffalo, Catawba, Concord, Delaware, Elvira, Niagara, Patricia and President.

Production/Maturation Most wineries have modern equipment with stainless steel fermentation and wood maturation in common use.

Longevity *Whites* can be aged for 1 to 4 years, *reds* for 3 to 8.

Top Producers *Arizona*: RW Webb. *Arkansas*: Wiederkehr Wine Cellars. *Mississippi*: Almarla Vineyards, Clairbone. *Missouri*: Mt Pleasant Vineyards. *New Mexico*: Anderson Valley Vineyards, La Vina *Texas*: Pheasant Ridge, Sanchez Creek. *Canada*: *British Columbia*: Calona Wines, Mission Hill, Andres Wines. *Ontario*: Andres Wines, Brights Wines, Chateau des Charmes, Inniskillin, Jordan & Ste Michelle Cellars.

The Pindar winery on Long Island is clearly proud of its nationality. Despite the growing success of wineries such as this one in New York and throughout the USA, far too many people imagine California to be the only state that produces wine.

The South-West

The wines of Texas and Arizona stand as tributes to the self-belief of the residents of these states; it's a brave man who'll tell a Texan that he can't do anything as well as a Californian. So, despite the hot climate of both states, cool, high-altitude sites have been found, where decent, if not great, wines can be made. In Arizona, look for Cabernet Sauvignon made near Tucson by Sonoita Vineyard and Riesling produced in the Four Corners region by RW Webb. The Bordeaux firm of Cordier has made successful Sauvignon Blanc in Texas and Pheasant Ridge and Llano Estacado have made good reds.

Hawaiian wine may sound like a joke, but the Tedeschi Vineyard makes sparkling wine using the Carnelian grape. It is not one of the world's greatest fizzes, but it's well made.

Canada

The readiness of Canadians to drink 'Canadian' wine made from imported grape concentrate has offered little incentive to quality-oriented producers to try to see what could be made. Besides, with temperatures cold enough to kill vines in the winter, prospects for vinifera seemed bleak. Fortunately, a few wineries in Ontario and British Columbia have persevered with vineyards situated in warmer micro-climates – and been rewarded with prize-winning sparkling wines, Rieslings and Chardonnays. The best wines – so far – are white and late harvested; wineries to look out for are Inniskillin, Hillebrand, Château des Charmes, Mission Hill, Gehringer and Gray Monk.

THE ESSENTIALS — ATLANTIC NORTH-EAST

Region Group of states – New York State, Pennyslvania, Maryland, Michigan, Ohio and Virginia – located between the Great Lakes and the Atlantic Ocean.

Quality AVAs are: Catoctin, Cayuga Lake, Central Delaware Valley, Cumberland Valley, Fennville, Finger Lakes, Grand River Valley, Hudson River Region, Isle St George, Kanawha River Valley, Lake Erie, Lake Michigan Shore, Lancaster Valley, Leelanau Peninsula, Linganore, Loramie Creek, Martha's Vineyard, Monticello, Northern Neck George Washington Birthplace, North Fork of Long Island, Ohio River Valley.

Style The white wines produced in the states of the Atlantic seaboard tend to be crisp and light, although the Hudson River area produces richer, toasty Chardonnays. Reds are similarly light in body and have plenty of acidity. The best wines come from Long Island, notably some lovely grassy Sauvignons and crisp, intense and oaky Chardonnays. Cabernet Sauvignons and Pinot Noirs tend to be rather green. Sound sparkling wines are produced along with tiny quantities of sweet wine made from Riesling or Gewürztraminer.

Climate Continental, with severe winters moderated by the tempering effects of the Atlantic Ocean and the large areas of inland waters, such as the Finger Lakes and Lake Michigan, to produce suitable vinegrowing micro-climates.

Cultivation Vines are mainly grown on the flat shores of lakes or the lower slopes of mountain ranges. Soils vary considerably with limestone-based soils in Pennyslvania, Ohio and Virginia, glacial scree in Michigan and a mixture of shale, slate and limestone in New York. Silty loams and gravel are also found, mainly in Virginia.

Grape Varieties *Vinifera*: Chardonnay, Cabernet Sauvignon, Gewürztraminer, Merlot, Pinot Noir, Riesling. *Labrusca:* Concord, Catawba, Delaware, Ives. *Hybrids:* Vidal Blanc, Aurore, Seyval Blanc, Baco Noir, Maréchal Foch and Chelois.

Production/Maturation New vinification technology and the use of sprays is resulting in a growing number of *vinifera* varieties being grown, although in some areas the vines have to be buried under several feet of earth in order to survive the harsh winters. Traditional methods are used for sparkling wine production.

Longevity Most wines are for early drinking although some can be kept for 3 to 7 years.

Top Producers *Maryland*: Elk Run. *Michigan*: Lakeside Vineyard, Tabor Hill. *New York Finger Lakes:* Gold Seal, Wagner, and Hermann Wiemer. *New York Long Island:* Hargrave, Bridgehampton, Pindar, Bidwell.

SOUTH AMERICA

1 MEXICO	5 CHILE
SOUTH AMERICA	North-Central
2 BRAZIL	Central Valley
Caxias do Sul	South-Central Valley
Garibaldi/Bento Gonçalves	Southern Region
3 URUGUAY	Central Secano
4 ARGENTINA	South-Central Secano
San Juan	6 PERU
La Rioja	7 COLOMBIA
Mendoza	8 PARAGUAY
Rio Negro	9 BOLIVIA

South and Central America

The winemaking countries of Central and South America are still chips off the old Iberian block. Attitudes and tastes remain very close to those that modernists such as Miguel Torres have had such difficulty in banishing from Spain. Old wines that have spent a long period oxidising in large barrels are still generally considered to be better than fresh and fruity ones.

Local economic problems have not only ensured that there is little opportunity to taste wines from other countries, but also that prices have remained low. Sadly, with the exception of the best wines from a few quality-conscious producers, standards are still set by the lowest common denominator.

Mexico

The country from which the first vines to be planted in California were imported is not an ideal place to make wine. Half of Mexico is within the tropics and wholly unsuitable for grape-growing; the rest is divided between areas that are too hot or too dry. Perhaps inevitably, the average Mexican is not a great wine lover; annual consumption currently stands at around a bottle a year – about a ninth of the amount drunk by the British or Americans. The Domecq winery does produce some reasonable soft reds, but little to set the world alight.

Chile

This, on the other hand, is what Miguel Torres has described as a viticultural paradise. A combination of mountains and sea have entirely escaped the attentions of the phylloxera louse and all kinds of other pest. The climate of the Central Valley, where the top-quality grapes are planted, is neither too warm, nor too

LEFT: Despite the size and age of its wine industry, Chile has suprisingly few wineries, and an even smaller number that make high quality wine. The Errazuriz Panquehue estate and winery is one of the best in the country. ABOVE: The Andes provide essential water for irrigation.

cool, and a lack of rain is amply compensated for by the ready availability of snow-melt irrigation from the Andes.

Unfortunately, Chile has only six wineries – Cousiño Macul, Santa Rita, Errazuriz Panquehue/Caliterra, Los Vascos, Montes/ Nogales and Concha y Toro – that are really doing much to develop the potential of Chilean wine. At their best, Chile's Cabernet Sauvignons can be wonderfully soft, rich, blackcurranty and smoky – like a cross between Bordeaux and Rioja. Unfortunately, some are dull, others are dilute. The whites are less impressive so far, but the Chardonnays of several wineries are improving.

Argentina

The fact that this is the fourth largest wine-producing country in the world comes as a surprise to most people. But, with the reopening of relations with Britain, and the thirst of the North Americans for inexpensive varietal wines, the picture is changing very quickly. At the Esmeralda *bodega* close to Mendoza, for example, advice from top-class Californian winemakers is already paying off in the shape of good Chardonnay and some impressive Cabernet, Merlot and Syrah. And the Weinert winery won a Silver Medal in the 1990 *WINE Magazine* International Challenge for its Cabernet Sauvignon.

The grape that may be among the most interesting in Argentina, though, is the Malbec, which, though not ideally suited to being used by itself, can give blends some wonderfully spicy flavours. Another Argentinian speciality is the Torrontes, a Muscat-like grape whose wines smell as though they are going to taste sweet but are, in fact, quite dry.

Brazil

Wine is made close to Porto Alegre around the towns of Bento Gonçalves and Garibaldi, and at Palomas on the southern border with Uruguay. The former region is too wet to be ideal, though companies such as Moët & Chandon and Martini & Rossi do their best. The Palomas winery offers greater possibilities but, so far, the wines are light and undistinguished.

Other Countries of South America

Despite a long history of winemaking, there are no good wines to be found yet in Peru or Uruguay, though when winemakers learn to avoid the effects of oxidation, both countries' vineyards have potential. Which is more than can be said for most of those of Bolivia, Paraguay, Ecuador and Colombia.

THE ESSENTIALS — SOUTH AND CENTRAL AMERICA

Quality Only Chile has a form of quality control.
Style Chile is best known for its slightly earthy, soft, fruity reds made from Cabernet Sauvignon, Merlot and Malbec. Clean but dull Sauvignons and some Chardonnay and Gewürztraminer are also made.
Argentina produces a large amount of inexpensive and generally well-made wine. The whites are soft and rounded and may lack acidity: the reds are better, medium-weight with good fruit. Mexico has a long history of wine production but much of it is distilled into brandy or tequila. Recent investment by European companies has produced red and white wines of decent quality. Brazil and Uruguay produce large amounts of wine; the whites tend to be rather dull but the reds show more promise.
Climate Widely varying in most countries with extreme fluctuations of temperature and either too much or too little rain causing great problems. Chile is particularly variable. The north is hot and arid while the south receives a great deal of rain. Around Santiago it is dry, frost-free and sunny. Argentina's Mendoza district has a semi-desert climate, with lower rain levels than Chile, although it is spread over the growing season.
Cultivation Vines are generally cultivated on flatter lands, notably coastal and valley plains, although some hillside sites are used in Chile. Soils vary considerably, although sand, clay and alluvial soils are common. Chile has good limestone-based soils.
Grape Varieties *Red*: Barbera, Bonarda, Cabernet Franc, Cabernet Sauvignon, Carignan, Grenache, Malbec, Merlot, Nebbiolo, Pinot Gris, Pinot Noir, Syrah, Tempranillo, Zinfandel. *White*: Chardonnay, Chenin Blanc, Riesling, Lambrusco, Sauvignon Blanc, Pinot Blanc, Sémillon, Ugni Blanc, Palomino.
Production/Maturation Recent interest in wine production in these regions means that modern equipment and methods are fairly widespread although Chile and Argentina still use traditional methods as well. Irrigation is widely used, as is cold fermentation, resulting in fresher, fruitier wines.
Longevity *Whites* are best drunk within two to three years and *reds* within four to five years, though some can develop for 10 years or more.
Top Producers *Chile*: Concha Y Toro, Cousino Macul, Santa Rita, Miguel Torres, Errazuriz Panquehue, Nogales/Montes, Los Vascos. *Argentina*: Esmeralda, Finca Flichman, San Telmo, Weinert.

Pollo Borracho

Chicken braised with ham, white wine and herbs

Although the chicken was only introduced into South America by the Spanish *conquistadores* it quickly became popular, as is this dish throughout the continent.

SERVES 4
1 onion, minced
3 garlic cloves, peeled and minced
2 tbsp olive or vegetable oil
3 oz/85 g ham, diced
4 chicken breast fillets, skinned
¹/₂ tsp cumin
¹/₂ tsp dried sage, crumbled
15 fl oz/450 ml dry white wine
10 fl oz/300 ml chicken stock

In a large flameproof casserole, sauté the onion and garlic in the oil until the onion is soft. Add half the ham in a layer, followed by the chicken in one layer, topped by the rest of the ham. Sprinkle with cumin and sage. Add the wine and enough stock to cover the chicken. Simmer for 30 minutes or until the chicken is cooked. Remove the chicken and ham to a warm serving dish. Heat the remaining sauce over a moderately high heat, stirring, until it thickens. Pour the sauce over the chicken and serve with rice or warmed pitta bread.

AUSTRALIA

In 1987, while teams of yachtsmen from Australia and the USA raced against each other off the coast for the Americas Cup, held in Perth, a group of internationally respected tasters took part in the Qantas Cup, a parallel challenge that set wines from both countries against each other in a blind tasting. On the water the Americans took the prize; when it came to the wine it was an Australian walkover.

The first reactions from the Californian winemakers was that their wines had fared badly because of the effect of the trip halfway across the world. The following year, the tasting was held in the Napa Valley; the Australian wines – clearly better long-distance travellers than their US counterparts – won an even more resounding victory. There was no Qantas Cup tasting in 1989 and 1990.

Despite their success in those tastings, and in others in Europe, where they did similarly well against some of the cream

of the crop of France and Germany, Australia's wines are still only beginning to receive international recognition. In California, for instance, there are still very few winemakers who acknowledge them to represent any kind of serious competition. In some ways, the Californians' point of view is quite understandable. For starters, by comparison with their wine industry, Australia produces a tiny amount of wine. And then there's the fact that the Aussies were relatively slow to promote their wines. While the world was growing familiar with names such as Mondavi and Heitz, few people outside Australia had so much as heard of Penfolds, Lindemans or Orlando.

Besides, to most outsiders, the Australians were far busier extolling the qualities of their beers. One of the most surprising things about the surprising continent of Australia is the way in which a nation of beer drinkers has fallen in love with wine. Today the Australians are some of the keenest of wine drinkers

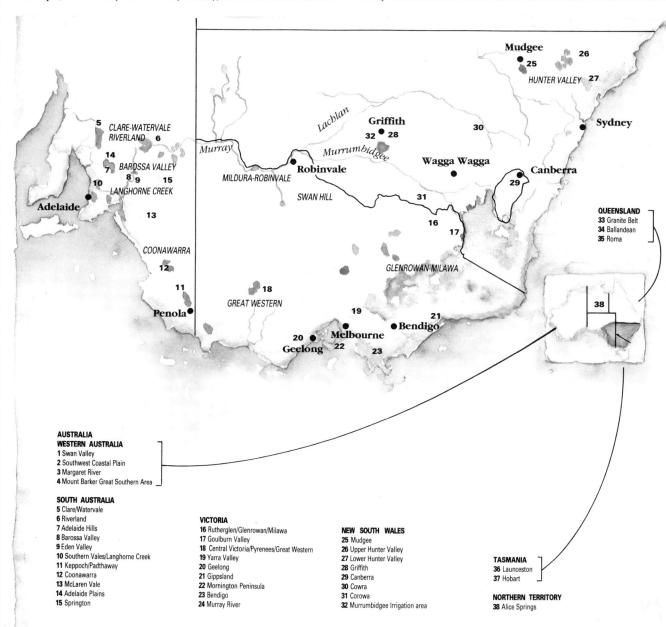

AUSTRALIA
WESTERN AUSTRALIA
1 Swan Valley
2 Southwest Coastal Plain
3 Margaret River
4 Mount Barker Great Southern Area

SOUTH AUSTRALIA
5 Clare/Watervale
6 Riverland
7 Adelaide Hills
8 Barossa Valley
9 Eden Valley
10 Southern Vales/Langhorne Creek
11 Keppoch/Padthaway
12 Coonawarra
13 McLaren Vale
14 Adelaide Plains
15 Springton

VICTORIA
16 Rutherglen/Glenrowan/Milawa
17 Goulburn Valley
18 Central Victoria/Pyrenees/Great Western
19 Yarra Valley
20 Geelong
21 Gippsland
22 Mornington Peninsula
23 Bendigo
24 Murray River

NEW SOUTH WALES
25 Mudgee
26 Upper Hunter Valley
27 Lower Hunter Valley
28 Griffith
29 Canberra
30 Cowra
31 Corowa
32 Murrumbidgee Irrigation area

QUEENSLAND
33 Granite Belt
34 Ballandean
35 Roma

TASMANIA
36 Launceston
37 Hobart

NORTHERN TERRITORY
38 Alice Springs

Australia is more of a continent than a country, and winegrowing conditions vary almost as much as they do in Europe. This Hill Smith Heggies Vineyard in South Australia's Barossa Valley looks very different from the slopes of the Rhine, but it still produces great 'Rhine Riesling'.

in the world, with an annual per capita intake of over 20 litres per person – around twice the figure for Britain or the USA. And they don't just drink a lot of the stuff, they take an enormous interest in what it tastes like, how it is made and where it comes from. Books on what most outsiders would consider to be such obscure Aussie wine regions as the Clare Valley can sell as many copies to a market of 16 million Australians as one on Bordeaux or California might to 270 million North Americans.

So what was it that turned the Australians on to wine? Travel must have played a part; this is a remarkably well-travelled nation; Europe is liberally scattered with Volkswagen busfuls of young Antipodeans eagerly working, eating and drinking their way from one part of the continent to the other before heading back home with a taste for the good life. Then, of course, there have been the immigrants who have brought with them all kinds of 'foreign' flavours that would have been quite unfamiliar to the Anglo-Saxon colonists.

A more mischievous explanation was provided by a cynical journalist who gave the credit to the sexual revolution, which led to young Australian males growing bored with the men-only, beer-swilling ethos of the bars and 'hotels' in which they used to do their drinking. Wine was a social drink that you could enjoy with the 'barbie' or take down to the beach (in a special, custom-designed cooler pack), or, in the case of two out of every three glasses drunk, pour at home from a four-litre box with a tap on the side.

None of this would have been possible, however, without the fundamental change that took place in the way wine was made. Even as recently as the early 1980s, Jack Mann, one of the veterans of the Western Australian wine industry, unblushingly told wine writer James Halliday that 'unless a wine can be diluted with an equal volume of water, it wasn't worth making in the first place...' Mann's ideal of big, thickly alcoholic red and white wine was shared by most of his contemporaries, and by a great many wine drinkers overseas. In the days when doctors took a rather different attitude to alcohol, they used to prescribe Guinness to pregnant women and Australian 'Burgundy' to anyone who was suffering from anaemia.

As Adam Wynn, one of the modern winemakers, says, 'Thirty years ago, 80% of consumption and production in Australia was of fortified wine. With the exception of Coonawarra, every wine region now existing was then geared to fortified wine. This meant they were in warmer areas, with rich soil, and produced

very, very ripe grapes'. In real terms this made for wines that were often strong enough to taste as though they were fortified even when they weren't. Today fortified wine has dropped to 15% of the annual production and wine growers have increasingly sought out new cooler areas, and ways of making lighter wines in the existing regions. Which is how Australia came to found two of the best wine schools in the world at Roseworthy and the improbably named Wagga Wagga.

But another reason for the phenomenal development of the industry lies in a particular Australian personality trait; this is one of the most competitive nations in the world and nowhere is this more true than in wine making. Every region has an annual show at which hundreds of wines compete against each other for medals and trophies. Tastings such as these are held in every winemaking country but it is the Australians who have elevated wine competitions to a level unknown elsewhere. Interestingly, France, which makes much more wine, has far fewer than Australia. Trophies are worth real money to their winners; a winery whose wine has been awarded the Jimmy Watson Trophy as the best young red can expect to sell a million dollars more wine than it might have done otherwise.

But where these competitions really set Australia's producers apart from their counterparts in other countries is the way in which they enter almost every wine they make, including their most basic bag-in-box reds and whites, and the technical expertise required of the tasters. Almost any French producer can be invited to taste at the major competitions in Paris and Mâcon; in Australia, wine 'judges' have to undergo an apprenticeship that can last several years.

Lastly, there has been a welcome Aussie resistance, so far at least, to hype of the kind with which California is riddled. Of course, there is a growing number of superstar wineries and one or two 'gurus', whose advice on what to buy is taken seriously, but, by and large, Australians are as unimpressed by highly priced, 'big name' wines as they are by old school ties. What they want is flavour and value for money – which is exactly what most Antipodean wineries have proved to be very capable of providing – both at home and abroad.

NEW SOUTH WALES

The Hunter Valley does not quite break all of the rules of wine-making, but it leaves very few unscathed. The two main problems that have always confronted winegrowers are the heat, which can be intense, and the rain, which falls at precisely the time when it is least wanted – during the harvest.

Almost from the beginning, the growing of vines in the new colony was seen to offer a way for the British to become vinously self-sufficient and to produce an alternative form of alcohol to rum. So, Australia's first vines – imported from the Cape of Good Hope – were planted in 1788, almost as soon as the ships dropped anchor. These first vineyards were situated around Sydney Harbour itself, but despite the keenest efforts of a band of would-be winemakers, almost all of the vines succumbed to the effects of pests or vine disease. In 1824, however, a 2,000 acre (800 hectares) plot of land in the Hunter Valley was granted to an immigrant engineer called John Busby whose 23-year-old son James, had briefly studied vinegrowing and winemaking in France. It was James Busby who would not only found the wine industry of Australia, but also, a few years later, that of New Zealand.

The Styles

The Lower Hunter

Visitors who today drive along smart tarmac roads, sleep in international-style motels and pay megabucks to go ballooning over the vineyards can hardly imagine the Hunter Valley of as recently as the 1950s and 1960s. It was farming country in which a few big companies made similarly big wines. Much of what they produced was pretty basic fare, but some of the whites made from the Semillon (described as Hunter Valley Riesling or Chablis) and the Shiraz (usually sold as 'Burgundy') by firms like Lindemans and McWilliams were very impressive in their unashamedly old-fashioned way. They weren't wines with

which a frail man would wish to argue. And, as anyone who has had the chance to taste old bottles that are occasionally released by Lindeman's in their 'Classic' series will have discovered, these were wines that were made to last.

The switch to more 'modern' winemaking came with the arrival of young individualists from Sydney. These men and women had, in many cases, travelled to Europe and tasted lighter, more delicate wines and saw no reason why they shouldn't produce some for themselves in vineyards that were a handy distance from the city.

Arriving in the Hunter Valley, most of the newcomers dismissed the dry, flat, northern part of the region, the Upper Hunter, as being better suited to bulk wine making than to the kind of wine they had in mind, and turned their attention to the Lower Hunter, to the south of the Hunter River itself.

Among the influential new arrivals was a surgeon called Max Lake and a Welshman called Len Evans who, not content with creating a name for himself as a wine producer (at the Rothbury Estate), went on to write books and columns galore, more or less run Australia's wine competitions (the team of judges is unofficially known as the 'Evans Eleven') and generally to kick the industry as a whole into the league of international quality winemaking. The Rothbury wines are not always the cream of the Hunter crop, but the Semillons and Shirazes are always worth looking out for.

Another winery that's rather more variable in quality, but also capable of occasional brilliance is Tyrrell's, whose Pinot Noir once outscored a range of Burgundies in a French tasting. If you haven't come across Tyrrell's two bottom-of-the-range wines: Long Flat Red and Long Flat White, you should give them a try. Not only are they good to drink, but also their names ought to rekindle any flagging dinner-party conversation.

For commercial, modern winemaking, Wyndham Estate is hard to fault, but my own soft spot is still for the large, quirky, family-owned firm of McWilliams. When I visited they had just put a substantial quantity of glorious 'Sauternes' into green-glass, claret-style bottles, 'because that's what we had to hand', they said disarmingly. Other wines I tasted that day included some wonderful old-fashioned, nutty, peachy Hunter Semillons named after members of the British royalty (the 'Anne Riesling' was stunning), and Shirazes with enough smoky, spicy, indescribable flavours to make you wonder whether the old Hunter description for this variety of 'sweaty saddle' doesn't make some sense after all.

The Upper Hunter

In the early 1980s, Australian wine experts who had never paid the region any heed were shocked to taste a wine that proved what the Upper Hunter grapes could do when treated properly. Rosemount was not the first winery to attempt to make quality wine in this part of the region – Penfolds had made some good reds here – but it was the first to demonstrate its potential for Chardonnay. Over the last decade, Rosemount, and Phil Shaw its winemaker, have more or less done for this grape in Australia what Mondavi did for it and for the Fumé Blanc in California. The Rosemount Fumé Blanc is not yet a truly successful wine (few Australian Sauvignons are), but the range of Chardonnays, from the 'basic', to the oaky, Show Reserve, to the individual vineyard Roxburgh are all in their individual ways, benchmark wines. Shaw has begun to hit the mark with Pinot Noir and with light fruity Shiraz, as well as with some very exciting Semillon. So far, Rosemount is still the only major quality player in the Upper Hunter.

Other (Lower) Hunter wineries to look out for are the traditional Tullochs and the modern Brokenwood, Hungerford Hill and Robson Vineyards.

Mudgee

Up in the hills, to the north-west of Sydney, Mudgee remains one of Australia's 'unknown' regions. But it deserves – and will one day get – greater recognition, because its cool conditions can permit producers like Montrose and organic specialists Botobolar to make wines that easily outclass some of the ones that bear the more commercially acceptable Hunter Valley label. In an attempt to thrust the region into the limelight, in 1979, Mudgee's growers created an appellation for themselves. So far, it has done more for their morale than for sales.

Cowra and Corowa

Corowa is fortified wine country where Lindemans once made traditional 'port' and 'sherry' just across the river and the state boundary from Rutherglen in Victoria. Cowra, by contrast is a 'new' region that is fast gaining a reputation for its cool-climate grapes, thanks in no small measure to the belief in its potential of Len Evans, whose Rothbury Winery has a vineyard here. The varieties to look out for are the Chardonnay and Traminer.

Riverina /Murrumbidgee Irrigation Area /Griffith-Leeton

Hot and isolated, this is great raisin country and, thanks to irrigation from the Murrumbidgee River, a very easy place to produce huge quantities of wine. In the past, most of the producers here remained true to their Italian roots by making Asti-style wines and vermouths. Recently, however, the De Bortoli winery startled everyone by making a botrytised Semillon that did well against top Sauternes.

FACING PAGE: Lindemans, which makes wines in several regions of Australia, was one of the pioneers of 'Hunter Valley Riesling' (Sémillon)
BELOW: The most successful of the new-wave Hunter Valley wineries has been Rosemount, whose Chardonnay has helped to introduce Australian wines to wine drinkers throughout the world

---

THE ESSENTIALS — NEW SOUTH WALES

Location On the south-east of the continent between Victoria and Queensland.

Quality No official designations exist, but the Mudgee region established its own appellation in 1979, and the Hunter Valley is creating an appellation system of its own. Other notable areas of production are: Upper Hunter Valley; Lower Hunter Valley; Griffith; Canberra; Cowra; Corowa and the Murrumbidgee Irrigation Area.

Style Generally warm, soft, ripe wines in all styles,with plenty of richness. The classic Hunter Valley Sémillon is rich and honeyed and frequently tastes oak-aged even when it has had no contact with wood at all. Rieslings and Gewürztraminers are aromatic and show good varietal flavour. Chardonnays are packed full of ripe tropical fruit, often with a good dose of sweet vanilla from ageing in new oak. The famous Hunter Valley Shiraz has a distinctive earthy, peppery style. Cabernet Sauvignon is frequently blended with the Shiraz to produce soft, jammy reds, but on its own the Shiraz produces some of Australia's best wines, all showing vibrant varietal character.

Climate The climate is sub-tropical, becoming progressively drier as one heads inland. **Cultivation** Sand and clay loams of varying fertility are widespread, with alluvial soils on the valley floors. Vines are grown on low-lying or flat valley sites although the slopes of the Brockenback range (up to 500m) and the Great Dunding Range in Mudgee (up to 800m) are also used.
Irrigation is widespread.

Grape Varieties *Red*: Cabernet Sauvignon, Grenache, Pinot Noir, Shiraz, Pedro Ximénez. *White*: Chardonnay, Chasselas, Colombard, Marsanne, Muscat, Palomino, Riesling, Sauvignon Blanc, Sémillon, Muscadelle, Gewürztraminer, Verdelho.

Production/Maturation Modern methods are employed with machine-harvesting, temperature-controlled fermentation in stainless steel and judicious use of new oak for finishing. A number of Chardonnays are barrel-fermented.

Longevity *Whites*: most are at their best between 2 to 4 years, but top examples will develop for up to 15 years. *Reds*: most are best drunk when 3 to 5 years old, but top examples will quite possibly improve over 8 to 12 years.

Vintage Guide Reds 79, 80, 83, 85, 86, 87
　　　　　　　Whites 79, 80, 81, 83, 85, 86, 87

Top Producers Brokenwood, Craigmoor, Hungerford Hill, Lake's Folly, Lindemans, Montrose, Rosemount, Rothbury, Tyrrells, McWilliams, Tulloch, de Bortoli, Murray Robson, Simon Whitlam.

VICTORIA AND TASMANIA

The one thing that almost everybody who has ever visited Australia knows is that, in Melbourne, you can live through four seasons' weather in the space of an hour; sensible day-trippers remember to pack an umbrella with the swim-suit. Victoria's wines are just as eclectic. Head up to the one-horse wine town of Rutherglen in the north-east and you can imagine yourself back in the days of the gold-rush, drinking precisely the same brew the prospectors would have enjoyed over a century ago. But visit the 'new' wine regions of the Mornington Peninsula, and the Yarra Valley, and you're Rip Van Winkled straight back to the world of the 1990s where all is modernity and clean, fresh flavours. The effect can be disconcerting - and very good fun.

The North-East

Rutherglen, Glenrowan and Milawa

If the Australian film industry ever gets around to making westerns, this is the part of the country to which they should bring their cameras. Rutherglen has a bar, a che ist, a barber, a milk bar and a bank – and a range of extraordinary 'sticky' Liqueur Muscats and Tokays (made from Bordeaux's Muscadelle). Both are – or should be – brilliant, long-aged wines, full of Christmas Puddingy intensity. The best are made by Mick Morris, but Campbells, Bullers and Stanton & Killeen are good too. Non-fortified wines, apart from some hefty reds, are less exciting, though Chris Pfeiffer and All Saints are both making progress.

Glenrowan is still a one-winery town, but what a winery. Baileys is, like Morris's a living museum of Australian vinous tradition. Try the Liqueur Muscats; then move on to the Shiraz. It's less beefy than it was, but it would still support a teaspoon. Top class Cabernet Sauvignon grapes are also grown in the Koombalah vineyard here. Follow them to the winery and you'll arrive at The Brown Brothers winery in Milawa.

John Brown Sr (a doyen of the industry whose experience rivals that of Robert Mondavi) and his wife head a team of Browns who divide up between them the responsibilities of growing, making and selling. Brown Brothers produce a wide range of wines, from Liqueur Muscat to lean dry whites from new, high altitude, vineyards in the King River Valley. They have yet to make a really stunning dry red or white, but they produce nothing that is less than good, and wines like the unusual marmaladey Late Harvest Orange Muscat and Flora have developed a cult following worldwide.

Central Victoria

Great Western, Bendigo and the Goulburn Valley

Say 'Great Western' to any Australian and he'll think bubbles. Seppelt created an enviable reputation for their commercial sparkling wines, recent vintages, and the new Salinger label, show class. There are some good reds here too – especially the Shiraz from Mount Langhi-Ghiran – while up in the cool foothills of the Pyrenees, the son of the former winemaker at Château Lafite makes impressive Shiraz and Cabernet and improving whites. Chateau Remy and Redbank are good too.

Three fairly traditional wineries fly the flag for the warm region of the Goulbourn Valley. Chateau Tahbilk, the oldest in the state (it was founded in 1860) can make big, old-fashioned reds that demand patient cellaring; the whites made from the Marsanne are sometimes spicily impressive. Mitchelton produces good Marsanne too, some rich Cabernet and Chardonnay and Tisdall's 'Mount Helen' efforts with these varieties can be impressive. Look out for the wines of Balgownie, Heathcote, Jasper Hill and Passing Clouds in Bendigo and Idyll's Cabernet Shiraz and Bannockburn's Pinot Noir from Geelong.

Murray Valley

This is Victoria's irrigated grape basket, where the river water permits producers in the sub-regions of the wonderfully named Sunraysia and Mildura to make copious amounts of grapes. The Mildara winery here never produces table wines that are remotely as good as the ones from its Coonawarra vineyards, or as impressive as the 'sherry' and 'port' made from ripe Mildura fruit, but they can be undemandingly appealing.

The South

The Yarra Valley and Mornington Peninsula

If the traditional Victorian rivalry is between Rutherglen and Glenrowan, the state's modernists have the choice of supporting the cool climate regions of the Yarra Valley or the Mornington Peninsula, both of which have almost simultaneously proved that they can make Pinot Noir that competes with the best in the world. The Yarra Valley was 'founded' in 1969 by Dr Bailey Carrodus whose Yarra Yering Dry Red No. 1 can be a great Bordeaux-style blend, beaten only by his pure Shiraz Dry Red No. 2. Dr Carrodus's Pinot Noir can be good too, but not as impressive as the example produced at the nearby Coldstream Hills winery by lawyer-turned-wine-writer-turned-winemaker, James Halliday. A plethora of star wineries here includes St Huberts, Yarra Burn Mount Mary (famous for its Pinot Noir), Domaine Chandon (who make some of Australia's best fizz), Tarrawarra (producers of some very complex Chardonnays), Seville Estate (source of glorious late-harvest sweeties).

The Yarra is now pretty well established as a region; Mornington Peninsula, a short drive from Melbourne, is still a region of part-time winemakers – men and women who earn good money in the city and play with their vineyards at the weekends. But there is a top-class consultant on hand, in the shape of Garry Crittenden, a man whose own Dromana Estate and Schinus Moller (its 'second label') Pinots, Cabernets and Chardonnays rival the best in the country. The Hickinbotham

LEFT: Wines from James Halliday's recently-planted Coldstream Hills vineyards in the Yarra Valley are among the most sought after in Australia

ABOVE: the traditional basket-press used by Mick Morris for his Rutherglen Liqueur Muscat and Tokay, some of the most gloriously sweet and traditional of all Australian wines

winery's Pinot Noir vineyard makes stunning Burgundy-style wine too while a specially developed system of fermenting grapes, uncrushed in polythene bags has yielded some very convincing freshly fruity alternatives to Beaujolais.

In neither region, but in no other clearly defined district, Delatite also benefits from cool conditions to make lean white wines with some style.

Tasmania

Tasmania has the same cool region vinous raison d'etre - and then some. It is either Australia's Oregon, or its Siberia. According to the island's supporters, it has the cool-climate conditions that are essential for lean, long-lived, Chablis-like sparkling wine and Burgundy-style Pinot Noir; for a large number of other Australian winemakers, it's a chilly wasteland where no one would ever voluntarily choose to grow grapes.

In fact, winemaking is no novelty here; vines were growing in Tasmania in the 1830s, some years before they were introduced to South Australia or Victoria. But the first flourish of Tasmanian winemaking did not last long and it was the 1950s before serious attempts were made to try again. Today Dr Andre Pirie is making some wonderful, long-lived Chardonnay and promising Pinot, while Louis Roederer is producing impressive fizz in a cooperative effort with the Heemskirk winery.

THE ESSENTIALS — VICTORIA AND TASMANIA

Location Victoria is on the south-eastern edge of Australia. The island of Tasmania is located 200 kms off the coast.

Quality Both Victoria and Tasmania have controlled appellations, although only the Tasmanian laws work effectively. Important Victorian areas of production are: Rutherglen; Glenrowan; Milawa; Goulborn Valley; Central Victoria; Pyrenees; Yarra Valley; Geelong and Mornington Peninsula; Great Western; Murray River; Macedon.

Style Good quality whites and reds, some sparkling wines and stunning dessert and fortified wines. Chardonnays are creamy with rich depth of flavour yet also have good acidity and balance. Rieslings show fine varietal character, and there are good examples of Sauvignon Blanc, Sémillon, Gewürztraminer, Chenin Blanc and Marsanne. Cabernet Sauvignons from the more temperate southerly regions exhibit classic blackcurrant and cedar flavours and have great balance. Elsewhere the style is slightly richer. Fine, spicy Shiraz, which generally requires some ageing, is produced, together with small quantities of improving Pinot Noir and Merlot. Glenrowan and Rutherglen produce some luscious and rich fortified Liqueur Muscat and Tokay. These traditional 'stickies' are of outstanding quality. Tasmania, with its cooler climate, produces some rich, elegant Chardonnays and vibrantly fruity Cabernet Sauvignons.

Climate Inland, conditions are hot and continental but towards the coast the climate is tempered by the maritime influence. Tasmania enjoys an even cooler climate.

Cultivation The better quality wines are produced at the cooler high-altitude sites (around 500m – 1,600 feet – above sea level). Wines of lesser quality are made from vines grown on all types of land. Soils vary widely, from the rich alluvial soils of the Murray Basin to the gravelly soils of the Pyrenees. North-east Victoria has red loams while Tasmania has clay soils.

Grape Varieties *Red*: Cabernet Franc, Cabernet Sauvignon, Cinsault, Dolcetto, Malbec, Merlot, Pinot Meunier, Pinot Noir, Shiraz. *White*: Chardonnay, Chasselas, Chenin Blanc, Gewürztraminer, Marsanne, Müller-Thurgau, Muscat, Riesling, Sauvignon Blanc, Sémillon, Tokay.

Production/Maturation Modern high-quality production methods are used with mechanical harvesting, temperature-controlled fermentation in stainless steel and early bottling common in most districts. The top wines, particularly the reds, are oak-aged. The fortified Muscats of Rutherglen are produced using a solera-type system. The winemakers of Tasmania are known for their experimentation with viticultural techniques.

Longevity *Reds*: The best can age for some 10 to 15 years. *Whites*: Most are excellent upon release but can develop in bottle for up to 8 years.

Vintage Guide Reds 79, 80, 82, 84, 85, 86, 88
　　　　　　　　Whites 79, 82, 84, 85, 87, 88, 89

Top Producers *Victoria*: Baileys, Brown Brothers, Morris, Mount Mary, Chambers, Bannockburn, Campbells, Stanton and Killeen, Chateau le Amon, Coldstream Hills, Hickinbotham, Mitchelton, St Huberts, Taltarni, Tisdall ,Yarra Yering, Delatite, Dromana/Scinus Molle, Yarra Burn, Yeringberg, Chateau Tahbilk, Mount Langhi Ghiran, Jasper Hill, Giaconda, Oakridge Seppelt, Domaine, Balgownie, Dalwhinnie. *Tasmania*: Pipers Brook, Murilla, Heemskerk

SOUTH AUSTRALIA

If Australia had to choose just one winemaking state, this would have to be it, both for quality and quantity. That is not to say that the other parts of the country don't make great wines too (the competitive spirit between states is so fierce that my dentist wouldn't allow me to suggest any such thing even if it were true) but none can combine the capacity to produce around two thirds of Australia's annual harvest with the ability to make huge quantities of good basic wine as well as the Antipodes' greatest reds and some of their most impressive whites.

The potential of this state was appreciated as early as 1849, the year in which a horticulturist called George McEwin predicted that 'Wine rivalling the most famous growths of the old world will be produced in South Australia as soon as we gain the requisite knowledge and the practical experience necessary to success...' It took just over a century for the winemakers of South Australia to justify what must have appeared to be McEwin's absurdly high-flown prediction.

No one knows who began it all. Walter Duffield, Richard Hamilton and John Reynell are all said to have planted vines near Adelaide in the 1830s, using in Reynell's case, cuttings from Tasmania, but it was a doctor from Sussex, Christopher Rawson Penfold, who was to found the company which would grow to become the largest in Australia and gain the reputation for consistently making the finest red wines in the continent.

Ironically, given the current medical aversion to alcohol in any form, Penfold's initial reason for making wine was as a tonic for his patients. South Australia's early success owes much to the efforts of men like Penfold, but it has also to thank the *Phylloxera vastatrix* which, though devastating most of the rest of Australia's vines, left this state alone. Which explains why visitors today have to pass through an anti-Phylloxera Check-Point-Charlie when crossing its borders.

The Regions

The Barossa Valley

Although the first vineyards were planted around Adelaide by Britons, the region that would become the most important in the state was more or less founded by 28 families of Lutherans from Silesia in Germany. The Barossa Valley, in which they settled in the 1840 is still a curious mixture of Australian, British and Germanic, where coachloads of wine-thirsty tourists pour out of the Kaiser Stuhl winery and into the 'Olde Englishe Tea Shoppe'.

Initially, as elsewhere, the first wines to be made were 'sherries' and 'port's; it did not take long, however, for the Germans to develop a market for the grape they were used to growing back home: the Riesling. Despite a climate that is less than ideal for white wines, Barossa Rhine Riesling from companies such as Orlando, Seppelt and Kaiser Stuhl soon became one of Australia's best known styles.

Many of the companies here also produced good reds – often from grapes grown in other parts of the state, but it was, another German, a pint-sized, bow-tied, showman known as Wolf Blass who taught the region and the rest of Australia a lesson in how to make and more importantly blend, red wine. Australia's reds, though often big and tasty, tended to need to be left to soften before drinking. It was Blass who, after a spell in Champagne, developed a skill at blending which enabled him to make well-balanced (not too big, not too light) wine that was ready to drink the day it was sold. Among the Barossa Valley names worth watching out for are Orlando (almost always good value for money, and producers of great Steingarten Riesling), Peter Lehman and Seppelt (makers of tremendous sparkling wines and some very good reds and fortified wines).

LEFT: The Berri-Renmano cooperative produces some of Australia's most reliable, inexpensive, commercial wines

ABOVE: The red 'terra rossa' soil of Coonawarra and the coolish climate of this region give wines made here an intensity and quality matched by few other regions in Australia

THE ESSENTIALS — SOUTH AUSTRALIA

Location In the south central part of Australia.
Official Quality Significant areas: Clare/Watervale; Southern Vales; Riverland; Adelaide Hills; Barossa Valley; Eden Valley; Langhorne Creek; Keppoch/Padthaway; Coonawarra; McLaren Vale; Adelaide; Springton.
Style Sauvignons and Sémillons are richly flavoured and Muscats are packed full of grapy fruit. Chardonnays have tended to be rich and buttery but are increasingly being made in a more elegant, balanced style combining rich fruit and good acidity. Of the reds the best known are the intensely-flavoured plummy Shirazes and the herbaceous Cabernet Sauvignons which have soft, juicy blackcurrant and stewed plum fruit flavours. Some top quality dessert, fortified and sparkling wines are also made, including honeyed – and occasionally botrytised – Rhine Rieslings, together with 'port' and 'sherries'.
Climate Temperatures range from the very hot continental conditions of the Riverland to the cooler areas of Coonawarra and the Adelaide plains.
Cultivation Soils are varied, but tend to be sand, loam or limestone topsoils over red earth and limestone subsoils.
Grape Varieties *Red*: Cabernet Sauvignon, Grenache, Malbec, Merlot, Pinot Noir, Shiraz, Pedro Ximénez. *White*: Chardonnay, Muscat, Rhine Riesling, Sémillon, Sauvignon Blanc, Gewürztraminer, Ugni Blanc.
Production/Maturation Mass-production methods are used to produce cheap and well-made basic wines. The producers of premium wines use traditional vinification methods. Oak-ageing is common for these wines.
Longevity Most quality *whites* will develop for 2 to 4 years, selected examples for up to 10 years. *Reds* improve for 5 to 15 years.
Vintage Guide Reds 76, 79, 80, 82, 84, 85, 86, 87, 88
　　　　　　　　Whites 79, 82, 84, 85, 86, 87, 88
Top Producers Wolf Blass, Penfolds, Petaluma, Wynns, Hollick, Mountadam, Seaview, Orlando, Rouge Homme, Henschke, Basedows, Seppelt, Hill Smith, Yalumba, Leo Buring, Berri-Renmano, Katnook, Woodstock, Tim Adams, Grossett, Lindeman, Hardys/Chateau Reynella, Peter Lehmann, Geoff Merrill, Shaw-Smith.

Eden Valley, Pewsey Vale and Springton

A number of producers have done the same as their counterparts in that other warm wine valley, the Napa in California; they have headed for the hills. So, up at the High Eden Ridge, over 500 metres above sea level, David Wynn, the man who is said to have 'invented' Coonawarra where he owned the Wynns winery, has launched Mountadam with his son, Adam. The wines – especially a Chardonnay – are among the most stylish and subtle in Australia. Up in Pewsey Vale, Hill Smith and its Yalumba sister company which make some of Australia's most reliable fizz, are producing similarly stylish Rhine Riesling, particularly from the grapes grown in its Heggies Vineyard.

Coonawarra

There is not a lot to Coonawarra: a couple of 'hotels' (pubs) and a few shops and a strip of very special, *terra rossa* soil that runs like a one-mile wide red carpet for about 10 miles. Australian wine buffs wax as lyrical about the qualities of this soil as Bordeaux fans talking about gravel, and there certainly is something rather magical about the richness of blackcurranty - minty fruit that is packed into the Conawarra Cabernet Sauvignons and Shirazes. But the climate plays a role too; judged by the Californian Winkler system of Heat Units, it is actually comparable to Champagne and Burgundy.

There is some top class winemaking here, both from local wineries such as Rouge Homme and Wynns (both of which belong to Penfolds) and by 'outsiders' such as Rosemount, Mildara and Lindemans (another Penfolds subsidiary).

Keppoch / Padthaway

So far, although some good Coonawarra whites have been made, like the Médoc, with which it likes to be compared, Coonawarra does best with its reds. For classy Chardonnay and Sauvignon Blanc, it is worth heading 40 miles north to the village of Padthaway. Dubbed 'poor man's Coonawarra' because it was partly developed in reaction to the rising cost of land and grapes in that area, this region has a small patch of red soil of its own. For a taste of the style here, try the ones made by Lindemans – but don't go searching for the town of Keppoch; it only exists on planners' maps and wine labels.

Clare Watervale

If the name puts you in mind of lush, green Irish meadows, think again. The country here is warm, dry and very woody - and about as far removed from the Emerald Isle as it could be. There are some good reds, but it is the ripe whites – especially the Semillons – that are the most impressive.

Southern Vales

The big company here is Hardy's, a family-owned firm that has spawned a number of classy winemakers as well as an improving range of reds and whites. An ex-Hardy's man to watch is Geoff Merrill, whose reds are acquiring cult status.

Adelaide / Adelaide Hills

The old and new coexist here. In vineyards surrounded by suburban housing, Penfolds makes its traditional Grange and more modern Magill wines, both of which, like the plethora of 'Bin Number' reds by this company (none of the numbers mean anything by the way) are not only big and concentrated, but also often surprisingly complex. At a higher altitude, however, in one of the buzziest of Australia's 'buzz' regions, the Adelaide Hills is the source of a growing range of cool-climate wines. The leader of the pack is Brian Croser, whose wines are all impeccably made but need time to develop.

Riverland

Around a third of Australia's grapes are harvested in this irrigated region. Much of the juice is distilled, but big cooperatives – particularly Berri-Renmano – make good value wines.

OTHER WINES OF AUSTRALIA

Western Australia

In the late 1980s, all of Western Australia's dreams seemed to have come true at the same time. The Americas Cup was being defended in the waters off Fremantle, money of every kind was pouring into Perth, and the rest of the world was finally beginning to acknowledge that this state really might have the potential to be Australia's own west-coast answer to California. Within a few years, many of the dreams had faded; Alan Bond, the brewery tycoon, property magnate and sponsor of the Australian yacht was fighting to save his business and Denis Horgan, his fellow millionaire businessman, had reportedly had to put his showcase Leeuwin Estate winery up for sale.

This temporary decline in Western Australia's fortunes should not have too significant an effect on the the state's best winemakers several of whom have achieved national and international renown, but it has helped to focus attention on the polarisation that has taken place between the 'old' region of the Swan Valley where most of the state's best-known wines were historically made, and the 'new' regions of the Margaret River, where the generally far better wines of today are being produced.

Winemaking began in Western Australia in 1829 at around the same time as it did in Tasmania, a few years before the first vineyards were planted in South Australia or Victoria. For nearly 150 years, although vineyards were started in the late 19th century at Mount Barker and in the Margaret River, almost all of the attention was paid to the wineries of the Swan Valley, where huge amounts of full-bodied red and white were made, by men like Jack Mann of Hougton who believed all wine should be intense enough to need diluting with water.

The Leeuwin Estate vineyards were the ones that Robert Mondavi originally selected when he planned to start a winery in Australia. They produce one of the best Chardonnays in the country

Swan Valley

This is the kind of hot, arid country most most foreigners imagine they'll find throughout the continent; a vast oven, ideally suited to the making of 'sherry' and 'port' and wholly inappropriate to the making of 'modern' table wines. In the past, this was of little concern to companies like Houghton that were doing very nicely thank you with the old fashioned stuff.

I find it difficult to become very enthusuastic about many of the wines being made in the Swan Valley today, even from such well-regarded wineries as Evans & Tate. The reds always seem to be too big for their boots while the whites, at their best, taste like triumphs of winemaking know-how over too hot a climate, though Houghton's 'White Burgundy' is a pleasant enough, rich blend. There is one winery that does produce wines that support the reputation of the region: Sandalford's 'port' styles can be wonderful – but their quality, like that of the fortified wines of Rutherglen, merely helps to demonstrate how warm the weather is here.

Margaret River

This cattle-and-sheep farming region saw its first vineyard planted in the late 19th century but for around 75 years its potential went largely unexplored; in those days, its (relatively) cooler climate and its wet winters seemed less suitable for winemaking than the well-established Swan Valley. But, in the 1970s, a number of doctors independently followed the advice of an encouraging report published in 1965 and planted vines here. Soon, Doctors Cullen, Cullity, Lagan, Pannel, Peterkin and

Sheridan had all established their vinous practices and were making wine to rival the best in Australia.

The Margaret River is often thought to be cool; in fact its climate is quite warm enough to ripen the Cabernet Sauvignon with no difficulty whatsoever. The only problems encountered by winegrowers are occasional shortage of rain, vine disease and the unwelcome attention of parrots and kangaroos. The list of star wineries is extraordinary, especially when one considers the youth of the region. The wines they make amply support the official recognition in 1978 of the region's right to be Australia's first appellation. Leeuwin Estate's claim to fame – apart from its Californian style winery, the big-name orchestral concerts held on its lawns, and the fact that its vineyards were originally selected by Robert Mondavi when he was thinking of making wine in Australia - lies in the quality of its Chardonnay. Vasse Felix's success has been with its rich, blackcurranty Cabernet Sauvignon, while Moss Wood has benefitted from its owners' Burgundian associates to make top class Pinot Noir and Bordeaux-style Semillon and Cabernet Sauvignon.

Leeuwin's Chardonnay has to fight hard to beat the one made by Vanya Cullen, a winemaker who also makes a balanced, improving Bordeaux-blend red. Cape Mentelle shares its owner, the charismatic David Hoehnen, with the legendary Cloudy Bay in New Zealand. The wines here are exemplary too, and there's a middle-weight spicy Zinfandel that's better than most examples from California, and a blend that interestingly includes the lime-flavoured Verdelho. Also worth looking out for are Chateau Xanadu (for its Semillon), Capel Vale and Redgate.

Great Southern Area / Mount Barker / Frankland

This cool(ish), dry region near Albany on the south coast, is best known for the high quality of the Plantagenet wines – especially its Shiraz. Houghton's make some good wine in Frankland, but the region remains under-exploited.

Canberra District

James Halliday evocatively described the winemaking of this region as being carried out 'on a doll's house scale' at weekends by civil servants. Until quite recently, this area was thought to be too cool to ripen grapes. Now, it has been appreciated that the climate is as warm as that of Bordeaux but that there is a problem of a lack of rainfall. None of the wines is easily obtainable outside the district or of particularly high quality; the best efforts so far have been by Doonkuna Estate and with red wines made from Bordeaux varieties and late harvest whites.

Queensland

The Granite Belt, as it is known because of its acidic decomposed granite soil, is cool, high altitude, apple-growing country. The grapes that are grown here are not generally used to make high-quality wine, though Bungawarra Vineyard and Robinsons Family try their best with such traditional varieties as the Shiraz and Rhine Riesling.

Northern Territory

Alice Springs is not a part of the country in which any winegrowing manual would advise you to try to make wine. Vines don't really like being asked to perform in the equivalent of a furnace. Denis Hornsby has overcome the climatic impediments by building an underground winery and a highly sophisticated system of year-round drip irrigation. The grapes – which include Cabernet Sauvignon, Shiraz, Riesling and Semillon ripen several weeks before those in most other parts of the country; indeed, if the harvest were a fortnight earlier the 1995s would be harvested just after Christmas 1994. Given these handicaps, Chateau Hornsby's wines are surprisingly palatable; the best though is probably the Beaujolais-style red.

THE ESSENTIALS — WESTERN AUSTRALIA, QUEENSLAND AND THE NORTHERN TERRITORY

Quality The Margaret River of Western Australia and Queensland's Granite Belt have controlled appellations. The Swan Valley, the Southwest Coastal Plain, the Great Southern Area and Mount Barker are important areas in Western Australia. Ballandean is significant while Alice Springs is the only notable region in the Northern Territory.

Style Western Australia, particularly the Margaret River, produces some of Australia's finest wines, notably some vibrantly fruity yet extremely elegant Chardonnays, Sauvignon, Sémillon, Shiraz and Pinot Noir. Queensland produces a wide range of styles from the fruity and delicate 'Ballandean Nouveau' a Beaujolais-style wine, to some rich Cabernets and Shirazes and traditional fortified wines. The Northern Territory has very few wineries but those that exist produce Shiraz–Cabernet blends of decent quality.

Climate The climate of Western Australia is very varied. Queensland is hot with moderate rainfall which can cause problems at vintage time. The Northern Territory has a very hot and dry continental climate.

Cultivation Most vineyards in Western Australia are on flat coastal plains or river valley basins, although higher altitude sites are being used in the hotter areas. Soils are rich, free-draining alluvial and clay loams. Queensland and Northern Territory vines are grown at altitude (600-900m) to temper the heat. Granite is common in Queensland.

Grape Varieties *Red*: Cabernet Franc, Cabernet Sauvignon, Malbec, Merlot, Pinot Noir, Shiraz, Zinfandel. *White*: Chardonnay, Chenin Blanc, Muscat, Riesling, Sémillon, Sauvignon, Verdelho, Traminer, Traminer.

Production/Maturation The winemakers of Western Australia employ modern viticultural and vinification techniques They are used in Queensland and Northern Territory to combat the problems of heat.

Longevity In Queensland and the Northern Territory most wines are for immediate consumption. The *whites* of Western Australia can develop for 2 to 4 years, the best for some 8 years; *reds* benefit from 3-6 years bottle age with selected examples requiring up to 15 years.

Vintage Guide Reds 77, 81, 82, 84, 85, 86, 87
Whites 80, 82, 84, 85, 86, 87

Top Producers *Western Australia*: Alkoomi, Capel Vale, Moss Wood, Cape Clairault, Cape Mentelle, Cullens, Houghton, Leeuwin Estate, Plantagenet, Vasse Felix. *Queensland*: Old Caves. *Northern Territory* Chateau Hornsby.

Barbecue Marinades

The 'barbie' has become synonymous with Australian cooking. Beacause food is being cooked at such searing temperatures, it is often useful first to marinate it for an hour or two so that it stays moist and tender.

BASIC MEAT MARINADE
3 tbsp white wine
2 tbsp soy sauce
3 tbsp olive or vegetable oil
2 tbsp Worcestershire sauce
1 tbsp tomato purée
4-5 drops Tabasco sauce
1 garlic clove, crushed
$\frac{1}{2}$ tsp salt
$\frac{1}{2}$ tsp sugar
Freshly ground black pepper to taste

BASIC FISH AND SHELLFISH MARINADE
3 tbsp dry white wine
3 tbsp olive or vegetable oil
2 tbsp lemon juice
1 garlic clove, crushed
1 tsp dried thyme
1 tbsp parsley, minced
$\frac{1}{2}$ tsp salt
$\frac{1}{2}$ tsp sugar
Freshly ground black pepper to taste

NEW ZEALAND

Until New Zealand's sudden emergence as the source of world-beating wines in the late 1980s, there was little reason for outsiders to argue with the image of this distant ex-colony as a shared annexe to Australia and Britain.

One visitor who was evidently taken by the idea of New Zealand as a cool country with moderate potential was the German wine and vine expert, the late Professor Helmut Becker who, on a trip to New Zealand, informed his hosts that they should plant a variety he was recommending for such cool European countries as Germany and England. This grape – the Müller-Thurgau – had the advantage, Becker explained, of ripening early and yielding generous crops of grapes which, with a little 'back-blending' (the addition of a little sweet juice), could produce an alternative to cheap German wine.

The New Zealand winemakers of the early 1970s saw little reason to argue. After all, the world was not exactly clamouring at the door to buy bottles of New Zealand 'port' or 'sherry'. So, within a decade, the Müller-Thurgau took over the industry.

To say that this was under-exploiting New Zealands vinous potential is something of an understatement. The arrival of the Müller-Thurgau set New Zealand's winemaking back a decade; it wasn't until the mid 1980s that a significant number of producers developed the confidence to follow the example of a few pioneers in trying their hands at more classic French grape varieties. Today, as an increasing number of sophisticated wine drinkers have discovered, New Zealand has been transformed from backwater into mainstream. At the beginning of the 1990s, firmly committed fans of Australian Chardonnay suddenly began to talk about the extraordinarily intense flavours of New Zealand Sauvignon Blanc, and about putting themselves on the waiting list for the next vintage from Cloudy Bay, the small winery that developed cult status with almost its very first wine.

As recently as 20 years ago, I doubt if anyone in or outside New Zealand could have imagined that winemaking would help to attract the international spotlight. In 1946 a Royal Commission on Licensing stated that: 'More than 60% of the wine made by the smaller winemakers is infected with bacterial

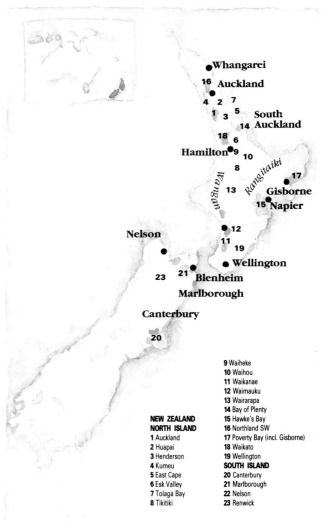

NEW ZEALAND	9 Waiheke
NORTH ISLAND	10 Waihou
1 Auckland	11 Waikanae
2 Huapai	12 Waimauku
3 Henderson	13 Wairarapa
4 Kumeu	14 Bay of Plenty
5 East Cape	15 Hawke's Bay
6 Esk Valley	16 Northland SW
7 Tolaga Bay	17 Poverty Bay (incl. Gisborne)
8 Tikitiki	18 Waikato
	19 Wellington
	SOUTH ISLAND
	20 Canterbury
	21 Marlborough
	22 Nelson
	23 Renwick

disorders... A considerable quantity of the wine made in New Zealand would be classified as unfit for human consumption in other wine-producing countries.' New Zealand-born winebar owner Don Hewitson ruefully admits that just 15 years ago he used to joke to his customers in London that there was nothing wrong with New Zealand wine – provided you didn't get it on your hands. In those days Hewitson had no New Zealand wine on offer in his bars. Today, his staff are pouring Montana Sauvignon Blanc and Chardonnay by the gallon.

Winemaking began in New Zealand 150 years earlier when the 'Father of Australian viticulture', James Busby, was made the 'British Resident' in New Zealand, planted vines 'between the house and the flagstaff' and made a white wine that in 1840 impressed the visiting French explorer Eumont d'Urville as 'light ... very sparkling, and delicious to taste'.

Busby's career as a winemaker was, however, curtailed by the ravaging of his vineyards by horses, sheep, cattle and pigs, and by soldiers during local clashes. Although settlers followed his example, it was not long before they realised that they would need to import winemaking expertise. While small groups of French and German winegrowers were persuaded to stay for a while, two shiploads of German vintners who had, as New Zealand author Michael Cooper narrates, 'been promised perfect conditions for viticulture by the New Zealand Company, arrived on our shores, contemplated the steep bush-clad hills surrounding Nelson and left for South Australia'.

Over the following years several New Zealanders attempted to make a living from winemaking, but only a handful suc-

FACING PAGE: The cypresses in the Mission Vineyards — some of the oldest in New Zealand — look almost Tuscan, while the palm tree (BELOW) in the Cooks vineyards seems positively tropical

THE ESSENTIALS — NEW ZEALAND

Location A pair of volcanic islands lying some 1,600 miles east of Melbourne.
Quality Designated regions are: *North Island*: Bay of Plenty; East Cape; Gisborne; Esk Valley; Hawke's Bay; Henderson; Huapai Valley; Ihumatao; Kumeu; Manawatu; Marigatawhiri Valley; Poverty Bay; Riverhead; Te Kauwhata; Tolaga Bay; Tikitiki; Waiheke; Waihou; Waikanae; Waikato; Waimauku; Wairarapa; Wellington. *South Island*: Canterbury; Marlborough; Nelson; Renwick.
Style Wines have crisp, varietal character with plenty of fruit but less heaviness than their Australian counterparts. Chardonnays are rich yet have an elegant freshness too. Sémillons can be rich and fat, or crisp with piercing fruit. Gewürztraminers, when made dry, have excellent spicy character but can also be lusciously sweet wines when late-picked, as can Rieslings. However, the most famous New Zealand wines are world-beating Sauvignon Blancs, packed full of green flavours – gooseberries, grass, asparagus and nettles – and occasionally oak-aged. Red wines have, until recently, enjoyed less acclaim but as vines grow older the Cabernets and Merlots are showing greater depth of clean blackcurrant and plummy fruit while some Pinot Noirs are showing greater varietal expression. These wines have potential.
Climate In general, a cool maritime climate prevails although the North Island has more tropical conditions, with higher temperatures and higher rainfall producing greater humidity. This, together with the heavy rains, can cause problems of rot and grape damage during harvest time.
Cultivation Vineyards are planted on a variety of clay and alluvial loams over volcanic subsoils. Drainage is often a problem, so some north-facing slopes have been cultivated on the North Island, although flatter land is used elsewhere.
Grape Varieties *Red*: Cabernet Sauvignon, Merlot, Pinot Noir, Pinotage, Pinot Gris. *White*: Chardonnay, Chenin Blanc, Gewürztraminer, Müller-Thurgau, Muscat, Pinot Blanc, Riesling, Sauvignon Blanc, Sylvaner, Sémillon.
Production/Maturation Very modern viticultural techniques are used for premium varieties; mechanical harvesting and temperature-controlled fermentation in stainless steel are widely employed. Barrel-fermentation is used to produce top-grade Chardonnays while new oak is frequently used for maturation.
Longevity While all wines can be drunk immediately the better-quality *whites* can benefit from 1 to 5 years' ageing. *Reds* can benefit from 3 to 8 years ageing, although they may last longer in future as the vines become older.
Vintage Guide Red 84, 85, 86, 87, 89
　　　　　　　　White 85, 86, 87, 89
Top Producers Babich, Cloudy Bay, Cooks, Corbans, Delegats, Hunters, Kumeu River, Matua Valley, Mission, Montana, Morton, Nobilos, St Helena, Te Mata, Vidal, Villa Maria, Martinborough, Weingut Seifried, Neudorf, Vavasour, Selaks, Collard, Coopers Creek.

ceeded. Furthermore, in the late-19th century, any who might have been tempted to take up vinegrowing were deterred by the arrival of powdery mildew in the vineyards, which prevented wine from being made, and a virulent set of temperance societies, which sought to prevent it being drunk.

The man who saved New Zealand from full-scale prohibition went by the wonderful name of Romeo Bragato, an Italian-trained winemaker born in Dalmatian Yugoslavia.

Thanks to Bragato, New Zealand's wine industry survived. Thanks to his countrymen, it began to flourish. Because, despite their efforts, it wasn't the early British settlers who really set New Zealand winemaking on its feet, but a group of Dalmatians who had come to tap gum from trees in the far north of the North Island. These men, isolated by racial prejudice, settled, planted vines and opened wine shops for their countrymen.

The peevish Anglo-Saxons, galled by this modest success, opened up yet another avenue of prejudice. As the 1916 Aliens Commission complained, 'A great deal of feeling against these men.... is due to many of them being wine growers, and the belief that Maori women are able to get, through them, intoxicating liquors.... Where young and vigorous men, attractive young women free from conventional social restraints, and abundance of intoxicating liquors are found together, debauchery will very certainly result...'

The Dalmatians, following the exhaustion of the gum trees, began to concentrate on wine growing, using expertise learned in Yugoslavia and from Romeo Bragato's *Viticulture in New Zealand*, and with the assistance of a government research station at Te Kauwhata on the North Island.

During the first two decades of this century, despite the

arrival of phylloxera (correctly identified by Bragato, whose initial warnings and advice were, needless to say, ignored by the authorities), both the winemakers and the prohibition lobby strengthened their position. In 1919 the temperance societies appeared to have won a conclusive victory when a national referendum voted for prohibition. Had it not been for a contingency of servicemen returning from the war just in time to swing the ballot, winemaking here might have undergone the same period of hibernation as it did in the USA.

By 1960 there were still less than 1,000 acres of vines planted. But within a few years, a rapid influx of money from outside New Zealand, partly fuelled by the beginnings of the Australian wine boom, encouraged heavy plantation. Between 1965 and 1970 the acreage under vines tripled; by 1983 it had risen to 15,000 acres; two years later the country found itself awash with wine. Today the acreage is rather smaller than in 1983, thanks to a government-funded 'vine-pull' scheme which encouraged growers to uproot uneconomical vineyards, but the grapes that are grown are more likely than ever to be high-quality varieties such as the Sauvignon Blanc and Chardonnay.

The newness, and often the slightly impermanent look of some of the wineries is explained by the fact that they may well have opened their doors last week.

The Regions

The New Zealand wine industry has developed – and is continuing to develop – at such an extraordinary speed that it is impossible to talk about regions without the frustrating knowledge that the map will have been re-drawn almost between one vintage and the next. New areas are being explored and old ones discarded and, to confuse matters further, regions are changing their names.

Northland, the region where winemaking really began in New Zealand, has been largely abandoned, although for two or three years it appeared as though this region might be the source of New Zealand's top red wine. Two lawyer brothers created a California-style mini-estate, grandly called it 'The Antipodean', planted Bordeaux-style grape varieties, and presented their first wine 'blind' to an audience of London wine experts, who were invited to compare it with a range of Bordeaux first growths. The experts all spotted the New Zealand wine, but generally acknowledged the potential quality of The Antipodean. The lawyers hyped the wine for all they were worth, sold every bottle they made for a very high price, had an argument and closed the winery.

Until about 25 years ago The North Island had only two other main wine regions: Auckland itself and Hawkes Bay. That number has now risen to five, plus Waiheke Island, where the Goldwater Estate winery has produced a very impressive Cabernet-Merlot. In and around Auckland, wineries such as Matua Valley, Kumeu River, Coopers Creek, Selaks and Nobilos are all variously hitting the mark with white wines, and the first two of these, in particular, are making some of New Zealand's most exciting reds.

At Henderson, 12 miles (20km) to the west of Auckland, Babich, Delegats and Collard are the names to look out for, while to the south of the city, St Nesbit is having some success with Bordeaux-style reds, as is winemaker Kym Milne at Villa Maria. Further south still, Te Kauwhata, site of New Zealand's wine research station, was once thought of as good red wine country – particularly by the giant Cooks who made Cabernet Sauvignon here. Today, as the winemaking potential of other, less rainy parts of New Zealand have been discovered, the black grapes have been replaced by white ones and few people are making any claims for this region. Three wineries that show what can be produced here are Morton Estate, de Redcliffe and Rongopai.

Out east, on the coast at Gisborne, there are only two wine estates – the organic Millton, where some terrific late-harvest wines and dry Chenin Blancs are being made, and Matawhero, source of New Zealand's best Gewürztraminer – but most grapes grown here are used by wineries elsewhere. This is great Chardonnay country – arguably the best in New Zealand.

Further down the east coast, Hawkes Bay boasts Mission Vineyards, New Zealand's oldest winery, as well as the Te Mata Estate at which John Buck has made Coleraine, the country's most successful Bordeaux-style red, and the similarly impressive Elston Chardonnay. To listen to the Hawkes Bay producers, you might believe that they could make any kind of wine here; this warm region certainly seems to offer some of the best hopes for red wines, though the whites have a hard time beating the competition from the South Island. Other names to look for here are Ngatarawa, Vidal, Esk Valley and Brookfields.

Perhaps the most exciting area of the North Island, though, is Martinborough. There are five wineries in this wide valley, one of which, Dry River, has produced New Zealand's best Pinot Gris, while another, Martinborough Vineyards, is making classy Pinot Noir and Chardonnay. Ata Rangi has also done the apparently impossible, by making raspberryish Pinot Noir and richly spicy Shiraz, thus producing Burgundy and Rhône-style wine from grapes grown in almost the same vineyard.

Across the water, on the South Island, the most famous region has to be Marlborough, where many of New Zealand's best Sauvignon Blancs have been made. Apart from Cloudy Bay and Montana, whose huge acreage of vines carpets the valley floor, there are Hunters, Cooks' Stoneleigh, Vavasour and, following the recent arrival of the Australian success story, Wolf Blass. The grape that has made this region famous is the Sauvignon Blanc, whose gooseberry freshness makes many Sancerres taste like last year's apples. The Riesling and Gewürztraminer do particularly well here too, but other varieties, including the Chardonnay and Pinot Noir, are also beginning to perform well – though some tend to be rather lean in style. Watch Kevin Judd of Cloudy Bay: his exiting reds – Cabernets Sauvignon and Franc, and Pinot Noir – could all become as famous as his Sauvignon Blanc.

One of the greatest bus rides in the world takes you from the increasingly famous vineyards of Marlborough westwards through the folds of the hills to the almost unknown wine region of Nelson. There are five wineries here, but only two that are producing good wine in any quantity. Tim and Judy Finn of Neudorf Vineyards and Hermann and Agnes Seifried of Weingut Seifried and Redwood Valley ruefully admit to having something of an inferiority complex. Years of being told by 'experts' that their region is less ideally suited to winegrowing than Marlborough or Hawkes Bay, for example, have had their effect; wines from Nelson tend to cost less than those of other regions. But taste them blind, taste Neudorf's Semillon (one of the few New Zealand successes with this variety), Chardonnay and Sauvignon Blanc, or Seifried's late-harvest Redwood Valley Rieslings, and you simultaneously want to buy up every bottle at its bargain-basement price, and to give these winemakers the confidence to charge what their wines are worth.

Further south, Canterbury became famous as the cool, dry region in which was situated St Helena, the winery at which, in 1982, a Burgundy-mad winemaker called Danny Schuster made New Zealand's first world-class Pinot Noir. Slightly less successful subsequent vintages and hotter competition from wineries in other parts of the country have shifted the spotlight of attention away from this southern region, but Canterbury remains a name to watch. Its future may lie less in the Pinot Noir than in the Riesling, a variety in which the German-born Giesen family, who own the region's largest estate, fervently believe. Other wineries to look out for here include Larcomb (for its Riesling), Amberley and Torlesse.

For most winegrowers in Marlborough and Nelson, let alone those on the North Island, Canterbury is too far south, and thus too cool, to ripen wine grapes. Mention Central Otago to these sceptics and they simply smile and shake their heads in sympathy at the thought of anyone trying to make wine in what, at 44° 36', is the southernmost wine region in the world. But a handful of producers think the attempt is worthwhile. It is too early to predict whether they are right.

Lamb and Kiwi Fruit Kebab

Along with dairy produce, lamb is New Zealand's largest export, and nothing could be more appropriate than teaming it with kiwi fruit in a delicious and quick kebab.

SERVES 4
3 tbsp olive or vegetable oil
1 tbsp lemon juice
1 garlic clove, peeled and crushed
1 tbsp soy sauce
Freshly ground black pepper
1 lb/500 g leg of lamb, boned, trimmed of fat and cut into chunks
6 kiwi fruit, peeled and cut into wedges

In a ceramic or glass bowl, combine 1 tbsp of oil, the lemon juice, garlic, soy sauce and pepper to taste. Add the lamb and marinate for at least an hour. Skewer the lamb and kiwi fruit alternately. Brush with the remaining oil and grill, turning occasionally, for about 8 minutes or until the meat is cooked. Serve with rice and a tomato and onion salad.

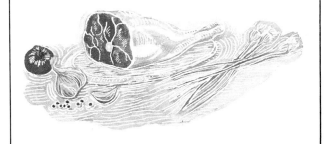

FACING PAGE: The vineyards of the Marlborough Valley in the South Island of New Zealand — home of some of the best Sauvignon Blanc in the world. ABOVE: John Buck, whose Te Mata estate wines have proved that New Zealand can make reds too

THE UNITED KINGDOM

The British are a strange race. Given a choice when buying anything – a car, a cheese, a beer, a computer – they all too frequently opt for an import; foreign is best. In no instance is this more true than that of wine. A growing number of English and Welsh men and women have thrown themselves body, soul and savings account into winemaking over the last few years, only to be rewarded with the almost total indifference of their countrymen.

Of course, Britain's characteristically grey skies and chilly temperatures do little to dispel prejudice; surely the climate here cannot be warm enough to ripen grapes? But the people who hold this view clearly have not spent much time in such classic wine regions as Champagne, Chablis and northern Germany, none of which offers much to entice holidaymaking sun-seekers but who still manage to use what seem to be inhospitable conditions to make very good wine indeed.

No, the problem facing England's wine industry is more a deadly blend of the cottage-industry mentality of many of the growers themselves and the unwillingness of British govern-ments to help them. Winemakers in other parts of Europe are feather-bedded in all sorts of ways; in Britain, they are told to stand on their own two feet – and, just for good measure, given a few hefty blows to the ankles by the revenue-gathering arms of the state.

Supporters of English wine never tire of proudly reminding those who scoff that the Romans and Normans made English wine, that Henry VIII probably drank it – until he dissolved the monasteries and put a stop to its production – and that Vine Street, the City of London thoroughfare familiar to generations of English Monopoly players, was once a place in which were grown good, ripe grapes.

My only retort to all this is – so what? The kind of wine mediaeval monks enjoyed would, I'm pretty certain, fare no better in most modern wine bars than the food they ate. No, the modern British wine industry dates firmly from the late 1960s

David Carr Taylor is one of England's most successful winemakers — both in terms of the quality of his wines, and of his skill at marketing them to customers who now include wine enthusiasts in France

and early '70s – at around the time when wine suddenly began to interest a broader range of Britons who previously thought of it as something exotic and 'foreign'.

In those early days, farmers all too often simply expelled a pony from its paddock and planted a few vines without applying any real thought – let alone expertise – to the question of whether the grape variety and the plot of land were remotely suited to each other. Hardly auspicious beginnings. But luckily, more sensible would-be winegrowers did seek advice, perhaps inevitably looking to Germany, a country they rightly saw as having similar climatic conditions and whose vinicultural tradi-tion seemed entirely appropriate to English conditions.

It was immediately clear that Germany's greatest grape, the Riesling, would not ripen in England, but the experts at the Geisenheim wine academy on the Rhine saw no reason why

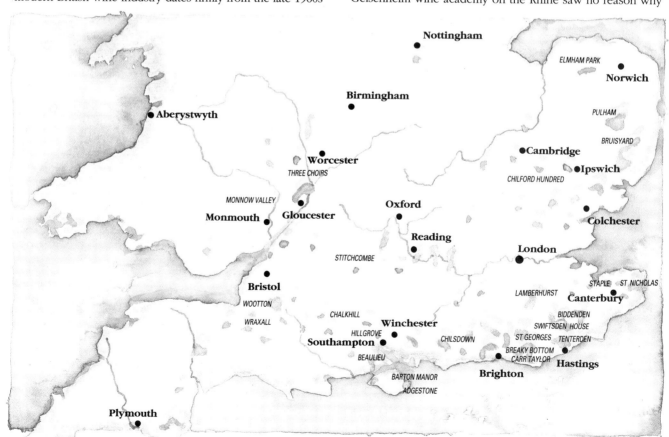

newer varieties developed for Germany's cold climate should not succeed. In particular, they set great store by the Müller-Thurgau, the variety which was rapidly supplanting the Riesling almost throughout Germany.

The combination of Germanic grapes and advice meant, inevitably, that most of the early efforts were semi-sweet versions of wines that were already being imported from the Rhine and Mosel. Like the producers of many of those wines, the English could only make their wines sweet by 'backblending', adding *süssreserve* – sweet grape juice – which they generally imported from Germany.

While the quality of these wines was often comparable to that of the German examples they were mimicking, the price was almost invariably higher than that, say, of a mass-produced Piesporter. Why then, English wine drinkers asked, with some justifiable logic, should we buy a local product instead of the cheaper import?

During the second half of the 1980s, however, the business of making English wine became more businesslike. Hobbyists tired of what no longer seemed such a romantic occupation; the vines grew older and, like all mature vines, began to produce richer wine; and, most importantly of all, many of the English winegrowers, who wre growing in confidence, decided to stop copying the Germans.

And when they did their own thing, hey presto! Their Germanic grapes began to produce dry and off-dry wines that seemed a whole lot closer in style to the Loire than to the Rhine. At their best – and that's an increasing proportion – these new styles are packed with the flavour of (ripe) grapefruit and gooseberries. The acidity – which was always their hallmark – is now balanced by a smokiness and a fatty richness that you'd never expect from cold climate vineyards. Most growers still add *süssreserve*, some most emphatically don't; both groups, thanks partly to (in German terms) tiny yields, partly to increasingly skilful winemaking and partly, ironically, to our cool climate, seem consistently to produce intensely flavoured, good-quality wine with a capacity to age that surprises even their makers.

Today there are nearly 2,000 acres of British vines – heading for over 200 times as many as there were when a dozen pioneers gathered, in 1967, to launch the English Vineyards Association, the body that still oversees the quality of English, Welsh and Channel Island wines through the allocation of its gold seals of approval.

However, of the hundred or so vineyards in production today, there are still less than two dozen that really make wine on a commercial basis, scattered all over the southern third of Britain. For this reason, it is still a little too early to say where the best areas for winemaking are located, and to define the styles of any particular regions (though I swear I can spot the smoky style of a Norfolk wine 'blind'). Even so, the news from Brussels is that sets of officially designated regions and internationally recognised criteria for English quality wine may well be established during the early 1990s.

The last decade of the century will be a fascinating time for English wines. The summer of 1989 gave them their best-ever vintage and the damp conditions in the autumn provided many with their first chance to make late-harvest wine – even, in some cases, from grapes affected by noble rot. This – and possibly the growing number of good sparkling wines – could be the style that will finally help to persuade Englishmen and women to take their country's wines as seriously as some French wine drinkers have already done.

THE FLAVOUR OF ENGLISH WINES
Schönburger Peachy aromas with soft acidity.
Müller-Thurgau Flowery, light, grapefruit/gooseberry fruit.
Seyval Blanc Lighter than Müller-Thurgau, grapefruity acidity.
Reichensteiner Floral aromas and Müller-Thurgau-like flavour.
Huxelrebe Fat, gently Germanic.
Scheurebe Very grapefruity – good in the late-harvest style.

Welsh Rarebit

Not every dish has to be grand enough for a royal banquet in order to enjoy it with a glass of wine. This classic would be as good with a well-chilled English Lamberhurst Reichensteiner as with a Côtes du Rhône. No-one seems to know whether the 'rarebit' is 'rabbit', but it is good as a starter, a lunch dish with salad or the savoury finale to an elegant dinner.

SERVES 6
8 oz/225 g Farmhouse Cheddar or Double Gloucester, grated
5 fl oz/150 ml milk
1oz/25g butter
Salt and freshly ground black pepper
1 tbsp prepared English mustard
1 tsp Worcestershire sauce
6 slices of toast
Chopped parsley to garnish

In a saucepan, melt the cheese in the milk, stirring over a low heat. Add the butter, salt and pepper, mustard and Worcestershire sauce. Simmer and stir until the mixture is quite thick and creamy. Taste and adjust seasoning if necessary. Put the toast in a shallow heatproof dish or on to a grill pan covered with tinfoil. Spread a good thick layer of the mixture on to each piece of toast and grill until golden brown. Sprinkle with the chopped parsley.

THE ESSENTIALS — THE UNITED KINGDOM

Location The majority of English vineyards lie south of Birmingham, all the way down to the Isle of Wight. Many of the areas now cultivating vines were the same area used for wine-making in the Middle Ages. Fertile Kent and Sussex are particularly well-populated with English winemakers. The handful of Welsh vineyards, particularly those around the Monnow Valley and usually lumped together with the English – should not be overlooked by any means.
Quality As yet recognised by the EC only as the equivalent of *vins de pays*. The English Vineyards Association awards seals of approval and various trophies to particularly good wines. Accept only 'English' wine: 'British wine' is simply foreign grape juice diluted with British water, and should be avoided.
Style Whites range from dry, even austere, through clean, fruity Loire-style to Germanic, medium-sweet wines. Many are made from a single grape, though blends can be very successful. *Süssreserve* is used by some producers to soften the high acidity, and chaptalization is essential to raise the alcohol level in grapes which can never produce enough sugar by themselves. There is proven potential for sparkling and, in warm years, dessert styles. A little light red is made.
Climate Maritime, at (cynics say beyond) the northerly extreme of table wine production. Even some warmer areas of south-west England can get 100in (254cm) of rain a year.
Cultivation Wide range of soils, including chalk, limestone, gravel and granite. Slopes play an important role as suntraps and windbreaks.
Grape Varieties Principally white and Germanic, though there is some experimentation with French varieties. Kerner, Müller-Thurgau, Seyval Blanc, Scheurebe, Reichensteiner, Schönburger, Huxelrebe and Madeleine Angevine are most commonly seen; (rare) reds are from the Pinot Noir.
Production/Maturation Stainless steel predominates. Occasional efforts with new oak – for example, Penshurst's Seyval Blanc – are quite promising.
Longevity Surprisingly high – 1 to 8 years, thanks to the wines' high acidity.
Vintage Guide 76, 88, 89
Top Producers Carr Taylor, Breaky Bottom, Lamberhurst, Three Choirs, Thames Valley, Ditchling, Astley, St Edmund, Pulham, Wootton, Penshurst, Adgestone, Bruisyard, Berwick Glebe, Pilton Manor, Staple, Nutbourne Manor, Chiltern Valley, Wickham, Bodenham, Biddenden, Headcorn, Shawsgate, Little Harps, Tenterden, Chilsdown, Swiftsden House, Beaulieu, Wraxall, Elmham Park, Bruisyard St Peter.

AUSTRIA, SWITZERLAND AND LUXEMBOURG

Austria

The sweetening, by a small number of Austrians, of their wine with an anti-freeze-like chemical called dyethylene glycol has had a long-term effect on the Austrian industry. And the irony is that if the Austrians had been making the wine they like to drink, rather than the stuff foreigners wanted to buy, no 'anti-freeze' would have been needed.

For far too long Austria was expected to provide inexpensive alternatives to Germany's finer sweet wines. Austria's warm

Switzerland has traditionally made little effort to send its wines beyond its borders, and the strength of the Swiss franc has not envouraged foreigners with weaker currencies to buy them. Noiw, however, there is a growing selection of Swiss wines on offer, including good Chardonnay and Fendant, made from the Chasselas.

climate allows it in some regions to ripen grapes more effectively and noble rot affects the grapes rather more reliably, than in Germany. And if those grapes were sometimes the intrinsically second-rate Welschriesling rather than the real Riesling,

SWITZERLAND
5 Graubunden
6 Neuchâtel
7 Thurgau
8 Ticino
9 Valais
10 Vaud
11 Zurich

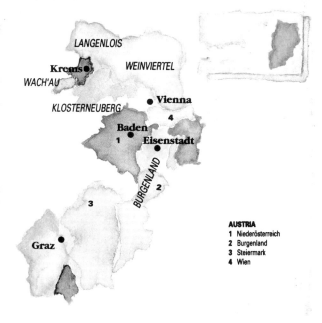

AUSTRIA
1 Niederösterreich
2 Burgenland
3 Steiermark
4 Wien

what did it matter? The wines tasted luscious and sweet enough. Unfortunately, they often cost more to produce well than anyone was prepared to pay for them – hence huge overproduction, compensated for by dollops of dyethylene glycol.

Today Austria is back on course with new, stricter wine laws and, more importantly, the will to sell Austrian wines rather than German taste-alikes. The way the Austrians like to drink their wine - red or white - is by the jugful in *Heurigen* ('nouveau') taverns, as young and cool as possible. Foreigners will have to make do with bottles of young Grüner Veltliner, the spicy white variety grown throughout Austria but almost nowhere else in the world. One of the best parts of the country to look for top-quality Grüner Veltliner is in Niederösterreich, in the the regions of Kamptal-Donauland and Wachau where some lovely, lean, grapey Riesling is made.

The Mittel and Sud Burgenland, to the east of the country, are the source of some surprisingly good reds (made from the local Blayfrankisch), while the warm climate and the humid atmosphere created by the huge, shallow Neusiedler See lake provide perfect conditions for botrytis to develop. This is the region in which to find Austria's most luscious sweet wines.

Switzerland

Switzerland is a country that is split into three sections, each of which speaks its own language and has its own names for just about everything. So the German-speakers call the Pinot Noir the Klevner or the Blauburgunder and have Räuschling as an alternative name for the Elbling. The French-speakers know the widely grown Chasselas as the Fendant, the Perlan (in the regions of Geneva and Neuchâtel) and the Dorin (in the Vaud). Another popular Swiss style, the red blend of Pinot Noir and Gamay, is variously called Dôle, Goron and Salvagnin (allowing further confusion with Sauvignon, which *isn't* grown here).

You will find that Swiss wines are precisely what you'd expect them to be: well made, meticulously clean – and expensive. Although they find it hard to compete on value-for-money terms with wines made in neighbouring France, Germany and Austria, Switzerland's wines offer a range of styles and flavours not often found in those countries.

The real success story has to be the Chasselas; French versions of the Chasselas are generally dull; in the hands of the meticulous Swiss, this grape can produce surprisingly refreshing and long-lived wines. Look out for the slightly sparkling examples that have been bottled *sur lie* – on their yeast.

Of Switzerland's other whites, try the Malvoisie (the local name in the Valais for sweet wines made from the Pinot Gris), the (quite rare) Riesling and the Müller-Thurgaus produced around Thurgau, the home of Dr Müller, who invented this Riesling/Sylvaner cross . In Geneva and Neuchâtel the Chardonnay is also producing some tastily pineappley wines not unlike the best examples from north-east Italy. If you like Beaujolais, you should enjoy Switzerland's reds, some of the best of which, such as Dôle, are made from blends of Pinot Noir and Gamay.

Luxembourg

Luxembourg is another of the world's more quietly efficient wine-producing countries: nearly three quarters of the annual production are drunk within the Duchy and most of the rest is exported to Belgium. The key grapes are the Elbling, the Riesling-Sylvaner (here often called the Rivaner), the Auxerrois, the Pinot Blanc and Pinot Gris (here, as in Germany, known as the Rulander), the Traminer and the Riesling. Of these, the most successful are probably the Riesling and the Pinot Gris, both of whose wines have more substance than the rather neutral ones made from the Elbling and Auxerrois. Even so, Luxembourg is not the place to come looking for full-flavoured wines; the key style, whatever the grape, is lightweight. Also beware of 'Luxembourg' sparkling wines, which, like 'British' wine, can be made from imported juices.

Gruyère Cheese Puffs

In the country that gave us fondue cooking, cheese has always played an important part. This recipe is very easy and will do wonders for a wine and cheese party. It uses one of the great Swiss cheeses, Gruyère, but any hard cheese can be substituted.

MAKES 16
5 fl oz/150 ml milk
5 tbsp water
4 oz/100 g butter
¹/₂ tsp salt
6 oz/175 g flour
4 eggs
8 oz/225 g Gruyère or other hard cheese, grated
1 tsp cayenne pepper (optional)

In a saucepan, combine the milk, water, butter and salt and bring to the boil. Reduce the heat to moderate and add the flour all at once. Mix vigorously with a wooden spoon until the mixture comes away from the side of the bowl and forms a ball. Put the mixture in a bowl and whisk in the eggs, one at a time. Mix the cheese and cayenne (if using) into the dough. Form 16 balls of dough (about 1 tbsp each ball), place them on a buttered baking sheet and bake in an oven preheated to 400°F/200°C/Gas mark 6 for 30 minutes, or until the puffs are golden.

THE ESSENTIALS — AUSTRIA, SWITZERLAND AND LUXEMBOURG

Quality Luxembourg and Switzerland have 'official appellation' (OA) systems used to protect certain names. OA's in Switzerland are: Dôle, Dorin, Fendant, Goron, Malvoisie, Perlan, Salvagnin and Viti. Austria uses the German classifications, the only different category being *ausbruch*, which falls between Beerenauslese and Trockenbeerenauslese.
Style In Switzerland, the Chasselas grape can produce dry, fragrant whites. White wines from Luxembourg and Austria are generally Germanic in style, those from Luxembourg being dry or off-dry and those from Austria covering the full range of sweetness levels. Luxembourg also produces dry to off-dry, quite full *méthode champenoise* sparkling wines. Austrian wines tend to have less acidity than their German counterparts but the best sweet wines, luscious yet elegant, do have ageing potential. Austria's fuller-flavoured white wines include the peppery Grüner Veltliner. Swiss red wines tend to have more weight in the southerly Italian-speaking cantons. All Swiss wines are soft and approachable in youth with good fruit. Austrian reds vary greatly between regions and draw from both their eastern and western neighbours. The fragrant, lightly sweet St Laurent is an Austrian speciality.
Climate In Switzerland, continental Alpine conditions mean early sun but late frosts. The Austrian climate is generally warm and quite dry. Burgenland, in the south-east, is the hottest area and here, in the autumn, botrytis often affects the vines.
Cultivation Vines are found mainly on the slopes above lakes and rivers, for example, the Danube in Austria and the Mosel in Luxembourg.
Grape Varieties *Switzerland*: Chasselas (here called the Fendant), Gamay, Pinot Noir, Cabernet Sauvignon. *Luxembourg*: Riesling, Gewürztraminer, Elbing, Müller-Thurgau, Pinot Gris, Auxerrois. *Austria*: Blauer Portugieser, Bouvier, Cabernet Sauvignon, Furmint, Gewürztraminer, Grüner Veltliner, Merlot, Müller-Thurgau, Muskateller, Muskat Ottonel, Neuberger, Pinot Blanc, Pinot Gris, Riesling, Rotgipfler, St Laurent, Welschriesling, Zierfandler.
Production/Maturation Almost all wines are naturally cool-fermented and bottled young. New oak is very rare.
Longevity All whites, apart from the sweeter Austrians, should be drunk within 4 years. Red wines are also for early drinking, although there is the occasional exception from Austria.
Vintage Guide Austria: 81, 83, 85, 86, 87, 88.
Top Producers *Switzerland*: Château de Vaumarcus, Andre Ruedin, Domaine du Mont d'Or, Testuz, Dubois. *Luxembourg*: Bernard Massard. *Austria*: Siegendorf, Lenz Moser, Schlumberger, Unger, Hopler.

EASTERN EUROPE

While the Soviet Union produces huge quantities of many styles of wine, its greatest export success is likely to lie in 'Champagnski' sparkling wines like these, here stacked in traditional pupitres

---

THE ESSENTIALS — EASTERN EUROPE/SOVIET UNION

Quality Quality control tends to be non-existent in these state-run industries, though as export possibilities widen the situation will doubtless improve. However, Bulgaria, in line with its success in Western markets, has established a system: 'Country Wine' is table wine from a particular area; DGO (declared geographical origin) indicates a specified village appellation and *Controliran* is wine from a designated grape from a specific DGO. A quality ladder, and one which is very ancient, exists for Hungarian Tokay: the higher the *puttonyo* number on the bottle, the sweeter the wine.
Style White wines are generally Germanic in style, from off-dry and medium with basic fresh fruit through to lusciously sweet wines, such as the Romanian *edelbeerenauslese*. Bulgaria produces some passable but dull Chardonnay. There are also several sparkling wines produced in these countries, particularly in Czechoslovakia and the USSR, the latter producing sweet, red sparkling wine called 'Champanski' and 'Krim'. From Hungary comes Tokay, made from *aszu* — semi-dried botrytis-affected grapes mixed, in varying quantities, with a dry base wine to make a variety of styles. Szamorodni is made in the Tokay region from the same grapes but is rarely botrytised. Although these wines are not in the same mythical league as the pure *aszu essencia* drunk by the Tsars, they can still be great and all are worth trying.
　Eastern European red wines are generally full-bodied and approachable with lots of ripe, rich fruit though they can be spoiled by sweetness and oxidation. Bulgarian red wines owe not a little to Bordeaux, both in terms of style and grape varieties: putting up spirited competition to these is the local Mavrud grape. Modern examples of the famous Bulls Blood from Eger in Hungary are lesser wines than their fiery, robust ancestors.
Climate The wine growing areas of Romania, Hungary, Bulgaria, Czechoslovakia, southern Yugoslavia and Russia have a warm continental climate. Hungary's climate is particularly affected by Lake Balaton, which is the largest in Europe.
Grape Varieties Aligoté, Cabernet Sauvignon, Chardonnay, Dingac, Furmint, Gamza, Gewürztraminer, Kratosija, Laski Rizling, Leányka, Mavrud, Melnik, Merlot, Misket, Muskat Ottonel, Pinot Gris, Pinot Noir, Plavac Mau, Plovdina, Prokupac, Riesling, Sauvignon Blanc, Ugni Blanc, Vranac, Zilavka.
Production/Maturation Varies from mediaeval to ultra-modern.
Longevity Dry and medium whites should be drunk within 3 years. Good quality sweet wines and Tokay will age at least 5 years. Red wines are often non-vintage and are released when ready to drink. Most will keep at least two years in bottle.
Vintage Guide 81, 84, 85, 86, 87

Even before the Iron Curtain was finally drawn at the end of the 1980s, winemakers throughout eastern Europe had already made friends with the West. Their reason was that they were responsible for one of the few forms of produce that could bring in large amounts of western currency.

USSR

There are three key areas of winemaking in the Soviet Union. Together, Crimea, Moldavia and Georgia contribute to an annual harvest that places the USSR at number five in the ranking of the world's wine producing nations. Today, Soviet winemakers – and now, one would have to say, those in the Balkan republics – are eagerly trying to modernise their wineries.

Hungary

Hungary's vines were first planted as a means of reclaiming sandy-soiled land. For this reason, there is less incidence of phylloxera than elsewhere in the world.

　The best-known wines here are Tokay and Bull's Blood – or

to give it its full name, 'Egri Bikaver' or 'Bull's Blood of Eger'. This wine, from Transdanubia in northern Hungary, is made from a blend of Kadarka, Kekfrankos, Cabernet Franc and Merlot (known here as 'Medoc Noir').

Of Hungary's other red wines, the best are probably the Merlot and the local Kadarka from the pre-Roman vineyards of Villanyi-Siklos where Kadarka and Blau Portuguiser are grown and where, more importantly, Villanyi Burgundi is made from the Pinot Noir and the indigenous Kekfrankos.

If the quality of Bull's Blood has slipped in recent years, so too has that of the Tokay that has been seen outside Hungary. At its best, however, this is one of the world's great sweet, honeyed wines.

Quite unrelated to the wines of the same name produced in Alsace and Australia, Hungarian Tokay is produced close to the River Bodrog, from a blend of the local Furmint, Harslevelu and Yellow Muscat all of which are regularly attacked by noble rot. Unlike Sauternes, most Tokay is made by turning the nobly rotted grapes into a paste – *aszu* – which is then blended by the 35-litre hodful – *puttonyo* – in varying proportions into 140-litre containers of dry – *Szamorodni* – wine. The sweetness of the Tokay is measured in *puttonyos*; the most intense, being a 'six *puttonyo*'. Even more intense are Tokay Aszu Essencia and Tokay Essencia. Both are phenomenally pricy and made exclusively from nobly rotted grapes. All styles of Tokay live almost for ever, because of the sherry-like process of oxidation that accompanies its slow fermentation.

Romania

The state research centres of Murfatlar and Valea Calugareasca have, over the last few years, made enormous progress in introducing Romania's winemakers to such western varietals as the Cabernet Sauvignon, Merlot and Pinot Noir. Previously, the vineyards which were first planted even before the arrival of the Greeks in the seventh century BC, tended to be planted with local grape varieties like the Babeasca de Nicoresti, Negru Virtos, Frincusa, Tamiiosca Romaesca, Feteasca Neagra and Kadarka. The climate, though northerly, is well suited to the production of both red and white wines, but the best regions for reds are Murfatlar, close to the Black Sea where both Pinot Noir and Cabernet Sauvignon have been successful; Banat, which makes Cabernet Sauvignon and the locally famous Kadarka de Banat; Vrancea where the Pinot Noir and Cabernet Sauvignon are grown as well as the Babeasca de Nicoresti and Feteasca Negra; and Deleal-Mare on the lower slopes of the Carpathians where the biggest, richest Cabernet Sauvignons and Pinot Noirs tend to be produced.

Bulgaria

Bulgaria is the success story of the eastern bloc thanks to the provision (by Pepsi Cola USA!) of Californian winemaking know-how. It has one of the oldest winemaking traditions in the world. The Black Sea is a crucial influencing factor on the land to the east of the Balkans, while the region to the west of the mountains is more affected by the influence of the Atlantic. Throughout the country, however, while conditions are typical of a continental climate, with warm summers and cool winters, local micro-climates are produced by hilly and mountainous regions.

The two most widely planted black grape varieties are the Gamza which is used to make daily-drinking lightweight reds, and the more serious Mavrud which is used to make long-lasting, hefty wines. Further south, the Pamid and Saperavi are both used to make daily-drinking reds, but the key red grapes for quality wines are now the Merlot and more particularly the Cabernet Sauvignon. The best wines from these varieties can be rich and almost Bordeaux-like. And very good value. Look out for the 'estate' wines, and the 'Mountain Cabernet' from Sakar in the south of the country. So far, the whites – principally the Chardonnay and Sauvignon Blanc – have been less successful.

Csirke Paprikas
Paprika chicken

This dish from Hungary combines two of the most popular ingredients used in Eastern Europe — paprika, made from dried sweet peppers, and the fresh sweet peppers themselves — in a typical goulash that goes equally well with the red and white wines of this and neighbouring countries.

Serves 4
1 medium onion, peeled and chopped
2 tbsp olive or vegetable oil
2 tbsp paprika
10 fl oz/300 ml chicken stock
8 chicken pieces
2 green peppers, seeded and cut into thin strips
3 tomatoes, skinned, seeded and chopped, or 3 tinned
tomatoes, drained and chopped
5 fl oz/150 ml sour cream
1 tbsp flour
Salt and freshly ground black pepper

In a flameproof pan, cook the onion in the oil until it is softened. Remove from the heat and stir in the paprika. Stir in the stock, return to the heat and cook, stirring occasionally, for 2-3 minutes. Add the chicken, peppers, tomatoes and salt to taste. Cook, covered, for about 30 minutes or until the chicken is cooked through. In a bowl, whisk together the cream and flour. Reduce the heat and remove the chicken pieces with tongs or a slotted spoon to a warmed serving dish. Stir the cream mixture into the vegetable mixture. Simmer and stir for 3-4 minutes. Add more salt if needed and pepper to taste and spoon over the chicken. Serve with rice or noodles.

Yugoslavia

Despite its reputation as a white wine producing country, Yugoslavia has a tradition of making a range of reds. Unfortunately, while the exported whites are feeble, the reds are thick, heavy and strong, with alcohol levels in some cases of over 14%.

Among the most typical of these heavyweights are the wines made from the local Mali Plavac in Dalmatia, from such regions as Pitovske Plaze, Bol, Vis, Brela, Postup, Dingac, Lastovo and Sveta. Another local variety that is popular in Yugoslavia is the Prokupac (once known as the 'national vine of Serbia'), but this too is now rapidly giving way to the Cabernet Sauvignon, Merlot, Gamay and Pinot Noir.

In Croatia, such western varieties as the Cabernet Sauvignon, Merlot and Pinot Noir are grown. In Serbia, the province of Kosmet on the Albanian border, makes full-bodied Cabernet Sauvignons and Merlots.

The potential of Yugoslavia to join Bulgaria and Hungary in competing with the rest of the world's red wines is clear – if there is a commitment to quality and a greater understanding of Western wine-drinkers' demands.

Albania and Czechoslovakia

Albania's isolation from the rest of the world has denied outsiders the opportunity to sample its wines of which there were reportedly once quite large quantities. Czechoslovakia is astonishingly second only to France as a producer of Gewürztraminer, and as maker of large quantities of 'Champagne' that will be familiar to many visitors.

THE EASTERN MEDITERRANEAN

LEFT: Serge Hochar, the brave Lebanese winemaker whose Château Musar is the most famous wine from the Eastern Mediterranean, picks out a bottle of his wine from the cellar of a London hotel

ABOVE: Winemaking in Cyprus – and the style of the wines themselves – has changed little in over 2,000 years; even the winegrowers' trucks look as though they have been in use for generations

The eastern Mediterranean and Levant deserve recognition for having been the birthplace of wine, the region where it all started. The trouble is that, having begun, winemaking never really developed. The general impoverishment of the region following the Mongol invasions of the 13th century and the non-vinous enthusiasm of the Turkish empire more or less put a halt to the evolution of winemaking. Visiting some wineries in this region can be rather like wandering around a wine museum.

Greece

This is one of the world's best examples of vinous arrested development. The problem here, as one of this country's modern, quality-conscious producers explained, is that very few Greeks have ever sent a wine back in a restaurant. If it's alcoholic and liquid enough to wash down a plateful of chilli peppers, it'll do. And if it's old and oxidised, so much the better.

Improvements are being made, but people who enjoy the flavour of fresh, clean fruit should still approach almost all Greek wine with circumspection. except for the excellent Cabernet-based reds of Château Carras in the Côtes de Meliton, the similarly impressive whites of Gentilini, made in Corfu from the Chardonnay, Sauvignon and the indigenous Tssaoussi, and the often wonderfully grapey Muscats of Samos and the sweet, red Mavrodaphne from Patras.

Cyprus

Sadly, Cyprus's reputation as a wine producing country has almost entirely been gained by its 'sherry' - a drink that few non-Cypriots with the price of a bottle of fino or Oloroso in their pocket would ever drink for pleasure. I say 'sadly' because this island does have a wine that deserves far greater recognition. Commandaria, one of the world's finest fortified wines, has been made here since the days of the Crusades. There are moves towards making clean, modern reds and whites too, but examples of these are still rare.

Turkey

It has sometimes been suggested that the only thing that has deterred non-Turks from buying Turkish wines, has been the fact that they have names like Buzbag and Dikmen. In fact, tired, oxidised flavours do tend to put people off too. The Tekel State Monopoly is trying to modernise the industry. We shall see.

Lebanon

If you were to ask most wine writers to name their favourite wines and winemakers, one name would almost certainly feature on almost all of the lists. To have produced any kind of wine in the war-torn Lebanon of the 1980s would be a considerable achievement; to have regularly made a world-beating red, is something else again. Hochar's wine, produced from grapes grown in the Bekaa Valley, varies from one vintage to the next, partly because of climatic variation, and partly because of the way that Hochar changes the proportions of Cabernet Sauvignon, Cinsault and Syrah in the blend. Whatever the mixture, however, Château Musar is reliably one of the world's most interesting wines.

Israel

One of the most treasured addresses among international travellers is that of a decent restaurant in Tel Aviv. Until the late 1980s, much the same might have been said of a good Israeli wine; orthodox jews who cared what their kosher wine tasted like had no alternative but to buy one that was made in Europe. Israel's winemakers seemed to be able to produce sweet Moscatel without too much difficulty; clean, fruity dry reds and whites seemed to be beyond their grasp; the Sauvignon Blanc produced by the Carmel winery proved in three blind tastings to be the least enjoyable example of this grape I had ever encountered.

Then, in the mid 1980s, The Yarden winery in the Golan Heights demonstrated that, if vines were planted at a sufficiently high altitude and were carefully made, good wines could be produced. In 1989, the quality of the Yarden wines was acknowledged by the awarding of a Gold medal to the 1985 Cabernet Sauvignon which beat a wide number of Californian and French wines at the WINE Magazine International Challenge. The Sauvignon Blanc and rosé are both good too.

Syria, Jordan, Egypt and Iran

There is some wine made in Syria - from Muscat grapes left over from this country's fairly sizeable table grape industry - and in Jordan. But far less than in the past.

One day, some charitable soul will remind the present generation of Egyptian winemakers of the care which their ancestors apparently devoted to winemaking. For the moment at least, modern Egyptian wines are best avoided.

In 1948, the wine writer Andre Simon wrote of what was then known as Persia that 'Once upon a time the country was famous for its wines; today the making and sale of wine is not allowed to Persians, but there are a few Armenians who make and Jews who sell wine'. 40 years later, the only wine being produced is made in secret. Which is a pity because there are at least a few lovers of Australian wine who would like to visit the hillside town of Shiraz, purported birthplace of the grape of that name.

THE ESSENTIALS — EASTERN MEDITERRANEAN AND THE LEVANT

Quality Greece alone has a broad Appellation of Origin system; the term Traditional Appellation is specific to Retsina.

Style Most wines, whether white or red, are flabby, alcoholic and frequently oxidised, suiting local tastes. Greek Muscats can have an attractive raisiny character. Some full-bodied, richly flavoured reds, notably from Macedonia, are made while Mavrodaphne can resemble Recioto della Valpolicella and Château Carras has made progress with Cabernet Sauvignon. Most Turkish wines are flabby and alcoholic but Trakya, a dry white Sémillon, and the reds, Buzbag and Hozbag, are better, as is the Gamay, Villa Doluca. Cyprus is starting to produce clean, fruity whites and reds as well as the traditional strong wines, such as Commandaria, and Cyprus 'sherry'. Good quality Israeli Sauvignons, Cabernets and Grenaches are now being made, while in Lebanon, though Domaine des Tourelles and Domaine de Kefrayya reds are improving, quality winemaking is restricted to Château Musar.

Climate Very hot and dry although moderated by the Mediterranean and by the mountain slopes of these countries.

Cultivation A variety of soils — volcanic, alluvial and gravelly — exist in this region, where vines are grown at all altitudes, from flat coastal plains to mountain slopes. The more innovative winemakers have grasped that sites enjoying cooler micro-climates produce better wine.

Grape Varieties *Greece*: Xynomavro, Agiorgitiko, Mavrodaphne, Cabernet Franc, Cabernet Sauvignon, Cinsault, Grenache, Vertzami, Mandilaria, Savatiano, Rhoditis, Assyritiko, Moschophilero, Muscat, Robola. *Turkey*: Papazkarasi, Hasandede, Gamay, Sémillon, Karalhana, Altintas, Cinsault, Carignan, Cabernet Sauvignon. *Cyprus*: Mavron, Maratheftikon, Xynisteri, Cabernet Sauvignon, Cabernet Franc, Grenache, Muscat, Ugni Blanc, Palomino, Mataro. *Lebanon*: Cabernet Sauvignon, Carignan, Cinsault, Pinot Noir, Muscat, Chasselas, Chardonnay, Sauvignon, Ugni Blanc, Aramon. *Israel*: Cabernet Sauvignon, Sauvignon, Grenache, Clairette, Muscat.

Production/Maturation Temperature-controlled fermentation and earlier bottling are being employed to produce lighter, fresher wines.

Longevity Most wines lack the acidity to be long-lasting although Musar and the best Greek reds can last for some 8 to 20 years.

Vintage Guide Vintages have less effect than winemaking on quality

Top Producers *Greece*: Château Carras, Union des Cooperatives Vinicoles de Samos, Union of Agricultural Cooperatives of Patras. *Lebanon*: Château Musar. *Israel*: Yarden, Gamla.

Kuzu Kapama

Leg of lamb baked with tomatoes, onions and coriander

This dish is traditional in Turkey, but its main ingredients — lamb, tomatoes, onion and olive oil — are used extensively throughout the Eastern Mediterranean, as is the practice of baking meat with vegetables.

SERVES 4-6
2-3 tbsp olive oil
12 spring onions, chopped
4 garlic cloves, peeled and minced
6 tomatoes, sliced
2 tbsp parsley, chopped fine
Salt and freshly ground black pepper
4 lb/2 kg leg of lamb
2 tsp coriander seeds, crushed
6 tbsp lamb or chicken stock

Coat a large roasting pan with the olive oil. Mix the spring onions with half the garlic and sprinkle the mixture over the bottom of the pan. Next, add the tomatoes in a layer. Top with the parsley and salt and pepper to taste. Rub the leg of lamb all over with the remaining garlic, the crushed coriander seeds and salt and pepper. Put the lamb on to the bed of vegetables and pour over the stock. Bake uncovered in an oven preheated to 350°F/180°C/ Gas mark 4 for about 1 hour 20 minutes (20 minutes per pound if you prefer your lamb pink), basting occasionally with the juices. Serve with potatoes or bulgar (cracked wheat).

AFRICA AND ASIA

Parts of Africa and Asia have vinous traditions that are almost as well-established as those of some of the well-known regions of Europe. The difference between most of these countries and Europe, though, has been the quality – or lack of it – of their winemaking.

North Africa

Like Greece, Egypt is a country whose winemaking has developed little since the days of the pharoes – principally because of a lack of demand for anything better.

Algeria's wine industry has long suffered from having been more or less established by the French to provide alcoholic reds that could be used to beef up anaemic Burgundy. There was little market among the mostly Muslim local population. More recent efforts in the Coteaux de Mascara to introduce modern winemaking methods and to overcome the natural disadvantage of the hot climate have produced some much more decent stuff. The most impressive reds are Chante Bled and Tarik, both of which are pretty muscular. Tunisia is Muscat country; few of its would-be Muscat de Beaumes de Venise wines are of brilliant quality, but all are better than most of the too-big-for-their-boots reds.

South Africa and Zimbabwe

In the early 1970s, most impartial observers would have placed South Africa at the forefront of the wine producing countries of the New World. The beautiful, Europe-like region of the Cape was decreed perfect winemsking country, Cabernet Sauvignons of the Cape were already compared to the best wines of Europe, and the name of the Groot Constantia winery was whispered in awe. Until quite recently, little has changed in South Africa. And therein lay the problem.

While Australia and California raced ahead, the South Africans developed very little. The political isolation, the unwillingness of some of the Afrikaners to adapt their winemaking and a level of quasi state control held by the KWV over the wine industry, all contributed to a state of stagnancy. South Africa still makes some top-class wines, but its vineyards are often in poor health and are still far too full of such poor-quality grapes as the Pinotage Welsch Riesling. There is some first-class Cabernet Sauvignon, and Sauvignon Blanc and a great deal of Chenin Blanc (here known as the Steen), but the quality of the winemaking is still surprisingly poor. Politically motivated subsidies intended to keep the members of the cooperatives acquiescent ensure that half of South Africa's annual grape harvest is distilled into brandy or industrial alcohol.

My advice would be to sidestep most of South Africa's basic wines and look out for the cream of the Cape's crop, such as Meerlust's Cabernet, the late-harvest wines from Nederburg, the Le Bonheur Sauvignon Blanc and the wines made by Tim Hamilton Russell.

The economic sanctions of the 1960s forced Zimbabwe in to winemaking. The stuff they have made has been a triumph of optimism, effort and ingenuity over climatic adversity. Every year, it rains at almost precisely the time when the grapes are ready to be picked, so rot and dilution are major problems. Nor have they been helped by the poor quality of many of the types of grapes and of the soil in which they have been grown.

India, China and Japan

In the late 1980s, a 'new' wine suddenly appeared on the dinner tables of would-be sophisticates in Britain and the USA. Described (erroneously) as 'Indian Champagne', the first spar-

kling wine from the Sub-Continent was also the first palatable wine any westerner had tasted from that country for several hundred years. Made a day's drive from Bombay, Omar Khayam benefits from high altitude vineyards, the winemaking skills of a consultant from Champagne and a blend of grapes that includes the Chardonnay. It is far from spectacular in quality but it is light years ahead of the truly apalling red and white 'wine' sold in screw-cap bottles in Bombay.

Wine and *vinifera* vines were imported into China in 128 BC, in the 13th century, Marco Polo described the Shangsi province as growing 'many excellent vines'. Sadly, over the succeeding years, the lines between distilled drink (the Chinese may have invented the process), grape wine and rice wine became quite blurred. When Rémy Martin announced the launch of its Great Wall co-production wine and rice wine in the 1970s, it was the first modern effort at Chinese winemaking to reach the rest.

The Japanese have known about wine since the 12th century when the Konshu *vinifera* grape was apparently grown here with some success. Today, however Japan is suddenly blossoming into a nation where keen wine drinkers can buy wine in daylight hours from vending machines. The problems for would-be Japanese wine makers are a lack of space and a climate – monsoon, earthquake, typhoons and general humidity – that encourages all kinds of bugs and diseases. This helps to explain why the Japanese import such huge quantities of concentrated grape juice from other countries which, adapting the tradition of 'British' wine, they blend with a little local juice and label the result as as Japanese. Its best wine is the Yquem lookalike Château Lion Noble Semillon, made with grapes whose bunches are protected from the elements by little paper hats. It costs Yquem-like prices, too.

ABOVE: The Monis winery in Zimbabwe has the tough job of trying to make good wine in a climate that is ill-suited to quality grape-growing.

BELOW: Outspoken winemaker Tim Hamilton Russell has no such problems in his vineyards at Hermanos, on the southern-most part of the Cape in South Africa. Conditions here are ideal for his classic varieties

THE ESSENTIALS — AFRICA AND ASIA

Style North Africa produces all styles of wine, not all particularly attractive to European palates, the best being the rich Algerian and Moroccan reds, full-bodied and rustic with a slightly coarse flavour, and Tunisian Muscats which range from the lusciously sweet Vin de Muscat de Tunisie to the dry, fragrant Muscat de Kelibia. Grenache-based Moroccan rosé can be pleasant. South Africa should be producing great wine, given the climate of the Cape. Unfortunately top-class Cabernets and Sauvignons are still the exceptions to a dull and isolated rule. Zimbabwe attempts to produce wine in former tobacco fields but is hindered by heavy rains during harvest. Marks for trying. In the Far East plenty of thick, sweet, very unpleasant wine is still produced but reasonable dry whites are made with French varieties under French or Australian supervision in China and Japan. The technically well-made Indian *méthode champenoise*, Omar Khayyam, has a good mousse and acidity and a pleasant Chardonnay character.

Climate Africa and India are, of course, extremely hot and dry, though South Africa's coastal region tends to be cool and fairly wet. China's wine-producing areas are generally cool, tempered by the Pacific and Indian oceans. Japan's wine production is at the whim of a climate of extremes with summer typhoons, spring and autumn monsoons and freezing winters, hence the readiness to use imported concentrate.

Cultivation Rich alluvial soils predominate in the flat coastal plains of North Africa, while the cooler hill sites inland have limestone, sand and volcanic soils. In India, lime-rich soils and east-facing hillslopes provide the best vineyard sites. South Africa's vary from the sandy gravels of the coastal area to the lime-rich soils inland, where irrigation is often necessary. China/Japan: the best vineyard sites are on south-facing slopes. China has good alluvial soils; those of Japan are more acidic.

Grape Varieties *North Africa*: Alicanté Bouschet, Cabernet Franc, Cabernet Sauvignon, Carignan, Cinsault, Clairette, Grenache, Merseguera, Mourvèdre, Morastel, Syrah, Pinot Noir, Ugni Blanc. *South Africa*: Cabernet Sauvignon, Pinotage, Syrah, Sauvignon Blanc, Chenin Blanc, Chardonnay, Muscat d'Alexandre. Very few *vinifera* plantings exist outside Africa, though Cabernet Sauvignon, Chardonnay, Ugni Blanc, Pinot Noir, Muscat and Merlot are being experimented with in the Far East, where local species include Ariab-e-Shahi, Arka Kanchan and Arka Shyam (*India*); Beichun, Dragon's Eye, Cow's Nipple and Cock's Heart (*China*). *Japan* favours *labrusca* vines such as Campbell's Early and Delaware, together with the native Koshu.

Production/Maturation In North Africa, a strong French influence persists, notably in grape varieties and appellations. The tendency for grapes to overripen in the African climate necessitates strict harvesting control and cool fermentation temperatures. To the east, a combination of government commitment to improved standards and Muslim religion has reduced yields and raised the quality of the wines. Recent developments in wine production have concerned the use of classic grape varieties under the auspices of French or Australian winemakers. Omar Khayyam is produced at a high-tech winery with technical assistance from the Champagne firm Piper-Heidsieck.

Top Producers *Algeria*: Cuvée du President. *South Africa*: Meerlust Rubicon, Hamilton Russell.

INDEX

ACKNOWLEDGMENTS

The writing and publication of this book would not have been possible without the encouragement and help of a large number of people. Of these, I should particularly like to thank Louise Abbott, John Clay, Dorn Hackett, Anne McDowall, Samantha Murphy, Jonathan Philips, Patrick Poritt, Mike and Sue Rose, Ruth Sheard and Simon Woods; David Gleave MW, Charles Metcalfe, Angela Muir MW and Anthony Rose; Jill Ford and Richard Raper; Nigel Elmer at Word Perfect and Laurie Hammond and Ian Thorpe at Jarrolds; Mike Trew, Margaret Rand and the editorial team at *WINE Magazine*; Steve Jackman and the wine department of Tesco.

PHOTOGRAPHIC CREDITS

Front cover: Bob Harris.

Back cover (author): John Heseltine; frontispiece: Steven Morris*; 8 (below): Charles Metcalfe*; 12 (above): Steven Morris*; 14: Joanna Simon*; 16: Charles Metcalfe*; 18 Martin Symington*; 20 (below): Irene Lenghui/Grants of St James's; 22 (below), 26: Margaret Rand*; 42: WINE Magazine; 43/44/45 (below): Steven Morris*; 48 (left, above): The Anthony Blake Photo Library; 49: Joanna Simon*; 54: Steven Morris*; 57: Restaurant St Quentin/Alan Crompton-Batt Associates; 59: Henri Cartier Bresson/ Magnum Photos Ltd; 61 (above): Charles Metcalfe; 71: Steven Morris*; 82: Steven Morris*; 94: Janet Price; 104 (bottom): Georges Duboeuf/Berkmann Wine Cellars; 110 (bottom): Susanna Bingham*; 129: Bollinger; 132, 136/137: Janet Price; 141 (below) Margaret Rand*; 144/145: Steven Morris*; 146 Martin Symington*; 147: Janet Price; 148 (top): Janet Price; (below): Fiona Wild*; 150: Steven Morris*; 151, 152/153 (above): Janet Price; (below): Steven Morris*; 154/155/156/157: Steven Morris*; 158 Mick Rock/Cephas Picture Library; 163/164/165: Grants of St. James's; 167: WINE Magazine; 168: John Lawlor/Grants of St James's; 169: Deinhard; 171: Charles Metcalfe*; 172: Grants of St James's; 173: Janet Price; 174: (above) Charles Metcalfe; 178: Percy Fox; 181, 185: Charles Metcalfe*; 186/187: Wines from Spain; 188: Margaret Rand*; 190 (bottom): Margaret Rand*; 195: WINE Magazine; 196: Douglas Amrine*; 199: Charles Metcalfe*; 201: WINE Magazine; 202: Margaret Rand*; 208/209 (below): Mick Rock/Cephas Picture Library; 210: Janet Price; 213: Mick Rock/Cephas Picture Library; 222: Joanna Simon*; 224: Charles Metcalfe*; 225: Joanna Simon*; 227, 232/233: Charles Metcalfe*; 236: Swiss Wine Growers Association; 240 (top): Charles Metcalfe*; (bottom): WINE Magazine; 242/243: Tim Hamilton Russell.

All other photographs: Robert Joseph*.

* All photographs from photographers whose names are marked with an asterisk are available from the WINE Magazine library, 60 Waldegrave Road, Twickenham, Middx TW11 8LG.